Lecture Notes in Computer Science 2595

Edited by G. Goos, J. Hartmanis, and J. van Leeuwen

T0216046

Springer

Berlin
Heidelberg
New York
Barcelona
Hong Kong
London
Milan
Paris
Tokyo

Kaisa Nyberg   Howard Heys (Eds.)

Selected Areas in Cryptography

9th Annual International Workshop, SAC 2002
St. John's, Newfoundland, Canada, August 15-16, 2002
Revised Papers

Springer

Series Editors

Gerhard Goos, Karlsruhe University, Germany
Juris Hartmanis, Cornell University, NY, USA
Jan van Leeuwen, Utrecht University, The Netherlands

Volume Editors

Kaisa Nyberg
Nokia Research Center
P.O. Box 407, 00045 Nokia Group, Finland
E-mail: kaisa.nyberg@nokia.com

Howard Heys
Memorial University of Newfoundland
Faculty of Engineering and Applied Science
St. John's, NF, A1B 3X5 Canada
E-mail: howard@engr.mun.ca

Cataloging-in-Publication Data applied for

A catalog record for this book is available from the Library of Congress.

Bibliographic information published by Die Deutsche Bibliothek
Die Deutsche Bibliothek lists this publication in the Deutsche Nationalbibliografie;
detailed bibliographic data is available in the Internet at <http://dnb.ddb.de>.

CR Subject Classification (1998): E.3, D.4.6, K.6.5, F.2.1-2, C.2, H.4.3

ISSN 0302-9743
ISBN 3-540-00622-2 Springer-Verlag Berlin Heidelberg New York

Springer-Verlag Berlin Heidelberg New York
a member of BertelsmannSpringer Science+Business Media GmbH

http://www.springer.de

© Springer-Verlag Berlin Heidelberg 2003
Printed in Germany

Typesetting: Camera-ready by author, data conversion by Boller Mediendesign
Printed on acid-free paper   SPIN: 10872522   06/3142   5 4 3 2 1 0

Preface

SAC 2002 was the Ninth Annual Workshop on Selected Areas in Cryptography. Previous workshops have been held at Queen's University in Kingston (1994, 1996, 1998, and 1999), Carleton University in Ottawa (1995 and 1997), University of Waterloo (2000), and the Fields Institute in Toronto (2001). The intent of the workshop is to provide a relaxed atmosphere in which researchers in cryptography can present and discuss new work on selected areas of current interest. The traditional themes for SAC workshops are:

- Design and analysis of symmetric key cryptosystems.
- Primitives for private-key cryptography, including block and stream ciphers, hash functions, and MACs.
- Efficient implementation of cryptographic systems in public- and private-key cryptography.

The special theme for SAC 2002 was:

- Cryptographic solutions for mobile and wireless network security.

The local historic connections can be described in three words: communications, transatlantic, and wireless. After John Cabot discovered Newfoundland at the end of the 15th century, sea communication was established between that eastern outpost of the Western Hemisphere and Europe. Also in Newfoundland is Hearts Content where the first successful transatlantic cable was landed in 1866. Most remarkably, on December 12, 1901, Guglielmo Marconi reported from Signal Hill near St. John's that he successfully received the first transatlantic wireless signals, three dots, the Morse coding of letter "S," sent from Cornwall, UK.

Communication, transatlantic, and wireless were also to become the keywords of the SAC 2002 workshop held at Memorial University of Newfoundland, St. John's. There were two invited talks given by two leading cryptographers from different sides of the Atlantic Ocean presenting their views on the security of mobile and wireless communications. The invited talks were: "Security Algorithms for Mobile Telephony" by Steve Babbage from Vodafone, UK, and "Cellphone Security" by David Wagner from University of California, Berkeley.

A total of 90 papers were submitted for consideration to the program committee and after an extensive review process, 25 were accepted for presentation. We would like to thank the authors of all submitted papers, including both those that were accepted and those which, unfortunately, could not be accommodated.

We appreciate the hard work of the SAC 2002 Program Committee. We are also very grateful to the many others that participated in the review process: Jee Hea An, Kazumaro Aoki, N. Asokan, Anne Canteaut, Paolo D'Arco, Jean-François Dhem, Yael Gertner, Shai Halevi, Martin Hirt, Tetsuya Ichikawa,

Yuval Ishai, Stanislaw Jarecki, Shaoquan Jiang, Thomas Johansson, Don Johnson, Pascal Junod, Mike Just, Charanjit Jutla, Jonathan Katz, Khoongming Kho, Hugo Krawczyk, Frederic Legare, Moses Liskov, Barbara Masucci, Luke McAven, David M'Raïhi, Valtteri Niemi, Christian Paquin, Béatrice Peirani, Benny Pinkas, Omer Reingold, Ari Renvall, Phil Rogaway, Markku-Juhani Saarinen, Hong-Yeop Song, Anton Stiglic, Dong To, Eric Verheul, Johan Wallén, Rebecca Wright, and Huapeng Wu.

The local arrangements for the conference was managed by a committee consisting of Howard Heys, Paul Gillard, David Pike, Nabil Shalaby, and Lu Xiao. In particular, we would like to thank Yvonne Raymond for her help with local arrangements and registration.

Lastly, we are very grateful for the financial support that the workshop has received from Entrust Technologies, Queen's University, and the Faculty of Engineering and Applied Science of Memorial University of Newfoundland.

On behalf of all those involved in organizing the workshop, we thank all the workshop participants for making SAC 2002 a success!

December 2002   Kaisa Nyberg and Howard Heys

Organization

Program Committee

Stefan Brands	Credentica Inc., Canada
Henri Gilbert	France Telecom, France
Guang Gong	University of Waterloo, Canada
Helena Handschuh	Gemplus, France
Howard Heys (Co-chair)	Memorial University of Newfoundland, Canada
Helger Lipmaa	Helsinki University of Technology, Finland
Tal Malkin	AT&T Research, USA
Mitsuru Matsui	Mitsubishi Electric, Japan
Kaisa Nyberg (Co-chair)	Nokia Research Center, Finland
Reihaneh Safavi-Naini	University of Wollongong, Australia
Douglas Stinson	University of Waterloo, Canada
Stafford Tavares	Queen's University, Canada
Serge Vaudenay	École Polytechnique Fédérale de Lausanne, Switzerland
Michael Wiener	Ottawa, Canada
Robert Zuccherato	Entrust, Inc., Canada

Local Arrangements Committee

Howard Heys, Paul Gillard, David Pike, Yvonne Raymond, Nabil Shalaby, Lu Xiao

Sponsoring Institutions

Entrust, Inc.
Memorial University of Newfoundland
Queen's University

Table of Contents

Elliptic Curve Enhancements

Modifications of ECDSA 1
John Malone-Lee and Nigel P. Smart

Integer Decomposition for Fast Scalar Multiplication on Elliptic Curves . . 13
Dongryeol Kim and Seongan Lim

Analysis of the Gallant-Lambert-Vanstone Method Based on Efficient
Endomorphisms: Elliptic and Hyperelliptic Curves 21
Francesco Sica, Mathieu Ciet, and Jean-Jacques Quisquater

SNOW

Guess-and-Determine Attacks on SNOW 37
Philip Hawkes and Gregory G. Rose

A New Version of the Stream Cipher SNOW 47
Patrik Ekdahl and Thomas Johansson

Encryption Schemes

Encryption-Scheme Security in the Presence of Key-Dependent Messages . 62
John Black, Phillip Rogaway, and Thomas Shrimpton

On the Security of CTR + CBC-MAC 76
Jakob Jonsson

Single-Path Authenticated-Encryption Scheme Based on Universal
Hashing 94
Soichi Furuya and Kouichi Sakurai

Differential Attacks

Markov Truncated Differential Cryptanalysis of Skipjack 110
Ben Reichardt and David Wagner

Higher Order Differential Attack of $Camellia(II)$ 129
Yasuo Hatano, Hiroki Sekine, and Toshinobu Kaneko

Square-like Attacks on Reduced Rounds of IDEA 147
Hüseyin Demirci

Full-Round Differential Attack on the Original Version of the Hash
Function Proposed at PKC'98 160
*Donghoon Chang, Jaechul Sung, Soohak Sung, Sangjin Lee, and
Jongin Lim*

Boolean Functions and Stream Ciphers

On Propagation Characteristics of Resilient Functions 175
Pascale Charpin and Enes Pasalic

Two Alerts for Design of Certain Stream Ciphers: Trapped LFSR and
Weak Resilient Function over $GF(q)$ 196
Paul Camion, Miodrag J. Mihaljević, and Hideki Imai

Multiples of Primitive Polynomials and Their Products over $GF(2)$ 214
Subhamoy Maitra, Kishan Chand Gupta, and Ayineedi Venkateswarlu

A New Cryptanalytic Attack for PN-generators Filtered by a Boolean
Function 232
Sabine Leveiller, Gilles Zémor, Philippe Guillot, and Joseph Boutros

Block Cipher Security

White-Box Cryptography and an AES Implementation 250
*Stanley Chow, Philip Eisen, Harold Johnson, and
Paul C. Van Oorschot*

Luby-Rackoff Ciphers: Why XOR Is Not So Exclusive 271
Sarvar Patel, Zulfikar Ramzan, and Ganapathy S. Sundaram

Signatures and Secret Sharing

New Results on Unconditionally Secure Distributed Oblivious Transfer .. 291
*Carlo Blundo, Paolo D'Arco, Alfredo De Santis, and
Douglas R. Stinson*

Efficient Identity Based Signature Schemes Based on Pairings 310
Florian Hess

The Group Diffie-Hellman Problems 325
Emmanuel Bresson, Olivier Chevassut, and David Pointcheval

MAC and Hash Constructions

Secure Block Ciphers Are Not Sufficient for One-Way Hash Functions
in the Preneel-Govaerts-Vandewalle Model 339
Shoichi Hirose

An Efficient MAC for Short Messages 353
Sarvar Patel

RSA and XTR Enhancements

Optimal Extension Fields for XTR 369
Dong-Guk Han, Ki Soon Yoon, Young-Ho Park, Chang Han Kim, and Jongin Lim

On Some Attacks on Multi-prime RSA 385
M. Jason Hinek, Mo King Low, and Edlyn Teske

Author Index 405

Modifications of ECDSA

John Malone-Lee and Nigel P. Smart

University of Bristol, Department of Computer Science,
Merchant Venturers Building,
Woodland Road,
Bristol, BS8 1UB, UK.
{malone, nigel}@cs.bris.ac.uk

Abstract. We describe two variants of ECDSA one of which is secure, in the random oracle model, against existential forgery but suffers from the notion of duplicate signatures. The second variant is also secure against existential forgery but we argue that it is likely to possess only four natural duplicate signatures. Our variants of ECDSA are analogous to the variants of DSA as proposed by Brickell *et al.* However, we show that the ECDSA variants have better exact security properties.

1 Introduction

In 1984, Goldwasser, Micali and Rivest [4], [5] introduced the notion of *existential forgery against adaptive chosen-message attack* for public key signature schemes. This notion has now become the *de facto* security definition for digital signature algorithms, against which all new schemes are measured. The definition involves a game in which the adversary is given a target user's public key and is asked to produce a valid signature, on any message, with respect to this public key. The adversary is given access to an oracle which will produce signatures on messages of the adversary's choice, in which case the signature output by the adversary at the end should clearly not have resulted from a query to its oracle.

Our work is motivated by the wish to create tighter security reductions for modified forms of ECDSA. This builds on the earlier work of Brickell *et al.* [2] who looked at the security of DSA and various minor modifications thereof. The work of Brickell *et al.* itself builds upon the earlier work of Pointcheval and Stern [7].

We shall describe a minor modification of ECDSA (which we call ECDSA-II), similar to the DSA-II variant of Brickell *et al.*, which is secure against existential forgery in the random oracle model. Our main contribution is that the tightness of our security reduction for ECDSA-II is better than that obtainable for DSA-II. However, ECDSA-II (just as ECDSA) suffers from the notion of duplicate signatures, as introduced in [8]. Duplicate signatures should not necessarily be considered a security weakness but they point out possible problems with the underlying design of the signature scheme.

The purpose of presenting ECDSA-II is to demonstrate the difference in the security result with DSA-II and to show why our final modification is better from

K. Nyberg and H. Heys (Eds.): SAC 2002, LNCS 2595, pp. 1–12, 2003.

the point of view of existential forgery. Finally we present ECDSA-III, which we shall show is secure against existential forgery in the random oracle model, with a tighter result than one could obtain for ECDSA-II. In addition we shall argue that ECDSA-III does not suffer from duplicate signatures. In fact by trying to remove the possibility of duplicate signatures we obtain a tighter security reduction. This demonstrates that removing anomalies in signature algorithms may lead to better provable security results, even when the anomalies are not security weaknesses.

The paper is structured as follows: we first define ECDSA and then we present DSA-II and ECDSA-II. Both schemes can be proved secure in the random oracle model against active adversaries. The proof technique requires *The Improved Forking Lemma* [2], and relies in the case of DSA-II on a heuristic assumption as to the distribution of the conversion function. No such heuristic is required for ECDSA-II and the resulting security reduction is also tighter than that for DSA-II. Subsequently we define ECDSA-III, which is another minor modification. We show that this is also secure, with an even tighter security reduction. Finally in the Appendix we give a uniform analogue of *The Improved Forking Lemma* that we call *The Uniform Multiple Forking Lemma*.

2 Definition of ECDSA

To use ECDSA, as defined in the ANSI [1] and other standards, one first picks an elliptic curve E over a finite field $\mathbb{F}_q$ whose order is equal to a prime n times a small cofactor c, i.e.

$$\#E(\mathbb{F}_q) = c \cdot n.$$

In addition, a base point $P \in E(\mathbb{F}_q)$ is chosen of order n. Note that, while users are free to choose their own individual base points, it is argued in [6] that they should be set by some central authority (alternatively one could generate the base point verifiably at random).

Each user has a private key $x \in \{1, \ldots, n-1\}$ and a public key

$$Z = xP.$$

ECDSA uses a hash function $H : \{0,1\}^* \to \{1, \ldots, n-1\}$. The algorithm itself is then given by:

Sign	**Verify**
1. $k \leftarrow \{1, \ldots, n-1\}$	1. $h \leftarrow H(m)$
2. $Q \leftarrow kP$	2. $a \leftarrow h/s \pmod{n}$
3. $r \leftarrow \text{xcoord}(Q) \pmod{n}$	3. $b \leftarrow r/s \pmod{n}$
4. $h \leftarrow H(m)$	4. $Q \leftarrow aP + bZ$
5. $s \leftarrow (h + x \cdot r)/k \pmod{n}$	5. $t \leftarrow \text{xcoord}(Q) \pmod{n}$
6. Output (r, s)	6. Accept iff $r = t$

A duplicate signature, see [8], for ECDSA is a pair of messages (m_1, m_2) and a signature (r, s) such that

$$H(m_1) \neq H(m_2)$$

and such that the pair (r, s) is a valid signature on both messages.

3   ECDSA - II

In [2] a modification of DSA is given, called DSA-II, which replaces the hash function evaluation $h = H(m)$ with $h = H(m\|r)$ where

$$r = (g^k \pmod{p}) \pmod{q}.$$

The authors of [2] claim that the map

$$k \rightarrow (g^k \pmod{p}) \pmod{q}$$

is likely to be $(\log q)$-collision free, in that it is impossible to find $\log q$ different values of $k \in \{1, \dots, q-1\}$ which map to the same number under the above map. Using this heuristic, and in the random oracle model, the authors of [2] prove the result below.

Theorem 1. *Suppose an adversary A against DSA-II exists which succeeds with probability $\epsilon > 4/q$ after Q queries to the random oracle H, then one can solve the discrete logarithm problem modulo p using fewer than*

$$25Q(\log q)(\log(2\log q))/\epsilon$$

replays of A with probability greater than $1/100$.

The proof uses a generalisation of *The Forking Lemma* from [7], *The Improved Forking Lemma* in [2], but it requires $\log q$ signatures on the same message with different random oracles to be produced.

The Improved Forking Lemma applies to *Trusted El Gamal Type Signature Schemes*, as defined in [2]. Here we define the analogous notion for schemes based on elliptic curves rather than finite fields: *Elliptic Curve Trusted El Gamal Type Signature Schemes* (ECTEGTSS).

Definition 1 (ECTEGTSS). A signature scheme is an ECTEGTSS if it has the following properties:

- The underlying group is from an elliptic curve E over a finite field $\mathbb{F}_q$ whose order is equal to a prime n times a small cofactor c, i.e. $\#E(\mathbb{F}_q) = c \cdot n$. A base point $P \in E(\mathbb{F}_q)$ of order n is given.
- It uses two functions G and H, with ranges $\mathcal{G}$ and $\mathcal{H}$ respectively. For security analysis the function H is modelled as a random oracle and G requires some practical properties such as (multi)-collision-resistance or (multi)-collision-freeness.
- There are three functions:

$$F_1(\mathbb{Z}_n, \mathbb{Z}_n, \mathcal{G}, \mathcal{H}) \rightarrow \mathbb{Z}_n, \ \ F_2(\mathbb{Z}_n, \mathcal{G}, \mathcal{H}) \rightarrow \mathbb{Z}_n, \ \ F_3 : (\mathbb{Z}_n, \mathcal{G}, \mathcal{H}) \rightarrow \mathbb{Z}_n$$

satisfying for all $(k, x, r, h) \in (\mathbb{Z}_n, \mathbb{Z}_n, \mathcal{G}, \mathcal{H})$,

$$\mathbb{F}_2(F_1(k, x, r, h), r, h) + x \cdot F_3(F_1(k, x, r, h), r, h) = k \bmod n.$$

- Each user has private and public keys x, Z such that $Z = xP$.
- To sign a message m, the signer Alice picks k at random from $\mathbb{Z}_n^*$, computes $Q = kP$ and $r = G(Q)$. She then gets $h = H(m\|r)$ and computes $s = F_1(k, x, r, h)$. The signature on m is (s, r, h), although (s, r) is enough in practice since h may be recovered from m and r.
- To verify the signature (s, r, h) on a message m the verifier Bob computes $e_P = F_2(s, r, h)$, $e_Z = F_3(s, r, h)$ and finally $W = e_P P + e_Z Z$. He then checks that $r = G(W)$ and $h = H(m\|r)$.
- The functions F_2 and F_3 must satisfy the following one-to-one condition: for given r, e_P and e_Z, there exists a unique pair (h, s) such that

$$e_P = F_2(s, r, h) \text{ and } e_Z = F_3(s, r, h).$$

Furthermore, this pair is easy to find.

∎

It is easily verified that the proof of *The Improved Forking Lemma* in [2] applies to ECTEGTSSs.

The analogue to ECDSA of DSA-II is the following signature algorithm, which we call ECDSA-II.

Sign
1. $k \leftarrow \{1, \ldots, n-1\}$
2. $Q \leftarrow kP$
3. $r \leftarrow \text{xcoord}(Q) \pmod{n}$
4. $h \leftarrow H(m\|r)$
5. $s \leftarrow (h + x \cdot r)/k \pmod{n}$
6. Output (r, s)

Verify
1. $h \leftarrow H(m\|r)$
2. $a \leftarrow h/s \pmod{n}$
3. $b \leftarrow r/s \pmod{n}$
4. $Q \leftarrow aP + bZ$
5. $t \leftarrow \text{xcoord}(Q) \pmod{n}$
6. Accept iff $r = t$

It is easily verified that ECDSA-II is an ECTEGTSS with:

$$F_1(k, x, r, h) = (h + x \cdot r)/k \bmod n = s$$
$$F_2(s, r, h) = h/s \bmod n$$
$$F_3(s, r, h) = r/s \bmod n$$

where $Q = kP$, $r = \text{xcoord}(Q) \bmod n$ and $h = H(m\|r)$.

The scheme still exhibits duplicate signatures because the function

$$G : k \rightarrow \text{xcoord}(kP) \pmod{n}$$

possesses trivial collisions, in that k and $-k$ always map to the same point. However, we also have that if

$$y = \lfloor q/n \rfloor + 1$$

and if

$$G(k_1) = G(k_2) = \ldots = G(k_y)$$

then there must exist $i, j \in \{1, \ldots, y\}$ with $i \neq j$ such that

$$k_i = \pm k_j.$$

Since we have

$$c \cdot n = \#E(\mathbb{F}_q) \geq q + 1 - 2\sqrt{q}$$

and for most elliptic curves used in "real life" we have $c \leq 4$, we deduce

$$y = \lfloor q/n \rfloor + 1 \leq \frac{4q}{q + 1 - 2\sqrt{q}} + 1 \leq 6.$$

This leads us to the following result:

Theorem 2. *Suppose an adversary A against ECDSA-II exists which succeeds with probability $\epsilon > 4/q$ after Q queries to the random oracle H, then one can solve the discrete logarithm problem in $E(\mathbb{F}_q)$ using fewer than*

$$150Q \log 12/\epsilon$$

replays of A with probability greater than $1/100$.

Proof. As in Theorem 1 we apply *The Improved Forking Lemma* from [2] to obtain 6 valid signatures on the same message m, each with a different random oracle. Denote these signatures

$$(r_i, h_i, s_i)$$

where

$$\begin{aligned}
r_i &= \mathrm{xcoord}(k_i P) \pmod{n}, \\
h_i &= H_i(m \| r_i), \\
s_i &= (h_i + x \cdot r_i)/k_i \pmod{n}.
\end{aligned}$$

We have for all these signatures that $r = r_i = r_j$, and so there exists two indices i and j, with $i \neq j$, such that

$$k_i = \pm k_j.$$

Then using the equality

$$(h_i + x \cdot r)/s_i = \pm(h_j + x \cdot r)/s_j \pmod{n}$$

we obtain two possibilities for the discrete logarithm x of the public key. The correct value of the discrete logarithm may then be determined using one point multiplication.

Notice how this only requires 6 different signatures as opposed to the $\log q$ different signatures in the result for DSA-II. In addition notice that it is the absence of collision resistance in G which makes the above security reduction tighter.

The above result holds for passive adversaries, a similar result for active adversaries can be deduced by providing the obvious signing simulator.

4   ECDSA - III

We now present a version of ECDSA which we call ECDSA-III. We shall show that it does not exhibit general duplicate signatures. In addition the security reduction against existential forgeries is tighter for ECDSA-III than for ECDSA-II. The alteration is to replace

$$r \leftarrow \text{xcoord}(kP) \pmod{n}$$

by

$$r \leftarrow X + Y$$

where $Q = (X, Y) = kP$. Notice how r is now treated as an element of $\mathbb{F}_q$ and not $\mathbb{F}_n^*$ and how the value of r depends on both the x and y coordinates of the point kP.

The precise details of ECDSA-III we give below, which one should notice is only marginally less efficient in terms of bandwidth and CPU time than standard ECDSA.

Sign
1. $k \leftarrow \{1, \ldots, n-1\}$
2. $Q = (X, Y) \leftarrow kP$
3. $r \leftarrow X + Y$
4. $h \leftarrow H(m\|r)$
5. $s \leftarrow (h + x \cdot r)/k \pmod{n}$
6. Output (r, s)

Verify
1. $h \leftarrow H(m\|r)$
2. $a \leftarrow h/s \pmod{n}$
3. $b \leftarrow r/s \pmod{n}$
4. $Q = (X, Y) \leftarrow aP + bZ$
5. Accept iff $r = X + Y$

It is easily verified that ECDSA-III is an ECTEGTSS with:

$$F_1(k, x, r, h) = (h + x \cdot r)/k \bmod n = s$$

$$F_2(s, r, h) = h/s \bmod n$$

$$F_3(s, r, h) = r/s \bmod n$$

where $Q = kP = (X + Y)$, $r = X + Y$ and $h = H(m\|r)$.

Notice that the equation $X + Y = t$ will intersect the curve in at most three points. This leads us to the following improved security reduction:

Theorem 3. *Suppose an adversary A against ECDSA-III exists which succeeds with probability $\epsilon > 4/q$ after Q queries to the random oracle H, then one can solve the discrete logarithm problem in $E(\mathbb{F}_q)$ using fewer than*

$$100Q \log 8/\epsilon$$

replays of A with probability greater than $1/100$.

Proof. Again we apply *The Improved Forking Lemma* from [2] to obtain four signatures with the same value of r. Two of these signatures correspond to points, $Q_1 = k_1 P$ and $Q_2 = k_2 P$, with $k_1 = \pm k_2$. We may now recover the discrete logarithm of the public key Z in the obvious way.

As usual one can simulate the signing oracles so as to obtain a similar result for active adversaries.

The way in which *The Improved Forking Lemma* uses the adversary A to produce multiple signatures on the same message depends on A's probability of success ϵ, and the number of oracle queries it makes Q. This makes the resulting reduction non-uniform. We give the following uniform reduction for ECDSA-III.

Theorem 4. *Suppose an adversary A against ECDSA-III exists which succeeds in time T and with probability $\epsilon > 14Q/q$ after Q queries to the random oracle H, then one can solve the discrete logarithm problem in $E(\mathbb{F}_q)$ using a probabilistic algorithm in expected time*

$$T' \leq 1984506 \cdot Q \cdot T/\epsilon.$$

Proof. We apply *The Uniform Multiple Forking Lemma* from the appendix with $y = 4$ and $2^k = q$ and reason as in the proof of Theorem 3.

Note that for schemes where we may usefully apply *The Uniform Multiple Forking Lemma*, the efficiency of the resulting security reduction depends very much on the parameter y, the number of signatures required on the same message. The smaller the value of y, the better the reduction. We require $\log q$ signatures for DSA-II, 6 signatures for ECDSA-II, and only 4 for ECDSA-III. Therefore, as in the non-uniform case, the uniform reduction given in Theorem 4 for ECDSA-III is the tightest among the reductions using this method for the three schemes considered in this paper.

We now turn to discussing whether ECDSA-III is resistant to duplicate signatures. We cannot give a security proof but give an informal argument.

We wish to show that it is hard to find two elliptic curve points $Q_1 = (x_1, y_1)$ and $Q_2 = (x_2, y_2)$ such that one knows the respective discrete logarithms $Q_i = k_i P$ and such that

$$x_1 + y_1 = x_2 + y_2.$$

Intuitively this can only happen when the line

$$L(t) : X + Y = t$$

for some constant t is geometrically related to the group law linking Q_1 and Q_2. If $L(t)$ is a tangent at Q_1 and we know the discrete logarithm k_1 then we know that $L(t)$ intersects the curve in one other point, say $Q_2 = k_2 P$, of the required form and that $k_2 = (-2k_1) \pmod{n}$. Hence we need to avoid points where $L(t)$ is a tangent. But for all possible values of t the line $L(t)$ is only a tangent for at most four points on any given elliptic curve.

In ECDSA all values of r could be members of a trivial duplicate signature, for ECDSA-III we see that only four possible values of r can be members of a trivial duplicate signature.

Now assume that we have a value of t such that $L(t)$ is not a tangent to the curve. Suppose it intersects the curve at Q_1 and that we know the discrete logarithm of Q_1 with respect to P. About fifty percent of the time there will be no other $\mathbb{F}_q$-point on the curve which lies on the line $L(t)$, in which case Q_1 cannot be part of a duplicate signature. For the other fifty percent of the time we obtain two other elliptic curve points Q_2 and Q_3. To use these points to obtain a duplicate signature it would appear we need to extract their discrete logarithm with respect to P. Although we cannot prove that this is the only way to obtain duplicate signatures it seems likely to be the case.

5   Conclusion

We have shown that a modified form of ECDSA has a tighter security reduction than a similarly modified form of DSA. In addition we have presented a second modified form of ECDSA which not only has an even tighter security reduction, it also does not suffer from the phenomenon of duplicate signatures.

6   Acknowledgements

Many thanks to David Pointcheval for helpful correspondence during this work.

References

1. ANSI X9.62. *Public Key Cryptography for the Financial Services Industry: The Elliptic Curve Digital Signature Algorithm* (ECDSA), 1999.
2. E. Brickell, D. Pointcheval, S. Vaudenay and M. Yung. Design validations for discrete logarithm based signature schemes. *Public Key Cryptography 2000*, Springer-Verlag LNCS 1751, 276–292, 2000.
3. D. Brown. Generic groups, collision resistance and ECDSA. Preprint, 2001.
4. S. Goldwasser, S. Micali and R. Rivest. A "paradoxical" solution to the signature problem. *Proc. 25th Symposium on Foundations of Computer Science*, 441–448, 1984.
5. S. Goldwasser, S. Micali and R. Rivest. A digital signature scheme secure against adaptive chosen ciphertext attacks. *SIAM J. Computing*, **17**, 28–308, 1988.
6. A. Menezes and N.P. Smart. Security of signature schemes in a multi-user setting. Preprint 2001.
7. D. Pointcheval and J. Stern. Security arguments for digital signatures and blind signatures. *J. Cryptology*, **13**, 361–396, 2000.
8. D. Pointcheval, J. Stern, J. Malone-Lee and N.P. Smart. Flaws in Security Proofs. To appear *Advances in Cryptology - CRYPTO 2002*.

Appendix

In this Appendix we prove a generalisation of the forking Lemma of [7]. Our result applies to *generic signature schemes*, as defined below.

Definition 2. *[7] A* **generic signature scheme** *is a signature scheme* (G, V, S) *such that on input of the message* m, *the signing algorithm* S *produces a signature* $(m, \sigma_1, h, \sigma_2)$, *where* σ_1 *randomly takes its values in a large set,* h *is the hash value of* $m\|\sigma_1$, *and* σ_2 *depends on* σ_1, m, *and* h. *Here and henceforth* $\|$ *denotes concatenation.*

Theorem 5 (The Uniform Multiple Forking Lemma). *Let* (G, S, V) *be a generic digital signature scheme with security parameter* k. *Let* A *be a probabilistic polynomial time Turing machine whose input consists of public data and which can make* $Q > 0$ *queries to a random oracle* $\mathcal{O}$. *Assume that, within time bound* T, *the attacker* A *produces a valid signature* $(m, \sigma_1, h, \sigma_2)$ *with probability* $\epsilon \geq xQ/2^k$. *Then, for* y *such that* $x - 1 > 4(y - 1)$, *there is a machine* M *that by using* A *can produce* y *valid signatures,*

$$(m, \sigma_1, h, \sigma_2) \text{ and } (m, \sigma_1, h^i, \sigma_2^i)$$

for $i = 1, \dots, y - 1$, *with* h, h^i *all distinct. The expected running time of* M *is upper bounded by*

$$21 \cdot \frac{x}{x-1} \cdot \sigma(x, y) \cdot \frac{(1 + \gamma(y))^3}{\gamma(y)(\gamma(y) - 1)^2} \cdot \frac{QT}{\epsilon},$$

where

$$\sigma(x, y) = \sum_{k=1}^{y-1} \frac{x}{x - 1 - 4k} \text{ and } \gamma(y) = 1 - \left(\frac{1}{4}\right)\left(\frac{3}{4}\right)\left(\frac{3}{5}\right)^{y-1}.$$

Our proof uses the following lemma from [7]:

Lemma 1 (The Splitting Lemma). *Let* $A \subset X \times Y$ *be such that* $\Pr[A] \geq \epsilon$. *Define*

$$B = \{(x, y) \in X \times Y : \Pr_{y' \in Y}[(x, y') \in A] \geq \epsilon/2\}.$$

We have the following:

1. $\forall (x, y) \in B, \Pr_{y' \in Y}[(x, y') \in A] \geq \epsilon/2.$
2. $\Pr[B|A] \geq 1/2.$

We now return to the proof of the main theorem.

Proof (Of Theorem 5). The attacker A is a probabilistic polynomial time Turing machine with random tape ω that mounts a no-message attack on (G, S, V). During the attack A makes a polynomial number of queries to the random oracle $\mathcal{O}$. Let us denote these queries $\mathcal{Q}_1, \dots, \mathcal{Q}_Q$, and the corresponding responses $\rho_1, \dots, \rho_Q$. We will assume that A stores the query and answer pairs in a table and so the queries are all distinct. Clearly a random choice of $\mathcal{O}$ corresponds to random choices for $\rho_1, \dots, \rho_Q$.

For a random choice of $(\omega, \mathcal{O})$, A outputs a valid signature $(m, \sigma_1, h, \sigma_2)$ with probability ϵ. Since $\mathcal{O}$ is random, the probability for h to be equal to $\mathcal{O}(m\|\sigma_1)$ is less than $1/2^k$ unless A made the query $m||\sigma_1$ during its attack. We let $Ind(\omega, \mathcal{O})$ be the index of the query $m||\sigma_1$ and we let $Ind(\omega, \mathcal{O}) = \infty$ if this query is never made. We define the sets

$$S = \{(\omega, \mathcal{O}) : A^{\mathcal{O}}(\omega) \text{ succeeds and } Ind(\omega, \mathcal{O}) \neq \infty\} \text{ and}$$
$$S_i = \{(\omega, \mathcal{O}) : A^{\mathcal{O}}(\omega) \text{ succeeds and } Ind(\omega, \mathcal{O}) = i\} \text{ for } i \in \{1, \dots, Q\}.$$

For index i let $\mathcal{O}|_i$ denote the restriction of $\mathcal{O}$ to queries of index strictly less than i, and let $\mathcal{O}|^i$ denote the restriction of $\mathcal{O}$ to queries of index greater or equal to i.

We define the parameter

$$\alpha(y) = \frac{1}{2\gamma(y)} + \frac{1}{2}. \tag{1}$$

The machine M is now described in figure 1.

Fig. 1. Machine M

```
algorithm M
 1. j = 1
 2. run A until, on input of a pair (ω, 𝒪) ∈ S, it outputs a forgery
    call such a forgery ''successful''
    denote the number of calls made to A to obtain a successful
    forgery by N_j, and denote Ind(ω, 𝒪) by β
 3. for k = 1, ..., y − 1 :
     i. run A until it produces a new successful forgery, or at most
        20N_jα(y)^jδ_k times, where δ_k = x/(x − 1 − 4k)
        for each run use the same ω as above and choose 𝒪^{j,k} randomly
        subject to 𝒪^{j,k}|_β = 𝒪|_β
     ii. if A has not produced a new successful forgery goto 4
         else increment k
 4. if A has produced y successful forged signatures return these
    else increment j and goto 2
```

The sets in $\{S_i : i \in \{1, \dots, Q\}\}$ form a partition of S. With our definitions we have

$$\nu = \Pr[S] \geq \epsilon - 1/2^k \geq \epsilon - \epsilon/xQ \geq \epsilon(x - 1)/x. \tag{2}$$

Also

$$\Pr[N_j \geq 1/5\nu] = (1 - \nu)^{\lceil 1/5\nu \rceil - 1} > 3/4. \tag{3}$$

Let I be the set of the most likely indices,

$$I = \{i : \Pr[S_i|S] \geq 1/2Q\}.$$

Define the sets

$$\Omega_i = \{(\omega, \mathcal{O}) : \Pr_{\mathcal{O}|^i} [(\omega, \mathcal{O}|_i, \mathcal{O}|^{i'}) \in S_i] \geq \nu/4Q\}.$$

For $i \in I$ we have

$$\Pr[S_i] = \Pr[S_i \cap S] = \Pr[S_i|S] \cdot \Pr[S] \geq \nu/2Q,$$

and so by the Splitting Lemma $\Pr[\Omega_i|S_i] \geq 1/2$.

Since all the subsets S_i are disjoint,

$$\Pr_{\omega, \mathcal{O}}[(\exists i \in I) \, (\omega, \mathcal{O}) \in \Omega_i \cap S_i|S]$$

$$= \Pr\left[\bigcup_{i \in I}(\Omega_i \cap S_i)|S\right] = \sum_{i \in I} \Pr[\Omega_i \cap S_i|S]$$

$$= \sum_{i \in I} \Pr[\Omega_i|S_i] \cdot \Pr[S_i|S] \geq \left(\sum_{i \in I} \Pr[S_i|S]\right)/2 \geq 1/4. \tag{4}$$

Define $l = \lceil \log_{\alpha(y)} Q \rceil$. For any $j \geq l$ and any $1 \leq k \leq y$, whenever $N_j \geq 1/5\nu$ we have

$$20N_j\alpha(y)^j \delta_k \geq 20 \cdot \frac{1}{5\nu} \cdot \alpha(y)^{\lceil \log_{\alpha(y)} Q \rceil} \cdot \frac{x}{x-1-4k}$$

$$> \frac{4xQ}{\epsilon(x-1-4k)}. \tag{5}$$

At step 3 of M when $(\omega, \mathcal{O}) \in \Omega_\beta \cap S_\beta$ we have

$$\Pr_{\mathcal{O}^{j,k}|\beta}[(\omega, \mathcal{O}^{j,k}) \in S_\beta \text{ and } \rho_\beta^{j,k} \neq \rho_\beta, \rho_\beta^{j,k} \neq \rho_\beta^{j,1}, \ldots, \rho_\beta^{j,k} \neq \rho_\beta^{j,k-1}]$$

$$\geq \Pr_{\mathcal{O}^{j,k}|\beta}[(\omega, \mathcal{O}^{j,k}) \in S_\beta] - \Pr_{\mathcal{O}^{j,k}|\beta}[\rho_\beta^{j,k} = \rho_\beta] - \sum_{i=1}^{k-1} \Pr_{\mathcal{O}^{j,k}|\beta}[\rho_\beta^{j,k} = \rho_\beta^{j,i}]$$

$$\geq \nu/4Q - k/2^k \geq \epsilon(x-1)/4xQ - \epsilon k/xQ = \epsilon(x-1-4k)/4xQ \tag{6}$$

From (5) and (6) we know that, for $j \geq l$ and $N_j \geq 1/5\nu$, the probability of getting $y-1$ successful forks after at most $\sum_{k=1}^{y-1} 4xQ/\epsilon(x-1-4k)$ runs of A at step 3 is greater or equal to

$$\prod_{k=1}^{y-1}\left(1 - \left(1 - \frac{\epsilon(x-1-4k)}{4xQ}\right)^{4xQ/\epsilon(x-1-4k)}\right)$$

$$\geq (1 - e^{-1})^{y-1} > \left(\frac{3}{5}\right)^{y-1}. \tag{7}$$

Recall from (4) that at step 2 of M when A produces a forgery using $(\omega, \mathcal{O}) \in S$ with $Ind(\omega, \mathcal{O}) = \beta$ then, with probability at least $1/4$, $(\omega, \mathcal{O}) \in \Omega_\beta \cap S_\beta$.

Combining this fact with (3) and (7) we have that for any $t \geq l$ the probability for J to be greater or equal to t is less than

$$\left(1 - \left(\tfrac{1}{4}\right)\left(\tfrac{3}{4}\right)\left(\tfrac{3}{5}\right)^{y-1}\right)^{t-l} = \gamma(y)^{t-l}. \tag{8}$$

Let J denote the final value of j during an execution of M and let N be the total number of calls made to A. We want to compute an upper bound on the expectation on N. We have

$$E[N|J = t] \leq \sum_{j=1}^{t} \left(E[N_j] + 20E[N_j]\alpha(y)^j \sum_{k=1}^{y-1} \delta_k\right)$$

$$= \sum_{j=1}^{t} \left(E[N_j] + 20E[N_j]\alpha(y)^j \sigma(x, y)\right),$$

and,

$$E[N_j] = \sum_{i=1}^{\infty} i \cdot \Pr[N_j = i] = \sum_{i=1}^{\infty} i(1 - \nu)^{i-1}\nu = \frac{1}{\nu},$$

so,

$$E[N|J = t] \leq \frac{1}{\nu} \sum_{j=1}^{t} \left(1 + 20\alpha(y)^j \sigma(x, y)\right)$$

$$< 21 \cdot \frac{\sigma(x, y)}{\nu} \sum_{j=1}^{t} \alpha(y)^j < 21 \cdot \frac{\sigma(x, y)}{\nu} \cdot \frac{\alpha(y)^{t+1}}{\alpha(y) - 1}. \tag{9}$$

Now, (1), (2), (8) and (9) give us

$$E[N] = \sum_{t=0}^{\infty} E[N|J = t] \cdot \Pr[J = t]$$

$$\leq \sum_{t<l} E[N|J = t] + \sum_{t \geq l} E[N|J = t] \cdot \Pr[J \geq t]$$

$$< 21 \cdot \frac{\sigma(x, y)}{\nu} \cdot \left(\sum_{t=0}^{l-1} \frac{\alpha(y)^{t+1}}{\alpha(y) - 1} + \sum_{t \geq l} \left(\frac{\alpha(y)^{t+1}}{\alpha(y) - 1} \cdot \gamma(y)^{t-l}\right)\right)$$

$$< 21 \cdot \frac{\sigma(x, y)}{\nu} \cdot \frac{\alpha(y)^{l+1}}{\alpha(y) - 1} \cdot \left(\frac{1}{\alpha(y) - 1} + \frac{1}{1 - \alpha(y)\gamma(y)}\right)$$

$$\leq 21 \cdot \frac{x}{x - 1} \cdot \sigma(x, y) \cdot \frac{\alpha(y)^2}{\alpha(y) - 1} \cdot \left(\frac{1}{\alpha(y) - 1} + \frac{1}{1 - \alpha(y)\gamma(y)}\right) \cdot \frac{Q}{\epsilon}$$

$$= 21 \cdot \frac{x}{x - 1} \cdot \sigma(x, y) \cdot \frac{(1 + \gamma(y))^3}{\gamma(y)(\gamma(y) - 1)^2} \cdot \frac{Q}{\epsilon}.$$

The result follows.

Integer Decomposition for Fast Scalar Multiplication on Elliptic Curves[*]

Dongryeol Kim and Seongan Lim

KISA (Korea Information Security Agency),
78, Garak-Dong, Songpa-Gu, Seoul 138-803, Korea
{drkim, seongan}@kisa.or.kr

Abstract. Since Miller and Koblitz applied elliptic curves to cryptographic system in 1985[3,6], a lot of researchers have been interested in this field and various speedup techniques for the scalar multiplication have been developed. Recently, Gallant *et al.* published a method that accelerates the scalar multiplication and is applicable to a larger class of curves[4]. In the process of their method, they assumed the existence of a special pair of two short linearly independent vectors. Once a pair of such vectors exists, their decomposition method improves the efficiency of the scalar multiplication roughly about 50%. In this paper, we state and prove a necessary condition for the existence of a pair of desired vectors and we also present an algorithm to find them.

Keywords. elliptic curve cryptosystem, scalar multiplication, integer decomposition, endomorphism

1 Introduction

Since the introduction of elliptic curve cryptosystem in 1985 by Miller and Koblitz, independently, cryptographic schemes using elliptic curves get lots of attention in the field of public key cryptography due to its low bandwidth and small space storage requirements. The scalar multiplication is the main operation in public key schemes using elliptic curves and it can be usually done by successive doubling and addition of points. The doubling and addition of points need a few inversions and multiplications over the underlying finite field.

Although the key size is small, the required complexity may still be relatively heavy and hence intensive researches have been done to improve its computational efficiency. Many different approaches to improve the computational efficiency for elliptic curve cryptography have been tried[1,2,3,5,7].

One of the approaches is to analyze the algebraic structure of elliptic curves and classify a class of special curves with better efficiency in the scalar multiplication. The most well-known and commonly used class is Koblitz curve. For

---

[*] This work was supported by R&D project 2002-s-073 of KISA.

K. Nyberg and H. Heys (Eds.): SAC 2002, LNCS 2595, pp. 13–20, 2003.

Koblitz curve, scalar multiplication does not need any point doubling by exploiting a feature of the Frobenious endomorphism[5,8,9,10]. When the underlying finite field is of characteristic 2, the Frobenious endomorphism can be efficiently computed since squaring is much faster than multiplication. The idea of using Frobenious endomorphism can be extended to elliptic curves with arbitrary characteristic, but the improvement of the efficiency can not be guaranteed.

Recently, a speedup idea of scalar multiplication kP using efficiently computable endomorphism of an elliptic curve E over a prime field F_q has been proposed by Gallant et $al.$ for a point $P \in E$ of prime order n. In their paper, they introduced an idea using decomposition of $k = k_1 + \lambda k_2 \pmod{n}$ where λ is an integer that satisfies $\phi(P) = \lambda P$ and ϕ is an endomorphism on E. If the endomorphism is efficiently computable and one can guarantee that each component k_1, k_2 in the decomposition is short enough, say both of them are bounded by $\sqrt{n}$, then their method improves the computational efficiency up to 50 percent to the general method of computing scalar multiplication in elliptic curves over the prime field.

In order to find such a decomposition of $k = k_1 + \lambda k_2 \pmod{n}$ with $-\sqrt{n} < k_1, k_2 < \sqrt{n}$, Gallant et $al.$ introduced a way to use two linearly independent short vectors v_1, v_2 in the kernel of the homomorphism $f : Z \times Z \rightarrow Z_n$ defined by $f(i, j) = i + j\lambda \pmod{n}$. For the simplicity of the notation, we call a set of such vectors v_1, v_2 by a GLV(R. Gallant, R. Lambert and S. Vanstone) generator that will be defined later. Gallant et $al.$ also suggested a specific way to find a GLV generator, but the completeness of their method is claimed heuristically without any proof. In fact, the gaps unproven in their claim are

- One cannot guarantee the existence of a GLV generator.
- One cannot guarantee the success of finding a GLV generator even if there is a GLV generator.

In this paper, we propose

- A necessary condition for the existence of a GLV generator
- A method of finding a GLV generator when a GLV generator exists.

Our paper is organized as follows. In Section 2, we review briefly how to speedup the scalar multiplication using a GLV generator proposed by Gallant et $al.$'s in [4]. In Section 3, we present a necessary condition for the existence of a GLV generator and a new algorithm to find a GLV generator. Finally, we conclude and discuss some further works in Section 4.

2   Preliminary

Let F_q be a finite field of q elements and E be an elliptic curve defined over F_q with the point at infinity O. An endomorphism of E is a rational map $\phi : E \rightarrow E$ with $\phi(O) = O$.

Let $P \in E$ be a rational point of a large prime order n. Let ϕ be an efficiently computable endomorphism of E and ϕ acts on the subgroup $\langle P \rangle$ as a multiplication by λ which is an integer root of the characteristic polynomial of ϕ modulo n. Let k be an integer and be selected uniformly at random from the interval $[1, n-1]$. We consider a set of two linearly independent vectors in $Z \times Z$ that will be used to speed up the computation of kP and name it a GLV generator. For given λ, n, Gallant et $al.$ introduced a homomorphism $f : Z \times Z \to Z_n$ defined by

$$f(i, j) = i + j\lambda \pmod{n}. \tag{1}$$

Here we define a GLV generator.

Definition A set $\{v_1, v_2\}$ of two linearly independent vectors v_1, v_2 in the kernel of the homomorphism f in (1) is called a GLV generator if each component of v_1, v_2 is bounded by $\sqrt{n}$.

2.1   How to Use a GLV Generator to Calculate kP

Now we briefly explain how Gallant et $al.$ used a GLV generator to speed up the computation of kP. Suppose that $\{v_1, v_2\}$ is a GLV generator. Since v_1, v_2 are linearly independent over $Q \times Q$, they span $Q \times Q$. Therefore we have

$$(k, 0) = \beta_1 v_1 + \beta_2 v_2,$$

for some $\beta_1, \beta_2 \in Q$. Let b_1, b_2 be the nearest integers to β_1, β_2, respectively. Finally, set

$$\begin{aligned} x = (k_1, k_2) &= (k, 0) - (b_1 v_1 + b_2 v_2) \\ &= (k, 0) - (\beta_1 v_1 + \beta_2 v_2) + (\beta_1 v_1 + \beta_2 v_2) - (b_1 v_1 + b_2 v_2) \\ &= (\beta_1 - b_1)v_1 + (\beta_2 - b_2)v_2. \end{aligned}$$

Then we have $f(x) = k \pmod{n}$ and $\|x\| \leq \frac{1}{2}(\|v_1\| + \|v_2\|)$. Since $\{v_1, v_2\}$ is a GLV generator, each component of v_1 and v_2 is bounded by $\sqrt{n}$ and we have $-\sqrt{n} < k_1, k_2 < \sqrt{n}$. Thus we see that one can always decompose $k = k_1 + k_2\lambda$ (mod n) with $-\sqrt{n} < k_1, k_2 < \sqrt{n}$ from any GLV generator $\{v_1, v_2\}$. Hence kP can be calculated by $k_1 P + k_2\phi(P)$ using the windowed simultaneous multiple point multiplication method for P and $\phi(P)$ and the efficiency improvement is roughly 50% to the general scalar multiplication method for the currently recommended key sizes [4].

2.2   A Method to Find a GLV Generator by Gallant et $al.$

Gallant et $al.$ suggested an algorithm of finding a GLV generator using extended Euclidean algorithm. In the procedure of extended Euclidean algorithm for n and λ, we have a sequence of equations,

$$s_i n + t_i \lambda = r_i, \quad i = 0, 1, 2, \cdots, \tag{2}$$

where $s_0 = 1$, $s_1 = 0$, $t_0 = 0$, $t_1 = 1$, $r_0 = n$, $r_1 = \lambda$ and s_i, t_i, r_i have the following properties,

$$\begin{aligned}
r_i > r_{i+1} \geq 0, & \quad i \geq 0, \\
|s_i| < |s_{i+1}|, & \quad i \geq 1, \\
|t_i| < |t_{i+1}|, & \quad i \geq 0, \\
r_{i-1}|t_i| + r_i|t_{i-1}| = n, & \quad i \geq 1.
\end{aligned}$$

Let m be the greatest index such that $r_m \geq \sqrt{n}$. Set $v_1 = (r_{m+1}, -t_{m+1})$ and take v_2 to be the shorter of $(r_m, -t_m)$ and $(r_{m+2}, -t_{m+2})$. From the above properties, it can be easily checked that each component of v_1 is less than $\sqrt{n}$. If each component of v_2 is also bounded by $\sqrt{n}$, then $\{v_1, v_2\}$ is a GLV generator. But Gallant *et al.* expected heuristically that v_2 would be also short without any proof. In addition, some cases could also occur so that there do not exist two linearly independent short vectors. Hence the method proposed by Gallant *et al.* only suggests a possible way of finding a GLV generator. For instance,

$$n = 85093, \quad \sqrt{n} \approx 291.707, \quad \lambda = 33206.$$

All solutions of the equation $f(i, j) = 0$, $|i| < \sqrt{n}, |j| < \sqrt{n}$ are

$$\pm(252, 246), \pm(210, 205), \pm(168, 164), \pm(126, 123), \pm(84, 82), \pm(42, 41), (0, 0).$$

Note that all of them are generated by one vector $(42, 41)$ over the field Q and v_2 does not exist under the assumption that each component of v_2 is bounded by $\sqrt{n}$.

In the next section, we shall present a necessary condition for the existence of a GLV generator and propose an algorithm to find the second vector v_2 whose components are bounded by $\sqrt{n}$ if it exists and compare with Gallant *et al.*'s algorithm.

3   Algorithm

3.1   A Necessary Condition for the Existence of a GLV Generator

As we've seen above, Gallant *et al.*'s method is not a complete solution of finding a GLV generator even though their method always gives the first small vector $v_1 = (r, t)$. In this subsection, we state and prove a necessary condition for the existence of a GLV generator.

Assume that $v_1 = (r, t)$ and $v_2 = (u, v)$ are two linearly independent integer vectors in the kernel of f such that $-\sqrt{n} < r, t, u, v < \sqrt{n}$. Then we have

$$r + t\lambda = sn, \quad u + v\lambda = wn, \tag{3}$$

for some $s, w \in Z$. By multiplying the first and the second equations in (3) by u and r, respectively, we get

$$(tu - rv)\lambda = (su - rw)n. \tag{4}$$

Similarly, we have

$$rv - tu = (sv - tw)n. \tag{5}$$

Note that $|tu - rv| < 2n$. If $tu - rv = 0$, (r,t) and (u,v) are linearly dependent. Thus $tu - rv = -n, n$ since n divides $tu - rv$. From (5) we have

$$sv - tw = -1, 1. \tag{6}$$

Therefore we conclude that t is relatively prime to s and v is also relatively prime to w. We shall state and prove the following Lemmas.

Lemma 1 *Let n be prime and $\lambda \in [1, n-1]$. Assume that $v_1 = (r,t)$, $v_2 = (u,v) \in kerf$ and $-\sqrt{n} < r,t,u,v < \sqrt{n}$. If v_1, v_2 are linearly independent, then r is relatively prime to t and u is relatively prime to v.*

Proof : Since $v_1, v_2 \in kerf$, we have $s, w \in Z$ which satisfy (3). Assume that the greatest common divisor of r and t is $\alpha > 1$. Then α becomes a common divisor of s and t from (3) since n is prime and this contradicts to (6). This completes the proof.   □

Lemma 1 shows a necessary condition for the existence of a GLV generator. If $(r,t) \in kerf$, $\gcd(r,t) \neq 1$ and $|r| < \sqrt{n}, |t| < \sqrt{n}$, then the second vector $v_2 = (u,v)$, $|u| < \sqrt{n}, |v| < \sqrt{n}$ never exists. In fact, Lemma 1 itself shows that if $\gcd(r,t) \neq 1$, there is no GLV generator that contains the vector (r,t).

Lemma 2 *Let n be prime and $\lambda \in [1, n-1]$. If there is a vector $v = (r,t)$ in the kernel of f such that $\gcd(r,t) \neq 1$ and $-\sqrt{n} < r,t < \sqrt{n}$, then there exists no GLV generator.*

Proof : Suppose that $\{v_1, v_2\}$ is a GLV generator. It is easy to see that either $\{v, v_1\}$ or $\{v, v_2\}$ is a GLV generator containing v. This contradicts to Lemma 1. Therefore, there exists no GLV generator from Lemma 1.   □

Suppose that $v = (r,t)$ is in the kernel of f and $-\frac{1}{2}\sqrt{n} < r,t < \frac{1}{2}\sqrt{n}$. Then $2v = (2r, 2t)$ is also contained in the kernel of f. Therefore, from Lemma 2, we know that at least one component of each vector in a GLV generator, say a, should satisfy either $\frac{1}{2}\sqrt{n} < a < \sqrt{n}$ or $-\sqrt{n} < a < -\frac{1}{2}\sqrt{n}$.

3.2   A Proposed Algorithm to Find a GLV Generator

Using the method proposed by Gallant *et al.* described in subsection 2.2, one can always get the first vector v_1 where each component of v_1 is bounded by $\sqrt{n}$. Now we present an algorithm of finding the second short vector v_2 after one gets the first vector v_1 if there is any such v_2.

Suppose we have the first vector $v_1 = (r_{m+1}, -t_{m+1})$ in the kernel of f as in Gallant *et al.*'s algorithm. We know that $|r_{m+1}|, |t_{m+1}|$ are already less than $\sqrt{n}$.

Finding v_2. Let $v_2 = (u, v)$ be the second vector so that $\{v_1, v_2\}$ is a GLV generator. Suppose $v_1 = (r, t), v_2 = (u, v)$ satisfy the equation (3) for some $s, w \in Z$. From the equation (6), we know that s is relatively prime to $-t$. We apply the extended Euclidean algorithm to find the greatest common divisor of s and $-t$. Then the algorithm returns v' and w' which satisfy

$$sv' - tw' = 1. \tag{7}$$

In general, every integer vector (v, w) which satisfies $sv - tw = 1$ can be represented by $(v' + \alpha t, w' + \alpha s), \alpha \in Z$. Our purpose is to find a suitable α. Set

$$v = v' + \alpha t, \qquad w = w' + \alpha s.$$

Since $|v| < \sqrt{n}$ and $t = -t_{m+1} \neq 0$, we have

$$-\frac{v'}{t} - \frac{\sqrt{n}}{t} < \alpha < -\frac{v'}{t} + \frac{\sqrt{n}}{t}, \quad t > 0, \tag{8}$$

$$-\frac{v'}{t} + \frac{\sqrt{n}}{t} < \alpha < -\frac{v'}{t} - \frac{\sqrt{n}}{t}, \quad t < 0.$$

Note that $u = wn - v\lambda$ and $r = r_{m+1} > 0$, then we also have

$$\frac{v'\lambda - w'n}{r} - \frac{\sqrt{n}}{r} < \alpha < \frac{v'\lambda - w'n}{r} + \frac{\sqrt{n}}{r}. \tag{9}$$

Therefore α has to be an integer in the intersection of (8) and (9). From Lemma 2, in order to seek α for the second vector v_2 of a GLV generator, it is sufficient to test only four integers at most since one of $|r|, |t|$ is greater than $\frac{1}{2}\sqrt{n}$. Now we give our algorithm of finding the second vector $v_2 = (u, v)$.

Algorithm 1 *Find a GLV generator* $v_1 = (r, t), v_2 = (u, v)$, *for given* n *and* λ *as above*

Input: n, λ
Output: v_1, v_2

Step 1. *Compute* $v_1 = (r_{m+1}, -t_{m+1})$ *such that* $s_{m+1}n + t_{m+1}\lambda = r_{m+1}$ *and* $|r_{m+1}|, |t_{m+1}| < \sqrt{n}$ *using the extended Euclidean algorithm to find the greatest common divisor of* n *and* λ. *(Gallant et al.'s algorithm)*
Step 2. *Check if each components of either* $(r_m, -t_m)$ *or* $(r_{m+2}, -t_{m+2})$ *is bounded by* $\sqrt{n}$, *stop and set the shorter of* $(r_m, -t_m)$ *and* $(r_{m+2}, -t_{m+2})$ *as the second vector* v_2. *Otherwise, go to step 3.*
Step 3. *Find any* v' *and* w' *such that*

$$s_{m+1}v' - t_{m+1}w' = 1.$$

For example, v' *and* w' *are obtained from the extended Euclidean algorithm since* s_{m+1} *is relatively prime to* $-t_{m+1}$.

Step 4. *Compute*

$$I_{11} = -\frac{v'}{t} - \frac{\sqrt{n}}{t}, \qquad I_{12} = -\frac{v'}{t} + \frac{\sqrt{n}}{t}.$$

Step 5. *Let $I_1 = [I_{11}, I_{12}]$, if $t > 0$, and $I_1 = [I_{12}, I_{11}]$ if $t < 0$.*
Step 6. *Compute*

$$I_{21} = \frac{v'\lambda - w'n}{r} - \frac{\sqrt{n}}{r}, \qquad I_{22} = \frac{v'\lambda - w'n}{r} + \frac{\sqrt{n}}{r}.$$

Step 7. *Let $I_2 = [I_{21}, I_{22}]$.*
Step 8. *Find all integers in the intersection of I_1 and I_2 and define them by α. Note that the number of α's is at most 4. If there does not exist any such integer, stop.*
Step 9. *Set $v_2 = (u, v)$, where*

$$u = w'n - v'\lambda + \alpha r, \qquad v = v' + \alpha t.$$

One can easily verify that $v_2 = (u, v)$ is in $ker\, f$ and $|u|, |v| < \sqrt{n}$. Therefore $\{v_1, v_2\}$ is a GLV generator.

3.3   Comparison with the Method of Gallant *et al.*

To compare our algorithm with Gallant *et al.*'s algorithm, consider the following example,

$$n = 1319399, \quad \lambda = 344894, \quad \sqrt{n} \approx 1148.65.$$

We have from the extended Euclidean algorithm,

$$(r_m, -t_m) = (1812, -329), \quad (r_{m+1}, -t_{m+1}) = (871, 570),$$
$$(r_{m+2}, -t_{m+2}) = (70, -1469).$$

Therefore the two vectors from Gallant *et al.*'s algorithms are $v_1 = (871, 570)$ and $v_2 = (70, -1469)$. To proceed our algorithm, let $\tilde{v}_1 = (r, t) = (871, 570)$. We have $v' = -241$, $w' = -63$ since $s_{m+1} = (r_{m+1} - t_{m+1}\lambda)/n = 149$ and $-t_{m+1} = 570$. Then

$$I_{11} \approx -1.59237, I_{12} \approx 2.43798, \quad I_{21} \approx 1.76159, I_{22} \approx 4.39914.$$

The integer intersection of I_1 and I_2 is $\{2\}$. Therefore we have $\tilde{v}_2 = (-941, 899)$ from Step 9. We note that each component of $\tilde{v}_2$ in our algorithm is bounded by $\sqrt{n}$ while the second component of vector v_2 from Gallant *et al.*'s algorithm exceeds $\sqrt{n}$.

From the above example, we see that Gallant *et al.*'s algorithm does not give a GLV generator even if there is a GLV generator. Since our proposed algorithm checks all the possibility of the existence of a GLV generator with the first vector v_1, we never miss a GLV generator if there is any. Our proposed algorithm needs only a few more real number arithmetic after one gets the first vector v_1.

4   Conclusion

We presented an algorithm to facilitate the use of Gallant *et al.*'s idea to speed up the scalar multiplication of elliptic curves over a prime field in a more concrete way. Their method gives the desired efficiency if there is a GLV generator which we named in this paper. The efficiency improvement of their method is still good if one can guarantee that each component of the two linearly independent vectors is bounded by a small constant multiple of $\sqrt{n}$, i.e., $c\sqrt{n}$ when c is small. Analyzing cases with $c > 1$ is more complicated than the case with $c = 1$ and can be an further interesting work.

Acknowledgment

We appreciate the anonymous referees of the SAC 2002 for their comments and suggestions.

References

1. D. Bailey and C. Paar : *'Optimal extention fields for fast arithmetic in public-key algorithms'*, Advances in Cryptology-Crypto'98, Lecture Notes in Computer Science, Vol 1462, 1998, pp.472–485.
2. H. Cohen, A. Miyaji, and T. Ono : *'Efficient Elliptic Curve Exponentiation using Mixed Coordinates'*, Advances in Cryptology-Asiacrypt'98, Lecture Notes in Computer Science, Vol 1514, 1998, pp.51–65.
3. V. Miller : *'Use of Elliptic Curves in Cryptography'*, Advances in Cryptology-Crypto'85, Lecture Notes in Computer Science, Vol 263, 1986, pp.417–426.
4. R. Gallant, R. Lambert, and L. Vanstone : *'Faster Point Multiplication on Elliptic Curves with Efficient Endomorphism'*, Advances in Cryptology-Crypto'2001, Lecture Notes in Computer Science, Vol 2139, 2001, pp.190–201.
5. N. Koblitz : *'CM-curves with Good Cryptographic Properties'*, Advances in Cryptology-Crypto'91, 1992, 48, pp.279–287.
6. N. Koblitz : *'Elliptic Curve Cryptosystems'*, Mathematics of Computation, 1987, 48, pp.203–209.
7. C. Lim and P. Lee : *'More Flexible Exponentiation with Precomputation'*, Advances in Cryptology-Crypto'94, Lecture Notes in Computer Science, Vol 839, 1994, pp.95–107.
8. J. Solinas : *'An Improved Algorithm for Arithmetic on a Family of Elliptic Curves'*, Advances in Cryptology-Crypto'97, Lecture Notes in Computer Science, Vol 1294, 1997, pp.357–371.
9. J. Solinas : *'Efficient Arithmetic on Koblitz Curves'*, Design, Codes and Crytography, 2000, 19, pp.195–249.
10. V. Müller : *'Fast Multiplication on Elliptic Curves over small fields of charactersitic two'*, J. of Cryptology, 1998, 11, pp.219–234.

Analysis of the Gallant-Lambert-Vanstone Method Based on Efficient Endomorphisms: Elliptic and Hyperelliptic Curves

Francesco Sica[*], Mathieu Ciet[*], and Jean-Jacques Quisquater

UCL Crypto Group
Place du Levant, 3. B-1348 Louvain-la-Neuve. Belgium
{sica, ciet, jjq}@dice.ucl.ac.be - http://www.dice.ucl.ac.be/crypto

Abstract. In this work we analyse the GLV method of Gallant, Lambert and Vanstone (CRYPTO 2001) which uses a fast endomorphism Φ with minimal polynomial $X^2 + rX + s$ to compute any multiple kP of a point P of order n lying on an elliptic curve.

First we fill in a gap in the proof of the bound of the kernel $\mathcal{K}$ vectors of the reduction map $f: (i, j) \mapsto i + \lambda j \pmod{n}$. In particular, we prove the GLV decomposition with explicit constant

$$kP = k_1 P + k_2 \Phi(P), \quad \text{with } \max\{|k_1|, |k_2|\} \leq \sqrt{1 + |r| + s}\sqrt{n} \ .$$

Next we improve on this bound and give the best constant in the given examples for the quantity $\sup_{k,n} \max\{|k_1|, |k_2|\}/\sqrt{n}$. Independently Park, Jeong, Kim, and Lim (PKC 2002) have given similar but slightly weaker bounds.

Finally we provide the first explicit bounds for the GLV method generalised to hyperelliptic curves as described in Park, Jeong and Lim (EUROCRYPT 2002).

Keywords. *Elliptic curve cryptography, fast performance, efficiently-computable endomorphisms, algebraic number fields.*

1 Introduction

Since elliptic curves made their entrance into cryptography in 1985 [8,13], it has become of vital importance to secure the same performance on the elliptic cryptosystems as on the traditional asymmetric ones such as RSA. For this, a key step is to be able to compute a scalar multiple kP of an elliptic curve point P of

---

[*] The work described in this paper has been supported [in part] by the Commission of the European Communities through the IST Programme under Contract IST-1999-12324, http://www.cryptonessie.org/. The information in this document is provided as is, and no guarantee or warranty is given or implied that the information is fit for any particular purpose. The user thereof uses the information at its sole risk and liability. The views expressed are those of the authors and do not represent an official view/position of the NESSIE project (as a whole).

K. Nyberg and H. Heys (Eds.): SAC 2002, LNCS 2595, pp. 21–36, 2003.

large prime order n (see [1,12] for background on elliptic curve cryptography). Various methods have been devised to this end [6], most of them adopting a binary setting (elliptic curves E over finite fields of characteristic 2). A group of methods cleverly employs a distinguished endomorphism $\Phi \in \mathrm{End}(E)$ to split a large computation into a sequence of cheaper ones so that the overall computational cost is lowered [17].

Recently, Gallant, Lambert and Vanstone [5] used such a technique, which, contrary to previous ones, also applies to curves defined over large prime fields. Their method uses an efficiently computable endomorphism $\Phi \in \mathrm{End}(E)$ to rewrite kP as

$$kP = k_1 P + k_2 \Phi(P), \quad \text{with } \max\{|k_1|, |k_2|\} = O(\sqrt{n}) \ . \tag{1}$$

Their key point is an algorithm (henceforth called the GLV algorithm) which inputs integers n and $0 < \lambda < n$ and produces for any $k \pmod{n}$, two residues $k_1, k_2 \pmod{n}$ such that

$$k \equiv k_1 + \lambda k_2 \pmod{n} \ .$$

However they fail to provide an upper bound on $\max\{|k_1|, |k_2|\}$ but only give a heuristic estimate that this should be $O(\sqrt{n})$ (but again no estimation of the involved constant appears in their paper). An upper bound was first demonstrated in [15] using an apparently different method.

In this work we first supply a proof that the original GLV algorithm works by producing a required upper bound and then we give the value for $\sup_{k,n} \max\{|k_1|, |k_2|\}/\sqrt{n}$ in the case where n is the norm of an element of $\mathbb{Z}[\Phi]$, which is the case in the examples given in [5,15]. This allows us to show that the class of elliptic curves susceptible to the GLV speedup is exceptional.

At the conference, we became aware of another contribution to the GLV method [7] where a necessary condition is developed to insure that in (1) the constant in $O(\sqrt{n})$ is 1. An algorithm alternative to the GLV algorithm is then presented.

A way to improve the GLV algorithm would be to find a decomposition

$$kP = k_1 P + k_2 \Phi(P) + \cdots + k_d \Phi^{d-1}(P), \quad \text{with } \max_{1 \le i \le d} |k_i| = O(n^{1/d}) \ .$$

This is not possible in general using the GLV paradigm, since the powers Φ^i are independent (over $\mathbb{Z}$) only when $i < 2$. However, in [14], a class of Φ's for which such a decomposition exists is found. Nevertheless this does not apply to our analysis since it is supposed that the norm of Φ is not too small (compared to n), whereas in our work it is fixed (denoted by s below).

On the other hand the previous decomposition can be applied to the generalisation of the GLV algorithm to hyperelliptic curves of genus at least $d/2$ as described in [16]: in this context we provide an explicit upper bound, of the same nature as (1).

2   Bridging the Logical Gaps of the GLV Algorithm

In this part, we will briefly summarize the Gallant-Lambert-Vanstone (GLV for short) computation method [5]. Let E be an elliptic curve defined over a finite field $\mathbb{F}_q$ and P be a point of this curve with order n such that the cofactor $h = \#E(\mathbb{F}_q)/n$ is small, say $h \leq 4$. Let us consider Φ a non trivial endomorphism defined over $\mathbb{F}_q$ and $X^2 + rX + s$ its characteristic polynomial. In all the examples r and s are actually small fixed integers and q is varying in some family. By the Hasse bound, since n is large, $\Phi(P) = \lambda P$ for some $\lambda \in [0, n-1]$. Indeed, there is only one copy of $\mathbb{Z}/n$ inside $E(\mathbb{F}_q)$ and $\Phi(P)$ has also order dividing n. We can easily exclude the case where $\lambda = 0$ which is exceptional (for instance in the examples we have $n \nmid s$, by the Hasse bound). In all cases, λ is obtained as a root of $X^2 + rX + s$ modulo n.

A crucial role of the GLV method lies in the definition of the group homomorphism

$$f \colon \mathbb{Z} \times \mathbb{Z} \to \mathbb{Z}/n$$
$$(i, j) \mapsto i + \lambda j \pmod{n} \ .$$

Let $\mathcal{K} = \ker f$. It is clearly a sublattice of $\mathbb{Z} \times \mathbb{Z}$. Let v_1, v_2 be two linearly independent vectors of $\mathcal{K}$ satisfying $\max\{\,|\,v_1\,|\,,\,|\,v_2\,|\,\} < M$ for some $M > 0$, where $|\cdot|$ denotes any metric norm. Express

$$(k, 0) = \beta_1 v_1 + \beta_2 v_2 \ ,$$

where $\beta_i \in \mathbb{Q}$. Then round β_i to the nearest integer $b_i = \lfloor \beta_i \rceil = \lfloor \beta_i + 1/2 \rfloor$ and let $v = b_1 v_1 + b_2 v_2$. Note that $v \in \mathcal{K}$ and that $u \overset{\text{def}}{=} (k, 0) - v$ is short. Indeed by the triangle inequality we have that

$$|\,u\,| \leq \left|\, \frac{v_1 + v_2}{2} \,\right| < M \ .$$

If we set $(k_1, k_2) = u$, then we get $k = k_1 + k_2 \lambda$ or equivalently $kP = k_1 P + k_2 \Phi(P)$, with $|\,(k_1, k_2)\,| < M$. Thus it is essential in the GLV method that M be as small as possible, keeping in mind that by a simple counting argument we must have $M \geq \sqrt{n}/2$.

Gallant, Lambert and Vanstone then claim without proof that in fact $M \leq \Bbbk\sqrt{n}$, for some constant $\Bbbk$.[1]

We overcome this omission in the next section.

2.1   A Value for $\Bbbk$

Recall that the GLV algorithm makes use of the extended Euclidean algorithm applied to n, λ to produce a sequence of relations

$$s_i n + t_i \lambda = r_i, \quad \text{for } i = 0, 1, 2, \dots \ , \tag{2}$$

---

[1] They actually also assume $\Bbbk = 1$ which is true in their examples from Corollary 1, but cannot be true in general, by our analysis on the optimal bound.

where $|s_i| < |s_{i+1}|$ for $i \geq 1$, $|t_i| < |t_{i+1}|$ and $r_i > r_{i+1} \geq 0$ for $i \geq 0$. Also, we have (cf. [5, Lemma 1(iv)])

$$r_i|t_{i+1}| + r_{i+1}|t_i| = n \quad \text{for all } i \geq 0 . \tag{3}$$

The GLV algorithm defines the index m as the largest integer for which $r_m > \sqrt{n}$. Then (3) with $i = m$ gives that $|t_{m+1}| < \sqrt{n}$, so that the kernel vector $v_1 = (r_{m+1}, -t_{m+1})$ has rectangle norm[2] bounded by $\sqrt{n}$. The GLV algorithm then sets v_2 to be the shorter between $(r_m, -t_m)$ and $(r_{m+2}, -t_{m+2})$ but does not give any estimate on the size of v_2. In fact, Gallant, Lambert and Vanstone claim that

$$\min \left(|(r_m, -t_m)| , |(r_{m+2}, -t_{m+2})| \right) \leq \Bbbk\sqrt{n} ,$$

which is what we will now show, with an explicit value of $\Bbbk$.

Let $\lambda, \mu \in [1, n-1]$ be the zeros of $X^2 + rX + s \pmod{n}$. For any $(x, y) \in \mathcal{K} - \{(0,0)\}$, we have

$$0 \equiv (x + \lambda y)(x + \mu y) \equiv x^2 - rxy + sy^2 \pmod{n} ,$$

hence since $X^2 + rX + s$ is irreducible in $\mathbb{Z}[X]$ we must have $x^2 - rxy + sy^2 \geq n$. This certainly implies that

$$\max(|x|, |y|) \geq \sqrt{\frac{n}{1 + |r| + s}} .$$

In particular, $|(r_{m+1}, -t_{m+1})| \geq \sqrt{n}/\sqrt{1 + |r| + s}$.

CASE 1: $|t_{m+1}| \geq \sqrt{n}/\sqrt{1 + |r| + s}$. Then (3) with $i = m$ implies that $r_m < \sqrt{1 + |r| + s}\sqrt{n}$, hence

$$|(r_m, -t_m)| < \sqrt{1 + |r| + s}\sqrt{n} . \tag{4}$$

CASE 2: $r_{m+1} \geq \sqrt{n}/\sqrt{1 + |r| + s}$. The same (3) with $i = m+1$ implies that $|t_{m+2}| < \sqrt{1 + |r| + s}\sqrt{n}$, hence

$$|(r_{m+2}, -t_{m+2})| < \sqrt{1 + |r| + s}\sqrt{n} . \tag{5}$$

We have thus proved the following

Theorem 1. *An admissible value for $\Bbbk$ is*

$$\Bbbk = \sqrt{1 + |r| + s} .$$

In particular any multiple kP can be decomposed as $kP = k_1P + k_2\Phi(P)$ with $\max\{|k_1|, |k_2|\} < \sqrt{1 + |r| + s}\sqrt{n}$.

We next revisit the GLV map f, following an idea already present in [15]. This will lead us to an improvement for $\Bbbk$ and in some instances, to the best possible constant.

---

[2] The rectangle norm of (x, y) is by definition $\max(|x|, |y|)$. We denote it by $|(x, y)|$.

3   An Algebraic Interpretation of the GLV Method

Let Φ be a non trivial endomorphism defined over $\mathbb{F}_q$, as in the GLV method, satisfying $\Phi^2 + r\Phi + s = 0$.

Consider the sequence of group homomorphisms:

$$\mathbb{Z} \times \mathbb{Z} \xrightarrow[\varphi]{\cong} \mathbb{Z}[\Phi] \xrightarrow[\text{mod } \mathfrak{n} \cap \mathbb{Z}[\Phi]]{\text{reduction}} \mathbb{Z}/n$$

$$(i,j) \longmapsto i + j\Phi \longmapsto i + \lambda j \pmod{n} .$$

Here $\mathfrak{n}$ is a specific prime lying above n in the quadratic field $\mathbb{Q}(\Phi)$ (remember that n splits in $\mathbb{Q}(\Phi)$). The composition of the two homomorphisms gives (for the appropriate $\mathfrak{n}$) the Gallant-Lambert-Vanstone map $f : (i,j) \mapsto i + \lambda j \pmod{n}$. We henceforth assume we made this choice of $\mathfrak{n}$.

Note that $\mathbb{Z}[\Phi]$ is actually a normed ring with norm

$$N_{\mathbb{Z}[\Phi]/\mathbb{Z}}(i + j\Phi) = i^2 + sj^2 - rij .$$

When embedding $\mathbb{Z}[\Phi]$ into $\mathbb{C}$, this norm actually becomes the square of the usual complex Euclidean norm. Therefore under the (group) isomorphism φ, we can define the *number theoretic norm* $\langle\langle(i,j)\rangle\rangle$ of $(i,j) \in \mathbb{Z} \times \mathbb{Z}$ to be

$$\langle\langle(i,j)\rangle\rangle = \sqrt{i^2 + sj^2 - rij} ,$$

different from (but equivalent to) the *rectangle norm* on $\mathbb{Z} \times \mathbb{Z}$, denoted by

$$|(i,j)| = \max(|i|, |j|) .$$

We will denote v_1 and v_2 two linearly independent vectors in the kernel $\mathcal{K}$ of the map f. We also require that v_1 and v_2 have rectangle norm $O(\sqrt{n})$.

We say a vector $v \in \mathbb{Z} \times \mathbb{Z}$ is the *shortest* if it has the smallest rectangle norm and that it is the *smallest* when it has the smallest number theoretic norm.

4   Examples

We quote here four examples, dubbed E_1, E_2, E_3 and E_4, appearing already in [5,15]. Note that in all these examples, $\mathbb{Z}[\Phi]$ is the maximal order and it is principal.

Example 1. Let $p \equiv 1 \pmod 4$ be a prime. Define an elliptic curve E_1 over $\mathbb{F}_p$ by

$$y^2 = x^3 + ax .$$

If β is an element of order 4, then the map Φ defined in the affine plane by

$$\Phi(x,y) = (-x, \beta y) ,$$

is an endomorphism of E_1 defined over $\mathbb{F}_p$ with $\mathbb{Z}[\Phi] = \mathbb{Z}[\sqrt{-1}]$. Moreover Φ satisfies the equation

$$\Phi^2 + 1 = 0 .$$

Example 2. Let $p \equiv 1 \pmod 3$ be a prime. Define an elliptic curve E_2 over $\mathbb{F}_p$ by

$$y^2 = x^3 + b \ .$$

If γ is an element of order 3, then the map Φ defined in the affine plane by

$$\Phi(x, y) = (\gamma x, y) \ ,$$

is an endomorphism of E_2 defined over $\mathbb{F}_p$ with $\mathbb{Z}[\Phi] = \mathbb{Z}[\frac{1+\sqrt{-3}}{2}]$. Moreover Φ satisfies the equation

$$\Phi^2 + \Phi + 1 = 0 \ .$$

Example 3. Let $p > 3$ be a prime such that -7 is a quadratic residue modulo p. Define an elliptic curve E_3 over $\mathbb{F}_p$ by

$$y^2 = x^3 - \frac{3}{4}x^2 - 2x - 1 \ .$$

If $\xi = (1 + \sqrt{-7})/2$ and $a = (\xi - 3)/4$, then the map Φ defined in the affine plane by

$$\Phi(x, y) = \left(\frac{x^2 - \xi}{\xi^2 (x - a)}, \frac{y(x^2 - 2ax + \xi)}{\xi^3 (x - a)^2} \right) \ ,$$

is an endomorphism of E_3 defined over $\mathbb{F}_p$ with $\mathbb{Z}[\Phi] = \mathbb{Z}[\frac{1+\sqrt{-7}}{2}]$. Moreover Φ satisfies the equation

$$\Phi^2 - \Phi + 2 = 0 \ .$$

Example 4. Let $p > 3$ be a prime such that -2 is a quadratic residue modulo p. Define an elliptic curve E_4 over $\mathbb{F}_p$ by

$$y^2 = 4x^3 - 30x - 28 \ .$$

The map Φ defined in the affine plane by

$$\Phi(x, y) = \left(-\frac{2x^2 + 4x + 9}{4(x + 2)}, -\frac{2x^2 + 8x - 1}{4\sqrt{-2}(x + 2)^2} \right) \ ,$$

is an endomorphism of E_4 defined over $\mathbb{F}_p$ with $\mathbb{Z}[\Phi] = \mathbb{Z}[\sqrt{-2}]$. Moreover Φ satisfies the equation

$$\Phi^2 + 2 = 0 \ .$$

In the next section, we will investigate an alternative way to construct the GLV vectors v_1 and v_2. We will then give an optimal result on smallest decompositions.

5   The GLV Method Revisited

Let $\Delta = r^2 - 4s < 0$ be the discriminant of the minimal polynomial of Φ and $\epsilon_r = (1 - (-1)^r)/2$. In order to find v_1 and v_2, the most natural method to use is Gaussian reduction,[3] which gives an optimal reduced basis v_1 and v_2 meaning:

$$\langle v_1 \rangle = \min_{v \in \mathcal{K} - \{(0,0)\}} \langle v \rangle \leq \frac{\sqrt{3|\Delta|}}{2} \sqrt{n} \ ,$$

$$\langle v_2 \rangle = \min_{v \in \mathcal{K} - \{\mathbb{Z} v_1\}} \langle v \rangle \leq \frac{\sqrt{\epsilon_r - \Delta}}{2} \langle v_1 \rangle \ .$$

The first inequality arises from Theorem 1, while the second comes from taking the norm of $\varphi(v_1)\Phi'$, with $\Phi' = \Phi - [\Re\Phi] = (\epsilon_r + \sqrt{\Delta})/2 \in \mathbb{Z}[\Phi]$.

Note that when n is the norm of an $element$ of $\mathbb{Z}[\Phi]$, one has

$$\langle v_1 \rangle = \sqrt{n} \qquad \text{and} \qquad \varphi(v_2) = \varphi(v_1)\Phi' \Longrightarrow \langle v_2 \rangle = \frac{\sqrt{\epsilon_r - \Delta}}{2} \sqrt{n} \ .$$

This is the case in the examples of the preceding section, because $\mathbb{Z}[\Phi]$ is maximal and principal (we already know that n is the norm of the ideal $\mathfrak{n}$). One can also easily prove the following geometric lemma.

Lemma 1. *The rectangle and number theoretic norms are related by the following optimal inequality: for any vector $u \in \mathbb{Z} \times \mathbb{Z}$ one has*

$$|u| \leq \frac{2\sqrt{s}}{\sqrt{|\Delta|}} \langle u \rangle \ .$$

Hence we deduce

Theorem 2. *Assume n is the norm of an element of $\mathbb{Z}[\Phi]$ then one can take*

$$\Bbbk = \frac{\sqrt{s}\sqrt{\epsilon_r - \Delta}}{\sqrt{|\Delta|}} \ .$$

This is already better than the first bound (Theorem 1) on the examples, although on the same assumptions one can improve on this.

---

[3] The standard Gaussian algorithm is sufficient here. It is deterministic and runs in average <u>constant</u> time, better than the Euclidean algorithm and with same order of magnitude for the worst case. We refer to [3] for all these facts and for the description of the algorithm. However in the examples we do not need this algorithm as Cornacchia's algorithm [2, Section 1.5.2] to find ν such that $N_{\mathbb{Z}[\Phi]/\mathbb{Z}}(\nu) = n$ gives us automatically $(\nu, \nu\Phi)$ as a reduced basis of $\mathcal{K}$ (see Section 7).

6   An Optimal Improvement

The idea, which already appears in [15], consists in working directly in the (Euclidean) space $\mathbb{C}$ where we have embedded $\mathbb{Z}[\Phi]$. We will denote $\mathcal{T}$ the triangle whose vertices are 0, 1 and Φ' and $\mathcal{P}$ the fundamental parallelogram with vertices 0, 1, Φ' and $\Phi' + 1$. The heart of our main result lies in the following lemma.

Lemma 2. *Let ABC be any triangle in $\mathbb{R}^2$ with vertices A, B and C. For any two points P, P', let PP' denote their distance. Let O be any point inside the closure of ABC maximising*

$$f(P) = \min\{PA, PB, PC\} \ ,$$

so that $R \overset{\text{def}}{=} f(O) = \max\limits_{P \in \overline{ABC}} f(P)$. In other terms, O is the farthest point from any vertex. Then

1. *if ABC is acutangle, $O = \mathcal{O}$ is the centre of the circumscribed circle and $R = r$ is its radius,*
2. *if $\widehat{BAC}$ (the angle abutting to A) has measure greater than $\pi/2$ radians, so that $[BC]$ is the largest side of the triangle, supposing that $[AC]$ is the smallest side, then O is obtained as the intersection of the axis of $[AB]$ with $[BC]$ (so that $OA = OB$) and $R = AB/(2\cos\widehat{CBA})$.*

Proof. Let $\mathcal{O}$ be the center of the circumscribed circle.

1. (See Figure 1). In the first case, since the triangle is acutangle, $\mathcal{O} \in \overline{ABC}$. Therefore ABC can be partitioned into three isosceles subtriangles $\mathcal{O}AB$, $\mathcal{O}BC$ and $\mathcal{O}CA$. Also, each of these three triangles can be subdivided into two symmetric right triangles, for instance, $\mathcal{O}CA$ is made up of $\mathcal{O}CB'$ and $\mathcal{O}B'A$, where B' is the midpoint of the segment $[AC]$ and similarly for the other two subtriangles.
   Suppose by absurd $O \neq \mathcal{O}$. Without loss of generality, we can suppose $O \in \overline{OB'A}$. Since the triangle is right-angled, $\mathcal{O}A$ is its diameter, which is unique,[4] therefore $OA < \mathcal{O}A = f(\mathcal{O})$. Hence $f(O) < f(\mathcal{O})$, contradicting the definition of O and $O = \mathcal{O}$.
2. (See Figure 2). In this case $\mathcal{O} \notin \overline{ABC}$, so we have to look for another point O. Let O be the point constructed as in the statement of the lemma, and let O' be the intersection of the axis of $[AC]$ with $[BC]$. Then ABC is partitioned into ABO, AOO' and $AO'C$, the first and the last being isosceles, since $AO = BO$ and $AO' = CO'$. We claim that $AB \geq AC$ is equivalent to $AO \geq AO'$, with equality holding simultaneously. By an argument of symmetry, it suffices to show that $AB > AC$ implies $AO > AO'$. We have

---

[4] The diameter of a set Σ is by definition $\sup\limits_{P,P'\ \Sigma} PP'$. We will say the diameter is unique if the sup is attained for exactly one pair $\{P, P'\}$.

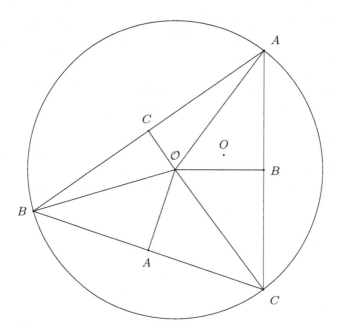

Fig. 1. Case 1 of Lemma 2

$$\begin{cases} BO &= \dfrac{AB}{2\cos\widehat{CBA}} \ , \\[2mm] CO' &= \dfrac{AC}{2\cos\widehat{ACB}} \ . \end{cases} \tag{6}$$

Indeed working in the right-angled triangle $OC'B$, where C' is the midpoint of $[AB]$, we have that $\cos\widehat{CBA} = BC'/BO = AB/(2BO)$ and similarly for the other equality. Notice that the well-known fact

$$\sin\widehat{CBA}/AC = \sin\widehat{ACB}/AB \tag{7}$$

together with $AB > AC$ implies that $\widehat{CBA} < \widehat{ACB}$ (we are measuring angles in $[0, \pi]$). Hence $\widehat{CBA} < \pi/4$. Using (7) in (6) we get

$$\begin{cases} BO\dfrac{AC}{\sin\widehat{CBA}} &= \dfrac{AB\,AC}{2\cos\widehat{CBA}\sin\widehat{CBA}} = \dfrac{AB\,AC}{\sin 2\widehat{CBA}} \ , \\[3mm] CO'\dfrac{AB}{\sin\widehat{ACB}} &= \dfrac{AC\,AB}{2\cos\widehat{ACB}\sin\widehat{ACB}} = \dfrac{AB\,AC}{\sin 2\widehat{ACB}} \ . \end{cases}$$

Hence

$$\frac{AO}{AO'} = \frac{\sin 2\widehat{ACB}}{\sin 2\widehat{CBA}} \ .$$

Notice that $\widehat{CBA} = x - \widehat{ACB}$ for some $0 < x < \pi/2$. Hence $2\widehat{CBA} = 2x - 2\widehat{ACB} = \pi - \theta$ with $\theta > 2\widehat{ACB}$. Finally, we have that $\sin 2\widehat{CBA} = \sin \theta < \sin 2\widehat{ACB}$, because $2\widehat{CBA} < 2\widehat{ACB} < \theta$ and $2\widehat{CBA} < \pi/2$. This proves the claim.

Any point $\Omega \neq O$ in $\overline{ABO}$ satisfies $\min\{\Omega A, \Omega B\} < OA = OB$ by the same kind of arguments (splitting into two right-angled triangles) used in Case 1. In that case, $f(\Omega) < f(O)$.

Similarly if $\Omega \in \overline{AOO'}$, then by the claim we have $A\Omega < AO$, except when $\Omega = O'$ and $AO = AO'$. Hence in this case $f(\Omega) < f(O)$ except when $AB = AC$ and $\Omega = O'$.

The remaining case $\Omega \in \overline{AO'C}$ can be treated like the case $\Omega \in \overline{ABO}$ and in this case $f(\Omega) < f(O') \leq f(O)$. □

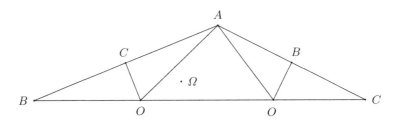

Fig. 2. Case 2 of Lemma 2

This lemma shows that any point lying inside $\mathcal{T}$ (or $\mathcal{P}$) will be at a distance $\leq R$ from one of the vertices, and that this R is optimal. Determining it is easy and we write here the final result.

$$
R = \begin{cases} \dfrac{\sqrt{6 - \Delta - \Delta^{-1}}}{4}, & \text{if } r \text{ is odd,} \\[2ex] \dfrac{\sqrt{4 - \Delta}}{4}, & \text{if } r \text{ is even.} \end{cases} \tag{8}
$$

Thus we get

Theorem 3. *In the above-defined notations, given a vector $(k, 0) \in \mathbb{Z} \times \mathbb{Z}$, there exists a vector $v = b_1 v_1 + b_2 v_2 \in \mathcal{K}$ such that the vector $u \stackrel{\text{def}}{=} (k, 0) - v$ has number theoretic norm bounded by*

$$
\langle u \rangle \leq R\sqrt{n} ,
$$

with R given by (8). Such a vector v is obtained as the closest vertex of the copy of $\varphi^{-1}(\nu \mathcal{P})$ (or $\varphi^{-1}(\nu \mathcal{T})$) inside which $(k, 0)$ lies.

Hence the main difference with previous methods is that b_i is not defined as $\lfloor \beta_i \rceil$ anymore when r is odd, but rather as either $\lfloor \beta_i \rfloor$ or $\lceil \beta_i \rceil$. In general one has to test three possible values but for each endomorphism ring there are shortcuts (conditions) that can be checked, so to avoid this probabilistic check. For even values of r Theorem 3 gives the same bound as [15].

Applying Lemma 1, one immediately gets

Theorem 4. *Assume n is the norm of an element of $\mathbb{Z}[\Phi]$ then one can take*

$$\Bbbk = \frac{2\sqrt{s}R}{\sqrt{|\Delta|}} \quad,$$

where R is given by (8). Furthermore, this constant cannot be improved.

Applying this theorem to Examples E_1 to E_4 we get:

Corollary 1. *In Examples E_1 to E_4, the optimal bounds for $|k_1|, |k_2|$ are:*

$$\max\{|k_1|, |k_2|\} \leq \begin{cases} \sqrt{n}/\sqrt{2}, & \text{for } E_1, \\ \sqrt{7\,n}/3, & \text{for } E_2, \\ \sqrt{46\,n}/7, & \text{for } E_3, \\ \sqrt{3\,n}/2, & \text{for } E_4. \end{cases}$$

This result ought to be compared to [15], where we improve $\Bbbk$ in the case when $r \neq 0$, that is in Examples 2 and 3.

7   On the Optimality of Theorems 3 and 4

We now discuss the optimality of this method. The first step is to show that the inequality in Theorem 3 is best possible, that is we have

$$R = \sup_{k,n} \langle (k_1, k_2) \rangle / \sqrt{n} \quad. \tag{9}$$

We begin with a number theoretic lemma.

Lemma 3. *In the notations of Section 3 the index $(\mathbb{Z} \times \mathbb{Z} : \mathcal{K})$ of $\mathcal{K}$ inside $\mathbb{Z} \times \mathbb{Z}$ is n. Furthermore, under the assumption that n is the norm of an element $\nu \in \mathbb{Z}[\Phi]$, we have $\mathcal{K} = \varphi^{-1}(\nu \mathbb{Z}[\Phi])$. In particular, a reduced fundamental domain of $\mathcal{K}$ is $\varphi^{-1}(\nu \mathcal{P})$, where $\mathcal{P}$ is the fundamental parallelogram described at the beginning of the last section.*

Proof. By the third isomorphism theorem of algebra and the group isomorphism given by φ we have

$$(\mathbb{Z} \times \mathbb{Z})/\mathcal{K} \cong \mathbb{Z}[\Phi]/(\mathfrak{n} \cap \mathbb{Z}[\Phi]) \cong (\mathbb{Z}[\Phi] + \mathfrak{n})/\mathfrak{n} \quad. \tag{10}$$

Since $\mathbb{Z}[\Phi] + \mathfrak{n}$ is contained in the ring of integers $\mathfrak{I}$ of $\mathbb{Q}(\Phi)$, the right-most quotient group is a subgroup of $\mathfrak{I}/\mathfrak{n} \cong \mathbb{Z}/n$. Hence its cardinality is 1 or n. But if it were 1, then $\mathbb{Z}[\Phi] \subset \mathfrak{n}$, hence $1 \in \mathfrak{n}$ which is impossible. The cardinality must therefore be n and the same is true for the left-most group, whose cardinality is $(\mathbb{Z} \times \mathbb{Z} \colon \mathcal{K})$. Notice that

$$\mathbb{Z}[\Phi] \supset \mathfrak{n} \cap \mathbb{Z}[\Phi] \supset \nu\mathbb{Z}[\Phi] \tag{11a}$$

or equivalently

$$\mathbb{Z} \times \mathbb{Z} \supset \mathcal{K} \supset \varphi^{-1}\bigl(\nu\mathbb{Z}[\Phi]\bigr) . \tag{11b}$$

Therefore, in order to prove the second statement, we have to prove that the right-most inclusions in Equations (11) are actually equalities, and it suffices to do so for the first one.

In view of (10), it suffice to prove $\bigl(\mathbb{Z}[\Phi] \colon \nu\mathbb{Z}[\Phi]\bigr) = n$. Note that $N_{\mathfrak{J}/\mathbb{Z}}(\nu) = n$ can be viewed as the determinant of the multiplication by ν map when viewed as a linear endomorphism of $\mathfrak{J}$. This determinant does not change under a linear change of variables with *rational* coefficients, hence n is also the determinant of multiplication by ν when viewed as a linear endomorphism of $\mathbb{Z}[\Phi]$. But the geometric interpretation of the determinant gives that this is also the index of $\nu\mathbb{Z}[\Phi]$ inside $\mathbb{Z}[\Phi]$.

The third statement is an immediate consequence of the second. □

Notice that the lemma tells us something more than we already knew from the last section, namely that $\varphi^{-1}(\nu\mathcal{P})$ is a fundamental domain for $\mathcal{K}$. Moreover ν and $\nu\Phi'$ form a Gaussian reduced (in the sense of Section 5) basis of $\mathcal{K}$. Furthermore, the cosets $(k, 0)$ modulo $\mathcal{K}$ for $0 \leq k \leq n - 1$ represent all cosets of $(\mathbb{Z} \times \mathbb{Z})/\mathcal{K}$. Their representatives (rather, their images under φ) are then uniformly spaced inside $\nu\mathcal{P}$.

This fact, coupled with the trivial remark that there are n such cosets and that the area in $\mathbb{C}$ of $\nu\mathcal{P}$ is $O(n)$, implies that any point in $\nu\mathcal{P}$ can be approximated by some $\varphi(k, 0)$ with an error $O(1)$. Hence since there is a point of $\nu\mathcal{P}$ distant as far as $R\sqrt{n}$ from a vertex of $\nu\mathcal{P}$, there exists some $\varphi(k, 0)$ which is at distance $R\sqrt{n} + O(1)$, implying (9).

To deduce that the constant in Theorem 4 is also optimal, we invoke the optimality of Lemma 1, together with the fact that any point in $\nu\mathcal{P}$ can be approximated by some $\varphi(k, 0)$ in a given angular sector (cone) stemming from that point with an error $O(1)$ (here, the constant may depend on the angle of the sector). In other words, points $\varphi(k, 0)$ tend to be distributed all around any point.

Theorem 4 implies in particular that $\Bbbk \geq \sqrt{-\Delta}/4$. A consequence of this fact is that one cannot hope to always get $\Bbbk \leq 1$ and that the GLV method is only effective for those exceptional elliptic curves that have complex multiplication by an order with small discriminant. We give a heuristic argument showing this: it is known by [18] that the number of elliptic curves E defined over $\mathbb{F}_p$ with Frobenius endomorphism σ_p of trace t is $H(t^2 - 4p)$, the Kronecker class number of $t^2 - 4p$. By Dirichlet's class number formula [4, p. 49], this is $O(\sqrt{4p - t^2})$. Hence there are few isomorphism classes with $4p - t^2$ small. But generally, the index $\bigl(\operatorname{End}(E) \colon \mathbb{Z}[\sigma_p]\bigr)$ is small [9, p. 41], so $4p - t^2$ is small if and only if the discriminant of $\mathrm{End}(E)$ is small. Thus there are few E's with $\mathrm{End}(E)$ of small discriminant. On the other hand, if $4p - t^2$ becomes large (say of order p), so does $-\Delta$, so that $\Bbbk \approx \sqrt{p} \approx \sqrt{n}$. But this implies that in the GLV decomposition we can only gain at most few bits, thus rendering the method ineffective.

8   The GLV Method Carries Over to Hyperelliptic Curves

In [16] it is shown[5] how to generalise the construction of the GLV method to hyperelliptic curves in two ways. The first one is a straightforward generalisation of the Gallant-Lambert-Vanstone arguments, which involve only lattice theory, to a higher dimensional setting (namely $d \leq 2g$ instead of 2 in the case of elliptic curves). In particular, one has to resort to the LLL algorithm to find small vectors $v_1, \ldots, v_d$ in the lattice given by a prime $\mathfrak{n}$ lying above n in some degree d extension of the rationals. We recall here this method and give an upper bound on $\max |v_i|$, where $|v|$ denotes the rectangle norm of v.

Let X be a hyperelliptic curve defined over a finite field $\mathbb{F}_q$ and $\mathrm{Jac}(X)$ its Jacobian variety. Suppose $\#\mathrm{Jac}(X)(\mathbb{F}_q) = hn$ with h "small" (say less than 4, but strictly less than n would theoretically suffice) and n prime. Let Φ be an efficiently computable endomorphism of $\mathrm{Jac}(X)$ defined over $\mathbb{F}_q$ and let $X^d + a_1 X^{d-1} + \cdots + a_{d-1} X + a_d$ be its minimal polynomial. Let $D \in \mathrm{Jac}(X)$ be a divisor defined over $\mathbb{F}_q$ of order n and $\lambda \in [1, n-1]$ defined by $\Phi(D) = \lambda D$.

Consider the generalised GLV reduction map f_d by

$$f_d \colon \mathbb{Z}^d \to \mathbb{Z}/n$$
$$(x_1, \ldots, x_d) \mapsto \sum_{j=1}^{d} x_j \lambda^{j-1} \pmod{n} \ .$$

If we can find linearly independent vectors $v_1, \ldots, v_d$ inside $\ker f_d$, say with $\max_i |v_i| < M$ for some small $M > 0$, then for any $k \in [1, n-1]$ we can write

$$(k, 0, \ldots, 0) = \sum_{j=1}^{d} \beta_j v_j \ ,$$

with $\beta_j \in \mathbb{Q}$. As in the GLV method one sets $v = \sum_{j=1}^{d} \lfloor \beta_j \rceil v_j$ and

$$u = (k, 0, \ldots, 0) - v = (k_1, \ldots, k_d) \ .$$

We then get

$$kD = \sum_{j=1}^{d} k_j \Phi^{j-1}(D) \quad \text{with } \max_j |k_j| < M \ .$$

The generalisation of GLV is completed if we find M of the smallest possible order, namely around $n^{1/d}$. This is what we will do next.

---

[5] However, we would like to stress that these ideas appear and have been extensively studied in Lange's PhD thesis [10].

Let $K = \mathbb{Q}(\varPhi)$. Its degree over $\mathbb{Q}$ is d. The key point of [16] is that there is a prime ideal $\mathfrak{n}$ in K dividing n, such that $\mathbf{N}\mathfrak{n} = n$. This follows from the fact that λ is a root of the minimal polynomial of $\varPhi$ modulo n, ensuring the existence of such a prime ideal $\mathfrak{n}$, generated as a $\mathbb{Z}$-algebra by n and $\varPhi - \lambda$.

Thus again as previously, we can factor the GLV map f_d as

$$
\mathbb{Z}^d \xrightarrow{\quad\varphi\quad} \mathbb{Z}[\varPhi] \xrightarrow[\text{mod } \mathfrak{n} \cap \mathbb{Z}[\varPhi]]{\text{reduction}} \mathbb{Z}/n
$$

$$
(x_1,\ldots,x_d) \longmapsto \sum_{j=1}^{d} x_j \varPhi^{j-1} \longmapsto \sum_{j=1}^{d} x_j \lambda^{j-1} \pmod{n} .
$$

Note that the index (hence the volume $\mathrm{Vol}(\mathcal{F})$ of a fundamental domain $\mathcal{F}$) of $\varphi^{-1}(\mathfrak{n} \cap \mathbb{Z}[\varPhi])$ inside $\mathbb{Z}^d$ is certainly bounded by $\mathbf{N}\mathfrak{n}$. It is equal to $\mathbf{N}\mathfrak{n}$ if $\mathbb{Z}[\varPhi]$ is the whole ring of integers of K.

The LLL algorithm [11] then finds, for a given basis $w_1,\ldots,w_d$ of $\varphi^{-1}(\mathfrak{n} \cap \mathbb{Z}[\varPhi])$, a reduced basis $v_1,\ldots,v_d$ in polynomial time (in d and the size of the w_i's) such that (cf. [2, Theorem 2.6.2 p.85])

$$
\mathrm{Vol}(\mathcal{F}) \leq \prod_{i=1}^{d} \|v_i\| \leq 2^{d(d-1)/4} n . \tag{12}
$$

Lemma 4. *Let*

$$
\mathcal{N}\colon \mathbb{Z}^d \to \mathbb{Z}
$$

$$
(x_1,\ldots,x_d) \longmapsto \sum_{\substack{i_1,\ldots,i_d \\ i_1+\cdots+i_d=d}} b_{i_1,\ldots,i_d} x_1^{i_1} \ldots x_d^{i_d}
$$

be the norm of an element $\sum_{j=1}^{d} x_j \varPhi^{j-1} \in \mathbb{Z}[\varPhi]$, where the $b_{i_1,\ldots,i_d}$'s lie in $\mathbb{Z}$. Then, for any nonzero $v_i \in \varphi^{-1}(\mathfrak{n} \cap \mathbb{Z}[\varPhi])$, one has

$$
|v_i| \geq \frac{n^{1/d}}{\left(\displaystyle\sum_{\substack{i_1,\ldots,i_d \\ i_1+\cdots+i_d=d}} |b_{i_1,\ldots,i_d}| \right)^{1/d}} . \tag{13}
$$

Proof. This is a straightforward generalisation of the argument given in the proof of Theorem 1. Indeed for $v_i \in \varphi^{-1}(\mathfrak{n} \cap \mathbb{Z}[\varPhi])$ we have $\mathcal{N}(v_i) \equiv 0 \pmod{n}$ and if $v_i \neq 0$ we must therefore have $|\mathcal{N}(v_i)| \geq n$. On the other hand, if we did not have (13), then every component of v_i would be strictly less than the right-hand side and plugging this upper bound in the definition of $\mathcal{N}(v_i)$ would yield a quantity $< n$, a contradiction. $\qquad\square$

Let B be the denominator of the right-hand side of (13), then (12) and (13) imply that

$$
|v_i| \leq B^{d-1} 2^{d(d-1)/4} n^{1/d} .
$$

Thus we have proved the following.

Theorem 5. *Let Φ be an endomorphism of $\mathrm{Jac}(X)$ and let d be the degree of its minimal polynomial. The hyperelliptic GLV method yields a decomposition*

$$kD = \sum_{j=1}^{d} k_j \Phi^{j-1}(D) \quad \text{with} \quad \max_j |k_j| \le B^{d-1} 2^{d(d-1)/4} n^{1/d} \;,$$

where B is the denominator of the right-hand side of (13), that is a polynomial expression in the coefficients of the minimal polynomial of Φ.

9   Examples

We quickly list some examples by producing the minimal polynomial $P(X)$ of Φ, which is all we need. For a complete description of the curves, we refer the reader to [16].

- In Example 2, we have $P(X) = X^2 + 1$. When $d = 2$, the discussion about elliptic curves applies (since it's not a matter of curves, but of rings $\mathbb{Z}[\Phi]$) and the first bound of Corollary 1 applies.
- In Examples 3 and 4, the minimal polynomial is of the form $P(X) = G(X^2)$, where $G(Y) = Y^2 + rY + s$ is the minimal polynomial of $\Psi = \Phi^2$. Then we have

$$B^d = 1 + r^2 + 9s^2 + \left| s^2(r-1)^2 + r^3 s \right| + 7s + 3r^2 s + 3rs + 3\left| r \right|$$
$$+ 9\left| r \right| s + \left| 2s(r-1) - r^3 \right| + \left| 4s - 2r^3 \right| + \left| 2s^2(r-1) + r^2 s \right|$$
$$+ \left| 4s^2(r-1) + 2r^2 s \right| \;.$$

In the case when $r = 0$, we get the simplified equation

$$B^d = 1 + 13s + 16s^2 \;.$$

10   Conclusion

This work does a careful analysis of the GLV method on fast scalar multiplication on elliptic curves. It improves on existing bounds [15] and produces in classical examples the best constants obtainable by this method. In particular we prove that the GLV method is not effective for a generic elliptic curve with complex multiplication by an order of large discriminant. This analysis can be generalised to the hyperelliptic variant of the GLV method [16] and we provide the first explicit bounds on the size of the decomposition, thus quantifying the effectiveness of the GLV method for higher genus curves.

11   Acknowledgements

The authors would like to thank Marc Joye, David Kohel and Takakazu Satoh for fruitful discussions and useful comments on preliminary versions of this paper. We are also grateful to the anonymous referees for their valuable remarks.

References

1. I. Blake, G. Seroussi, and N. Smart. *Elliptic Curves in Cryptography*, volume 265 of *London Mathematical Society*. Cambridge University Press, 2000.
2. H. Cohen. *A Course in Computational Algebraic Number Theory*, volume 138 of *Graduate Texts in Mathematics*. Springer, 1996.
3. H. Daudé, P. Flajolet, and B. Vallée. An Average-case Analysis of the Gaussian Algorithm for Lattice Reduction. Technical Report 2798, INRIA, February 1996.
4. H. Davenport. *Multiplicative Number Theory*, volume 74 of *Graduate Texts in Mathematics*. Springer Verlag, 1980.
5. R. P. Gallant, J. L. Lambert, and S. A. Vanstone. Faster Point Multiplication on Elliptic Curves with Efficient Endomorphisms. In J. Kilian, editor, *Advances in Cryptology - Proceedings of CRYPTO 2001*, volume 2139 of *Lecture Notes in Computer Science*, pages 190–200. Springer, 2001.
6. D. M. Gordon. A Survey of Fast Exponentiation Methods. *Journal of Algorithms*, 27(1):129–146, 1998.
7. D. Kim and S. Lim. Integer Decomposition for Fast Scalar Multiplication on Elliptic Curves. In Howard Heys and Kaisa Nyberg, editors, *Selected Areas in Cryptography, 9th Annual International Workshop, SAC 2002*, Lecture Notes in Computer Science. Springer, 2002. (this volume).
8. K. Koblitz. Elliptic Curve Cryptosystems. *Mathematics of Computation*, 48(177):203–209, 1987.
9. D. Kohel. *Endomorphism Rings of Elliptic Curves over Finite Fields*. PhD thesis, UC Berkeley, 1996.
10. T. Lange. *Efficient Arithmetic on Hyperelliptic Koblitz Curves*. PhD thesis, University of Essen, 2001.
11. A. K. Lenstra, H. W. Lenstra Jr., and L. Lovász. Factoring polynomials with rational coefficients. *Mathematische Ann.*, 261:513–534, 1982.
12. A.J. Menezes. *Elliptic Curve Public Key Cryptosystems*. Kluwer Academic Publishers, 1995.
13. V. Miller. Use of Elliptic Curves in Cryptography. In A. M. Odlyzko, editor, *Advances in Cryptology - Proceedings of CRYPTO 1986*, volume 263 of *Lecture Notes in Computer Science*, pages 417–426. Springer, 1986.
14. V. Müller. Efficient Point Multiplication for Elliptic Curves over Special Optimal Extension Fields. In Walter de Gruyter, editor, *Public-Key Cryptography and Computational Number Theory*, pages 197–207, Warschau, Poland, September 11-15, 2000 (2001).
15. Y-H. Park, S. Jeong, C. Kim, and J. Lim. An Alternate Decomposition of an Integer for Faster Point Multiplication on Certain Elliptic Curves. In D. Naccache and P. Paillier, editors, *Advances in Cryptology - Proceedings of PKC 2002*, volume 2274 of *Lecture Notes in Computer Science*, pages 323–334. Springer, 2002.
16. Y-H. Park, S. Jeong, and J. Lim. Speeding Up Point Multiplication on Hyperelliptic Curves with Efficiently-computable Endomorphisms. In L. Knudsen, editor, *Advances in Cryptology - Proceedings of EUROCRYPT 2002*, volume 2332 of *Lecture Notes in Computer Science*, pages 197–208. Springer, 2002.
17. J. A. Solinas. An Improved Algorithm for Arithmetic on a Family of Elliptic Curves. In Burton S. Kaliski Jr., editor, *Advances in Cryptology - Proceedings of CRYPTO 1997*, volume 1294 of *Lecture Notes in Computer Science*, pages 357–371. Springer, 1997.
18. E. Waterhouse. Abelian varieties over finite fields. *Ann. Sci. École Norm. Sup.*, 2:521–560, 1969.

Guess-and-Determine Attacks on SNOW

Philip Hawkes and Gregory G. Rose

Qualcomm Australia, Level 3, 230 Victoria Rd, Gladesville, NSW 2111, Australia
{phawkes, ggr}@qualcomm.com

Abstract. This paper describes guess-and-determine attacks on the stream cipher SNOW. The first attack has a data complexity of $O(2^{64})$ and a process complexity of $O(2^{256})$. The second attack has process complexity of $O(2^{224})$, and a data complexity of $O(2^{95})$.

1 Introduction

SNOW is synchronous stream cipher proposed by Patrik Ekdahl and Thomas Johansson [3]. The cipher accepts both 128-bit and 256-bit keys. SNOW has been selected as a contender in the second phase of the NESSIE crypto-algorithm evaluation project (see www.cryptonessie.org).

This paper presents *guess-and-determine attacks* (GD attacks) on SNOW. GD attacks have proven effective in analyzing word-oriented stream ciphers. For example, the best known attacks on the SOBER family of stream ciphers (SOBER-t16 [5] and SOBER-t32 [6] are also contenders in the NESSIE project), are GD attacks [1,2,4]. These attacks exploit the relationships between internal values (such as the recurrence relationship in a shift register), and the relationship used to construct the key-stream values from the internal values. A GD attack *guesses* some internal values and then exploits the relationships to *determine* other internal values; hence the name. The cipher is "broken" when a complete internal state has been determined from the guessed values. The basic attack on SNOW has a data complexity of $O(2^{64})$ and a process complexity of $O(2^{256})$. The other attack is based on this first attack; reducing the process complexity at the cost of increased data complexity. The second attack has process complexity of $O(2^{224})$, and a data complexity of $O(2^{95})$.

The paper is arranged as follows. Section 2 describes the SNOW algorithm. Section 3 summarizes the basic attack and describes a "tricks" used in the attack. Section 3.2 describes the steps involved in the third phase of the attack. Section 3.3 discusses the complexity. The second attack is described in Section 4.

2 SNOW

SNOW is based on a *Linear Feedback Shift Register* (LFSR) with a recurrence defined over the Galois field of order 2^{32}, denoted $GF(2^{32})$. The state of the LFSR at time t is denoted $(s_{t+15}, ..., s_t)$, where the values s_{t+i} are 32-bit words.

K. Nyberg and H. Heys (Eds.): SAC 2002, LNCS 2595, pp. 37–46, 2003.

The next state of the LFSR is $(s_{t+16}, ..., s_{t+1})$, where s_{t+16} is defined using a recurrence over $GF(2^{32})$:

$$s_{t+16} = \alpha(s_t \oplus s_{t+3} \oplus s_{t+9}), \tag{1}$$

where $\oplus$ denotes the field addition (equivalent to the bit-wise exclusive-OR operation), α is a specified field element and multiplication is performed in the field. The values of α and the basis for the field are chosen so that for $X = (x_{31}, .., x_0) \in GF(2^{32})$,

$$\alpha X = (x_{30}, .., x_0, 0) \oplus (x_{31} \cdot \text{0x80421009}).$$

Values from the LFSR are combined with values in a *Finite State Machine* (FSM) to generate the key-stream. The FSM contains two 32-bit values; these values (at time t) are denoted by $(R1_t, R2_t)$. The 32-bit output of the FSM at time t is

$$f_t = (s_{t+15} \boxplus R1_t) \oplus R2_t,$$

where $\boxplus$ denotes addition modulo 2^{32}. The 32-bit output of the cipher at time t is computed as

$$z_t = f_t \oplus s_t.$$

The next state of the FSM is computed as

$$R1_{t+1} = R1_t \oplus ROT(f_t \boxplus R2_t, 7)$$
$$R2_{t+1} = S(R1_t),$$

where $ROT(A, B)$ denotes the cyclic rotation of A by B bits towards the most-significant bit (MSB), and $S()$ is defined by four invertible 8-bit S-boxes and a bit permutation. In this document, S is treated as a single, invertible 32-bit S-box.

3   The Basic Attack

It is assumed that the attacker has observed a portion of key-stream $\{z_t\}$, $t = 1..N$, where N is large enough to give a high probability of the attack succeeding. The GD attack has four "phases":

Phase One The attacker make the following assumptions regarding the internal values of the FSM at time t:

Assumption 1 $R2_t = S(R1_t \oplus (2^{32} - 1))$,
Assumption 2 $R2_{t+14} = S(R1_{t+14} \oplus (2^{32} - 1))$.

Phase Two The attacker *guesses* the values of s_t, s_{t+1}, s_{t+2}, s_{t+3}, $R1_t$ and $R1_{t+14}$, (32-bits each: a total of 192 bits).

Phase Three The attacker *determines* the LFSR state $(s_{t+15}, \ldots, s_t)$ from the values guessed in Phase Two, based on the assumptions in Phase One (the details of Phase Three are discussed in Section 3.2).

Phase Four The attacker tests the correctness of the LFSR state $(s_{t+15}, \ldots, s_t)$ and FSM state $(R1_t, R2_t)$ by producing a key-stream using these states and comparing this with the observed key-stream. If the streams agree, then the states are correct. If the streams do not agree, and the attacker can try further guesses (Phase Two) for that values of t (Phase One) then return to Phase Two. If all guesses have been tried for that value of t, then the assumptions in Phase One must be incorrect, so the attacker increases t and returns to Phase One.

The probability that both assumptions in Phase One are correct is 2^{-64}. Thus, around 2^{64} values of t will be tried before finding internal states where $R2_t = S(R1_t \oplus (2^{32} - 1))$ and $R2_{t+14} = S(R1_{t+14} \oplus (2^{32} - 1))$. If the assumptions are incorrect, then none of the guesses in Phase two will result in the correct LFSR state and FSM state in Phase Three, so none of the guesses will produce the correct key-stream in Phase Four.

The bulk of the detail of the attack is in Phase Three. The remainder of Section 3 describes a "trick" exploited in Phase Three.

3.1 A Trick

The "assumed" relationship between $R2_t$ and $R1_t$ (in Phase One) is specially chosen to allow s_{t+14} to be determined from $R1_t$. Note that due to the assumed form of $R2_t = (R1_t \oplus (2^{32} - 1))$):

$$R1_{t-1} = invS(R2_t)$$
$$= invS(\ S(R1_t \oplus (2^{32} - 1))\ )$$
$$= R1_t \oplus (2^{32} - 1),$$
$$\Rightarrow R1_{t-1} \oplus R1_t = (2^{32} - 1),$$

where $invS$ is the inverse of the S mapping. Furthermore,

$$R1_{t-1} = R1_t \oplus (2^{32} - 1) = -R1_t - 1 \,(\mathrm{mod}\ 2^{32}),$$

for all values of $R1_t$. The FSM internal state is updated by computing $R1_t$ from $R1_{t-1}$, f_{t-1} and $R2_{t-1}$ as

$$R1_t = R1_{t-1} \oplus ROT(f_{t-1} \boxplus R2_{t-1}, 7),$$
$$\Rightarrow \quad (R2_{t-1} \boxplus f_{t-1}) = ROT(R1_{t-1} \oplus R1_t, -7)$$
$$= ROT((2^{32} - 1), -7)$$
$$= (2^{32} - 1).$$

Note that since $(R2_{t-1} \boxplus f_{t-1}) = (2^{32} - 1)$, this implies that

$$(R2_{t-1} \oplus f_{t-1}) = (2^{32} - 1).$$

Now that the attacker knows that $(R2_{t-1} \oplus f_{t-1})$, the attacker can "reverse" the FSM to compute s_{t+14}:

$$\begin{aligned} s_{t+14} &= (R2_{t-1} \oplus f_{t_1}) - R1_{t-1} \pmod{2^{32}} \\ &= (2^{32} - 1) - (-R1_t - 1) \pmod{2^{32}} \\ &= R1_t. \end{aligned}$$

The assumed relationship between $R2_t$ and $R1_t$ is especially chosen to allow s_{t+14} to be determined from $R1_t$. Similarly, the assumed relationship between $R2_{t+14}$ and $R1_{t+14}$ is especially chosen to allow s_{t+28} to be determined from $R1_{t+14}$:

$$s_{t+28} = R1_{t+14}.$$

The assumptions are specially designed to allow s_{t+14} and s_{t+28} to be determined "for free". This is discussed in more detail in Section 3.3.

3.2   Details of Phase Three

This section concerns the details or Phase Three: determining a full LFSR state from the values guessed in Phase Two and based on the assumptions in Phase One. Phase Three is divided into 29 "steps". In the following description, a value s_{t+i} in the LFSR is often represented using the value "i": for example, 0 represents s_t and 6 represents s_{t+6}. Also, the following notation is used:

"$F \rightarrow$" denotes exploiting the relationship between s_{t+i+15}, $R1_{t+i}$, $R2_{t+i}$ and f_{t+i};

"$G \rightarrow$" denotes exploiting the relationship between $R1_{t+i+1}$, f_{t+i}, $R1_{t+i}$ and $R2_{t+i}$;

"$S \rightarrow$" denotes exploiting the relationship $R2_{t+i+1} = S(R1_{t+i})$.

After guessing the values in Phase Two, the attacker has guessed all the bits in the values for 0, 1, 2, 3 (that is, s_t, s_{t+1}, s_{t+2}, s_{t+3}), and $R1_t$, $R2_t$ $R1_{t+14}$, $R2_{t+14}$. For a given guess, all the bits of the following values can be immediately determined by exploiting the relationships in the FSM:

> **Step 0.a** $s_t \oplus z_t$ $\quad\quad = f_t.$
> **Step 0.b** $f_t, R1_t, R2_t$ $F \rightarrow s_{t+15}.$
> **Step 0.c** $f_t, R1_t, R2_t$ $G \rightarrow R1_{t+1}.$
> **Step 0.d** $R1_t$ $\quad\quad\quad S \rightarrow R2_{t+1}.$

These four steps can be repeated for $i = 1, 2, 3$, to determine (among other values) s_{t+16}, s_{t+17} and s_{t+18}.

> **Step 1/2/3.a** $s_{t+i} \oplus z_{t+i}$ $\quad\quad = f_{t+i}.$
> **Step 1/2/3.b** $f_{t+i}, R1_{t+i}, R2_{t+i}$ $F \rightarrow s_{t+i+15}.$
> **Step 1/2/3.c** $f_{t+i}, R1_{t+i}, R2_{t+i}$ $G \rightarrow R1_{t+i+1}.$
> **Step 1/2/3.d** $R1_{t+i}$ $\quad\quad\quad S \rightarrow R2_{t+i+1}.$

The attacker can also utilize the "trick" described in Section 3.1.

$$\textbf{Step 4}\ s_{t+14} = R1_t.$$
$$\textbf{Step 5}\ s_{t+28} = R1_{t+14}.$$

The attacker has now guessed or determined all the bits in the values:

$$0\text{-}3,\ 14\text{-}18, 28, R1_{t+i}, R2_{t+i},\ i \in \{0\text{-}4, 14\}.$$

The four basic steps are now repeated for $i = 14,\ldots,18$.

$$
\begin{aligned}
&\textbf{Step 6/../10.a}\ s_{t+i} \oplus z_{t+i} &&= f_{t+i}.\\
&\textbf{Step 6/../10.b}\ f_{t+i}, R1_{t+i}, R2_{t+i}\ F \to s_{t+i+15}.\\
&\textbf{Step 6/../10.c}\ f_{t+i}, R1_{t+i}, R2_{t+i}\ G \to R1_{t+i+1}.\\
&\textbf{Step 6/../10.d}\ R1_{t+i} &&S \to R2_{t+i+1}.
\end{aligned}
$$

(Step 6 has $i = 14$, Step 7 has $i = 15$, and so forth). The attacker has now guessed or determined all the bits of the values:

$$0\text{-}3,\ 14\text{-}18,\ 28\text{-}33, R1_{t+i}, R2_{t+i},\ i \in \{0\text{-}4, 14\text{-}19\}.$$

The attacker can exploit linear relationships between state words s_t, that result from the linear recurrence. The linear relationships exploited in this attack correspond to the linear recurrence (1), denoted by "$L \to$", and the linear relationship corresponding to the "square" of the linear recurrence:

$$s_{t+32} = \alpha^2(s_t \oplus s_{t+6} \oplus s_{t+18}),$$

denoted by "$L2 \to$". The attacker determines more internal values using the following steps:

Step 11 $14, 17, 30$	$L \to 23.$	
Step 12 $0, 3, 16$	$L \to 9.$	
Step 13 $0, 18, 32$	$L2 \to 6.$	
Step 14 $6, 9, 15$	$L \to 22.$	
Step 15 $15, 18, 31$	$L \to 24.$	
Step 16 $16, 22, 29$	$L \to 13.$	
Step 17 $1, 17$	$L2 \to (s_{t+4} \oplus s_{t+10}).$	
Step 18 $(s_{t+4} \oplus s_{t+10}), 22$	$L2 \to 36.$	
Step 19 $23, 29, 36$	$L \to 20.$	
Step 20 $17, 20, 33$	$L \to 26.$	
Step 21 $2, 14, 28$	$L2 \to -4.$	
Step 22 $17, 31$	$L2 \to (s_{t-1} \oplus s_{t+5}).$	
Step 23 $-4, (s_{t-1} \oplus s_{t+5})$	$L \to 12.$	
Step 24 $3, 6, 12$	$L \to 19.$	
Step 25 $12, 15, 28$	$L \to 21.$	
Step 26 $9, 12, 18$	$L \to 25.$	
Step 27 $s_{t+19} \oplus z_{t+19}$	$= f_{t+19}.$	
Step 28 $f_{t+19}, R1_{t+19}, R2_{t+19}\ F \to s_{t+34}.$		
Step 29 $18, 21, 34$	$L \to 27.$	

The attacker has now determined a full LFSR state $(s_{t+27}, \ldots s_{t+12})$. The LFSR is "rewound" to determine $(s_{t+15}, \ldots, s_t)$.

3.3   Complexity

Recall the assumptions that $R2_t = S(R1_t \oplus (2^{32} - 1))$ and $R2_{t+14} = S(R1_{t+14} \oplus (2^{32} - 1))$. The probability that both of these assumptions are correct is 2^{-64}. The attacker will have to try around 2^{64} values of t before finding internal states where $R2_t = S(R1_t \oplus (2^{32} - 1))$ and $R2_{t+14} = S(R1_{t+14} \oplus (2^{32} - 1))$. That is, the attacker will need $O(2^{64})$ outputs. For each value of t, the attack requires guessing 192 bits (all 32 bits of $s_t, s_{t+1}, s_{t+2}, s_{t+3}, R1_t, R2_{t+14}$). This corresponds to 2^{192} guesses for each value of t. Thus, the data complexity of the attack is 2^{64} and the process complexity is $2^{64} \cdot 2^{192} = 2^{256}$.

Note that the effect of forcing $R2_t$ to be related to $R1_t$ (rather than guessing $R2_t$ independently of $R1_t$) is to increase the data complexity by a factor of 2^{32}, while not changing the process complexity. However, by choosing the relationship between $R1_t$ and $R2_t$, the attacker is able to determine more information about s_{t+14}. If attacker had simply guessed $R2_t$, then the attacker could determine

$$(R_{t-1} \boxplus f_{t-1}) = ROT((R1_{t-1} \oplus R1_t), -7)$$
$$= ROT(invS(R2_t) \oplus R1_t, -7).$$

However, the attacker may be unable to determine much information about $(R2_{t-1} \oplus f_{t-1})$ (required to obtain s_{t+14}). For example, if $(R_{t-1} \boxplus f_{t-1}) = 0$, then two possible "solutions" for $(R1_{t-1}, f_{t-1})$ are $(R1_{t-1}, f_{t-1}) = (0, 0)$ and $(R1_{t-1}, f_{t-1}) = (2^{32} - 1, 1)$. If $(R1_{t-1}, f_{t-1}) = (0, 0)$, then $(R_{t-1} \oplus f_{t-1}) = 0$, while if $(R1_{t-1}, f_{t-1}) = (2^{32} - 1, 1)$, then $(R_{t-1} \oplus f_{t-1}) = (2^{32} - 2)$. This uncertainty in the value of $(R_{t-1} \oplus f_{t-1})$ means that the attacker determines less information about s_{t+14}. This is why the attacker assumes the value of $R2_t$, rather than guessing it. The same argument applies to $R2_{t+14}$.

3.4   Observation

This attack is aided by the choice of inputs to the recurrence relation:

$$s_{t+16} = \alpha(s_t \oplus s_{t+3} \oplus s_{t+9}).$$

There is a gap of 3 words between the inputs s_t and s_{t+3}, and gap of $6 = 2 \times 3$ words between the inputs s_{t+3} and s_{t+9}. This difference of 6 words is unfortunate because it is the same gap as between the first two inputs to the square of the linear recurrence:

$$s_{t+32} = \alpha^2(s_t \oplus s_{t+6} \oplus s_{t+18}).$$

Thus the value of $(s_{t+i} \oplus s_{t+6+i})$ can be considered as a single input to either equation. For example, in Step 17, the values of s_{t+1} and s_{t+17} are used to determine the value of $(s_{t+4} \oplus s_{t+10})$ by exploiting the linear recurrence. In Step 18, the value of $(s_{t+4} \oplus s_{t+10})$ is then combined with the value of s_{t+22} to obtain s_{t+36}, by exploiting the square of the linear recurrence. The value of s_{t+36} is determined despite the attacker being unable to determine the values of s_{t+4} and s_{t+10}. If the linear recurrence did not have this property, then it is likely that fewer state words could be derived from the guessed words, and the attacker would be unable to derive a full state from the guessed words. This may force the attacker to guess more internal values before being able to derive a full state, thus increasing the complexity. That is, it is likely that guess-and-determine attacks could be forced to have a larger complexity by the use of a different linear recurrence.

4   Reducing the Process Complexity

The process complexity of the attack can be reduced if the attacker can avoid guessing all of s_{t+3}. We have explored various ways of achieving this: as of yet we have been unable to decrease the complexity significantly without increasing the data complexity.

It is assumed that the attacker has observed a portion of key-stream $\{z_t\}$, $t = 1..N$, where N is large enough to give a high probability of the attack succeeding. Like the first attack, this GD attack has four "phases":

Phase One The attacker make the following assumptions regarding the internal values of the FSM at time t:

$$\textbf{Assumption 1} \quad R2_t = S(R1_t \oplus (2^{32} - 1)),$$
$$\textbf{Assumption 2} \ R2_{t+14} = S(R1_{t+14} \oplus (2^{32} - 1)),$$
$$\textbf{Assumption 3} \ \ R1_{t+3} \in \{0, 2^{31}\}.$$

Phase Two The attacker *guesses* the values of s_t, s_{t+1}, $R1_t$, $R1_{t+14}$, (32-bits each: a total of 128 bits), and $R1_{t+3} \in \{0, 2^{31}\}$) (1 bit).

Phase Three The attacker *determines* the LFSR state $(s_{t+15}, \ldots, s_t)$ from the values guessed in Phase Two, based on the assumptions in Phase One (the details of Phase Three are discussed below).

Phase Four The attacker tests the correctness of the LFSR state $(s_{t+15}, \ldots, s_t)$ and FSM state $(R1_t, R2_t)$ by producing a key-stream using these states and comparing this with the observed key-stream.

The probability that both assumptions in Phase One are correct is 2^{-95}. Thus, around 2^{95} values of t will be tried before finding internal states where $R2_t = S(R1_t \oplus (2^{32} - 1))$, $R2_{t+14} = S(R1_{t+14} \oplus (2^{32} - 1))$, and $R1_{t+3} \in \{0, 2^{31}\}$. If the assumptions are incorrect, then none of the guesses in Phase two will result in the correct LFSR state and FSM state in Phase Three, so none of the guesses will produce the correct key-stream in Phase Four.

After guessing the values in Phase Two, the attacker has values for 0, 1, and $R1_t$, $R2_t$, $R1_{t+3}$, $R1_{t+14}$, $R2_{t+14}$ (using the assumptions in Phase One). For a given guess, all the bits of the following values can be immediately determined for $i = 0, 1$;

$$\textbf{Step i.a } s_{t+i} \oplus z_{t+i} \qquad = \ f_{t+i}.$$
$$\textbf{Step i.b } f_{t+i}, R1_{t+i}, R2_{t+i} \ F \rightarrow s_{t+i+15}.$$
$$\textbf{Step i.c } f_{t+i}, R1_{t+i}, R2_{t+i} \ G \rightarrow R1_{t+i+1}.$$
$$\textbf{Step i.d } R1_{t+i} \qquad\qquad S \rightarrow R2_{t+i+1}.$$

Recall that $R1_{t+3}$ has been guessed to be either 0 or $2^{31} = \text{0x80000000}$. The attacker uses the function G to compute f_{t+2}.

Step 2.a $R1_{t+3}, R1_{t+2}, R2_{t+2}\ G \rightarrow f_{t+2}$.

Now that the attacker has computed f_{t+2}, they can compute s_{t+2}, s_{t+17} and $R2_{t+3}$.

Step 2.b $f_{t+2} \oplus z_{t+2}$ $\qquad = \quad s_{t+2}$.
Step 2.c $f_{t+2}, R1_{t+2}, R2_{t+2}\ F \rightarrow s_{t+17}$.
Step 2.d $R1_{t+2}$ $\qquad\qquad\qquad S \rightarrow R2_{t+3}$.

The attacker can utilize the "trick" described in Section 3.1.

Step 3 $s_{t+14} = R1_t$.
Step 4 $s_{t+28} = R1_{t+14}$.

The attacker has now guessed or determined all the bits in the values:

$$0\text{-}2,\, 14\text{-}17, 28,\, R1_{t+i}, R2_{t+i},\ i \in \{0\text{-}3, 14\}.$$

The four basic steps are now repeated for $i = 14, \ldots, 17$.

Step 5/../8.a $s_{t+i} \oplus z_{t+i}$ $\qquad = \quad f_{t+i}$.
Step 5/../8.b $f_{t+i}, R1_{t+i}, R2_{t+i}\ F \rightarrow s_{t+i+15}$.
Step 5/../8.c $f_{t+i}, R1_{t+i}, R2_{t+i}\ G \rightarrow R1_{t+i+1}$.
Step 5/../8.d $R1_{t+i}$ $\qquad\qquad\qquad\ S \rightarrow R2_{t+i+1}$.

(Step 5 has $i = 14$, Step 6 has $i = 15$, and so forth). The attacker has now guessed or determined all the bits of the values:

$$0\text{-}2,\, 14\text{-}17, 28\text{-}32,\, R1_{t+i}, R2_{t+i},\ i \in \{0\text{-}3, 14\text{-}18\}.$$

Exploiting the linear recurrence and the linear relationships corresponding to the square of the connection polynomial, allows the attacker to determine more internal values:

Step 9 $14, 17, 30$ $\qquad L \rightarrow 23$.
Step 10 $2, 14, 28$ $\qquad L2 \rightarrow -4$.
Step 11 $17, 31$ $\qquad\ L2 \rightarrow (s_{t-1} \oplus s_{t+5})$.
Step 12 $-4, (s_{t-1} \oplus s_{t+5})\ L \rightarrow 12$.
Step 13 $12, 15, 28$ $\qquad L \rightarrow 21$.
Step 14 $0, 16$ $\qquad\quad L \rightarrow (s_{t+3} \oplus s_{t+9})$.
Step 15 $(s_{t+3} \oplus s_{t+9}), 21\ L2 \rightarrow 35$.

Note that if $R1_{t+3} \in \{0, 2^{31}\}$, then

$$f_{t+3} = (s_{t+18} \boxplus R1_{t+3}) \oplus R2_{t+3}$$
$$= (s_{t+18} \oplus R1_{t+3}) \oplus R2_{t+3},$$
$$\Rightarrow \qquad z_{t+3} = s_{t+3} \oplus f_{t+3}$$
$$= s_{t+3} \oplus (s_{t+18} \oplus R1_{t+3} \oplus R2_{t+3}),$$
$$\Rightarrow \qquad (s_{t+3} \oplus s_{t+18}) = z_{t+3} \oplus R1_{t+3} \oplus R2_{t+3}.$$

The attacker can use the value of $(s_{t+3} \oplus s_{t+18})$ to compute other values of s_{t+i} by exploiting linear relationships. For example, that attacker can combine the two equations

$$s_{t+19} = \alpha \cdot (s_{t+3} \oplus s_{t+6} \oplus s_{t+12}),$$
$$s_{t+6} = s_t \oplus s_{t+18} \oplus \alpha^{-2} s_{t+32},$$
$$\Rightarrow \quad s_{t+19} = \alpha \cdot ((s_{t+3} \oplus s_{t+18}) \oplus s_t \oplus s_{t+12} \oplus \alpha^{-2} s_{t+32}).$$

Since the attacker knows $(s_{t+3} \oplus s_{t+18})$, 0, 12 and 32, the attacker can perform the: following step

Step 16 $s_{t+19} = \alpha \cdot ((s_{t+3} \oplus s_{t+18}) \oplus s_t \oplus s_{t+12} \oplus \alpha^{-2} s_{t+32}).$

The attacker has now guessed or determined all the bits of the values:

0-2, 12,14-17,19,21,23, 28-32,35, $R1_{t+i}, R2_{t+i}, \ i \in \{0\text{-}3,14\text{-}18\}.$

Now that the attacker knows s_{t+19}, there are many other values that the attacker can compute.

Step 17 $16, 19, 32$	$L \to 25.$	
Step 18 $19, 28, 35$	$L \to 22.$	
Step 19 $16, 22, 29$	$L \to 13.$	
Step 20 $s_{t+13} \oplus z_{t+13}$	$=$	$f_{t+13}.$
Step 21 $R2_{t+14}$	$S \to R1_{t+13}.$	
Step 22 $s_{t+28}, R1_{t+13}, f_{t+13}$	$F \to R2_{t+13}.$	
Step 23 $R2_{t+13}$	$S \to R1_{t+12}.$	
Step 24 $s_{t+12} \oplus z_{t+12}$	$=$	$f_{t+12}.$
Step 25 $R1_{t+12}, R1_{t+13}, f_{t+12}$	$G \to R2_{t+12}.$	
Step 26 $R1_{t+12}, R2_{t+12}, f_{t+12}$	$F \to 27.$	

As an update, the attacker has now guessed or determined the values:

0-2, 12-17,19,21-23, 25, 27-32,35, $R1_{t+i}, R2_{t+i}, \ i \in \{0\text{-}3,12\text{-}18\}.$

The final steps are:

Step 27 $1, 13, 27$	$L2 \to -5.$	
Step 28 $16, 30$	$L2 \to (s_{t-2} \oplus s_{t+4}).$	
Step 29 $-5, (s_{t-2} \oplus s_{t+4})$	$L \to 11.$	
Step 30 $11, 14, 27$	$L \to 20.$	
Step 31 $s_{t+11} \oplus z_{t+11}$	$=$	$f_{t+11}.$
Step 32 $R2_{t+12}$	$S \to R1_{t+11}.$	
Step 33 $R1_{t+11}, R1_{t+12}, f_{t+11}$	$G \to R2_{t+11}.$	
Step 34 $R1_{t+11}, R2_{t+11}, f_{t+11}$	$F \to 26.$	
Step 35 $17, 20, 26$	$L \to 33.$	
Step 36 $s_{t+33}, R1_{t+18}, R2_{t+18}$	$F \to f_{t+18}.$	
Step 37 $z_{t+18} \oplus f_{t+18}$	$=$	$s_{t+18}.$
Step 38 $15, 18, 31$	$L \to 24.$	

The attacker has now determined a full LFSR state $(s_{t+26}, \ldots s_{t+11})$. The LFSR is "rewound" to determine $(s_{t+15}, \ldots, s_t)$.

The probability that the three Phase One assumptions are correct is 2^{-95}. The attacker will have to try around 2^{95} values of t before finding internal states where the assumptions are correct; that is, the attacker will need $O(2^{95})$ outputs. For each value of t, the attack requires guessing 129 bits (the MSB of $R1_{t+3}$ and all 32 bits of s_t, s_{t+1}, $R1_t$, $R2_{t+14}$). This corresponds to 2^{129} guesses for each value of t. Thus, the data complexity of the attack is 2^{95} and the process complexity is $2^{95} \cdot 2^{129} = 2^{224}$.

It is possible to reduce the data complexity of the second attack by allowing other values of $R1_{t+3}$. However, if $R1_{t+3}$ is no longer either 0 or 2^{31}, then there will be more than one possible value for $(s_{t+3} \oplus s_{t+18})$. The attacker can test the possible combinations of $(R1_{t+3}, (s_{t+3} \oplus s_{t+18}))$, starting with the most probable combinations and leading down to the less probable combinations. This results in an increase in the process complexity. We have not conducted a detailed analysis of the expected complexity using this approach.

5   Conclusion

This paper demonstrates two guess-and-determine attacks on SNOW. The first attack has a process complexity of $O(2^{256})$ and a data complexity of $O(2^{64})$. The second attack has a process complexity of $O(2^{224})$ and a data complexity of $O(2^{95})$. It is likely that guess-and-determine attacks could be forced to have a larger complexity if the linear recurrence were changed, as discussed in Section 3.4.

References

1. S. Blackburn, S. Murphy, F. Piper, and P. Wild. A SOBERing remark. Technical report, Information Security Group, Royal Holloway University of London, Egham, Surrey TW20 0EX, U.K., 1998.
2. D. Bleichenbacher and S Patel. SOBER cryptanalysis. *Fast Software Encryption, FSE'99 Lecture Notes in Computer Science, vol. 1636, L. Knudsen ed., Springer-Verlag*, pages 305–316, 1999.
3. P. Ekdahl and T. Johansson. SNOW - a new stream cipher, 2000. This paper is found in the NESSIE webpages:
   http://www.cosic.esat.kuleuven.ac.be/nessie/workshop/submissions/snow.zip.
4. P. Hawkes and G. Rose. Exploiting multiples of the connection polynomial in word-oriented stream ciphers. *Advances in Cryptology, ASIACRYPT2000, Lecture Notes in Computer Science, vol. 1976, T. Okamoto ed., Springer-Verlag*, pages 302–316, 2000.
5. P. Hawkes and G. Rose. Primitive specification and supporting documentation for SOBER-t16 submission to NESSIE, 2000. See:
   http://www.cosic.esat.kuleuven.ac.be/nessie/workshop/submissions/sober-t16.zip.
6. P. Hawkes and G. Rose. Primitive specification and supporting documentation for SOBER-t32 submission to NESSIE, 2000. See:
   http://www.cosic.esat.kuleuven.ac.be/nessie/workshop/submissions/sober-t32.zip.

A New Version of the Stream Cipher SNOW

Patrik Ekdahl and Thomas Johansson

Dept. of Information Technology
Lund University, P.O. Box 118, 221 00 Lund, Sweden
{patrik,thomas}@it.lth.se

Abstract. In 2000, the stream cipher SNOW was proposed. A few attacks followed, indicating certain weaknesses in the design. In this paper we propose a new version of SNOW, called SNOW 2.0. The new version of the cipher does not only appear to be more secure, but its implementation is also a bit faster in software.

Keywords. SNOW, Stream ciphers, summation combiner, correlation attacks.

1 Introduction

A stream cipher is a cryptographic primitive used to ensure privacy on a communication channel. A common way to build a stream cipher is to use a pseudo-random length-increasing function (or keystream generator) and mask the plaintext using the output from the keystream generator. Typically, the masking operation is the XOR operation, and the keystream output is thus used as a one-time-pad to produce the ciphertext.

A number of stream ciphers have been proposed during the history of cryptology. Most of them have been bit-oriented stream ciphers based on linear feedback shift registers (LFSRs). These range from the simple and very insecure Geffe generator, nonlinear combination generators, filter generators, to the more interesting clock-controlled generators like the (self-) shrinking generator and the alternating step generator [13].

Apart from security, the main characteristic of a stream cipher is its performance. Performance can be the speed of an implemented cipher on different platforms, but also chip area, power consumption etc. for hardware implementations.

A general research topic for any cryptographic primitive is to try to optimize the trade-off between security and performance. Bit-oriented stream ciphers do not perform very well in software implementations. This is the reason why we have recently seen word-oriented stream ciphers. A word-oriented stream cipher outputs a sequence of words of a certain word size (like 32 bits). Such a cipher can provide a very good performance, typically 5-10 times faster than a block cipher in a software implementation.

Several word-oriented stream ciphers have recently been proposed, e.g., RC4 [14], SEAL [15], different versions of SOBER [9,10], SNOW [5], SSC2 [17],

K. Nyberg and H. Heys (Eds.): SAC 2002, LNCS 2595, pp. 47–61, 2003.

SCREAM [2], MUGI [16]. It can be noted that essentially all of the proposed stream ciphers have documented weaknesses of varying strength (this does not include SCREAM and MUGI that were proposed in 2002).

The purpose of this paper is to propose a new version of the SNOW cipher. The original version, now denoted SNOW 1.0, was submitted to the NESSIE project. It has excellent performance, several times faster than AES. However, a few attacks have been reported. One attack is a key recovery attack requiring a known output sequence of length 2^{95} having expected complexity 2^{224} [7]. Another attack is a distinguishing attack [1] also requiring a known output sequence of length 2^{95} and about the same complexity. Although one might argue about the relevance of such a distinguishing attacks, the attacks do demonstrate some weaknesses in the design.

In this paper we propose a new version of SNOW, called SNOW 2.0, which appears to be more secure. Moreover, SNOW 2.0 can be implemented even faster than SNOW 1.0 in software. Our optimized C implementation reports a speed of about 5-6 clock cycles per byte.

The paper is organized as follows. In Section 2 we describe the original design, in the sequel referred to as SNOW 1.0. In Section 3 we describe the weaknesses found in SNOW 1.0. In Section 4 we present the new version SNOW 2.0, and in Section 5 we discuss the design differences between the two versions. In Section 6 we then focus on implementation aspects.

2   First Version of SNOW

In this section we give a short description of the original SNOW design. SNOW 1.0 is a word oriented stream cipher with a word size of 32 bits.

The cipher is described with two possible key sizes, 128 and 256 bits. As usual, the encryption starts with a key initialization, giving the components of the cipher their initial key values. In this description we will only concentrate on the cipher in operation. The details of the key initialization can be found in [5].

The generator is depicted in Figure 1. It consists of a length 16 linear feedback shift register over $\mathbb{F}_{2^{32}}$, feeding a finite state machine. The FSM consists of two 32 bit registers, called R1 and R2, as well as a some operations to calculate the output and the next state (the next value of R1 and R2).

The operation of the cipher is as follows. First, key initialization is done. This procedure provides initial values for the LFSR as well as for the R1,R2 registers in the finite state machine. Next, the first 32 bits of the keystream is calculated by bitwise adding the output of the FSM and the last entry of the LFSR. After that the whole cipher is clocked once, and the next 32 bits of the keystream is calculated by again bitwise adding the output of the finite state machine and the last entry of the LFSR. We clock again and continue in this fashion.

Returning to Figure 1, the LFSR has a primitive feedback polynomial over $\mathbb{F}_{2^{32}}$ which is

$$p(x) = x^{16} + x^{13} + x^7 + \alpha^{-1},$$

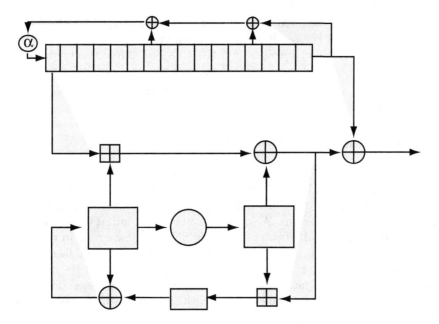

Fig. 1. A schematic picture of SNOW 1.0

where $\mathbb{F}_{2^{32}}$ is generated by the irreducible polynomial

$$\pi(x) = x^{32} + x^{29} + x^{20} + x^{15} + x^{10} + x + 1,$$

over $\mathbb{F}_2$, and $\pi(\alpha) = 0$. Furthermore let $s(1), s(2), \ldots s(16) \in \mathbb{F}_{2^{32}}$ be the state of the LFSR.

The output of the FSM, called FSM_{out}, is calculated as follows.

$$FSM_{\text{out}} = (s(1) \boxplus R1) \oplus R2.$$

The output of the FSM is XORed with $s(16)$ to form the keystream, i.e.,

$$\text{running key} = FSM_{\text{out}} \oplus s(16).$$

The keystream is finally XORed with the plaintext, producing the ciphertext. Inside the FSM, the new values of R1 and R2 are given as follows,

$$newR1 = ((FSM_{\text{out}} \boxplus R2) \lll) \oplus R1,$$
$$R2 = S(R1),$$
$$R1 = newR1.$$

By the notation $x \boxplus y$, we mean the integer addition of x and y mod2^{32}. The notation $x \lll$ is a cyclic shift of x 7 steps to the left, and the addition sign in $x \oplus y$ represents bitwise addition (XOR) of the words x and y.

Finally, the S-box, denoted $S(x)$, consists of four identical 8-to-8 bit S-boxes and a permutation of the resulting bits. The input x is split into 4 bytes, each byte enters a nonlinear mapping from 8 bits to 8 bits. After this mapping, the bits in the resulting word are permuted to form the final output of the S-box. A comprehensive description of the original design, including the key setup and modes of operation can be found in [5].

3   Weaknesses in SNOW 1.0

In this section we describe the weaknesses found in the original construction. In February 2002, Hawkes and Rose described a guess-and-determine attack on SNOW 1.0 [7,8]. The attack has data complexity of 2^{95} words and a process complexity of 2^{224} operations. Apart from some clever initial choices made by Hawkes and Rose, basically two properties in SNOW 1.0 are used to reduce the complexity of the attack below exhaustive key search. First, the fact that the FSM has only *one* input $s(1)$. This enables an attacker to invert the operations in the FSM and derive more unknowns from only a few guesses. The second property is an unfortunate choice of feedback polynomial in SNOW 1.0. The linear recurrence equation is given by

$$s_{t+16} = \alpha(s_{t+9} + s_{t+3} + s_t). \tag{1}$$

There is a distance of 3 words between s_t and s_{t+3} and a distance of $6 = 2 \cdot 3$ between s_{t+3} and s_{t+9}. Thus, by squaring (1)

$$s_{t+32} = \alpha^2(s_{t+18} + s_{t+6} + s_t) \tag{2}$$

we see that $(s_{t+i} \oplus s_{t+i+6})$ can be considered as a single input to either equation. Hence, the attacker does not need to determine both s_{t+i} and s_{t+i+6} explicitly, but only the XOR sum to use in (1) and (2).

A second weakness in the choice of the feedback polynomial emerges when considering *bitwise* linear approximations. Using the same technique as in [6], we can take the 2^{32}th power of the feedback polynomial $p(x) = x^{16} + x^{13} + x^7 + \alpha^{-1} \in \mathbb{F}_{2^{32}}[x]$, giving us

$$p^{2^{32}}(x) = x^{16 \cdot 2^{32}} + x^{13 \cdot 2^{32}} + x^{7 \cdot 2^{32}} + \alpha^{-1 \cdot 2^{32}} \in \mathbb{F}_{2^{32}}[x]. \tag{3}$$

Since $\alpha \in \mathbb{F}_{2^{32}}$ we have $\alpha^{-1 \cdot 2^{32}} = \alpha^{-1}$, and summation of $p(x) + p^{2^{32}}(x)$ yields

$$x^{16 \cdot 2^{32}} + x^{13 \cdot 2^{32}} + x^{7 \cdot 2^{32}} + x^{16} + x^{13} + x^7. \tag{4}$$

Dividing (4) with x^7 gives us a linear recurrence equation satisfying

$$s_{t+16 \cdot 2^{32}-7} + s_{t+13 \cdot 2^{32}-7} + s_{t+7 \cdot 2^{32}-7} + s_{t+9} + s_{t+6} + s_t = 0 \tag{5}$$

In (5) we have derived a linear recurrence equation that holds for *each single bit position*. Hence, any bitwise correlation found in the FSM can be turned into a distinguishing attack. In a recent paper by Coppersmith, Halevi and Jutla [1], they find such a correlation and for the resulting distinguishing attack they need about 2^{95} words of output and the computational complexity is about 2^{100}. By computer search we have also found other smaller correlations, often involving similar bit positions. The strong correlations seem to be caused by an interaction between the permutation in the S-box and the cyclic shift by 7 in the FSM.

Even if this indeed is a security flaw unpredicted by the authors, one could argue about the relevance of such a distinguishing attack. Using e.g. AES (or any other block cipher with block length 128 bits) in counter mode, there is an almost trivial distinguishing attack after seeing about 2^{64} ciphertext blocks. However, as we regard security as the outmost important design criteria, we addressed all known weaknesses in SNOW 1.0 and propose a slightly modified design, SNOW 2.0.

4   SNOW 2.0

As we now turn to describe the new version SNOW 2.0, we want to emphasize that the notations from the previous sections are no longer valid and will be redefined in the following. The new version is schematically a small modification of the original construction, see Figure 2. The word size is unchanged (32 bits) and the LFSR length is again 16, but the feedback polynomial has been changed. The Finite State Machine (FSM) has two input words, taken from the LFSR, and the running key is formed as the XOR between the FSM output and the last element of the LFSR, as done in SNOW 1.0. The operation of the cipher is as follows. First, a key initialization is performed. This operation provides the LFSR with a starting state as well as giving the internal FSM registers $R1$ and $R2$ there initial values. Next the cipher is clocked once and the first keystream symbol is read out[1]. Then the cipher is clocked again and the second keystream symbol is read, etcetera.

Let us give a detailed description of the cipher, starting with the LFSR. The main reason for the specific feedback polynomial chosen in SNOW 1.0, was to have a fast realization in software. By choosing a multiplication with the same primitive element as the base is constructed from, we can realize the multiplication with just one left shift and a possible XOR with a known pattern. However, this choice opens up possible weaknesses, as discussed in Section 3. In SNOW 2.0, we have two different elements involved in the feedback loop, α and α^{-1}, where α now is a root of a primitive polynomial of degree 4 over $\mathbb{F}_{2^8}$. To be more precise, the feedback polynomial of SNOW 2.0 is given by

$$\pi(x) = \alpha x^{16} + x^{14} + \alpha^{-1} x^5 + 1 \in \mathbb{F}_{2^{32}}[x], \qquad (6)$$

where α is a root of $x^4 + \beta^{23} x^3 + \beta^{245} x^2 + \beta^{48} x + \beta^{239} \in \mathbb{F}_{2^8}[x]$, and β is a root of $x^8 + x^7 + x^5 + x^3 + 1 \in \mathbb{F}_2[x]$.

---

[1] Observe the change from the original version where the first symbol was read out *before* the cipher was clocked.

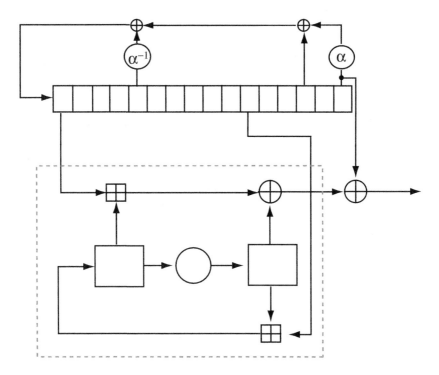

Fig. 2. A schematic picture of SNOW 2.0

Let the state of the LFSR at time $t \geq 0$ be denoted $(s_{t+15}, s_{t+14}, \ldots, s_t)$, $s_{t+i} \in \mathbb{F}_{2^{32}}$, $i \geq 0$. The element s_t is the rightmost element (or first element to exit) as indicated in Figure 2, and the sequence produced by the LFSR is $(s_0, s_1, s_2, \ldots)$. By time $t = 0$, we mean the time instance directly after the key initialization. Then the cipher is clocked once before producing the first keystream symbol, i.e., the first keystream symbol, denoted z_1, is produced at time $t = 1$. The produced keystream sequence is denoted $(z_1, z_2, z_3, \ldots)$.

The Finite State Machine (FSM) has two registers, denoted $R1$ and $R2$, each holding 32 bits. The value of the registers at time $t \geq 0$ is denoted $R1_t$ and $R2_t$ respectively. The input to the FSM is (s_{t+15}, s_{t+5}) and the output of the FSM, denoted F_t, is calculated as

$$F_t = (s_{t+15} \boxplus R1_t) \oplus R2_t, \quad t \geq 0 \tag{7}$$

and the keystream is given by

$$z_t = F_t \oplus s_t, \quad t \geq 1. \tag{8}$$

Here we use the notation $\boxplus$ for integer addition modulo 2^{32} and $\oplus$ for bitwise addition (XOR). The registers $R1$ and $R2$ are updated with new values according to

$$R1_{t+1} = s_{t+5} \boxplus R2_t \quad \text{and} \qquad (9)$$
$$R2_{t+1} = S(R1_t) \quad t \geq 0. \qquad (10)$$

4.1   The S-box

The S-box, denoted by $S(w)$, is a permutation on $\mathbb{Z}_{2^{32}}$ based on the round function of Rijndael [4]. Let $w = (w_3, w_2, w_1, w_0)$ be the input to the S-box, where $w_i, i = 0...3$ is the four bytes of w. Assume w_3 to be the most significant byte. Let

$$w = \begin{pmatrix} w_0 \\ w_1 \\ w_2 \\ w_3 \end{pmatrix} \qquad (11)$$

be a vector representation of the input to the S-box. First we apply the Rijndael S-box, denoted S_R to each byte, giving us the vector

$$\begin{pmatrix} S_R[w_0] \\ S_R[w_1] \\ S_R[w_2] \\ S_R[w_3] \end{pmatrix}. \qquad (12)$$

In the *MixColumn transformation* of Rijndael's round function, each 4 byte word is considered a polynomial in y over $\mathbb{F}_{2^8}$, defined by the irreducible polynomial $x^8 + x^4 + x^3 + x + 1 \in \mathbb{F}_2[x]$. Each word can be represented by a polynomial of at most degree 3. Next we consider the vector in (12) as representing a polynomial over $\mathbb{F}_{2^8}$ and multiply with a fixed polynomial $c(y) = (x+1)y^3 + y^2 + y + x \in \mathbb{F}_{2^8}[y]$ modulo $y^4 + 1 \in \mathbb{F}_{2^8}[y]$. This polynomial multiplication can (as done in Rijndael) be computed as a matrix multiplication,

$$\begin{pmatrix} r_0 \\ r_1 \\ r_2 \\ r_3 \end{pmatrix} = \begin{pmatrix} x & x+1 & 1 & 1 \\ 1 & x & x+1 & 1 \\ 1 & 1 & x & x+1 \\ x+1 & 1 & 1 & x \end{pmatrix} \begin{pmatrix} S_R[w_0] \\ S_R[w_1] \\ S_R[w_2] \\ S_R[w_3] \end{pmatrix}, \qquad (13)$$

where (r_3, r_2, r_1, r_0) are the output bytes from the S-box. These bytes are concatenated to form the word output from the S-box, $r = S(w)$.

4.2   Key Initialization

SNOW 2.0 takes two parameters as input values; a secret key of either 128 or 256 bits and a publicly known 128 bit *initialization variable IV*. The IV value is considered as a four word input $IV = (IV_3, IV_2, IV_1, IV_0)$, where IV_0 is the least significant word. The possible range for IV is thus $0 \dots 2^{128} - 1$. This means that for a given secret key K, SNOW 2.0 implements a *pseudo-random length-increasing* function from the set of IV values to the set of possible output sequences. The use of a IV value is optional and applications requiring a IV value typically reinitialize the cipher frequently with a fixed key but the IV value is changed. This could be the case if two parties agreed on a common secret key but wish to communicate multiple messages, e.g. in a frame based setting. Frequent reinitialization could also be desirable from a resynchronization perspective in e.g. a radio based environment.

The key initialization is done as follows. Denote the registers in the LFSR by $(s_{15}, s_{14}, \ldots, s_0)$ from left to right in Figure 2. Thus, s_{15} corresponds to the element holding s_{t+15} during normal operation of the cipher. Let the secret key be denoted by $K = (k_3, k_2, k_1, k_0)$ in the 128 bit case and by $K = (k_7, k_6, k_5, k_4, k_3, k_2, k_1, k_0)$ in the 256 bit case, where each k_i is a word and k_0 is the least significant word. First, the shift register is initialized with K and IV according to

$$s_{15} = k_3 \oplus IV_0, \quad s_{14} = k_2, \qquad s_{13} = k_1, \qquad s_{12} = k_0 \oplus IV_1,$$
$$s_{11} = k_3 \oplus \mathbf{1}, \quad s_{10} = k_2 \oplus \mathbf{1} \oplus IV_2, \quad s_9 = k_1 \oplus \mathbf{1} \oplus IV_3, \quad s_8 = k_0 \oplus \mathbf{1},$$

and for the second half,

$$s_7 = k_3, \qquad s_6 = k_2, \qquad s_5 = k_1, \qquad s_4 = k_0,$$
$$s_3 = k_3 \oplus \mathbf{1}, \quad s_2 = k_2 \oplus \mathbf{1}, \quad s_1 = k_1 \oplus \mathbf{1}, \quad s_0 = k_0 \oplus \mathbf{1},$$

where $\mathbf{1}$ denotes the all one vector (32 bits).

In the 256 bit case, the LFSR initialization is correspondingly,

$$s_{15} = k_7 \oplus IV_0, \quad s_{14} = k_6, \qquad s_{13} = k_5, \qquad s_{12} = k_4 \oplus IV_1,$$
$$s_{11} = k_3, \qquad s_{10} = k_2 \oplus IV_2, \quad s_9 = k_1 \oplus IV_3, \quad s_8 = k_0,$$
$$s_7 = k_7 \oplus \mathbf{1}, \quad s_6 = k_6 \oplus \mathbf{1} \quad \ldots, \qquad\qquad s_0 = k_0 \oplus \mathbf{1}.$$

After the LFSR has been initialized, R1 and R2 are both set to zero. Now, the cipher is clocked 32 times without producing any output symbols. Instead, the output of the FSM is incorporated in the feedback loop, see Figure 3. Thus, during the 32 clocks in the key initialization, the next element to be inserted into the LFSR is given by

$$s_{t+16} = \alpha^{-1} s_{t+11} \oplus s_{t+2} \oplus \alpha s_t \oplus F_t. \qquad (14)$$

After the 32 clockings the cipher is shifted back to normal operation (Figure 2) and clocked once before the first keystream symbol is produced. The maximum number of keystream words allowed is set to 2^{50}, then the cipher must be rekeyed. This limit provides a bound for cryptanalysis and implies no practical limits to the operation of the cipher. The need for producing more than 2^{50} words using the same key, is quite unlikely.

5   Design Differences from SNOW 1.0

In this section we highlight the differences between SNOW 2.0 and SNOW 1.0 and their expected security improvements. We start with the choice of feedback

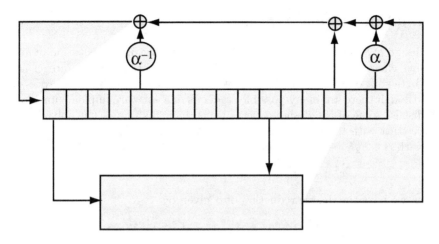

Fig. 3. Cipher operation during key initialization.

polynomial. In SNOW 1.0 the multiplication could be implemented by a single left shift of the word followed by a possible XOR with a known pattern of weight 6. This means that the resulting word was in many positions only a shift of the original word. In SNOW 2.0 we define $\mathbb{F}_{2^{32}}$ as an extension field over $\mathbb{F}_{2^8}$ and each of the two multiplications can be implemented as a *byte* shift together with a unconditional XOR with one of 256 possible patterns. This results in a better spreading of the bits in the feedback loop, and improves the resistance against certain correlation attack, as discussed in [6]. The use of *two* constants in the feedback loop also improves the resistance against bitwise linear approximation attacks, as discussed in Section 3. To the authors, there is no known method to manipulate the feedback polynomial such that the resulting linear recurrence hold for each bit position and have reasonably low weight. The unconditional XOR also seems to improve speed, by removing the possible branch prediction error in a pipelined processor.

The FSM in SNOW 2.0 now takes *two* inputs. This makes a guess-and-determine type of attack more difficult. Given the output of the FSM, together with $R1$ and $R2$ it is no longer possible to deduce the next FSM state directly. The update of $R1$ does not depend on the output of the FSM, but on a word taken from the LFSR. This also suggests that similar correlations as those found in [1] would be much weaker.

The S-box in SNOW 1.0 was also byte oriented but the final bit permutation did not diffuse as much as the new design. In SNOW 1.0, each input byte to the S-box affected only 8 bits of the output word. The choice of the new S-box, based on the round function of Rijndael, provides a much stronger diffusion. Each output bit now depends on each input bit.

6   Implementation Aspects

The design of SNOW 2.0 was done with a fast software implementation in mind. We have chosen a minimum number of different operations; XOR, integer addition, byte shift of a word, and table lookups, all available on modern processors. Even though there are many possible tradeoffs in a software implementation, we will discuss some of the design aspects which have high impact in software.

   We start with the LFSR. The field $\mathbb{F}_{2^{32}}$ is defined as an extension field over $\mathbb{F}_{2^8}$, with $\alpha \in \mathbb{F}_{2^{32}}$ being the root of the degree 4 polynomial

$$x^4 + \beta^{23}x^3 + \beta^{245}x^2 + \beta^{48}x + \beta^{239} \in \mathbb{F}_{2^8}[x] \tag{15}$$

Hence, we have the degree reduction of α given by

$$\alpha^4 = \beta^{23}\alpha^3 + \beta^{245}\alpha^2 + \beta^{48}\alpha + \beta^{239} \tag{16}$$

In the feedback loop, multiplication with α and α^{-1} can be implemented as a simple byte shift plus an additional XOR with one of 256 possible patterns. This can be seen from the representation of a word as a polynomial in $\mathbb{F}_{2^8}[x]$ using $(\alpha^3, \alpha^2, \alpha, 1)$ as base. Thus, any element w in $\mathbb{F}_{2^{32}}$ can be written as

$$w = c_3\alpha^3 + c_2\alpha^2 + c_1\alpha + c_0, \tag{17}$$

where (c_3, c_2, c_1, c_0) are the bytes of w, c_0 being the least significant byte. Multiplying w with α, will yield a reduction according to (16) as follows

$$\alpha w = c_3\alpha^4 + c_2\alpha^3 + c_1\alpha^2 + c_0\alpha \tag{18}$$
$$= (c_3\beta^{23} + c_2)\alpha^3 + (c_3\beta^{245} + c_1)\alpha^2 + (c_3\beta^{48} + c_0)\alpha + c_3\beta^{239}. \tag{19}$$

Similar calculations can be done for the multiplication with α^{-1}. Thus, to get a fast implementation of the LFSR feedback, one can use precomputed tables

$$MUL_\alpha[c] = (c\beta^{23}, c\beta^{245}, c\beta^{48}, c\beta^{239}) \tag{20}$$
$$MUL_{\alpha^{-1}}[c] = (c\beta^{16}, c\beta^{39}, c\beta^6, c\beta^{64}), \tag{21}$$

where c runs through all elements in $\mathbb{F}_{2^8}$. The pseudo-code for the multiplication would be

```
// Multiplication w*alpha ("<<" is left shift,">>" is right shift)
result=(w<<8) XOR MUL_a[w>>24];
// Multiplication  w*alpha^-1
result=(w>>8) XOR MUL_ainverse[w and 0xff];
```

   The S-box are implemented using the same techniques as done in Rijndael [4] and SCREAM [2]. Recall the expression for the S-box, $r = S(w)$

$$\begin{pmatrix} r_0 \\ r_1 \\ r_2 \\ r_3 \end{pmatrix} = \begin{pmatrix} x & x+1 & 1 & 1 \\ 1 & x & x+1 & 1 \\ 1 & 1 & x & x+1 \\ x+1 & 1 & 1 & x \end{pmatrix} \begin{pmatrix} S_R[w_0] \\ S_R[w_1] \\ S_R[w_2] \\ S_R[w_3] \end{pmatrix}. \tag{22}$$

The matrix multiplication can be split up into a linear combinations of the columns

$$\begin{pmatrix} r_0 \\ r_1 \\ r_2 \\ r_3 \end{pmatrix} = S_R[w_0] \begin{pmatrix} x \\ 1 \\ 1 \\ x+1 \end{pmatrix} + S_R[w_1] \begin{pmatrix} x+1 \\ x \\ 1 \\ 1 \end{pmatrix} +$$

$$S_R[w_2] \begin{pmatrix} 1 \\ x+1 \\ x \\ 1 \end{pmatrix} + S_R[w_3] \begin{pmatrix} 1 \\ 1 \\ x+1 \\ x \end{pmatrix}.$$

By using four tables of words, each of size 256, defined by

$$T_0[a] = \begin{pmatrix} xS_R[a] \\ S_R[a] \\ S_R[a] \\ (x+1)S_R[a] \end{pmatrix}, T_1[a] = \begin{pmatrix} (x+1)S_R[a] \\ xS_R[a] \\ S_R[a] \\ S_R[a] \end{pmatrix},$$

$$T_2[a] = \begin{pmatrix} S_R[a] \\ (x+1)S_R[a] \\ xS_R[a] \\ S_R[a] \end{pmatrix}, T_3[a] = \begin{pmatrix} S_R[a] \\ S_R[a] \\ (x+1)S_R[a] \\ xS_R[a] \end{pmatrix},$$

we can easily implement the S-box by addressing the tables with the bytes (w_3, w_2, w_1, w_0) of the input word w. In pseudo-code we can write

```
// Calculate r=S-box(w)
r=T0[byte0(w)] XOR T1[byte1(w)] XOR T2[byte2(w)] XOR T3[byte3(w)];
```

where byte0(w) means the least significant byte of w, etcetera.

We have two different C implementations, both using tables for feedback multiplication and S-box operations. The first version (*version 1*) implements the LFSR with an array using the *sliding window* technique, see e.g. [10]. This version is considered an "easy to read" standard reference version. The second version (*version 2*) implements the cipher with "hard coded" variables for the LFSR. This version produces $16 \cdot 32 = 512$ bits of keystream in each procedure call, corresponding to 16 consecutive clockings. Table 1 indicates the speed of the two implementations versions. For the key setup in SNOW 1.0, the IV mode is used as reference, since it also uses 32 clockings in the initialization phase. This accounts for a more reasonable comparison. The tests where run on an PC with Intel 4 processor running at 1.8GHz, 512 Mb of memory. Each program was compiled using gcc with optimization parameter "-O3" and *inline* directives in the code.

7 Conclusions

We have proposed a new stream cipher SNOW 2.0. The design is based on the NESSIE proposal SNOW 1.0 and addresses all weaknesses found in the original

Operation	SNOW 1.0		SNOW 2.0	
	version 1	version 2	version 1	version 2
Key setup	925	-	937	-
Keystream generation	47	34	38	18

Table 1. Number of cycles needed for key setup and cycles per word for keystream generation on a Pentium 4 @1.8GHz.

construction. The implementation is easier and encryption is faster than SNOW 1.0. Typical encryption speed is over 3Gbits/sec on a Intel Pentium 4 running at 1.8GHz.

A complete description of SNOW 2.0 was given and the design differences from SNOW 1.0 and how they apply to the known attacks were discussed. Some implementation aspects of the new design were discussed, in particular how to get a fast implementation of the LFSR and the S-box.

References

1. D. Coppersmith, S. Halevi, C. Jutla, "Cryptanalysis of stream ciphers with linear masking", To appear in *Advances in Cryptology - CRYPTO 2002*, Lecture Notes in Computer Science, Springer, 2002.
2. D. Coppersmith, S. Halevi, C. Jutla, "Scream: a software-efficient stream cipher", In *Fast Software Encryption (FSE) 2002*, Lecture Notes in Computer Science, vol. 2365, Springer 2002, 195-209.
3. D. Coppersmith, P. Rogaway, "Software-efficient pseudorandom function and the use thereof for encryption", US Patent 5,454,039, 1995.
4. J. Daemen, V. Rijmen, "The design of Rijndael", Springer Verlag Series on Information Security and Cryptography, Springer Verlag, 2002, ISBN 3-540-42580-2.
5. P. Ekdahl, T. Johansson, "SNOW - a new stream cipher", *Proceedings of first NESSIE Workshop*, Heverlee, Belgium, 2000.
6. P. Ekdahl, T. Johansson, "Distinguishing attacks on SOBER", In *Fast Software Encryption (FSE) 2002*, Lecture Notes in Computer Science, vol. 2365, Springer 2002, 210-224.
7. P. Hawkes, "Guess-and-determine attacks on SNOW", private correspondence, 2002.
8. P. Hawkes, G. Rose, "Guess-and-determine attacks on SNOW", Preproceedings of Selected Areas in Cryptography (SAC), August 2002, St John's, Newfoundland, Canada.
9. P. Hawkes, G. Rose "Primitive Specification and supportion documentation for SOBER-t16 submission to NESSIE", *Proceedings of first NESSIE Workshop*, Heverlee, Belgium, 2000.
10. P. Hawkes, G. Rose "Primitive Specification and supportion documentation for SOBER-t32 submission to NESSIE", *Proceedings of first NESSIE Workshop*, Heverlee, Belgium, 2000.
11. L. Knudsen, W. Meier, B. Preneel, V. Rijmen, S. Verdoolaege, "Analysis methods for (alleged) RC4", *Lecture Notes in Computer Science*, vol. 1514 , pp. 327–341., (Asiacrypt'98).

12. I. Mantin, A. Shamir, "A practical attack on RC4", In *Fast Software Encryption (FSE) 2001*, Lecture Notes in Computer SCience, vol. 2355, Springer 2002.
13. A. Menezes, P. van Oorschot, S. Vanstone, *Handbook of Applied Cryptography*, CRC Press, 1997.
14. R. Rivest, "The RC4 encryption algorithm", RSA Data Security, Inc. Mar. 1992.
15. P. Rogaway, D. Coppersmith, "A software optimized encryption algorithm". *Journal of Cryptology*, 11(4):273-287, 1998.
16. D. Watanabe, S. Furuya, H. Yoshida, B. Preneel, "A new keystream generator MUGI", In *Fast Software Encryption (FSE) 2002*, Lecture Notes in Computer Science, vol. 2365, Springer 2002, 179-194.
17. M. Zhang, C. Caroll, A. Chan, "The software-oriented stream cipher SSC2", In *Fast Software Encryption (FSE) 2000*, Lecture Notes in Computer Science, vol. 1978, Springer 2001, 31-48.

8   Appendix A. Test Vectors

```
Test vectors for SNOW 2.0, 128 bit key
Each key is given in bigendian format (MSB...LSB) in hexadecimal
==================

    (IV3,IV2,IV1,IV0)=(0,0,0,0)
    key=80000000000000000000000000000000
Keystream output 1...5:
        keystream=8D590AE9
        keystream=A74A7D05
        keystream=6DC9CA74
        keystream=B72D1A45
        keystream=99B0A083
==================

    (IV3,IV2,IV1,IV0)=(0,0,0,0)
    key=AAAAAAAAAAAAAAAAAAAAAAAAAAAAAAAA
Keystream output 1...5:
        keystream=E00982F5
        keystream=25F02054
        keystream=214992D8
        keystream=706F2B20
        keystream=DA585E5B
==================

    (IV3,IV2,IV1,IV0)=(4,3,2,1)
    key=80000000000000000000000000000000
Keystream output 1...5:
        keystream=D6403358
        keystream=E0354A69
        keystream=57F43FCE
        keystream=44B4B13F
        keystream=F78E24C2
==================

    (IV3,IV2,IV1,IV0)=(4,3,2,1)
    key=AAAAAAAAAAAAAAAAAAAAAAAAAAAAAAAA
Keystream output 1...5:
        keystream=C355385D
        keystream=B31D6CBD
        keystream=F774AF53
        keystream=66C2E877
        keystream=4DEADAC7
=========== End of test vectors =========
```

```
Test vectors for SNOW 2.0, 256 bit key
Each key is given in bigendian format (MSB...LSB) in hexadecimal
==================
(IV3,IV2,IV1,IV0)=(0,0,0,0)
key=
80000000000000000000000000000000000000000000000000000000000000
Keystream output 1...5:
        keystream=0B5BCCE2
        keystream=0323E28E
        keystream=0FC20380
        keystream=9C66AB73
        keystream=CA35A680
==================
(IV3,IV2,IV1,IV0)=(0,0,0,0)
key=
AAAAAAAAAAAAAAAAAAAAAAAAAAAAAAAAAAAAAAAAAAAAAAAAAAAAAAAAAAAAAAAAAA
Keystream output 1...5:
        keystream=D9CC22FD
        keystream=861492D0
        keystream=AE6F43FB
        keystream=0F072012
        keystream=078C5AEE
==================
(IV3,IV2,IV1,IV0)=(4,3,2,1)
key=
80000000000000000000000000000000000000000000000000000000000000000
Keystream output 1...5:
        keystream=7861080D
        keystream=5755E90B
        keystream=736F1091
        keystream=6ED519B1
        keystream=2C1A3A42
==================
(IV3,IV2,IV1,IV0)=(4,3,2,1)
key=
AAAAAAAAAAAAAAAAAAAAAAAAAAAAAAAAAAAAAAAAAAAAAAAAAAAAAAAAAAAAAAAAAA
Keystream output 1...5:
        keystream=29261FCE
        keystream=5ED03820
        keystream=1D6AFAF8
        keystream=B87E74FE
        keystream=D49ECB10
=========== End of test vectors =========
```

Encryption-Scheme Security in the Presence of Key-Dependent Messages

John Black[1], Phillip Rogaway[2], and Thomas Shrimpton[3]

[1] Dept. of Computer Science, University of Colorado, Boulder CO 80309, USA,
jrblack@cs.colorado.edu, www.cs.colorado.edu/~jrblack
[2] Dept. of Computer Science, University of California, Davis, CA 95616, USA, and
Dept. of Computer Science, Fac of Science, Chiang Mai University, 50200 Thailand,
rogaway@cs.ucdavis.edu, www.cs.ucdavis.edu/~rogaway
[3] Dept. of Electrical and Computer Engineering, University of California,
Davis, CA 95616, USA,
teshrim@ucdavis.edu, www.ece.ucdavis.edu/~teshrim

Abstract. Encryption that is only semantically secure should not be used on messages that depend on the underlying secret key; all bets are off when, for example, one encrypts using a shared key K the value K. Here we introduce a new notion of security, KDM security, appropriate for key-dependent messages. The notion makes sense in both the public-key and shared-key settings. For the latter we show that KDM security is easily achievable within the random-oracle model. By developing and achieving stronger notions of encryption-scheme security it is hoped that protocols which are proven secure under "formal" models of security can, in time, be safely realized by generically instantiating their primitives.

1 Introduction

BACKGROUND. This paper defines and begins to investigate a new notion for encryption-scheme security: KDM security. KDM stands for *key-dependent messages*. This is a new attack model, one that allows requested plaintexts to depend on the underlying decryption key. Our definitions are strictly stronger than indistinguishability under chosen-plaintext attacks (IND-CPA) [3, 11], and the idea is orthogonal to strengthenings in the direction of non-malleability [8], chosen-ciphertext security [18], and anonymity [10]. We show that, in the symmetric-key setting, KDM security is achievable, and by simple means, within the random-oracle model [5].

Why, at this time, do we put forth a new definition for encryption-scheme security? Our goal has been to nudge the computational treatment of encryption in a direction that makes it closer to simplistic intuition about what an *idealized* encryption scheme does. We have done this to facilitate smoothly linking up "real" encryption with "formal" encryption. Let us elaborate.

THE FORMAL VIEWS VS. THE COMPUTATIONAL VIEW. In designing high-level protocols many users of cryptography prefer to take an "abstract" or "formal" view of what they're given. They don't view encryption as a transformation

K. Nyberg and H. Heys (Eds.): SAC 2002, LNCS 2595, pp. 62–75, 2003.

on strings at all. Instead, typically, they see encryption as a formal symbol, the properties of which are modeled (not defined) by the manner in which this formal symbol may be manipulated. There are many such formal views towards cryptography; see, for example, [1, 6, 9, 15]

Quite recently, some work has emerged which starts to bridge the computational view and the formal one. Lincoln, Mitchell, Mitchell and Scedrov [13] develop a formal model that blends in computational aspects. Pfitzmann, Schunter and Waidner [16], and then Pfitzmann and Waidner [17], consider security, in the computational sense, of general reactive systems, which are modeled formally. Abadi and Rogaway [2] give a formal treatment of encryption and then prove that formally-equivalent expressions give rise to computationally indistinguishable ensembles, as long as the expressions contain no "encryption cycles" (a generalization of encrypting ones own key) and as long as the encryption scheme has the right (computational) properties.

Consider the last of these works. To the computational cryptographer the technical restriction just mentioned might be understood as a warning: formal cryptography easily permits its users to ignore an essential restriction (the necessity of avoiding encryption cycles). But there is another viewpoint—and the one that motivates us. Maybe the formal view of cryptography is already doing a nice job to capture strong intuition and it is incumbent on computational cryptography to find definitions and schemes which support formal cryptography. From this viewpoint, there is nothing obviously and intuitively "wrong" with encrypting ones decryption key, and so one had better find definitions and realizations that make this allowable. In this view, a mandate to avoid encryption cycles might seem to be an artifact of inessential definitional choices.

CONTRIBUTIONS. At a technical level, the current paper does several things:

 − We present a new, and very strong, definition of security—a definition that allows the adversary indirect access to hidden keys. One can think of this as a new attack model, KDM, and we leave the goal, IND, alone. We define KDM security for both the symmetric and asymmetric settings.

 − We separate KDM security from other notions of security. We show that KDM security implies but is not implied by CPA security. We show that some conventional means to achieve CPA security, in particular those that employ stateful encryption (e.g., counter-mode with a fixed initial counter), do *not* achieve KDM security.

 − At the same time, we show that KDM security is easy to achieve within the random-oracle model [5]: we give a simple scheme that is KDM secure.

Most of this paper focuses on the symmetric model for KDM security, but there would seem to be no essential differences between the symmetric and asymmetric settings. We define KDM security in the public-key trust model and discuss achieving it.

CONCURRENT WORK. A recent paper by Camenisch and Lysyanskaya defines a notion of *circular security* for the asymmetric setting [7, p. 17]. Their notion would seem to be strictly weaker than our (asymmetric-model) notion of KDM security. Camenisch and Lysyanskaya were interested in anonymous credential systems and saw encryption schemes satisfying circular security as a tool. Their work highlights the possibility that KDM-secure encryption schemes may be a useful primitive in designing higher-level protocols. Our own work and that of [7] were independent and cross-reference each other.

AN INTERESTING OPEN PROBLEM. This paper proposes a new privacy notion and then answers some simple questions about it. We leave unanswered the question as to whether KDM security, either for the symmetric or the asymmetric trust model, can be provably achieved in the *standard* model of computation (no random oracle) under a standard complexity assumption.

2   The Peril of Encrypting Ones Key

Goldwasser and Micali were the first to recognize the potential problems surrounding encryption cycles [11, 14]. Let us assume the symmetric setting. Given an encryption scheme that is secure in any of a number of standard senses (say IND-CPA), one can trivially modify it to construct a similarly secure encryption scheme (still IND-CPA secure, say) that is rendered completely *insecure* were the adversary somehow handed an encryption of the underlying key. (For example, modify $\mathcal{E}_K(M, R)$ to $0 \parallel \mathcal{E}_K(M, R)$ if $M \neq K$, and $1 \parallel K$ otherwise.) We call an encryption of the decryption key *an encryption cycle of length one.*

More generally, an encryption cycle involves the encryption of some function of the key. For example, the encryption the bitwise complement of K and the encryption of $M \parallel K$ (for some plaintext M) are both cycles. Some cycles pose no threat to security; other cycles do. There is no known characterization of the cases that cause problems for the standard definitions.

Informally, an encryption scheme will be called "KDM secure" if it is secure (in the sense of indistinguishability) despite an adversary's ability to obtain the encryption under key K_i of some function $g(\mathbf{K})$ of the vector $\mathbf{K}$ of underlying secret keys. (We have to think of a vector of keys because the assumption that there is just a single key would seem to entail a loss of generality.) Through the function g the adversary has indirect access to the keys, but this information is only surfaced after encryption. As examples, function g might request a particular key K_i, or it might xor various keys.

We note that one can also give a notion for key-dependent chosen-ciphertext attack, KDC, where a function of the keys can be surfaced through decryption as well as through encryption. We do not pursue this at this time.

Well-designed protocols rarely employ encryption cycles (a fact that certainly does limit the applicability of this paper!). Some encrypting backup systems may encrypt their own key (blithely encrypting the entire system image, which may include the encryption key). Some key-distribution protocols allow the adversary to effectively create an encryption cycle: having recorded a message M which includes the encryption of a session key K, the adversary may now be able to replay this message M (perhaps pretending it is a nonce) in a context in which the principal will now encrypt it under K. This gives a cycle, though not a troublesome one. The recently proposed credential system of [7] uses encryption cycles in the asymmetric setting.

We comment that there are multiple properties (beyond the ability to safely encrypt ones key) implicit in formal models and not guaranteed by IND-CPA security. These properties include protecting the integrity of messages, concealing the length of a plaintext, and concealing which pairs of ciphertexts were encrypted under the same key. But the most bothersome and most ignored problem seems to be key-dependent plaintexts.

3   Background Notions

NOTATION. Let $\{0,1\}^*$ be the space of (finite) binary strings, let $\{0,1\}^\infty$ be the space of infinite binary strings, and let S^∞ be the set of tuples $(K_1, K_2, \ldots)$ where each $K_i \in S$. If $Pad \in \{0,1\}^\infty$ and $M \in \{0,1\}^*$ then $Pad \oplus M$ and $M \oplus Pad$ are the xor of M and the first $|M|$ bits of Pad. Let $x_1, x_2, \ldots \xleftarrow{\$} \Omega$ mean that $x_1, x_2, \ldots$ are assigned values independently from the distribution Ω. (Use the uniform distribution when Ω is a finite set.) If A is a probabilistic algorithm then $a \xleftarrow{\$} A(x_1, x_2, \ldots)$ denotes running A on the given inputs and letting a be the outcome. An *adversary* is a probabilistic algorithm that may access one or more oracles. The running time of A is the actual running time of A plus its description size. If A makes oracle queries that specify functions $g_1, g_2, \ldots$ then the running time of A also includes the (worst case) time to compute each queried function g_i.

SYMMETRIC ENCRYPTION. We recall the syntax for a symmetric-encryption scheme as given (in a slightly modified form) by [3]. Let Plaintext and Ciphertext be nonempty sets of strings. We assume that Plaintext has the property that if $M \in$ Plaintext then $M' \in$ Plaintext for every M' of the same length as M. Let Key $= \{0,1\}^k$ for some $k \geq 1$ and let Coins $= \{0,1\}^r$ for some $r \geq 1$. Let String $= \{0,1\}^*$ be the set of all (finite) strings. Then a *symmetric encryption scheme* is a triple of algorithms $\Pi = (\mathcal{K}, \mathcal{E}, \mathcal{D})$ where: $\mathcal{K}$: Coins $\rightarrow$ Key and $\mathcal{E}$: Key $\times$ String $\times$ Coins $\rightarrow$ Ciphertext $\cup \{*\}$ and $\mathcal{D}$: Key $\times$ String $\rightarrow$ Plaintext $\cup \{*\}$. Algorithm $\mathcal{K}$ is called the *key-generation* algorithm, $\mathcal{E}$ is called the *encryption* algorithm, and $\mathcal{D}$ is the *decryption* algorithm. We call k (the length of any string K output by $\mathcal{K}$) the *key length* of Π and we call r (the number of random bits used by $\mathcal{E}$) the *coin length* of Π. We usually write the first argument to $\mathcal{E}$ and $\mathcal{D}$ as a subscript. We call $\mathcal{E}_K(M, R)$ the encryption of the *plaintext* M under key K and coins R. Usually we omit specific reference to the final argument to $\mathcal{E}$, the random string R, thinking of $\mathcal{E}_K$ as a probabilistic algorithm. Likewise, we usually omit mention of the argument to $\mathcal{K}$, thinking of $\mathcal{K}$ as a probabilistic algorithm, or else the induced probability space. We require that for all $K \in$ Key and $R \in$ Coins, if $M \notin$ Plaintext then $\mathcal{E}_K(M, R) = *$ and if $M \in$ Plaintext then $\mathcal{E}_K(M, R) \in$ Ciphertext and, what's more, $\mathcal{D}_K(\mathcal{E}_K(M, R)) = M$.

The syntax above is for encryption schemes in the *standard model*. To define encryption schemes in the *random-oracle model* we allow that $\mathcal{K}$, $\mathcal{E}$ and $\mathcal{D}$ are given an oracle $H \in \Omega$ where Ω is the set of all functions from $\{0,1\}^*$ to $\{0,1\}^\infty$.

IND-CPA SECURITY. We review the notion of indistinguishability under a chosen-plaintext attack [3, 11]. Let $\Pi = (\mathcal{K}, \mathcal{E}, \mathcal{D})$ be a symmetric encryption scheme and let A be an adversary. For $K \in \mathsf{Key}$ let

> Real_K be the oracle that on input M returns $C \overset{\$}{\leftarrow} \mathcal{E}_K(M)$ and let
>
> Fake_K be the oracle that on input M returns $C \overset{\$}{\leftarrow} \mathcal{E}_K(0^{|M|})$

The **IND-CPA advantage** of A is defined as

$$\mathsf{Adv}_{\Pi}^{\mathrm{cpa}}(A) \overset{\mathrm{def}}{=} \left| \Pr\left[K \overset{\$}{\leftarrow} \mathcal{K} : A^{\mathsf{Real}_K} = 1 \right] - \Pr\left[K \overset{\$}{\leftarrow} \mathcal{K} : A^{\mathsf{Fake}_K} = 1 \right] \right|$$

4   The Notion of Symmetric KDM Security

The notion of IND-KDM security strengthens the IND-CPA notion just given. We again imagine two experiments. Both experiments begin by selecting a vector of keys $\mathbf{K} = (K_1, K_2, \ldots)$ where each key K_i is determined by running the key-generation algorithm $\mathcal{K}$. Independent coins are used in each run. We denote this step by $\mathbf{K} \overset{\$}{\leftarrow} \mathcal{K}$ and it is the same as: **for** $i \in \{1, 2, \ldots\}$ **do** $K_i \overset{\$}{\leftarrow} \mathcal{K}$. Then:

- **Real**: the adversary is given an oracle $\mathsf{Real}_{\mathbf{K}}$ that takes two inputs: a number $j \in \{1, 2, \ldots\}$ and a function g. The function g is described by a (deterministic) RAM program, encoded according to some fixed conventions. Function g maps $\mathbf{K} \in (\{0, 1\}^*)^\infty$ to $g(\mathbf{K}) \in \{0, 1\}^*$. When oracle $\mathsf{Real}_{\mathbf{K}}$ is asked (j, g) it probabilistically encrypts $M = g(\mathbf{K})$ under key K_j.
- **Fake**: the adversary is given an oracle $\mathsf{Fake}_{\mathbf{K}}$ that, when similarly asked (j, g), probabilistically encrypts $|g(\mathbf{K})|$ zero-bits under key K_j.

The adversary should output a 1 if it believes it has participated in experiment **Real** and 0 if it believes it has participated in experiment **Fake**. We insist that for any (j, g) queried by an adversary, $|g(\mathbf{K})|$ does not depend on $\mathbf{K}$. To describe this condition we say that g is *fixed-length*. We call g the *plaintext-construction function*.

Definition 1 (IND-KDM — standard model — symmetric setting). Let $\Pi = (\mathcal{K}, \mathcal{E}, \mathcal{D})$ be a symmetric encryption scheme and let A be an adversary. For $\mathbf{K} \in (\{0, 1\}^*)^\infty$, let

> $\mathsf{Real}_{\mathbf{K}}$ be the oracle that on input (j, g) returns $C \overset{\$}{\leftarrow} \mathcal{E}_{K_j}(g(\mathbf{K}))$ and let
>
> $\mathsf{Fake}_{\mathbf{K}}$ be the oracle that on input (j, g) returns $C \overset{\$}{\leftarrow} \mathcal{E}_{K_j}(0^{|g(\mathbf{K})|})$

The **IND-KDM advantage** of an adversary A is defined as

$$\mathsf{Adv}_{\Pi}^{\mathrm{kdm}}(A) \overset{\mathrm{def}}{=} \left| \Pr\left[\mathbf{K} \overset{\$}{\leftarrow} \mathcal{K} : A^{\mathsf{Real}_{\mathbf{K}}} = 1 \right] - \Pr\left[\mathbf{K} \overset{\$}{\leftarrow} \mathcal{K} : A^{\mathsf{Fake}_{\mathbf{K}}} = 1 \right] \right| \qquad \Diamond$$

We often omit the quantifier IND in IND-KDM.

Informally, an encryption scheme Π is KDM secure if for any "reasonable" adversary A we have that $\mathsf{Adv}_{\Pi}^{\mathrm{kdm}}(A)$ is "small." We shall make precise statements along these lines. However, there is also an asymptotic way of defining this notion. For it one parameterizes the encryption scheme by a security parameter k and provides k to the adversary, in unary. Then one demands that for any polynomial time adversary A we have that $\mathsf{Adv}_\Pi^{\mathrm{kdm}}(A)$ is negligible (i.e., it vanishes faster than the inverse of any polynomial). One includes in A's running time the running time of the plaintext-construction functions g.

IND-KDM IN THE RO MODEL. KDM security is an extremely strong notion. It is easily seen to imply "standard" notions, like IND-CPA, and it is easily seen not to be implied by IND-CPA (that is, if there exists an IND-CPA secure encryption scheme then there exists an IND-CPA secure encryption scheme that is not IND-KDM secure). The IND-KDM notion is so strong, in fact, that we are unaware of any scheme, regardless of complexity, that demonstrably meets the definition we have given (for the standard model of computation). Here we will instead be giving an efficient scheme in the random-oracle model. Before giving our scheme, we must define KDM security in the random-oracle model.

Recall that Ω is the set of all functions H from $\{0,1\}^*$ to $\{0,1\}^\infty$. This set is provided with a probability measure by saying that a random H from Ω assigns to each $X \in \{0,1\}^*$ an infinite sequence of bits each of which is selected uniformly at random. Though $H(X)$ is defined to be an infinite string, algorithms that use H necessarily make use of only a finite-length prefix. We provide algorithms $\mathcal{K}, \mathcal{E}, \mathcal{D}, A$, and g with oracle access to $H \in \Omega$. We write a question-mark superscript, as in $g^?$, if we wish to emphasize that an algorithm calls out to an (unspecified) oracle.

For the RO model we must update the notion of g being fixed-length: for any (j,g) asked by an adversary, $|g^H(\mathbf{K})|$ must be independent of both H and $\mathbf{K}$. This means that $|g^H(\mathbf{K})| = |g^H(\mathbf{K}')|$ for any $H, H' \in \Omega$ and $\mathbf{K}, \mathbf{K}' \in (\{0,1\}^*)^\infty$.

Definition 2 (IND-KDM — RO-model — symmetric setting). Let $\Pi = (\mathcal{K}, \mathcal{E}, \mathcal{D})$ be a symmetric encryption scheme for the RO model, and let A be an adversary. For $\mathbf{K} \in (\{0,1\}^*)^\infty$, let

$\mathsf{Real}_\mathbf{K}^H$ be the oracle that on input $(j, g^?)$ returns $C \xleftarrow{\$} \mathcal{E}_{K_j}^H(g^H(\mathbf{K}))$ and let

$\mathsf{Fake}_\mathbf{K}^H$ be the oracle that on input $(j, g^?)$ returns $C \xleftarrow{\$} \mathcal{E}_{K_j}^H(0^{|g^H(\mathbf{K})|})$

The **KDM-advantage** of A in the random-oracle model is defined as

$$\mathsf{Adv}_\Pi^{\mathrm{kdm}}(A) \stackrel{\mathrm{def}}{=} \left| \Pr\left[\mathbf{K} \xleftarrow{\$} \mathcal{K}; H \xleftarrow{\$} \Omega : A^{H, \, \mathsf{Real}_\mathbf{K}^H} = 1 \right] \right.$$
$$\left. - \Pr\left[\mathbf{K} \xleftarrow{\$} \mathcal{K}; H \xleftarrow{\$} \Omega : A^{H, \, \mathsf{Fake}_\mathbf{K}^H} = 1 \right] \right| \qquad \Diamond$$

COMMENTS. We emphasize that for KDM security in the RO model, the adversary A can effectively access the random oracle H in two different ways: in a *direct* query the adversary asks X and receives $H(X)$; while in an *indirect* query the adversary asks for the encryption under key K_i of $M = g^H(\mathbf{K})$ and the computation of $g^H(\mathbf{K})$ does *itself* involve some number of calls to H.

The assumption that the plaintext-construction function g is fixed-length is a necessary one; without making this assumption, KDM-secure schemes would not exist. Consider, for example, the function $g_{i,j}$ where $g_{i,j}(\mathbf{K}) = 1$ if the i-th bit of K_j is 1 and $g_{i,j}(\mathbf{K}) = 00$ if the i-th bit of K_j is 0. If encryption function $\mathcal{E}$ reveals the length of the plaintext (which our definition allows) then an adversary can ask for $g_{i,j}(\mathbf{K})$-values as a way to learn any key, bit by bit. Once a key K_j is determined by the adversary it can use this knowledge to distinguish experiments **Real** and **Fake**. Basically, having allowed encryption to be the length-revealing, one must not permit the length of $M = g^H(\mathbf{K})$ to act as "covert channel" for the adversary to learn information about $\mathbf{K}$.

The role of the plaintext-construction function g can be thought of like this: it's as though A and g are in cahoots (after all, A chooses g) and g knows all of the keys. If only g could get some information back to its buddy A, then A would win. But g's output is forced to go through an encryption operation before it is sent back to A. In a KDM-secure scheme, the plaintext-construction function g, poor thing, has no way to get anything useful back to A.

5   Achieving KDM Security in the Symmetric Setting

We now provide a simple and efficient technique to achieve an IND-KDM secure symmetric encryption scheme in the RO model. Several natural methods would seem to accomplish this goal (see the discussion at the end of this section); we give a particularly simple one.

THE **ver** CONSTRUCTION. For $k \geq 1$ an integer, the symmetric encryption scheme that we denote $\mathbf{ver}[k] = (\mathcal{K}, \mathcal{E}, \mathcal{D})$ works as follows. Key-generation algorithm $\mathcal{K}$ outputs a random k-bit string K. Encryption algorithm $\mathcal{E}$ is defined by $\mathcal{E}_K(M, R) = R \parallel (H(K \parallel R) \oplus M)$ where $R \in \{0,1\}^k$ is the $r = k = |K|$ random coins used for encryption. Decryption algorithm $\mathcal{D}$ is defined by $\mathcal{D}_K(\mathcal{C}) = *$ if $|\mathcal{C}| < |K| = k$ and, otherwise, $\mathcal{D}_K(\mathcal{C}) = H(K \parallel R) \oplus C$ where $R = \mathcal{C}[1..k]$ is the first $k = |K|$ bits of $\mathcal{C}$ and $C = \mathcal{C}[k+1..]$ is the rest of $\mathcal{C}$.

We now show that scheme **ver** is KDM secure (in the RO model).

Theorem 1 (KDM security of the ver construction). Let $k \geq 1$ be a number and let A be an adversary that attacks $\mathbf{ver}[k]$. Suppose that A asks at most q oracle queries (encryption queries + direct RO queries + indirect RO queries). Then $\mathsf{Adv}^{\mathrm{kdm}}_{\mathbf{ver}[k]}(A) \leq q^2/2^{k-2}$. $\qquad\qquad\diamondsuit$

Proof: The proof is an application of the game-playing paradigm as used, for example, in [12].

We begin by making some without-loss-of-generality assumptions about the behavior of A. Let $N < q$ be the number of different keys referenced by adversary A (that is, referenced as j-values in $(j, g^?)$-queries). First, we assume that the keys referenced by A are keys $j = 1, 2, \ldots, N$. This entails no loss of generality: an adversary that uses a key with a name other than $j \in [1..N]$ can easily be modified not to do this by renaming to j the j-th new key accessed by A. Such a renaming does not impact A's advantage. Second, we assume that A makes no H-queries, either direct or indirect, having length other than $2k$. Such queries are clearly irrelevant to A's mission and any adversary A making such queries is easily modified to an adversary A which does not. Finally, we assume that A

```
INITIALIZATION:
10    for j ← 1 to N do K_j ←$ {0, 1}^k
11    bad ← false;   X ← ∅
12    for all X ∈ {0, 1}^{2k} do H(X) ← undefined

ON RO QUERY K ‖ R:
20    if K ‖ R ∈ X then bad ← true
21    if K ‖ R ∉ Domain(H) then H(K ‖ R) ←$ {0, 1}
22    return H(K ‖ R)

ON ENCRYPTION QUERY (j, g^?):
30    Compute M ← g^?(K). To do this, run g.
31    When g makes a RO query of K ‖ R:
32         if K ‖ R ∉ Domain(H) then H(K ‖ R) ←$ {0, 1}
33         Answer g's RO query with H(K ‖ R)
34    R ←$ {0, 1}^k
35    C ←$ {0, 1}^{|M|}
36    if K_j ‖ R ∈ Domain(H) then
37       bad ← true
38       C ← H(K_j ‖ R) ⊕ M          ⟵ use this line in game R
38       C ← H(K_j ‖ R) ⊕ 0^{|M|}     ⟵ use this line in game F
39    else
40       H(K_j ‖ R) ← C ⊕ M           ⟵ use this line in game R
40       H(K_j ‖ R) ← C ⊕ 0^{|M|}      ⟵ use this line in game F
41    X ← X ∪ {K_j ‖ R}
42    return R ‖ C
```

Fig. 1. Definition for game R and F. We define Domain(H) to be the set of points X where $H(X)$ is not equal to undefined.

never repeats a direct RO query $K ‖ R$. The adversary has no need to repeat RO queries since it already knows the answer.

To prove that $\mathsf{Adv}^{\mathrm{kdm}}_{\mathbf{ver}[k]}(A)$ is small we are going to present A not with a Real or Fake oracle to distinguish, but an R or F oracle, instead, where these oracles are defined in Fig. 1. We refer to these oracles as specifying different *games* that the adversary plays. The games (oracle behavior) depends on the parameter k but we omit this from the notation.

We first claim that the R-labeled code in Fig. 1 provides A an identical view as a Real $\mathbf{ver}[k]$-oracle, while the F-labeled code provides A an identical view as a Fake $\mathbf{ver}[k]$-oracle. This is apparent by inspecting the code. Ignore all statements involving variable *bad* since these statements do not result in any change visible to adversary A (they are used only for accounting purposes). The code simulates a random oracle H by assigning a uniform and independent range point $H(X)$ to each domain point X for which a value is needed. The code chooses C at random and then defines $H(K_j‖R)$ from it, rather than choosing $H(K_j‖R)$ at random and then defining C from it. These are clearly equivalent as far as the view provided to adversary A. With the natural abbreviations in notation we then have the following:

Claim 1. $\mathsf{Adv}^{\mathrm{kdm}}_{\mathbf{ver}[k]}(A) = \left|\Pr[A^{\mathsf{R}} = 1] - \Pr[A^{\mathsf{F}} = 1]\right|$

To proceed with our analysis we introduce in Fig. 2 a third game, game C. Let "A^{R} sets *bad*" be the event that flag *bad* gets set to true (at some point in the execution) when A runs with an R oracle, and similarly define events "A^{F} sets *bad*" and "A^{C} sets *bad*". We have the following:

Claim 2. $\left|\Pr[A^{\mathsf{R}} = 1] - \Pr[A^{\mathsf{C}} = 1]\right| = \Pr[A^{\mathsf{C}} \text{ sets } bad]$ and
$\left|\Pr[A^{\mathsf{F}} = 1] - \Pr[A^{\mathsf{C}} = 1]\right| = \Pr[A^{\mathsf{C}} \text{ sets } bad]$ and so
$\left|\Pr[A^{\mathsf{R}} = 1] - \Pr[A^{\mathsf{F}} = 1]\right| \leq 2 \cdot \Pr[A^{\mathsf{C}} \text{ sets } bad]$

Let us show the the first equality. First imagine eliminating line 38 from the code for game R. Call the new game R'. The change does not impact the probability that flag *bad* is set to true (that is, $\Pr[A^{\mathsf{R}} \text{ sets } bad] = \Pr[A^{\mathsf{R}'} \text{ sets } bad]$) because *bad* has already been set to true when line 38 executes. Now that line 38 is gone, in game R', also eliminate line 40. This too does not change the probability that *bad* gets set to true. The reason is that the value stored at $H(K_j \parallel R)$ by line 40 can only influence what the adversary sees by a subsequent execution of line 22, and when the assignment statement at line 40 does so influence line 22, the book-keeping done at line 41 will have caused *bad* to be set to true at line 20 anyway. (Why can't the assigning of a value to $H(K_j \parallel R)$ at line 40 influence values returned at a subsequent execution of line 42 in game R'? Because the use made of the $H(\cdots)$-values in lines 30–42 of game R' is only in defining $M = g^H(\mathbf{K})$, but then all that we use of M (in lines 34–42 of game R') is $|M|$ (at line 35), and we have *assumed* that $|g^H(\mathbf{K})|$ is independent of both H and $\mathbf{K}$, our "fixed-length" assumption on g.) We conclude that $\Pr[A^{\mathsf{R}} \text{ sets } bad] = \Pr[A^{\mathsf{C}} \text{ sets } bad]$. The exact same reasoning tells us that $\Pr[A^{\mathsf{F}} \text{ sets } bad] = \Pr[A^{\mathsf{C}} \text{ sets } bad]$. The final inequality of Claim 2 then follows by the triangle inequality.

Next we show the following:

Claim 3. $\Pr[A^{\mathsf{C}} \text{ sets } bad] \leq q^2/2^{k-1}$

To prove this claim we separately consider the two places in game C where *bad* can be set to true. The probability that *bad* gets set to true at line 36 is at most $q^2/2^k$ since during each of the at most q times that line 36 is executed the value R is randomly chosen just before (line 34) from a set of size 2^k and then we test if *something* $\parallel R$ is in a set of size at most q. Similarly, we claim that the probability that *bad* gets set to true at line 20 is at most $qN/2^k \leq q^2/2^k$. This statement would be clear if only the adversary were given no information about the values $(K_1, \ldots, K_N)$ selected at line 10; in such a case, we are testing at most q times if $K \parallel something$ (where K is supplied by the adversary) is in a random, secret set of size at most $N/2^k$. But, in fact, the view provided to the adversary A in game C *is* independent of $(K_1, \ldots, K_N)$. Note that every encryption query

```
INITIALIZATION:
10    for j ← 1 to N do K_j ←$ {0,1}^k
11    bad ← false;   X ← ∅
12    for all X ∈ {0,1}^{2k} do H(X) ← undefined

ON RO QUERY K ∥ R:
20    if K ∥ R ∈ X then bad ← true
21    if K ∥ R ∉ Domain(H) then H(K ∥ R) ←$ {0,1}
22    return H(K ∥ R)

ON ENCRYPTION QUERY (j, g^?):
30    Compute M ← g^?(K). To do this, run g.
31    When g makes a RO query of K ∥ R:
32        if K ∥ R ∉ Domain(H) then H(K ∥ R) ←$ {0,1}
33        Answer g's RO query with H(K ∥ R)
34    R ←$ {0,1}^k
35    C ←$ {0,1}^{|M|}
36    if K_j ∥ R ∈ Domain(H) then bad ← true
41    X ← X ∪ {K_j ∥ R}
42    return R ∥ C
```

Fig. 2. Game C. This game has similar behavior, as far as the adversary can tell, to games R and F.

returns a random string whose length is independent of $(K_1, \ldots, K_N)$ (by the fixed-length assumption on g) while every RO query returns a random infinite string, independent of $(K_1, \ldots, K_N)$ (whether that random string is selected in line 21 or in line 32 is irrelevant).

Putting together the three claims completes the proof. ∎

ALTERNATIVE CONSTRUCTIONS. There are a number of natural constructions for a KDM-secure symmetric encryption scheme in the RO model. For example, one might start with an arbitrary symmetric encryption scheme $\Pi = (\mathcal{K}, \mathcal{E}, \mathcal{D})$ for which the coins R used to encrypt can be recovered from the ciphertext. (Standard modes like CBC with a random IV have this property.) Then modify Π to a symmetric encryption scheme $\bar{\Pi} = (\mathcal{K}, \bar{\mathcal{E}}, \bar{\mathcal{D}})$ by setting $\bar{\mathcal{E}}_K(M, R) = \mathcal{E}_{H(K \parallel R)}(M, R)$ and correspondingly modifying $\mathcal{D}$. It seems reasonable to expect that $\bar{\Pi}$ will be IND-KDM secure (in the RO model) when Π is IND-CPA secure (in the standard model).

6   KDM Insecurity for Stateful Symmetric Encryption

A *stateful* encryption scheme is like the (probabilistic, symmetric) encryption schemes we have defined except that the encryption function $\mathcal{E}$ is deterministic and takes as input a hidden variable, the *state*. Every time a message M is encrypted under $\mathcal{E}_K$ the current state S of the encryption algorithm is modified to a new state $S' = f(S, M)$. (It is fine to allow this update to depend on K as well.) The initial state, S_0, is specified as part of the scheme. We write $\mathcal{E}_K^S(M)$ for the encryption of message M using key K and state S.

An example of a stateful encryption scheme is the form of CBC mode where the IV is $E_K(S)$ and S, initially the zero-block, is incremented with every message that is encrypted. This scheme is IND-CPA secure.

It is straightforward to adapt the definitions we have given for KDM security to deal with stateful schemes. However, one will soon notice that there can not exist a stateful KDM-secure encryption scheme. Let us explain the problem.

Since the function $\mathcal{E}$ is deterministic and and the plaintext-construction function g depends on $\mathbf{K}$, the plaintext-construction function g "knows" everything that $\mathcal{E}$ knows and so, in particular, g can determine what ciphertext $\mathcal{E}$ will produce next for any given message. The function g can generate a plaintext such that its encryption conveys to A some information about $\mathbf{K}$. For example, one could define a plaintext-construction function $g_{i,j,k,S,V}$ that returns the first k-bit message M (or 0^k if no such message exists) such that the inner product of V and ciphertext $C = \mathcal{E}_K^S(M)$ is the ith bit of K_j. Using such functions the adversary can easily extract an underlying key, bit-by-bit, and use this key to break the scheme's KDM security.

7   KDM Security in the Public-Key Setting

PRELIMINARIES. We recall the syntax of an asymmetric encryption scheme, as given (in a slightly modified form) in [4]. Let String, Plaintext, and Ciphertext all be as before. Also, let Parameter $= 1^*$ and let Coins $= \{0, 1\}^\infty$, PublicKey $\subseteq$ String, and SecretKey $\subseteq$ String. Then an *asymmetric encryption scheme* is a triple of algorithms $\Pi = (\mathcal{K}, \mathcal{E}, \mathcal{D})$ where $\mathcal{K}$: Parameter $\times$ Coins $\rightarrow$ PublicKey $\times$ SecretKey and $\mathcal{E}$: PublicKey $\times$ String $\times$ Coins $\rightarrow$ Ciphertext $\cup \{*\}$ and $\mathcal{D}$: SecretKey $\times$ String $\rightarrow$ Plaintext $\cup \{*\}$. As for symmetric encryption, we usually omit the last argument to both $\mathcal{K}$ and $\mathcal{E}$, thinking of both as probabilistic algorithms, and we write the second argument to $\mathcal{E}$ and $\mathcal{D}$ as a subscript. Upon input 1^k the key-generation algorithm returns a pair (pk, sk) of matching public and secret keys. We require that for all (pk, sk) which can be output by $\mathcal{K}(1^k)$, for all $M \in$ Plaintext, and for all strings C that can be output by $\mathcal{E}_{pk}(M)$, we have that $\mathcal{D}_{sk}(C) = M$.

DEFINITION OF KDM SECURITY IN THE PUBLIC-KEY SETTING. The intuition behind the definition of KDM security in the asymmetric setting is just like that for the symmetric setting. The adversary A is given access to an oracle that will encrypt under a specific public key pk a specified function g that may depend on a vector of secret keys $\mathbf{sk}$. Notice that A can compute encryptions of standard plaintext messages on its own, but still requires the oracle for computation of g when it accesses $\mathbf{sk}$. After interacting with its oracle, adversary A outputs a "1" if it believes its oracle returns real encryptions, and it outputs a "0" otherwise. If a reasonable adversary can not do a good job at this game, then the scheme is KDM secure. We let $(\mathbf{pk}, \mathbf{sk}) \xleftarrow{\$} 1^k$ denote: **for** $i \in \{1, 2, \ldots\}$ **do** $(pk_i, sk_i) \xleftarrow{\$} \mathcal{K}(1^k)$.

Definition 3 (IND-KDM — standard model — asymmetric setting).
Let $\Pi = (\mathcal{K}, \mathcal{E}, \mathcal{D})$ be an asymmetric encryption scheme, and let A be an adversary. For $(\mathbf{pk}, \mathbf{sk}) \in (\mathsf{PublicKey} \times \mathsf{SecretKey})^\infty$ let

Real$_{\mathbf{sk}}$ be the oracle that on input (i, g) returns $C \xleftarrow{\$} \mathcal{E}_{pk_i}(g(\mathbf{sk}))$

Fake$_{\mathbf{sk}}$ be the oracle that on input (i, g) returns $C \xleftarrow{\$} \mathcal{E}_{pk_i}(0^{|g(\mathbf{sk})|})$.

The **IND-KDM advantage** of an adversary A for security parameter k is

$$\mathsf{Adv}^{\mathrm{kdm}}_{\Pi, k}(A) \stackrel{\mathrm{def}}{=} \left| \Pr\left[(\mathbf{pk}, \mathbf{sk}) \xleftarrow{\$} \mathcal{K}(1^k) : A^{\mathsf{Real}_{\mathbf{sk}}}(1^k, \mathbf{pk}) = 1 \right] \right.$$
$$\left. - \Pr\left[(\mathbf{pk}, \mathbf{sk}) \xleftarrow{\$} \mathcal{K}(1^k) : A^{\mathsf{Fake}_{\mathbf{sk}}}(1^k, \mathbf{pk}) = 1 \right] \right|. \qquad \Diamond$$

The plaintext-construction function g must, as usual, be fixed-length: $|g(\mathbf{sk})|$ may not depend on $\mathbf{sk}$.

The definition for KDM security within the RO model is exactly analogous to what we have done already. Here one insists that $|g^H(\mathbf{sk})|$ be independent of both H and $\mathbf{sk}$.

THE **VER** CONSTRUCTION. We recall a simple encryption scheme specified in [5]. Let $\mathcal{F}$ be a trapdoor permutation generator: on input 1^k the probabilistic algorithm $\mathcal{F}$ returns (the encodings of) functions (f, f^{-1}) where $f: \{0, 1\}^k \to \{0, 1\}^k$ and $f^{-1}: \{0, 1\}^k \to \{0, 1\}^k$ is its inverse. (We do not bother to distinguish between functions and their encodings.) Mirroring our construction for the symmetric-key setting, define the (random-oracle model) asymmetric encryption scheme $\mathbf{VER}[\mathcal{F}] = (\mathcal{K}, \mathcal{E}, \mathcal{D})$ as follows. The key-generation algorithm $\mathcal{K}$ is identical to $\mathcal{F}$. Encryption algorithm $\mathcal{E}_f(M, R) = f(R) \parallel (H(R) \oplus M)$ where $k = |R|$ is the domain length of f (assumed to be apparent f and f^{-1}) and R is the random coins used by the encryption algorithm and H is the random oracle. Decryption algorithm $\mathcal{D}_{f^{-1}}(\mathcal{C}) = *$ if $|\mathcal{C}| < k$ and $\mathcal{D}_{f^{-1}}(\mathcal{C}) = H(f^{-1}(Y)) \oplus C$ otherwise, where Y is the first k bits of $\mathcal{C}$ and C is the remaining bits.

One expects that $\mathbf{VER}[\mathcal{F}]$ is a KDM-secure encryption scheme if $\mathcal{F}$ is a secure trapdoor permutation. At the time of this writing, we have not written up a proof of this.

The above is only one natural construction; others would seem to work. In [7] Camenisch and Lysyanskaya give a different scheme which they claim is "circular secure" (in the RO model), a notion that they define. One would expect their scheme to be KDM secure as well, though we have not written up a proof of this.

Acknowledgments

Thanks to the anonymous reviewers for their comments.

John Black received support from NSF CAREER award CCR-0133985. Part of this work was carried out while John was at the University of Nevada, Reno.

Phil Rogaway and his student Tom Shrimpton received support from NSF grant CCR-0085961 and a gift from CISCO Systems. Many thanks for their kind support.

References

[1] M. Abadi and A. Gordon. A calculus for cryptographic protocols: The spi calculus. *Information and Computation*, 148(1):1–70, January 1999. An extended version appeared as Digital Equipment Corporation Systems Research Center report No. 149, January 1998.

[2] M. Abadi and P. Rogaway. Reconciling two views of cryptography: The computational soundness of formal encryption. In *IFIP International Conference on Theoretical Computer Science*, August 2000.

[3] M. Bellare, A. Desai, E. Jokipii, and P. Rogaway. A concrete security treatment of symmetric encryption: analysis of the DES modes of operation. In *Proceedings of 38th Annual Symposium on Foundations of Computer Science (FOCS 97)*, 1997.

[4] M. Bellare, A. Desai, D. Pointcheval, and P. Rogaway. Relations among notions of security for public-key encryption schemes. In H. Krawczyk, editor, *Advances in Cryptology – CRYPTO '98*, volume 1462 of *Lecture Notes in Computer Science*, pages 232–249. Springer-Verlag, 1998.

[5] M. Bellare and P. Rogaway. Random oracles are practical: A paradigm for designing efficient protocols. In *Proceedings of the 1st ACM Conference on Computer and Communications Security*, pages 62–73, 1993.

[6] M. Burrows, M. Abadi, and R. Needham. A logic of authentication. *Proceedings of the Royal Society of London A*, 426:233–271, 1989. A preliminary version appeared as Digital Equipment Corporation Systems Research Center report No. 39, February 1989.

[7] J. Camenisch and A. Lysyanskaya. "Efficient non-transferable anonymous multi-show credential system with optional anonymity revocation". In *Advances in Cryptology – EUROCRYPT '01*, Lecture Notes in Computer Science. Springer-Verlag, 2001.

[8] D. Dolev, C. Dwork, and M. Naor. Non-malleable cryptography. To appear in *SIAM J. on Computing*. Earlier version in STOC 91, 1998.

[9] D. Dolev and A. Yao. On the security of public key protocols. *IEEE Transactions on Information Theory*, IT-29(12):198–208, March 1983.

[10] M. Fischlin. "Pseudorandom function tribe ensembles based on one-way permutations: Improvements and applications". In *Advances in Cryptology – EUROCRYPT '99*, Lecture Notes in Computer Science. Springer-Verlag, 1999.

[11] S. Goldwasser and S. Micali. Probabilistic encryption. *Journal of Computer and System Sciences*, 28:270–299, April 1984.

[12] J. Kilian and P. Rogaway. How to protect DES against exhaustive key search. *Journal of Cryptology*, 14(1):17–35, 2001. Earlier version in CRYPTO '96.

[13] P. Lincoln, J. Mitchell, M. Mitchell, and A. Scedrov. A probabilistic poly-time framework for protocol analysis. In *Proceedings of the Fifth ACM Conference on Computer and Communications Security*, pages 112–121, 1998.

[14] S. Micali. Personal communication, circa 1985.

[15] L. Paulson. The inductive approach to verifying cryptographic protocols. *Journal of Computer Security*, 6(1–2):85–128, 1998.

[16] B. Pfitzmann, M. Schunter, and M. Waidner. Cryptographic security of reactive systems (extended abstract). *Electronic Notes in Theoretical Computer Science*, 32, April 2000.

[17] B. Pfitzmann and M. Waidner. "Composition and integrity preservation of secure reactive systems". *IBM Research Report RZ 3234, #93280*, June 2000.

[18] C. Rackoff and D.Simon. Non-interactive zero-knowledge proof of knowledge and chosen ciphertext attack. In *Advances in Cryptology – CRYPTO '94*, Lecture Notes in Computer Science. Springer-Verlag, 1994.

On the Security of CTR + CBC-MAC

Jakob Jonsson[*]

jakob_jonsson@yahoo.se

Abstract. We analyze the security of the CTR + CBC-MAC (CCM) encryption mode. This mode, proposed by Doug Whiting, Russ Housley, and Niels Ferguson, combines the CTR ("counter") encryption mode with CBC-MAC message authentication and is based on a block cipher such as AES. We present concrete lower bounds for the security of CCM in terms of the security of the underlying block cipher. The conclusion is that CCM provides a level of privacy and authenticity that is in line with other proposed modes such as OCB.

Keywords: AES, authenticated encryption, modes of operation.

1 Introduction

Background. Block ciphers are popular building blocks in cryptographic algorithms intended to provide information services such as privacy and authenticity. Such block-cipher based algorithms are referred to as *modes of operation*. Examples of encryption modes of operation are Cipher Block Chaining Mode (CBC) [21], Electronic Codebook Mode (ECB) [21], and Counter Mode (CTR) [8]. Since each of these modes provides privacy only and not authenticity, most applications require that the mode be combined with an authentication mechanism, typically a MAC algorithm [20] based on a hash function such as SHA-1 [22].

As it turns out, there are secure and insecure ways of combining a secure encryption mode with a secure MAC algorithm; certain constructions are easily broken due to bad interactions between the components (see [4,18] for discussion). While there are generic constructions with a provable security in terms of the underlying components (e.g., schemes based on the first-encrypt-then-authenticate paradigm as described in [18]), implementers tend to pick other combinations for reasons that are beyond the scope of this paper. Some of these combinations have turned out to be secure for the specific components chosen, while other combinations have been broken (see again [18]).

An interesting line of research the last couple of years has been the development of block cipher modes of operation that simultaneously provide privacy and authenticity. We will refer to such modes of operation as *combined modes* (a less ambiguous and frequently used term is *authenticated-encryption modes*). Ideally, such a mode should be *provably* secure, roughly meaning that there exists a mathematical proof that the scheme cannot be broken unless a weakness can be found in the underlying block cipher.

---

[*] This work was completed at RSA Laboratories Europe in Stockholm.

K. Nyberg and H. Heys (Eds.): SAC 2002, LNCS 2595, pp. 76–93, 2003.

Our goal. In this paper we provide a formal analysis of a combined mode denoted CCM, which is shorthand for **CTR + CBC-MAC**. As the full name indicates, CCM combines the CTR encryption mode with the CBC-MAC [13] authentication mode; it does so using one single block cipher encryption key. CCM is proposed for IEEE 802.11 [27] and NIST Modes of Operation [28].

Some attractive properties of CCM mode are as follows.

1. CCM readily handles arbitrary messages in which certain parts are intended to be authenticated only and not encrypted; this is done without any additional ciphertext overhead. Many other combined modes require certain enhancements to fully achieve this property.
2. The underlying block cipher is used only in the forward "encryption" direction and not in the reverse "decryption" direction; this is true both for CCM encryption and CCM decryption. This feature makes CCM an attractive candidate for applications where a small code size is desirable. Also, this makes it possible to define CCM in terms of an arbitrary pseudo-random function that is not necessarily reversible. In this respect, CCM is more versatile than many other proposed modes.
3. CCM is based on well-known technology; CTR and CBC-MAC were introduced long ago. The two modes being widely scrutinized and documented may help avoid potential implementation loopholes. Also, highly optimized and well-trusted implementations of CBC have been around for years.
4. According to [27], all intellectual property rights to CCM have been released into the public domain.

As is pointed out in [25], CCM being based on well-trusted components is not in itself an argument for the security of CCM: While the underlying modes CTR and CBC-MAC are known to be provably secure under certain assumptions (see [2] and [3,24]), the two modes share the same block cipher encryption key within CCM. In particular, the results in [18] do not apply. Our object is to demonstrate that CCM is as secure as the two-key variant covered in [18]. We stress that our analysis applies to the typical situation where messages of variable length (as opposed to a fixed prescribed length as in [3]) are to be processed.

Property 2 turns out to be of significant help in the analysis; thanks to this property we can give a security proof for CCM in terms of a pseudo-random function that does not necessarily have a well-defined inverse. By standard arguments, the proof is then easily translated into a security proof for CCM in terms of a pseudo-random permutation (i.e., a block cipher) that does have an inverse. A direct proof in terms of a block cipher would most certainly be very tricky due to biases caused by the absence of output collisions in permutations.

Related work and further directions. A number of different combined modes have been proposed; these modes have in common that they add "redundancy" to the message to be encrypted. The approach, employed in proposals such as IAPM [16], OCB [26], IACBC [15], and IGE [10], is to concatenate the message with a non-cryptographic checksum before encryption. In some cases the checksum is an xor sum of the blocks in the message, while in other cases a constant block will do. The encryption method is typically a refinement of a standard mode such as CBC (e.g., IACBC and IGE) or ECB (e.g., IAPM and OCB). See [1] for a general treatment of the "encrypt-with-redundancy" paradigm.

The purpose of concatenating a checksum to the message is to make it hard for an adversary to modify a ciphertext in a manner consistent with the underlying message. The above mentioned modes of operation are all equipped with security proofs assuring that this is indeed hard. CCM employs the same paradigm but uses a cryptographic tag rather than a checksum. This makes CCM less efficient than the other variants, but instead CCM achieves benefits such as properties 1 and 2 listed above.

While our definition of a combined mode is in terms of a block cipher, another possibility would be to use a hash function such as SHA-1 as the underlying primitive. It has been demonstrated [11] that certain standard hash functions (e.g., SHA-1) are easily turned into block ciphers with attractive properties. Also, any hash function can be used as a building block in a stream cipher; consider the MGF construction in [12] based on ideas from [5]. We will not pursue this discussion further in this context and confine ourselves with acknowledging the problem as an interesting area of research.

Notation

For each integer $k > 0$, $\{0,1\}^k$ denotes the set of bit strings of length k. The length of a bit string X is denoted $|X|$. For integers $j \geq 0$ and $k > 0$ $(j < 2^k)$, $(j)_k$ is the k-bit representation of j (e.g., $(13)_6 = 001101$). For a bit string X of bit length k, we will sometimes write $(X)_k$ instead of X to indicate explicitly that the bit length of X is k. For any set S, define S^* as the union $\bigcup_{k \geq 0} S^k$; S^* is the set of all finite sequences (including the empty sequence) of elements from S. The concatenation of two bit strings X and Y is denoted $X . Y$.

2   Scheme Description

CTR + CBC-MAC [27] (from now on denoted CCM) is a combined mode providing privacy and authenticity. We stress that CCM as defined in this section is a generalization of the proposal [27]; the special case defined in [27] is described in Section 2.3. CCM is based on a pseudo-random function

$$E : \{0,1\}^{k_0} \times \{0,1\}^{k_b} \to \{0,1\}^{k_b} ;$$

E takes as input a key of bit length k_0 and a block to be encrypted of bit length k_b and outputs an encrypted block of the same bit length k_b. We will write $E_K(X) = E(K, X)$.

We anticipate that most practical applications of CCM will be based on a traditional block cipher E, which means that E_K is a permutation (thus invertible) for each K. For example, in the proposal [27] the underlying function is AES [7,23]. However, as we have already pointed out, E_K does not have to be a permutation; the function is used only in the forward encryption direction and never in the reverse decryption direction.

2.1   Overview of CCM

Before the CCM encryption scheme can be used, the parties that are going to exchange secret information must agree on a secret key K. A detailed description of possible key exchange methods is beyond the scope of this paper, but it is assumed that the key is selected uniformly (or close to uniformly) at random from the set $\{0, 1\}^{k_0}$ of all possible keys.

The CCM encryption operation takes as input a *nonce* N of fixed bit length $k_n < k_b$, a *message* m, and *additional data* a to be authenticated.[1] The additional data a is only authenticated and not encrypted, whereas the message m is both authenticated and encrypted; an authentication *tag* is derived from (N, m, a) via CBC-MAC and encrypted together with m in CTR mode. The tag is of fixed length $k_t \leq k_b$. The encryption operation outputs a ciphertext c of bit length $|m| + k_t$.

The nonce N is *non-repeating* ("fresh") in the sense that it must not have been used as a nonce in a previous application of the CCM encryption operation during the lifetime of a key. Typically, there are certain restrictions on the inputs to the CCM encryption operation. For example, the lengths of the message and the additional data might be upper-bounded by some constant. Also, some applications may require that the bit length of the message and the additional data be a multiple of 8 or the block length. An input (N, m, a) satisfying all requirements is *valid*; the set of all valid inputs is a subset $\mathcal{V}$ of the set of all possible triples (N, m, a) of bit strings.

CBC-MAC computation. In the first step of the encryption operation, we compute a CBC-MAC tag of a string derived from the input. Since CBC-MAC acts on blocks of bit length k_b, it cannot be applied directly to the CCM input (which is a triple of bit strings with lengths not necessarily multiples of k_b). For this reason we need to introduce an *encoding function*

$$\beta : \mathcal{V} \to \mathcal{W}^*,$$

where $\mathcal{W} = \{0, 1\}^{k_b}$ ($\mathcal{W}$ is the set of *blocks*); the output from β is a string of blocks. On a valid input $(N, m, a) \in \mathcal{V}$, the encoding function β derives a string

$$B_0 . B_1 . \cdots . B_r$$

of *CBC-MAC blocks* $B_0, \ldots, B_r$. A tag T is derived by applying CBC-MAC to these blocks; see the algorithm description in Section 2.2 for details. The first block B_0 is the *CBC-MAC pre-IV*.[2]

We require that the following hold for the encoding function β.

1. N is uniquely determined by the first block B_0 of $\beta(N, m, a)$.
2. For any two valid and distinct inputs (N, m, a) and (N', m', a') with corresponding CBC-MAC blocks

---

[1] As a convention, upper-case letters denote fixed-length strings, whereas lower-case letters denote variable-length strings.

[2] We may view T as the CBC-MAC tag of $B_1 . \cdots . B_r$ with IV $E_K(B_0)$.

$$\beta(N, m, a) = B_0 . B_1 . \cdots . B_r \ ,$$
$$\beta(N', m', a') = B'_0 . B'_1 . \cdots . B'_s \ ,$$

B_i and B'_i are distinct for some $i \leq \min\{r, s\}$; the function β is *prefix-free*.

While maybe not absolutely necessary for security (compare to [3,24,14]), the first condition is a convenient way of making the security analysis more stream-lined; each new application of the CCM encryption operation will employ a fresh CBC-MAC pre-IV B_0. The second condition is not arbitrarily chosen; Petrank and Rackoff [24] have observed that CBC-MAC has attractive security properties when applied to a prefix-free message space. Note that this condition implies that (N, m, a) is uniquely determined by $\beta(N, m, a)$.

CTR encryption. In the second step of the encryption operation, we encrypt the message m and the CBC-MAC tag T in CTR mode. We use a *CTR block generator* π with four arguments $(i, N, |m|, a)$ such that the nonce N and the *counter* i (but not necessarily the message length $|m|$ and the the additional data a) are uniquely determined by the CTR block $\pi(i, N, |m|, a)$. Here, $N \in \{0, 1\}^{k_n}$ and $0 \leq i \leq \mu_{\max}$, where $\mu_{\max}$ is a scheme-specific parameter bounding the maximal number of blocks in a message (note that $(\mu_{\max} + 1) \cdot 2^{k_n} \leq 2^{k_b}$). This gives the theoretical upper bound $\mu_{\max} \cdot 2^{k_n}$ on the total number of message blocks that can be encrypted during the lifetime of a key. There might be scheme-specific restrictions on the nonce that make the actual upper bound considerably smaller than the theoretical upper bound.

On input (N, m, a), the CTR input blocks $A_0, A_1, A_2, \ldots$ are defined as

$$A_i = \pi(i, N, |m|, a) \ .$$

The k_t leftmost bits of $E_K(A_0)$ are used for encryption of the CBC-MAC tag T, while the $|m|$ leftmost bits of the string $E_K(A_1) . E_K(A_2) . E_K(A_3) . \cdots$ are used for encryption of the message m. Let $\beta_0(N, m, a)$ be equal to the first block B_0 of $\beta(N, m, a)$. We require that

$$\pi(i, N, |m|, a) \neq \beta_0(N', m', a')$$

for all valid $(N, m, a), (N', m', a')$ and $0 \leq i \leq \mu_{\max}$. This is achieved if, e.g., the leftmost bit of the output from π is always 0, whereas the leftmost bit of the output from β_0 is always 1.

The nonce being non-repeating implies that *all CTR input blocks A_i and all CBC-MAC pre-IVs B_0 used during the lifetime of a key are distinct.*

2.2   CCM Specification

CCM encryption can be summarized as follows. First, the CBC-MAC tag T of $\beta(N, m, a)$ is computed. Second, the message m is encrypted in CTR mode with CTR blocks generated from the nonce N via π. Finally, the tag T is encrypted with a single CTR block.

Formally, CCM encryption is defined as follows.

CCM-ENCRYPT(N, m, a)

1. CBC-MAC computation:
   - Let $B_0 . B_1 . \cdots . B_r = \beta(N, m, a)$.
   - Let $Y_0 = E_K(B_0)$.
   - For $1 \leq i \leq r$, let $Y_i = E_K(Y_{i-1} \oplus B_i)$.
   - Let T be equal to the k_t leftmost bits of Y_r.
2. CTR encryption:
   - Let $\mu = \lceil |m|/k_b \rceil$.
   - For $0 \leq i \leq \mu$, let $A_i = \pi(i, N, |m|, a)$.
   - For $0 \leq i \leq \mu$, let $S_i = E_K(A_i)$.
   - Let s_m be equal to the $|m|$ leftmost bits of $S_1 . S_2 . \cdots . S_\mu$ and let S_T be equal to the k_t leftmost bits of S_0.
   - Let $c = [m \oplus s_m] . [T \oplus S_T]$.
3. Output c.

CCM decryption of a ciphertext c with the nonce N and the additional data a is defined in the obvious manner: First, apply the reverse of step 2 to c to obtain a message m and a CBC-MAC tag T (the CTR block generator π is applied to $(i, N, |c| - k_t, a)$). Next, apply CBC-MAC to $\beta(N, m, a)$ as in step 1 to obtain a CBC-MAC tag T' equal to the k_t leftmost bits of Y_r. If $T = T'$, then c is valid and m is output. Otherwise, c is not valid and an error is output. Note that the decryption operation must not release the message or any part of it until the tag has been verified. This is to prevent a chosen-ciphertext adversary from deriving useful information from invalid decryption queries.

2.3   Example

In the proposals [27] to IEEE 802.11 and [28] to NIST, CCM is based on AES with block length $k_b = 128$ and key length k_0 equal to 128, 192, or 256. All strings are assumed to be of length a multiple of 8. Before CCM can be used, we need to fix k_t, k_n, and $\mu_{\max}$. In [27,28], the tag length k_t is a multiple of 16 between 32 and 128, while the nonce length k_n is a multiple of 8 between 56 and 112. For formatting reasons, the number of octets in a message must not exceed $2^{120-k_n} - 1$; put $k_{\max} = 120 - k_n$. Note that $\mu_{\max} = 2^{k_{\max}-4}$; each block contains 2^4 octets. An input (N, m, a) is valid if and only if $N \in \{0, 1\}^{k_n}$, $0 \leq |a|/8 < 2^{16}$, and $0 \leq |m|/8 < 2^{k_{\max}}$. [3]

The encoding function β is defined as follows on input (N, m, a). The first block B_0 is equal to

$$(0b)_2 . (k_t/16 - 1)_3 . (k_{\max}/8 - 1)_3 . (N)_{k_n} . (|m|/8)_{k_{\max}} .$$

---

[3] For simplicity, we assume that the octet length of the additional data a is small enough to fit within two octets; the proposal can handle larger values as well.

The bit b is equal to 0 if a is the empty string and 1 otherwise. If $b = 1$, then the two leftmost octets of B_1 are equal to $(|a|/8)_{16}$. Let L_a be $(|a|/8)_{16}$ if $|a| > 0$ and the empty string otherwise. Then

$$\beta(N, m, a) = B_0 . L_a . a . Z_1 . m . Z_2 .$$

Here, Z_1 and Z_2 are short (possibly empty) strings of zeros such that $|L_a . a . Z_1|$ and $|m . Z_2|$ are multiples of the block length 128. Note that N is uniquely determined by B_0 and that β is prefix-free; no proper prefix of $\beta(N, m, a)$ is a valid output from β, and the input (N, m, a) is uniquely determined by $\beta(N, m, a)$. Namely, the inclusion of the exact octet length of a and m in $\beta(N, m, a)$ makes it possible to extract a and m from $a . Z_1 . m . Z_2$ in an unambiguous manner.

The CTR block generator π depends only on the nonce and the counter and is defined as

$$\pi(i, N) = (00000)_5 . (k_{\max}/8 - 1)_3 . (N)_{k_n} . (i)_{k_{\max}} .$$

This cannot be equal to a CBC-MAC pre-IV B_0; the first five bits in B_0 are not all zeros since $k_t/16 - 1$ is nonzero.

3   Security Analysis of CCM

In this section we analyze the security of CCM. There are two aspects of security in our setting:

- Privacy: It should be infeasible for an adversary to derive any information from the ciphertexts without access to the secret key.
- Authenticity: It should be infeasible for an adversary to forge a valid ciphertext without access to the secret key.

In Section 3.1 we argue heuristically for the security of CCM. Formal definitions are provided in Section 3.2, while the main theorems are given in Section 3.3.

3.1   Heuristic Security Argument

Before analyzing CCM in greater detail, we provide a rough outline of the security properties of CCM; see next section for a detailed description of the attack models. Note that the discussion in this section is only heuristic and leaves out quite a few technical details that must not be ignored in a formal analysis. Throughout this section, we assume that the underlying permutation E_k is chosen uniformly at random from the set of all permutations.

First, consider privacy. In our setting, the goal for the adversary is to distinguish the ciphertexts from "random gibberish" (a bit string chosen uniformly at random from the set of all possible bit strings of a specified length). Let (N, m, a) be an input to the encryption operation. This operation first computes a tag T and then encrypts the message m and the tag in CTR mode. Since N is required to be fresh, the CTR input blocks and the CBC-MAC pre-IVs are new.

In particular, the output ciphertext will be very close to random gibberish even if the adversary knows the plaintext.

As we will see in the formal analysis, there are only two ways for the adversary to be successful. First, the adversary may mount a "birthday" attack against the CTR output blocks. Namely, since E_k is a block cipher and since all input blocks are distinct, there are no collisions among the CTR output blocks. However, with probability approximately $O(q^2) \cdot 2^{-b}$ (q is the number of applications of the underlying block cipher), true random gibberish will contain such block collisions. Second, the adversary may hope for an anomaly to occur within the CBC-MAC computations (e.g., an internal collision or a CBC-MAC tag that coincides with some CTR output block). In our formal analysis, we will demonstrate that the probability of any such anomaly is bounded by $O(q^2) \cdot 2^{-b}$.

Next, consider authenticity. We have already concluded that it is hard to distinguish the ciphertexts from random gibberish. In addition, it turns out that it is hard to tell anything nontrivial about the internal CBC-MAC input and output blocks even if all plaintexts are known. We will prove later that the probability that the adversary is able to extract any useful information about the internal blocks is bounded by $O(q^2) \cdot 2^{-b}$.

Unless q is very large, the adversary knows close to nothing about the internal blocks, which implies that it is close to impossible to modify any previous encryption query without having the encrypted tag modified in an unpredictable manner. Namely, since β is prefix-free, any forgery attempt is uniquely determined by the corresponding sequence $B_0 . B_1 . \cdots$ of CBC-MAC blocks. Specifically, if there is a previous encryption query with the same initial blocks as the present forgery attempt, it is still the case that there is some position on which the CBC-MAC blocks differ. The conclusion is that it is hard to guess the tag with probability better than 2^{-k_t}; whatever modification the adversary tries to make, she cannot predict the consequences.

3.2   Security Concepts

Our definitions are based on work in [2,4,6,17] and are analogous to those in [26]. CCM is a member of the family of *nonce-using symmetric encryption schemes*. Such a scheme is defined by a 4-tuple $(\mathcal{K}, \mathcal{E}, \mathcal{D}, k_n)$. Here, k_n is an integer (the nonce length) and $\mathcal{K}$ is the *key space*. In our setting, $\mathcal{E}$ and $\mathcal{D}$ are functions

$$\mathcal{K} \times \{0,1\}^{k_n} \times \{0,1\}^* \times \{0,1\}^* \to \{0,1\}^* \cup \{\phi\}$$

($\phi =$ "Error") such that

$$\mathcal{D}(K, N, c, a) = \begin{cases} m & \text{if } c = \mathcal{E}(K, N, m, a) \text{ for some (unique) } m; \\ \phi & \text{if } c \neq \mathcal{E}(K, N, m, a) \text{ for all } m. \end{cases}$$

We will write $\mathcal{E}_K(N, m, a) = \mathcal{E}(K, N, m, a)$ and similarly for $\mathcal{D}$. We assume that the bit length of $\mathcal{E}_K(N, m, a)$ is uniquely determined by the bit lengths of m and a (the bit length of N is fixed to k_n).

We define privacy and authenticity of a nonce-using symmetric encryption scheme $\Pi = (\mathcal{K}, \mathcal{E}, \mathcal{D}, k_n)$ in terms of two attack experiments. In each of the two experiments, a key K is first chosen uniformly at random from $\mathcal{K}$. We proceed as follows in a manner similar to the approach in [26], except that we allow the adversary against authenticity to make several forgery attempts.

Privacy. In the privacy experiment, the adversary $\mathcal{A}$ has access to an encryption oracle $\mathcal{O}$ that on input (N, m, a) returns a ciphertext c. $\mathcal{A}$ may send arbitrary queries to the oracle, except that the same nonce must not be used in more than one query; such a query is immediately rejected by the oracle. Thus we restrict our attention to *nonce-respecting* adversaries.

The encryption oracle is chosen from a set of two possible oracles via a fair coin flip $b \in \{0, 1\}$. If $b = 1$, then the oracle is the true oracle $\mathcal{E}_K$. If $b = 0$, then the oracle is a random oracle $\mathcal{R}$ that on input (N, m, a) returns a string of length $|\mathcal{E}_K(N, m, a)|$ chosen uniformly at random. By assumption, $|\mathcal{E}_K(N, m, a)|$ depends only on $|m|$ and $|a|$. The goal for $\mathcal{A}$ is to guess the bit b; a correct guess would mean that she is able to distinguish $\mathcal{E}_K$ from a true random number generator. We define the advantage of $\mathcal{A}$ against the privacy of Π as

$$\mathrm{Adv}_{\Pi}^{\mathrm{priv}}(\mathcal{A}) = \left| \Pr_{K \leftarrow \mathcal{K}} (1 \leftarrow \mathcal{A}^{\mathcal{E}_K}) - \Pr(1 \leftarrow \mathcal{A}^{\mathcal{R}}) \right| \; ;$$

$1 \leftarrow \mathcal{A}^{\mathcal{O}}$ denotes the event that $\mathcal{A}$ outputs 1 conditioned that the underlying oracle is $\mathcal{O}$. $\square$

Authenticity. In the authenticity experiment, $\mathcal{A}$ has access to the true encryption oracle $\mathcal{E}_K$ and to the true decryption oracle $\mathcal{D}_K$. Queries to the decryption oracle will be referred to as *forgery attempts*. As in the privacy experiment, we assume that the adversary is nonce-respecting when making encryption queries. However, there are no such restrictions on forgery attempts. The goal for $\mathcal{A}$ is to produce a forgery attempt (N^*, c^*, a^*) such that $\mathcal{D}_K(N^*, c^*, a^*) \neq \phi$; if this is true, then $\mathcal{A}$ *forges*. The only restriction on (N^*, c^*, a^*) is that there must not be any previous encryption query (N^*, m, a^*) with response c^*. However, N^* may well be part of a previous encryption query and one or several previous forgery attempts. $\mathcal{A}$ may send her encryption queries and forgery attempts in any order and at any time during the experiment. We define the advantage of $\mathcal{A}$ against the authenticity of Π as

$$\mathrm{Adv}_{\Pi}^{\mathrm{auth}}(\mathcal{A}) = \Pr_{K \leftarrow \mathcal{K}} (\mathcal{A}^{\mathcal{E}_K} \text{ forges}) . \; \square$$

The reason for accepting several forgery attempts (as opposed to one single forgery attempt at the end of the experiment) is that we want to analyze how the number of forgery attempts affects the success probability of an adversary. Specifically, we want to show that the adversary does not gain more than negligibly from making multiple forgery attempts if the tag length is considerably larger than $k_b/2$.

Our goal is to relate the security of CCM to the hardness of distinguishing the underlying function E_K from a random function (and, if E is a block cipher, from a random permutation). Let $\mathsf{Rand}(k_b)$ be the set of all functions $f : \{0,1\}^{k_b} \to \{0,1\}^{k_b}$ and let $\mathsf{Perm}(k_b)$ be the subset of $\mathsf{Rand}(k_b)$ consisting of all permutations. First consider indistinguishability from a random function.

PRF indistinguishability. The attack experiment for E_K is very similar to the privacy experiment for Π above. In the first step of the experiment a key K is chosen uniformly at random from $\mathcal{K}$ and an oracle $\mathcal{O}$ is chosen via a fair coin flip b. If $b = 0$, then $\mathcal{O}$ is a function ρ selected uniformly at random from $\mathsf{Rand}(k_b)$. If $b = 1$, then $\mathcal{O}$ is E_K. The adversary $\mathcal{B}$ is given access to the oracle $\mathcal{O}$ and is allowed to send arbitrary queries. The goal for the adversary is to guess the bit b. We define

$$\mathrm{Adv}_E^{\mathrm{prf}}(\mathcal{B}) = \left| \Pr_{K \leftarrow \mathcal{K}}(1 \leftarrow \mathcal{B}^{E_K}) - \Pr_{\rho \leftarrow \mathsf{Rand}(k_b)}(1 \leftarrow \mathcal{B}^{\rho}) \right| . \ \square$$

PRP indistinguishability. We now consider indistinguishability from a random permutation. The only modification from the previous experiment is that ρ is selected from $\mathsf{Perm}(k_b)$ instead of $\mathsf{Rand}(k_b)$; we define

$$\mathrm{Adv}_E^{\mathrm{prp}}(\mathcal{B}) = \left| \Pr_{K \leftarrow \mathcal{K}}(1 \leftarrow \mathcal{B}^{E_K}) - \Pr_{\rho \leftarrow \mathsf{Perm}(k_b)}(1 \leftarrow \mathcal{B}^{\rho}) \right| . \ \square$$

Before we proceed, we state a useful result regarding the correspondence between PRF and PRP indistinguishability; see [3] for a proof.

Lemma 1. *Let E be a block cipher; E_K is a permutation for each key $K \in \mathcal{K}$. Then for any PRF distinguisher $\mathcal{B}$ making q queries to his oracle, there is a PRP distinguisher $\hat{\mathcal{B}}$ making q queries to his oracle such that*

$$Adv_E^{\mathrm{prf}}(\mathcal{B}) \leq Adv_E^{\mathrm{prp}}(\hat{\mathcal{B}}) + q(q-1) \cdot 2^{-k_b - 1} .$$

The running time for $\hat{\mathcal{B}}$ is the running time for $\mathcal{B}$ plus the time needed to transport q queries and q responses between $\mathcal{B}$ and $\hat{\mathcal{B}}$'s oracle. $\square$

3.3   Security Results

We now present lower bounds for the security of CCM in terms of the underlying function E_K. First consider authenticity. For an encryption query $Q = (N, m, a)$, define

$$l_Q = \left\lceil \frac{|\beta(N, m, a)| + |m|}{k_b} \right\rceil + 1 ;$$

l_Q is the total number of applications of the block cipher needed to respond to the query Q. For a forgery attempt $Q^* = (N^*, c^*, a^*)$ corresponding to the message m^*, define

$$l_Q = \left\lceil \frac{|\beta(N^*, m^*, a^*)| + |c^*|}{k_b} \right\rceil + 1 ;$$

l_Q is the total number of applications of the block cipher needed to decrypt c^* and check whether c^* is valid.

Theorem 1. *Let $\mathcal{A}$ be an adversary against the authenticity of CCM. Let q_E be the number of encryption queries and let $Q_1, Q_2, \ldots, Q_{q_E}$ denote the queries. Let q_F be the number of forgery attempts and let $Q_1^*, Q_2^*, \ldots, Q_{q_F}^*$ denote the attempts. Put*

$$l_E = \sum_i l_{Q_i} \quad and \quad l_F = \sum_i l_{Q_i} .$$

Then there is a PRF distinguisher $\mathcal{B}$ such that

$$\mathrm{Adv}_{\mathsf{CCM}}^{\mathsf{auth}}(\mathcal{A}) \leq \mathrm{Adv}_E^{\mathsf{prf}}(\mathcal{B}) + q_F \cdot 2^{-k_t} + (l_E + l_F)^2 \cdot 2^{-k_b - 1} .$$

Thus, by Lemma 1, if E is a block cipher, then there is a PRP distinguisher $\hat{\mathcal{B}}$ such that

$$\mathrm{Adv}_{\mathsf{CCM}}^{\mathsf{auth}}(\mathcal{A}) \leq \mathrm{Adv}_E^{\mathsf{prp}}(\hat{\mathcal{B}}) + q_F \cdot 2^{-k_t} + (l_E + l_F)^2 \cdot 2^{-k_b} .$$

Both distinguishers have an additional running time equal to the time needed to process the queries from $\mathcal{A}$. This includes making $l_E + l_F$ oracle queries and xoring $l_E - q_E + l_F - q_F$ pairs of blocks of size k_b.

The proof of Theorem 1 is given in Appendix A.

Now consider privacy.

Theorem 2. *Let $\mathcal{A}$ be an adversary against the privacy of CCM. Let q_E and l_E be defined as in Theorem 1. Then there is a PRF distinguisher $\mathcal{B}$ such that*

$$\mathrm{Adv}_{\mathsf{CCM}}^{\mathsf{priv}}(\mathcal{A}) \leq \mathrm{Adv}_E^{\mathsf{prf}}(\mathcal{B}) + l_E^2 \cdot 2^{-k_b - 1} .$$

Thus, by Lemma 1, if E is a block cipher, then there is a PRP distinguisher $\hat{\mathcal{B}}$ such that

$$\mathrm{Adv}_{\mathsf{CCM}}^{\mathsf{priv}}(\mathcal{A}) \leq \mathrm{Adv}_E^{\mathsf{prp}}(\hat{\mathcal{B}}) + l_E^2 \cdot 2^{-k_b} .$$

Both distinguishers have an additional running time equal to the time needed to process the queries from $\mathcal{A}$. This includes making l_E oracle queries and xoring $l_E - q_E$ pairs of blocks of size k_b.

The proof of Theorem 2 is given in Appendix B.

3.4   Possible Extensions Beyond the Birthday Paradox

The security bounds in the previous section include a term of the form $c \cdot l^2 \cdot 2^{-k_b}$, where c is a small constant, l is the number of applications of the underlying block cipher, and k_b is the block size. This term is closely related to the "birthday paradox", which states that a collision $X_i = X_j$ is likely to be found among l uniformly random bit strings $X_1, \ldots, X_l$ of length k_b if l is approximately $2^{k_b/2}$.

In some situations, it would be desirable to have assurance that CCM remains secure beyond the birthday paradox bound. While this cannot be true for the confidentiality of CCM, we still hope to find an authenticity bound that is linear rather than quadratic in the number of applications of the block cipher.

As a comparison, consider the recent paper [14], which elaborates on a variant of CBC-MAC called RMAC. The RMAC construction is a message authentication code based on CBC-MAC that is provably secure against birthday paradox attacks. RMAC is similar to CCM in that both schemes encrypt the CBC-MAC tag. While the encryption method in RMAC is substantially stronger than that in CCM, we still conjecture that the CTR encryption of the CBC-MAC tag is strong enough to thwart birthday attacks.

We summarize the problem to be solved as follows.

Problem 1 *Let notations be as in Theorem 1 with $\mathcal{A}$ being an adversary against the authenticity of CCM, and assume that E is a block cipher. Is there a PRP distinguisher $\hat{\mathcal{B}}$ with approximately the same running time as $\mathcal{A}$ such that*

$$\mathrm{Adv}_{\mathrm{CCM}}^{\mathrm{auth}}(\mathcal{A}) \leq \mathrm{Adv}_E^{\mathrm{prp}}(\hat{\mathcal{B}}) + q_F^{1+o(1)} \cdot 2^{-k_t} + (l_E + l_F)^{1+o(1)} \cdot 2^{-k_b} \ ?$$

Ferguson [9] has demonstrated that the corresponding conjecture for OCB mode [26] is false; there is an attack against the authenticity of OCB with complexity very close to the lower security bound established in [26]. In this context, it is worth mentioning TAE, an interesting variant of OCB with excellent security bounds based on a "tweakable" block cipher; see [19] for details. It remains to be examined whether there exists a variant of CCM based on a "tweakable" block cipher with just as good security bounds.

Acknowledgments

I thank Burt Kaliski, Tadayoshi Kohno, and the CCM designers Niels Ferguson, Russ Housley, and Doug Whiting for valuable comments and fruitful discussions.

References

1. J. H. An and M. Bellare. Does Encryption with Redundancy Provide Authenticity? *Advances in Cryptology – EUROCRYPT 2001*, pp. 512 – 528, Springer Verlag, 2001.
2. M. Bellare, A. Desai, E. Jokipii, and P. Rogaway. A Concrete Security Treatment of Symmetric Encryption: Analysis of the DES Modes of Operation. *Proceedings of 38th Annual Symposium on Foundations of Computer Science (FOCS 97)*, IEEE, 1997.
3. M. Bellare, J. Kilian, P. Rogaway. The Security of the Cipher Block Chaining Message Authentication Code. *Journal of Computer and System Sciences*, 61 (3), 362 – 399, 2000.
4. M. Bellare and C. Namprempre. Authenticated Encryption: Relations Among Notions and Analysis of the Generic Composition Paradigm. *Advances in Cryptology – ASIACRYPT 2000*, pp. 531 – 545, Springer-Verlag, 2000.
5. M. Bellare and P. Rogaway. Optimal Asymmetric Encryption – How to Encrypt with RSA. *Advances in Cryptology – Eurocrypt '94*, pp. 92 – 111, Springer Verlag, 1994.

6. M. Bellare and P. Rogaway. Encode-Then-Encipher Encryption: How to Exploit Nonces or Redundancy in Plaintexts for Efficient Encryption. *Advances in Cryptology – ASIACRYPT 2000*, pp. 317 – 330, Springer-Verlag, 2000.

7. J. Daemen and V. Rijmen. *AES Proposal: Rijndael.* Contribution to NIST, September 1999. Available from csrc.nist.gov/encryption/aes/rijndael/.

8. W. Diffie and M. Hellman. Privacy and Authentication: An Introduction to Cryptography. *Proceedings of the IEEE*, 67, pp. 397 – 427, 1979.

9. N. Ferguson. *Collision Attacks on OCB.* Preprint, February 2002.

10. V. Gligor, P. Donescu. *Infinite Garble Extension.* Contribution to NIST, 2000. Available from csrc.nist.gov/encryption/modes/proposedmodes/.

11. H. Handschuh and D. Naccache. *SHACAL.* Contribution to the NESSIE project, 2000.

12. IEEE Std 1363-2000. *Standard Specifications for Public Key Cryptography.* IEEE, 2000.

13. *ISO/IEC 9797: Information Technology – Security Techniques – Data Integrity Mechanism Using a Cryptographic Check Function Employing a Block Cipher Algorithm.* Second edition, 1994.

14. É. Jaulmes, A Joux and F. Valette. On the Security of Randomized CBC-MAC Beyond the Birthday Paradox Limit – A New Construction. *Fast Software Encryption, 9th International Workshop, FSE 2002*, to appear.

15. C. S. Jutla. *Encryption Modes with Almost Free Message Integrity.* Contribution to NIST, 2000. Available from csrc.nist.gov/encryption/modes/proposedmodes/.

16. C. S. Jutla. *Parallelizable Encryption Mode with Almost Free Message Integrity.* Contribution to NIST, 2000. Available from csrc.nist.gov/encryption/modes/proposedmodes/.

17. J. Katz and M. Yung. Unforgeable Encryption and Chosen-Ciphertext-Secure Modes of Operation. *Fast Software Encryption 2000*, pp. 284-299, 2000.

18. H. Krawczyk. The Order of Encryption and Authentication for Protecting Communications (or: How Secure Is SSL?). *Advances in Cryptology – CRYPTO 2001*, pp. 310 – 331, Springer Verlag, 2001.

19. M. Liskov, R. L. Rivest and D. Wagner. *Tweakable Block Ciphers. Advances in Cryptology – CRYPTO 2002*, Springer Verlag, 2002.

20. A. Menezes, P. van Oorschot and S. Vanstone. *Handbook of Applied Cryptography.* CRC Press, 1996.

21. National Institute of Standards and Technology (NIST). *FIPS Publication 81: DES Modes of Operation.* December 1980.

22. National Institute of Standards and Technology (NIST). *FIPS Publication 180-1: Secure Hash Standard (SHS).* April 1995.

23. National Institute of Standards and Technology (NIST). *FIPS Publication 197: Advanced Encryption Standard (AES).* November 2001.

24. E. Petrank, C. Rackoff. CBC MAC for Real-Time Data Sources. *Journal of Cryptology*, 13 (3), pp. 315–338, 2000.

25. P. Rogaway. *IEEE 802.11-01/156r0: Some Comments on WHF Mode.* March 2002. Available from www.cs.ucdavis.edu/~rogaway/ocb/ocb-doc.htm.

26. P. Rogaway, M. Bellare, J. Black and T. Krovetz. OCB: A Block-Cipher Mode of Operation for Efficient Authenticated Encryption. *8th ACM Conference on Computer and Communications Security (CCS-8)*, pp. 196-205. ACM Press, 2001.

27. D. Whiting, R. Housley and N. Ferguson. *IEEE 802.11-02/001r2: AES Encryption & Authentication Using CTR Mode & CBC-MAC.* March 2002.

28. D. Whiting, R. Housley and N. Ferguson. *Counter with CBC-MAC (CCM), AES Mode of Operation*. Contribution to NIST, May 2002. Available from http://csrc.nist.gov/encryption/modes/proposedmodes/.

A   Proof of Theorem 1

We want to relate an adversary $\mathcal{A}$ against the authenticity of CCM to a PRF distinguisher $\mathcal{B}$ attacking the underlying function E_K. $\mathcal{B}$ is given access to an oracle $\mathcal{O}$ equal to either E_K or a random function ρ, each with probability $1/2$. $\mathcal{B}$ is able to respond to encryption queries from $\mathcal{A}$ if $\mathcal{O} = E_K$. In this case $\mathcal{B}$ provides a perfect simulation of $\mathcal{E}_K$; the responses are exactly the same as those provided by the true encryption oracle $\mathcal{E}_K$.

However, if $\mathcal{O} = \rho$, then the simulation is no longer perfect. Still, the experiment can be run; $\mathcal{A}$ may or may not be able forge at the end. Let $\mathcal{B}$ output 1 if $\mathcal{A}$ forges (with respect to an oracle based on $\mathcal{O}$) and 0 otherwise. Note that

$$\mathrm{Adv}^{\mathrm{auth}}_{\mathrm{CCM}}(\mathcal{A}) = \Pr_{K \leftarrow \mathcal{K}}(1 \leftarrow \mathcal{B}^{E_K}) \leq \mathrm{Adv}^{\mathrm{prf}}_{E}(\mathcal{B}) + \Pr_{\rho \leftarrow \mathrm{Rand}(k_b)}(1 \leftarrow \mathcal{B}^{\rho})$$

$$= \mathrm{Adv}^{\mathrm{prf}}_{E}(\mathcal{B}) + \Pr_{\rho \leftarrow \mathrm{Rand}(k_b)}(\mathcal{A}^{\rho} \text{ forges}) \ ;$$

$\mathcal{A}^{\rho}$ denotes $\mathcal{A}$ with a CCM encryption oracle based on ρ. Thus we need to give a bound for the probability that an adversary $\mathcal{A}$ forges conditioned that the underlying function is selected uniformly at random from $\mathrm{Rand}(k_b)$. To achieve such a bound, we need to demonstrate how to simulate $\mathcal{A}$'s encryption oracle. This is achieved if we are able to simulate the underlying random function ρ. We will also need to simulate the decryption oracle to check whether the forgery attempts by the adversary are valid or not. However, for the moment we restrict our attention to the encryption oracle simulation.

A true simulation of the function ρ would be as follows. The algorithm RF-SIMULATION (RF = Random Function) takes as input the block X to be processed and a list $\mathcal{L}$ containing all pairs (X', Y') corresponding to previous applications of ρ; $Y' = \rho(X')$.

RF-SIMULATION$(X, \mathcal{L})$

1. If X is the first block in some entry on the list $\mathcal{L}$, then $Y = \rho(X)$ is already defined; output Y and exit.
2. Generate a string Y uniformly at random.
3. Add (X, Y) to the list $\mathcal{L}$ and output Y.

To simplify analysis, we introduce a modified simulation by skipping step 1 and the list $\mathcal{L}$; RO-SIMULATION (RO = Random Output) is defined as follows, in the easiest possible manner.

RO-SIMULATION(X)

1. Generate a string Y uniformly at random and output Y.

This simulation fails if and only if some block appears twice as input to RO-Simulation and the two corresponding outputs are distinct (this makes the definition of ρ inconsistent). Let RO-InColl be the even that some input X appears twice; $\Pr(\text{RO-InColl})$ is at least the probability of a simulation failure. Before we can estimate the probability of RO-InColl, we need to examine the structure of the input blocks to RO-Simulation. This is done as follows.

Let $\mathcal{X}$ be the multi-set of all input blocks to ρ needed when responding to encryption queries. $\mathcal{X}$ being a multi-set means that if some input block appears several times during the simulation, then this block appears just as many times in $\mathcal{X}$. We claim that the following holds for RO-Simulation.

Claim. The set $\mathcal{X}$ of input blocks can be divided into two sets $\mathcal{X}_1$ and $\mathcal{X}_2$. $\mathcal{X}_1$ is the set of input blocks derived from the nonces (i.e., the CTR blocks and the CBC-MAC pre-IV), while $\mathcal{X}_2$ is the set of input blocks occurring in the internal CBC-MAC computations. All blocks in the first set $\mathcal{X}_1$ are distinct and known to the adversary. All blocks in the second set $\mathcal{X}_2$ are, from the view of the adversary, mutually independent and uniformly distributed among all possible blocks. Also, the sets $\mathcal{X}_1$ and $\mathcal{X}_2$ are independent. In particular, the ciphertexts given to the adversary leak no information about the blocks in the set $\mathcal{X}_2$.

Proof of Claim. We use induction over the number of encryption queries to prove that the claim holds. Thus assume that after a certain number $q \geq 0$ of queries, the set $\mathcal{X}'$ containing the corresponding input blocks can be divided into two sets $\mathcal{X}_1'$ and $\mathcal{X}_2'$ as above. Consider a new encryption query (N, m, a) with blocks $A_0, \ldots, A_\mu, B_0$ derived from N. Since N is a new nonce never used before, the set $\mathcal{X}_1'$ does not contain any of the blocks $A_0, \ldots, A_\mu, B_0$. Also, N is independent from all elements in $\mathcal{X}_2'$ since these are completely unknown to the adversary and since N is generated in a predetermined fashion. Thus adding $A_0, \ldots, A_\mu, B_0$ to $\mathcal{X}_1'$ does not violate the desired properties.

Now, consider the CBC-MAC computation of

$$\beta(N, m, a) = B_0 . B_1 . \cdots . B_r .$$

By construction, the first output block Y_0 in the CBC-MAC computation is a uniformly distributed string. Namely, RO-Simulation does not check for input collisions (with the true simulation, Y_0 would not necessarily be uniformly distributed). In particular, Y_0 is independent from B_1, which implies that $Y_0 \oplus B_1$ is independent from other input blocks and uniformly distributed. Similarly, Y_{i-1} is uniformly distributed for $i > 1$, which implies that $Y_{i-1} \oplus B_i$ is independent from other input blocks and uniformly distributed. Also, the CBC-MAC tag T (which is Y_r truncated to k_t bits) and the part of the CTR output stream to which T is xored are both uniformly distributed and do not leak any information about the internal blocks. Hence, all internal CBC-MAC input blocks can be added to $\mathcal{X}_2'$ without violating the desired properties.

Using induction, we conclude that $\mathcal{X}$ has the desired property. $\square$

As a consequence, we may now compute the probability of the event RO-InColl. Let $x_1 = |\mathcal{X}_1|$ and $x_2 = |\mathcal{X}_2|$ (the sets are still viewed as multi-sets); $x_1 + x_2 = l_E$. The probability that there is an input block that appears twice in the simulation is bounded by

$$\mathsf{RO\text{-}InColl} \leq (x_1 x_2 + x_2(x_2 - 1)/2) \cdot 2^{-k_b} \leq l_E(l_E - 1)/2 \cdot 2^{-k_b} ; \qquad (1)$$

This follows immediately from the facts that the elements in $\mathcal{X}_1$ are all different and that the elements in $\mathcal{X}_2$ are uniformly distributed, mutually independent, and independent from $\mathcal{X}_1$. Thus, from the view of the adversary, every two elements in $\mathcal{X}$ coincide with probability either 0 (if both elements are in $\mathcal{X}_1$) or 2^{-k_b} (otherwise).

Note that total secrecy of the elements in $\mathcal{X}_2$ is essential for the proof; otherwise the adversary might be able to increase the failure probability for the simulation by selecting new encryption queries on the basis of leaked information about $\mathcal{X}_2$.

Now consider forgery attempts. We may assume that $\mathcal{B}$ always responds with ϕ on any forgery attempt, even if the forgery attempt turns out to be valid with respect to $\mathcal{B}$'s oracle. Namely, if $\mathcal{A}$ forges with a specific query Q^*, then $\mathcal{A}$ wins, so $\mathcal{B}$'s response does not matter. If Q^* is invalid, then $\mathcal{B}$'s response coincides with the true oracle.

Using this flawed simulation of the decryption oracle, we obtain a model where the actual success of a specific forgery attempt does not depend on the responses to other forgery attempts (as these are always ϕ), only on the responses to the encryption queries. The conclusion is that we may analyze each forgery attempt separately. In addition, we may assume that all forgery attempts are made at the end of the attack (see [14] for further discussion), with the following exception:

In case $\mathcal{A}$ makes a forgery attempt Q^* corresponding to a certain triple (N, m, a) and later queries the very same triple (N, m, a) at the encryption oracle (e.g., by pure coincidence or by choosing a very short m that can be guessed), we cannot make the assumption that $\mathcal{A}$ waits until the end before she queries Q^*. Namely, she is not allowed to make forgery attempts corresponding to previous encryption queries in this manner. Still, by construction, the responses to later encryption queries are completely unpredictable, which implies that Q^* cannot be valid with better probability than 2^{-k_t}; all encrypted tags are equally likely.

From now on, consider forgery attempts that do not correspond to later encryption queries in the manner just described. For such forgery attempts, we may assume that all encryption queries are already made. We need to compute the probability that a specific forgery attempt is successful. Let $Q^* = (N^*, c^*, a^*)$ be such an attempt and let m^* be the corresponding message (note that we may not know m^* yet).

If N^* is not part of any encryption query, then we may apply the decryption operation in the same manner as we applied the encryption operation on encryption queries, thus generating a uniformly distributed output block for each application of ρ. With the same argument as before, it is easily seen that this simulation will fail with probability at most

$$(l_Q (l_Q - 1)/2 + l_E l_Q) \cdot 2^{-k_b} . \tag{2}$$

Namely, each of the input blocks in the decryption computation is equal to some input block appearing in an encryption query with probability at most $l_E \cdot 2^{-k_b}$; there are l_Q such blocks. With probability at most $l_Q (l_Q - 1)/2 \cdot 2^{-k_b}$, there is an input collision within the decryption computation. The success probability for the adversary is obviously 2^{-k_t} since each encrypted tag has the same probability.

Now, assume that N^* is part of an encryption query $Q = (N^*, m, a)$. Extract m^* from c^* by applying ρ to the relevant CTR blocks derived from N^*. Some of these blocks might be part of the computations needed to respond to the encryption query Q; ρ is already defined on these blocks. Define E_k on the other blocks in the usual manner as uniformly distributed output blocks. The resulting message m^* is clearly independent from the set $\mathcal{X}_2$.

We identify two cases; the first block B_0 in $\beta(N^*, m, a)$ and the first block B_0^* in $\beta(N^*, m^*, a^*)$ are either equal or different.

- First, assume that $B_0 \neq B_0^*$. This implies that B_0^* is not part of $\mathcal{X}_1$. In particular, we may simulate the CBC-MAC computation in the same random manner as usual. Again, the error probability for this simulation is bounded by (2) and the success probability for the adversary is 2^{-k_t}. Namely, the CBC-MAC tag is uniformly distributed and independent from the block that is xored to it to form the encrypted tag T.
- Second, assume that $B_0 = B_0^*$. Write

$$\beta(N^*, m, a) = B_0 . \cdots . B_r ;$$
$$\beta(N^*, m^*, a^*) = B_0^* . \cdots . B_r^* .$$

Let $i \leq \min\{r, r^*\}$ be the smallest index such that B_i and B_i^* are different; such an i exists since β is prefix-free. Let Y_{i-1} be the corresponding block that is xored to B_i and B_i^*, respectively, within the CBC-MAC computation. Put $X_i = Y_{i-1} \oplus B_i$ and $X_i^* = Y_{i-1} \oplus B_i^*$. By assumption, X_i is an element in $\mathcal{X}_2$ that is completely unknown to the adversary and independent from all other elements in $\mathcal{X}$. Also, B_i^* is independent from all elements in $\mathcal{X}_2$ (namely, the adversary has no information about $\mathcal{X}_2$). In particular, X_i^* is uniformly distributed and independent from all elements in $\mathcal{X} \setminus \{X_i\}$ and different from X_i. Thus we may proceed in the usual manner from this point with the CBC-MAC computation of $B_0^* . B_1^* . \cdots . B_r^*$, generating random output blocks $Y_i^*, \ldots, Y_r^*$. As before, the error probability for this simulation is bounded by (2), and the success probability for the adversary is 2^{-k_t}.

Summing over all forgery attempts, we conclude that the success probability for the adversary within this model based on RO-SIMULATION is at most $q_F \cdot 2^{-k_t}$ and that the probability of decryption oracle simulation failure is bounded by

$$\sum_i \left(l_{Q_i}(l_{Q_i} - 1)/2 + l_E l_{Q_i}\right) \cdot 2^{-k_b} \leq (l_F(l_F - 1)/2 + l_E l_F) \cdot 2^{-k_b} ; \tag{3}$$

this follows from (2). The total probability of simulation failure is bounded by the sum of (1) and (3), from which we conclude that the probability of success for the adversary within the true model based on RF-SIMULATION is bounded by

$$q_F \cdot 2^{-k_t} + l_E(l_E - 1)/2 \cdot 2^{-k_b} + (l_F(l_F - 1)/2 + l_E l_F) \cdot 2^{-k_b}$$
$$< q_F \cdot 2^{-k_t} + (l_E + l_F)^2 \cdot 2^{-k_b - 1} \;,$$

which is the desired bound. $\square$

B   Proof of Theorem 2

We want to relate an adversary $\mathcal{A}$ against the privacy of CCM to a PRF distinguisher $\mathcal{B}$ attacking the underlying function E_K. The prerequisites are the same as in the proof of Theorem 1. In addition, introduce a random oracle $\mathcal{R}'$ for $\mathcal{B}$ that on any input block X outputs a uniformly random output block Y (without checking for consistency with previous queries). This oracle is the oracle simulated by RO-SIMULATION in the proof of Theorem 1. It is easily seen that $\mathcal{B}$ is able to provide a perfect simulation of $\mathcal{R}$ with probability 1 using the oracle $\mathcal{R}'$. Thus we obtain that

$$\mathrm{Adv}_{\mathsf{CCM}}^{\mathrm{priv}}(\mathcal{A}) = \left| \Pr_{K \leftarrow \mathcal{K}}(1 \leftarrow \mathcal{B}^{E_K}) - \Pr(1 \leftarrow \mathcal{B}^{\mathcal{R}}) \right|$$

$$\leq \mathrm{Adv}_E^{\mathrm{prf}}(\mathcal{B}) + \left| \Pr_{\rho \leftarrow \mathsf{Rand}(k_b)}(1 \leftarrow \mathcal{B}^{\rho}) - \Pr(1 \leftarrow \mathcal{B}^{\mathcal{R}}) \right| \;.$$

Hence we need to compute the probability that ρ, selected uniformly at random from $\mathsf{Rand}(k_b)$, does not provide a perfect simulation of the random oracle $\mathcal{R}'$. This is the case only if $\mathcal{B}$ is asked to query the same input block twice. From the proof of Theorem 1 we learn that this happens with probability at most $l_E^2 \cdot 2^{-k_b}$, which gives the desired bound. $\square$

Single-Path Authenticated-Encryption Scheme Based on Universal Hashing

Soichi Furuya[1] and Kouichi Sakurai[2]

[1] Systems Development Laboratory, Hitachi, Ltd.,
292 Yoshida-cho, Totsuka-ku, Yokohama, 244-0817 Japan
soichi@sdl.hitachi.co.jp
[2] Dept. of Computer Science and Communications Engineering, Kyushu University,
6-10-1 Hakozaki, Higashi-ku, Fukuoka 812-8581 Japan
sakurai@csce.kyushu-u.ac.jp

Abstract. An authenticated-encryption scheme is frequently used to provide a communication both with confidentiality and integrity. For stream ciphers, i.e., an encryption scheme using a cryptographic pseudo-random-number generator, this objective can be achieved by the simple combination of encryption and MAC generation. This naive approach, however, introduces the following drawbacks; the implementation is likely to require two scans of the data, and independent keys for the encryption and MAC generations must be exchanged. The single-path construction of an authenticated-encryption scheme for a stream cipher is advantageous in these two aspects but non-trivial design.

In this paper we propose a single-path authenticated-encryption scheme with provable security. This scheme is based on one of the well-known ϵ-almost-universal hash functions, the evaluation hash. The encryption and decryption of the scheme can be calculated by single-path operation on a plaintext and a ciphertext. We analyze the security of the proposed scheme and give a security proof, which claims that the security of the proposed scheme can be reduced to that of an underlying PRNG in the *indistinguishability from random bits*. The security model we use, *real-or-random*, is one of the strongest notions amongst the four well-known notions for confidentiality, and an encryption scheme with *real-or-random* sense security can be efficiently reduced to the other three security notions. We also note that the security of the proposed scheme is tight.

Keywords: Stream cipher, mode of operation, provable security, message authentication, real-or-random security.

1   Introduction

A symmetric-key encryption is a cryptographic primitive that is mainly used to provide confidentiality to communicated (or stored) data against adversaries who do not possess the secret key. However, many cryptographic protocols implicitly use symmetric-key encryption to provide not only data confidentiality but also data integrity [R97].

K. Nyberg and H. Heys (Eds.): SAC 2002, LNCS 2595, pp. 94–109, 2003.

Although a secure communication in terms of data confidentiality can be achieved by using an encryption scheme, use of an encryption scheme does not always provide data integrity at the same time. Typically, data integrity is achieved by making use of an independent mechanism to generate a message authentication code (MAC).

A naive solution to achieve the two securities is a simple combination of two mechanisms, namely, an encryption and a MAC generation. However, we note that this simple approach does have some drawbacks. One is that the encoding and decoding mechanisms must manage two keys independently, e.g., random generation, exchange, storage, and discarding of the two keys. More importantly, there is another drawback in that the typical software implementation encoding and decoding processes are not single-path operation. This potential drawback is critical even for modern computers when they are dealing with, for example, streaming multimedia data. A construction to void those two drawbacks is not a trivial problem.

For the block cipher, there are reports of recent studies where an efficient mode of operation providing data authenticity as well as data confidentiality was provided [GD01, J01, RBBK01]. The modes in all cases demonstrated that they can provide the two securities independently if the underlying block cipher is treated as a pseudorandom permutation. On the other hand, there have been fewer reports on stream ciphers, i.e., an encryption scheme based on a secure key stream.

In this paper, we present an approach to construct an encryption scheme based on a key stream and analyze its security. Our main objectives of the construction are: *1.* An encryption scheme that operates with single-path calculation on a plaintext or ciphertext; and *2.* An encryption scheme using only one initialized key stream without compromising any security.

Our start point is a typical stream cipher; that is a bitwise xor operation of a key stream and a plaintext stream. The security of this scheme can be proven in terms of the confidentiality in the strongest sense. The information theoretic approach of Shannon's theorem proves this fact [S49]. For the computational approach, a similar technique that proves the security of CTR mode can be used to provide four major notions of confidentiality [BDJR97].

On the other hand, there is a well-known construction for MAC schemes that fits a stream cipher. We chose the Wegman-Carter construction [WC81] to embed the integrity mechanism into the Vernam cipher. The Wegman-Carter construction is a provably secure approach to the generation of a MAC, using universal hashing [CW79] and one-time paddness. Because there are a number of (almost) universal hash functions using a pseudorandom sequence, the adoption of an additional Wegman-Carter's MAC mechanism to a stream cipher looks less expensive[1].

The design of universal hashing is important not only for MAC generation but also for operations on databases. There are many reports of extensive re-

---

[1] Golić proposed primitive-converting constructions based on a PRNG [G00]. These are rather theoretical works and less efficient than dedicated universal hash functions.

search on the construction of a universal hashing. The evaluation hash analyzed by Shoup [S96] has piqued our interest for three reasons. *R1:* The required length of random bits is constant and short. *R2:* All the operations used in the evaluation hash are invertible, the hash achieves sufficient performance both in software and hardware implementations. *R3:* Security reduction is very small with comparison to the hash length. These characteristics play important roles in making the proposed scheme practical. Because of *R1*, the output length of the PRNG required for encryption (or decryption) can be reduced by a factor of two in comparison with the most inefficient construction, such as the combination of a stream cipher and MMH [HK97]. *R2* enables the proposed scheme to become a single-path operation both for encryption and decryption. The security bound of *R3* is critically important for the security bound of the proposed scheme.

In the latter part of this paper, we analyze the security of a scheme based on the studied construction. We mainly use the security notion in terms of *real-or-random* sense [BDJR97]. The reason we use this notion is that the notion can be efficiently reduced to three other well-known notions. This means that a scheme with a provable security of the *real-or-random* sense can be said to be as secure as the currently known strongest schemes.

The proof consists of two independent parts, i.e., security proofs for data confidentiality and data authenticity. In both proofs, we use *indistinguishability of PRN from random bits*. This notion of security can be also efficiently reduced to other notions of security, *left-or-right* sense, *semantic* security, and *find-then-guess* security [BDJR97].

There are known results on single-path authenticated-encryption schemes. Especially for the modes of block ciphers, there are designs and security analyses on XCBC [GD01], XIAPM [J01] and OCB [RBBK01]. As for stream ciphers, there are also results of authenticated-encryption schemes. Taylor's work [T93] is one of the practical message authentication mechanisms that is based on a PRNG. Although Taylor also describes the enhancement of his MAC scheme to achieve both confidentiality and integrity in [T93], the required additional length pseudorandom sequence over Vernam cipher is not a constant. Therefore, for a longer message the additional cost to a Vernam cipher cannot be negligible.

The chain and sum primitive [JV98] is another efficient scheme to achieve authenticity with an encryption based only on a PRNG. Moreover, the additional pseudorandom number consumption is constant. However, the scheme mandatorily requires a sequential two-path process. The scheme initially calculates the chain and sum of the plaintext, then it encrypts the Vernam cipher with a PRNG keyed by the resultant value of the chain and sum. This means that the intermediate value, which must not be disclosed for security, is as big as the size of message. Therefore, if this scheme deals a very long message, the same size of secure storage is required.

Many reports on the design of universal hashing are relevant to our past work and future problems. The MMH [HK97] and the Square hash [PR99] are efficient universal hashing schemes based on a PRNG. However, either of the two modes consumes a pseudorandom sequence increasingly proportional to a message's

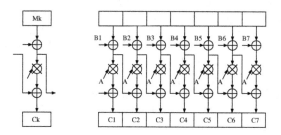

Fig. 1. Encryption block diagram (S01).

length. NMH universal hashing is used in UMAC [BHKKR99] and NMH is an extremely efficient universal hashing scheme. Also we note that whether or not the UMAC construction (instead of Wegman-Carter's) can be used to embed the message authenticity into a stream cipher is an open problem to us.

This paper is organized as follows: We introduce the studied encryption scheme S01 in Section 2 followed by two security discussions. The confidentiality is discussed in Section 3 and the integrity is in Section 4. In Section 5, summarize the feasibility of implementing the proposed scheme from the practical point of view. Finally, we offer our concluding remarks in Section 6.

2   Studied Model

Let n be a parameter that specifies the block length. The encryption takes two input data: an mn-bit message M and an n-bit redundancy R; using n-bit non-zero key stream and $(m+3)n$ key stream, the encryption generates $(m+2)n$-bit ciphertext. The decryption also takes two input data: an $c'n$-bit ciphertext C' and an n-bit redundancy R; using n-bit non-zero key stream and $(c'+1)n$-bit key stream, the decryption outputs either a forgery detection signal ϕ or $(c'-2)n$-bit message M'. If the length of a ciphertext does not change, $m+2 = c'$.

For both encryption and decryption, three key streams are used, namely S_A, S_B, and S_P. The key streams are generated as follows:

Key stream generation:

S_A n-bit Non-zero key stream: Generate n-bit pseudorandom number. If the generated number is zero, discard it and generate n-bit random number again until n-bit non-zero key stream is obtained.

S_B $(m+2)n$-bit key stream: Generate $(m+2)n$-bit pseudorandom number following the S_A generation.

S_P n-bit key stream: Generate n-bit pseudorandom number following the S_B generation.

The encryption consists of three processes: data padding, data masking and data randomization. This is depicted in Fig. 1.

Encryption process

Padding Append S_P and R at the end of the message M. Therefore, the padded message M' is $(m+2)n$-bit length.

Masking Generate $F = M' \oplus S_B$.

Data randomization Divide F into n-bit blocks. Each block is multiplied by S_A over a finite field $\mathbf{F}2^n$. Each block of the resultant data is XORed by the previous block of F. Then concatenate all blocks to generate the ciphertext C.

We describe the mathematical description of S01 encryption scheme [FS01].

$$M' = M|S_P|R,$$
$$M' = (M'_1, \ldots, M'_{m+2}),$$
$$F_0 = 0,$$
$$F_i = M_i \oplus S_{Bi}, \tag{1}$$
$$C_i = (S_A \otimes F_i) \oplus F_{i-1}, \tag{2}$$
$$C = C_1|C_2|\cdots|C_{m+2}.$$

For Equations (1) and (2), $1 \le i \le m+2$.

The decryption is a combination of the inverse of encryption and message authentication. We leave only its mathematical description.

$$F_0 = 0,$$
$$C' = (C'_1, C'_2, \ldots, C'_c),$$
$$F_i = (C_i \oplus F_{i-1}) \otimes S_A^{-1}, \tag{3}$$
$$M'_i = F_i \oplus S_{Bi}, \tag{4}$$
$$M' = M'_1|M'_2|\cdots|M'_{c-2},$$
$$S'_P = M'_{c-1},$$
$$R' = M'_c. \tag{5}$$

The last two blocks of M', i.e., S'_P and R', are used to check the integrity of the ciphertext. If and only if $S'_P = S''_P$ and $R' = R$, the decryption outputs M'. Otherwise output the forgery detection signal ϕ.

3   Confidentiality

In this section, we prove the confidentiality of the S01 scheme. To discuss the security, we have to determine the notion of confidentiality. There are four major notions of confidentiality in the symmetric-key setting. We study the confidentiality in the *real-or-random* sense, since the security in the *real-or-random* sense can be efficiently reduced to that of the other three notions. That means that the *real-or-random* sense is one of the strongest security notions.

Real-or-random setting The encryption oracle tosses a coin $(= \{0, 1\})$ to decide which game to play. There are two games in this setting. In Game 1, in response to an input message M, the oracle (ignores the message and) generates a secret random string with the same length to M and encrypts it under a randomly-chosen key $\mathcal{K}$. In Game 2, in response to an input message M, the oracle encrypts M under a randomly-chosen key $\mathcal{K}$. The adversary is a deterministic algorithm. He is allowed to generate a message and make oracle calls so that the adversary obtains the oracle outputs. Based on the knowledge of these oracle queries and oracle outputs, the adversary outputs one bit value $J^{rr} = \{0, 1\}$. The advantage of the adversary is defined as

$$\mathrm{Adv}^{rr} \stackrel{\mathrm{def}}{=} \left| \Pr(J^{rr} = 1 | \mathrm{Game\ 1}) - \Pr(J^{rr} = 1 | \mathrm{Game\ 2}) \right|.$$

We call that encryption scheme $(t, \mu; \epsilon)$-secure if $\mathrm{Adv}^{rr} \leq \epsilon$ holds for any adversary with computational time $t_A \leq t$ and total oracle-query length $\mu_A \leq \mu$. Following these definitions we introduce the main theorem concerning the security of the S01 scheme.

Theorem 1. *A pseudorandom number generator (PRNG)π is $(t_\pi, \mu_\pi; \epsilon_\pi)$-secure in the indistinguishability from random bits, i.e.,*

$$\mathrm{Adv}^{rr}_\pi = \Pr(J^{rr}_\pi = 1 | \mathrm{Game}(\pi)) - \Pr(J^{rr}_\pi = 1 | \mathrm{Game}(\$)) \leq \epsilon_\pi,$$

with computational time t_π and amount of query μ_π, where $\mathrm{Game}(\pi)$ and $\mathrm{Game}(\$)$ are games with the oracle outputting the π sequence and random sequence, respectively.

The encryption scheme S01 with π, i.e., $S01_\pi$ is $(t_{S01 \cdot \pi}, \mu_{S01 \cdot \pi}; \epsilon_{S01 \cdot \pi})$ secure in the real-or-random sense, where $(t_{S01 \cdot \pi}, \mu_{t_{S01 \cdot \pi}}; \epsilon_{S01 \cdot \pi}) = (t_\pi - c_1 \mu_\pi + c_2, \mu_\pi - c_1 c_2, \epsilon_\pi)$.

Proof: We prove this through contradiction. Assume that an adversary $A^{rr}_{S01 \cdot \pi}$ can $(t_{S01 \cdot \pi}, \mu_{S01 \cdot \pi}; \epsilon_{S01 \cdot \pi})$-break $S01_\pi$ in the real-or-random sense. We construct a new adversary A^{rr}_π that can $(t_\pi, \mu_\pi; \epsilon_\pi)$-break π in the indistinguishability from random bits.

Let $\mathcal{O}_\pi(\cdot)$ be A^{rr}_π's oracle. A^{rr}_π will run $A^{rr}_{S01 \cdot \pi}$, using $\mathcal{O}_\pi(\cdot)$ to provide an appropriate simulation of $A^{rr}_{S01 \cdot \pi}$'s oracle $\mathcal{O}_{S01 \cdot \pi}(\cdot)$ as indicated below.

Algorithm A^{rr}_π

1. Invoke $A^{rr}_{S01 \cdot \pi}$, and obtain $A^{rr}_{S01 \cdot \pi}$'s outputs a message, M and a redundancy R,
2. (Gen. S_A) Obtain n-bit oracle output to generate S_A. If $S_A = 0$, repeat the generation until $S_A \neq 0$.
3. (Gen. S_B) Calculate the length of M (the number of n-bit blocks in M, m) and obtain $(m + 2)$-block (or equivalently $(m + 2)n$-bit) oracle output.
4. (Gen. S_P) Obtain n-bit oracle output to generate S_P.
5. Using S_A, S_B, S_P, and R, encrypt M to generate the ciphertext C.

6. Send C to $A_{S01 \cdot \pi}^{rr}$.
7. Obtain $J_{S01 \cdot \pi}^{rr} = \{0, 1\}$, the output of $A_{S01 \cdot \pi}^{rr}$.
8. Output $J_{\pi}^{rr} = J_{S01 \cdot \pi}^{rr}$, and terminate this run.

Let $\Pr[E]$ stand for the probability of event E occuring. Then, $\mathrm{Adv}_{A_{S01 \cdot \pi}}^{rr}$ is defined as follows:

$$
\begin{aligned}
\mathrm{Adv}_{A_{S01 \cdot \pi}}^{rr} &= \Pr[J_{S01 \cdot \pi}^{rr} = 1 | \mathrm{Game}(S01 \cdot \pi)] \\
&\quad - \Pr[J_{S01 \cdot \pi}^{rr} = 1 | \mathrm{Game}(\$)] \\
&\geq \epsilon_{S01 \cdot \pi}.
\end{aligned}
$$

$\mathcal{O}_{\pi}(\cdot)$ outputs either (Game π) the output sequence of π, or (Game $\$$) the random sequence.

We now compute A_{π}^{rr}'s advantage, $\mathrm{Adv}_{A_{\pi}}^{rr}$.

$$
\begin{aligned}
\mathrm{Adv}_{A_{\pi}}^{rr} &= \Pr[J_{\pi}^{rr} = 1 | \mathrm{Game}(\pi)] \\
&\quad - \Pr[J_{\pi}^{rr} = 1 | \mathrm{Game}(\$)] \\
&= \Pr[J_{S01 \cdot \pi}^{rr} = 1 | \mathrm{Game}(S01 \cdot \pi)] \\
&\quad - \Pr[J_{\pi}^{rr} = 1 | \mathrm{Game}(\$)] \qquad (6) \\
&= \Pr[J_{S01 \cdot \pi}^{rr} = 1 | \mathrm{Game}(S01 \cdot \pi)] \\
&\quad - \Pr[J_{S01 \cdot \pi}^{rr} = 1 | \mathrm{Game}(\$)] \qquad (7) \\
&\geq \epsilon_{S01 \cdot \pi}.
\end{aligned}
$$

Equations (6) and (7) are obtained because of Lemma 1 and 2. Therefore, we have

$$
\begin{aligned}
t_{\pi} &= t_{S01 \cdot \pi} + c_1 \cdot \mu_{S01 \cdot \pi}, \\
\mu_{\pi} &= \mu_{S01 \cdot \pi} + 4n + \frac{n}{2^n} + \frac{n}{2^{2n}} + \cdots \\
&= \mu_{S01 \cdot \pi} + c_2, \\
\epsilon_{\pi} &= \epsilon_{S01 \cdot \pi}.
\end{aligned}
$$

where $c_2 = 3n + \frac{n}{1 - 2^{-n}}$. Therefore, we solve $\mu_{S01 \cdot \pi}$, $t_{S01 \cdot \pi}$, and $\epsilon_{S01 \cdot \pi}$.

$$
\begin{aligned}
\mu_{S01 \cdot \pi} &= \mu_{\pi} - c_2, \\
t_{S01 \cdot \pi} &= t_{\pi} - c_1 \cdot \mu_{S01 \cdot \pi} \\
&= t_{\pi} - c_1 \cdot (\mu_{\pi} - c_2) \\
&= t_{\pi} - c_1 \cdot \mu_{\pi} + c_1 c_2, \\
\epsilon_{S01 \cdot \pi} &= \epsilon_{\pi}.
\end{aligned}
$$

Therefore, A_{π}^{rr} can $(t_{S01 \cdot \pi}, \mu_{S01 \cdot \pi}; \epsilon_{S01 \cdot \pi})$-break π in the indistinguishability from random bits. $\qquad \square$

Lemma 1. *In the proof of Theorem 1, the following equation holds.*

$$
\Pr[J_{\pi}^{rr} = 1 | \mathrm{Game}(\pi)] = \Pr[J_{S01 \cdot \pi}^{rr} = 1 | \mathrm{Game}(S01 \cdot \pi)].
$$

In other words, in Game(π), i.e., a game with $\mathcal{O}_\pi$ outputting π sequence, the probability that A_π^{rr} outputs $J_\pi^{rr} = 1$ is equal to the probability that $A_{S01\cdot\pi}^{rr}$ outputs $J_{S01\cdot\pi}^{rr} = 1$ in Game(π).

Proof: In the game with $\mathcal{O}_\pi$ outputting π sequence, $A_{S01\cdot\pi}^{rr}$ (invoked by A_π^{rr}) receives a ciphertext C encrypted by $S01 \cdot \pi$. Therefore the operations of $A_{S01\cdot\pi}^{rr}$ are exactly the same as $A_{S01\cdot\pi}^{rr}$ playing in Game ($S01 \cdot \pi$). Because A_π^{rr} always outputs $J_{S01\cdot\pi}^{rr}$ such that $J_{S01\cdot\pi}^{rr} = J_\pi^{rr}$,

$$\Pr[J_\pi^{rr} = 1|\text{Game}(\pi)] = \Pr[J_{S01\cdot\pi}^{rr} = 1|\text{Game}(S01 \cdot \pi)].$$

□

Lemma 2. *In the proof of Theorem 1, the following equation holds.*

$$\Pr[J_\pi^{rr} = 1|\text{Game}(\$)] = \Pr[J_{S01\cdot\pi}^{rr} = 1|\text{Game}(\$)]. \tag{8}$$

In other words, in Game($\$$), i.e., a game with $\mathcal{O}_\pi$ outputting a random sequence, the probability that A_π^{rr} outputs $J_\pi^{rr} = 1$ is equal to the probability that $A_{S01\cdot\pi}^{rr}$ outputs $J_{S01\cdot\pi}^{rr} = 1$ in Game(π).

Proof: At first we evaluate the left-hand-side term of Equation (8), i.e., $\Pr[J_\pi^{rr} = 1|\text{Game}(\$)]$. As we mentioned in the proof of Lemma 1, the relation $J_\pi^{rr} = J_{S01\cdot\pi}^{rr}$ always holds. Therefore,

$$\Pr[J_\pi^{rr} = 1|\text{Game}(\$)] = \Pr[J_{S01\cdot\pi}^{rr} = 1|\text{Game}(S01 \cdot \$)]. \tag{9}$$

Note that $A_{S01\cdot\pi}^{rr}$ is a deterministic algorithm that generates a message M and output $J_{S01\cdot\pi} = 0$(random number)/1(ciphertext) in response to a ciphertext C. There exist a function $f_{A_{S01\cdot\pi}^{rr}}$ such that for $\forall (P, C)$, $f_{A_{S01\cdot\pi}^{rr}}(P, C) = J_{S01\cdot\pi}^{rr}$. Let $\mathbb{C}_{A_{S01\cdot\pi},0} = \{C : f_{A_{S01\cdot\pi}^{rr}}(C) = 0\}$ and we have following equations.

$$\Pr(J_\pi^{rr} = 0|\text{Game}(\$)) = \sum_{C \in \mathbb{C}} \Pr(C)$$
$$= \sum_{C \in \mathbb{C}} \frac{1}{2^{|C|}} \tag{10}$$
$$= \frac{|\mathbb{C}|}{2^{|C|}}.$$

Because of the uniformity of a random number as the input C, Equation (10) can be evaluated as $\Pr(C) = \frac{1}{2^{|C|}}$.

We now evaluate the right-hand-side term of Equation (8), i.e., $\Pr[J_{S01\cdot\pi}^{rr} = 1|\text{Game}(\$)]$.

$$\Pr(J_{S01\cdot\pi}^{rr} = 0|\text{Game}(\$)) = \sum_{C \in \mathbb{C}} \Pr(C)$$
$$= \sum_{C \in \mathbb{C}} \frac{1}{2^{|C|}} \tag{11}$$
$$= \frac{|\mathbb{C}|}{2^{|C|}}.$$

Because of the uniformity of the ciphertext that $A_{S01 \cdot \pi}^{rr}$ receives (stated and proven in Proposition 1), Equation (11) is obtained.

Hence, Equation (9) holds and the following relation also holds.

$$\Pr[J_\pi^{rr} = 1 | \text{Game}(\$)] = \Pr[J_{S01 \cdot \pi}^{rr} = 1 | \text{Game}(\$)].$$

□

We now show Proposition 1 and its proof.

Proposition 1. *Uniformity of ciphertext of* $S01 \cdot \$$: *If the scheme* $S01 \cdot \$$ *uses random number, ciphertexts distributes uniformly. The distribution is independent of a message.*

Proof: Let M' be the padded message. More specifically a secret random padding S_P and redundancy data R are appended to M in order to generate M'. Because of Proposition 2 shown in the latter part of the paper, for an arbitrary M', the number of key streams (S_A, S_B) that maps a message M' on to a ciphertext C, is $2^n - 1$, which is independent of M'. Therefore, for an arbitrary M' the probability that the corresponding ciphertext coincides with C is $(2^n - 1)/2^{mn}$ (over possible key streams).

Remember that the way to generate M' out of M is independent of (S_A, S_B). Hence, for an arbitrary message M, M's ciphertext distributes uniformly, as well.

□

Proposition 2. *For a arbitrary* (M', C) *pair there are exactly* $2^n - 1$ *key streams of* (S_A, S_B) *that maps a message* M' *to a ciphertext* C. *Moreover each key-stream candidate for a fixed* (M', C) *has distinct* S_A *value. Hence,* S_A *value cannot be determined only from a* (M', C).

Proof: From Equations (1) and (2), we solve S_{Bi}'s recursively.

$$S_{B1} = (C_1 \oplus F_0) \otimes S_A^{-1} \oplus M_1', \tag{12}$$
$$S_{Bi} = (C_i \oplus M_{i-1}' \oplus S_{Bi-1}) \otimes S_A^{-1} \oplus M_i'. \tag{13}$$

For an arbitrary S_A, S_B sequence is uniquely determined. Therefore, (S_A, S_B) pairs that map M' to C exist at least as many as S_A's, i.e., $2^n - 1$.

We then fix S_A value and prove that only one S_B sequence maps M' to C. In total we conclude there exist $(2^n - 1)$ key streams (S_A, S_B) that map M' to C.

We assume two different key streams, (S_A, S_B') and (S_A, S_B''). Note that these two share common S_A value. When these two key streams encrypt M',

$$F_{i+1}' = P_i \oplus S_{Bi}',$$
$$C_i' = (F_{i+1}' \otimes S_A) \oplus F_i',$$
$$F_{i+1}'' = P_i \oplus S_{Bi}'',$$
$$C_i'' = (F_{i+1}'' \otimes S_A) \oplus F_i''.$$

Let j be the least index where S'_B and S''_B differs. From Equations (1) and (2), we have $F'_j = F''_j$, $S'_B \neq S''_B$ and $F'_{j+1} \neq F''_{j+1}$. Therefore, $C'_j \neq C''_j$.

Hence, there is no message M' that is mapped to the same C under two different keys streams that shares the same S_A.

We therefore conclude that the number of key streams (S_A, S_B) that encrypts M' and generates ciphertext C is $2^n - 1$.   □

4 Integrity

In this section we study security in terms of message integrity. We first define an model of the adversary. We assume the adversary that can choose a message and the redundancy and obtain the corresponding ciphertext. Because the studied model is a stream cipher, the key stream is used in the one-time-pad manner, or equivalently any part of the key stream is never re-used. An adversary forges a ciphertext out of the knowledge of a message, the redundancy and the corresponding ciphertext. The adversary is capable of altering even the length of the ciphertext. The aim of this study is to give an upperbound probability of a successful forgery. We give Theorem 2 about the security of the studied encryption scheme.

Theorem 2. *A pseudorandom number generator (PRNG)π is $(t_\pi, \mu_\pi; \epsilon_\pi)$-secure in the indistinguishability from random bits, i.e.,*

$$\mathrm{Adv}_\pi^{rr} = \Pr(J_\pi^{rr} = 1 | \mathrm{Game}(\pi)) - \Pr(J_\pi^{rr} = 1 | \mathrm{Game}(\$)) \leq \epsilon_\pi,$$

with computational time t_π and amount of query μ_π, where $\mathrm{Game}(\pi)$ and $\mathrm{Game}(\$)$ are games with the oracle outputting the π sequence and random sequence, respectively.

The encryption scheme S01 with π, $S01_\pi$ is $(t_{S01 \cdot \pi}^{alter}, \mu_{S01 \cdot \pi}^{alter}; p_{S01 \cdot \pi}^{alter})$ secure against the adversary, i.e., an adversary cannot generate a successful forgery with computational time $(t_{S01 \cdot \pi}^{alter}$ data complexity $\mu_{S01 \cdot \pi}^{alter}$ and the upperbound of the successful probability $p_{S01 \cdot \pi}^{alter}$, where $(t_{S01 \cdot \pi}^{alter}, \mu_{S01 \cdot \pi}^{alter}, p_{S01 \cdot \pi}^{alter}) = (t_\pi - c_3 \cdot \mu_\pi + c_3 c_4, \mu_\pi - c_4, \epsilon_\pi + (m+1)/(2^n - 1))$.

Proof: We prove this through contradiction. Assume that an adversary $A_{S01 \cdot \pi}^{alter}$ can $(t_{S01 \cdot \pi}^{alter}, \mu_{S01 \cdot \pi}^{alter}; p_{S01 \cdot \pi}^{alter})$-forge $S01_\pi$. We construct a new adversary A_π^{rr} that can $(t_\pi^{rr}, \mu_\pi^{rr}; \epsilon_\pi^{rr})$-break π in the indistinguishability from random bits.

Let $\mathcal{O}_\pi(\cdot)$ be A_π^{rr}'s oracle. A_π^{rr} will run $A_{S01 \cdot \pi}^{alter}$, using $\mathcal{O}_\pi(\cdot)$ to provide an appropriate simulation of $A_{S01 \cdot \pi}^{alter}$'s oracle $\mathcal{O}_{S01 \cdot \pi}(\cdot)$. More specifically, $A_{S01 \cdot \pi}^{alter}$ is a deterministic algorithm that generates a message and a redundancy. In response to the ciphertext C, or equivalently the output of the oracle $\mathcal{O}_{S01 \cdot \pi}(\cdot)$, $A_{S01 \cdot \pi}^{alter}$ outputs the forged ciphertext C', which is different from C. The probability that C' passes the integrity check of the decryption is $p_{S01 \cdot \pi}^{alter}$.

We indicate the algorithm of the constructed adversary below.

Algorithm A_π^{rr}

1. Invoke $A_{S01\cdot\pi}$, and obtain $A_{S01\cdot\pi}$'s outputs. The output consists of a message M and a redundancy R,
2. (Gen. S_A) Obtain n-bit oracle output to generate S_A. If $S_A = 0$, repeat the generation until $S_A \neq 0$.
3. (Gen. S_B) Calculate the length of M (the number of n-bit blocks in M, m) and obtain $(m + 2)$-block (or equivalently $(m + 2)n$-bit) oracle output.
4. (Gen. S_P) Obtain n-bit oracle output to generate S_P.
5. Using S_A, S_B, S_P, and R, encrypt M to generate the ciphertext C.
6. Send C to $A_{S01\cdot\pi}^{alter}$.
7. Obtain C', the output of $A_{S01\cdot\pi}^{alter}$.
8. Check the validity of C'. If the decryption result is the forgery detection signal ϕ, output $J_\pi^{rr} = 0$. Otherwise, output $J_\pi^{rr} = 1$.
9. Terminate this run.

Let $\mathcal{O}_\pi(\cdot)$ be the oracle of A_π^{rr}. $\mathcal{O}_\pi(\cdot)$ outputs either (Game π) the output sequence of π, or (Game \$) the random sequence.

We now compute A_π^{rr}'s advantage, $\mathrm{Adv}_{A_\pi}^{rr}$.

$$\mathrm{Adv}_{A_\pi}^{rr} = \Pr(J_\pi^{rr} = 1|\mathrm{Game}(\pi))$$
$$- \Pr(J_\pi^{rr} = 1|\mathrm{Game}(\$)).$$

Because of the following Lemma 3, the following equation holds.

$$\mathrm{Adv}_{A_\pi}^{rr} = p_{S01\cdot\pi}^{alter} - \Pr(J_\pi^{rr} = 1|\mathrm{Game}(\$)).$$

From Lemma 4, we have

$$\mathrm{Adv}_{A_\pi}^{rr} \geq p_{S01\cdot\pi}^{alter} - (m + 1)/(2^n - 1).$$

Therefore, we can evaluate the cost and advantage of A_π^{rr} as follows:

$$t_\pi^{rr} = t_{S01\cdot\pi}^{alter} + c_3 \cdot \mu_{S01\cdot\pi}^{alter}$$
$$\mu_\pi^{rr} = \mu_{S01\cdot\pi}^{alter} + 4n + \frac{n}{2n} + \frac{n}{2^{2n}} + \cdots$$
$$= \mu_{S01\cdot\pi}^{alter} + c_4,$$
$$\epsilon_\pi = p_{S01\cdot\pi}^{alter} - (m + 1)/2^n,$$

where $c_4 = 3n + \frac{n}{1-2^{-n}}$. We finally solve $t_{S01\cdot\pi}^{alter}, \mu_{S01\cdot\pi}^{alter}, p_{S01\cdot\pi}^{alter}$ and obtain the following relations:

$$\mu_{S01\cdot\pi}^{alter} = \mu_\pi - c_4,$$
$$t_{S01\cdot\pi}^{alter} = t_\pi - c_3 \cdot \mu_{S01\cdot\pi}$$
$$= t_\pi - c_3 \cdot (\mu_\pi - c_4)$$
$$= t_\pi - c_3 \cdot \mu_\pi + c_3 c_4,$$
$$p_{S01\cdot\pi}^{alter} = \epsilon_\pi + (m + 1)/2^n.$$

$\square$

Lemma 3. *In the proof of Theorem 2, the following equation holds.*

$$\Pr[J_\pi^{rr} = 1 | \text{Game}(\pi)] = p_{S01 \cdot \pi}^{alter}.$$

In other words, in $\text{Game}(\pi)$*, i.e., a game with* $\mathcal{O}_\pi$ *outputting* π *sequence, the probability that* A_π^{rr} *outputs* $J_\pi^{rr} = 1$ *is equal to the probability that* $A_{S01 \cdot \pi}^{alter}$ *outputs a valid forged ciphertext in* $\text{Game}(\pi)$.

Proof: In the game with $\mathcal{O}_\pi$ outputting π sequence, $A_{S01 \cdot \pi}^{alter}$ (invoked by A_π^{rr}) receives a ciphertext C encrypted by $S01 \cdot \pi$. Therefore, the operations of $A_{S01 \cdot \pi}^{alter}$ are exactly the same as $A_{S01 \cdot \pi}^{alter}$ playing in $\text{Game}(S01 \cdot \pi)$. Note that A_π^{rr} outputs $J_{S01 \cdot \pi} = 1$ if and only if $A_{S01 \cdot \pi}^{alter}$ outputs the successful forgery C'. Therefore, we have the following equation.

$$\Pr[J_\pi^{rr} = 1 | \text{Game}(\pi)] = p_{S01 \cdot \pi}^{alter}.$$

$\square$

Lemma 4. *In the proof of Theorem 2, the following equation holds.*

$$\Pr[J_\pi^{rr} = 1 | \text{Game}(\$)] \leq (m + 1)/(2^n - 1).$$

In other words, in $\text{Game}(\$)$*, i.e., a game with* $\mathcal{O}_\pi$ *outputting a random sequence, the probability that* A_π^{rr} *outputs* $J_\pi^{rr} = 1$ *is at most* $(m + 1)/(2^n - 1)$.

Proof: We first consider attacks without changing the length of the ciphertext (namely, the attack is limited only to changing the ciphertext value). The proofs for the cases of (1) eliminating the length of the ciphertext and (2) appending new ciphertext blocks will be discussed in the latter part of the proof.

Assuming that $A_{S01 \cdot \pi}^{alter}$ with known-plaintext tries to alter ciphertext and the decryptor receives the maliciously altered ciphertext, C', instead of C. The one of the necessary objective of the attacker is to alter a message such that the recovered (modified) message has the same redundancy. Due to the algebraic structure of the scheme, a successful forgery must have special relation that includes an unknown S_A value. The proof of the S_A's uncertainty out of a known plaintext is given in Proposition 2.

We construct the necessary condition to match R. From Equations (3) and (4), the recovered message M' of the forged ciphertext is:

$$F_1' = F_1,$$
$$F_i' = (C_i' \oplus F_{i-1}') \otimes S_A^{-1},$$
$$M_i' = F_i' \oplus S_{Bi}.$$

$A_{S01 \cdot \pi}^{alter}$ also knows the original message, so that he has following equations:

$$F_1 = F_1,$$
$$F_i = (C_i \oplus F_{i-1}) \otimes S_A^{-1},$$
$$M_i = F_i \oplus S_{Bi}.$$

From these equations, we solve R and R'. Consequently we have

$$R = M_{m+2} = S_{Bm+2} \oplus \bigoplus_{i=1}^{m+2} C_{m+3-i}S_A^{-i} \oplus F_0 S_A^{-(m+2)},$$

$$R' = M'_{m+2} = S_{Bm+2} \oplus \bigoplus_{i=1}^{m+2} C'_{m+3-i}S_A^{-i} \oplus F_0 S_A^{-(m+2)}.$$

The necessary condition is to hold $R = R'$. Then we have a condition.

$$0 = \delta_{m+2}S_A^{-1} \oplus \delta_{m+1}S_A^{-2} \oplus \delta_m S_A^{-3} \oplus \ldots \oplus \delta_2 S_A^{-(m+1)} \oplus \delta_1 S_A^{-(m+2)}. \qquad (14)$$

Remember that $A_{S01\cdot\pi}^{alter}$ is a deterministic algorithm and $A_{S01\cdot\pi}^{alter}$ determines δ without the knowledge of S_A (Proposition 2). Then for a fixed δ value, there exist at most $m+1$ roots for non-zero S_A of Equation (14). Because S_A is random and independent of the $A_{S01\cdot\pi}^{alter}$'s actions, the probability of a successful forgery is upperbounded by $(m+1)/(2^n - 1)$.

Eliminating ciphertext length: In this part of the proof, we concentrate on the case in which the ciphertext is shortened. Here we use $S_P = S'_P$ as a necessary condition for the successful forgery.

Let c' be the length of the forged ciphertext ($c' < m+2$). Then the decryptor will identify $M'_{c'-1}$ as S_P. More specifically,

$$S'_P = M'_{c'-1} = S_{Bc'-1} \oplus \bigoplus_{i=1}^{c'-1} C'_{c'-i}S_A^{-i} \oplus F_0 S_A^{-(c'-1)}. \qquad (15)$$

On the other hand, the decryption scheme generates S_P as the next pseudorandom block after $S_{Bc'}$. Therefore,

$$S_P = S_{Bc'+1} = M_{c'+1} \oplus \bigoplus_{i=1}^{c'+1} C'_{c'+2-i}S_A^{-i} \oplus F_0 S_A^{-(c'+1)}. \qquad (16)$$

From Equations (12), and (13), $S_{Bc'-1}$ can be expressed only by the public value and S_A as follows:

$$S_{Bc'-1} = M_{c'-1} \oplus S_A^{-1}C_{c'-1} \oplus S_A^{-2}C_{c'-2} \oplus \cdots \oplus S_A^{-(c'-1)}C_1 \oplus F_0 S_A^{-(c'-1)}$$

$$= M_{c'-1} \oplus F_0 S_A^{-(c'-1)} \oplus \bigoplus_{i=1}^{c'-1} C_{c'-i}S_A^{-i}. \qquad (17)$$

From Equations (15), (16) and (17), the necessary condition for matching S_P and S'_P is expressible only with known values (M, C, C'), and an unknown independent value S_A as follows:

$$0 = M_{c'+1} \oplus M_{c'-1} \oplus F_0 S_A^{-(c'+1)} \oplus C'_2 S_A^{-c'} \oplus C'_1 S_A^{-(c'+1)} \oplus \bigoplus_{i=1}^{c'-1}(\delta_{c'-i} \oplus C_{c'+2-i})S_A^{-i}.$$

$$(18)$$

Being similar to the previous case of attack, $A_{S01 \cdot \pi}^{alter}$ determines δ, c', and C' without the knowledge of S_A (Proposition 2). Then for a fixed set of (δ, c', C'), there exist at most $c' + 1$ roots for non-zero S_A of Equation (18). Because S_A is random and independent of the $A_{S01 \cdot \pi}^{alter}$'s actions, the probability of a successful forgery is upperbounded by $(c' + 1)/(2^n - 1) \leq m/(2^n - 1)$.

Appending new ciphertext blocks: We briefly describe the proof of the case in which the adversary appends a new ciphertext block (in addition to changing the existing ciphertext blocks). Let c' be the length of the appended ciphertext $(c' > c)$.

In this case we consider the difficulty of controlling R'. From Equation (5), R' can be expressed by

$$R' = S_{Bc} \oplus M_c \oplus F_c . \tag{19}$$

Note that what $A_{S01 \cdot \pi}$ can control is limited to something about F_c. S_{Bc} is a new value that has never appeared in the encryption process, i.e., S_{Bc} is independently random from any public value. Therefore, although he can control the actual value of F_c, the probability that $R' = R$ is $1/2^n$.   □

5   Implementation and Efficiency

In this section, we discuss the implementation and efficiency of the proposed scheme. For the practical parameters, we set the block length to be 64 bits for all evaluations.

In terms of software implementation, we implemented the proposed scheme together with the PANAMA stream cipher [DC98]. As a result, we have performances of 202 Mbps (encryption) and 207 Mbps (decryption) on a 600-MHz Alpha processor. The code is written in C-language and compiled by a DEC cc compiler.

The hardware suitability of our scheme is very high because of operations in $\mathbf{F2}^{64}$. We estimated additional hardware cost to the PRNG. Generally speaking, there are considerable trade-offs between performance and hardware size. Our evaluation demonstrates two instances: the maximum throughput model and the smallest gate size model. All estimations were evaluated with a 0.35-μm CMOS process.

For the maximum throughput, the multiplication is implemented with full logical expression, and is estimated by the size (the number of gates) and the propagation delay. As a result of an estimation with Verilog-HDL, the multiplication in $\mathbf{F2}^{64}$ is implemented in a 36-K gate and its propagation delay is 5.4 ns. This is an optimized circuit in the sense of the propagation delay. The circuit performs up to 150 MHz and encrypts a block (64-bit) with a clock. Thus, the maximum throughput is estimated to be 9.6 Gbps (when the PRNG performs fast enough).

Similarly we estimated the smallest gate count implementation, in which a multiplication in a finite field is realized very cheaply with a linear feedback shift register. we found that the additional circuit to the PRNG can be implemented with no more than 3 K gate. This circuit works with clocks up to 800 MHz. Since a block en(de)cryption takes 65 clocks, this smallest gate count instance practically performs about 200 Mbps at 200 MHz.

6   Concluding Remarks

We proposed an encryption scheme both for data confidentiality and data integrity that uses a $n(m+4)$-bit random number stream, where n is the length of a block and m is the number of blocks in a message. We proved the probability of a forgery in known-plaintext environments.

The proposed scheme is practical as we demonstrated implementations both on software and hardware. In particular, hardware suitability is very high since operations in the scheme are suitable for a hardware platform. Therefore, either the additional gate count is very small, or the maximum throughput can be very high with acceptable gate counts. Because of the possibility of parallel PRNG, the maximum throughput of 9.6 Gbps is a reasonably realistic estimation.

As for efficiency, the scheme has two more advantages. First of all, the scheme achieves single-path encryption scheme so that streaming data can be also dealt with using a limited hardware resource. Secondly, the PRNG is independent of either the intermediate value or the message. This means that parallel computation and precomputation are very easy and effective for increasing the maximum throughput.

An additional issue regarding security is that any part of an actual key stream value cannot be determined by an adversary so that the most likely target to crack, the PRNG, is unreachable directly from the attacker. This cannot be construed to mean any concrete additional security. However, in a cryptographic attack on a PRNG, the attacker must make use of the actual value, then the scheme itself may bring a certain hedge against attacks.

References

[BDJR97] M. Bellare, A. Desai, E. Jokipii, and P. Rogaway, "A Concrete Security Treatment of Symmetric Encryption: Analysis of the DES Modes of Operation," *Proceedings of the 38th Symposium on Foundations of Computer Science, IEEE,* 1997, full paper is available at http://www-cse.ucsd.edu/users/mihir/.

[BGV96] A. Bosselaers, R. Govaerts, and J. Vandewalle, "Fast Hashing on the Pentium," *Advances in Cryptology, —CRYPTO'96, LNCS Vol. 1109, Springer-Verlag,* 1996.

[BKR94] M. Bellare, J. Kilian, and P. Rogaway, "The Security of Cipher Block Chaining," *Advances in Cryptology, —CRYPTO'94, LNCS Vol. 839, Springer-Verlag,* 1994.

[BHKKR99] J. Black and S. Halevi, H. Krawczyk, T. Krovets, P. Rogaway, "UMAC: Fast and Secure Message Authentication," *Advances in Cryptology, — CRYPTO'99, LNCS Vol. 1666, Springer-Verlag,* 1999.

[CW79] L. Carter and M. Wegman, "Universal Hash Functions," *Journal of Computer and System Sciences, Vol. 18,* 1979.

[DC98] J. Daemen and C. Clapp, "Fast Hashing and Stream Encryption with PANAMA," *Fast Software Encryption, 5th International Workshop, FSE'98, Proceedings, LNCS Vol. 1372, Springer-Verlag*, 1998.

[FS01] S. Furuya, D. Watanabe, Y. Seto, and K. Takaragi, "Integrity-Aware Mode of Stream Cipher," *IEICE Transactions on Fundamentals of Electronics, Communications and Computer Sciences*, Vol. E85-A No.1, pp.58–65, 2002.

[HK97] S. Halevi and H. Krawczyk, "MMH: Software Message Authentication in the Gbit/second Rates," *Fast Software Encryption, 4th International Workshop, FSE'97, LNCS Vol. 1267, Springer-Verlag*, 1997.

[GD01] V. D. Gligor and P. Donescu, "Fast Encryption and Authentication: XCBC Encryption and XECB Authentication Modes," In *Preproceedings of FSE 2001, 8th Fast Software Encryption Workshop*, Yokohama Japan, 2001.

[G00] J. D. Golić, "Modes of Operation of Stream Ciphers," *Selected Areas in Cryptography, 7th Annual International Workshop, SAC 2000 Proceedings, LNCS Vol. 2012, Springer-Verlag*, 2001.

[JV98] M. H. Jakubowski and R. Venkatesan, "The Chain & Sum Primitive and Its Applications to MACs and Stream Ciphers," *Advances in Cryptology, — EUROCRYPT'98, LNCS Vol. 1403, Springer-Verlag*, 1998.

[J97] T. Johansson, "Bucket Hashing with Small Key Size," *Advances in Cryptology, —EUROCRYPT'97, LNCS Vol. 1233, Springer-Verlag*, 1997.

[J01] C. S. Jutla, "Encryption Modes with Almost Free Message Integrity," *Advances in Cryptology, —EUROCRYPT2001, LNCS Vol. 2045, Springer-Verlag*, 2001.

[KY00] J. Katz and M. Yung, "Unforgeable Encryption and Chosen Cipher Secure Modes of Operation," *Fast Software Encryption, 7th International Workshop, FSE2000, LNCS Vol. 1978, Springer-Verlag*, 2001.

[NP99] W. Nevelsteen and B. Preneel, "Software Performance of Universal Hash Functions," *Advances in Cryptology, —EUROCRYPT'99, LNCS Vol. 1592, Springer-Verlag*, 1999.

[PR99] S. Patel and Z. Ramzan, "Square Hash: Fast Message Authentication via Optimized Universal Hash Functions," *Advances in Cryptology, —CRYPTO'99, LNCS Vol. 1666, Springer-Verlag*, 1999.

[PvO96] B. Preneel and P. van Oorschot, "On The Security of Two MAC Algorithms," *Advances in Cryptology, —EUROCRYPT'96, LNCS Vol. 1070, Springer-Verlag*, 1996.

[R97] M. Roe, "Cryptography and Evidence," *Doctoral Dissertation with the University of Cambridge*, 1997. available at http://www.ccsr.cam.ac.uk/techreports/index.html.

[RBBK01] P. Rogaway, M. Bellare, J. Black, and T. Krovetz, "OCB: A Block-Cipher Mode of Operation for Efficient Authenticated Encryption," *Eights ACM conference on computer and communications security CCS-8, ACM Press*, 2001.

[S49] C. E. Shannon, "A Mathematical Theory of Communication," *Bell Systems Technical Journal*, Vol.28, No.4, 1949.

[S96] V. Shoup, "On Fast And Provably Secure Message Authentication Based on Universal Hashing," *Advances in Cryptology, —CRYPTO'96, LNCS Vol. 1109, Springer-Verlag*, 1996.

[T93] R. Taylor, "An Integrity Check Value Algorithm for Stream Ciphers," *Advances in Cryptology, —CRYPTO'93, LNCS Vol. 773, Springer-Verlag*, 1993.

[WC81] M. Wegman and L. Carter, "New Hash Functions And Their Use in Authentication And Set Equality," *Journal of Computer and System Sciences*, Vol. 22, 1981.

Markov Truncated Differential Cryptanalysis of Skipjack

Ben Reichardt and David Wagner

UC Berkeley, Berkeley CA 94720, USA,
{breic,daw}@cs.berkeley.edu

Abstract. Using Markov chains, we systematically compute all the truncated differentials of Skipjack, assuming the nonlinear G boxes are random permutations. We prove that an attacker with one random truncated differential from each of 2^{128} independently-keyed encryption oracles has advantage of less than 2^{-16} in distinguishing whether the oracles are random permutations or the Skipjack algorithm.

1 Introduction

Skipjack encrypts a 64-bit plaintext by applying eight type-A rounds, followed by eight type-B rounds, then eight more A rounds and eight more B rounds [8]. The A and B rounds, given in Fig. 1, are feedback shift registers on four 16-bit words, with a nonlinear permutation G (a four-round Feistel network). B rounds, when keyed correctly and with w_1 swapped with w_2, w_3 swapped with w_4, invert the A rounds. Compare the "Fibonacci" form of the A-round shift register to that of a Feistel cipher shown in Fig. 2; they differ in the placement of the nonlinear function.

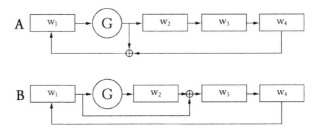

Fig. 1. Skipjack consists of eight rounds through the type A shift register, followed by eight rounds of the reversed shift register type B, then eight further rounds each of types A and B. G is a keyed bijection. A round counter is also input to the exor

A differential for a cipher consists of a set Δ of differences of plaintexts, a set Δ^* of differences of ciphertexts, and a probability p that two randomly chosen

K. Nyberg and H. Heys (Eds.): SAC 2002, LNCS 2595, pp. 110–128, 2003.

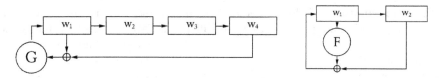

Fig. 2. The "Fibonacci" form of the Skipjack A round (left) has its nonlinear permutation G in a different position than the nonlinear function F of a Feistel shift register (right)

plaintexts with difference in Δ will be encrypted to ciphertexts with difference in Δ^*, for a fixed key. For Skipjack, the appropriate definition of the "difference" between texts t and t' is the exor $t \oplus t'$. Differentials with p significantly different – either more or less – than the same probability for a random permutation can be used as distinguishers, and often to build key-recovery attacks [4]. For traditional differentials, the sets Δ, Δ^* are singletons [2]; so-called truncated differentials deal with larger sets [5].

There are no known attacks on all 32 rounds of Skipjack better than exhaustive search over the 80-bit key space. However, the unbalanced structure of the Skipjack network, in which the nonlinear permutation affects only a quarter of the bits at each round, slows diffusion of nonlinearities, and makes it easy to follow differentials across multiple rounds. The best known attacks on up to 31 rounds of Skipjack are truncated differential attacks by Biham et al. [1] and Knudsen et al. [6]. They found differentials either by tracing through by hand an unrolled diagram of Skipjack rounds, or by having a computer search for differentials across a similar form cipher with fewer bits per word – e.g., a 32-bit cipher with 8-bit words. However, Granboulan [4] found several errors in the probability calculations of [6].

We here apply the Markov techniques of [7] to systematically and efficiently calculate correct probabilities for all the truncated differentials of Skipjack, under the assumption that the G boxes are random permutations. We verify Granboulan's corrected differential probabilities. We verify the 24-round impossible differential (i.e., a differential with $p = 0$) used in the attack of [1], and find three mistaken differentials they state but do not use in their attack. We also describe several new "distinguishers", for instance a 30-round truncated differential. We show that there are no good truncated differentials for the full 32 rounds of Skipjack. Additionally, we estimate the best distinguishing advantage gained by considering multiple differentials, instead of just a single one. We prove that an attacker with one random truncated differential from each of 2^{128} independently-keyed encryption oracles has advantage of less than 1.0003×2^{-17} in distinguishing whether the oracles are random permutations or the Skipjack algorithm. Since no attack on Skipjack can obtain more than $2^{64}(2^{64} - 1)/2$ plaintext pairs, this provides heuristic evidence that Skipjack may be secure against truncated differential distinguishing attacks.

The contributions of this paper are twofold. First, we carefully develop a framework for the analysis of truncated differential attacks, and we introduce new mathematical tools for precisely characterizing the strength of a cipher against truncated differential attacks. Notably, we give methods for calculating the exact probability of truncated differentials (many trails), in contrast to many previous works which only looked at truncated differential characteristics (a single trail), and we show how to bound the distinguishing advantage of any truncated differential attack, even one that uses several truncated differentials simultaneously. Second, we apply these methods to Skipjack, and we characterize its strength against truncated differential cryptanalysis. We hope that these investigations will yield new insight into the structure of Skipjack and more generally into the analysis of security against truncated differential attacks.

In Sect. 2 we define Markov ciphers, for which round applications correspond to a Markov process. In Sect. 3, we introduce our methods and use them to compute truncated differentials for a simple two-word Skipjack variant. In Sect. 4, we compute truncated differentials for a three-word Skipjack variant and give a criterion for weak key classes. In Sect. 5, we give the Markov transition matrices for full, four-word Skipjack's A and B rounds. We correct some differential probability calculations. In Sect. 6, we bound the advantage an attacker gains from using multiple (independent) differentials. Finally, in Sect. 7 we list the best truncated differentials for Skipjack. We also show that it is unlikely that there exist any weak key classes for which a truncated differential attack would be significantly improved.

2   Markov Ciphers

Let Λ be a collection of nonempty, pairwise-disjoint subsets of $\Gamma \times \Gamma$ covering $\Gamma \times \Gamma$. For $f : \Gamma \to \Gamma$, define $\tilde{f} : \Gamma \times \Gamma \to \Gamma \times \Gamma$ by $\tilde{f}(x, y) = (f(x), f(y))$. If F is a random distribution over functions $\Gamma \to \Gamma$, we call F *Markov* with respect to Λ, or Λ-Markov, if for all $\Delta, \Delta' \in \Lambda$, for f sampled according to F and δ uniformly distributed in Δ such that $\tilde{f}(\delta) \in \Delta'$, $\tilde{f}(\delta)$ is uniformly distributed in Δ'. That is, using $\in_R$ to mean sampling according to the uniform distribution, $\Pr[\tilde{f}(\delta) = (x, y) | \delta \in_R \Delta, f(\delta) \in \Delta']$ is independent of $(x, y) \in \Delta'$.

For F, G distributions over functions $\Gamma \to \Gamma$, we define the distribution $G \circ F$ as given by that of $g \circ f$, where g, f are sampled from G, F, respectively. Then for F, G independent Λ-Markov function distributions, the distribution $G \circ F$ is also Λ-Markov, and for $\Delta, \Delta', \Delta'' \in \Lambda$, $\Pr_{G \circ F}[(\tilde{g} \circ \tilde{f})(\delta) \in \Delta'', \tilde{f}(\delta) \in \Delta' | \delta \in_R \Delta] = \Pr_G[\tilde{g}(\delta') \in \Delta'' | \delta' \in_R \Delta'] \cdot \Pr_F[\tilde{f}(\delta) \in \Delta' | \delta \in_R \Delta]$.

We can associate to any Λ-Markov distribution F a corresponding transition matrix $[F]$ with a row and a column for each $\Delta \in \Lambda$, defined by $[F]_{\Delta, \Delta} = \Pr_F[\tilde{f}(\delta) \in \Delta' | \delta \in_R \Delta]$. Then the above property implies $[G \circ F] = [G][F]$, i.e., functional composition corresponds to matrix multiplication.

When Γ is the set of texts, an iterated round block cipher is a Λ-Markov cipher if its round functions are independent Λ-Markov function distributions, where the probability is taken over the round key. For example, if its rounds were keyed independently, DES would be a Markov cipher with respect to the exor operation $\oplus$, i.e., with respect to Λ consisting of sets $\{(x,y)|x \oplus y = z\}$ for every z [7], [2].

3   Two-Word Skipjack Variant

To introduce our techniques, we'll consider an adaptation of Skipjack into a two-word cipher with A and B rounds as shown in Fig. 3. As with full Skipjack, the A round is inverted by the B round with G^{-1} and swapped words. By analogy with full Skipjack, two-word Skipjack begins with four A rounds, then has four B rounds, then four more of each of the A and B rounds: $SJ_2(x) = B^4A^4B^4A^4(x)$ for $x \in \{0,1\}^{2n}$. Assume the G boxes are uniformly random permutations $\{0,1\}^n \rightarrow \{0,1\}^n$, chosen independently for each round.

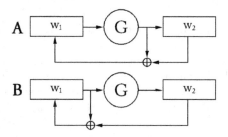

Fig. 3. Our two-word Skipjack variant consists of four A rounds (above), then four B rounds (below), then four more A rounds and four more B rounds

If α is an arbitrary plaintext, then the encryption $SJ_2(\alpha)$ will be drawn uniformly at random from $\{0,1\}^{2n}$. We ask the following natural question: for any given β, what is the distribution of $SJ_2(\beta)$ given $SJ_2(\alpha)$? Since $SJ_2 : \{0,1\} \rightarrow \{0,1\}^{2n}$ is a permutation, $SJ_2(\alpha) = SJ_2(\beta)$ if and only if $\alpha = \beta$. But even for $\alpha \neq \beta$, the distribution of $SJ_2(\alpha) \oplus SJ_2(\beta)$ is *not* uniformly distributed across the nonzero elements of $\{0,1\}^{2n}$. If this distribution – of course depending on the relationship between α and β – is sufficiently non-uniform, it may indicate exploitable weaknesses in the cipher. In practice, a noticeably non-uniform distribution of β's encryption given α's encryption across fewer than all the rounds can often give attacks.

To make our calculations, we'll consider each round separately, and then combine the rounds using the round-independence assumption. For $x \in \{0,1\}^{2n}$ we call its first word $x_1 \in \{0,1\}^n$ and its second word x_2, so $x = (x_1, x_2)$. Note $A(x) = (G(x_1) \oplus x_2, G(x_1))$ and $B(x) = (x_1 \oplus x_2, G(x_1))$.

For a pair of words α_1 and β_1, the joint distribution of their images $G(\alpha_1)$, $G(\beta_1)$ through a G box depends only on whether the two words are the same. Indeed, if $\alpha_1 = \beta_1$ then $G(\alpha_1) = G(\beta_1)$ is uniformly distributed across $\{0,1\}^n$.

If $\alpha_1 \neq \beta_1$ then $G(\alpha_1) \in_R \{0,1\}^n$ and $G(\alpha_1) \oplus G(\beta_1) \in_R \{0,1\}^n \setminus \{0\}$. The minimum amount of information needed to keep track of whether the input difference to a G box is zero or nonzero is given by the *truncated differential class* of the pair α, β. For two-word Skipjack, there are five truncated differential classes of text pairs:

$$[(a,b)] \equiv \{(\alpha,\beta)|\alpha_1 \oplus \beta_1, \alpha_2 \oplus \beta_2, (\alpha_1 \oplus \beta_1) \oplus (\alpha_2 \oplus \beta_2) \neq 0\},$$
$$[(a,a)] \equiv \{(\alpha,\beta)|\alpha_1 \oplus \beta_1 = \alpha_2 \oplus \beta_2 \neq 0\},$$
$$[(a,0)] \equiv \{(\alpha,\beta)|\alpha_2 \oplus \beta_2 \neq 0, \alpha_2 \oplus \beta_2 = 0\},$$
$$[(0,b)] \equiv \{(\alpha,\beta)|\alpha_1 \oplus \beta_1 = 0, \alpha_2 \oplus \beta_2 \neq 0\},$$
$$[(0,0)] \equiv \{(\alpha,\beta)|\alpha = \beta\} \ .$$

We will henceforth omit the brackets around an equivalence class, and write, e.g., (a,b) for $[(a,b)]$. Our notation deviates slightly from previous work in that we require truncated differential classes to be pairwise disjoint. Earlier authors would typically consider the classes (a,a), $(a,0)$ and $(0,b)$ to be subclasses of (a,b), whereas in our setting every text pair belongs to exactly one truncated differential class.

We treat the evolution of a differential across cipher rounds as a Markov process on the truncated differential classes. Let $\delta = (\alpha_\delta, \beta_\delta) \in \{0,1\}^{2n} \times \{0,1\}^{2n}$ denote a pair of texts, and define $\tilde{A} : \{0,1\}^{2n} \to \{0,1\}^{2n}$ by $\tilde{A}(\delta) = (A(\alpha_\delta), A(\beta_\delta))$. Then if $\delta \in_R (0,0)$, $\tilde{A}(\delta) \in_R (0,0)$. If $\delta \in_R (0,a)$, $\tilde{A}(\delta) \in_R (a,0)$. If $\delta \in_R (a,0)$, $\tilde{A}(\delta) \in_R (a,a)$. If $\delta \in_R (a,a)$ or $\delta \in_R (a,b)$, then with probability $\frac{1}{2^n-1}$, $\tilde{A}(\delta) \in_R (a,0)$, and with probability $1 - \frac{1}{2^n-1}$, $\tilde{A}(\delta) \in_R (a,b)$. Figure 4 shows the matrix $[A]$, as well as $[B]$, which can be calculated similarly.

$$
\begin{pmatrix}
1 - \frac{1}{2^n-1} & 1 - \frac{1}{2^n-1} & 0 & 0 & 0 \\
0 & 0 & 1 & 0 & 0 \\
0 & 0 & 0 & 1 & 0 \\
\frac{1}{2^n-1} & \frac{1}{2^n-1} & 0 & 0 & 0 \\
0 & 0 & 0 & 0 & 1
\end{pmatrix}
\qquad
\begin{pmatrix}
1 - \frac{1}{2^n-1} & 0 & 1 - \frac{1}{2^n-1} & 0 & 0 \\
\frac{1}{2^n-1} & 0 & \frac{1}{2^n-1} & 0 & 0 \\
0 & 0 & 0 & 1 & 0 \\
0 & 1 & 0 & 0 & 0 \\
0 & 0 & 0 & 0 & 1
\end{pmatrix}
$$

Fig. 4. The transition matrices for two-word A (left) and B (right). The row and column order is $[(a,b)], [(a,a)], [(a,0)], [(0,b)], [(0,0)]$

The rounds A, B are Markov with respect to $\{(a,b), (a,a), (a,0), (0,b), (0,0)\}$, so we can compute the transition probabilities for any sequence of A and B rounds simply by multiplying the matrices appropriately. So, for example, the entry in row (a,a) and column (a,b) of $([B]^4[A]^4)^2$ gives the probability that a pair of plaintexts $\delta \in_R (a,b)$ is sent by the sixteen rounds of two-word Skipjack to a pair of ciphertexts in (a,a); and all output differences in (a,a) are equally likely.

For comparison, a random permutation takes a nonzero difference to a random nonzero difference. Since $|(0,0)| = 2^{2n}$, $|(0,b)| = |(\alpha,0)| = |(a,a)| =$

$2^{3n} - 2^{2n}$, $|(a,b)| = 2^{4n} - 3 \cdot 2^{3n} + 2 \cdot 2^{2n}$, the probability that a nonzero difference is sent to (a,b) is $|(a,b)|/(2^{4n} - 2^{2n}) = \frac{2^n - 2}{2^n + 1}$, and the probability that a nonzero difference is sent to, e.g., (a,a) is $|(a,a)|/(2^{4n} - 2^{2n}) = \frac{1}{2^n + 1}$.

This technique of computing the transition matrix can be applied to any cipher consisting of exors, linear operations, and components that can be modeled as a random permutation or random function – in particular to Feistel ciphers. Figure 5 shows the transition matrices between these equivalence classes for a two-word Feistel network in which the nonlinear function is either a random function, or a random permutation.

$$
\begin{pmatrix}
1 - \frac{2}{2^n} & 1 - \frac{2}{2^n} & 1 - \frac{2}{2^n} & 0 & 0 \\
\frac{1}{2^n} & \frac{1}{2^n} & \frac{1}{2^n} & 0 & 0 \\
0 & 0 & 0 & 1 & 0 \\
\frac{1}{2^n} & \frac{1}{2^n} & \frac{1}{2^n} & 0 & 0 \\
0 & 0 & 0 & 0 & 1
\end{pmatrix}
\qquad
\begin{pmatrix}
1 - \frac{2}{2^n} & 1 - \frac{1}{2^n} & 1 - \frac{1}{2^n} & 0 & 0 \\
\frac{1}{2^n} & 0 & \frac{1}{2^n} & 0 & 0 \\
0 & 0 & 0 & 1 & 0 \\
\frac{1}{2^n} & \frac{1}{2^n} & 0 & 0 & 0 \\
0 & 0 & 0 & 0 & 1
\end{pmatrix}
$$

Fig. 5. The transition matrix for a two-word Feistel cipher $(x_1, x_2) \mapsto (F(x_1) \oplus x_2, x_1)$, for $F : \{0,1\}^n \rightarrow \{0,1\}^n$ a random function (left), and for F is a random permutation (right). Once again, the row and column order is $(a,b), (a,a), (a,0), (0,b), (0,0)$.

4   Three-Word Skipjack Variant

We adapt Skipjack into a three-word cipher with A and B rounds as shown in Fig. 6. Similarly to full Skipjack, the A round is inverted by the B round with G^{-1} and swapped words w_1 and w_2. By analogy with full Skipjack, three-word Skipjack begins with six A rounds, then has six B rounds, then six more of each of the A and B rounds: $SJ_3(x) = B^6 A^6 B^6 A^6(x)$ for $x \in \{0,1\}^{3n}$. Assume the G boxes are uniformly random permutations $\{0,1\}^n \rightarrow \{0,1\}^n$, chosen independently for each round.

As for two-word Skipjack, to compute long enough differentials we can restrict our attention to sixteen truncated differential classes, corresponding to the sixteen linear subspaces of $GF(2)^3$:

$$(a, b, c),$$
$$(0, b, c), (a, 0, c), (a, b, 0), (a, a, c), (a, b, a), (a, b, b), (a, b, a \oplus b),$$
$$(a, 0, 0), (0, b, 0), (0, 0, c), (a, a, 0), (a, 0, a), (0, b, b), (a, a, a),$$
$$(0, 0, 0) \ .$$

This notation captures exactly which exor relationships between the words hold. For example, $(a, b, a \oplus b)$ contains all plaintext pairs of the form $\big((x_1, x_2, x_3), (x_1 \oplus a', x_2 \oplus b', x_3 \oplus (a' \oplus b'))\big)$ with $x \in \{0,1\}^{3n}$ and $a', b', a' \oplus b' \neq 0$. Every pair of

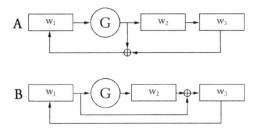

Fig. 6. Our three-word Skipjack variant consists of six A rounds (above), then six B rounds (below), then six more A rounds and six more B rounds

texts in $\{0,1\}^{6n}$ belongs to exactly one truncated differential equivalence class. The equivalence class (a,b,c) contains $2^{3n}(2^n - 1)(2^n - 2)(2^n - 4)$ text pairs, the next seven classes each contain $2^{3n}(2^n - 1)(2^n - 2)$ text pairs, the next four classes each contain $2^{3n}(2^n - 1)$ pairs, and $|(0,0,0)| = 2^{3n}$ of course.

It is an easy exercise to compute the matrices $[A]$, $[B]$ as for two-word Skipjack, so we'll compute them in a slightly different manner here. Define $G_3 : \{0,1\}^{3n} \rightarrow \{0,1\}^{3n}$ by $G_3(x_1, x_2, x_3) = (G(x_1), x_2, x_3)$. We'll compute $[G_3]$. Then, since wordwise permutations and exors just permute the differential classes and A, B just differ from G_3 by wordwise permutations and xors, $[G_3]$ differs from $[A]$, $[B]$ only by left- and right-multiplication by some permutation matrices.

Consider for example a text pair in (a,a,a). If G_3 fixes the difference in the first word, then $\tilde{G}_3$ will map the text pair into another pair in (a,a,a); otherwise it will be sent to (a,b,b). Hence the total number of text pairs mapped from (a,a,a) to (a,a,a) is exactly $2^{2n}\theta$, where $\theta = |\{(x,y) \in \{0,1\}^n \times \{0,1\}^n | G(x) \oplus G(y) = x \oplus y\}|$ denotes the number of exor differences fixed by G (the factor of 2^{2n} comes in because it doesn't matter what the last two words of the texts are, as long as their differences are correct). The total number of text pairs mapped from (a,a,a) to (a,b,b) is $2^{3n}(2^n - 1) - 2^{2n}\theta = 2^{2n}(2^n(2^n - 1) - \theta)$. Similar arguments show that the number of text pairs mapped from any of $(0,b,b)$, $(a,0,a)$, or $(a,a,0)$ to themselves is also $2^{2n}\theta$.

Consider next a text pair in (a,a,c). G_3 maps the text pair to another in (a,a,c) if and only if the difference in the first words is fixed, so the number of text pairs mapped from (a,a,c) to itself is exactly $2^{2n}(2^n - 2)\theta$; the factor of $2^n - 2$ comes in because the difference in the third words can be anything except 0 or the difference in the first words. If, however, the difference in the first words is not fixed, then we can *choose* the third words so that their difference is the difference in the first words after applying G_3. Hence exactly $2^{2n}(2^n(2^n - 1) - \theta)$ text pairs are mapped from (a,a,c) to (a,b,a), and, similarly, the same number is mapped to $(a,b,a \oplus b)$. All the remaining pairs are mapped to (a,b,c).

With similar arguments, we compute for any pair of truncated differential classes the exact number of difference pairs mapped between them, depending only on θ. By dividing through by the size of the source truncated differential classes, we get the matrix $[G_3]$ conditional on θ, shown in Fig. 7.

$$
\left(\begin{array}{cccccccccccccccc}
r_1 & 0 & 0 & 0 & r_3 & r_3 & 0 & r_3 & 0 & 0 & 0 & 0 & 0 & 0 & 0 & 0 \\
0 & 1 & 0 & 0 & 0 & 0 & 0 & 0 & 0 & 0 & 0 & 0 & 0 & 0 & 0 & 0 \\
0 & 0 & r_2 & 0 & 0 & 0 & 0 & 0 & 0 & 0 & 0 & 0 & r_4 & 0 & 0 & 0 \\
0 & 0 & 0 & r_2 & 0 & 0 & 0 & 0 & 0 & 0 & 0 & r_4 & 0 & 0 & 0 & 0 \\
\tfrac{1}{2^n}\tfrac{\bar\theta}{2} & 0 & 0 & 0 & \bar\theta & \tfrac{1}{2^n}\tfrac{\bar\theta}{2} & 0 & \tfrac{1}{2^n}\tfrac{\bar\theta}{2} & 0 & 0 & 0 & 0 & 0 & 0 & 0 & 0 \\
\tfrac{1}{2^n}\tfrac{\bar\theta}{2} & 0 & 0 & 0 & \tfrac{1}{2^n}\tfrac{\bar\theta}{2} & \bar\theta & 0 & \tfrac{1}{2^n}\tfrac{\bar\theta}{2} & 0 & 0 & 0 & 0 & 0 & 0 & 0 & 0 \\
0 & 0 & 0 & 0 & 0 & 0 & r_2 & 0 & 0 & 0 & 0 & 0 & 0 & r_4 & 0 & 0 \\
\tfrac{1}{2^n}\tfrac{\bar\theta}{2} & 0 & 0 & 0 & \tfrac{1}{2^n}\tfrac{\bar\theta}{2} & \tfrac{1}{2^n}\tfrac{\bar\theta}{2} & 0 & \bar\theta & 0 & 0 & 0 & 0 & 0 & 0 & 0 & 0 \\
0 & 0 & 0 & 0 & 0 & 0 & 0 & 0 & 1 & 0 & 0 & 0 & 0 & 0 & 0 & 0 \\
0 & 0 & 0 & 0 & 0 & 0 & 0 & 0 & 0 & 1 & 0 & 0 & 0 & 0 & 0 & 0 \\
0 & 0 & 0 & 0 & 0 & 0 & 0 & 0 & 0 & 0 & 1 & 0 & 0 & 0 & 0 & 0 \\
0 & 0 & 0 & \tfrac{1}{2^n}\tfrac{\bar\theta}{2} & 0 & 0 & 0 & 0 & 0 & 0 & 0 & \bar\theta & 0 & 0 & 0 & 0 \\
0 & 0 & \tfrac{1}{2^n}\tfrac{\bar\theta}{2} & 0 & 0 & 0 & 0 & 0 & 0 & 0 & 0 & 0 & \bar\theta & 0 & 0 & 0 \\
0 & 0 & 0 & 0 & 0 & 0 & 0 & 0 & 0 & 0 & 0 & 0 & 0 & 1 & 0 & 0 \\
0 & 0 & 0 & 0 & 0 & 0 & \tfrac{1}{2^n}\tfrac{\bar\theta}{2} & 0 & 0 & 0 & 0 & 0 & 0 & 0 & \bar\theta & 0 \\
0 & 0 & 0 & 0 & 0 & 0 & 0 & 0 & 0 & 0 & 0 & 0 & 0 & 0 & 0 & 1
\end{array}\right)
$$

Fig. 7. $[G_3]$ conditional on the number θ of pairs in $\{0,1\}^n \times \{0,1\}^n$ whose exor difference is fixed by G $(0 \le \theta \le 2^{2n})$. For convenience, in this figure we define $\bar\theta \equiv \frac{\theta/2^n}{2^n-1}$ and the remainders r_1, r_2, r_3, r_4 are such that the columns sum to one. The row and column order is $(a, b, c), (0, b, c), (a, 0, c), (a, b, 0), (a, a, c), (a, b, a), (a, b, b), (a, b, a \oplus b), (a, 0, 0), (0, b, 0), (0, 0, c), (a, a, 0), (a, 0, a), (0, b, b), (a, a, a), (0, 0, 0)$

The expected value of θ is 2^n; this follows since, for example, the probability that a difference in (a, a, a) is mapped to (a, a, a) is $\frac{1}{2^n-1} = \frac{2^n E[\theta]}{|(a,a,a)|}$. Round functions distributed so that θ is significantly above or below its mean spread the differential classes less uniformly. Knowing $[G_3]$ conditioned on θ lets us compute exactly what cipher weaknesses this may imply. Letting $n_i = |\{x \in \{0,1\}^n | G(x) = x \oplus i\}|$, for $i \in \{0,1\}^n$, we see that $\theta/2 = \sum_{i\in\{0,1\}^n} \binom{n_i}{2}$. Some intensive calculation using indicator variables and taking advantage of the many symmetries among the n_i gives $\mathrm{Var}[\theta] = 2^{n+1}\left(1 + \frac{1}{2^n-3}\right)$. This is a tight enough distribution that weak key classes seem unlikely when the G boxes are random permutations; we'll examine this further for the actual G boxes of full Skipjack in Sect. 7.2.

5   Four-Word Skipjack

Recall the specification of full four-word Skipjack from Fig. 1. Assume the G boxes are uniformly random permutations $\{0,1\}^n \to \{0,1\}^n$, chosen independently for each round; we'll consider the actual 16-bit G boxes in Sect. 7.2.

Corresponding to the 67 linear subspaces of $GF(2)^4$, we consider 67 different truncated differential classes for four n-bit words, listed in Fig. 8. A truncated differential represents the set of pairs in $\{0,1\}^{4n} \times \{0,1\}^{4n}$ where the wordwise exor differences satisfy a given pattern. For example, the class $(0, b, c, b \oplus c)$ contains $\left(w, w \oplus (0, b', c', b' \oplus c')\right)$ for all $w \in \{0,1\}^{4n}$ and all $b', c' \in \{0,1\}^n$ with $b', c' \neq 0$ and $b' \neq c'$. Every pair of texts belongs to exactly one truncated differential class.

$$(a, b, c, d);$$
$$(0, b, c, d), (a, 0, c, d), (a, b, 0, d), (a, b, c, 0), (a, a, c, d), (a, b, a, d), (a, b, c, a), (a, b, b, d), (a, b, c, b),$$
$$(a, b, c, c), (a, b, a \oplus b, d), (a, b, c, a \oplus b), (a, b, c, a \oplus c), (a, b, c, b \oplus c), (a, b, c, a \oplus b \oplus c);$$
$$(0, 0, c, d), (0, b, 0, d), (0, b, c, 0), (a, 0, 0, d), (a, 0, c, 0), (a, b, 0, 0),$$
$$(a, a, a, d), (a, a, c, a), (a, b, a, a), (a, b, b, b), (a, a, 0, d), (a, a, c, 0), (a, 0, a, d), (a, b, a, 0),$$
$$(a, 0, c, a), (a, b, 0, a), (0, b, b, d), (a, b, b, 0), (0, b, c, b), (a, b, 0, b), (0, b, c, c), (a, 0, c, c),$$
$$(0, b, c, b \oplus c), (a, 0, c, a \oplus c), (a, b, 0, a \oplus b), (a, b, a \oplus b, 0), (a, a, c, c), (a, b, a, b), (a, b, b, a);$$
$$(a, a, c, a \oplus c), (a, b, a, a \oplus b), (a, b, a \oplus b, a), (a, b, b, a \oplus b), (a, b, a \oplus b, b), (a, a \oplus c, c, c),$$
$$(0, 0, 0, d), (0, 0, c, 0), (0, b, 0, 0), (a, 0, 0, 0), (0, b, b, b), (a, 0, a, a), (a, a, 0, a), (a, a, a, 0),$$
$$(a, a, 0, 0), (a, 0, a, 0), (a, 0, 0, a), (0, b, b, 0), (0, b, 0, b), (0, 0, c, c), (a, a, a, a);$$
$$(0, 0, 0, 0)$$

Fig. 8. There are 67 different truncated differential classes for four n-bit words, listed here in the basis order we use for our transition matrices. There are $2^{4n}(2^n - 1)(2^n - 2)(2^n - 4)(2^n - 8)$ ordered difference pairs of the first type, $2^{4n}(2^n - 1)(2^n - 2)(2^n - 4)$ of each of the next 15 types, $2^{4n}(2^n - 1)(2^n - 2)$ of each of the next 35 types, $2^{4n}(2^n - 1)$ of each of the next 15 types, and, of course, 2^{4n} trivial difference pairs

Figure 9 shows the truncated differential transition matrices $[A]$ and $[B]$ for the A and B rounds, computed as in Sect. 4. The entry in column j and row i is the probability that a truncated differential of type j, as ordered in Fig. 8, is brought to one of type i. For example, the entry in the eighth row and first column indicates that with probability $\frac{1}{2^{16}-1}$ a difference in (a, b, c, d) is taken to (a, b, c, a). The columns sum to one, and the random distribution is an eigenvector.

Composing these matrices $([B]^8[A]^8)^2$ gives the truncated differential transition matrix for the entire 32-round Skipjack cipher. We used Mathematica to calculate the matrix product to 256 decimal digit precision for $n = 16$. As a sanity check we also verified the twenty-four round impossible differential through $[B]^4[A]^8[B]^8[A]^4$ [1], which in fact continues to give a good, improbable differential through the last round.

The matrix for the full 32-round Skipjack is too large to show here, but it appears to be quite close to the matrix obtained from a random permutation, for which any nonzero differential is sent to a random nonzero differential. To quantify the "closeness" between the two transition distributions, Fig. 10 shows the columnwise total variation distances. An optimal distinguishing algorithm given the truncated differential equivalence classes of exactly *one* pair of plaintexts and

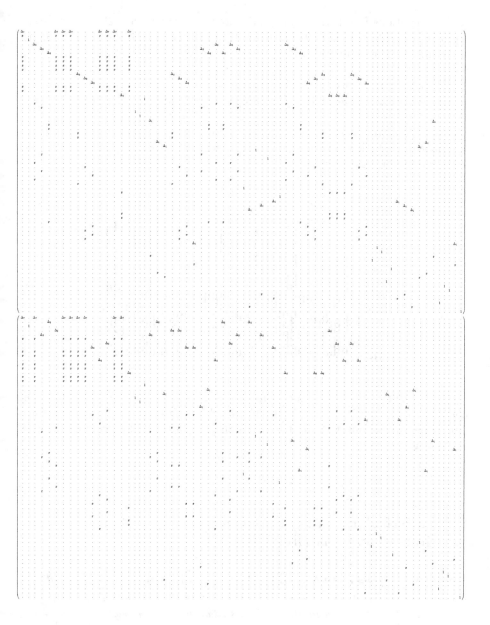

Fig. 9. The truncated differential matrices for the A (top) and the B rounds. $\Delta_j \equiv 1 - \frac{j}{2^n - 1}$ and $x \equiv \frac{1}{2^n - 1}$, while 0 entries are written "." to expose the structure

their encryptions has distinguishing advantage less than 1.5×2^{-79}, and is best for plaintext differences in $(0, b, c, 0)$ or $(0, b, b, 0)$ (the 19th and 63rd columns in the figure). Unfortunately, dependencies invalidate the transition matrices as soon as more than two encryptions are sent through the same keyed cipher. ("Impossible" differentials remain valid, however, and for small numbers of differentials the transition probabilities are probably still approximately accurate.) Our model requires the independence of each differential, equivalent to re-keying the cipher for every pair of encryptions. We turn now to some statistics in order to bound an attacker's advantage using *many* truncated differentials with this independence assumption.

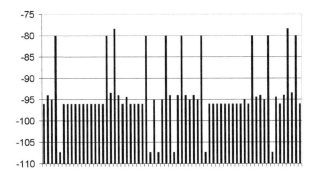

Fig. 10. The total variation norm distance, shown here on a $\log_2$ scale, between columns of the Skipjack truncated differential transition matrix and those for a truly random permutation is always less than 1.5×2^{-79}. The column order is given in Fig. 8

6   Statistical Bounds on Distinguishing Multiple Multinomial Distributions

Definition 1 (Decision Multiple Multinomial Game). *Let SJ be m' different multinomial distributions over m categories, with probabilities $p_1^{(i)}, \ldots, p_m^{(i)}$, $i = 1, \ldots, m'$. Let R be a multinomial distribution over the same m categories, with probabilities $p_1, p_2, \ldots, p_m$, $\sum_{i=1}^m p_i = 1$. With equal probabilities $\frac{1}{2}$, take N_i independent samples over the ith multinomial distribution of SJ, or take N_i samples over R, $i = 1, \ldots, m'$; $\sum_{i=1}^m N_i = N$. The results of the samples are $n_1^{(i)}, n_2^{(i)}, \ldots, n_m^{(i)}$, $\sum_{j=1}^m n_j^{(i)} = N_i$, $i = 1, \ldots, m'$, denoted individually $S^{(i)}$ or collectively S. An adversary $\mathcal{A}$ has advantage ϵ in this game if $\mathcal{A}$ chooses the correct multiple multinomial distribution when given S with probability at least $\frac{1}{2}(1 + \epsilon)$.*

We note that the problem of distinguishing Skipjack from an ideal cipher, given the truncated differential classes of many known text pairs, is exactly given by the Decision Multiple Multinomial Game. The multinomial distributions SJ for Skipjack are given by $p_j^{(i)} = M_{ji}$, where $M = ([B]^8[A]^8)^2$ and R is the multinomial distribution for an ideal cipher. We turn now to the problem of giving good bounds on the maximum advantage of any attacker at the Decision Multiple Multinomial Game. This will provide the mathematical tools needed to analyze cryptanalysis with multiple truncated differentials. Those readers uninterested in the statistical details may safely skip ahead to Theorem 5 at the end of this section.

Assume $p_1, p_2, \ldots, p_m > 0$, $p_1^{(i)}, p_2^{(i)}, \ldots, p_m^{(i)} > 0$, $i = 1, \ldots, m'$, so the ratio $\frac{\Pr[S|SJ]}{\Pr[S|R]}$ is well-defined. By Neyman's Lemma, the optimum algorithm for the decision multiple multinomial game decides SJ if this ratio is greater than one, and R if the ratio is less than one. Since

$$\Pr[SJ|S] - \frac{1}{2} = \frac{\Pr[S|SJ]\Pr[SJ]}{\Pr[S|SJ]\Pr[SJ] + \Pr[S|R]\Pr[R]} - \frac{1}{2} = \frac{1}{2}\frac{\frac{\Pr[S|SJ]}{\Pr[S|R]} - 1}{\frac{\Pr[S|SJ]}{\Pr[S|R]} + 1}, \quad (1)$$

this is equivalent to deciding based on the sign of $\Pr[SJ|S] - \frac{1}{2}$.

Lemma 2. *The advantage of an optimal algorithm for the Decision Multiple Multinomial Game is $\epsilon = 2\,\mathrm{E}_S\left|\Pr[SJ|S] - \frac{1}{2}\right|$.*

Proof. Let $Q = \{S : \Pr[SJ|S] \geq \frac{1}{2}\}$.

$$\Pr[\text{correct}] = \overbrace{\Pr[SJ]\sum_S \Pr[S|SJ]\,\chi_Q(S)}^{\text{prob. correctly guesses } SJ} + \overbrace{\Pr[R]\sum_S \Pr[S|R]\,(1 - \chi_Q(S))}^{\text{prob. correctly guesses } R}$$

$$= \sum_S \Pr[S]\left(\Pr[SJ|S]\chi_Q(S) + (1 - \Pr[SJ|S])(1 - \chi_Q(S))\right), \quad (2)$$

since $\Pr[S] - \Pr[S, SJ] = \Pr[S, R]$. Now $\Pr[SJ|S] = \frac{1}{2} + |\Pr[SJ|S] - \frac{1}{2}|$ when $\chi_Q(S) = 1$ and $1 - \Pr[SJ|S] = \frac{1}{2} + |\Pr[SJ|S] - \frac{1}{2}|$ when $\chi_Q(S) = 0$, so

$$\Pr[\text{correct}] = \sum_S \Pr[S]\left(\frac{1}{2} + \left|\Pr[SJ|S] - \frac{1}{2}\right|\right)(\chi_Q(S) + (1 - \chi_Q(S)))$$

$$= \frac{1}{2} + \mathrm{E}_S\left|\Pr[SJ|S] - \frac{1}{2}\right|. \quad (3)$$

$\square$

Lemma 3. $|\ln x| \geq 2\left|\frac{x-1}{x+1}\right|$, *with equality only at $x = 1$.*

Proof. $\lim_{x \to 1} \ln x\, \frac{x+1}{x-1} = 2$, by l'Hôpital's rule. Differentiating the ratio gives the equivalent condition that $\frac{1}{x} + \ln\left(\frac{1}{x+1} - \frac{1}{x-1}\right) > 0$. This simplifies to a sign condition on $x - 2\ln x - \frac{1}{x}$, which another differentiation directly proves. $\square$

Proposition 4. *The advantage of an optimal algorithm for the Decision Multiple Multinomial Game is bounded by*

$$\frac{1}{2} \mathrm{E}_S \left| \ln \left(\frac{\Pr[S|SJ]}{\Pr[S|R]} \right) \right|$$

$$\leq \frac{1}{4} \sqrt{\sum_{i=1}^m N_i \left(\sum_{j=1}^m {\epsilon_j^{(i)}}^2 p_j^{(i)} - \left(\sum_{j=1}^m \epsilon_j^{(i)} p_j^{(i)} \right)^2 \right) + \left(\sum_{i=1}^m N_i \sum_{j=1}^m \epsilon_j^{(i)} p_j^{(i)} \right)^2}$$

$$+ \frac{1}{4} \sqrt{\sum_{i=1}^m N_i \left(\sum_{j=1}^m {\epsilon_j^{(i)}}^2 p_j - \left(\sum_{j=1}^m \epsilon_j^{(i)} p_j \right)^2 \right) + \left(\sum_{i=1}^m N_i \sum_{j=1}^m \epsilon_j^{(i)} p_j \right)^2} , \quad (4)$$

where $\epsilon_j^{(i)} = \ln \frac{p_j^{(i)}}{p_j}$.

Proof. The bound on the advantage

$$\epsilon \leq \frac{1}{2} \mathrm{E}_S \left| \ln \left(\frac{\Pr[S|SJ]}{\Pr[S|R]} \right) \right| \quad (5)$$

follows directly from Lemmas 2 and 3. We need to compute the bound on $\mathrm{E}_S \left| \ln \left(\frac{\Pr[S|SJ]}{\Pr[S|R]} \right) \right|$.

Since

$$\Pr[S|SJ] = \prod_{i=1}^m \Pr[S^{(i)}|SJ] = \prod_{i=1}^m N_i! \prod_{j=1}^m (p_j^{(i)})^{n_j^{(i)}} / n_j^{(i)}! , \quad (6)$$

$$\Pr[S|R] = \prod_{i=1}^m \Pr[S^{(i)}|R] = \prod_{i=1}^m N_i! \prod_{j=1}^m p_j^{n_j^{(i)}} / n_j^{(i)}! , \quad (7)$$

the log of their ratio is

$$\ln \frac{\Pr[S|SJ]}{\Pr[S|R]} = \sum_{i=1}^m \sum_{j=1}^m \epsilon_j^{(i)} n_j^{(i)} . \quad (8)$$

Let $\Delta_k^{(i)} = \sum_{j=1}^k \epsilon_j^{(i)} n_j^{(i)}$ and $\Delta^{(i)} = \Delta_m^{(i)}$. Take the multinomial probabilities to be $q_j^{(i)}$, either $p_j^{(i)}$ from SJ or p_j from R. Then $\mathrm{E}\Delta^{(i)} = N_i \sum_{j=1}^m \epsilon_j^{(i)} q_j^{(i)}$. We remark that $\mathrm{Var}(n_j^{(i)}) = N_i q_j^{(i)}(1 - q_j^{(i)})$ and $\mathrm{Cov}(n_j^{(i)}, n_k^{(i)}) = -N_i q_j^{(i)} q_k^{(i)}$, $j \neq k$. For $k > 1$,

$$\mathrm{Var}\Delta_k^{(i)} = \mathrm{Var}(\epsilon_k n_k) + 2 \mathrm{Cov}(\epsilon_k n_k, \Delta_{k-1}) + \mathrm{Var}\Delta_{k-1}$$

$$= \epsilon_k^2 N_i q_k (1 - q_k) - 2 \epsilon_k N_i q_k \sum_{j=1}^{k-1} \epsilon_j q_j + \mathrm{Var}\Delta_{k-1} , \quad (9)$$

where we have begun to suppress excessive i superscripts. By induction,

$$
\frac{\mathrm{Var}\Delta^{(i)}}{N_i} = \sum_{j=1}^{m} \epsilon_j^2 q_j (1-q_j) - 2 \sum_{j<k} \epsilon_j \epsilon_k q_j q_k
$$
$$
= \sum_{j=1}^{m} \epsilon_j^2 q_j - \left(\sum_{j=1}^{m} \epsilon_j q_j \right)^2 . \tag{10}
$$

Note that $\mathrm{E}\Delta = \sum_{i=1}^{m} \mathrm{E}\Delta^{(i)}$ and $\mathrm{Var}\Delta = \sum_{i=1}^{m} \mathrm{Var}\Delta^{(i)}$ since $\mathrm{Cov}(\Delta^{(i)}, \Delta^{(i')}) = 0$ for $i \neq i'$ by independence. Now for a random variable X, $\mathrm{Var}X = \mathrm{E}X^2 - (\mathrm{E}X)^2 \geq 0$, so $\mathrm{E}X = \sqrt{\mathrm{E}X^2 - \mathrm{Var}X} \leq \sqrt{\mathrm{E}X^2}$. Hence,

$$
\mathrm{E}\left(\left| \sum_{i=1}^{m} \Delta^{(i)} \right| \right) = \mathrm{E}\left(\sqrt{\left(\sum_{i=1}^{m} \Delta^{(i)} \right)^2} \right)
$$
$$
\leq \sqrt{ \mathrm{E}\left(\left(\sum_{i=1}^{m} \Delta^{(i)} \right)^2 \right) }
$$
$$
= \sqrt{ \mathrm{Var}\left(\sum_{i=1}^{m} \Delta^{(i)} \right) + \left(\mathrm{E}\sum_{i=1}^{m} \Delta^{(i)} \right)^2 } \tag{11}
$$
$$
= \sqrt{ \sum_{i=1}^{m} N_i \left(\sum_{j=1}^{m} \epsilon_j^{(i)2} q_j^{(i)} - \left(\sum_{j=1}^{m} \epsilon_j^{(i)} q_j^{(i)} \right)^2 \right) + \left(\sum_{i=1}^{m} N_i \sum_{j=1}^{m} \epsilon_j^{(i)} q_j^{(i)} \right)^2 } .
$$

The result follows from averaging the above bound over the $q_j^{(i)}$ being $p_j^{(i)}$ from SJ or p_j from R. □

Proposition 4 gives a bound for distinguishing the multiple multinomials of a block cipher's truncated differentials from those of a random permutation's truncated differentials. From the transition matrix calculated in Sect. 5 we obtain a bound for Skipjack, with G boxes given by independent random permutations.

Theorem 5. *An adversary who sees the truncated differential classes for one pair of plaintexts and corresponding ciphertexts from each of 2^{128} independently keyed oracle ciphers, such that each input truncated differential class appears exactly the size of that class times (sizes given in Fig. 8), has advantage less than 7.63103×10^{-6} in distinguishing whether the oracle ciphers are truly random permutations or Skipjack (with G boxes independent random permutations).*

7   Truncated Differentials for Full Skipjack

7.1   Best Differentials

Table 1 shows the longest impossible differentials starting at each round from 1 to 16. The longest impossible differential goes through 24 rounds, from rounds

5 to 28, inclusive: $(0, b, 0, 0) \nrightarrow (a, 0, 0, 0)$. Biham et al. use this differential to mount an attack on 31-round Skipjack which is slightly faster than exhaustive key-search [1]. On the same differential path is one impossible differential from rounds 5 to 27, $(0, b, 0, 0) \nrightarrow (0, 0, 0, d)$, and also four from rounds 5 to 26:

$$(0, b, 0, 0) \nrightarrow (a, 0, c, 0), \qquad (0, b, 0, 0) \nrightarrow (0, 0, c, 0),$$
$$(0, b, 0, 0) \nrightarrow (a, 0, 0, 0), \qquad (0, b, 0, 0) \nrightarrow (a, 0, a, 0) \ .$$

While [1] found these latter four impossible differentials, they did not find the impossible differential from rounds 5 to 26. Additionally, the impossible differentials they list from rounds 5 to 27, $(0, b, 0, 0) \nrightarrow (a, 0, 0, 0)$ and $(0, b, 0, 0) \nrightarrow (0, b, 0, 0)$, are *incorrect*, as is another impossible differential they list from rounds 5 to 26, $(0, b, 0, 0) \nrightarrow (0, b, 0, 0)$.

Along the same differential path are several other long impossible differentials, one from rounds 6 to 28 – $(0, 0, c, 0) \nrightarrow (a, 0, 0, 0)$ – four from rounds 7 to 28, and seven from rounds 5 to 25. Other long impossible differentials include $(0, b, 0, 0) \nrightarrow (a, 0, 0, 0)$ from rounds 4 to 24, and $(0, b, 0, 0) \nrightarrow (a, 0, 0, 0)$ from rounds 9 to 29.

Table 2 shows the best differentials for distinguishing attacks based on an attacker seeing all 2^{64} possible plaintext encryptions. The distinguishing bound is from Proposition 4, using just the stated differential ($m' = 1$, $m = 2$). We assume that the G boxes are independent random permutations, and that each text pair (2^{128} total) is encrypted independently.

For example, the best differential through all of Skipjack, rounds 1 to 32, is $(a, b, 0, d) \rightarrow (a, b, c, 0)$. An attacker with access to the encryptions of all 2^{64} plaintexts has a distinguishing advantage of at most 7.62980×10^{-6} from considering just this differential. By Theorem 5, the distinguishing advantage an attacker gains from considering *all* truncated differentials is only 7.63103×10^{-6}, so most of that advantage is from just this one differential. In general, it appears that counting other differentials besides the single best one does not often significantly increase the distinguishing power.

The differential $(0, b, c, 0) \rightarrow (a, 0, 0, d)$ through rounds 2 to 31 has probability about $(1 - 2^{-32})2^{-32}$, compared to a probability of about 2^{-32} for a random permutation. The $2^{64}(2^{16} - 1)(2^{16} - 2) \approx 2^{96}$ difference pairs of this type can conceivably distinguish between Skipjack and a random permutation using this differential, since the difference in the expected number of pairs satisfying the differential for Skipjack versus for a random permutation is about 2^{32}, and the standard deviation of the number of satisfying pairs is also about $\sqrt{2^{64}} = 2^{32}$.

7.2   Existence of Weak Key Classes

As shown in Sect. 4, G boxes giving an unusually low or high θ – the number of n-bit input pairs whose exor difference is fixed by G – can lead to poor mixing of the truncated differential classes. Figure 11 shows the distribution of θ for the actual 16-bit G boxes of official Skipjack. θ is quite tightly distributed and it seems unlikely that there exist *any* weak keys or key classes for this level of

Table 1. Longest impossible differentials starting at each round from 1 to 16

Start	End	Impossible differentials
1	14	$(0,b,c,0) \nrightarrow (a,0,0,0)$, $(0,0,0,d) \nrightarrow (a,0,0,0)$, $(0,0,c,0) \nrightarrow (a,0,0,0)$, $(0,b,0,0) \nrightarrow (a,0,0,0)$, $(0,b,b,0) \nrightarrow (a,0,0,0)$
2	14	$(0,b,c,d) \nrightarrow (a,0,0,0)$, $(0,0,c,d) \nrightarrow (a,0,0,0)$, $(0,b,0,d) \nrightarrow (a,0,0,0)$, $(0,b,c,0) \nrightarrow (a,0,0,0)$, $(0,b,b,d) \nrightarrow (a,0,0,0)$, $(0,b,c,b) \nrightarrow (a,0,0,0)$, $(0,b,c,c) \nrightarrow (a,0,0,0)$, $(0,b,c,b \oplus c) \nrightarrow (a,0,0,0)$, $(0,0,0,d) \nrightarrow (a,0,0,0)$, $(0,0,c,0) \nrightarrow (a,0,0,0)$, $(0,b,0,0) \nrightarrow (a,0,0,0)$, $(a,0,0,0) \nrightarrow (a,0,0,0)$, $(0,b,b,b) \nrightarrow (a,0,0,0)$, $(0,b,b,0) \nrightarrow (a,0,0,0)$, $(0,b,0,b) \nrightarrow (a,0,0,0)$, $(0,0,c,c) \nrightarrow (a,0,0,0)$
3	21	$(0,b,0,0) \nrightarrow (a,a,0,0)$
4	24	$(0,b,0,0) \nrightarrow (a,0,0,0)$
5	28	$(0,b,0,0) \nrightarrow (a,0,0,0)$
6	28	$(0,0,c,0) \nrightarrow (a,0,0,0)$
7	28	$(0,b,0,d) \nrightarrow (a,0,0,0)$, $(0,0,0,d) \nrightarrow (a,0,0,0)$, $(0,b,0,0) \nrightarrow (a,0,0,0)$, $(0,b,0,b) \nrightarrow (a,0,0,0)$
8	28	$(a,0,c,0) \nrightarrow (a,0,0,0)$, $(0,0,c,0) \nrightarrow (a,0,0,0)$, $(0,b,0,0) \nrightarrow (a,0,0,0)$, $(a,0,0,0) \nrightarrow (a,0,0,0)$, $(a,0,a,0) \nrightarrow (a,0,0,0)$
9	29	$(0,b,0,0) \nrightarrow (a,0,0,0)$
10	29	$(0,0,c,0) \nrightarrow (a,0,0,0)$
11	29	$(a,a,0,d) \nrightarrow (a,0,0,0)$, $(0,0,0,d) \nrightarrow (a,0,0,0)$, $(a,a,0,a) \nrightarrow (a,0,0,0)$, $(a,a,0,0) \nrightarrow (a,0,0,0)$
12	30	$(a,a,0,0) \nrightarrow (a,0,0,0)$
13	30	$(0,b,0,0) \nrightarrow (a,0,0,0)$
14	30	$(0,0,c,0) \nrightarrow (a,0,0,0)$, $(a,a,0,0) \nrightarrow (a,0,0,0)$
15	30	$(a,a,0,d) \nrightarrow (a,0,0,0)$, $(0,0,0,d) \nrightarrow (a,0,0,0)$, $(0,b,0,0) \nrightarrow (a,0,0,0)$, $(a,a,0,a) \nrightarrow (a,0,0,0)$, $(a,a,0,0) \nrightarrow (a,0,0,0)$
16	30	$(a,b,0,0) \nrightarrow (a,0,0,0)$, $(0,0,c,0) \nrightarrow (a,0,0,0)$, $(0,b,0,0) \nrightarrow (a,0,0,0)$, $(a,0,0,0) \nrightarrow (a,0,0,0)$, $(a,a,0,0) \nrightarrow (a,0,0,0)$

Table 2. Best differentials starting from rounds 1–5 (rows) and ending in rounds 28–32 (columns). Beneath each differential is the full-codebook, distinguishing-advantage bound, and also one minus the ratio between the differential probability for Skipjack and that for a random permutation on $\{0,1\}^{64}$

	28	29	30	31	32
1	$(a,b,0,d) \to (a,0,0,0)$ $.56, 2^{32}$	$(a,b,0,d) \to (0,b,c,0)$ $.0020, 2^{48}$	$(a,b,0,d) \to (0,0,c,d)$ $.0020, 2^{48}$	$(a,b,0,d) \to (a,0,0,d)$ $.0020, 2^{48}$	$(a,b,0,d) \to (a,b,c,0)$ $7.63 \cdot 10^{-6}, 2^{64}$
2	$(0,b,c,0) \to (a,0,0,0)$ $16385, 2^{16}$	$(0,b,c,0) \to (0,b,c,0)$ $.56, 2^{32}$	$(0,b,c,0) \to (0,0,c,d)$ $56, 2^{32}$	$(0,b,c,0) \to (a,0,0,d)$ $.56, 2^{32}$	$(0,b,c,0) \to (a,b,c,0)$ $.0020, 2^{48}$
3	$(0,0,c,d) \to (a,0,0,0)$ $16385, 2^{16}$	$(0,0,c,d) \to (0,b,c,0)$ $.56, 2^{32}$	$(0,0,c,d) \to (0,0,c,d)$ $.56, 2^{32}$	$(0,0,c,d) \to (a,0,0,d)$ $.56, 2^{32}$	$(0,0,c,d) \to (a,b,c,0)$ $.0020, 2^{48}$
4	$(a,0,0,d) \to (a,0,0,0)$ $16385, 2^{16}$	$(a,0,0,d) \to (0,b,c,0)$ $..56, 2^{32}$	$(a,0,0,d) \to (0,0,c,d)$ $.56, 2^{32}$	$(a,0,0,d) \to (a,0,0,d)$ $.56, 2^{32}$	$(a,0,0,d) \to (a,b,c,0)$ $.0020, 2^{48}$
5	$(0,b,0,0) \nrightarrow (a,0,0,0)$ $\infty, 1$	$(0,b,0,0) \to (0,b,c,0)$ $16385, 2^{16}$	$(0,b,0,0) \to (0,0,c,d)$ $16385, 2^{16}$	$(0,b,0,0) \to (a,0,0,d)$ $16385, 2^{16}$	$(0,b,0,0) \to (a,b,c,0)$ $.56, 2^{32}$

attack. With our independence assumptions, a successful attack will not be able to assume that the G boxes are random permutations, nor that they are random permutations with a given θ distribution, but will need to look more closely at the exact distribution of G-box permutations.

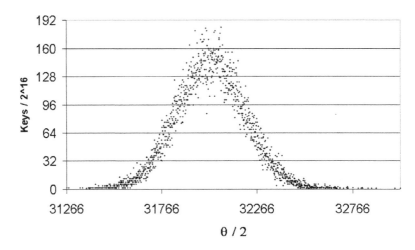

Fig. 11. The distribution of θ, the number of fixed differences, is tighter for Skipjack's true G boxes than for random permutations $\{0,1\}^{16} \to \{0,1\}^{16}$. This histogram shows for each θ value the number of keys which give that θ (always a multiple of 2^{16})

7.3   Interpretation

Our calculations were intended to give us insight into the power of truncated differential attacks on Skipjack. However, to enable explicit calculation, we were forced to abstract away a few features of Skipjack in our theoretical model. Our theoretical model is still fairly close to the real Skipjack, but the differences could potentially affect the correctness of our figures. Consequently, our results must be interpreted with care.

We will try to enumerate to all potential ways that our abstract model could fail to accurately represent the behavior of the real Skipjack, and so Theorem 5 could overestimate Skipjack's security.

1. We only consider standard truncated differential attacks. Obviously, other attacks – exact differentials, higher-order differentials, integrals, boomerang attacks, the Yoyo game, and so on – might have lower complexity.
2. We consider only the possibility of building distinguishers, and ignore methods for guessing key material at the outer rounds. In particular, our model does not account for the possibility of attacks that guess, say, the 32 key bits

determining the G permutation used in the last round. Consequently, any attack that succeeds in distinguishing Skipjack for r rounds in our model can likely be extended to a key-recovery attack on the real Skipjack for $r + r'$ rounds for some small r' (the best attack on Skipjack currently known achieves $r' = 7$ [1]).

3. Our model ignores the Skipjack key schedule. In our model we assume that round keys are independent, while in the real Skipjack round subkeys have a simple relationship to each other. For instance, G boxes separated by a multiple of five rounds are identical. This might make our truncated differential distinguishing bound too optimistic, and – since the first two round subkeys match the last two round subkeys – could also aid key-recovery attacks.

4. Our model ignores the internal structure of the G box, and simply treats it as a random permutation. There might plausibly be some way to take advantage of the internal structure of the G box to build a more efficient attack. For instance, it is known that there are four differential characteristics with probability $2^{-10.42}$ for the Skipjack G box [3], while for a random permutation the chances of encountering such characteristics is remote. As another example, one can see that the parameter θ for the real Skipjack G boxes differs what one would expect for a random permutation: the difference is small but statistically significant (see Fig. 11). It is conceivable that it might be possible to exploit these or other properties of the real G box somehow, but we do not see any obvious way to do so. More convincing is that the strongest existing attacks on Skipjack all treat the G box as though it were a random permutation, and ignore its internal structure.

5. Our model is overly generous with the text pairs given to the attacker. We are trying to model the case of an attacker who is given the entire codebook for Skipjack, i.e., the encryption of all 2^{64} possible plaintexts. Such an attacker can obtain $2^{64} \times (2^{64} - 1)/2 \approx 2^{127}$ text pairs, and this is obviously an upper bound on the number of pairs available to the attacker. If Skipjack is secure against all truncated differential attacks using 2^{127} pairs, then it will also be secure against all truncated differential attacks using less than the whole codebook.

For technical reasons, to rigorously analyze the advantage of such an attack, we needed to assume that each pair behaves independently. This assumption is embodied by modeling each pair as coming from an independently keyed instantiation of the cipher. This seems to be a clean way to model the heuristic assumptions made in previous work on truncated differential attacks on Skipjack. However, this assumption may be too generous to the attacker. The assumption implies that each of the 2^{127} pairs gives new information to the attacker. However, when we obtain 2^{127} text pairs from 2^{127} texts, the pairs definitely do not behave independently, and some are redundant. For instance, if c, c', c'' represent three ciphertexts with the differences $c \oplus c'$ and $c' \oplus c''$ both in the truncated class $(a, 0, 0, 0)$, then the difference $c \oplus c''$ is surely in the same class, and hence the third pair gives no new information.

The independence issue may well be the most troubling aspect of our model. Characterizing the appropriateness of this assumption is an interesting problem for future research.

References

1. Biham, E., Biryukov, A., Shamir, A.: Cryptanalysis of Skipjack reduced to 31 rounds using impossible differentials. Technical report CS0947, Computer Science Department, Technion – Israel Institute of Technology (1998)
2. Biham, E., Shamir, A.: Differential cryptanalysis of DES-like cryptosystems. Journal of Cryptology, **4** (1991) 3–72
3. Biham, E., Biryukov, A., Dunkelman, O., Richardson, E., Shamir, A.: Initial observations on Skipjack: Cryptanalysis of Skipjack-3XOR. Technical report CS0946, Computer Science Department, Technion – Israel Institute of Technology (1998)
4. Granboulan, L.: Flaws in differential cryptanalysis of Skipjack. Fast Software Encryption, 8th International Workshop (2001)
5. Knudsen, L.: Truncated and higher-order differentials. Fast Software Encryption, 2nd International Workshop Proceedings, Springer LNCS 1008 (1995)
6. Knudsen, L., Robshaw, M., Wagner, D.: Truncated differentials and Skipjack. Advances in Cryptology – CRYPTO'99, Springer LNCS 1666 (1999)
7. Lai, X., Massey, J., Murphy, S.: Markov ciphers and differential cryptanalysis. Advances in Cryptology – EUROCRYPT'91, Springer LNCS 547 (1991)
8. Skipjack and KEA algorithm specifications, Version 2.0, 29 May 1998. Available from the National Institute of Standards and Technology, `http://csrc.nist.gov/encryption/skipjack/skipjack.pdf`

Higher Order Differential Attack of *Camellia*(II)

Yasuo Hatano, Hiroki Sekine, and Toshinobu Kaneko

Department of Electrical Engineering,
Tokyo University of Science
2641, Yamazaki, Noda, Chiba, 278-8510, Japan
{j7302656,j7301625}@ed.noda.tus.ac.jp
kaneko@kaneko01.ee.noda.tus.ac.jp

Abstract. *Camellia* is a 128-bit block cipher, proposed by NTT and Mitsubishi in 2000. It has been shown that 10 round variant without FL function under a 256-bit secret key is attackable by Higher Order Differential Attack and even if FL function is included, 9 round variant is attackable by Square Attack. In this paper, we present a new attack of *Camellia* using 16-th order differential and show that 11 round variant without FL function is attackable. Moreover, we show that 11 round variant with FL function is attackable, if we use chosen ciphertexts for this attack.

1 Introduction

Camellia[1] is a 128-bit block cipher proposed by NTT and Mitsubishi in 2000. Designers have evaluated it's strength against various attacks and insist that it is secure against Truncated Differential and Truncated Linear Cryptanalysis, if it consists of at least 12 rounds (without FL function) or 11 rounds (with FL function). Also, Shirai et. al. have shown that it is secure against these cryptanalysis in the case of 11 round variant (without FL function) or 10 round variant (with FL function) in FSE2002[12].

On the other hand, we have already shown that 10 round variant without FL function, under a 256-bit secret key, is attackable by a new attack, which we call "Controlled Higher Order Differential Attack"[7][1]. Furthermore, Yeom et. al. have shown that 9 round variant can be attacked by Square Attack, even if FL function is included[15].

In this paper, we present an attack of *Camellia* using 16-*th* Order Differential and show that 11 round variant without FL function, under a 256-bit secret key, is attackable. Moreover, we show that 11 round *Camellia* with FL function is attackable, if we use chosen ciphertexts. Table.1(a)[15] summarizes known attacks of *Camellia* and Table.1(b) shows our results in this paper.

This paper is organized as follows. Section 2 shows the structure of *Camellia*. Section 3 describes Higher Order Differential and leads an attack equation for *Camellia* without FL function. Section 4 shows the results of computer experiments and these analyses. In section 5, we conduct a basic attack on *Camellia*

---

[1] We call that paper "Higher Order Differential Attack of *Camellia* (I)"

K. Nyberg and H. Heys (Eds.): SAC 2002, LNCS 2595, pp. 129–146, 2003.
© Springer-Verlag Berlin Heidelberg 2003

Table 1. The necessary number of chosen plaintexts and complexity for attacks

(a) Previous results

Round	FL	Method	Plaintexts	Complexity	Authors
5R	×	SA	$2^{10.3}$	2^{48}	Y.He et.al[4]
	×	SA	2^{16}	2^{16}	Y.Yeom et.al.[15]
6R	×	HODA	2^{17}	$2^{19.4}$	T.Kawabata et.al.[7]
	×	SA	$2^{11.7}$	2^{112}	Y.He et.al[4]
	×	SA	2^{56}	2^{56}	Y.Yeom et.al.[15]
7R	×	HODA	2^{19}	$2^{51.2}$	T.Kawabata et.al.[7]
	×	TDC	$2^{82.6}$	192	S.Lee et.al.[10]
	○	SA	$2^{58.5}$	$2^{80.2}$	Y.Yeom et.al.[15]
8R	×	HODA	2^{20}	2^{126}	T.Kawabata et.al.[7]
	×	TDC	$2^{83.6}$	$2^{55.6}$	S.Lee et.al.[10]
	○	SA	$2^{59.7}$	$2^{138.6}$	Y.Yeom et.al.[15]
9R	×	HODA	2^{21}	$2^{190.8}$	T.Kawabata et.al.[7]
	○	SA	$2^{50.5}$	$2^{202.2}$	Y.Yeom et.al.[15]
10R	×	HODA	2^{21}	$2^{254.7}$	T.Kawabata et.al.[7]

HODA : Higher Order Differential Attack
SA   : Square Attack
TDC : Truncated Differential Cryptanalysis
Complexities are based on the number of encryptions.

(b) Our results[‡]

Round	ET	$K1/K2/K3$	Plaintexts	Complexity	FL
6R	+1R	8/0/0	2^{17}	2^{18}	×
7R	+2R	48/40/0	2^{19}	2^{57}	×
	−1 + 1R	24/0/16	2^{34}	2^{34}	×
8R	+3R	112/104/0	2^{20}	2^{120}	×
	−1 + 2R	64/40/16	2^{36}	2^{71}	×
	−2 + 1R	80/0/72	2^{92}	2^{93}	×
9R	+4R	176/168/0	2^{21}	2^{188}	×/○
	−1 + 3R	128/104/16	2^{37}	2^{136}	×
	−2 + 2R	120/40/72	2^{92}	2^{111}	×
10R	+5R	240/232/0	2^{21}	2^{252}	×
	−1 + 4R	176/168/16	2^{37}	2^{201}	×/○
	−2 + 3R	184/104/72	2^{92}	2^{186}	×
11R	−2 + 4R	248/168/72	2^{93}	$2^{255.6}$	×/○

Computer Simulation $*: 0.2[sec]$, $**: 1.5[h]$

[‡] Complexities are based on the number of encryptions. ET column shows an "Elimination Technique", in which we call $+nR$ when we guess the last n round keys and $-nR$ when we guess the first n round keys for the attack. $K1$ denotes the total number of guessed key bits. $K2$ and $K3$ denote the number of guessing key bits, for which we perform simple brute-force search, in the last $(n-1)$ round, and the first n round, respectively.

without FL function using 16-*th* order differential, and expand the attack in section 6,7. Section 8 shows some computer experiments, which gives an attack of 11 round *Camellia* with FL function by the chosen ciphertext. Section 9 summarizes this paper.

2 *Camellia*[1]

Camellia is a 128-bit block cipher and supports 3 kinds of secret key size, 128, 192, and 256 bits. It's number of rounds are 18 (128-bit secret key) and 24 (192, 256-bit secret key), respectively. It has a Feistel structure with SPN type round function, called F function. Additionally, FL/FL^{-1} function is inserted every 6 round.

Fig.1,2 and Fig.3 shows the main structure of *Camellia* and its components. For simplicity, we call *Camellia* without FL function as *Camellia*. Note that we omit key inputs of KW_i in the following explanation, since these have no influence on our attacks.

Let P_L, P_R be the left and right half of a plaintext P, and C_L, C_R be those of the ciphertext, respectively. Let X_{Li}, X_{Ri} be the left and right half of an *i-th* round input variables, and Y_{Li}, Y_{Ri} be these outputs, respectively. Note that in r round *Camellia*,

$$X_{Li} = Y_{L(i-1)} , X_{Ri} = Y_{R(i-1)} \tag{1}$$
$$X_{L1} = P_L , X_{R1} = P_R \tag{2}$$
$$C_L = Y_{Lr} , C_R = Y_{Rr}. \tag{3}$$

Let X_i, Y_i be the input and output variable of *i-th* round F function, respectively. And K_i denotes an input key to the function.

$$Y_i = F(X_i; K_i) \tag{4}$$

$$\begin{cases} X_i = {}^t(x_{i1}, \cdots, x_{i8}) \ x_{ij} \in \mathrm{GF}(2)^8 \ (j = 1 \sim 8) \\ Y_i = {}^t(y_{i1}, \cdots, y_{i8}) \ y_{ij} \in \mathrm{GF}(2)^8 \ (j = 1 \sim 8) \\ K_i = {}^t(k_{i1}, \cdots, k_{i8}) \ k_{ij} \in \mathrm{GF}(2)^8 \ (j = 1 \sim 8) \end{cases} \tag{5}$$

Let Z_i be the intermediate variable in the function.

$$Z_i = {}^t(z_{i1}, \cdots, z_{i8}) \ z_{ij} \in \mathrm{GF}(2)^8 \ (j = 1 \sim 8) \tag{6}$$

Fig.2 illustrates these variables in *i-th* round F function. F function is composed of two function layers. One is S function, the other is P function.
[S Function]

$$Z_i = S(X_i \oplus K_i) \tag{7}$$

$$\begin{cases} z_{i1} = s_1(x_{i1} \oplus k_{i1}) \\ z_{i2} = s_2(x_{i2} \oplus k_{i2}) \\ z_{i3} = s_3(x_{i3} \oplus k_{i3}) \\ z_{i4} = s_4(x_{i4} \oplus k_{i4}) \\ z_{i5} = s_2(x_{i5} \oplus k_{i5}) \\ z_{i6} = s_3(x_{i6} \oplus k_{i6}) \\ z_{i7} = s_4(x_{i7} \oplus k_{i7}) \\ z_{i8} = s_1(x_{i8} \oplus k_{i8}) \end{cases} \tag{8}$$

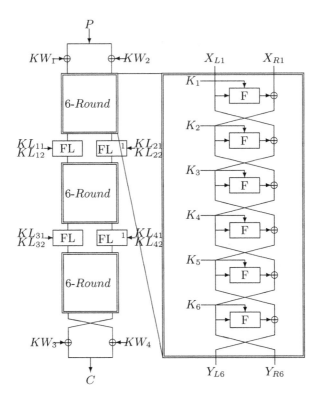

Fig. 1. *Camellia*(128-bit secret key)

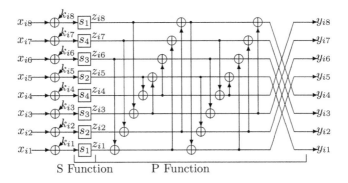

Fig. 2. F function

(a) FL   (b) FL $^{-1}$

Fig. 3. FL function

where $s_1()$, $s_2()$, $s_3()$, and $s_4()$ denote S-Boxes, which are bijective functions over GF(2^8).

[P Function]

$$Y_i = \mathbf{P}Z_i, \tag{9}$$

where $\mathbf{P}$ is a regular matrix as follows.

$$\mathbf{P} = \begin{pmatrix} 1 & 0 & 1 & 1 & 0 & 1 & 1 & 1 \\ 1 & 1 & 0 & 1 & 1 & 0 & 1 & 1 \\ 1 & 1 & 1 & 0 & 1 & 1 & 0 & 1 \\ 0 & 1 & 1 & 1 & 1 & 1 & 1 & 0 \\ 1 & 1 & 0 & 0 & 0 & 1 & 1 & 1 \\ 0 & 1 & 1 & 0 & 1 & 0 & 1 & 1 \\ 0 & 0 & 1 & 1 & 1 & 1 & 0 & 1 \\ 1 & 0 & 0 & 1 & 1 & 1 & 1 & 0 \end{pmatrix} \tag{10}$$

3 Higher Order Differential Attack

3.1 Higher Order Differential[9]

Let $E()$ be a function that transforms an input $X \in \mathrm{GF}(2)^n$ to the output $Y \in \mathrm{GF}(2)^m$ under a key $K \in \mathrm{GF}(2)^s$.

$$Y = E(X;K) \tag{11}$$

Let $\{A_1, \cdots, A_i\}$ be a set of linear independent vectors in GF($2)^n$ and $V^{(i)}$ be the vector sub-space spanned by these vectors. Then, *i-th* order differential is defined as follows.

$$\Delta_{V^{(i)}}^{(i)} E(X;K) = \bigoplus_{A \in V^{(i)}} E(X \oplus A; K), \tag{12}$$

where $\bigoplus_{A \in V^{(i)}}$ denotes the ex-OR sum over $V^{(i)}$. In the following, we denote $\Delta_{V^{(i)}}^{(i)}$ as $\Delta^{(i)}$, when it is clearly understood.

In this paper, we use the following properties of Higher Order Differential:
[Property 1]
    If the degree of $E(X; K)$ equals N, then

$$deg_X E(X; K) = \begin{cases} \Delta^{(N+1)} E(X; K) = 0 \\ \Delta^{(N)} E(X; K) = const. \end{cases}$$

[Property 2]
    Higher order differential operation has a linear property.

$$\Delta^{(i)} \{E_1(X; K_1) \oplus E_2(X; K_2)\} = \Delta^{(i)} E_1(X; K_1) \oplus \Delta^{(i)} E_2(X; K_2)$$

[Property 3]
    If a set of 2^n vectors in $GF(2)^n$, which are outputs of $E(X; K)$, has the following properties, the value of n-th order differential becomes to 0.

$$\begin{aligned} all & \quad : \text{each possible output value appears only once.} \\ balance^2 & : \text{every output value appears even times.} \\ constant & : \text{the output remains a constant value.} \end{aligned}$$

3.2   Attack Equation

Fig.4 shows the structure of 6 round Feistel type block cipher with SPN type round function. In the figure, the following equation holds.

$$\begin{aligned} P_L \oplus Y_2 \oplus Y_4 \oplus Y_6 &= C_L \\ \Longleftrightarrow P_L \oplus C_L &= \mathbf{P}Z_2 \oplus \mathbf{P}Z_4 \oplus \mathbf{P}Z_6 \\ \Longleftrightarrow \mathbf{P}^{-1}\{P_L \oplus C_L\} &= Z_2 \oplus Z_4 \oplus Z_6 \end{aligned} \qquad (13)$$

For an i-th byte, the above equation is

$$\{\mathbf{P}^{-1} P_L\}_i \oplus \{\mathbf{P}^{-1} C_L\}_i = z_{2i} \oplus z_{4i} \oplus z_{6i}, \qquad (14)$$

where $\{\bullet\}_i$ denotes the i-th byte of variable $\bullet$.

   Let $V^{(N)}$ be a vector sub-space in P_R. Consider N-th order differential of Eq.(14) with respect to $V^{(N)}$. Since P_L has $constant$ property, from Property2 and 3, it can be calculated as

$$\bigoplus_{P_R \in V^{(N)}} \{\mathbf{P}^{-1} C_L\}_i = \Delta^{(N)} z_{2i} \oplus \Delta^{(N)} z_{4i} \oplus \Delta^{(N)} z_{6i}. \qquad (15)$$

On the other hand, by guessing the key k_{6i}, N-th order differential of z_{6i} with respect to $V^{(N)}$ can be calculated as

$$\Delta^{(N)} z_{6i} = \bigoplus_{P_R \in V^{(N)}} s_j(c_{Ri} \oplus k_{6i}), \qquad (16)$$

where c_{Ri} denotes i-th byte of right half of the ciphertext C_R(see Fig.4).

---

[2] This definition is different from that in Square Attack[15].

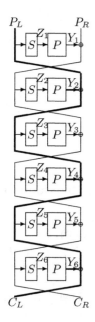

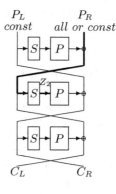

Fig. 5. Path : $P_R \to Z_2$

Fig. 4. Feistel Type Block Cipher with
SPN Type Round Function

From Eq.(15) and Eq.(16), the following equation holds.

$$\bigoplus_{P_R \in V^{(N)}} \{P^{-1}C_L\}_i = \bigoplus_{P_R \in V^{(N)}} s_j(c_{Ri} \oplus k_{6i}) \oplus \Delta^{(N)} z_{2i} \oplus \Delta^{(N)} z_{4i} \qquad (17)$$

If the following condition holds

$$\Delta^{(N)} z_{2i} \oplus \Delta^{(N)} z_{4i} = 0, \qquad (18)$$

then we have the following attack equation.

$$\bigoplus_{P_R \in V^{(N)}} \{P^{-1}C_L\}_i = \bigoplus_{P_R \in V^{(N)}} s_j(c_{Ri} \oplus k_{6i}) \qquad (19)$$

The above equation(19) always holds when the guessed key k_{6i} is true, and holds
probabilistically when it is false. Thus, we can determine the true key k_{6i} by an
adequate number of N-th order differential. Table.2 summarizes our basic attack.

In the explanation above, we guess the last one round key and check its
correctness by the attack equation(19). We call this +1R elimination technique.
In the same manner, we call +nR elimination technique if we guess the last n
round keys and −nR elimination technique if we guess the first n round keys.

Table 2. Basic 6R Attack

Chosen Plaintext	P_L has a *constant* property. A variable for which Eq.(18) holds are chosen in P_R.
Guessing Key	k_{6i}
Attack Equation	$\displaystyle\bigoplus_{P_R\ V^{(N)}} \{\mathbf{P}^{-1}C_L\}_i = \bigoplus_{P_R\ V^{(N)}} s_j(c_{Ri} \oplus k_{6i})$ (Eq.(19))

4   Effective Chosen Plaintext

4.1   Search for the Effective Chosen Plaintext by Computer Experiment

Camellia encrypts a plaintext in a byte oriented manner. So we perform the byte wise search for the variable sub-block with which Eq.(18) holds.

Let's consider 8-*th* order differential with respect to one byte of P_R. As shown in Fig.5, if we choose i_1-*th* byte of P_R as a variable, z_{2i_1} has *all* property, and z_{2i} ($i \neq i_1$) has *constant* property. Thus $\Delta^{(8)}z_{2i} = 0$. Therefore if $\Delta^{(N)}z_{4i} = 0$, then Eq.(18) holds. So we conducted a computer search for such variable sub-blocks. However, we could not find any one-byte variable to meet the condition.

If we select two bytes as variables for Higher Order Differential, we still have $\Delta^{(16)}z_{2i} = 0$. So we searched for such byte pairs by a computer experiment that make $\Delta^{(16)}z_{4i} = 0$. We show the result in Table.3. For example, the first entry in the table (1,2) means that if we choose the first and second byte pairs as variable sub-blocks for 16-*th* order differential, then $\Delta^{(16)}z_{46} = 0$. With 16-*th* order differential, the attack equation to determine a 6-*th* round key is as follows.

$$\bigoplus_{(i_1,i_2)} \{\mathbf{P}^{-1}C_L\}_i = \bigoplus_{(i_1,i_2)} s_j(c_{Ri} \oplus k_{6i}) \tag{20}$$

where $\bigoplus_{(i_1,i_2)}$ denotes the sum over the variable, i_1-*th* and i_2-*th* byte in P_R.

4.2   The Pattern Whose 16-*th* Order Differential Equal to 0

If we select pairs (i_1, i_2) as variable sub-blocks, only z_{2i_1}, z_{2i_2}, which are outputs of S-Boxes in the second round, are affected by these variables. In the third round, the input of each S-Boxes are among the following, $c, z_{2i_1}\oplus c, z_{2i_2}\oplus c, z_{2i_1}\oplus z_{2i_2}\oplus c$, where c are some constant values. These outputs in third round S-Boxes are process by P function to make fourth round inputs. These inputs are converted by the corresponding S-Boxes in the fourth round to make z_{4i}.

We analyzed these processes. We found that the condition for $\Delta^{(16)}z_{4i} = 0$ is classified into following three patterns:
[*pattern*1]

$$z_{4i} = s_{j_1}(s_{j_2}(z_{2i_1} \oplus c_1) \oplus f(z_{2i_1} \oplus z_{2i_2}) \oplus c_2)$$

Table 3. Input variables sub-block byte pairs for $\Delta^{(16)} z_{4i} = 0$

$(i_1 i_2)$	observation byte
$(1, 2)$	$z_{46}[1]$
$(1, 4)$	$z_{45}[1]$
$(1, 6)$	$z_{43}[1], z_{47}[1], z_{48}[2]$
○ $(1, 7)$	$z_{42}[1], z_{43}[3], z_{45}[1], z_{46}[1]$
$(2, 3)$	$z_{47}[1]$
$(2, 7)$	$z_{44}[1], z_{45}[2], z_{48}[1]$
● $(2, 8)$	$z_{43}[1], z_{44}[3], z_{46}[1], z_{47}[1]$
$(3, 4)$	$z_{48}[1]$
○ $(3, 5)$	$z_{41}[3], z_{44}[1], z_{47}[1], z_{48}[1]$
$(3, 8)$	$z_{41}[1], z_{45}[1], z_{46}[2]$
$(4, 5)$	$z_{42}[1], z_{46}[1], z_{47}[2]$
● $(4, 6)$	$z_{41}[1], z_{42}[2], z_{45}[1], z_{48}[1]$

[ ] denotes the *pattern*.
Two ● pairs (or two ○ pairs) gives the minimum number of
chosen plaintexts to solve all 6-*th* round keys.

[*pattern2*]

$$z_{4i} = s_{j_1}(s_{j_2}(z_{2i_1} \oplus c_1) \oplus s_{j_2}(z_{2i_1} \oplus c_2) \oplus f(z_{2i_1} \oplus z_{2i_2}) \oplus c_3)$$

[*pattern3*]

$$z_{4i} = s_{j_1}(s_{j_2}(z_{2i_1} \oplus c_1) \oplus s_{j_2}(z_{2i_2} \oplus c_2) \oplus f(z_{2i_1} \oplus z_{2i_2}) \oplus c_3)$$
$$(j_1, j_2 = 1, 2, 3, 4),$$

where c_1, c_2, c_3 are constant values, calculated from round keys and plaintext
bytes except i_1-*th* and i_2-*th* in P_R. $f()$ denotes some function having $z_{2i_1} \oplus z_{2i_2}$
as an input.

These patterns are shown in Table.3 as a number in the bracket[ ]. For example, when we select pairs $(1, 2)$ as variable sub-blocks, z_{46} is expressed as
follows.

$$z_{46} = s_3(s_1(z_{21} \oplus c_1) \oplus s_2(z_{21} \oplus z_{22} \oplus c_2) \oplus$$
$$s_2(z_{21} \oplus z_{22} \oplus c_3) \oplus s_3(z_{21} \oplus z_{22} \oplus c_4) \oplus c_5) \qquad (21)$$

Then, if we choose $f()$ as

$$f(z_{21} \oplus z_{22}) = s_2(z_{21} \oplus z_{22} \oplus c_2) \oplus s_2(z_{21} \oplus z_{22} \oplus c_3) \oplus s_3(z_{21} \oplus z_{22} \oplus c_4),$$
$$(22)$$

z_{46} is classified to *pattern1*.
The proofs for $\Delta^{(16)} z_{4i} = 0$ are described in Appendix.

5   Attack of 6 Round *Camellia* (Basic Attack)

Based on the previous discussion, we can derive an attack equation to determine the 6-*th* round key. For example, when we choose pairs $(1, 2)$ as variable sub-blocks, the attack equation is as follows.

$$\bigoplus_{(1,2)} s_3(c_{R6} \oplus k_{66}) = \bigoplus_{(1,2)} \{\mathbf{P}^{-1}C_L\}_6 \tag{23}$$

Eq.(23) is a vector equation over $\mathrm{GF}(2)^8$. It holds with probability 2^{-8} for a false key k_{66}, and always holds for the true key. Let $K1$ be the number of key bits on which we must perform a brute-force search in the attack. To remove all false keys, the necessary number M of 16-*th* order differential is the one satisfying the following.

$$(2^{-8})^M \times 2^{K1} \ll 1 \tag{24}$$

Here, we have $K1 = 8$. So we choose $M = 2$. This attack requires $2^{16} \times M = 2^{17}$ chosen plaintexts.

In the straight forward calculation, the computational complexity to determine the left side of Eq.(23) is 2^{16} S-Box operations for each supposed key k_{66}. However we can reduce its cost to 2^8 S-Box operations by an occurrence table for c_{R6}. Because an even time ex-OR sum always becomes 0.

We have M sets of 16-*th* order differentials for checking the correctness of supposed key. On the first check, we can expect 2^8 possible values of k_{66} to check. On the *i*-*th* check, there are $2^8 \times 2^{-8i}$ survived false key values, which we must check for its correctness. Thus the complexity is

$$T_s = \sum_{i=0}^{M-1} \left(2^8 \times 2^8 \times 2^{-8i}\right) < 2^8 \times 2^8 \times 2 = 2^{17} \tag{25}$$

S-Box operations.

In addition, we have to consider the complexity to prepare the occurrence table [3]. It equals the complexity of encrypting 2^{16} plaintexts in 6 round *Camellia*. So it is estimated as

$$T_b = M \times 2^{16} \times 8 \times 6 \simeq 2^{23} \tag{26}$$

S-Box operations. The complexity to complete this task is $T = \dfrac{T_s + T_b}{8 \times 6} < 2^{20}$ encryptions. We did computer experiments. It(CPU:alpha 21264A 667MHz) took about $0.1[sec]$, which is an average value for 10,000 experiments.

To determine all the 6-*th* round keys, we need 8 attack equations. It needs $8 \times T$ encryptions. If we choose pairs $(1,7)$ and $(3,5)$ as variables, which are marked $\circ$ in Table.3, we can have 4 attack equations for each pairs. So the necessary number of chosen plaintexts are $2 \times M \times 2^{16} = 2^{18}$. We can also use two $\bullet$ made pairs to make such attack equations.

---

[3] In general, it can be ignored because it is far smaller than the complexity to solve the attack equation. In this case, however, we can not ignore it.

6   Expansion of Attack (I)

We expand the attack described in the previous section. Let's consider the +2R elimination technique. In this case, we have to guess 5 byte keys in 7-*th* round and 1 byte key in 6-*th* round. So $K1 = 48$.

From Eq.(24), we choose $M = 7$ and $m = 2^{16} \times M \simeq 2^{19}$. As previously mentioned, the complexity to determine k_{6i} can be reduced if we use an occurrence table method. In this paper, for the first test, we check the all-possible value of 6-*th* round key k_{6i} using the occurrence table under one guessed keys in 7-*th* round. In the consecutive test, we check the survived keys by a brute-force search, because the expected number of survived keys k_{6i} are $|k_{6i}| = 2^{-8} \times 2^8 = 1$ and the occurrence table method does not work effectively.

The complexity to prepare all ciphertexts for this attack is $T_e = M \times 2^{16} \times 7 \times 8 < 2^{25}$ S-Box operations, because each ciphertext requires the encryption of 7 round *Camellia*. And the complexity for the brute-force search for each guessed key in 7-*th* round is $T_{b1} = 2^{16} \times 5$ and that for each guessed key in 6-*th* and 7-*th* round is $T_{b2} = 2^{16} \times 6$. Let $K2$ be the number of key bits which we have to guess the last n round except the round in which we apply the occurrence table method. In this case, $K2 = 40$. And let T_1 be the complexity for the first test, and T_2 be the complexity for consecutive test. These are calculated as follows.

$$T_1 = 2^{K2} \times (T_{b1} + 2^8 \times 2^8) = 2^{K2} \times T_{b2} \tag{27}$$

$$T_2 = \sum_{i=0}^{M-2} \left\{ 2^{K2} \times |k_{6i}| \times T_{b2} \times 2^{-8i} \right\} < 2^{K2} \times |k_{6i}| \times T_{b2} \times 2 \tag{28}$$

The complexity to complete this task is

$$T_s = T_1 + T_2 + T_e < 3 \times 2^{K2} \times T_{b2} \simeq 2^{61}. \tag{29}$$

S-Box operations. This is $T = T_s/(8 \times 7) = 2^{57}$ encryptions.

Similarly, we can conduct +3R elimination technique. In this case, $K2 = 104$, because we have to guess 64-bit round keys at 8-*th* round in addition to the guessed keys on +2R elimination technique. Therefore, we choose $M = 15$ from Eq.(24) and $m = 2^{16} \times M = 2^{20}$. It's complexity is

$$T_{b2} = 2^{16} \times 14 \tag{30}$$

$$T_s < 3 \times 2^{K2} \times T_{b2} < 2^{126} \tag{31}$$

S-Box operations, which is equal to $T = T_s/(8 \times 8) = 2^{120}$ encryptions.

The necessary number of plaintexts and complexity for +4R,+5R elimination technique can also be calculated similarly(see Table.1).

7   Expansion of Attack (II)

Our attack can also be improved by eliminating the first n round. For *Camellia*, this kind of technique was used by Yeom et. al.[15].

7.1 Attack of 7 Round *Camellia* Using −1R Elimination Technique

In this section, we present an attack of 7 round *Camellia*, which needs to guess 2 bytes of first round keys. Although we can adopt any sub-block pairs in Table.3, we choose pairs (1,2) as variables as an example.

Let's review the attack of 6 round using +1R elimination technique. In that attack, to determine the 6-*th* round key k_{66}, we use the plaintext, which has *constant* property except first and the second byte in P_R, which has *all* property. We express this condition as

$$\begin{cases} P_L = (\text{"}c\text{"}, \cdots, \text{"}c\text{"}) \\ P_R = (\text{"}v_1\text{"}, \text{"}v_2\text{"}, \text{"}c\text{"}, \cdots, \text{"}c\text{"}) \end{cases} \tag{32}$$

where $\text{"}v_1\text{"}, \text{"}v_2\text{"}$ denote a variable sub-block, and $\text{"}c\text{"}$ denote a constant sub-block.

To apply −1R elimination technique, the input of the second round X_{L2}, X_{R2} must satisfy the following condition.

$$\begin{cases} X_{L2} = (\text{"}c\text{"}, \cdots, \text{"}c\text{"}) \\ X_{R2} = (\text{"}v_1\text{"}, \text{"}v_2\text{"}, \text{"}c\text{"}, \cdots, \text{"}c\text{"}) \end{cases} \tag{33}$$

Let v_1, v_2 be the actual values of $\text{"}v_1\text{"}, \text{"}v_2\text{"}$, respectively. Note that X_{R2} is also an input for the first round F function. The output of the first round F function can be expressed as follows by using k_{11}, k_{12}, which are the first and second byte of the first round keys, and some constants $c_i (i = 0 \sim 8)$.

$$\begin{cases} y_{11} = s_1(v_1 \oplus k_{11}) \oplus c_1 \\ y_{12} = s_1(v_1 \oplus k_{11}) \oplus s_2(v_2 \oplus k_{12}) \oplus c_2 \\ y_{13} = s_1(v_1 \oplus k_{11}) \oplus s_2(v_2 \oplus k_{12}) \oplus c_3 \\ y_{14} = s_2(v_2 \oplus k_{12}) \oplus c_4 \\ y_{15} = s_1(v_1 \oplus k_{11}) \oplus s_2(v_2 \oplus k_{12}) \oplus c_5 \\ y_{16} = s_2(v_2 \oplus k_{12}) \oplus c_6 \\ y_{17} = c_7 \\ y_{18} = s_1(v_1 \oplus k_{11}) \oplus c_8 \end{cases} \tag{34}$$

In the above formula, independent variables are

$$\begin{cases} \alpha_1 = s_1(v_1 \oplus k_{11}) \\ \alpha_2 = s_2(v_2 \oplus k_{12}) \\ \alpha_3 = s_1(v_1 \oplus k_{11}) \oplus s_2(v_2 \oplus k_{12}). \end{cases} \tag{35}$$

From the guessed key k_{11}, k_{12}, the right half of the plaintext P_R can be calculated as follows.

$$P_R = (\alpha_1, \alpha_3, \alpha_3, \alpha_2, \alpha_3, \alpha_2, c_9, \alpha_1) \tag{36}$$

If the guessed keys k_{11}, k_{12} are true, the input of the second round satisfies the condition(Eq.(33)) and the attack equation is

$$\bigoplus_{v_1, v_2} s_3(c_{R6} \oplus k_{76}) = \bigoplus_{v_1, v_2} \left\{ \mathbf{P}^{-1} C_L \right\}_6, \tag{37}$$

where $\bigoplus_{v_1, v_2}$ denote the sum over variables v_1, v_2.

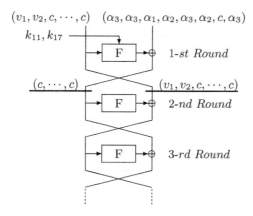

Fig. 6. −1R elimination technique

7.2 The Number of Plaintext and Complexity

Let $K3$ be the number of key bits to determine the chosen plaintext. In this attack, we have to guess keys, k_{11}, k_{12} in first round and k_{76} in the attack equation. Therefore $K1 = 24, K3 = 16$, respectively. The number of 16-*th* order differential pairs M have to satisfy $(2^{-8})^M \times 2^{K1} \ll 1$ from Eq.(24). Here, we choose $M = 4$. We need $2^{16} \times M$ chosen plaintexts for each candidate keys in the first round. So the necessary number of chosen plaintexts are $m = 2^{K3} \times 2^{16} \times M = 2^{36}$.

Since it needs 2 S-Box operations to choose the plaintext, the complexity to make the occurrence table is $T_b = 2^{16} \times (8 \times 7 + 2) < 2^{22}$ S-Box operations. At the beginning, we must determine a chosen plaintext by guessing first round keys k_{11}, k_{12}. Since we have to conduct a brute-force search for those 2 byte keys, the complexity for this attack is

$$T_s < 2^{K3} \times \left(M \times T_b + 2^8 \times 2^8 \times 2 \right) \simeq 2^{40} \tag{38}$$

S-Box operations, and $T = T_s/(8 \times 7) < 2^{34}$ encryptions. We conducted computer experiments. It took about 1.5[*h*], which is an average value of 30 trials(CPU:alpha 21264A 667MHz).

7.3 −2R Elimination Technique

It is possible to expand the above technique to −2R elimination one. In this case, we have to guess first round keys, $k_{11}, \cdots, k_{16}, k_{18}$ and first and second byte keys k_{21}, k_{22} in the second round, and control the plaintext so that the input of the second round equals to the plaintext for +1R elimination technique(Fig.6). As shown in Fig.7, let $\beta_1, \cdots, \beta_8$ be sub-blocks, which are calculated from $\alpha_1, \alpha_2, \alpha_3$, when we guess the first round keys, $k_{11}, \cdots, k_{16}, k_{18}$. The chosen plaintext can be expressed as

$$\begin{cases} P_R = (\alpha_1, \alpha_3, \alpha_3, \alpha_2, \alpha_3, \alpha_2, c_7, \alpha_1) \\ P_R = (\beta_1, \cdots, \beta_8). \end{cases} \tag{39}$$

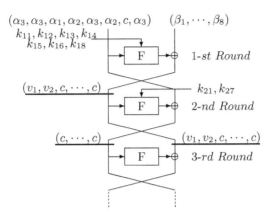

Fig. 7. $-2R$ elimination technique

In this attack, $K1 = 80, K3 = 72$, because it needs to guess 9 byte keys in the first and the second round, and 1 byte key in the 7-*th* round. Therefore $M = 11$, because it must hold $(2^{-8})^M \times 2^{80} \ll 1$. The necessary number of plaintexts are $m = 2^{72} \times 2^{16} \times M = 2^{93}$. And the complexity for this attack is

$$T_b = 2^{16} \times (8 \times 8 + 9) < 2^{23} \tag{40}$$
$$T_s < 2^{K3} \times (M \times T_b + 2^8 \times 2^8 \times 2) < 2^{99} \tag{41}$$

S-Box operations, and $T = T_s/(8 \times 8) = 2^{93}$ encryptions.

7.4 $+nR$ and $-nR$ Elimination Technique

$-nR$ technique can be used with $+nR$ elimination technique simultaneously. From Eq.(24), the number M of 16-*th* order differential to complete an attack satisfies $(2^{-8})^M \times 2^{K1}$ and it needs $m = 2^{K3} \times 2^{16} \times M$ chosen plaintexts. For each supposed key in the first n round, we must conduct $+nR$ elimination technique. Thus the complexity to complete this attack is

$$T_s < 3 \times 2^{K2+K3} \times T_{b2} \tag{42}$$

S-Box operations.

Now, we estimate the attack of 11 round *Camellia*. When $-2+4R$ elimination technique is applied, it needs to guess 9 byte keys in the first 2 rounds and 22 byte keys in the last 4 rounds. Thus $K1 = 248, K2 = 168, K3 = 72$. From Eq.(24), we choose $M = 32$ and $m = 2^{16} \times 2^{K3} \times M = 2^{93}$ chosen plaintexts. The complexity to calculate the left side of the attack equation from ciphertexts is $T_{b2} = 2^{16} \times (8 \times 2 + 5 + 1) = 2^{16} \times 22$ S-Box operations. The complexity to complete this attack is

$$T_s < 3 \times 2^{K2+K3} \times T_{b2} \simeq 2^{262.1} \tag{43}$$

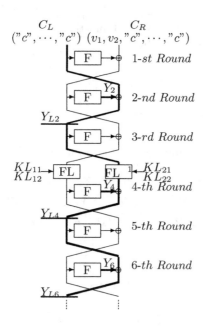

Fig. 8. 9 round *Camellia*(From a ciphertext)

S-Box operations and so $T = T_s/(8 \times 11) = 2^{255.6}$ encryptions[4]. Therefore, 11 round *Camellia* under a 256 bit secret key can be attacked with less complexity than brute-force search for a secret key.

8   Attack of *Camellia* with FL Function Using Chosen Ciphertexts

In this section, we analyze *Camellia* with FL function using chosen ciphertexts. Let $KL_{11}, KL_{12}, KL_{21}$, and KL_{22} be keys, which are inputs to FL/FL^{-1} function as shown in Fig.3 and 8. X_{Li}, X_{Ri} denote i-th round inputs, and Y_{Li}, Y_{Ri} denote these outputs.

Let's consider +4R elimination technique. Then, FL function is inserted between the third and the fourth round since it is inserted every 6 round from the plaintext.

---

[4] If we adopt precise value for T_2 in Eq.(28) as

$$T_2 = \sum_{i=0}^{M\ 2} \left\{ 2^{K2} \times |k_{6i}| \times T_{b2} \times 2^{\ 8i} \right\},$$

this complexity is slightly less than 2^{255} encryptions.

Table 4. Input variable sub-block bytes pair for $\Delta^{(16)}z_{4i} = 0$
(With FL function)

$(i_1 i_2)$	observation byte ! !	$(i_1 i_2)$	observation byte ! !
$(1,6)$	z_{48}	$(3,5)$	z_{47}
$(1,7)$	z_{45}	$(3,8)$	z_{46}
$(2,7)$	z_{45}	$(4,5)$	z_{47}
$(2,8)$	z_{46}	$(4,6)$	z_{48}

As shown in Fig.8, the following equation holds.

$$Y_{L6} = Y_6 \oplus Y_4 \oplus FL^{-1}(Y_{L2}; KL_{21}, KL_{22})$$
$$\iff Z_6 \oplus Z_4 = \mathbf{P}^{-1}\{Y_{L6} \oplus FL^{-1}(Y_{L2}; KL_{21}, KL_{22})\}$$
$$\iff z_{6i} = z_{4i} \oplus \{\mathbf{P}^{-1}Y_{L6}\}_i \oplus \{\mathbf{P}^{-1}FL^{-1}(Y_{L2}; KL_{21}, KL_{22})\}_i$$
$$(i = 1 \sim 8) \qquad (44)$$

Since $z_{6i} = s_j(x_{6i} \oplus k_{6i})$, when we choose pairs (i_1, i_2) as a variable sub-blocks and calculate 16-*th* order differential of the above equation, it gives as

$$\bigoplus_{(i_1,i_2)} s_j(x_{6i} \oplus k_{6i}) = \bigoplus_{(i_1,i_2)} \{\mathbf{P}^{-1}Y_{L6}\}_i \oplus \Delta^{(16)}z_{4i} \oplus$$
$$\Delta^{(16)}\{\mathbf{P}^{-1}\{FL^{-1}(Y_{L2}; KL_{21}, KL_{22})\}\}_i, \qquad (45)$$

where

$$Y_{L2} = Y_2 \oplus C_L = \mathbf{P}Z_2 \oplus C_L. \qquad (46)$$

Let's consider 8-*th* order differential for *i*-*th* byte in C_R. Then each byte of Z_2 has *all* or *constant* property and C_L has *constant* property. Since P and FL functions are linear functions, the third term in Eq.(45) become 0 for any 16-*th* order differential. Thus if $\Delta^{(16)}z_{4i} = 0$, we have

$$\bigoplus_{(i_1,i_2)} s_j(x_{6i} \oplus k_{6i}) = \bigoplus_{(i_1,i_2)} \{\mathbf{P}^{-1}Y_{L6}\}_i. \qquad (47)$$

This is the same attack equation as Eq.(19), which is the attack equation without FL function.

We searched for variable sub-block pairs, which satisfy $\Delta^{(16)}z_{4i} = 0$. Eight pairs satisfy such condition, which are shown in Table.4. Therefore, with Eq.(47) and +4R elimination technique, we can conduct the attack of 9 round *Camellia* with FL function when we choose one of these pairs as a variable. The complexity and the necessary number of chosen plaintexts are the same as that for without FL function because Eq.(47) is the same attack equation for the case of without FL function. Using $-1, -2R$ elimination technique, 10 round and 11 round *Camellia* with FL function is attackable with the same complexity as the attack of variant without FL function, respectively(see Table.1).

9   Conclusion

In this paper, we present a new attack of *Camellia* using 16-*th* order differential. We have shown that 11 round *Camellia* without FL function can be attacked. Moreover, we did computer experiments of attacks for 6 round and 7 round *Camellia*. They took about 0.2[*sec*] and 1.5[*h*], respectively. Using chosen ciphertexts, we have shown that 11 round *Camellia* with FL function is attackable with less complexity than a brute-force search for a 256-bit secret key.

References

1. K.Aoki, T.Ichikawa, M.Kanda, M.Matsui, S.Moriai, J.Nakajima, and T.Tokita, "The 128-Bit Block Cipher *Camellia*," IEIEC Trans. Fundamentals, Vol.E85-A, No.1, pp.11-24, Jan, 2002.
2. K.Aoki, T.Ichikawa, M.Kanda, M.Matsui, S.Moriai, J.Nakajima, and T.Tokita, "*Camellia* −A 128-Bit Block Cipher *Camellia*,"Technical Report of IEICE, ISEC2000.
3. N.Furguson, J.Kelsey, S.Luck, B.Schneier, M.Stay, D.Wagner, and D.Whiting, "Improved Cryptanalysis of Rijndael," Seventh Fast Software Encryption Workshop, 2000.
4. Y.He, and S.Quing, "Square Attack on Reduced Round *Camemllia* Cipher," ICISC 2001, LNCS 2229, Springer-Verlag, pp.213-230, 2000.
5. T.Iwata, and K.Kurosawa,"Probabilistic Higher Order Differential Attack and Secure Boolean Functions",The 2000 Symposium on Cryptography and Information Security, SCIS2000-A-46, Okinawa, Japan, Jan.26-28, 2000.
6. M.Kanda, and T.Matsumoto, "On the Security of Feistel Cipher with SPN Round Function against Differential, Linear, and Truncated Differential Cryptanalysis," IEIEC Trans. Fundamentals, Vol.E85-A, No.1, pp.25-37, Jan, 2002.
7. T.Kawabata, and T.Kaneko, "A Study on Higher Order Differential Attack of *Camellia*," Second Open, NESSIE Workshop, Londom, U.K, Sep. 2001.
8. Lar R. Knudsen "The Interpolation Attack on Block Cipher," Fast Software Encryption 4-th International Workshop, LNCS.1008, Springer-Verlag. Berlin, 1996.
9. X.Lai, "Higher Order Derivatives and Differential Cryptanalysis," Communications and Cryptography, pp.227-233, Kluwer Academic Publishers, 1994.
10. S.Lee, S.Hong, S.Lee, J.Lim, and S.Yoon, "Truncated Differential Cryptanalysis of *Camellia*," ICISC2001.
11. T.Shimoyama, S.Moriai, and T.Kaneko, "Higher Order Differential Attack of a CAST Cipher," Fast Software Encryption 4-th International Workshop, LNCS.1372, Springer-Verlag. Berlin, 1996.
12. T.Shirai, S,Kanamaru, and G.Abe, "Improved Upper Bounds of Differential and Linear Characteristic Probability for *Camellia*" Fast Software Encryption 2002, FSE2002, pp.123-137, Lenven, Belgium, Feb, 2002.
13. M.Takeda, and T.Kaneko, "A Study for Controled Higher Order Differential Cryptanalysis of *Camellia*," The 2002 Symposium on Cryptography and Information Security, SCIS2002, Shirahama, Japan, Jan.29-Feb.1, 2002. (in Japanese).
14. H.Tanaka, K.Hisamatsu, and T.Kaneko, "Strength of MISTY1 without FL function for Higher Order Differential Attack," Applied Algebra, Algebraic Algorithm and Error Correcting Codes Symposium(AAECC13), LNCS.1719 pp.221-230, 1999.

15. Y.Yeom, S.Park, and I.Kim, "On the Security of *Camellia* against the Square Attack," Fast Software Encryption 2002, FSE2002, pp.84-93, Lenven, Belgium, Feb, 2002.

A   Proof of $\Delta z_{4i}^{(16)} = 0$

The reason for $\Delta z_{4i}^{(16)} = 0$ can be shown as follows.

Proof for *pattern*1

When we choose i_1, i_2-*th* byte in the plaintext P_R as variable sub-blocks, 16-*th* order differential of z_{4i} can be expressed as follows.

$$\Delta^{(16)} z_{4i} = \bigoplus_{(i_1, i_2)} \{ s_{j_1}(s_{j_2}(z_{2i_1} \oplus c_1) \oplus f(z_{2i_1} \oplus z_{2i_2}) \oplus c_2 \}, \tag{48}$$

where

$$z_{2i_1} = s_j(p_{Ri_1} \oplus c_8), z_{2i_2} = s_j(p_{Ri_2} \oplus c_9).$$

Since S-Boxes of *Camellia* are bijective functions, the sum over i_1, i_2-*th* byte in P_R $\bigoplus_{(i_1, i_2)}$ equals to the sum over z_{2i_1}, z_{2i_2}. Futhermore, let

$$\alpha = z_{2i_1} \oplus c_1, \beta = z_{2i_1} \oplus z_{2i_2}. \tag{49}$$

We can replace the sum over z_{2i_1} and z_{2i_2} with the sum over α and β.

$$\Delta^{(16)} z_{4i} = \bigoplus_{\alpha, \beta} \{ s_{j_1}(s_{j_2}(\alpha) \oplus f(\beta) \oplus c_2 \}$$

$$= \bigoplus_{\beta} \left\{ \bigoplus_{\alpha} s_{j_1}(s_{j_2}(\alpha) \oplus f(\beta) \oplus c_2) \right\} \tag{50}$$

Let's estimate the value in parentheses{ }. For a constant β, this is the sum over α for the function $g(\alpha, \beta)$ expressed as follows.

$$g(\alpha, \beta) = s_{j_1}(s_{j_2}(\alpha) \oplus f(\beta) \oplus c_2) \tag{51}$$

From Eq.(49), α has *all* property as inputs $s_{j_2}()$. Thus the value equals to 8-*th* order differential of $g()$ with respect to α.

$$\bigoplus_{\alpha} \{ s_{j_1}(s_{j_2}(\alpha) \oplus f(\beta) \oplus c_2) \} = \Delta^{(8)} g(\alpha, \beta) \tag{52}$$

Since β, c_2 are constant values and S-Boxes of *Camellia* are bijective functions, the output from $g()$ has *all* property. From Property3, we have $\Delta^{(8)} g(\alpha, \beta) = 0$. Therefore, we have the following.

$$\Delta^{(16)} z_{4i} = \bigoplus_{\beta} \left\{ \Delta^{(8)} g(\alpha, \beta) \right\}$$

$$= 0 \tag{53}$$

$$\square$$

Due to the limited space, we omit the proof for *pattern*2 and *pattern*3. With a similar procedure, they can also be easily proven.

Square-like Attacks on Reduced Rounds of IDEA

Hüseyin Demirci

Tübitak UEKAE, 41470 Gebze, Kocaeli, Turkey,
huseyind@uekae.tubitak.gov.tr

Abstract. In this paper we develop two new chosen plaintext attacks on reduced rounds of the IDEA block cipher. The attacks exploit the word structure of the algorithm and are based on the observation that suitable chosen plaintexts give rise to some special kind of distributions which provide a way to distinguish reduced round IDEA output from a random permutation with very few plaintexts. As a result, we develop an attack for 3.5 rounds of IDEA which requires only 103 chosen plaintexts. We have reduced the number of required plaintexts significantly up to 4 rounds. We also present some interesting properties of the reduced round variants of the cipher which have not been published before. The properties and the attacks bring a different approach to analyse the cipher.

1 Introduction

The IDEA block cipher is a modified version of the algorithm PES [9], [10]. The main design concept is "mixing operations from different algebraic groups". The authors have developed the idea of Markov ciphers to evaluate the cipher against differential cryptanalysis. IDEA is an original example of a non Feistel cipher with beautiful mathematical ideas and it has been widely used in commercial environment.

Since its description the process of cryptanalysing IDEA has developed slowly. In [13] and [4], differential cryptanalysis was applied to IDEA reduced to 2 and 2.5 rounds. In [3], 3 and 3.5 round IDEA were cryptanalysed using differential-linear and truncated-differential techniques respectively. Finally in [1], Biham, Biryukov and Shamir used impossible differential technique to sieve the key space for 3.5, 4 and 4.5 rounds. These are currently the best known attacks on IDEA, and the 4.5 round attack requires the encryption of the whole plaintext space.

Recently we are aware of a paper [14] which uses the square attack technique to analyse 2.5 rounds of PES and IDEA. The authors have also developed a related key square attack on 2.5 rounds of IDEA using 2 chosen plaintexts and 2^{17} related keys which recovers 32 key bits.

In this paper we describe some distribution properties of the cipher. Some of these properties are "saturation properties "[12], [7]. Also there are properties which are similar to the ones used in square attacks [5]. We preferred the name "square-like attack" rather than square or integral attack since we exploit the word structure of the algorithm in a different sense. Mainly we are interested

K. Nyberg and H. Heys (Eds.): SAC 2002, LNCS 2595, pp. 147–159, 2003.
© Springer-Verlag Berlin Heidelberg 2003

in the distribution of some variables more than taking sum (or integral) of the variables [5], [8]. Using these distributions we are able to attack the cipher up to 4 rounds. Our main contribution is that we are able to cryptanalyse the cipher with very few chosen plaintexts. This is a result of the powerful eliminating properties of the distributions. As time complexity, our attacks are not better than the known attacks, but we consider that the distribution properties and the reduction of the number of required plaintexts are surprising. We compare our results with the existing ones in Table 1.

Author	Rounds	No of C. Plaintexts	Total Complexity
[13]	2	2^{10}	2^{42}
[13]	2.5	2^{10}	2^{106}
[4]	2.5	2^{10}	2^{32}
[14]	2.5	3.2^{16}	$3.2^{63} + 2^{48}$
[14], Related Key	2.5	2	$2^{37} + 2^{23}$
[3]	3	2^{29}	2^{44}
[3]	3.5	2^{56}	2^{67}
[1]	3.5	$2^{38.5}$	2^{53}
[1]	4	2^{37}	2^{70}
[1]	4.5	2^{64}	2^{112}
This paper Attack 1	2	23	2^{64}
This paper Attack 1	2.5	55	2^{81}
This paper Attack 1	3	71	2^{71}
This paper Attack 1	3.5	103	2^{103}
This paper Attack 2	3	2^{33}	2^{82}
This paper Attack 2	3.5	2^{34}	2^{82}
This paper Attack 2	4	2^{34}	2^{114}

Table 1. Plaintext and time complexity of the attacks on reduced rounds of IDEA

1.1   Notation

Throughout this paper we will use the following notation. The plaintext is denoted by $(P1, P2, P3, P4)$ and ciphertext is denoted by $(C1, C2, C3, C4)$ where the seperated parts show the 16 bit subblocks. The round numbers are denoted by subindices. Therefore $C_2 1$ denotes the first subblock of the ciphertext after 2 rounds. For convenience we denote the subkeys of the MA-box by $K5$ and $K6$, the inputs of the MA-box by p and q and outputs by t and u. We call p as the first input, q the second input, t the first output and u the second output of the MA-box.

Following [12] and [7] we will call a variable "saturated" if it takes every possible value once. For instance if in the plaintext set $\{(P1, P2, P3, P4)\}$ the element $P4$ takes every 16-bit value once, we say $P4$ is saturated. A variable is said to be "k-saturated" if every possible element of the variable is observed exactly k times.

For the least significant bit of a variable we use the abbreviation lsb. Finally $K_21[97...112]$ means that the subkey subblock K_21 uses the key bits from 97 to 112 of the master key, including the boundaries.

2   Some Distributions in the IDEA Block Cipher

2.1   IDEA Block Cipher

IDEA is a 8.5 round block cipher which uses 3 different group operations on 16 bit subblocks: XOR, modular addition and IDEA multiplication. This multiplication can be described as $z = x \odot y$, where if any of x or y is 0, we convert that element to 2^{16} and calculate $z = (x \times y)$ modulo $2^{16} + 1$. If z is calculated as 2^{16}, we convert z to 0. Since $2^{16} + 1$ is prime, this multiplication is invertible. In [11] Lai suggests that the cipher satisfies "confusion" by using the fact that these operations are incompatible: there are no general commutativity, associativity or distributivity properties when different operations are used respectively. IDEA multiplication provides a strong non-linear component against linear attacks.

The round function of IDEA consists of two parts: first there is a transformation part of each plaintext subblock with the subkey subblocks, i.e. T : $(P1, P2, P3, P4) \rightarrow (P1 \odot K1, P2 \boxplus K2, P3 \boxplus K3, P4 \odot K4)$. In the second part we have the MA-box. MA-box has two inputs $p = (P1 \odot K1) \oplus (P3 \boxplus K3)$ and $q = (P2 \boxplus K2) \oplus (P4 \odot K4)$. Using p, q and the subkey subblocks $K5, K6$ we produce two output subblocks t and u. The outputs are calculated as $t = ((p \odot K5) \boxplus q) \odot K6$ and $u = (p \odot K5) \boxplus t$. The outputs of the MA-box are XORed with the outputs of the transformation part, and the two middle subblocks are exchanged. After 1 round the ciphertext is of the form $(C1, C2, C3, C4)$ where $C1 = (P1 \odot K1) \oplus t$, $C2 = (P3 \boxplus K3) \oplus t$, $C3 = (P2 \boxplus K2) \oplus u$, $C4 = (P4 \odot K4) \oplus u$. The cipher is composed of 8 full rounds and 1 extra transformation round. The 128 bit master key is cyclically shifted left 25 bits a few times to fill an array. Then we get the bits for subkey subblocks from this array respectively. Since $2^2 + 1, 2^4 + 1$ and $2^8 + 1$ are also prime, it is possible to build smaller variants of IDEA with similiar properties. IDEA with block size 8, 16 and 32 bits can be built with subblock size 2, 4 and 8 respectively.

Remark From [9] we observe that if $x, y \notin \{0, 1\}$, $(x \odot y) + (x \odot (2^{16} + 1 - y)) = 2^{16} + 1$. Therefore for $x, y \notin \{0, 1\}$, $\text{lsb}(x \odot y) = \text{lsb}(x \odot (2^{16} + 1 - y)) \oplus 1$. Also for any z we have $(0 \odot z) \boxplus (1 \odot z) = 1$. As a result for any value of i, there exists a j value, which satisfies $\text{lsb}(i \odot k) = \text{lsb}(j \odot k) \oplus 1$ for all k. This observation will be important during our key elimination process.

2.2   Some Distributions

With the diffusion properties of the MA-box, a single bit change in the plaintext is able to change every bit of the ciphertext after 1 round. Therefore classical

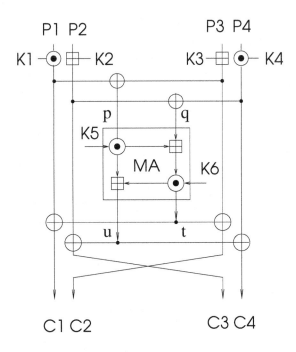

Fig. 1. One Round of IDEA

differential and linear attacks become greatly expensive after a few rounds. But
we have observed that the word (16 bit) structure of the cipher result some
distribution properties. To observe these, we begin with analysing the MA-box.

In [11], Lai claims that MA-box has complete diffusion: each output subblock
depends on every input subblock. But this dependency is exact in the following
sense:

Lemma 1. *Let p and q be the inputs of the MA-box respectively. If p is fixed and
q is saturated, then both of the outputs t and u of the MA-box are also saturated.*

Proof. If p is fixed and q changes over every value, then $p \odot K5$ is fixed and
$t = ((p \odot K5) \boxplus q) \odot K6$ changes over every element in 16 bits. Therefore
$u = t \boxplus (p \odot K5)$ changes over every element.

Now using this lemma, we have the following result on 1 round distribution
of the cipher.

Corollary 1. *Consider the set of plaintexts $(P1, P2, P3, P4)$ where we fix $P1$,
$P2, P3$ and $P4$ is saturated. Encrypt this set with 1 or 1.5 round IDEA. Then in
the ciphertexts $(C1, C2, C3, C4)$, each of the subblocks $C1, C2$ and $C3$ are also
saturated.*

Proof. After the first transformation part, $P1 \odot K1, P2 \boxplus K2, P3 \boxplus K3$ are fixed and since $\odot$ is invertible, $P4 \odot K4$ varies on every element. Therefore the first input to the MA-box is fixed, whereas the other varies on every element. By Lemma 1, the outputs of the MA-box take every value once. XOR of a fixed value with all the possible values gives the result.

This distribution can be selected as a distinguisher of 1 or 1.5 round cipher output from a random permutation. The probability of such an event in a random permutation is:

$$\left(2^{16}! / (2^{16})^{(2^{16})} \right)^3.$$

This number is approximately $2^{-281720}$. This is a strong indicator for one round. We note that such kind of distributions were used in structural cryptanalysis [2], the square attack [5], [6] applied on the ciphers Square and Rijndael by the designers, and the saturation attacks[12], [7].

The following property of the MA-box is crucial for us in the development of our attacks.

Lemma 2. $\mathrm{lsb}(t \oplus u) = \mathrm{lsb}(p \odot K5)$.

Proof. Since $u = t \boxplus (p \odot K5)$ and for the least significant bit XOR is the same as addition, we have $\mathrm{lsb}(t \oplus u) = \mathrm{lsb}(p \odot K5)$.

This property is useful for us because 1 bit of information related with MA-box outputs can be got using only one input and one subkey subblock. Therefore in our attacks we consider only the key bits of $K5$ and the ones acting on $p = C1 \oplus C2$.

As a result of Lemma 2, we observe the following fact:

Corollary 2. *Consider the set of plaintexts obtained by fixing the first 3 subblocks, and letting the last subblock take distinct values. Apply 1 round of IDEA to this set. Then in the ciphertexts $(C_1 1, C_1 2, C_1 3, C_1 4)$ the variables $C_1 1 \oplus C_1 2$ and $\mathrm{lsb}(C_1 2 \oplus C_1 3)$ are constant. Therefore as the last subblock takes every 2^{16} value, the first input to the MA-box and the last bit of the XOR of middle subblocks are constant.*

Proof. We have that $p = C_1 1 \oplus C_1 2 = (P1 \odot K_1 1) \oplus (P3 \boxplus K_1 3)$, therefore the first input of the MA-box is fixed. By Lemma 2, this gives that the last bit of XORs of the MA-box outputs is fixed. But $C_1 2 \oplus C_1 3 = (P3 \boxplus K_1 3) \oplus t \oplus (P2 \boxplus K_1 2) \oplus u$. Since for the last bit addition is the same as XOR and the last bit of $K_1 2 \oplus K_1 3$ is constant, we have that $\mathrm{lsb}(C_1 2 \oplus C_1 3)$ is the same for all ciphertexts.

We now extend this result to the second round with the use of Lemma 2. This observation is the basis of our first attack on IDEA block cipher.

Lemma 3. *Consider the set of plaintexts obtained by fixing the first 3 subblocks, and letting the last subblock take distinct values. Apply 2 rounds of IDEA to this set. Then, in the ciphertexts $(C_2 1, C_2 2, C_2 3, C_2 4)$ the variable $\mathrm{lsb}(C_2 2 \oplus C_2 3 \oplus K5 \odot (C_2 1 \oplus C_2 2))$ takes the same value for all ciphertexts.*

Proof. In the second round we have that $C_2 2 = (C_1 3 \boxplus K_1 3) \oplus t_2$ and $C_2 3 = (C_1 2 \boxplus K_1 2) \oplus u_2$. Then $\mathrm{lsb}(C_2 2 \oplus t_2 \oplus C_2 3 \oplus u_2) = \mathrm{lsb}((C_1 3 \boxplus K_1 3) \oplus (C_1 2 \boxplus K_1 2))$. By Lemma 2, $\mathrm{lsb}(t_2 \oplus u_2) = \mathrm{lsb}(K_2 5 \odot (C_2 1 \oplus C_2 2))$ and we have $\mathrm{lsb}(C_2 2 \oplus C_2 3 \oplus (K_2 5 \odot (C_2 1 \oplus C_2 2))) = \mathrm{lsb}(C_1 2 \oplus C_1 3 \oplus K_1 2 \oplus K_1 3)$. Since the first 3 subblocks are fixed, by Corollary 2 $\mathrm{lsb}(C_1 2 \oplus C_1 3)$ is constant, and we have the result.

Another consequence of Lemma 2 about the behaviour of 1 round cipher is the following corollary.

Corollary 3. *Fix the plaintext subblocks $P1, P3, P4$ and let $P2$ take different values. If we apply 1 round IDEA to these plaintexts, then the variable $\mathrm{lsb}(C_1 2 \oplus C_1 3)$ takes the same value for all plaintexts such that $\mathrm{lsb}(P2) = 0$, and takes the complement of that value for the plaintexts where $\mathrm{lsb}(P2) = 1$.*

Proof. Again by Lemma 2, $t \oplus u$ is constant. But $C_1 2 \oplus C_1 3 = (P3 \boxplus K3) \oplus t \oplus (P2 \boxplus K2) \oplus u$. Since for the last bit XOR is the same as addition, we have the result.

2.3 An Attack on IDEA

Lemma 3 leads to an attack for 2 rounds. We know that the correct value of $K_2 5$ satisfies the condition that $\mathrm{lsb}(C_2 2 \oplus C_2 3 \oplus K_2 5 \odot (C_2 1 \oplus C_2 2))$ is constant for all ciphertexts when we fix the first 3 subblocks of the plaintexts, where as the wrong key values will behave randomly. To eliminate the key candidates for $K_2 5$ continue the following steps.

1. Take a set of plaintexts by fixing the first three subblocks and changing the last subblock. Encrypt these plaintexts with 2 rounds of IDEA.
2. For any value of $K_2 5$, calculate the value of $\mathrm{lsb}(C_2 2 \oplus C_2 3 \oplus K_2 5 \odot (C_2 1 \oplus C_2 2))$ for all ciphertexts.
3. Eliminate the keys where the variable $\mathrm{lsb}(C_2 2 \oplus C_2 3 \oplus K_2 5 \odot (C_2 1 \oplus C_2 2))$ does not give the same value for all ciphertexts.
4. If more than 2 keys stay after elimination, take another plaintext where the first three subblocks are the same as previous ones, and the last subblock is different. Repeat step 3 for this ciphertext.

Repeat step 4 until only two key values stay. Recall from Remark in Section 2.1 that, for any value of $K_2 5$, there exists a K' which satisfies $\mathrm{lsb}(K_2 5 \odot x) = \mathrm{lsb}(K' \odot x) \oplus 1$ for all x. If $K_2 5 \notin \{0, 1\}$, this attack eliminates all keys except the correct subkey value $K_2 5$ and $2^{16} + 1 - K_2 5$. If $K_2 5 \in \{0, 1\}$, this attack eliminates all keys except 0 and 1. Therefore it is enough to search half of the key space, but at the end we will have 2 candidates for the subkey subblock $K_2 5$.

The probability that a wrong key has the property that $\mathrm{lsb}(C_2 2 \oplus C_2 3 \oplus K_2 5 \odot (C_2 1 \oplus C_2 2))$ is constant for m ciphertexts is $1/2^{m-1}$. Therefore with probability $(1 - 1/2^{m-1})^{N_k/2}$, all but 2 of the candidates for the key from a key space of N_k elements would be eliminated. Then 2 candidates for $K_2 5$ may be decided with only 23 chosen plaintexts with a probability about 0.99.

We may use Corollary 2 to decide the subkey values K_26, K_21, K_22 and the correct choice of K_25 from the two candidates. Since the first inputs of the MA-box for all the chosen ciphertexts should be equal in the first round, we can easily decide the values of K_26, K_21 and K_22 with the ciphertexts that we used to decide K_25. We may decide the remaining 64 bits of the key by exhaustive search. Therefore the total complexity of this attack is about 2^{64}.

Consider 2.5 rounds of IDEA. The least significant bit of XOR of the middle blocks is $\mathrm{lsb}(C_22 \oplus C_23 \oplus K_32 \oplus K_33)$, therefore for any ciphertext set, there are two possible sequences for the variable $\mathrm{lsb}(C_23 \oplus C_23)$ where one is the complement of the other. Also we may calculate the values of C_21 and C_22 by trying every possible value for K_31 and K_32. Then we may check $\mathrm{lsb}(C_22 \oplus C_23 \oplus K_25 \odot (C_21 \oplus C_22))$. We continue the steps above and eliminate the subkey values where $\mathrm{lsb}(C_22 \oplus C_23 \oplus K_25 \odot (C_21 \oplus C_22))$ is not constant for all chosen plaintexts. To decide the correct 48 bit subkey subblock, about 55 chosen plaintexts will be enough to eliminate all the keys with a probability near to 1. As above two keys will survive after the elimination process.

For the 3 round version of this attack, we have to search the subkey subblocks of the MA-box, K_35 and K_36 also. This requires 2^{64} trials for the key and needs about 71 chosen plaintexts. Total complexity of the elimination process is about 2^{71} decryptions.

Finally, for the attack on 3.5 rounds, we have to search for K_41, K_42, K_43 and K_44 additionally. As a result of the key schedule this attack requires 96 bit key search and needs about 103 chosen plaintexts. The work load of the elimination process is about 2^{103} decryptions.

This is a divide and conquer attack, after finding the key bits by the elimination process, we find the remaining key bits by exhaustive search. For the 2.5 round attack, after finding two candidates for the subkey subblocks K_25, K_31 and K_32, we decide the remaining subblocks by trying every possible combination of 80 bits. Then total complexity of the attack is about 2^{81}. For the 3 and 3.5 round attacks, the work done to decide the remaining key bits is negligible near the work done during the elimination process. The results are summarised in Table 1.

For this type of attacks, we have considered the following subkey subblocks:

$$K_21[97...112], K_22[113...128], K_25[58...73], K_26[74...89],$$

$$K_31[90...105], K_32[106...121], K_35[51...66], K_36[67...82],$$

$$K_41[83...98], K_42[99...114], K_43[115...2], K_44[3...18].$$

2.4   More Distributions

Using the word structure of the algorithm, we want to extend our observations to the third round. For this reason we need the following lemma and corollary.

Lemma 4. *Consider the two plaintext sets P and P' defined as: $P = \{(P1, P2, P3, P4)\}$ and $P' = \{(P1, P2', P3, P4)\}$ where $P1, P2, P2', P3$ are fixed, $P2 \neq$*

P2' and P4 is saturated. Let E and E' denote the sets obtained by encrypting P and P' with 1 round IDEA respectively. Then if (x, y, z, s) is an element in E, there is exactly one element in E' of the form (x, y, z', s') where $z \neq z'$, $s \neq s'$ and $z \oplus s = z' \oplus s'$.

Proof. Recall from Corollary 1 that, if we fix the first 3 subblocks of the plaintext and change the last subblock over every possible 16 bit value, then after 1 round, the variables $C_1 1, C_1 2, C_1 3, t_1, u_1$ are all saturated. On the other hand if we change $P2$ to $P2'$ and repeat this procedure again, we will obtain the same set of $(t_1, u_1)'s$. Therefore, if (x, y, z, s) is a ciphertext in E, then there will be exactly one element in E' with the first two subblocks x and y, respectively. To produce the same t_1, u_1, we should have $z \oplus s = z' \oplus s'$.

Observe that although there is a great similarity between the sets E and E', it is not possible to see this using classical differential analysis. Because where the similiar ciphertext pairs, i.e. (x, y, z, s) and (x, y, z', s') occur is not certain directly from the plaintext differences. This relation can be seen if we compare a set of ciphertexts with respect to another one.

For different values of the second subblock we obtain distinct z' and s' values. As a result we have the following:

Corollary 4. *Let $P = \{(P1, P2, P3, P4)\}$ where P1 and P3 are fixed and P2 and P4 take every possible combination. Encrypt P with 1 round IDEA and denote the resulting set by E. Then the sets $M_x = \{(x, y, z, s)\}$ where x and y are fixed and z and s are saturated, form a partition for the set E.*

Corollary follows from the Lemma 4, and Corollary 1.

The outputs of 2 round IDEA seem to be randomly distributed, but the following interesting properties are again result of the word structure of the algorithm.

Corollary 5. *Let the set P be defined as in Corollary 4 and let E_2 denote the set obtained when P is encrypted with 2 round IDEA. Let r_i denote the XOR of the i-th subblocks of the ciphertexts, r_5 denote the XOR of the first outputs, and r_6 denote the XOR of the second outputs of the MA-box of all the elements of E_2. Then we have $r_1 = r_2 = r_5$ and $r_3 = r_4 = r_6$.*

Proof. When P is encrypted with 1 round IDEA, for each value of x, there is a set M_x defined as in Corollary 4. In each of these sets, the third and fourth subblocks visit each 16 bit value once. Therefore after 1 round each subblock of the ciphertext will take every value 2^{16} times. In the second round we have $C_2 1 = (C_1 1 \odot K_2 1) \oplus t_2$, $C_2 2 = (C_1 3 \boxplus K_2 3) \oplus t_2$, $C_2 3 = (C_1 2 \boxplus K_2 2) \oplus u_2$ and $C_2 4 = (C_1 4 \odot K_2 4) \oplus u_2$. The terms in paranthesis repeat equal times so their XOR is 0 and we have the result.

This is very similiar to the result used in the square attack [5]. It is trivial that an attack can also be developed using this property, but we skip this as it neither decreases the number of plaintexts nor the total complexity. Instead, we use this property as a part of our second attack on 3 rounds.

Corollary 6. *If we fix the first and third subblocks of the plaintexts and range the second and fourth ones over all 2^{32} values, then in the second round we have that the first input of the MA-box takes is 2^{16}-saturated.*

Proof. By Lemma 4, the ciphertext set after 1 round may be decomposed into sets $M_x = (x, y, z, s)$ where x and y are fixed, and z and s change over every possible element. For a ciphertext (x, y, z, t) in M_x, the first input to the MA-box in the second round is $p = (x \odot K_21) \oplus (z \boxplus K_23)$. Since x is fixed and z changes over every element, for one set, p visits every element exactly once. For every different value of x, we have such a set, therefore we have the result.

This distribution may also be used as a distinguisher of the cipher from a random permutation. The probability of such an event in a random permutation is:

$$\frac{2^{32}!}{(2^{16}!)^{2^{16}} (2^{16})^{2^{32}}}.$$

This is approximately $\frac{2^{16}\sqrt{2\pi}}{((2^{2^{19}+2^{15}})\pi^{2^{15}})} \approx 2^{-611154}$.

Our main result which is used in the attack for 4 rounds is the following:

Theorem 1. *Let $P = \{(P1, P2, P3, P4)\}$ and $P' = \{(P1', P2, P3', P4)\}$ denote the sets of plaintexts where $P1, P3, P1', P3'$ are fixed, and $P2$ and $P4$ take every possible value. Encrypt these sets with 3 rounds of IDEA. Denote the resulting sets by E_3 and E'_3 respectively. Let n_0 denote the number of 0's of the variable $\mathrm{lsb}(C_32 \oplus C_33 \oplus K_35 \odot (C_31 \oplus C_32))$ for the set E_3. Then the number of 0's of the variable $\mathrm{lsb}(C_32 \oplus C_33 \oplus K_35 \odot (C_31 \oplus C_32))$ for E'_3 is either n_0 or $2^{32} - n_0$.*

Proof. By Lemmma 2, $\mathrm{lsb}(C_32 \oplus C_33 \oplus K_35 \odot (C_31 \oplus C_32)) = \mathrm{lsb}(C_22 \oplus C_23 \oplus K_32 \oplus K_33)$. Since $\mathrm{lsb}(K_32 \oplus K_33)$ is constant, it is enough to consider the variable $\mathrm{lsb}(C_22 \oplus C_23)$ in the second round. Now let E and E' denote the resulting ciphertext sets when P and P' are encrypted with 1 round IDEA, respectively. By Corollary 4, E and E' can be written as a union of sets $M_x = \{(x, y, z, s)\}$ and $M'_x = \{(x, y', z', s')\}$, where x, y, y' are fixed and z, z', s, s' change over every 16 bit value. Therefore if (x, y, z, s) is an element in E, then there exists an element in E' of the form (x, y', z, s'). The variable $(C_22 \oplus C_23)$ is of the form $(K_23 \boxplus z) \oplus t_2 \oplus (K_22 \boxplus y) \oplus u_2$ for (x, y, z, s) and $(K_23 \boxplus z) \oplus t'_2 \oplus (K_22 \boxplus y') \oplus u'_2$ for (x, y', z, s') for some t_2, u_2, t'_2, u'_2. But since the first input of the MA-box in the second round is $p = (x \odot K_21) \oplus (z \boxplus K_23)$ for both (x, y, z, s) and (x, y', z, s'), Lemma 2 implies $\mathrm{lsb}(t_2 \oplus u_2) = \mathrm{lsb}(t'_2 \oplus u'_2)$. Therefore it is enough to show that $\mathrm{lsb}(y \oplus y')$ is constant for every value of y and y'. But $y = (P3 \boxplus K_13) \oplus t_1$ and $y' = (P3' \boxplus K_13) \oplus t'_1$ for some t_1, t'_1. The first subblocks are equal in the first round, so we have $x = (P1 \odot K_11) \oplus t_1 = (P1' \odot K_11) \oplus t'_1$ which implies $t_1 \oplus t'_1 = (P1 \odot K_11) \oplus (P1' \odot K_11)$. Since $P3$ and $P3'$ are constant and $t_1 \oplus t'_1$ depends only on $P1$ and $P1'$, we have the result.

After observing the distributions as a result of the word structure, it is natural to ask the question what happens if we fix one subblock only, and change the remaining three subblocks over every possible element. We would like to conclude this section with the answer of this question.

Theorem 2. *Let us fix one of the subblocks $P1$ or $P3$ in the plaintexts $(P1, P2, P3, P4)$ and change the other three subblocks over all possible values. Encrypt these plaintexts with 3 round IDEA. Then in the ciphertexts (C_31, C_32, C_33, C_34), the variable $\mathrm{lsb}(C_32 \oplus C_33 \oplus K_35 \odot (C_31 \oplus C_32))$ takes the value 0 and 1, exactly equal, i.e. 2^{47} times.*

This follows from the fact that in the proof of Theorem 1, $\mathrm{lsb}(t \oplus t')$ and $\mathrm{lsb}(P3 \oplus P3')$ take the value of 0 and 1 equal times when ranging over one of $P1$ or $P3$ and keeping the other constant.

This is also a strong distinguisher from random. The probability of having equal number of 0's and 1's in a random binary sequence of 2^{48} elements is:

$$\frac{\binom{2^{48}}{2^{47}}}{2^{2^{48}}} = \frac{2^{48}!}{\left((2^{47}!)^2 2^{2^{48}}\right)}.$$

Using Stirling's Approximation, this number is approximately 2^{-24}.

Theorem 1 and Theorem 2 both consider the same variable. Theorem 2 is a much stronger distinguisher than Theorem 1, but we prefer to use the first one in an attack since it requires less number of plaintexts.

2.5   Another Attack on IDEA

Using Theorem 1, we may develop an attack on 3 rounds of the cipher. The attack proceeds as follows.

1. Take two plaintext sets of 2^{32} elements where the first and third subbloks are different fixed values and the second and fourth subblocks change over every possible element. Encrypt these sets with 3 rounds of IDEA.
2. For every possible value of the subkey K_35, count the number of 0's and 1's of the variable $\mathrm{lsb}(C_32 \oplus C_33 \oplus K_35 \odot (C_31 \oplus C_32))$ for both sets.
3. Let us denote the number of 0's and 1's of the first set by n_0 and n_1 and the second set r_0 and r_1 respectively. Eliminate the keys where the sets $\{n_0, n_1\}$ and $\{r_0, r_1\}$ do not coincide.
4. If more than 2 key values stay, then change the fixed part and take another set of 2^{32} plaintexts by ranging the second and fourth subblocks over every possible element. Continue the elimination by the same way.

Consider two random binary sequences of 2^{32} elements. The probability that the number of 0's of the first sequence is equal to either the number of 0's or the number of 1's of the second sequence is:

$$\frac{\left(4 \sum_{i=0}^{i=2^{31}-1} \binom{2^{32}}{i}^2 + \binom{2^{32}}{2^{31}}^2\right)}{2^{2^{33}}}.$$

We may approximate this probability as follows. Since we are counting the number of 0's, this is a binomial distribution. We have the parameters $N = 2^{32}$ and

$p = 1/2$. Therefore this distribution has mean $\mu = 2^{31}$ and variance $\sigma^2 = 2^{30}$. Since N is large and $p = 1/2$, we may assume that the number of 0's are normally distributed for both sets. Define a new variable as the difference of the number of 0's of two sets, i.e. $X_0 = n_0 - r_0$. Then X_0 is normally distributed with mean $\mu = 0$ and variance $\sigma^2 = 2^{31}$. Now for any value of ϵ we may calculate the probability that X_0 lies between $-\epsilon$ and ϵ.

$$P(-\epsilon \leq X_0 \leq \epsilon).$$

For instance for $\epsilon = 512$ this probability is about 2^{-25}. Since $P(n_0 = c \text{ or } n_0 = 2^{32} - c) = 2P(n_0 = c)$, our probability is 2 times this probability. Therefore only 2 plaintext sets will be enough to decide the two candidates of K_35. By Remark in Section 2.1, there is a K' value which satisfies $\text{lsb}(K35 \odot x) = \text{lsb}(K' \odot x) \oplus 1$ and as in the previous one, this attack eliminates all but 2 keys. This attack requires about 2^{33} chosen plaintexts and 2^{16} key search, and the work load in the elimination process is about 2^{49}. We may use Corollary 5 or Corollary 6 to decide the subkey blocks K_36, K_31, K_32 and the correct choice of K_35. Using these subkey values, we decrypt the ciphertexts and find the values of C_21 and C_22 to check if the conditions of the corollaries are satisfied. To decide the correct combination of K_33 and K_34 we may use Corollary 5 similarly with the values of C_23 and C_24. After finding these subkey subblocks, the remaining bits can be found by exhaustive search. Therefore the total work done in this attack is about 2^{49} decryptions for 2^{33} plaintexts, 2^{82}.

To extend the attack on 3.5 rounds, we shall search for the keys K_35, K_41 and K_42 since K_41 and K_42 are the subkey subblocks which affect the first two subblocks in the transformation part of the fourth round. Therefore we have to do 2^{48} trials for key search, and on the average $48/24 = 2$ comparisons will be enough to find 2 candidates for the correct key combination. About 3 plaintexts sets are required for the elimination process. The remaining 80 bits can be found by trying every possible combination. The total complexity of this attack is about 2^{82}.

We continue this way. For a 4 round attack we have to search for K_45 and K_46 also. This brings extra 32 bits search. Therefore totally we will search for 80 bits of the key. About 4 sets will be enough to eliminate all the keys in this case. The remaining subkey values are found by an exhaustive search.

For a 4.5 round attack, we have to search K_51, K_52, K_53 and K_54 additionally. But as a result of the key schedule, some of the bits we are searching are common and indeed we have to search for 114 bits. Again about 4 sets will be enough to find out the correct 114 bit combination. It is trivial that the attack for 4.5 rounds is slower than exhaustive search, but it is interesting to see that the number of required plaintexts do not change significantly as the number of rounds increase. This is a result of the strong distinguishing properties of the distributions.

The subkey subblocks we have used for this version of the attack are the following:

$$K_31[90...105], K_32[106...121], K_33[122...9], K_34[10...25], K_35[51...66],$$

$$K_36[67...82], K_41[83...98], K_42[99...114], K_45[19...34], K_46[35...50],$$

$$K_51[76...91], K_52[92...107], K_53[108...123], K_54[124...11].$$

3   Conclusion

We have observed some interesting distribution properties of the IDEA block cipher reduced to 1, 2 and 3 rounds as a result of the word structure of the algorithm. With the use of these properties, we have developed two chosen plaintext attacks. Up to 4 rounds, we are able to decrease the number of required plaintexts for an attack, but our total time complexities are not smaller than the known attacks. We consider that the distribution properties bring a different view to analyse the cipher, and they can be useful in the future attacks with more rounds. As an open question we remark that, if any distinguishing property related with the distribution of the last bits of the middle blocks of ciphertexts in the third round is found, this will immediately give rise to attacks for 4.5 or more rounds using the ideas in this paper.

4   Acknowledgements

We are very thankful to Ali Aydın Selçuk for his valuable comments and suggestions. We would also like to thank to Erkan Türe and Ali Doğanaksoy for their help on calculating and approximating the probabilities. We also thank to reviewers of SAC 2002 for pointing out integral cryptanalysis and saturation attacks.

References

1. E. Biham, A. Biryukov, A. Shamir, *Miss in the Middle Attacks on IDEA and Khufu*, LNCS 1636, Proceedings of Fast Software Encryption - 6th International Workshop, FSE' 99, pp. 124-138, Springer-Verlag, 1999.
2. A. Biryukov, A. Shamir, *Structural Cryptanalysis of SASAS,* LNCS 2045, Advances in Cryptology - Proceedings of EUROCRYPT'2001, pp. 394-405, Springer-Verlag, 2001.
3. J. Borst, L. R. Knudsen, V. Rijmen, *Two Attacks on Reduced IDEA (extended abstract)*, LNCS 1223, Advances in Cryptology - Proceedings of EUROCRYPT'97, pp. 1-13, Springer-Verlag, 1997.
4. J. Daemen, R. Govaerts, J. Vandewalle, *Cryptanalysis of 2.5 round of IDEA (extended abstract),* Technical Report ESAC-COSIC Technical Report 93/1, Department Of Electrical Engineering, Katholieke Universiteit Leuven, March 1993.

5. J. Daemen, L. Knudsen and V. Rijmen, *The Block Cipher SQUARE,* LNCS 1267, FSE'97, pp. 149-165, Springer-Verlag, 1997.

6. FIPS PUB 197, NIST.

7. K. Hwang, W. Lee, S. Lee, S. Lee, J. Lim, *Saturation Attacks on Reduced Round Skipjack,* FSE'2002, Pre-Proceedings.

8. L. Knudsen, D. Wagner, *Integral Cryptanalysis,* FSE'2002, Pre-Proceedings.

9. X. Lai, J. L. Massey, *A Proposal for a New Block Encryption Standard,* LNCS 473, Advances in Cryptology - Proceedings of EUROCRYPT'90, pp. 389-404, Springer-Verlag, 1991.

10. X. Lai, J. L. Massey and S. Murphy, *Markov Ciphers and Differential Cryptanalysis,* LNCS 547, Advances in Cryptology - Proceedings of EUROCRYPT'91, pp. 17-38,Springer-Verlag, 1991.

11. X. Lai, *On the Design and Security of the Block Ciphers,* ETH Series in Information Processing, Volume 1, Hartung-Gorre Verlag Konstanz, 1995.

12. S. Lucks, *The Saturation Attack - a Bait for Twofish,* LNCS 1039, FSE'2001, pp. 189-203, Springer-Verlag, 2001.

13. W. Meier, *On the Security of the IDEA Block Cipher,* LNCS 765, Advances in Cryptology - Proceedings of EUROCRYPT'93, pp. 371-385, Springer-Verlag, 1994.

14. J. Nakahara Jr., P.S.L.M. Barreto, B. Preneel, J. Vandewalle, H.Y. Kim, *SQUARE Attacks Against Reduced-Round PES and IDEA Block Ciphers,* IACR Cryptology ePrint Archive, Report 2001/068, 2001.

Full-Round Differential Attack on the Original Version of the Hash Function Proposed at PKC'98

Donghoon Chang[1*], Jaechul Sung[2], Soohak Sung[3], Sangjin Lee[1], and Jongin Lim[1]

[1] Center for Information Security Technologies(CIST),
Korea University, Anam Dong, Sungbuk Gu, Seoul, Korea
{pointchang, sangjin, jilim}@cist.korea.ac.kr
[2] Korea Information Security Agency(KISA),
Karag-dong, Songpa-gu, Seoul, Korea
sjames@kisa.or.kr
[3] Paichai University, Daejeon, Korea,
sungsh@mail.paichai.ac.kr

Abstract. Shin et al.[4] proposed a new hash function with 160-bit output length at PKC'98. Recently, at FSE 2002, Han et al.[5] cryptanalyzed the hash function proposed at PKC'98 and suggested a method finding a collision pair with probability 2^{-30}, supposing that boolean functions satisfy the SAC(Strict Avalanche Criterion). This paper improves their attack and shows that we can find a collision pair from the original version of the hash function with probability $2^{-37.13}$ through the improved method. Furthermore we point out a weakness of the function comes from shift values dependent on message.

1 Introduction

MD4, MD5, RIPEMD-160, HAVAL, SHA-1 are well known dedicated hash functions. Dobbertin[2][3] showed that there are serious weakness in MD4 and MD5. Haval[11] was attacked partially. Shin et al.[4] proposed a new hash function with 160-bit output length at PKC'98.

Recently, at FSE 2002, Han et al.[5] pointed out that, unlike the designer's attention, some of the boolean functions of the hash function proposed at PKC'98 do not satisfy the SAC(Strict Avalanche Criterion). And they analyzed the hash function proposed at PKC'98 and found a collision pair with probability 2^{-30}, supposing that the boolean functions satisfy the SAC. However only one of boolean functions used in the hash function satisfies the SAC. So, their attack introduced at FSE 2002 can not be applied to the hash function itself.

This paper improves the method proposed at FSE 2002 and shows that we can find a collision pair "from the original version" of the hash function with

---

* This work was supported by both Ministry of Information and Communication and Korea Information Security Agency, Korea, under project 2002-130

K. Nyberg and H. Heys (Eds.): SAC 2002, LNCS 2595, pp. 160–174, 2003.

probability $2^{-37.13}$ through the improved method. And we point out the problem of the hash function comes from shift values dependent on message. Next, we show that reduced versions for 3-pass HAVAL are attacked by our attack method.

2   The Hash Function Proposed at PKC'98

In this section, we briefly describe the hash function proposed at PKC'98, and we introduce notations used in this paper.

word	32-bit string
block	512-bit string used as input of compression function in the hash function
$+$	addition modulo 2^{32} operation between two words
$X^{<<s}$	left rotation X by s bits
$X \wedge Y$	bitwise logical AND operation of X and Y
$X \vee Y$	bitwise OR operation of X and Y
$X \oplus Y$	bitwise XOR operation of X and Y

2.1   Input Block Length and Padding

An input message is processed by 512-bit block. The proposed hash function pads a message by appending a single bit 1 next to the least significant bit of the message, followed by zero or more bit 0s until the length of the message is 448 modulo 512, and then appends to the message the 64-bit original message length modulo 2^{64}.

2.2   Initial Value(IV)

The initial values of five chaining variables (A,B,C,D,E) used in processing message are as follows.

A	B	C	D	E
0x67452301	0xefcdab89	0x98badcef	0x10325476	0xc3d2e1f0

2.3   Constants

The following numbers are used as constants(K_i is used in round i).

$$K_1 = 0 \quad K_2 = 0\text{x}5a827999 \quad K_3 = 0\text{x}6ed9eba1 \quad K_4 = 0\text{x}8f1bbcdc$$

2.4   Expansion of Message Variables

Eight message variables, $X_{16}, X_{17}, \cdots, X_{23}$ are additionally generated from original sixteen input message words, $X_0, X_1, \cdots, X_{15}$ as follows. So twenty-four message words are applied to the compression function.

$$X_{16+i} = (X_{0+i} \oplus X_{2+i} \oplus X_{7+i} \oplus X_{12+i})^{<<1} \quad (i = 0, 1, \cdots, 7) \qquad (1)$$

2.5 Ordering of Message Words

This hash function consists of four rounds. Each round has 24 steps.

Table 1. The definition of permutation ρ

i	0	1	2	3	4	5	6	7	8	9	10	11	12	13	14	15	16	17	18	19	20	21	22	23
$\rho(i)$	4	21	17	1	23	18	12	10	5	16	8	0	20	3	22	6	11	19	15	2	7	14	9	13

The ordering of message words is determined by ρ as follows.

Round	1	2	3	4
Permutation	id	ρ	ρ^2	ρ^3

2.6 Boolean Functions

The boolean functions used at each round are as follows. Only the function f_2 satisfies the SAC, while it is not the case for f_0 and f_1.

$$f_0(x_1, x_2, x_3, x_4, x_5) = (x_1 \wedge x_2) \oplus (x_3 \wedge x_4) \oplus (x_2 \wedge x_3 \wedge x_4) \oplus x_5 \qquad (2)$$
$$f_1(x_1, x_2, x_3, x_4, x_5) = x_2 \oplus ((x_4 \wedge x_5) \vee (x_1 \wedge x_3)) \qquad (3)$$
$$f_2(x_1, x_2, x_3, x_4, x_5) = x_1 \oplus (x_2 \wedge (x_1 \oplus x_4)) \oplus (((x_1 \wedge x_4) \oplus x_3) \wedge x_5) \qquad (4)$$

2.7 Operation in One Step

The operation in one step is defined as follows. The function f_0 is applied to the first round(0~23 step), the function f_1 is applied to the second round(24~47 step), the function f_2 is applied to the third round(48~71 step) and the function f_1 is applied to the fourth round(72~95 step).

$$A_i = (f(A_i, B_i, C_i, D_i, E_i) + X + K)^{<<S_i}, \quad B_i = B_i^{<<10} \qquad (5)$$
$$A_{i+1} = E_i, B_{i+1} = A_i, C_{i+1} = B_i, D_{i+1} = C_i, E_{i+1} = D_i \qquad (6)$$

The operation in one step can be described in the figure 1.

2.8 Shift Operation

The shift values used in each step, $S_i(i = 0, 1, 2, \cdots, 95)$, are determined depending on message words as follows.

$$S_i = X_{R(i \bmod 24)} \bmod 32 \qquad (7)$$

Next table shows R function per round.

Round	1	2	3	4
R function	ρ^3	ρ^2	ρ	id

For example, let's solve S_{20}, shift value at step 20. The step 20 is in the first round, so R function is ρ^3. Therefore $S_{20} = X_{\rho^3(20)} \bmod 32 = X_8 \bmod 32$.

Fig. 1. The operation in one step

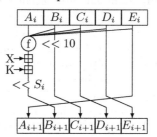

2.9   Each Step Operation through the Table

The following table shows each step operation from step 0 to step 6. A_i,B_i,C_i,D_i,E_i mean chaining variables after a equation (5) and before a equation (6) at i step.

Table 2. The message input order, shift value and chaining values per step

step	A	B	C	D	E	Input	Shift value(mod 32)
0	A_0	B_0	C_0	D_0	E_0	X_0	X_{13}
1	A_1	B_1	C_1	D_1	E_1	X_1	X_{22}
2	A_2	B_2	C_2	D_2	E_2	X_2	X_2
3	A_3	B_3	C_3	D_3	E_3	X_3	X_{14}
4	A_4	B_4	C_4	D_4	E_4	X_4	X_3
5	A_5	B_5	C_5	D_5	E_5	X_5	X_6
6	A_6	B_6	C_6	D_6	E_6	X_6	X_7

□ : The updated part per step

3   The Analysis of the Original Version of the Hash Function Proposed at PKC'98

3.1   The Analysis of Input and Output Difference for Boolean Functions

Boolean function f_2 satisfies the SAC. This means that when it has a difference at only one bit, output bit becomes zero with $1/2$ probability. At FSE 2002, under supposing that three boolean functions satisfy the SAC, Han et al. proposed a method finding a collision pair with probability 2^{-30}. But in fact, boolean functions f_0 and f_1 do not satisfy the SAC. In case of f_0, when only last input bit has a difference, output difference becomes always 1(table 3-5). Also, in case of f_1, when only second input bit has a difference, output difference becomes always 1(table 3-13). These mean the followings: if a message word having a difference is an input of a round using the function f_0, the difference avalanche occurs after four steps because fifth chaining variable have a difference. If message word having a difference is input of a round using the function f_1, the difference avalanche occurs after one step because second chaining variable have a difference. And the effect of difference avalanche is larger according as the number of steps increases. Therefore the method proposed by Han et al. at FSE 2002 cannot be applied to the original version of the hash function. But, in case of f_0, if we give simultaneously differences to fifth chaining variable and other chaining variable, the output bit becomes zero with some probability(table 3-8,9,11). This is similar to f_1. We will use this fact to attack the original version of the hash function proposed at PKC'98.

Table 3. The probability that output difference bit becomes 0 with the change of location of input difference bit of boolean function f_i

No.	Func.	Input	Prob.	No.	Func.	Input	Prob.
1	f_0	x_1	1/2	17	f_1	x_2, x_3	3/8
2	f_0	x_2	1/2	18	f_1	x_2, x_5	3/8
3	f_0	x_3	3/4	19	f_1	x_1, x_4	3/8
4	f_0	x_4	3/4	20	f_1	x_1, x_2	3/8
5	f_0	x_5	0	21	f_1	x_1, x_3	5/8
6	f_0	x_1, x_2	1/2	22	f_1	x_2, x_4	3/8
7	f_0	x_1, x_4	1/4	23	f_1	x_3, x_5	3/8
8	f_0	x_3, x_5	1/4	24	f_1	x_4, x_5	5/8
9	f_0	x_1, x_5	1/2	25	f_1	x_3, x_4	3/8
10	f_0	x_3, x_4	3/4	26	f_1	x_1, x_5	3/8
11	f_0	x_4, x_5	1/4	27	f_1	x_2, x_3, x_4	5/8
12	f_1	x_1	5/8	28	f_2	x_1	1/2
13	f_1	x_2	0	29	f_2	x_2	1/2
14	f_1	x_3	5/8	30	f_2	x_3	1/2
15	f_1	x_4	5/8	31	f_2	x_4	1/2
16	f_1	x_5	5/8	32	f_2	x_5	1/2

3.2   The Analysis of Input and Output Difference for Step Operation

At each step, such as equation (5), message word(X) having a difference has influence on a updating chaining variable(A_i). Therefore, we need to take the following facts into consideration for difference analysis. The step operation uses addition modulo 2^{32}. If addition modulo 2^{32} is substituted by $\oplus$, we must consider a probability according to a carry. If $k=31$, with respect to most significant bit, addition modulo 2^{32} and $\oplus$ play the same role. If $k \neq 31$, a carry happens with probability $1/2$. So, the analysis of input and output difference of step operation is done by equations (8), (9), (10), (11). α and β denote arbitrary words, and p denotes the probability satisfying a equation.

case 1 : $k = 31$

$$((\alpha \oplus 1^{<<k}) + \beta) \oplus (\alpha + \beta) = 1^{<<k} \qquad (p = 1) \qquad (8)$$
$$((\alpha \oplus 1^{<<k}) + (\beta \oplus 1^{<<k})) \oplus (\alpha + \beta) = 0 \qquad (p = 1) \qquad (9)$$

case 2 : $k \neq 31$

$$((\alpha \oplus 1^{<<k}) + \beta) \oplus (\alpha + \beta) = 1^{<<k} \qquad (p = 1/2) \qquad (10)$$
$$((\alpha \oplus 1^{<<k}) + (\beta \oplus 1^{<<k})) \oplus (\alpha + \beta) = 0 \qquad (p = 1/2) \qquad (11)$$

3.3 The Analysis of Expansion of Message Words

By (1), (12)$\sim$(19) are obtained as follows.

$$X_{16} = (X_0 \oplus X_2 \oplus X_7 \oplus X_{12})^{<<1} \qquad (12)$$
$$X_{17} = (X_1 \oplus X_3 \oplus X_8 \oplus X_{13})^{<<1} \qquad (13)$$
$$X_{18} = (X_2 \oplus X_4 \oplus X_9 \oplus X_{14})^{<<1} \qquad (14)$$
$$X_{19} = (X_3 \oplus X_5 \oplus X_{10} \oplus X_{15})^{<<1} \qquad (15)$$
$$X_{20} = (X_4 \oplus X_6 \oplus X_{11} \oplus X_{16})^{<<1} \qquad (16)$$
$$X_{21} = (X_5 \oplus X_7 \oplus X_{12} \oplus X_{17})^{<<1} \qquad (17)$$
$$X_{22} = (X_6 \oplus X_8 \oplus X_{13} \oplus X_{18})^{<<1} \qquad (18)$$
$$X_{23} = (X_7 \oplus X_9 \oplus X_{14} \oplus X_{19})^{<<1} \qquad (19)$$

Through the expansion of message words, message words which are affected by each $X_i (0 \leqslant i \leqslant 15)$ are shown on Table 4 below. This fact was shown by Han et al. at FSE 2002. When we take a look at the table 4, if we give a difference to X_0, X_{16} and X_{20} also have some differences.

Table 4. The effect of expansion of message words

X_0	X_1	X_2	X_3	X_4	X_5	X_6	X_7	X_8	X_9	X_{10}	X_{11}	X_{12}	X_{13}	X_{14}	X_{15}
X_{16}	X_{17}	X_{16}	X_{17}	X_{18}	X_{19}	X_{20}	X_{16}	X_{17}	X_{18}	X_{19}	X_{20}	X_{16}	X_{17}	X_{18}	X_{19}
X_{20}	X_{21}	X_{18}	X_{19}	X_{20}	X_{21}	X_{22}	X_{20}	X_{21}	X_{22}	X_{23}		X_{20}	X_{21}	X_{22}	X_{23}
		X_{20}	X_{21}	X_{22}	X_{23}		X_{21}	X_{22}	X_{23}			X_{21}	X_{22}	X_{23}	
		X_{22}	X_{23}				X_{23}								

3.4 The Analysis of Weakness of Shift Value Dependent on Message Words

Generally, in case of MDx-hash functions, shift values are fixed. If shift values can be selected arbitrarily by attacker, a hash function using these shift values can be attacked easily by our attack method (described in Appendix A), regardless of the expansion of message words and ordering of message words and boolean functions and step operation. The original version of the hash function proposed at PKC'98 uses shift values dependent on message words. This principle of the design makes an attacker select shift values. So, in section 5, based on this fact, we will attack the original version of the hash function proposed at PKC'98.

4   The Selection of Message Blocks and Shift Values for Maximizing an Attack Probability

4.1   The Selection of Message Block Pair

When we take a look at the table 4, for the expansion of message words, it is impossible to give a difference to only one message word pair. But we can give differences to two message word pairs. Four cases exist.

$(X_8, X_{13}), (X_9, X_{14}), (X_{10}, X_{15}), (X_{11}, X_{20})$. Out of four cases, we select (X_{11}, X_{20}) for maximizing the probability of attack, because (X_{11}, X_{20}) makes the smallest sum of four cases–the sums of the differences of steps of inputting $(X_8, X_{13}), (X_9, X_{14}), (X_{10}, X_{15}), (X_{11}, X_{20})$ per round. The table of four cases is as follows.

Table 5. The differences of steps of inputting each word pair per round

Round	(X_8, X_{13})	(X_9, X_{14})	(X_{10}, X_{15})	(X_{11}, X_{20})
1 Round	5	5	5	9
2 Round	13	1	11	4
3 Round	3	13	13	3
4 Round	20	18	4	7
Sum	41	37	33	23

4.2   The Selection of Differences of Message Block Pair and Shift Values

The first standard giving differences to block pair is to give a difference to most significant bit for changing a modular addition with XOR operation. The second is to apply the same shift values to message block pair.

We select message block pair and shift values as follows.

$$\cdot \; X = (X_i)_{0 \le i \le 15} \; , \; \widetilde{X} = (\widetilde{X_i})_{0 \le i \le 15} : \text{message block pair}$$
$$\cdot \; X_{11} \oplus \widetilde{X_{11}} = 1^{<<30} (\widetilde{X_{20}} \oplus 1^{<<31} = X_{20})$$
$$\cdot \; \widetilde{X_i} = X_i (i \ne 11, 20)$$
$$\cdot \; \text{Value of 5 low-order bits of message words}$$
$$lsb_5(X_1, X_4, X_7, X_{12}, X_{15}, X_{16}, X_{17}, X_{20}, X_{23}) = (10, 0, 21, 21, 11, 0, 10, 0, 13)$$

4.3   Input Order of Message Words and Shift Values per Round through the Table

Table 6 shows input order of message words and shift values per step.(M: order of message words, · : non-fixed value)

Table 6. The message input order and shift values per step

step	M	shift	step	M	shift	step	M	shift	step	M	shift
0	0	.	24	4	13	48	23	0	72	13	.
1	1	.	25	21	.	49	14	.	73	22	10
2	2	.	26	17	.	50	19	10	74	2	.
3	3	.	27	1	.	51	21	10	75	14	.
4	4	.	28	23	.	52	13	13	76	3	0
5	5	.	29	18	11	53	15	.	77	6	.
6	6	21	30	12	0	54	20	21	78	7	.
7	7	.	31	10	.	55	8	.	79	5	21
8	8	11	32	5	.	56	18	.	80	15	.
9	9	.	33	16	.	57	11	0	81	0	.
10	10	.	34	8	.	58	5	.	82	18	.
11	11	13	35	0	0	59	4	.	83	23	.
12	12	.	36	20	21	60	7	0	84	10	21
13	13	.	37	3	10	61	1	.	85	21	.
14	14	0	38	22	.	62	9	.	86	16	.
15	15	0	39	6	21	63	12	.	87	20	11
16	16	0	40	11	.	64	0	.	88	4	0
17	17	10	41	19	.	65	2	.	89	17	10
18	18	21	42	15	.	66	6	11	90	12	.
19	19	.	43	2	10	67	17	.	91	19	.
20	20	.	44	7	.	68	10	21	92	8	0
21	21	.	45	14	.	69	22	.	93	9	.
22	22	.	46	9	0	70	16	.	94	11	.
23	23	10	47	13	.	71	3	.	95	1	13

5   Full-Round Differential Attack

From now on, we start to attack the original version of the hash function proposed at PKC'98 based on sections 3 and 4. Table 7 shows the full-round differential attack. Concretely we analyze steps generating differences. See Appendix A. $\triangle A_i$, $\triangle B_i$, $\triangle C_i$, $\triangle D_i$, $\triangle E_i$ mean the differences of chaining variables after a equation (5) and before a equation (6) at i step.

The total probability is about $2^{-37.13}$. Therefore we can find a collision pair of the original version of the hash function proposed at PKC'98 with probability $2^{-37.13}$.

6   Finding a Collision Pair in Practice by Simulation

For finding a collision pair, we executed a program written in visual C 6.0 and running on a set of 10 PCs under Windows. From this, we found a collision pair in one computer with about 10 hours. The collision pair is as follows.

Table 7. The Full-Round Differential Attack

Step	A	B	C	D	E	X	p	Step	A	B	C	D	E	X	p
0	0	0	0	0	0	0	1	48	0	0	0	0	0	0	1
1	0	0	0	0	0	0	1	49	0	0	0	0	0	0	1
2	0	0	0	0	0	0	1	50	0	0	0	0	0	0	1
3	0	0	0	0	0	0	1	51	0	0	0	0	0	0	1
4	0	0	0	0	0	0	1	52	0	0	0	0	0	0	1
5	0	0	0	0	0	0	1	53	0	0	0	0	0	0	1
6	0	0	0	0	0	0	1	54	0	$1^{<20}$	0	0	0	$1^{<31}$	1
7	0	0	0	0	0	0	1	55	0	$1^{<30}$	0	0	0	0	1/2
8	0	0	0	0	0	0	1	56	0	$1^{<30}$	0	0	0	0	1/2
9	0	0	0	0	0	0	1	57	0	$1^{<30}$	0	0	0	$1^{<30}$	1/4
10	0	0	0	0	0	0	1	58	0	$1^{<30}$	0	0	0	0	1/2
11	0	0	0	0	$1^{<11}$	$1^{<30}$	1/2	59	0	0	0	0	0	0	1/2
12	0	0	0	0	$1^{<21}$	0	1/2	60	0	0	0	0	0	0	1
13	0	0	0	0	$1^{<21}$	0	3/4	61	0	0	0	0	0	0	1
14	0	0	0	0	$1^{<21}$	0	3/4	62	0	0	0	0	0	0	1
15	$1^{<21}$	0	0	0	$1^{<21}$	0	1/2	63	0	0	0	0	0	0	1
16	$1^{<31}$	0	0	0	$1^{<21}$	0	1/4	64	0	0	0	0	0	0	1
17	$1^{<31}$	0	0	0	$1^{<31}$	0	3/8	65	0	0	0	0	0	0	1
18	$1^{<31}$	0	0	0	$1^{<31}$	0	3/4	66	0	0	0	0	0	0	1
19	$1^{<31}$	0	0	0	$1^{<31}$	0	1/4	67	0	0	0	0	0	0	1
20	0	0	0	0	$1^{<31}$	$1^{<31}$	1/2	68	0	0	0	0	0	0	1
21	0	0	0	0	0	0	1/2	69	0	0	0	0	0	0	1
22	0	0	0	0	0	0	1	70	0	0	0	0	0	0	1
23	0	0	0	0	0	0	1	71	0	0	0	0	0	0	1
24	0	0	0	0	0	0	1	72	0	0	0	0	0	0	1
25	0	0	0	0	0	0	1	73	0	0	0	0	0	0	1
26	0	0	0	0	0	0	1	74	0	0	0	0	0	0	1
27	0	0	0	0	0	0	1	75	0	0	0	0	0	0	1
28	0	0	0	0	0	0	1	76	0	0	0	0	0	0	1
29	0	0	0	0	0	0	1	77	0	0	0	0	0	0	1
30	0	0	0	0	0	0	1	78	0	0	0	0	0	0	1
31	0	0	0	0	0	0	1	79	0	0	0	0	0	0	1
32	0	0	0	0	0	0	1	80	0	0	0	0	0	0	1
33	0	0	0	0	0	0	1	81	0	0	0	0	0	0	1
34	0	0	0	0	0	0	1	82	0	0	0	0	0	0	1
35	0	0	0	0	0	0	1	83	0	0	0	0	0	0	1
36	0	0	0	0	$1^{<20}$	$1^{<31}$	1	84	0	0	0	0	0	0	1
37	0	0	0	$1^{<30}$	$1^{<30}$	0	1/2	85	0	0	0	0	0	0	1
38	0	0	0	$1^{<8}$	$1^{<30}$	0	3/8	86	0	0	0	0	0	0	1
39	0	0	0	$1^{<8}$	$1^{<30}$	0	25/64	87	0	0	0	$1^{<10}$	0	$1^{<31}$	1
40	0	0	0	$1^{<8}$	$1^{<30}$	$1^{<30}$	15/128	88	0	0	$1^{<10}$	$1^{<20}$	0	0	1/2
41	0	0	0	$1^{<8}$	0	0	25/64	89	0	$1^{<20}$	$1^{<20}$	$1^{<20}$	0	0	5/16
42	0	0	0	0	0	0	5/8	90	0	$1^{<30}$	$1^{<20}$	$1^{<20}$	0	0	5/8
43	0	0	0	0	0	0	1	91	0	$1^{<30}$	$1^{<20}$	$1^{<20}$	0	0	25/64
44	0	0	0	0	0	0	1	92	0	$1^{<30}$	$1^{<20}$	0	0	0	15/64
45	0	0	0	0	0	0	1	93	0	$1^{<30}$	0	0	0	0	25/64
46	0	0	0	0	0	0	1	94	0	0	0	0	0	$1^{<30}$	3/16
47	0	0	0	0	0	0	1	95	0	0	0	0	0	0	1

□ : The updated part per step

$X_0 = \text{0xdf407f1a}$	$X_1 = \text{0x99c0464a}$	$X_2 = \text{0x3380a1fa}$	$X_3 = \text{0x0d40be50}$
$X_4 = \text{0x6580c1c0}$	$X_5 = \text{0xb8803020}$	$X_6 = \text{0xf5c09a9e}$	$X_7 = \text{0x388077d5}$
$X_8 = \text{0x1f005106}$	$X_9 = \text{0xb080db94}$	$X_{10} = \text{0xb700244c}$	$X_{11} = \text{0x3480cc5e}$
$X_{12} = \text{0xb5c00895}$	$X_{13} = \text{0xa9405c59}$	$X_{14} = \text{0x28c04748}$	$X_{15} = \text{0xba008ecb}$
$\widetilde{X_{11}} = X_{11} \oplus 1^{<<30}, \widetilde{X_i} = X_i (i \neq 11)$			

The output of compression function for two message blocks is as follows.

0xfe684dca   0x33524aa4   0x15ce9f59   0xd200e689   0x7b01f656

And a collision pair on the compression function leads to a collision on the full hash function by simply appending identical blocks or the padding fields for same-length messages.

7   On the Security of Reduced Versions of 3-Pass HAVAL

HAVAL is a dedicated hash function of the MD family which was proposed by Zheng et al[11]. Kasselman et al. found collisions for the last two passes of 3-pass HAVAL[6]. Park et al., at ACISP 2002, found a 256-bit collision of the first two passes of 3-pass HAVAL and of the last two passes of 3-pass HAVAL[7]. In this paper, we attack reduced versions of 3-pass HAVAL using our method different from two previous attack methods(1-2 round: attack probability is 2^{-18}, 2-3 round: attack probability is 2^{-50}). Concretely, we select two messages as follow. For 1-2 round of HAVAL, $W_{29} \oplus \widetilde{W_{29}} = 1^{<<31}, \widetilde{W_{31}} \oplus 1^{<<20} = W_{31}$. For 2-3 round of HAVAL, $W_7 \oplus \widetilde{W_7} = 1^{<<31}, \widetilde{W_{31}} \oplus 1^{<<30} = W_{31}$.(See Appendix B: Table 8, 9)

8   Conclusion

This paper shows that we can find a collision pair from the original hash function with probability $2^{-37.13}$ not transforming boolean functions. This means that a weakness of the hash function proposed at PKC'98 comes from the shift values of the hash function. That is, shift values depending on messages can be a factor of reducing the security of hash functions. Also, our attack method is applied to the reduced version of HAVAL because HAVAL has the weakness of message input order.

Therefore shift values have to be carefully chosen for the security of hash functions. And in case that shift values are fixed, the message input order have to be carefully chosen, also.

Acknowledgements

We thank to the anonymous referees for their useful comments.

References

1. F. Chabaud and A. Joux, *Differential Collisions in SHA-0*, Advances in CRYPTO'98, LNCS 1462, Springer-Verlag, 1998, pp. 56–71.
2. H. Dobbertin, *Cryptanalysis of MD4*, Fast Software Encryption, LNCS 1039, Springer-Verlag,1996, pp. 53–69.
3. H. Dobbertin, *Cryptanalysis of MD5 Compress*, May. 1996.
   www-cse.ucsd.edu/users/bsy/dobbertin.ps
4. Sanguk Shin, Kyunghyune Rhee, Daehyun Ryu, Sangjin Lee, *A New Hash Function Based on MDx-family and Its Application to MAC*, Public Key Cryptography'98, pp. 234–246. 1998.
5. Daewan Han, Sangwoo Park, Seongtaek Chee, *Cryptanalysis of a Hash Function Proposed at PKC'98*, Fast Software Encryption 2002, LNCS 2365, pp. 252–262.
6. P.R. Kasselman and W.T. Penzhorn, *Cryptanalysis of reduced version of HAVAL*, Electronics Letters 6th January 2000 Vol.36 No.1, pp. 30–31.
7. S.W. Park, S.H. Sung, S.T. Chee, J.I. Lim, *On the Security of Reduced Versions of 3-Pass HAVAL*, ACISP 2002, LNCS 2384, pp. 406–419.
8. R. Rivest, *The MD4 message digest algorithm*, RFC 1320, Internet Activities Board, Internet Privacy Task Force, Apr. 1992.
9. R. Rivest, *The MD5 message digest algorithm*, RFC 1321, Internet Activities Board, Internet Privacy Task Force, Apr. 1992.
10. Federal Information Processing Standards Publication 180-1, April 17, 1995.
11. Y. Zheng, J. Pieprzyk and J. Sebberry, *HAVAL - A one-way hashing algorithm with variable length of output*, Advances in Cryptology-Auscrypt'92, LNCS 718, Springer-Verlag, 1993, pp. 83–104.

Appendix A

1. The Analysis of 11∼21 Steps of Table 7

The first round use the function f_0. The values of Table 7 are calculated as follows.

$$\triangle E_{11} = [f_0(E_{10}, A_{10}, B_{10}, C_{10}, D_{10}) + X_{11} + K_1]^{<<S_{11}=13} \oplus [f_0(E_{10}, A_{10}, B_{10}, C_{10}, D_{10}) + (X_{11} \oplus 1^{<<30}) + K_1]^{<<S_{11}=13} = 1^{<<11} \qquad (p = 1/2)$$

Above equality holds with probability $1/2$ by (10).

$$\triangle D_{12} = [f_0(D_{11}, E_{11}, A_{11}, B_{11}, C_{11}) + X_{12} + K_1]^{<<S_{12}} \oplus [f_0(D_{11}, E_{11} \oplus 1^{<<11}, A_{11}, B_{11}, C_{11}) + X_{12} + K_1]^{<<S_{12}} = 0 \qquad (p = 1/2)$$

Above equality holds with probability $1/2$ by 2 of Table 3.

$$\triangle C_{13} = [f_0(C_{12}, D_{12}, E_{12}, A_{12}, B_{12}) + X_{13} + K_1]^{<<S_{13}} \oplus [f_0(C_{12}, D_{12}, E_{12} \oplus 1^{<<21}, A_{12}, B_{12}) + X_{13} + K_1]^{<<S_{13}} = 0 \qquad (p = 3/4)$$

Above equality holds with probability $3/4$ by 3 of Table 3.

$$\triangle B_{14} = [f_0(B_{13}, C_{13}, D_{13}, E_{13}, A_{13}) + X_{14} + K_1]^{<<S_{14}=0} \oplus [f_0(B_{13}, C_{13}, D_{13}, E_{13} \oplus 1^{<<21}, A_{13}) + X_{14} + K_1]^{<<S_{14}=0} = 0 \qquad (p = 3/4)$$

Above equality holds with probability $3/4$ by 4 of Table 3.

$$\triangle A_{15} = [f_0(A_{14}, B_{14}, C_{14}, D_{14}, E_{14}) + X_{15} + K_1]^{<<S_{15}=0} \oplus [f_0(A_{14}, B_{14}, C_{14}, D_{14},$$
$$E_{14} \oplus 1^{<<21}) + X_{15} + K_1]^{<<S_{15}=0} = 1^{<<21} \qquad (p = 1/2)$$

Above equality holds with probability $1/2$ by (10) and by 5 of Table 3.

$$\triangle E_{16} = [f_0(E_{15}, A_{15}, B_{15}, C_{15}, D_{15}) + X_{16} + K_1]^{<<S_{16}=0} \oplus [f_0(E_{15} \oplus 1^{<<21}, A_{15} \oplus$$
$$1^{<<21}, B_{15}, C_{15}, D_{15}) + X_{16} + K_1]^{<<S_{16}=0} = 1^{<<21} \qquad (p = 1/4)$$

Above equality holds with probability $1/4$ by (10) and by 6 of Table 3.

$$\triangle D_{17} = [f_0(D_{16}, E_{16}, A_{16}, B_{16}, C_{16}) + X_{17} + K_1]^{<<S_{17}=10} \oplus [f_0(D_{16}, E_{16} \oplus$$
$$1^{<<21}, A_{16} \oplus 1^{<<31}, B_{16}, C_{16}) + X_{17} + K_1]^{<<S_{17}=10} = 0 \qquad (p = 3/8)$$

Above equality holds with probability $3/8$ by 2, 3 of Table 3.

$$\triangle C_{18} = [f_0(C_{17}, D_{17}, E_{17}, A_{17}, B_{17}) + X_{18} + K_1]^{<<S_{18}=21} \oplus [f_0(C_{17}, D_{17}, E_{17} \oplus$$
$$1^{<<31}, A_{17} \oplus 1^{<<31}, B_{17}) + X_{18} + K_1]^{<<S_{18}=21} = 0 \qquad (p = 3/4)$$

Above equality holds with probability $3/4$ by 10 of Table 3.

$$\triangle B_{19} = [f_0(B_{18}, C_{18}, D_{18}, E_{18}, A_{18}) + X_{19} + K_1]^{<<S_{19}} \oplus [f_0(B_{18}, C_{18}, D_{18}, E_{18} \oplus$$
$$1^{<<31}, A_{18} \oplus 1^{<<31}) + X_{19} + K_1]^{<<S_{19}} = 0 \qquad (p = 1/4)$$

Above equality holds with probability $1/4$ by 11 of Table 3.

$$\triangle A_{20} = [f_0(A_{19}, B_{19}, C_{19}, D_{19}, E_{19}) + X_{20} + K_1]^{<<S_{20}} \oplus [f_0(A_{19} \oplus 1^{<<31}, B_{19}, C_{19},$$
$$D_{19}, E_{19} \oplus 1^{<<31}) + (X_{20} \oplus 1^{<<31}) + K_1]^{<<S_{20}} = 0 \qquad (p = 1/2)$$
$$\triangle E_{21} = [f_0(E_{20}, A_{20}, B_{20}, C_{20}, D_{20}) + X_{21} + K_1]^{<<S_{21}} \oplus [f_0(E_{20} \oplus 1^{<<31}, A_{20}, B_{20},$$
$$C_{20}, D_{20}) + X_{21} + K_1]^{<<S_{21}} = 0 \qquad (p = 1/2)$$

2. The Analysis of 36~42 Steps of Table 7

The probabilities of following equalities also are calculated like the above method.

$$\triangle E_{36} = [f_1(E_{35}, A_{35}, B_{35}, C_{35}, D_{35}) + X_{20} + K_2]^{<<S_{36}=21} \oplus [f_1(E_{35}, A_{35}, B_{35}, C_{35},$$
$$D_{35}) + (X_{20} \oplus 1^{<<31}) + K_2]^{<<S_{36}=21} = 1^{<<20} \qquad (p = 1)$$
$$\triangle D_{37} = [f_1(D_{36}, E_{36}, A_{36}, B_{36}, C_{36}) + X_3 + K_2]^{<<S_{37}=10} \oplus [f_1(D_{36}, E_{36} \oplus 1^{<<20}, A_{36},$$
$$B_{36}, C_{36}) + X_3 + K_2]^{<<S_{37}=10} = 1^{<<30} \qquad (p = 1/2)$$
$$\triangle C_{38} = [f_1(C_{37}, D_{37}, E_{37}, A_{37}, B_{37}) + X_{22} + K_2]^{<<S_{38}} \oplus [f_1(C_{37}, D_{37} \oplus 1^{<<30}, E_{37}$$
$$\oplus 1^{<<30}, A_{37}, B_{37}) + X_{22} + K_2]^{<<S_{38}} = 0 \qquad (p = 3/8)$$
$$\triangle B_{39} = [f_1(B_{38}, C_{38}, D_{38}, E_{38}, A_{38}) + X_6 + K_2]^{<<S_{39}=21} \oplus [f_1(B_{38}, C_{38}, D_{38}$$
$$\oplus 1^{<<8}, E_{38} \oplus 1^{<<30}, A_{38}) + X_6 + K_2]^{<<S_{39}=21} = 0 \qquad (p = 25/64)$$
$$\triangle A_{40} = [f_1(A_{39}, B_{39}, C_{39}, D_{39}, E_{39}) + X_{11} + K_2]^{<<S_{40}} \oplus [f_1(A_{39}, B_{39}, C_{39}, D_{39}$$
$$\oplus 1^{<<8}, E_{39} \oplus 1^{<<30}) + (X_{11} \oplus 1^{<<30}) + K_2]^{<<S_{40}} = 0 \qquad (p = 15/128)$$
$$\triangle E_{41} = [f_1(E_{40}, A_{40}, B_{40}, C_{40}, D_{40}) + X_{19} + K_2]^{<<S_{41}} \oplus [f_1(E_{40} \oplus 1^{<<30}, A_{40}, B_{40},$$
$$C_{40}, D_{40} \oplus 1^{<<8}) + X_{19} + K_2]^{<<S_{41}} = 0 \qquad (p = 25/64)$$
$$\triangle D_{42} = [f_1(D_{41}, E_{41}, A_{41}, B_{41}, C_{41}) + X_{15} + K_2]^{<<S_{42}} \oplus [f_1(D_{41} \oplus 1^{<<8}, E_{41}, A_{41},$$
$$B_{41}, C_{41}) + X_{15} + K_2]^{<<S_{42}} = 0 \qquad (p = 5/8)$$

3. The Analysis of 54~59 Steps of Table 7

The probabilities of following equalities also are calculated like the above method.

$$\triangle B_{54} = [f_2(B_{53}, C_{53}, D_{53}, E_{53}, A_{53}) + X_{20} + K_3]^{<<S_{54}=21} \oplus [f_2(B_{53}, C_{53}, D_{53}, E_{53},$$
$$A_{53}) + (X_{20} \oplus 1^{<<31}) + K_3]^{<<S_{54}=21} = 1^{<<20} \qquad (p=1)$$
$$\triangle A_{55} = [f_2(A_{54}, B_{54}, C_{54}, D_{54}, E_{54}) + X_8 + K_3]^{<<S_{55}} \oplus [f_2(A_{54}, B_{54} \oplus 1^{<<20}, C_{54},$$
$$D_{54}, E_{54}) + X_8 + K_3]^{<<S_{55}} = 0 \qquad (p=1/2)$$
$$\triangle E_{56} = [f_2(E_{55}, A_{55}, B_{55}, C_{55}, D_{55}) + X_{18} + K_3]^{<<S_{56}} \oplus [f_2(E_{55}, A_{55}, B_{55} \oplus 1^{<<30},$$
$$C_{55}, D_{55}) + X_{18} + K_3]^{<<S_{56}} = 0 \qquad (p=1/2)$$
$$\triangle D_{57} = [f_2(D_{56}, E_{56}, A_{56}, B_{56}, C_{56}) + X_{11} + K_3]^{<<S_{57}=0} \oplus [f_2(D_{56}, E_{56}, A_{56}, B_{56}$$
$$\oplus 1^{<<30}, C_{56}) + (X_{11} \oplus 1^{<<30}) + K_3]^{<<S_{57}=0} = 0 \qquad (p=1/4)$$
$$\triangle C_{58} = [f_2(C_{57}, D_{57}, E_{57}, A_{57}, B_{57}) + X_5 + K_3]^{<<S_{58}} \oplus [f_2(C_{57}, D_{57}, E_{57}, A_{57}, B_{57}$$
$$\oplus 1^{<<30}) + X_5 + K_3]^{<<S_{58}} = 0 \qquad (p=1/2)$$
$$\triangle B_{59} = [f_2(B_{58}, C_{58}, D_{58}, E_{58}, A_{58}) + X_4 + K_3]^{<<S_{59}} \oplus [f_2(B_{58} \oplus 1^{<<30}, C_{58}, D_{58},$$
$$E_{58}, A_{58}) + X_4 + K_3]^{<<S_{59}} = 0 \qquad (p=1/2)$$

4. The Analysis of 87~95 Steps of Table 7

The probabilities of following equalities also are calculated like the above method.

$$\triangle D_{87} = [f_1(D_{86}, E_{86}, A_{86}, B_{86}, C_{86}) + X_{20} + K_4]^{<<S_{87}=11} \oplus [f_1(D_{86}, E_{86}, A_{86}, B_{86},$$
$$C_{86}) + (X_{20} \oplus 1^{<<31}) + K_4]^{<<S_{87}=11} = 1^{<<10} \qquad (p=1)$$
$$\triangle C_{88} = [f_1(C_{87}, D_{87}, E_{87}, A_{87}, B_{87}) + X_4 + K_4]^{<<S_{88}=0} \oplus [f_1(C_{87}, D_{87} \oplus 1^{<<10}, E_{87},$$
$$A_{87}, B_{87}) + X_4 + K_4]^{<<S_{88}=0} = 1^{<<10} \qquad (p=1/2)$$
$$\triangle B_{89} = [f_1(B_{88}, C_{88}, D_{88}, E_{88}, A_{88}) + X_{17} + K_4]^{<<S_{89}=10} \oplus [f_1(B_{88}, C_{88} \oplus 1^{<<10}, D_{88}$$
$$\oplus 1^{<<20}, E_{88}, A_{88}) + X_{17} + K_4]^{<<S_{89}=10} = 1^{<<20} \qquad (p=5/16)$$
$$\triangle A_{90} = [f_1(A_{89}, B_{89}, C_{89}, D_{89}, E_{89}) + X_{12} + K_4]^{<<S_{90}} \oplus [f_1(A_{89}, B_{89} \oplus 1^{<<20}, C_{89}$$
$$\oplus 1^{<<20}, D_{89} \oplus 1^{<<20}, E_{89}) + X_{12} + K_4]^{<<S_{90}} = 0 \qquad (p=5/8)$$
$$\triangle E_{91} = [f_1(E_{90}, A_{90}, B_{90}, C_{90}, D_{90}) + X_{19} + K_4]^{<<S_{91}} \oplus [f_1(E_{90}, A_{90}, B_{90} \oplus 1^{<<30},$$
$$C_{90} \oplus 1^{<<20}, D_{90} \oplus 1^{<<20}) + X_{19} + K_4]^{<<S_{91}} = 0 \qquad (p=25/64)$$
$$\triangle D_{92} = [f_1(D_{91}, E_{91}, A_{91}, B_{91}, C_{91}) + X_8 + K_4]^{<<S_{92}=0} \oplus [f_1(D_{91} \oplus 1^{<<20}, E_{91}, A_{91},$$
$$B_{91} \oplus 1^{<<30}, C_{91} \oplus 1^{<<20}) + X_8 + K_4]^{<<S_{92}=0} = 0 \qquad (p=15/64)$$
$$\triangle C_{93} = [f_1(C_{92}, D_{92}, E_{92}, A_{92}, B_{92}) + X_9 + K_4]^{<<S_{93}} \oplus [f_1(C_{92} \oplus 1^{<<20}, D_{92}, E_{92}, A_{92},$$
$$B_{92} \oplus 1^{<<30}) + X_9 + K_4]^{<<S_{93}} = 0 \qquad (p=25/64)$$
$$\triangle B_{94} = [f_1(B_{93}, C_{93}, D_{93}, E_{93}, A_{93}) + X_{11} + K_4]^{<<S_{94}} \oplus [f_1(B_{93} \oplus 1^{<<30}, C_{93}, D_{93}, E_{93},$$
$$A_{93}) + (X_{11} \oplus 1^{<<30}) + K_4]^{<<S_{94}} = 0 \qquad (p=3/16)$$
$$\triangle A_{95} = [f_1(A_{94}, B_{94}, C_{94}, D_{94}, E_{94}) + X_1 + K_4]^{<<S_{95}=13} \oplus [f_1(A_{94}, B_{94}, C_{94}, D_{94}, E_{94})$$
$$+ X_1 + K_4]^{<<S_{95}=13} = 0 \qquad (p=1)$$

Appendix B

Table 8. Attack on the first two passes of 3-pass HAVAL

Step	A	B	C	D	E	F	G	H	X	p	Step	A	B	C	D	E	F	G	H	X	p
0	0	0	0	0	0	0	0	0	0	1	32	0	0	0	0	0	0	0	0	0	1
1	0	0	0	0	0	0	0	0	0	1	33	0	0	0	0	0	0	0	0	0	1
2	0	0	0	0	0	0	0	0	0	1	34	0	0	0	0	0	0	0	0	0	1
3	0	0	0	0	0	0	0	0	0	1	35	0	0	0	0	0	0	0	0	0	1
4	0	0	0	0	0	0	0	0	0	1	36	0	0	0	0	0	0	0	0	0	1
5	0	0	0	0	0	0	0	0	0	1	37	0	0	0	0	0	0	0	0	0	1
6	0	0	0	0	0	0	0	0	0	1	38	0	$1^{<31}$	0	0	0	0	0	0	$1^{<31}$	1
7	$1^{<31}$	0	0	0	0	0	0	0	$1^{<31}$	1	39	0	$1^{<31}$	0	0	0	0	0	0	0	1/2
8	$1^{<31}$	0	0	0	0	0	0	0	0	1/2	40	0	$1^{<31}$	0	0	0	0	0	0	0	1/2
9	$1^{<31}$	0	0	0	0	0	0	0	0	1/2	41	0	$1^{<31}$	0	0	0	0	0	0	0	1/2
10	$1^{<31}$	0	0	0	0	0	0	0	0	1/2	42	0	$1^{<31}$	0	0	0	0	0	0	0	1/2
11	$1^{<31}$	0	0	0	0	0	0	0	0	1/2	43	0	$1^{<31}$	0	0	0	0	0	0	0	1/2
12	$1^{<31}$	0	0	0	0	0	0	0	0	1/2	44	0	$1^{<31}$	0	0	0	0	0	0	0	1/2
13	$1^{<31}$	0	0	0	0	0	0	0	0	1/2	45	0	$1^{<31}$	0	0	0	0	0	0	0	1/2
14	$1^{<31}$	0	0	0	0	0	0	0	0	1/2	46	0	$1^{<20}$	0	0	0	0	0	0	0	1/2
15	$1^{<20}$	0	0	0	0	0	0	0	0	1/2	47	0	$1^{<20}$	0	0	0	0	0	0	0	1/2
16	$1^{<20}$	0	0	0	0	0	0	0	0	1/2	48	0	$1^{<20}$	0	0	0	0	0	0	0	1/2
17	$1^{<20}$	0	0	0	0	0	0	0	0	1/2	49	0	$1^{<20}$	0	0	0	0	0	0	0	1/2
18	$1^{<20}$	0	0	0	0	0	0	0	0	1/2	50	0	$1^{<20}$	0	0	0	0	0	0	0	1/2
19	$1^{<20}$	0	0	0	0	0	0	0	0	1/2	51	0	$1^{<20}$	0	0	0	0	0	0	0	1/2
20	$1^{<20}$	0	0	0	0	0	0	0	0	1/2	52	0	$1^{<20}$	0	0	0	0	0	0	0	1/2
21	$1^{<20}$	0	0	0	0	0	0	0	0	1/2	53	0	$1^{<20}$	0	0	0	0	0	0	0	1/2
22	$1^{<20}$	0	0	0	0	0	0	0	0	1/2	54	0	$1^{<9}$	0	0	0	0	0	0	0	1/2
23	$1^{<9}$	0	0	0	0	0	0	0	0	1/2	55	0	$1^{<9}$	0	0	0	0	0	0	0	1/2
24	$1^{<9}$	0	0	0	0	0	0	0	0	1/2	56	0	$1^{<9}$	0	0	0	0	0	0	0	1/2
25	$1^{<9}$	0	0	0	0	0	0	0	0	1/2	57	0	$1^{<9}$	0	0	0	0	0	0	0	1/2
26	$1^{<9}$	0	0	0	0	0	0	0	0	1/2	58	0	$1^{<9}$	0	0	0	0	0	0	0	1/2
27	$1^{<9}$	0	0	0	0	0	0	0	0	1/2	59	0	$1^{<9}$	0	0	0	0	0	0	0	1/2
28	$1^{<9}$	0	0	0	0	0	0	0	0	1/2	60	0	$1^{<9}$	0	0	0	0	0	0	0	1/2
29	$1^{<9}$	0	0	0	0	0	0	0	0	1/2	61	0	$1^{<9}$	0	0	0	0	0	0	0	1/2
30	$1^{<9}$	0	0	0	0	0	0	0	0	1/2	62	0	0	0	0	0	0	0	0	$1^{<30}$	1/4
31	0	0	0	0	0	0	0	0	$1^{<30}$	1/4	63	0	0	0	0	0	0	0	0	0	1

□ :The updated part per step

Table 9. Attack on the last two passes of 3-pass HAVAL

Step	A	B	C	D	E	F	G	H	X	p	Step	A	B	C	D	E	F	G	H	X	p
32	0	0	0	0	0	0	0	0	0	1	64	0	0	0	0	0	0	0	0	0	1
33	0	0	0	0	0	0	0	0	0	1	65	0	0	0	0	0	0	0	0	0	1
34	0	0	0	0	0	0	0	0	0	1	66	0	0	0	0	0	0	0	0	0	1
35	0	0	0	0	0	0	0	0	0	1	67	0	0	0	0	0	0	0	0	0	1
36	0	0	0	0	0	0	0	0	0	1	68	0	0	0	0	0	0	0	0	0	1
37	0	0	0	0	0	0	0	0	0	1	69	0	0	0	0	0	0	0	0	0	1
38	0	0	0	0	0	0	0	0	0	1	70	0	0	0	0	0	0	0	0	0	1
39	0	0	0	0	0	0	0	0	0	1	71	0	0	0	0	0	0	0	0	0	1
40	0	0	0	0	0	0	0	0	0	1	72	0	0	0	0	0	0	0	$1^{<31}$	$1^{<31}$	1
41	0	0	0	0	0	0	0	0	0	1	73	0	0	0	0	0	0	0	$1^{<31}$	0	1/2
42	0	0	0	0	0	0	0	0	0	1	74	0	0	0	0	0	0	0	$1^{<31}$	0	1/2
43	0	0	0	0	0	0	0	0	0	1	75	0	0	0	0	0	0	0	$1^{<31}$	0	1/2
44	0	0	0	0	0	0	0	0	0	1	76	0	0	0	0	0	0	0	$1^{<31}$	0	1/2
45	0	0	0	0	0	0	0	0	0	1	77	0	0	0	0	0	0	0	$1^{<31}$	0	1/2
46	0	0	0	0	0	0	0	0	0	1	78	0	0	0	0	0	0	0	$1^{<31}$	0	1/2
47	0	0	0	0	0	0	0	0	0	1	79	0	0	0	0	0	0	0	$1^{<31}$	0	1/2
48	0	0	0	0	0	0	0	0	0	1	80	0	0	0	0	0	0	0	0	$1^{<20}$	1/4
49	0	0	0	0	0	0	0	0	0	1	81	0	0	0	0	0	0	0	0	0	1
50	0	0	0	0	0	0	0	0	0	1	82	0	0	0	0	0	0	0	0	0	1
51	0	0	0	0	0	0	0	0	0	1	83	0	0	0	0	0	0	0	0	0	1
52	0	0	0	0	0	0	0	0	0	1	84	0	0	0	0	0	0	0	0	0	1
53	0	0	0	0	0	0	0	0	0	1	85	0	0	0	0	0	0	0	0	0	1
54	0	$1^{<31}$	0	0	0	0	0	0	$1^{<31}$	1	86	0	0	0	0	0	0	0	0	0	1
55	0	$1^{<31}$	0	0	0	0	0	0	0	1/2	87	0	0	0	0	0	0	0	0	0	1
56	0	$1^{<31}$	0	0	0	0	0	0	0	1/2	88	0	0	0	0	0	0	0	0	0	1
57	0	$1^{<31}$	0	0	0	0	0	0	0	1/2	89	0	0	0	0	0	0	0	0	0	1
58	0	$1^{<31}$	0	0	0	0	0	0	0	1/2	90	0	0	0	0	0	0	0	0	0	1
59	0	$1^{<31}$	0	0	0	0	0	0	0	1/2	91	0	0	0	0	0	0	0	0	0	1
60	0	$1^{<31}$	0	0	0	0	0	0	0	1/2	92	0	0	0	0	0	0	0	0	0	1
61	0	$1^{<31}$	0	0	0	0	0	0	0	1/2	93	0	0	0	0	0	0	0	0	0	1
62	0	0	0	0	0	0	0	0	$1^{<20}$	1/4	94	0	0	0	0	0	0	0	0	0	1
63	0	0	0	0	0	0	0	0	0	1	95	0	0	0	0	0	0	0	0	0	1

□ :The updated part per step

On Propagation Characteristics
of Resilient Functions

Pascale Charpin[1] and Enes Pasalic[2]

[1] INRIA, projet CODES, Domaine de Voluceau, Rocquencourt, BP 105,
78153 Le Chesnay Cedex, France.
Pascale.Charpin@inria.fr
[2] Department of Information Technology, Lund University
P.O. Box 118, 221 00 Lund, Sweden.
enes@it.lth.se

Abstract. [1] In this paper we derive several important results towards a better understanding of propagation characteristics of resilient Boolean functions. We first introduce a new upper bound on nonlinearity of a given resilient function depending on the propagation criterion. We later show that a large class of resilient functions admit a linear structure; more generally, we exhibit some divisibility properties concerning the Walsh-spectrum of the derivatives of any resilient function. We prove that, fixing the order of resiliency and the degree of propagation criterion, a high algebraic degree is a necessary condition for construction of functions with good autocorrelation properties. We conclude by a study of the main constructions of resilient functions. We notably show how to avoid linear structures when a linear concatenation is used and when the recursive construction introduced in [11] is chosen.

Keywords: Boolean functions, nonlinearity, propagation characteristics, resiliency, linear space.

1 Introduction

The security of most conventional cryptographic systems is based on some properties of Boolean functions – currently called *cryptographic criteria*. This paper deals with well-known such criteria. The *nonlinearity*, the distance from a Boolean function to the set of all affine functions, prevents linear attacks in block ciphers [9]. *Correlation-immune* functions were first introduced by Siegenthaler [14] in order to construct running-key generators for stream ciphers which resist to correlation attack. A balanced such function is said to be *resilient*; resiliency appears as the main criterion in several systems (see, for instance, [1]). The *propagation criterion* (PC) was introduced by Preneel [12], generalizing the *strict avalanche criterion* [17]. More generally, the *propagation characteristics* of

---

[1] More detailed explanations, examples and full proofs can be found in the extended version of this paper, see [6].

K. Nyberg and H. Heys (Eds.): SAC 2002, LNCS 2595, pp. 175–195, 2003.
© Springer-Verlag Berlin Heidelberg 2003

any Boolean function refer to certain properties of its derivatives [19]. A function which has constant derivatives is said to have a nontrivial *linear space*, the space of its *linear structures*. The distance from a Boolean function to the set of functions with linear structures was explained by Meier and Staffelbach in [10].

Recently, the relationships between propagation characteristics, nonlinearity, and correlation-immunity were investigated (see notably [2], [13], [15],[20], [4]). Generally, in all recent works, it appears that good cryptographic properties imply that the given function belongs to some well-structured class. It is especially true for resilient functions; a few effective constructions are known and the main of these are based on concatenations [7,16]. Our main purpose is the study of the consequences of high resiliency for other cryptographic criteria. How high resiliency could lead to some weakness ? In accordance with [10], such weakness has to be considered up to any simple transformation (for instance, any affine transformation).

In Section 2, we present the main tools for the study of Boolean functions on $\mathbb{F}_2^n$, the basic definitions and some recent results concerning the cryptographic criteria. In Section 3 we consider resilient functions which satisfy a certain propagation criterion. We introduce a new nontrivial upper bound on the nonlinearity of t-resilient functions satisfying PC with respect to some subspace of dimension p (Theorem 3). We then emphasize that for a fixed order of resiliency, the upper bound on nonlinearity of f, is smaller for larger p. Section 4 is devoted to the characterization of the linear space of functions. Different criteria regarding the functions with linear structures are addressed here. We then deduce that high resiliency leads to the existence of linear structures (Corollary 2). In Section 5, we study the weights of the derivatives of resilient functions which satisfy (or not) some propagation criterion. Our results reinforce those of the previous section. Namely, high resiliency leads to high divisibility for the weights of derivatives; moreover, taking into account the degree of propagation and the degree of the function, this divisibility increases (Theorem 5). In Section 6 we discuss the main known constructions of resilient functions. We first characterize resilient functions, obtained by linear concatenation, which have no linear structure (Proposition 3). We later study two recursive constructions [16],[11]. We prove that the first one provides resilient functions which have a linear space not reduced to 0, while the second one preserves the lack of linear structure (Proposition 7).

2   Definitions and Basic Properties

2.1   Boolean Functions

We denote by $\mathcal{B}_n$ the set of Boolean functions of n variables. Thus $f \in \mathcal{B}_n$ is a function from $\mathbb{F}_2^n$ to $\mathbb{F}_2$; it is generally represented by its *algebraic normal form*:

$$f(x_1, \ldots, x_n) = \sum_{u \in \mathbb{F}_2^n} \lambda_u \left(\prod_{i=1}^{n} x_i^{u_i} \right) , \quad \lambda_u \in \mathbb{F}_2 .$$

The *degree* of f is the maximal value of the Hamming weight of u such that $\lambda_u \neq 0$. The linear functions will be represented by means of the scalar product, with respect to the standard basis. They will be denoted as follows: for any $\alpha \in \mathbb{F}_2^n$, $\varphi_\alpha : x \in \mathbb{F}_2^n \longmapsto \alpha \cdot x = \sum_{i=1}^n \alpha_i x_i$.

The *Walsh transform* of $f \in \mathcal{B}_n$ in point α is denoted $\mathcal{F}(f + \varphi_\alpha)$ and calculated as,

$$\alpha \in \mathbb{F}_2^n \longmapsto \mathcal{F}(f + \varphi_\alpha) = \sum_{x \in \mathbb{F}_2^n} (-1)^{f(x) + \varphi_\alpha(x)} .$$

The values of these coefficients form the *Walsh-spectrum* of f. For convenience, $\mathcal{F}(f)$ will denote the Walsh transform in $\alpha = 0$. The *nonlinearity* $\mathcal{N}_f$ of $f \in \mathcal{B}_n$ is related to the Walsh transform via following expression:

$$\mathcal{N}_f = 2^{n-1} - \frac{\mathcal{L}(f)}{2} \quad \text{where} \quad \mathcal{L}(f) = \max_{\alpha \in \mathbb{F}_2^n} \mid \mathcal{F}(f + \varphi_\alpha) \mid.$$

The *propagation characteristics* of f are described by the behavior of its derivatives. The *derivative* of $f \in \mathcal{B}_n$ with respect to any direction $a \in \mathbb{F}_2^n$, is the mapping $D_a f : x \longmapsto f(x) + f(a + x)$. Thus, the *auto-correlation function* of f refers to the function $a \mapsto \mathcal{F}(D_a f)$. The main indicators of propagation characteristics are the *absolute indicator* and the *sum-of-square indicator* [19]:

$$\mathcal{M}(f) = \max_{a \in \mathbf{F}_2^m, a \neq 0} \mid \mathcal{F}(D_a f) \mid \quad \text{and} \quad \mathcal{V}(f) = \sum_{a \in \mathbf{F}_2^m} \mathcal{F}^2(D_a f) .$$

For any linear subspace V of $\mathbb{F}_2^n$, its dual $V^\perp$ will be the subspace of elements $x \in \mathbb{F}_2^n$ such that $x \cdot y = 0$ for all $y \in V$. The next formula provides a link between the Walsh and autocorrelation spectra of f. The proof can be found in [3, Lemma V.2].

Lemma 1 *Let V be a linear subspace of $\mathbb{F}_2^n$ of dimension k. Then for any function f in $\mathcal{B}_n$ we have for any $\beta \in \mathbb{F}_2^n$,*

$$\sum_{v \in V} \mathcal{F}^2(f + \varphi_{\beta + v}) = 2^k \sum_{u \in V} (-1)^{\beta \cdot u} \mathcal{F}(D_u f). \tag{1}$$

For $V = \{0\}$, (1) becomes the well-known relation:

$$\mathcal{F}^2(f + \varphi_\beta) = \sum_{u \in \mathbb{F}_2^n} (-1)^{\beta \cdot u} \mathcal{F}(D_u f) .$$

2.2 Resiliency and Propagation Characteristics

The next definitions are now classical. They were introduced in [10,12] (for the propagation characteristics) and in [14,18] (for the resiliency). Recall that the Hamming weight of any binary vector y is $wt(y) = \#\{i \mid y_i = 1\}$, where $\#A$ denotes the cardinality of any set A. By convention, the weight of $f \in \mathcal{B}_n$ is the Hamming weight of its corresponding codeword, where the codeword of $f(x)$

is the sequence of values $f(x)$, when x runs through $\mathbb{F}_2^n$. Any function $f \in \mathcal{B}_n$ is *balanced* when $wt(f) = 2^{n-1}$ or, equivalently, $\mathcal{F}(f) = 0$. A function exhibits *good propagation characteristics* when its autocorrelation function takes "small" (absolute) values; therefore the related indicators have to be "small" [19].

Definition 1 *The* linear space *of any Boolean function f is the linear subspace of those elements a such that the function $D_a f$ is constant. Such nonzero a is called a* linear structure *of f.*

The function $f \in \mathcal{B}_n$ has a linear structure if and only if $\mathcal{M}(f)$ takes its maximal value 2^n. On the other hand the sum-of-square indicator provides a bound for the nonlinearity.

Theorem 1 [2] *Let $f \in \mathcal{B}_n$. Then we have $\mathcal{V}(f) \leq 2^n \mathcal{L}^2(f)$ with equality if and only if the Walsh spectrum of f takes at most three values, 0, $\mathcal{L}(f)$ and $-\mathcal{L}(f)$.*

The propagation criterion of f concerns the set of balanced derivatives.

Definition 2 *Let $E \subset \mathbb{F}_2^n$. The function $f \in \mathcal{B}_n$ satisfies the propagation criterion (PC) with respect to E if for all $e \in E$ the function $D_e f$ is balanced. The function f satisfies PC of degree p (PC(p)) for some positive integer p when $D_a f$ is balanced for any $a \in \mathbb{F}_2^n$ such that $1 \leq wt(a) \leq p$.*

The correlation-immunity is characterized by the set of zero values in the Walsh spectrum.

Definition 3 *Let $f \in \mathcal{B}_n$ and let t be some positive integer. The function f is said to be* correlation-immune *of order t if and only if $\mathcal{F}(f + \varphi_\alpha) = 0$ for any $a \in \mathbb{F}_2^n$ such that $1 \leq wt(\alpha) \leq t$. Moreover, when f is balanced, it is said to be* t-resilient. *A balanced function is said to be 0-resilient.*

Besides its maximum value, the whole Walsh spectrum of a Boolean function has a great cryptographic significance. Several recent works are devoted to the divisibility of the Walsh coefficients of resilient functions. Sarkar and Maitra proved in [13] that any t-resilient function $f \in \mathcal{B}_n$ satisfies for all α: $\mathcal{F}(f+\varphi_\alpha) \equiv 0 \pmod{2^{t+2}}$. This result has been independently obtained by Tarannikov [15]. It was improved by Carlet in [4] by including the algebraic degree d of the function:

$$\mathcal{F}(f + \varphi_\alpha) \equiv 0 \pmod{2^{t+2+\lfloor \frac{n-t-2}{d} \rfloor}}, \ \forall \, \alpha \in \mathbb{F}_2^n \tag{2}$$

(where $\lfloor r \rfloor$ denotes the integer part of r). Carlet then derived a new upper bound on $\mathcal{N}_f$,

$$\mathcal{N}_f \leq 2^{n-1} - 2^{t+1+\lfloor \frac{n-t-2}{d} \rfloor}. \tag{3}$$

This bound is lose for small t, since there is a tighter upper bound derived from the nonlinearity of bent functions. However, for $t > \frac{n}{2} - 2$ the bound above is tighter for any n.

3   On Resilient Boolean Functions Satisfying PC

In this section, we focus on an improvement of the bound (3) when considering any t-resilient function which moreover satisfies some propagation criterion.

3.1   Preliminary

In a recent paper, Zhang and Zheng introduced several properties regarding the relationship between the correlation-immunity and propagation criteria [20]. They begin by giving a lower bound for the nonlinearity of functions satisfying PC(p). The following result is given in [20, Theorem 1].

Theorem 2 *Let f be a non-bent function in $\mathcal{B}_n$ satisfying PC(p). Then the nonlinearity of f satisfies*

$$\mathcal{N}_f \geq 2^{n-1} - 2^{n-\frac{p}{2}-1} \quad \text{or, equivalently,} \quad \mathcal{L}(f) \leq 2^{n-\frac{p}{2}} . \tag{4}$$

Moreover, if $\mathcal{L}(f) = 2^{n-\frac{p}{2}}$, then $p = n - 1$ and n is odd.

Actually this lower bound can be established more generally.

Proposition 1 *Let f be a non-bent function in $\mathcal{B}_n$. Assume that f satisfies PC with respect to $U \setminus \{0\}$, where U is a subspace of $\mathbb{F}_2^n$ of dimension p. Then the nonlinearity of f satisfies (4). This especially holds when f satisfies PC(p). When $p = n - 1$, for odd n, or $p = n - 2$, for even n, then $\mathcal{L}(f) = 2^{n-\frac{p}{2}}$.*

Proof: We apply (1) with $k = n - p$ and $V = U^\perp$. Then for any β,

$$\sum_{v \in U} \mathcal{F}^2(f + \varphi_{\beta+v}) = 2^{n-p}\mathcal{F}(D_0 f) = 2^{2n-p} .$$

This implies that $\mathcal{L}^2(f) \leq 2^{2n-p}$ or, equivalently, that $\mathcal{N}_f \geq 2^{n-1} - 2^{\frac{2n-p}{2}-1}$. When the function f satisfies PC(p), it satisfies PC with respect to $U_a \setminus \{0\}$ for any a where

$$U_a = \{ u \in \mathbb{F}_2^n \mid u \preccurlyeq a \} \quad \text{with} \quad wt(a) = p . \tag{5}$$

Note that $u \preccurlyeq a$ means that a *covers* u, i.e., $u_i \leq a_i$ for all i in the range $[1, n]$.

The cases $p = n - 1$ and $p = n - 2$ were explained in [3, § V.C]. Note that, according to the previous theorem, it is impossible to have: f satisfies PC($n-2$) and $\mathcal{L}(f) = 2^{n-\frac{p}{2}}$.

□

With the hypothesis of Theorem 2, $\mathcal{L}(f) = 2^{n-\frac{p}{2}}$ implies that $p = n - 1$ for odd n (and that f is bent for even n). The functions satisfying PC($n-1$) were fully-characterized in [2]. Such a function f admits one and only one linear structure, say e, and is such that $D_a f$ is balanced unless $a \in \{0, e\}$. Moreover it cannot be 1-resilient, with respect to any basis. In the case of Proposition 1, it is possible to have $\mathcal{L}(f) = 2^{n-\frac{p}{2}}$ for any even p. Furthermore for $p = n - 1$, when f is balanced it is generally 1-resilient, with respect to some basis (see [2], Corollary 2, Theorems 4 and 7).

In the sequel of this section, we will consider functions which are t-resilient with respect to the standard basis. We will fix the basis for the definitions of the t-resiliency; for the PC property we consider particular subspaces which are defined by means of this standard basis. We first indicate some restriction on the sum $p + t$.

Lemma 2 *Let f be a t-resilient function satisfying PC with respect to the non-zero elements of U_a, $wt(a) = p$, defined as in (5). Denote by $\bar{a}$ the vector $(1 + a_1, \ldots, 1 + a_n)$.*
Then $p + t \leq n - 1$. If $p + t = n - 1$ and $\mathcal{F}(f + \varphi_{\bar{a}}) \neq 0$ then $\mathcal{L}^2(f) = \mathcal{F}^2(f + \varphi_{\bar{a}}) = 2^{2n-p}$. When $p + t = n - 1$ and f satisfies PC(p) then $p = n - 1$, n is odd and $t = 0$.

Proof: We apply (1) with $k = n - p$, $V = U_a^\perp$ and $\beta = 0$: $\sum_{v \preccurlyeq \bar{a}} \mathcal{F}^2(f + \varphi_v) = 2^{2n-p}$.

Since $wt(\bar{a}) = n - p$ and f is t-resilient, $t \geq n - p$ would imply that each term in the sum above is zero, a contradiction. Now, assuming that $t = n - p - 1$, there is only one possible non-zero term in this sum (for $v = \bar{a}$). According to Proposition 1, $\mathcal{F}^2(f + \varphi_{\bar{a}}) = 2^{2n-p}$ provides $\mathcal{L}^2(f) = 2^{2n-p}$. The proof is completed by means of Theorem 2. □

3.2   A New Upper Bound

We will show that there exists a nontrivial upper bound on the nonlinearity of t-resilient functions satisfying PC with respect to the nonzero elements of some subspace of dimension p. According to the previous discussion we will assume that $p + t = n - k$ with $k \geq 2$. Recall that the degree d of any t-resilient function in $\mathcal{B}_n$ satisfies $d \leq n - t - 1$ [14].

Theorem 3 *Let $f \in \mathcal{B}_n$ be a t-resilient function of degree d with $d \geq 2$. Assume that f satisfies PC with respect to $U_a \setminus \{0\}$ where $U_a = \{u \in \mathbb{F}_2^n | u \preccurlyeq a\}$ with $wt(a) = p$. Let $p + t = n - k$ with $2 \leq k \leq n - 2$. Then the upper bound on nonlinearity of f is given by,*

$$\mathcal{N}_f \leq 2^{n-1} - \ell \, 2^{t+1+\lfloor \frac{n-t-2}{d} \rfloor}, \tag{6}$$

where ℓ is the minimum integer among all positive integers i satisfying

$$i^2 \sum_{j=1}^{k} \binom{t+k}{t+j} \geq 2^{p+2k-4-2\lfloor \frac{n-t-2}{d} \rfloor}. \tag{7}$$

This is especially true when f satisfies PC(p).

Proof: From Lemma 1, since $\mathcal{F}(D_u f) = 0$ for any nonzero $u \in U_a$, we have:

$$\sum_{v \in U_a} \mathcal{F}^2(f + \varphi_v) = 2^{n-p} \mathcal{F}(D_0 f) = 2^{2n-p}, \tag{8}$$

On the other hand we know that, as any t-resilient function, f satisfies for all α: $\mathcal{F}(f + \varphi_\alpha) \equiv 0 \pmod{2^{t+2+\epsilon}}$, where $\epsilon = \lfloor \frac{n-t-2}{d} \rfloor$ (see (2)). Combining this result with (8), we conclude that for any $v \in U_a^\perp$ there is an integer i such that $0 \leq i^2 \leq 2^{p+2k-4-2\epsilon}$ and $\mathcal{F}^2(f + \varphi_v) = i^2 2^{2(t+2+\epsilon)}$.

Remark that $2n - p - 2(t+2+\epsilon) = p + 2k - 4 - 2\epsilon$, since $p + t = n - k$, providing the upper bound on i^2. Moreover, the equality (8) implies $p + 2k - 4 - 2\epsilon \geq 0$. Now we set for any i:

$$\lambda_i = \text{card} \left\{ v \in U_a^\perp : |\mathcal{F}(f + \varphi_v)| = i 2^{t+2+\epsilon} \right\} .$$

Then we may rewrite (8) in terms of λ_i. We obtain (where $c = 2^{p+2k-4-2\epsilon}$):

$$\sum_{i=1}^{c} \lambda_i i^2 2^{2t+4+2\epsilon} = 2^{2n-p} , \quad i.e., \quad \sum_{i=1}^{c} \lambda_i i^2 = 2^{p+2k-4-2\epsilon},$$

On the other hand, we consider the number Λ of nonzero coefficients $\mathcal{F}(f + \varphi_v)$ when v describes $U_a^\perp$. Since f is t-resilient, then $\Lambda \leq \sum_{j=1}^{k} \binom{t+k}{t+j}$. Thus we claim that from a certain positive value of i, say for all $i \geq i_0$, we have :

$$\sum_{j=1}^{c} \lambda_j j^2 \leq \Lambda i^2 \leq i^2 \sum_{j=1}^{k} \binom{t+k}{t+j} . \tag{9}$$

Therefore, we can define ℓ as the smallest integer such that $2^{p+2k-4-2\epsilon} \leq \ell^2 \sum_{j=1}^{k} \binom{t+k}{t+j}$. Moreover we are sure that there is some $v \in U_a^\perp$ such that $|\mathcal{F}(f + \varphi_v)| \geq \ell\, 2^{t+2+\epsilon}$, because if this is not true then we can define $i < \ell$ such that $|\mathcal{F}(f + \varphi_v)| \leq i 2^{t+2+\epsilon}$ for all v ; such i satisfies (9) contradicting the assumption. Thus we have proved that the maximal absolute value of the coefficients $\mathcal{F}(f + \varphi_v)$ is at least $\ell\, 2^{t+2+\epsilon}$ or, equivalently, that $\mathcal{N}_f$ satisfies (6).
□

According to the previous theorem, it is easy to see that for a fixed order of resiliency the upper bound on nonlinearity becomes smaller as p increases. Note that the lower bound (4), which has concern with propagation criterion only, increases with p. The next example clearly indicate the trade-off between the nonlinearity and propagation. Another illustration is the following corollary, directly deduced from Theorem 3 (for $k = 2$).

Corollary 1 *Let f be a Boolean function in $\mathcal{B}_n$ of degree d satisfying the hypothesis of Theorem 3. Furthermore, let $p + t = n - 2$, $p > 0$. Then the upper bound on nonlinearity is given by, $\mathcal{N}_f \leq 2^{n-1} - \ell\, 2^{t+1+\lfloor \frac{p}{d} \rfloor}$, where ℓ is the minimum integer among all positive integers i satisfying*

$$i^2(t+3) \geq 2^{p-2\lfloor \frac{p}{d} \rfloor}. \tag{10}$$

Example 1 Let f be a 4-resilient function in $\mathcal{B}_{10}$. Assume there is $a \in \mathbb{F}_2^{10}$ of weight $wt(a) = 3$ such that $D_u f$ is balanced for any nonzero $u \preccurlyeq a$, i.e., $t = 4$

and $p = 3$ in Theorem 3. We suppose that the degree d of f is such that $\epsilon = 0$; for instance $d = 5$.

We have $p + t = 7$ and $k = 3$. Thus ℓ is the smallest integer i satisfying $i^2 \sum_{j=1}^{3} \binom{7}{4+j} \geq 32$; so $\ell = 2$. Then the nonlinearity of f is less than or equal to $2^{n-1} - 2 \cdot 2^{t+1} = 448$, for $n = 10, t = 4, p = 3$. We conclude that $\mathcal{N}_f \leq 448$, while the upper bound (3) gives $\mathcal{N}_f \leq 480$. Such a function, with these parameters, was firstly constructed in [11].

4   On Functions with(out) Linear Structure

To construct effectively functions with high resiliency remains an important open problem. However, high resiliency could imply some property which leads to some cryptographic weakness. This section is devoted to the existence of linear structures. We propose some general tools characterizing linear structures; then we can show that high resiliency provides linear structures. Recall that an attack on block ciphers, based on the existence of linear structures, was proposed by Evertse [8].

4.1   On Distance to Linear Structures

In [10], the propagation criterion was defined as the *nonlinearity* of f with respect to a linear structure. Since this criterion is invariant under the general affine group, it was considered as a *useful criterion*. It allows us to quantify the distance of f to any linear structure as we explain briefly.

Definition 4 *Let $LS(n)$ denote the subset of Boolean functions having linear structures:*

$$LS(n) = \{ \, g \in \mathcal{B}_n \mid \exists \, a \text{ such that } D_a g \in \{0,1\} \, \}.$$

The nonlinearity of f with respect to the functions with linear structures is defined as,

$$\sigma(f) = \min_{g \in LS(n)} wt(f + g) \ .$$

Note that $LS(n)$ properly contains the set of all affine functions. Moreover, it contains quadratic functions which are not bent. Thus, this kind of nonlinearity is much stronger than the usual nonlinearity. In [10], it was also proved that $\sigma(f) \leq 2^{n-2}$ for $f \in \mathcal{B}_n$ with equality if and only if f is bent. More precisely, *the minimum distance of f to the set of the functions which have a linear structure a is less than or equal to 2^{n-2} with equality if and only if $D_a f$ is balanced.*

4.2   Criteria for Linear Structure

A priori, there is no criteria to decide upon whether a Boolean function has a linear structure except of checking for all possible linear structures. However, as we will show, this problem for any function f, is strongly related with some properties of its Walsh-spectrum.

Lemma 3 *Let f be a Boolean function in $\mathcal{B}_n$. Then f has a linear structure, say a, if and only if either the hyperplane $\{0,a\}^\perp$ (if $D_a f = 1$) or its complement (if $D_a f = 0$) is contained in the set*

$$Z_f = \{\alpha \mid \mathcal{F}(f + \varphi_\alpha) = 0\} \ . \tag{11}$$

In particular, if the cardinality of Z_f does not exceed $2^{n-1} - 1$ then f has no linear structure.

Proof: For any $a \neq 0$ we consider the hyperplane $H = \{0,a\}^\perp$; then we can write (1) as follows:

$$\sum_{u \in H} \mathcal{F}^2(f + \varphi_u) = 2^{n-1}(\mathcal{F}(D_0 f) + \mathcal{F}(D_a f)) = 2^{2n-1} + 2^{n-1}\mathcal{F}(D_a f) \ . \tag{12}$$

Note that a is a linear structure of f if and only if either $\mathcal{F}(D_a f)) = 2^n$ (when $D_a f = 0$) or $\mathcal{F}(D_a f)) = -2^n$ (when $D_a f = 1$). We deduce from (12) that $D_a f = 1$ if and only if $\mathcal{F}(f + \varphi_u) = 0$ for all u in H ; on the other hand, $D_a f = 0$ if and only if $\sum_{u \in H} \mathcal{F}^2(f + \varphi_u) = 2^{2n}$. But this last property means $\sum_{u \in \mathbb{F}_2^n \setminus H} \mathcal{F}^2(f + \varphi_u) = 0$, because of Parseval's relation. So we have proved that $D_a f$ is constant if and only if the set Z_f contains either H or $\mathbb{F}_2^n \setminus H$. Therefore, the cardinality of Z_f must be at least 2^{n-1} when f has a linear structure, completing the proof.

$\square$

Note that any t-resilient function $f \in \mathcal{B}_n$, with $t \geq \lfloor \frac{n}{2} \rfloor$, is such that the number of zero values in its Walsh spectrum is greater than or equal to 2^{n-1}. Thus, for such a function, we cannot apply the previous lemma. An important consequence is that the design rule for $t < \frac{n}{2}$ may be formulated as: *Construct a Boolean function $f \in \mathcal{B}_n$ by selecting an optimum choice of the design parameters of concern (nonlinearity, order of resiliency, PC degree) such that its Walsh spectrum contains less than 2^{n-1} zeros.* Now the previous lemma yields a more practical condition.

Theorem 4 *Let $f \in \mathcal{B}_n$. Then $D_a f \neq 0$ for any nonzero a if and only if f satisfies $S(f)$: there exists a basis $(e_1, \ldots, e_n)$ of $\mathbb{F}_2^n$ such that $\mathcal{F}(f + \varphi_{e_i}) \neq 0$, $1 \leq i \leq n$. Moreover*

(i) *when f is not balanced, f has no linear structure if and only if the condition $S(f)$ is satisfied;*

(ii) *when f is balanced, f has no linear structure if and only if there is $e \neq 0$ in $\mathbb{F}_2^n$ such that the function $g = f + \varphi_e$ is not balanced and the condition $S(g)$ is satisfied.*

Proof: We assume that f is neither affine nor constant. In accordance with Lemma 3, $D_a f = 0$ for some nonzero a if and only if Z_f contains the complement of the hyperplane $\{0, a\}^\perp$. Let

$$NZ_f = \{ \alpha \mid \mathcal{F}(f + \varphi_\alpha) \neq 0 \} \tag{13}$$

be the complement of Z_f in $\mathbb{F}_2^n$. Denote by $\overline{H}$ the complement of some hyperplane H. Clearly, Z_f contains $\overline{H}$ if and only if NZ_f is contained in H. More generally, Z_f contains the complement of some hyperplane if and only if the rank of the set NZ_f is at most $n-1$ (*i.e.*, $S(f)$ cannot be satisfied), completing the first part of the proof.

Now, when f is not balanced then $D_a f$ cannot be equal to 1 for some a. So "*f not balanced and $D_a f \neq 0$ for any nonzero a*" is equivalent to "*f has no linear structure*", completing the proof of (i). When f is balanced, there exists some function in the spectrum of f which is not balanced. Moreover to prove that f has no linear structure is equivalent to prove that $f + \varphi_e$ has no linear structure, for some e. When e is such that $g = f + \varphi_e$ is not balanced, g has no linear structure if and only if $S(g)$ is satisfied, as remarked above.

$\square$

Corollary 2 *Let $f \in \mathcal{B}_n$ be a t-resilient function of degree d. Then $\# NZ_f \leq 2^{2(n-t-\epsilon-2)}$, where NZ_f is defined by (13) and $\epsilon = \lfloor \frac{n-t-2}{d} \rfloor$. Moreover, for $n \geq 2^{2(n-t-\epsilon-2)}$, f admits a linear structure.*

Proof: By Parseval's equality and according to (2), we have: $2^{2n} = \sum_{v \in \mathbb{F}_2^n} \mathcal{F}^2(f + \varphi_v) = 2^{2(t+2+\epsilon)} \Lambda$, where clearly $\Lambda \geq \# NZ_f$. This implies $\# NZ_f \, 2^{2(t+2+\epsilon)} \leq 2^{2n}$ or, equivalently, $\# NZ_f \leq 2^{2(n-t-\epsilon-2)}$. This proves the first part of the corollary.

To prove the second part we notice that f is balanced but there always exists some $\alpha \neq 0$ such that $\mathcal{F}(f + \varphi_\alpha) \neq 0$. In accordance with Theorem 4, we need at least n other nonzero elements, say $(e_1, \ldots, e_n)$, such that $\mathcal{F}(f + \varphi_{\alpha+e_i}) \neq 0$, for any i. But this is impossible when $n + 1 > \# NZ_f$, completing the proof.

$\square$

The previous corollary implies that for certain fixed values of the parameters n, d and t, it is impossible to construct a resilient function without linear structure. As an illustration, set $t = n - 5$ and $d = 3$ in Corollary 2. Then $\epsilon = 1$ and $2^{2(n-t-\epsilon-2)} = 2^4 = 16$. We can conclude as follows.

Corollary 3 *For $n \geq 16$, any $(n-5)$-resilient function $f \in \mathcal{B}_n$ which is of degree 3 has a linear structure.*

We conclude this section by giving a simple algorithm for checking that a function has no derivative equal to the constant function 1.

Proposition 2 *Let $f \in \mathcal{B}_n$. Suppose that there are u and v in $\mathbb{F}_2^n$ such that $u \neq v \neq 0$ and the four coefficients $\mathcal{F}(f)$, $\mathcal{F}(f + \varphi_u)$, $\mathcal{F}(f + \varphi_v)$ and $\mathcal{F}(f + \varphi_{u+v})$ are such that only one of them is zero. Then f has no linear structure a such that $D_a f = 1$.*

Proof: The sets Z_f and NZ_f are respectively defined by (11) and (13). We proved that $D_a f \neq 1$ for all a if and only if Z_f does not contain any hyperplane (see Lemma 3). Let H be any hyperplane and let $\overline{H}$ its coset. The intersection of H with any subspace $< u, v >$, $u \neq v \neq 0$, is either of dimension 2 or of dimension 1.

If $H \subset Z_f$ for some H, then $\mathcal{F}(f) = 0$ and $NZ_f \subset \overline{H}$. Thus, for any $u, v \in NZ_f$, $u+v \in Z_f$. We conclude that if a pair (u, v) satisfies the hypothesis, it is impossible to have $H \subset Z_f$ for any H.   □

5   Resilient Functions and Their Derivatives

In this section, we focus on the values of the auto-correlation function of $f \in \mathcal{B}_n$ when f is t-resilient. Actually we want to obtain some bounds for the absolute indicator $\mathcal{M}(f)$ (defined in § 2.1) of such a function. We first give a general property, whose proof is given in the Appendix.

Lemma 4 Let $f \in \mathcal{B}_n$, $n \geq 3$. Assume that the weight of f is even. Then

$$\mathcal{F}(D_a f) \equiv 0 \ (\mathrm{mod} \ 8) \quad \text{for any } a \in \mathbb{F}_2^n. \tag{14}$$

Remark 1 One might expect that an arbitrary t-resilient function satisfies the following congruence, $\mathcal{F}(D_a f) \equiv 0 \ (\mathrm{mod} \ 2^{t+3})$. This congruence holds for $t = 0$, but we easily found a 1-resilient function f such that $\mathcal{F}(D_a f) \equiv 0 \ (\mathrm{mod} \ 16)$ is not true for some a (by computer).

Next we investigate how the divisibility of derivatives is related to the resiliency order, PC degree, and algebraic degree.

Theorem 5 Let $f \in \mathcal{B}_n$ be a t-resilient function of degree d satisfying $PC(p)$. Set $\epsilon = \lfloor \frac{n-t-2}{d} \rfloor$. Then for $p, t \geq 0$ and for any $a \in \mathbb{F}_2^n$ we have:

$$\mathcal{F}(D_a f) \equiv 0 \quad (\mathrm{mod} \ 2^{2t+p+2\epsilon+5-n}) . \tag{15}$$

This property is significant for $2t + p + 2\epsilon + 2 > n$ only.

Proof: Let $a \in \mathbb{F}_2^n$ such that $wt(a) = p + 1$. Let $U_a = \{v \in \mathbb{F}_2^n \mid v \preccurlyeq a\}$ and $\overline{a} = (1 + a_1, \ldots, 1 + a_n)$. Then, since f satisfies $PC(p)$, we can write (1) (setting $\beta = 0$ and $V^\perp = U_a$) in the following form:

$$\sum_{\alpha \preccurlyeq \overline{a}} \mathcal{F}^2(f + \varphi_\alpha) = 2^{n-(p+1)}(2^n + \mathcal{F}(D_a f)),$$

where $\mathcal{F}^2(f + \varphi_\alpha) \equiv 0 \ (\mathrm{mod} \ 2^{2(t+2+\epsilon)})$ because f is t-resilient (see (2)). Since $|\mathcal{F}(D_a f)| \leq 2^n$, it is easily verified that $\mathcal{F}(D_a f)$ is congruent to 0 modulo $2^{2t+p+2\epsilon+5-n}$. Thus, we have proved that (15) holds for any a such that $wt(a) = p + 1$. Now, we proceed by induction on the weight of a. Assuming that (15) holds for $wt(a) \leq p + s - 1$, $s \geq 2$ we rewrite (1) for $wt(a) = p + s$:

$$\sum_{\alpha \preccurlyeq \overline{a}} \mathcal{F}^2(f + \varphi_\alpha) = 2^{n-(p+s)}(2^n + \sum_{u \preccurlyeq a, \ wt(u) \geq p+1} \mathcal{F}(D_u f)) . \tag{16}$$

For convenience, let $\rho = 2t + p + 2\epsilon + 5 - n$. The sum on the left is congruent to 0 modulo $2^{2(t+2+\epsilon)}$. In the sum on the right, all $\mathcal{F}(D_u f)$ are known to be congruent to 0 modulo 2^ρ (by induction hypothesis) unless $u = a$. Hence the formula (16) has the following form: $2^{2(t+2+\epsilon)}\lambda = 2^{n-(p+s)}(2^\rho \lambda' + \mathcal{F}(D_a f))$, for some integers λ and λ'. This leads to: $\mathcal{F}(D_a f) = 2^{2(t+2+\epsilon)-n+p+s}\lambda - 2^\rho \lambda' = 2^{\rho+s-1}\lambda - 2^\rho \lambda'$, since $\rho = 2(t + 2 + \epsilon) - n + p + 1$. Then we deduce that $\mathcal{F}(D_a f)$ is congruent to 0 modulo 2^ρ and conclude that this property holds for any a. Thus $\mathcal{F}(D_a f)$ is of the form $\pm 2^\rho \lambda$, for some integer $\lambda \geq 0$. Due to Lemma 4, this property is significant for $2t + p + 2\epsilon + 5 - n > 3$, completing the proof.

$\square$

Remark 2 The first consequence of Theorem 5 is that for high order of resiliency the autocorrelation properties becomes rather poor. We proved actually that the indicators related with the propagation criterion satisfy here: $\mathcal{M}(f) \geq 2^\rho$ and $\mathcal{V}(f) \geq 2^{2m} + 2^{2\rho} \times \mu$, where $\rho = 2t + p + 2\epsilon + 5 - n$ and μ denotes the number of $a \neq 0$ such that $\mathcal{F}(D_a f) \neq 0$.

Note that for fixed p and t the divisibility of derivatives depends entirely on algebraic degree d via $\epsilon = \lfloor \frac{n-t-2}{d} \rfloor$. Hence the overall good cryptographic properties are exhibited only by functions of high algebraic degree. Furthermore, the congruence relation above clearly indicates that the size of derivatives is more sensitive to the changes of resiliency order t, than to the changes of p.

Now, we want to illustrate that *due to the previous result a large class of resilient functions cannot be used in the design of Boolean functions having good propagation properties.*

Example 2 With notation of Theorem 5, take $n = 11$ and $t = 3$. Then $d \leq 7$ and $\epsilon = \lfloor \frac{6}{d} \rfloor$. For any $a \in \mathbb{F}_2^{11}$, $\mathcal{F}(D_a f) \equiv 0 \pmod{2^\rho}$, where $\rho = 2t+p+2\epsilon+5-n$. If $d = 3$ then $\epsilon = 2$. Applying Theorem 5, we obtain respectively for $p = 0, 1, \ldots, 6$ the values $\rho = 4, 5, \ldots, 10$.
If $3 < d \leq 6$ then $\epsilon = 1$. We obtain respectively for $p = 0, 1, \ldots, 6$ the values $\rho = 2, 3, \ldots, 8$. Note that by Lemma 4 the results for $p = 0, 1$, are not significant.

Corollary 4 *Let $f \in \mathcal{B}_n$ be a t-resilient function of degree 3. Assume that $t = n - 4$. Then the derivatives of f satisfy: $\mathcal{F}(D_a f) \equiv 0 \pmod{2^{n-3}}$ for any $a \in \mathbb{F}_2^n$.*
    Moreover, if f satisfies PC(1), then $\mathcal{F}(D_a f) \equiv 0 \pmod{2^{n-2}}$ for any a.

Proof: Due to the Siegenthaler's upper bound, $d \leq 3$ for $t = n - 4$. By setting $t = n - 4$, $p = 0$ and $d = 3$ in Theorem 5, we have $\epsilon = 0$ and then $2t + p + 2\epsilon + 5 - n = n - 3$.
If f satisfies PC(1) then $2t + p + 2\epsilon + 5 - n = n - 2$.

$\square$

Note that for $p + t = n - 2$, the result of Theorem 5 is significant for any $t \geq 0$. Taking a such that $wt(a) = p + 1$, we have $wt(\bar{a}) = t + 1$. So (1) gives here:

$$\sum_{\alpha \preceq \bar{a}} \mathcal{F}^2(f + \varphi_\alpha) = \mathcal{F}^2(f + \varphi_{\bar{a}}) = 2^{n-(p+1)}(2^n + \mathcal{F}(D_a f)) .$$

Hence $\mathcal{F}^2(f + \varphi_{\overline{a}}) = 0$ if and only if $\mathcal{F}(D_a f) = -2^n$, i.e., a is a linear structure of f with $D_a f = 1$.

Corollary 5 *Let $f \in \mathcal{B}_n$ satisfying the hypothesis of Theorem 5, with $p + t = n - 2$. Then*

- *for any a: $\mathcal{F}(D_a f) \equiv 0 \pmod{2^{t+3+2\lfloor \frac{p}{2} \rfloor}}$;*
- *for any a such that $wt(a) = p + 1$: $\mathcal{F}^2(f + \varphi_{\overline{a}}) = 0$ if and only if $D_a f = 1$.*

The proof of the next corollary is given in the Appendix.

Corollary 6 *Let $f \in \mathcal{B}_n$, $f(x_1, \ldots, x_n) = (1 + x_n)f_1(x_1, \ldots, x_{n-1}) + x_n f_2(x_1, \ldots, x_{n-1})$, where f_1, f_2 in $\mathcal{B}_{n-1}$. Assume that f is t-resilient and satisfies $PC(p)$ with $p = n - t - 2$.*
Then for any $\beta \in \mathbb{F}_2^{n-1}$ such that $wt(\beta) = t$ and $\mathcal{F}(f_1 + \varphi_\beta) = \mathcal{F}(f_2 + \varphi_\beta)$, $(\beta, 1)$ is a linear structure of f. Furthermore, if both f_1 and f_2 are t-resilient, then f is affine or constant.

6   The Main Classes of Resilient Functions

6.1   Linear Concatenation

The class of t-resilient functions, described by the next theorem, is actually a subclass of the Maiorana-McFarland class. It provides one of a few designs that guarantees a moderate value of nonlinearity for a given order of resiliency. We first need to introduce some notation. Let us denote by L_k the set of all linear functions on $\mathbb{F}_2^k$; note that $\#L_k = 2^k$. We define for any $0 \le t < k$:

$$L_k^t = \{\, \varphi_c(x) = c \cdot x \mid c \in \mathbb{F}_2^k, wt(c) > t \,\}. \tag{17}$$

The cardinality of L_k^t is equal to $\sum_{i=0}^{k-(t+1)} \binom{k}{t+1+i}$. For fixed integers t and n, $0 \le t < n$, we define

$$\mathbf{k} = \min_{t < k} \left\{ k \mid \sum_{i=0}^{k-(t+1)} \binom{k}{t+1+i} \ge 2^{n-k} \right\}. \tag{18}$$

Theorem 6 [7] *For any $0 \le t < n$, let $\mathbf{k}$ be defined by (18) and $L_{\mathbf{k}}^t$ by (17). Let us choose $2^{n-\mathbf{k}}$ linear functions in $L_{\mathbf{k}}^t$, each being labelled by an element of $\mathbb{F}_2^{n-\mathbf{k}}$ as follows:*

$$\tau \in \mathbb{F}_2^{n-\mathbf{k}} \quad \longleftrightarrow \quad \ell_{[\tau]} \in L_{\mathbf{k}}^t, \text{ where } [\tau] = \sum_{i=0}^{n-\mathbf{k}-1} \tau_i 2^i.$$

Then the Boolean function defined for all $(y, x) \in \mathbb{F}_2^{n-\mathbf{k}} \times \mathbb{F}_2^{\mathbf{k}}$ by

$$f(y, x) = \sum_{\tau \in \mathbb{F}_2^{\mathbf{k}}} (y_1 + \tau_1 + 1) \cdots (y_{n-\mathbf{k}} + \tau_{n-\mathbf{k}} + 1)\ell_{[\tau]}(x), \tag{19}$$

is a t-resilient function with nonlinearity $\mathcal{N}_f = 2^{n-1} - 2^{k-1}$. In general $\deg(f) \leq n - k + 1$ with equality if there exists a variable x_i, $i = 1, \ldots, k$, which occurs an odd number of times in $\ell_{[\tau]}(x)$ when τ runs through $\mathbb{F}_2^{n-k}$.

The proof of this theorem is due to Chee et al. [7]. Note that the linear functions $\ell_{[\tau]}$ in (19) are two-by-two distinct, and that, obviously, $k > n/2$. Any resilient function defined above has a simple algebraic structure, since it can be viewed as a concatenation of the linear functions $\ell_{[\tau]}$: for any fixed value of y, we get $f(y, x) = \ell_{[\tau]}(x)$, where $\tau = y$. Moreover it is easy to characterize the zeros of its Walsh-spectrum and its propagation characteristics (see the next Lemma whose proof is given in the Appendix). On the one hand, these properties can be considered as a weakness. However it allows us to define precisely the cryptographic properties. We will show that a well-chosen set of functions $\ell_{[\tau]}$ insures that such a function has no linear structure.

Lemma 5 *Let f be a function in $\mathcal{B}_n$ constructed by means of Theorem 6; let (α, β) be any element in $\mathbb{F}_2^{n-k} \times \mathbb{F}_2^k$. Then f satisfies:*

(i) $\mathcal{F}(f + \varphi_{(\alpha,\beta)}) = \pm 2^k$ *if and only if $\varphi_{(\alpha,\beta)} = \sum_{i=1}^{n-k} \alpha_i y_i + \ell_{[\tau]}(x)$ for some τ. Otherwise $f + \varphi_{(\alpha,\beta)}$ is balanced.*

(ii) $D_{(\alpha,\beta)}f$ *is balanced if and only if $\alpha \neq 0$ or $\alpha = 0$ and $D_\beta \ell_{[\tau]} = 0$ for 2^{n-k-1} values of τ exactly. Moreover $\mathcal{F}(D_{(0,\beta)}) \equiv 0 \pmod{2^k}$.*

(iii) (α, β) *is a linear structure of f if and only if $\alpha = 0$ and $\ell_{[\tau]}(\beta) = c$ for all τ, where $c \in \mathbb{F}_2$.*

Remark 3 The functions defined by means of Theorem 6 are said to be three-valued, since their Fourier-spectrum has three values only, i.e., 0 and $\pm 2^k$. They are also called three-valued almost optimal when $k = (n + 1)/2$ for odd n or $k = (n + 2)/2$ for even n; in this case, the nonlinearity is maximal (for three-valued functions). Concerning the propagation characteristics, the value of the sum-of-squares indicator is known: $\mathcal{V}(f) = 2^n \mathcal{L}^2(f) = 2^{n+2k}$. The value of the absolute indicator depends on the choice of the functions $\ell_{[\tau]}$. More about this kind of functions can be found in [2,3].

So, it turns out that the choice of the set $\{\ell_0, \ldots, \ell_{2^n-k}\}$ is crucial for propagation characteristics, especially if we want to construct resilient functions without linear structure. For clarity, we begin by giving a small example. By the next proposition, we indicate how this set can be chosen.

Example 3 Let $n = 5$ and $t = 0$. Thus $\sum_{i=0}^{k-1} \binom{k}{1+i} = 2^k - 1$ and we have to choose the smallest k such that $2^k - 1 \geq 2^{5-k}$. Clearly $k = 3$ and we have to select $S = \{\ell_0, \ldots, \ell_4\}$, four linear functions from the set L_3^0. Note that $\#L_3^0 = 7$.

We first choose $S = \{x_1, x_2, x_3, x_1 + x_2 + x_3\}$. Then the function

$$f(y, x) = \sum_{\tau \in \mathbb{F}_2^2} (y_1 + \tau_1 + 1)(y_2 + \tau_2 + 1)\ell_{[\tau]}(x)$$

is a balanced function with $\mathcal{N}_f = 12$ – according to Theorem 6. But $(0,0,1,1,1)$ is a linear structure of f, since $\ell_i(1,1,1) = 1$ for all i, $i = 0,\ldots,3$. Now we take $S = \{x_1 + x_2, x_1 + x_3, x_2 + x_3, x_1 + x_2 + x_3\}$. It is easy to check that in this case we cannot have: $\ell_i(\beta) = c$ for all i, $0 \le i \le 3$, and for any $\beta \in \mathbb{F}_2^3$ (where c is a binary constant). Thus, f has no linear structure. Furthermore, since the linear functions ℓ_i are of weight greater than one, f is 1-resilient with $\mathcal{N}_f = 12$.

Notice that the set L_k^t defined by (17) has always rank k. Indeed, since $k > t + 1$, at least the all-one vector and the k vectors of weight $(k-1)$ are in L_k^t. By adding the all-one vector to each vector of weight $(k-1)$ we obtain the standard basis.

Proposition 3 *Let f be a function in $\mathcal{B}_n$ constructed by means of Theorem 6; so $\mathbf{k}$ and t are fixed (and $\mathbf{k} > t+1$). Let us denote by S the set of the $2^{n-\mathbf{k}}$ linear functions $\ell_{[\tau]}$ which have to be chosen in $L_{\mathbf{k}}^t$. Then, there is at least one choice S such that f has no linear structure if and only if $\mathbf{k} < 2^{n-\mathbf{k}}$. In this case, S can be chosen as follows:*
— $\ell_0(x) = \lambda \cdot x$, where λ is the all-one vector;
— for every i, $1 \le i \le \mathbf{k}$, $\ell_i(x) = (\lambda + e_i) \cdot x$ where $e_i = (0,\ldots,0,\overset{i}{1},0,\ldots,0)$, i.e., $(e_1,\ldots,e_{\mathbf{k}})$ is the standard basis;
— $(\ell_{\mathbf{k}+1},\ldots,\ell_{2^n \mathbf{k}-1})$ are some other elements of $L_{\mathbf{k}}^t$.

Proof: It is a direct application of Theorem 4, **(ii)**. Indeed f is balanced and here we know exactly the nonzero coefficients of the Fourier-spectrum of f. So f has no linear structure if and only if we can construct one S such that the corresponding function f satisfies the hypothesis of this theorem. From Lemma 5, we know that $f + \varphi_{(\alpha,\beta)}$ is not balanced if and only if the function $\beta \cdot x$ is in S. Now we proceed as it is indicated in the proposition, and we have:

- $\ell_0 = \lambda \cdot x$ with $wt(\lambda) = \mathbf{k}$;
- so for any basis of $\mathbb{F}_2^{n-\mathbf{k}}$, say $(\alpha_1,\ldots,\alpha_{n-\mathbf{k}})$, the functions $f + \varphi_{(\alpha_j,\lambda)}$ are not balanced ;
- set $\ell_i(x) = \lambda \cdot x + e_i \cdot x$, $1 \le i \le \mathbf{k}$ (note that $wt(\lambda + e_i) = \mathbf{k} - 1$); complete the set S with any other functions in $L_{\mathbf{k}}^t$.

Now f is fully defined and we can check that, according to Theorem 4, it has no linear structure. Set $g = f + \varphi_{(0,\lambda)}$; so g is not balanced. Our construction is such that there is a basis of $\mathbb{F}_2^{n-\mathbf{k}} \times \mathbb{F}_2^{\mathbf{k}}$, $(\alpha_1,0),\ldots,(\alpha_{n-\mathbf{k}},0),(0,e_1),\ldots,(0,e_{\mathbf{k}})$, such that the functions $g + \varphi_{(\alpha_j,0)}$ and $g + \varphi_{(0,e_i)}$, which are respectively the functions $f + \varphi_{(\alpha_j,\lambda)}$ and $f + \varphi_{(0,\lambda+e_i)}$, are not balanced. Applying Theorem 4, f has no linear structure.

Since the rank of $L_{\mathbf{k}}^t$ is always equal to $\mathbf{k}$, such a construction is possible if and only if the cardinality of S is strictly greater than $\mathbf{k}$, i.e., $\mathbf{k} < 2^{n-\mathbf{k}}$.
□

Example 4 Let $n = 9$. For $t = 4$, we obtain $\mathbf{k} = 7$ (see (18)). But, in this case, $2^{n-\mathbf{k}} = 4$, implying that f has always a linear structure.

Now for $t = 3$, we obtain $\mathbf{k} = 6$ with $2^{n-\mathbf{k}} = 8$. So we can choose $S = \{\ell_0, \ldots, \ell_8\}$ in L_6^3, the set of linear functions $x \mapsto \beta \cdot x$ such that $\beta \in \mathbb{F}_2^6$ and $wt(\beta) \geq 4$, in such a manner that f has no linear structure. According to the previous proposition, $\ell_0(x) = x_1 + x_2 + x_3 + x_4 + x_5 + x_6$, and $\ell_i(x) = \ell_0(x) + x_i$, $1 \leq i \leq 6$. We can choose ℓ_7 to be any other function from L_6^3.

Corollary 7 *For any odd* $\mathbf{k} \geq 3$ *it is possible to construct a* $\lfloor \mathbf{k}/2 \rfloor$-*resilient Boolean function* f *of* $n = 2\mathbf{k} - 1$ *variables of degree* $\mathbf{k}$ *without linear structure and with nonlinearity* $\mathcal{N}_f = 2^{n-1} - 2^{\frac{n-1}{2}}$.

Proof: Since $\mathbf{k}$ is odd it is well-known that $\sum_{i=\lfloor \mathbf{k}/2 \rfloor+1}^{\mathbf{k}} \binom{\mathbf{k}}{i} = 2^{\mathbf{k}-1}$. Thus, by choosing $t = \lfloor \mathbf{k}/2 \rfloor$ the cardinality of $L_{\mathbf{k}}^t$ is $2^{\mathbf{k}-1}$. Thus, we can construct a t-resilient function f in $n = 2\mathbf{k} - 1$ variables, with $\mathcal{N}_f = 2^{n-1} - 2^{\frac{n-1}{2}}$. Also, $deg(f) = n - \mathbf{k} + 1 = \mathbf{k}$ since each variable x_i, $i = 1, \ldots, \mathbf{k}$ occurs an odd number of times in $L_{\mathbf{k}}^t$. By Proposition 3, f is without linear structure.

$\square$

Example 5 Let us construct f by means of Corollary 7 for $\mathbf{k} = 5$. So we take $t = \lfloor \mathbf{k}/2 \rfloor = 2$. Since $\sum_{i=0}^{2} \binom{5}{3+i} = 2^4$, $\#L_5^2 = 2^4$, and we must take all sixteen linear functions from L_5^2 to construct f. By Corollary 7, f is a 2-resilient function with nonlinearity $\mathcal{N}_f = 2^{n-1} - 2^{\mathbf{k}-1} = 240$, and without linear structure. Furthermore, the degree of f is 5.

6.2   Linear Structures in Recursive Constructions of Optimal Resilient Functions

We are going to discuss two recursive constructions of resilient functions given respectively in [16] and [11]. The main interest of these constructions is that they provide *optimal* functions, in the sense that they have the best nonlinearity with respect to the upper bound [4]. Both constructions are based on a concatenation of resilient functions with high nonlinearity. We will prove that the first construction leads to functions with linear structure while the second construction allows to avoid linear structures.

In this section, we assume that for any t-resilient function in $\mathcal{B}_n$, t satisfies $t \geq \frac{n}{2} - 2$. For this range of t the upper bound on nonlinearity is $\mathcal{N}_f \leq 2^{n-1} - 2^{t+1}$. This bound is achieved by the functions meeting the Siegenthaler's bound. Since we focus here on the existence of linear structure, we give the iterative formula proposed in [16] and indicate the nonlinearity without more explanations. By Proposition 5 (see the proof in the Appendix), we claim that such a construction in which each f_i appears several times in the concatenation, provides functions with linear space.

Proposition 4 [16] *Assume that* $f_0(x), \ldots, f_{2^k-1}(x)$ *are all* t-*resilient functions in* $\mathcal{B}_m$. *Let* (y, z) *in* $\mathbb{F}_2^k \times \mathbb{F}_2^s$, *where* $k \geq s$. *Then the function* f *defined by*

$$f(x, y, z) = \left(\sum_{\tau \in \mathbb{F}_2^k} \left(\prod_{i=1}^{s}(y_i + z_i + \tau_i) \right) \left(\prod_{i=s+1}^{k} (y_i + \tau_i) \right) f_{[\tau]}(x) \right) + \sum_{i=1}^{s} z_i, \quad (20)$$

is an $(t + s)$-resilient function on $\mathbb{F}_2^{m+k+s}$ (where the label $[\tau]$ is computed as in Theorem 6). Furthermore, if the nonlinearity of $f_0, \ldots, f_{2^k-1}$ is at least ν_0 and the functions $f_{[\tau]}$ satisfy certain properties (see [16]) then $\mathcal{N}_f \geq 2^s(2^{n-1}(2^k - 1) + \nu_0)$.

Proposition 5 Let $f \in \mathcal{B}_{m+k+s}$ be a function constructed by means of Proposition 4. Then the subspace $\{ (\alpha, \beta, \gamma) \in \mathbb{F}_2^m \times \mathbb{F}_2^k \times \mathbb{F}_2^s \mid \alpha = 0, \beta = (\gamma_1, \ldots, \gamma_s, 0, \ldots, 0) \}$ is contained in the linear space of f. The linear space of f has dimension at least s.

By an $(n, t, d, \mathcal{N}_f)$ function we mean an n-variable, t-resilient function f with degree d and nonlinearity $\mathcal{N}_f$. The construction introduced in [11] is a recursive one and starts with a suitable input function f^0 of type $(n, t, d, \mathcal{N}_f)$, which is said to be in *desired form*.

Definition 5 An $(n, t, d, -)$ function f is in desired form if it is of the form $f = (1 + x_n)f_1 + x_n f_2$, where f_1, f_2 are $(n - 1, t, d - 1, -)$ functions.

An infinite sequence f^i of $(n + 3i, t + 2i, d + i, \mathcal{N}_{f^i} = 2^{n+3(i-1)+1} + 4\mathcal{N}_{f^{i-1}})$ functions is then obtained for $i \geq 1$. Furthermore, if $t \geq \frac{n}{2} - 2$ and $\mathcal{N}_{f^0} = 2^{n-1} - 2^{t+1}$ then any function in this sequence will be optimal in the sense that its nonlinearity attains the upper bound on nonlinearity (see [11] for more details). We next describe one step of the algorithm.

Proposition 6 [11] Let $f = (1 + x_n)f_1 + x_n f_2$ be an $(n, t, d, \mathcal{N}_f)$ function in desired form, where f_1, f_2 are both $(n - 1, t, d - 1, -)$ functions. Let the functions F and G on $\mathbb{F}_2^{n+2}$ be defined by,

$$F = x_{n+2} + x_{n+1} + f$$
$$G = (1 + x_{n+2} + x_{n+1})f_1 + (x_{n+2} + x_{n+1})f_2 + x_{n+2} + x_n. \qquad (21)$$

Then the function $H \in \mathcal{B}_{n+3}$, $H = (1 + x_{n+3})F + x_{n+3}G$ is an $(n + 3, t + 2, d + 1, 2^{n+1} + 4\mathcal{N}_f)$ function in desired form.

Proposition 7 Let $f = (1 + x_n)f_1 + x_n f_2$ be an $(n, t, d, \mathcal{N}_f)$ function in desired form. Assume that f has no linear structure. Then, the function H constructed by means of Proposition 6 has no linear structure.

Proof: Considering the restrictions of H to the hyperplane defined by $x_{n+3} = 0$ and to its coset, we note $H = (F, G)$. We will consider the restrictions of $D_\beta H$ to the same hyperplane and to its coset. When $\beta_{n+3} = 0$, then we look at $D_\beta H$ with $\beta = (a, 0)$, where $a = (\beta_1, \ldots, \beta_{n+2})$. But in this case $D_\beta H = (D_a F, D_a G)$. Thus $D_\beta H = c$, $c \in \{0, 1\}$, if and only if $D_a F = D_a G = c$.

The derivative of F is as follows, where $\beta' = (\beta_1, \ldots, \beta_n)$: $D_{(\beta', \beta_{n+1}, \beta_{n+2})}F = \beta_{n+1} + \beta_{n+2} + D_{\beta'} f$. Since f has no linear structure, the linear structures of F

are of the form $(0, \ldots, 0, \beta_{n+1}, \beta_{n+2})$. So we have to compute the derivatives of G with respect to $a = (0, \ldots, 0, \beta_{n+1}, \beta_{n+2})$:

$$D_a G = (\beta_{n+2} + \beta_{n+1})(f_1 + f_2) + \beta_{n+2} \ .$$

Since f has no linear structure, then $f_1 + f_2$ cannot be constant because $D_{(0,\ldots,0,1)}f = f_1 + f_2$. Therefore $D_a G = c$ if and only if $\beta_{n+2} = \beta_{n+1} = 1$ (since $a \neq 0$). But, in this case, $D_a G = 1$ and $D_a F = 0$; we conclude that $(a, 0)$ cannot be a linear structure of H.

When $\beta_{n+3} = 1$, we use the general formula

$$D_{(a,1)}H = D_{(a,0)}H + D_{(0,\ldots,0,1)}H + D_{(a,0)}D_{(0,\ldots,0,1)}H \ .$$

We obtain: $D_{(a,1)}H = (F(x) + G(x + a), F(x + a) + G(x))$. But the function $x \mapsto F(x) + G(x + a)$ cannot be constant. Indeed F is of degre d, where d is the degree of f. By definition of F and G (see (21)) it is clear that the terms of degree d in F cannot be canceled in the expression of type $F(x) + G(x + a)$. Thus, $D_{(a,1)}H$ is not constant completing the proof. $\qquad\square$

References

1. A. Canteaut and M. Trabbia, "Improved fast correlation attacks using parity-check equations of weight 4 and 5." In *Advances in Cryptology - EUROCRYPT 2000*, number 1807 in Lecture Notes in Computer Science, pp. 573–588, Springer-Verlag, 2000.
2. A. Canteaut, C. Carlet, P. Charpin, and C. Fontaine, "Propagation characteristics and correlation-immunity of highly nonlinear Boolean functions." In *Advances in Cryptology - EUROCRYPT 2000*, number 1807 in Lecture Notes in Computer Science, pp. 507–522, Springer-Verlag, 2000.
3. A. Canteaut, C. Carlet, P. Charpin, and C. Fontaine. "On cryptographic properties of the cosets of $R(1, m)$." *IEEE Trans. Inform. Theory*, 47(4):1494–1513, 2001.
4. C. Carlet, "On the coset weight divisibility and nonlinearity of resilient and correlation-immune functions." In *Sequences and their Applications - SETA '01*, Discrete Mathematics and Theoretical Computer Science, pp. 131–144. Springer-Verlag, 2001.
5. C. Carlet, "On cryptographic propagation criteria for Boolean functions." *Information and Computation*, number 151, pp. 32–56, 1999.
6. P. Charpin, and E. Pasalic, "On propagation characteristics of resilient functions." In *Research-report RR-4537*, INRIA, September 2002.
7. S. Chee, S. Lee, D. Lee, and S.H. Sung, "On the correlation immune functions and their nonlinearity." In *Advances in Cryptology - ASIACRYPT'96*, number 1163 in Lecture Notes in Computer Science, pp. 232–243, Springer-Verlag, 1996.
8. J. H. Evertse, "Linear structures in block ciphers." In *Advances in Cryptology - EUROCRYPT' 87*, number 304 in Lecture Notes in Computer Science, pp. 249–266, Springer Verlag, 1987.
9. M. Matsui, "Linear cryptanalysis method for DES cipher." In *Advances in Cryptology - EUROCRYPT'93*, number 765 in Lecture Notes in Computer Science, pp. 386–397, Springer-Verlag, 1993.

10. W. Meier, and O. Staffelbach., "Nonlinearity criteria for cryptographic functions." In *Advances in Cryptology - EUROCRYPT'93*, number 434 in Lecture Notes in Computer Science, pp. 549–562, Springer-Verlag, 1988.
11. E. Pasalic, T. Johansson, S. Maitra, and P. Sarkar., "New constructions of resilient and correlation immune Boolean functions achieving upper bounds on nonlinearity." In *Cryptology ePrint Archive, eprint.iacr.org, No. 2000/048*, September, 2000.
12. B. Preneel, W.V. Leekwijck, L.V. Linden, R. Govaerts, and J. Vandewalle, "Propagation characteristics of Boolean functions." In *Advances in Cryptology - EUROCRYPT'90*, number 437 in Lecture Notes in Computer Science, pp. 155–165, Springer-Verlag, 1990.
13. P. Sarkar and S. Maitra, "Nonlinearity bounds and constructions of resilient Boolean functions." In *Advances in Cryptology - EUROCRYPT 2000*, number 1807 in Lecture Notes in Computer Science, pp. 515-532, Springer-Verlag, 2000.
14. T. Siegenthaler, "Correlation-immunity of nonlinear combining functions for cryptographic applications." *IEEE Trans. Inform. Theory*, IT-30(5): 776-780, 1984.
15. Y. Tarannikov, "On resilient Boolean functions with maximal possible nonlinearity." In *Proceedings of Indocrypt 2000*, number 1977 in Lecture Notes in Computer Science, pp. 19–30 , Springer Verlag, 2000.
16. Y. V. Tarannikov, "New constructions of resilient Boolean functions with maximal nonlinearity." In *Fast Software Encryption - FSE 2001*, to be published in Lecture Notes in Computer Science, pp. 70–81 (in preproceedings). Springer Verlag, 2001.
17. A.F. Webster and S.E. Tavares, "On the design of S-boxes." In *Advances in Cryptology - CRYPTO'85*, number 219 in Lecture Notes in Computer Science, pp. 523–534, Springer-Verlag, 1985.
18. G. Xiao and J.L. Massey. "A spectral characterization of correlation-immune combining functions." *IEEE Trans. Inform. Theory*, IT-34(3):569–571, 1988.
19. X.-M. Zhang and Y. Zheng, "GAC - the criterion for global avalanche characterics of cryptographic functions." *Journal of Universal Computer Science*, vol. 1, no. 5, pp. 320–337, 1995.
20. X.-M. Zhang and Y. Zheng, "On relationship among avalanche, nonlinearity, and propagation criteria," In *Advances in Cryptology - Asiacrypt 2000*, number 1976 in Lecture Notes in Computer Science, pp. 470–483, Springer-Verlag, 2000.

Appendix

Proof of Lemma 4: Let a be any nonzero word in $\mathbb{F}_2^n$, and $D_a f(x) = f(x) + f(x+a)$. The Boolean functions $D_a f(x), f(x), (x+a)$ can be associated to codewords of length 2^n denoted respectively $D_a f, f, f_a$. Then we have,

$$wt(D_a f) = wt(f) + wt(f_a) - 2wt(f f_a).$$

We note that $wt(f) = wt(f_a)$ for any a since f_a can be seen as a permutation of f. Thus the equation above may be rewritten to yield $wt(D_a f) = 2wt(f) - 2wt(f f_a)$. Since by assumption f is of even weight it remains to prove that $wt(f f_a)$ is even. We note that $\alpha \in \mathbb{F}_2^n$ satisfies $f(x)f(x+a) = 1$ if and only if $\alpha+a$ satisfies it too. Thus we conclude that $wt(f f_a) \equiv 0 \pmod{2}$ and consequently $wt(D_a f) \equiv 0 \pmod{4}$. This completes the proof.

Proof of Lemma 5: **(i)** For every fixed value of y, we get

$$f(y,x) + \varphi_{(\alpha,\beta)}(y,x) = \ell_{[y]}(x) + \sum_{i=1}^{n-k} \alpha_i y_i + \sum_{i=1}^{k} \beta_i x_i \ .$$

This function is balanced unless $\beta \cdot x = \ell_{[y]}(x)$. When it is not balanced, it is constant and this happens for this value of y only. Indeed, assuming that it is constant for y, we know that $\ell_{[y']}(x) \neq \ell_{[y]}(x)$, for all $y' \neq y$, providing $\mathcal{F}(f + \varphi_{(\alpha,\beta)}) = \pm 2^k$.

(ii) We compute the derivative of f with respect to (α,β):

$$D_{(\alpha,\beta)}f = f(y,x) + f(y+\alpha, x+\beta) = \sum_{\tau \in \mathbb{F}_2^n \ k} (y_1 + \tau_1 + 1) \cdots (y_{n-k} + \tau_{n-k} + 1)\ell_{[\tau]}(x)$$

$$+ \sum_{\tau \in \mathbb{F}_2^n \ k} (y_1 + \tau_1 + \alpha_1 + 1) \cdots (y_{n-k} + \tau_{n-k} + \alpha_{n-k} + 1)\ell_{[\tau]}(x+\beta) =$$

$$\sum_{\tau \in \mathbb{F}_2^n \ k} (y_1 + \tau_1 + 1) \cdots (y_{n-k} + \tau_{n-k} + 1)(\ell_{[\tau]}(x) + \ell_{[\tau+\alpha]}(x+\beta)). \quad (22)$$

For any nonzero α, each sum $\ell_{[\tau]}(x) + \ell_{[\tau+\alpha]}(x+\beta)$ is a linear (affine) function for any β in $\mathbb{F}_2^k$ – since it is not constant by construction. So $D_{(\alpha,\beta)}f$ is balanced for any nonzero α. When $\alpha = 0$, (22) becomes,

$$D_{(0,\beta)}f(y,x) = \sum_{\tau \in \mathbb{F}_2^n \ k} (y_1 + \tau_1 + 1) \cdots (y_{n-k} + \tau_{n-k} + 1)\ell_{[\tau]}(\beta),$$

since $\ell_{[\tau]}(x+\beta) = \ell_{[\tau]}(x) + \ell_{[\tau]}(\beta)$. Thus $D_{(0,\beta)}f(y,x)$ is constant for any fixed y. We deduce: $\mathcal{F}(D_{(0,\beta)}f) = 2^k \times \sum_{\tau}(-1)^{\ell_{[\tau]}(\beta)}$.

We directly obtain **(iii)** from this last equality, since we have proved that (α,β) can be a linear structure when $\alpha = 0$ only.

Proof of Corollary 6 Every Boolean function f in $\mathcal{B}_n$ can be viewed as a concatenation of two functions from $\mathcal{B}_{n-1}$, called *subfunctions of f of dimension* $n - 1$. More precisely, f can be written as,

$$f(x_1, \ldots, x_n) = (1 + x_n)f_1(x_1, \ldots, x_{n-1}) + x_n f_2(x_1, \ldots, x_{n-1}),$$

for some f_1, f_2 in $\mathcal{B}_{n-1}$. Note that if f is t-resilient then either both f_1 and f_2 are $(t-1)$-resilient or both f_1 and f_2 are t-resilient.

Let β be a vector satisfying the condition above. The Walsh transform of f in the point $(1, \beta) \in \mathbb{F}_2^n$ is calculated as,

$$\mathcal{F}(f + \varphi_{(1,\beta)}) = \mathcal{F}(f_1 + \varphi_\beta) - \mathcal{F}(f_2 + \varphi_\beta). \quad (23)$$

Then, $\mathcal{F}(f + \varphi_{(1,\beta)}) = 0$ due to the assumption. Since the weight of $(1, \beta)$ is $t + 1$, by Corollary 5 f has a linear structure.

Assume now that f_1 and f_2 are t-resilient. Then for any $\beta \in \mathbb{F}_2^{n-1}$ such that $wt(\beta) = t$ we have $\mathcal{F}(f_1 + \varphi_\beta) = \mathcal{F}(f_2 + \varphi_\beta) = 0$. Applying Corollary 5, we conclude that, for all such β, $(1, \beta)$ belongs to the linear space of f. Then the subspace V, generated by all these elements in contained in the linear space of f. Since $0 \le t \le n-2$ the dimension of V is at least $n-1$, completing the proof.

Proof of Proposition 5: The derivative of f with respect to any direction $(0, \beta, \gamma)$ with $\beta = (\gamma_1, \dots, \gamma_s, 0, \dots, 0)$ is

$$D_{(0,\beta,\gamma)}f = f(x, y, z) + f(x, y + \beta, z + \gamma)$$

$$= \left(\sum_{\tau \in \mathbb{F}_2^k} \left(\prod_{i=1}^{s} (y_i + z_i + \tau_i) \right) \left(\prod_{i=s+1}^{k} (y_i + \tau_i) \right) f_{[\tau]}(x) \right) + \sum_{i=1}^{s} z_i$$

$$+ \left(\sum_{\tau \in \mathbb{F}_2^k} \left(\prod_{i=1}^{s} (y_i + \gamma_i + z_i + \gamma_i + \tau_i) \right) \left(\prod_{i=s+1}^{k} (y_i + \tau_i) \right) f_{[\tau]}(x) \right)$$

$$+ \sum_{i=1}^{s} (z_i + \gamma_i) = \sum_{i=1}^{s} z_i + \sum_{i=1}^{s} (z_i + \gamma_i) = \sum_{i=1}^{s} \gamma_i .$$

Thus each such derivative is constant implying that the space of linear structures of f has dimension at least s.

Two Alerts for Design of Certain Stream Ciphers: Trapped LFSR and Weak Resilient Function over GF(q)

Paul Camion[1], Miodrag J. Mihaljević[2,3], and Hideki Imai[4]

[1] Centre National de la Recherche Scientifique, Universite Pierre et Marie Curie,
UMR 7090, Combinatoire, 175 rue du Chevaleret, 75013 Paris, France
paul.camion@wanadoo.fr
[2] SONY Corporation, 6-7-35 Kitashinagawa, Shinagawa-ku, Tokyo, 141-0001 Japan
[3] Mathematical Institute, Serbian Academy of Sciences and Arts,
Kneza Mihaila 35, 11001 Belgrade, Yugoslavia
miodragm@turing.mi.sanu.ac.yu
[4] University of Tokyo, Institute of Industrial Science,
4-6-1 Komaba, Meguro-ku, Tokyo, 153-8505, Japan
imai@iis.u-tokyo.ac.jp

Abstract. This paper points out: (i) a possibility for *malicious* selection of the LFSRs feedback polynomials in order to install a trap-door for the cryptanalysis; and (ii) a weakness of the construction of the resilient functions over GF(q) proposed at CRYPTO'96. Two corresponding methods for cryptanalysis are proposed. It is shown that although certain keystream generators over GF(q) are resistant against correlation and linear complexity based attacks, they are vulnerable by some novel attacks. The efficiency of these attacks depends on characteristics of the employed LFSRs and resilient functions. The developed attacks imply that LFSRs with certain characteristic polynomials and certain resilient functions are inappropriate as the building components for nonlinear combination generators and related schemes. They imply certain design criteria for employment of LFSRs and resilient functions over GF(q) in the nonlinear combination keystream generators and related schemes.

Keywords: linear feedback shift registers over GF(q), keystream generators, nonlinear combination generator, resilient functions, cryptanalysis.

1 Introduction

A number of the published keystream generators are based on linear feedback shift registers (LFSRs) assuming that parts of the secret key are used to load the LFSRs initial states (see [12], for example). Particularly, LFSRs over GF(q) appear as the interesting building blocks for certain keystream generators.

The unpredictability request, which is one of the main cryptographic requirements, implies that the linearity inherent in LFSRs should not be "visible" in the generator output. One general technique for destroying the linearity is to use

K. Nyberg and H. Heys (Eds.): SAC 2002, LNCS 2595, pp. 196–213, 2003.
© Springer-Verlag Berlin Heidelberg 2003

several LFSRs which run in parallel, and to generate the keystream as a nonlinear function of the outputs of the component LFSRs. Such keystream generators are called nonlinear *combination generators*. In this paper we consider nonlinear combination generators where the only unknown elements to a cryptanalyst are the initial states of the LFSRs.

It has been shown that nonlinearity which prevent the linear complexity based attacks (see [11], for example) can not provide resistance against the correlation attack initially proposed in [19], improved by developing fast correlation attack method in [13], and further improved in a number of papers including the following most recent ones [5], [6], [14], [9], [16], [17] and [7]. A very important issue related to the combination function is that a trade-off exists between the correlation-immunity order and the nonlinearity order (see [20], for example).

In a general case the combination generators can be constructed over $GF(q)$, $q > 2$. This assumes employment of LFSRs over $GF(q)$, as well as combining functions over $GF(q)$. Certain results related to this topic are reported in [8], [2], [3], [10], and [4], for example.

A particular class of the functions relevant for the combination generator are the *resilient functions*. f is t-resilient function over $GF(q)$ if f is t-th order correlation-immune over $GF(q)$ and balanced. A (n, m, t)-resilient function is an n-input m-output function f with the property that it runs through every possible output m-tuple an equal number of times when t arbitrary inputs are fixed and the remaining $n - t$ inputs runs through all q^{n-t} input tuples. Resilient functions are particularly appropriate for combining the outputs of linear feedback shift registers since such combination leads to pseudo-random generator which resists certain correlation attack. Knowing that a high correlation-immunity order is not sufficient for ensuring the security of the resulting generator the second important parameter, the nonlinearity order of the resilient function should be taken into account, as well, to ensure that linear-complexity attack can not be employed.

Motivation for the work.
Main intention of this paper is to point out certain issues which should be taken into account related to design of the nonlinear combination or filter like keystream generators over $GF(q)$: Otherwise these schemes, although resistant on the all reported attacks could be vulnerable by the developed specialized attacks. Recall that the previously reported results on the considered topic were focused on the correlation and linear complexity issues. Accordingly, it appears interesting to consider if certain schemes, which are resistant on the correlation attacks and the linear-complexity attacks, are at the same time vulnerable by some other attacks. A goal of this paper is to point out the novel approaches for cryptanalysis of certain nonlinear combination keystream generators over $GF(q)$, and to employ it in a context of the design criteria.

Our results.
This paper points out: (i) a possibility for *malicious* selection of the LFSRs feedback polynomials in order to install a trap-door for the cryptanalysis; (ii) a

weakness of the construction of the resilient functions over GF(q) proposed at CRYPTO'96.

Particularly, this paper presents two methods for cryptanalysis of certain nonlinear combination generators over GF(q). It is shown that the property of "resilience" is not sufficient for security, and a few concrete examples are given. Although, the previous is not entirely unexpected, the paper gives a precise support to the heuristic, and a particular importance of the results is that they show a way in which some previously proposed constructions can fail.

Certain characteristics of LFSRs over GF(q) based on the matrix characterization are discussed related to the behaviour of the different powers of the LFSR state transition matrix and it is pointed out the possibility of choosing the feedback polynomial, among all primitive polynomials of a given degree over $GF(q)$, which has a behaviour very far from the expected one, yielding the way for construction of a keystream generator with the trapped LFSRs which have the feedback polynomial with a hidden trap-door for a cryptanalysis. These characteristic are used for developing the algorithm (Algorithm A) for cryptanalysis of certain nonlinear combination keystream generators. These generators show all characteristics of a secure one but are however trapped and breakable. (As a trapped cryptographic component we assume the component which shows the characteristics of a secure one but however hides a previously unconsidered property that allows a cryptanalysis.) The derived characteristics and the developed algorithm for cryptanalysis imply a design criterion for employment of LFSRs over GF(q) in certain nonlinear combination keystream generators. The criterion requires check of the patterns distribution in a sequence of successive powers of the LFSR state transition matrix. Violation of the criterion can result in employment of an LFSR which is the trapped one so that the keystream is breakable when its very short output segment is available.

The second proposed methods for cryptanalysis (Algorithm B) points out weaknesses in the construction of the resilient functions over GF(q) with optimal nonlinearity order reported in [2]-[3]. It is shown that this method for construction opens a door for attacking the nonlinear combination generator which employs such resilient function based on the method for cryptanalysis proposed in this paper. The developed attack shows how a particular failure of the avalanche property of a function over GF(q) can be employed for the cryptanalysis, and accordingly the attack implies a particular condition necessary for the good avalanche characteristic of the combining function over GF(q).

The developed algorithms for cryptanalysis directly imply the design alerts and restrictions on LFSRs characteristic polynomials and resilient functions which are appropriate for nonlinear combination generators over GF(q) and the related schemes.

Organization of the paper.
Section 2 considers matrix characterization and certain characteristics of LFSRs over GF(q). The related security implications and a design criterion are pointed out in Section 3. The first algorithm for cryptanalysis, as well as an illustrative

example of cryptanalysis based on the proposed algorithm are given in Section 4. The second developed algorithm for cryptanalysis and its consequences, as well as an illustrative example, are discussed in Section 5. Finally, the conclusions are given in Section 6.

2   Matrix Characterization and Certain Characteristics of LFSRs over GF(q)

An LFSR can be considered as a linear finite state machine. Let us recall how a linear finite state machine is a realization or an implementation of certain linear operators. The characteristic polynomial or feedback polynomial of the LFSR is

$$b(u) = 1 + b_1 u + \ldots + b_L u^L \tag{1}$$

and the recursion implemented by the LFSR is then

$$X_{L+t} = -b_1 X_{L+t-1} - \ldots - b_L X_t = b_1 X_{L+t-1} + \ldots + b_L X_t, \tag{2}$$

since q here is a power of 2. The reader is referred to [18], for example, for more details.

When the LFSR feedback polynomial being given by (1), then the **state transition q-ary matrix A** can be written as:

$$\mathbf{A} = \begin{bmatrix} b_1 & b_2 & b_3 & \ldots & b_L \\ 1 & 0 & 0 & \ldots & 0 \\ 0 & 1 & 0 & \ldots & . \\ . & . & . & \ldots & . \\ 0 & & & \ldots & 1 & 0 \end{bmatrix} = \begin{bmatrix} \mathbf{A}_1 \\ \mathbf{A}_2 \\ \mathbf{A}_3 \\ . \\ \mathbf{A}_L \end{bmatrix}, \tag{3}$$

where each $\mathbf{A}_i$, $i = 1, 2, \ldots, L$, represents a $1 \times L$ matrix (a row-vector). Having denoted by $\mathbf{X}_0$ the vector $[X_{L-1}, \ldots, X_0]$ representing the initial contents or initial state and by $\mathbf{X}_t = [X_{L+t-1}, \ldots, X_t]$ the L-dimensional vector over GF(q) representing the LFSR state after t clocks, then in the matrix form (2) writes

$$\mathbf{X}_t = \mathbf{A}\mathbf{X}_{t-1}^T = \mathbf{A}^t \mathbf{X}_0^T, \ t = 1, 2, \ldots, \tag{4}$$

where $\mathbf{A}^t$ is the t-th power over GF(q) of the $L \times L$ state transition binary matrix $\mathbf{A}$ and $\mathbf{X}^T$ denotes the transpose of the L-dimensional vector $\mathbf{X}$. Accordingly, a state of a length-L LFSR after t clocks is given by the matrix-vector product over GF(q) in relations (4).

Relations (4) show that powers of the matrix $\mathbf{A}$ determine algebraic replica of the LFSR initial state.

The next two parts of this section show two important characteristics relevant for specification of a design criterion for a nonlinear combination keystream generator over GF(q). At the first we show the behaviour of different powers of the matrix $\mathbf{A}$ assuming a random primitive characteristic polynomial. In the next, we point out the possibility of choosing the characteristic polynomial, among all primitive polynomials of a given degree over $GF(q)$, which has a behaviour very far from the expected one, yielding a way for construction of the trapped keystream generator. These issues are the origins for specification of a design criterion for employment of LFSRs over GF(q) as the building blocks for keystream generators.

2.1   The Expected Behaviour

Proposition 2.1 *In a sequence of N different powers of the matrix $\mathbf{A}$, corresponding to an L-length LFSR with primitive characteristic polynomial, we can expect that Nq^{-L+B} of the vectors $\mathbf{A}_1^{(\cdot)}$, take a specific pattern of values (say all zero pattern) in certain $L - B$ coordinates, assuming arbitrary values in the remained B coordinates, $B < L$.*

Sketch of the Proof. Recall that an LFSR with a primitive characteristic polynomial of order L generates the sequences $\{X_i\}$ of period equal to $q^L - 1$, and note that since $X_{L+i} = \mathbf{A}_1^{(i)}\mathbf{X_0}$, where $\mathbf{X_0}$ is a vector constant, the sequences $\{X_i\}$ and $\{\mathbf{A}_1^{(i)}\}$ have the same period. Accordingly, the sequence $\mathbf{A}_1^{(i)}$, $i = 1, 2, ..., q^L - 1$, consists of all possible $q^L - 1$ different L-dimensional vectors over GF(q), except the all-zero vector. As a result, in a statistical model, any vector $\mathbf{A}_1^{(i)}$ could be considered as a realization of a random L-dimensional vector source of L-dimensional patterns over GF(q), and accordingly, we have the proposition statement.

Proposition 2.1 directly implies the following corollary.

Corollary 2.1. *In a sequence of N elements generated by an L-length LFSR over GF(q), we can expect that Nq^{-L+B} symbols depend only on certain $B < L$ symbols of the LFSR initial state assuming that the LFSR characteristic polynomial is a primitive one.*

As an illustration we consider the following particular example over GF(2^3). Let the coefficients of the primitive characteristic polynomial be $b_1 = 1$, $b_2 = 1$, $b_3 = \alpha$, $b_4 = 0$, $b_5 = 1 + \alpha^2$, where α is a root of $x^3 + x + 1$ over $GF(2)$. Here $L = 5$ and according to Corollary 2.1, for $B = 2$ and $N = 4000$ we can expect $4000/512 = 7.81$ occurrences of the i-th power $\mathbf{A}^i$ of the transition q-ary matrix $\mathbf{A}$ such that the first row of $\mathbf{A}^i$ has a 0 entry in any fixed three positions. When the first row of $\mathbf{A}$ is $[1, 1, \alpha, 0, 1 + \alpha^2]$, the first row of $\mathbf{A}^i$ for $i = 25, 161, 197,$ $1007, 1510, 2565$ and 3910, respectively, has the following forms: $[0, 0, 0, 1 + \alpha^2, \alpha]$, $[0, 0, 0, \alpha^2, \alpha]$, $[0, 0, 0, 1, \alpha]$, $[0, 0, 0, \alpha, \alpha + \alpha^2]$, $[0, 0, 0, 1 + \alpha + \alpha^2, 1 + \alpha]$, $[0, 0, 0, \alpha^2, \alpha^2]$, and $[0, 0, 0, 1 + \alpha, 1]$.

Accordingly, the LFSR output sequence symbols on the positions $i = 25$, 161, 197, 1007, 1510, 2565 and 3910, depend only on two symbols of the LFSR initial state.

2.2   The Probability of a High Deviation from the Expected Behaviour

Proposition 2.2 *In a set of R different LFSRs over $GF(q)$ of length L and primitive characteristic polynomial, the probability P that an LFSR exits such that at least M from its first N output symbols depends only on certain $B < L$ elements of the LFSR initial state is given by the following:*

$$P = 1 - [\sum_{m=0}^{M-1} P(m)]^R , \qquad (5)$$

where

$$P(m) = \binom{q^B}{m} \binom{q^L - 1 - q^B}{N - m} / \binom{q^L - 1}{N} . \qquad (6)$$

Sketch of the Proof. We consider the set of all primitive polynomial of degree L over $GF(q)$ and the corresponding roots over $GF(q^L)$. Any power α^i of such a root α can be expressed as $\alpha^i = \sum_{j=0}^{L-1} a_j \alpha^j$. It can be directly shown that the probability that exactly m patterns, such that $a_j = 0$ for any j out of certain set of B indices, appear in the first N powers of α is given by (6). On the other hand, $Pr = \sum_{i=0}^{M-1} P(i)$ is the probability that at most $M - 1$ powers of α with the specified pattern appear in the first N powers of α. Accordingly, the probability for the desired root is $1 - Pr^R$ where R is the number of primitive polynomials of degree L over $GF(q)$ that we consider.

The statement of Proposition 2.2 is illustrated by the following example. We consider the set of all primitive polynomial of degree $L = 6$ over $GF(q = 2^7)$ and the corresponding roots over $GF(q^L)$. Any power α^i of such a root α can be expressed as $\alpha^i = \sum_{j=0}^{5} a_j \alpha^j$. We are interested of the probability to have in the first N powers of the primitive root a subset I of elements such that $a_5 = a_4 = 0$ in the expression of $\alpha^\ell, \ell \in I$. The length of the generator output sequence is assumed to be N, which will here range from 10 to 50, maybe somewhat larger but not more than 100. Then $P = \sum_{i=0}^{2} P(i)$ is the probability that at most two powers of α with the specified pattern appear in the first N powers of α. The probability for the desired root is $1 - P^{R_N}$ where R_N is the number of primitive polynomials of degree 6 over $GF(q)$ that we need to go through for $1 - P^{R_N}$ to be at least 99%. Here the total number R of primitive polynomials is the number of integers prime to $128^6 - 1$ divided by 6. Then $R = 404620054272 \simeq 4 \cdot 10^{11}$. Since $P \simeq .999999995952$, then for $N = 50$ we need R_N to be 1.2 10^9 and the probability for the desired root is $1 - P^{R_N} \simeq .992$. For $N = 10$ we need R_N to be $1.9 \cdot 10^{11}$ and the probability for the desired root is $1 - P^{R_N} \simeq .99$.

3   Security Implications and Design Criterion

Proposition 2.1 and Corollary 2.1 open a door for a part-by-part recovery of a LFSR initial state employed in certain keystream generators. The critical observation is that if you can identify some output locations that depend on only a subset of the key, then you can speed-up exhaustive keysearch by guessing only that subset of the key.

Proposition 2.2 opens a door for a *malicious* selection of the characteristic polynomial so that the LFSR initial state recovery, in certain keystream generators, can be performed assuming availability of very short keystream output sequence. This malicious selection of the LFSRs feedback polynomials yields a possibility to install a trap-door for the cryptanalysis in certain keystream generators.

Accordingly, this section proposes the following design criterion for employment of LFSRs over $GF(q)$ in order to prevent the cryptanalysis using only a very short segment of the output keystream sequence.

– Check the patterns distribution of the first N powers of the LFSR state transition matrix, and do not employ the considered candidate if the distribution significantly deviates from the expected one given by Proposition 2.1.

Violation of the proposed rule for selection of the LFSR characteristic polynomial can result in a scheme vulnerable based on very short segments from the keystream generator.

4   An Algorithm for Cryptanalysis and Its Characteristics

As an illustration of the statements given in the previous section, this section proposes a particular approach for the cryptanalysis.

We assume a nonlinear combination keystream generator over $GF(q)$ which consists of two LFSRs and a 1-resilient nonlinear function $f(\cdot)$ which inverse is $f^{-1}(\cdot)$. The lengths of the LFSRs, $L1$ and $L2$, are co-prime, $L1 < L2$, and the secret key determines only the LFSRs initial states. Accordingly the considered keystream generator is resistant on the correlation attack and the linear complexity attack.

4.1   Underlying Ideas

The developed technique for cryptanalysis is based on the **divide and conquer** approach. This approach is widely used in cryptanalysis, and particularly it has been employed for initial state reconstruction of an LFSR as it is reported in [1], [6] and [9], for example, but these techniques are inappropriate in the cases under our consideration due to the following. The technique reported in [1] requires that the LFSR feedback taps are highly concentrated, and so it is inefficient or can not work in the general cases under our consideration. The techniques reported in [6], [9], [14], [17] and [7], are based on certain sums of the LFSR output symbols so that the relevant inversions can not be performed. In this paper we propose a novel divide and conquer approach which is suitable for the problem under our consideration.

Two main underlying ideas for the cryptanalytic method are the following:
- recovering of complete secret key by independent recovering of its certain parts;
- employment of a technique based on the linear finite state machine model of an LFSR over $GF(q)$ for autonomous reconstruction of the secret key parts using appropriate subsequence of an LFSR output sequence which depend on a part of the LFSR initial state only.

Characterization of an LFSR over $GF(q)$ by the state transition matrix, and the characteristics of a sequence of powers of the state transition matrix, derived in Section 2, are the main origins for construction of the algorithm for the cryptanalysis.

4.2   Algorithm A

– *INPUT.*
  Output sequence from the keystream generator, $\{Z_i\}_{i=1}^N$, and parameter ℓ.
– *PREPROCESSING.*
  Denote by $\mathbf{Aj}$ the state transition matrix of LFSRj, $j = 1, 2$, and by $\mathbf{Aj}_1^i$ the first row of the i-th power $\mathbf{Aj}^i$ of $\mathbf{Aj}$. Let $P_{(\ell)}$ be a subset of $\{1, 2, ..., L1\}$, and let N be large enough for having a set $S_{(\ell)}$ of indices with the size $L2 - \ell$ such that:
    • the first row of $\mathbf{A1}^i$, $i \in S_{(\ell)}$, has nonzero components only for the indices which belong to $P_{(\ell)}$;
    • the vectors $\mathbf{A2}_1^i$, $i \in S_{(\ell)}$ are linearly independent.
– *PROCESSING.*
  1. Suppose previously unconsidered hypothesis about the initial state part $\mathbf{X1}_{(0,\ell)}$ which components belong to the set $P_{(\ell)}$, and generate $L2 - \ell$ output elements of $LFSR1$, $X1_i$, $i \in S_\ell$ according to the following:
  $$X1_i = \mathbf{A1}_1^i (\mathbf{X1}_{(0,\ell)})^T \ , \quad i \in S_{(\ell)} \ .$$
  2. For each $(X1_i, Z_i)$, $i \in \{P_{(\ell)}, S_{(\ell)}\}$, calculate
  $$X2_i = f^{-1}(X1_i, Z_i) \ , \quad i \in \{P_{(\ell)}, S_{(\ell)}\} \ ,$$
  and solve the system
  $$\mathbf{A2}_1^i (\mathbf{X2}_0)^T = X2_i \ , \quad i \in S_{(\ell)} \ ,$$
  for $\mathbf{X2}_0$ where it is a candidate for the initial state of LFSR2.
  3. Based on the current candidate for $\mathbf{X2}_0$ and $\{Z_i\}$, recover complete candidate for $\mathbf{X1}_0$.
  4. For the established LFSRs states calculate the generator output sequence $\tilde{Z}_i$, $i = 1, 2, ..., L1 + L2$.
     If $\tilde{Z}_i = Z_i$, $i = 1, 2, ..., L1 + L2$, accept current hypothesis of the LFSR1 and LFSR2, as the true one; otherwise go to the step 1.
– *OUTPUT.*
  Secret key recovered from the reconstructed initial states.

4.3   Complexity and Required Input

The structure of Algorithm A directly implies the following statement.

Corollary 4.1. *The time complexity of Algorithm A is proportional to q^ℓ, $\ell < L1$, and it is smaller for a factor equal to $2^{L1-\ell}$ than a brute force attack, $L2 > L1 > \ell$.*

The required sample for the cryptanalysis strongly depends on the characteristic polynomial of employed LFSRs.

The algorithm preprocessing phase requires enough long output sequence from the generator to make possible collection of the suitable powers of the state transition matrix. Also note that, according to Proposition 2.2, the required length can be extremely small if an LFSR with certain characteristic polynomial is employed.

Table 1 gives a numerical illustration of the algorithm time complexity, according to Corollary 4.1, and assuming operations over $GF(2^3)$.

Table 1. Time complexity and required imput sample of the algorithm for cryptanalysis as the functions of the algorithm parameters L_1, L_2 and method of the characteristic polynomial selection assuming the combination generator over $GF(2^3)$ with two LFSRs and 1-resilient function.

secret key length (in bits)	LFSR lengths $L2$, $L1$ and the parameter ℓ (over $GF(8)$)	order of time complexity	order of required sample dependent on selection of the characteristic polynomial	
			random	malicious
63	11, 10, 5	8^5	8^5	100
96	17, 15, 8	8^8	8^8	100
156	27, 25, 15	8^{15}	8^{15}	1000
183	31, 30, 15	8^{15}	8^{15}	1000

4.4   Illustrative Example

Key Ideas

Our aim is to conceive a nonlinear combination keystream generator over $GF(q)$ with two LFSRs which shows all characteristics of a secure one but is however trapped and breakable. The key statements are as follows.

1. The nonlinear combining function is 1-resilient with maximal non-linearity order, and it combines LFSR1 and LFSR2 over $GF(2^7)$ of lengths 6 and 7,

respectively. We have chosen $GF(2^7)$ in order to produce ASCII symbols which are bytes as generator output symbols.

2. We first choose the feedback polynomial from the

$$\phi(2^{42} - 1)/6 = 404620054272 \simeq 4 \cdot 10^{11}$$

ones with the following property: Among the first 50 powers of the corresponding primitive root α a set I of at least 3 have the same pattern with 4 nonzero components and 2 zero components in its expression with 6 components over the ground field. It is established that the probability is larger than 99.2% so that a primitive polynomial for $LFSR1$ exists among $1.2 \cdot 10^9$ of them with the desired property. What we have in mind is to complete the crytanalysis with the knowledge of only 50 bytes of the generator output sequence. It is still feasible to find a primitive polynomial with the desired property such that among the first 10 powers of the corresponding primitive root α a set I of at least 3 have the same pattern with 4 nonzero components and 2 zero components in its expression with 6 components over the ground field. Here the probability of finding such a polynomial still is close to 99% but at the condition however to be able to go through $1.9 \cdot 10^{11}$ primitive polynomials, and this would allow to complete the cryptanalysis with only 10 bytes of the generator output sequence, corresponds to an attack with a known plaintext of only 10 characters.

3. Let I be the set of three powers of the transition matrix $\mathbf{A1}$ of LFSR1 for which the first row of $\mathbf{A1}^\ell$, $\ell \in I$ has 0 in the first two positions. For LFSR2 we need to choose independently a feedback polynomial such that the first rows of $\mathbf{A2}^\ell$, $\ell \in I$ together with the first four unit vectors of length 6 forms of a set of linearly independent vectors. This reduces to considering the probability that a 3×3 matrix over $GF(128)$ be invertible. That probability is $\simeq .99126$. Thus, such a feedback polynomial can be easily found.

Example of a Vulnerable 1-Resilient Function

We give an explicit form of the inversion of f when it is given as in [2, Proof of Proposition 14] by

$$f(x, y) = (x^{q-2} + y^{\frac{q-2}{2}} + 1)^{q-5}, \tag{7}$$

where $q > 4$ is a power of 2. This is an example of a 1-resilient function with optimal nonlinearity order over a finite field GF(q), q a power of 2.

It can be shown that the following statement holds.

Proposition 1. *Over the finite field* $GF(q)$, $q > 2$, q *a power of 2, if* $z = f(x, y) = (x^{q-2} + y^{\frac{q-2}{2}} + 1)^{q-5}$, *then* $y = (z^{q-2} + x^{4(q-2)} + 1)^{\frac{q-2}{2}}$.

Details of the Attack

The LFSRi state transition q-ary matrix is denoted by $\mathbf{Ai}$, $i = 1, 2$. The unknown initial state of $LFSR1$ is $[x_5, x_4, x_3, x_2, x_1, x_0]$ and that of $LFSR2$ is $[y_6, y_5, y_4, y_3, y_2, y_1, y_0]$. We recall that we have the feedback polynomial of LFSR1 such that there is a set I of size 3 of integers and that the first row of $\mathbf{A1}^\ell$, $\ell \in I$ has 0 for its first two entries. Our aim is to reduce the number of candidates to be checked for the whole initial state: $[x_5, x_4, x_3, x_2, x_1, x_0]$, $[y_6, y_5, y_4, y_3, y_2, y_1, y_0]$ to at most q^4. By considering the $128^4 = 2^{28}$ possible partial initial states $[x_3, x_2, x_1, x_0]$ of LFSR1, we are able to recover the complete initial states of LFSR1 and LFSR2 as follows. We first have the set of equations

$$y_\ell = g(x_\ell, z_\ell), \ell = 3, 2, 1, 0. \tag{8}$$

By those equations every choice of $[x_3, x_2, x_1, x_0]$ forces the partial initialization $[y_3, y_2, y_1, y_0]$. By our assumption on the matrices $\mathbf{A1}^\ell$, $\ell \in I$, we have that

$$x_\ell = \mathbf{A1}^\ell [0, 0, x_3, x_2, x_1, x_0]^T, \ \ell \in I \tag{9}$$

We are then able to solve for y_ℓ the equations

$$y_\ell = g(x_\ell, z_\ell), \ell \in I \tag{10}$$

Let us denote by $[e_1], [e_2], [e_3], [e_4]$ the row vectors $(1, 0, \ldots, 0), (0, 1, 0, \ldots, 0), (0, 0, 1, 0, \ldots, 0), (0, 0, 0, 1, 0, \ldots, 0)$, respectively. We then denote by $[\mathbf{A2}^\ell]$, $\ell \in I$ the first row of the matrix $\mathbf{A2}^\ell$, $\ell \in I$.

We finally have the set of equations

$$[e_{\ell+1}][y_6, y_5, y_4, y_3, y_2, y_1, y_0]^T = y_\ell, \ \ell = 0, 1, 2, 3. \tag{11}$$

and

$$\mathbf{A2}^\ell [y_6, y_5, y_4, y_3, y_2, y_1, y_0]^T = y_\ell, \ \ell \in I \tag{12}$$

We have chosen the feedback polynomial of LFSR2 in order that the vectors $[e_\ell]$, $\ell = 1, 2, 3, 4$, and $\mathbf{A2}^\ell$, $\ell \in I$ are linearly independent. We thus can solve (11) and (12) for $y_6, y_5, y_4, y_3, y_2, y_1, y_0$. The complete initial state of LFSR2 is then entirely recovered though only the assumed partial initial state $[x_3, x_2, x_1, x_0]$ of LFSR1. Now we can solve

$$x_\ell = h(y_\ell), \ \ell = 4, 5.$$

What we have just seen is that exploiting the property of the function $f(x_\ell, y_\ell) = z_\ell$ and the fact that we can choose the feedback polynomial, first for LFSR1 and then independently for LFSR2, so that every partial initialization x_3, x_2, x_1, x_0 of LFSR1 completely determines the whole initialization of both LFSR. We are then able to produce the keystream sequence corresponding to that initialization which eventually will match the keystream sequence used. Cryptanalysis will be achieved in an average of $\frac{q^4}{2} = 2^{27}$ steps with negligible memory space, whereas a straightforward brute force attack requires $\frac{q^7}{2} = 2^{48}$ steps.

5   A Weak Resilient Function over GF(q)

This section points out vulnerability of certain resilient functions over GF(q). The developed method for cryptanalysis applies when some input variables x of the combining function over GF(q) only appear as x^{q-1} in the algebraic normal form. A particular class of the functions which have certain optimal characteristics but fulfill this condition, as well, is proposed at CRYPTO'96, [2].

5.1   Keystream Generator Under Consideration

We assume that the nonlinear combination generator consists of the following:
• n LFSRs over GF(q): LFSR1, LFSR2, ..., LFSRn, with lengths L_1, L_2, ..., L_n, respectively, and known characteristic polynomials;
• 1-resilient function of n variables with the optimal nonlinearity order constructed as it is proposed in [2] employing the following Proposition 2 and (7);
• and that the secret key determine the LFSRs initial states only.

Proposition 2. *(Proposition 15, [2]) Let $q \neq 2$ or $t \neq n - 1$. Let f_1, f_2 : $GF(q)^n \rightarrow GF(q)$ be two t-resilient functions with optimal nonlinearity, such that $degree(f_1 - f_2) = degree(f_1)$. Then $g : GF(q)^{n+1} \rightarrow GF(q)$ defined by*

$$g(x_1, \ldots, x_{n+1}) = x_{n+1}^{q-1} f_1(x_1, \ldots, x_n) + (1 - x_{n+1}^{q-1}) f_2(x_1, \ldots, x_n) \qquad (13)$$

is a t-resilient function with optimal nonlinearity.

Finally, note the following. By Proposition 14 of [2] there exists a t-resilient function $f : GF(q)^{t+1} \rightarrow GF(q)$ with optimal nonlinearity order. Applying Proposition 2 with $f_1 = f$ and $f_2 = \alpha f$, where $\alpha \in GF(q) \setminus \{0, 1\}$ leads to a t-resilient function with $t + 2$ variables and optimal nonlinearity order. If we iterate this construction $n + t - 2$ times, we obtain a t-resilient function with n variables and optimal nonlinearity order. Siegenthaler [20] proved this result in Boolean case.

5.2   Underlying Ideas for Cryptanalysis

The algebraic normal form of the considered t-resilient function with optimal nonlinearity order has a monomial (with highest possible degree) that should have t variables with degree $q - 2$ and all other variables with degree $q - 1$. This is naturally brought to the attention of the cryptanalyst since a variable x raised to the power $q - 1$ takes the value 1 for every nonzero x.
The following statement points out an underlying result relevant for the cryptanalysis.

Proposition 3. *The probability $P(n, t)$ of at least t consecutive ones in a length n string of zeros and ones with independent probabilities p for zero and $1 - p = q$ for one is given by*

$$P(n, t) = 0 \text{ for } n < t, \ q^t \text{ for } n = t \text{ and}$$

$$P(n, t) = q^t + \sum_{i=2}^{n-t+1} pq^t(1 - P(i - 2, t)) \text{ for } n > t.$$

Sketch of the Proof. The probability of at least t consecutive *ones* starting in the first position is q^t. Next the probability of at least t consecutive *ones* appearing for the first time with the first one in the i-th position, $i > 1$ is $pq^t - P(i-2, t)pq^t$. Such a string has a *zero* in the $(i - 1)$-th position and there is no t consecutive ones in the first $i - 2$ positions.

5.3   Algorithm for Cryptanalysis

Algorithm B

- *INPUT.*
  Characteristic polynomials of the employed n LFSRs of lengths $L1, L2, ..., Ln$, assuming (without loosing generality) that $L1 < L2 < ... < Ln$, the combining function, assuming that the outputs from LFSR3-LFSRn appear only as x^{q-1} in the algebraic normal form of the combining function, and an output sequence from the keystream generator, $\{Z_i\}_{i=1}^I$,
- *PROCESSING.*
  Joint recovering of the LFSR1-LFSR2 initial states, and than sequential recovering of the LFSR3-LFSRn initial states.
  1. Recovering of the LFSR1-LFSR2 initial states.
     For each output sequence index $i = 1, 2, ..., I1$, where $I1 < I - (L1 + L2)$, do the following:
     (a) Assume that $L1 + L2$ successive output bits from each of LFSR3 to LFSRn are nonzero, implying that the keystream generator output depends only on the output sequences from LFSR1 and LFSR2;
     (b) Employ the following procedure for recovering of the initial states of LFSR1 and LFSR2.
        i. Suppose a previously unconsidered initial state $X_1, X_2, ..., X_{L1}$, of $L1$-length LFSR1 which generates the sequence $X_{L1+1}, X_{L1+2}, ..., X_K, K < I$.
        ii. Using the sequences $X_{L1+1}, X_{L1+2}, ..., X_{L1+L2}$ and $\{Z_i\}$ calculate $Y_k = f^{-1}(X_k, Z_k)$, $k = L1 + 1, L1 + 2, ..., L1 + L2$, where f^{-1} denotes inversion of f, and generate $Y_{L2+1}, Y_{L2+2}, ..., Y_K$.
        iii. Calculate $\tilde{Z}_k = f(X_k, Y_k)$, $k = L2+1, L2+2, ..., K$, where $K \leq I$ provides an unique solution in the next step test.
        If $\tilde{Z}_k = Z_k$, $k = L2+1, L2+2, ..., K$, go to Step iv; otherwise go to Step i.

    iv. Memorize the recovered initial states of LFSR1 and LFSR2. (i.e. the corresponding secret key parts), and go to the next step.
2. Recovering of the LFSR3-LFSRn initial states based on the recovered initial states of LFSR1-LFSR2.

For $j = 3, 4, ..., n$, based on the recovered initial states LFSR1-LFSR($j - 1$), reconstruct LFSRj employing the following:
  (a) assume previously unconsidered initial state of LFSRj
  (b) generate the output sequence $\{\tilde{Z}_i\}$ based on the recovered initial states of LFSR1-LFSRj, assuming that the outputs of LFSR($j+1$)-LFSRn are always nonzero
  (c) Calculate $d = \sum_{i=1}^{I} \delta(\tilde{Z}_i, Z_i)$ where $\delta(\tilde{Z}_i, Z_i) = 0$ for $\tilde{Z}_i = Z_i$ and $\delta(\tilde{Z}_i, Z_i) = 1$ for $\tilde{Z}_i \neq Z_i$, assuming that the algorithm parameter I provides the relevant separability.
  (d) if d is smaller than a certain threshold accept the current hypothesis as the true one; otherwise go to Step 2.(a).
 – *OUTPUT.*
Secret key recovered from the reconstructed initial states.

5.4   Required Sample and Complexity of Algorithm B

According to Algorithm B structure, it can be directly shown that the following is valid.

When available keystream output sequence is $O(256^2(\frac{256}{255})^{n-3})$, assuming $n \geq 3$, the complexity of attack is $O(q^{L1} + \sum_{j=3}^{n} q^{Lj})$.

Recall that a direct exhaustive search over all possible secret keys has complexity $O(q^{\sum_{j=1}^{n} Lj})$.

5.5   Illustrative Example: A Nonlinear Combination Generator with Five LFSRs

We assume that the generator under cryptanalysis consists of:
- 5 LFSRs, LFSR1, LFSR2, LFSR3, LFSR4, LFSR5, of respective lengths $L1 = 7$, $L2 = 11$, $L3 = 5$, $L4 = 9$, $L5 = 8$, over GF(256) with primitive characteristic polynomials;
- A known 1-resilient function of 5 variables $(x_1, x_2, x_3, x_4, x_5)$, corresponding to the LFSR1, LFSR2, LFSR3, LFSR4, LFSR5. It has been constructed according to the following: a 1−resilient function $f_2(x_1, x_2)$ defined by (7) is first obtained. Then three more variables x_3, x_4, x_5 are introduced in three steps with the recurrence (13).
Also, for the first step, we assume that 174 bytes of keystream are at our disposal. Under this condition, the attack succeeds with probability 0.97. If enough long sequence is available, the reconstruction can be completed.

The attack consists of the following two distinct parts:
• Recovering the initial states of LFSR1 and LFSR2 with probability 0.97, based on a search over no more than 8^7 hypothesis;

• Assuming that a long sequence of the generator output (or very long sequence of the ciphertext) is available, recovering the initial states of LFSR3, LFSR4 and LFSR5 based on three successive independent search which employ testing of 8^5, 8^9 and 8^8 hypothesis, respectively.

Starting steps of the algorithm for complete cryptanalysis are the following:
- Assume that the values of x_3, x_4, x_5 all are nonzero for 18 successive bytes of the keystream by taking those bytes starting from the first, the second, . . . , and the 156-th (156=174-18) byte.
- For each of the previous assumptions that the values of x_3, x_4, x_5 are nonzero for 18 successive bytes perform the cryptanalysis on what is now essentially function $f(x_1, x_2)$ defined by (7).

Considering relation (13), we see that the probability of a successful attack is that of having simultaneously 18 ones in three strings of length 174 of *zeros* and *ones*, where each *zero* appears with independent probability $p = \frac{1}{256}$ and *one* with probability $q = \frac{255}{256}$.

When the initial states of LFSR1 and LFSR2 are recovered, long segments of the keystream sequence can be generated, since, for any t, the probability that the output byte of the generator at time t is equal to $f_2(x_1, x_2)$ is $\left(\frac{255}{256}\right)^3 = 0.9883$. If a sufficiently long generator output (or even ciphertext only) is at disposal it is possible to recover the initial state of LFSR3, LFSR4 and LFSR5 using the following approach.
- Suppose previously unconsidered initial state of LFSR3. If the assumption is correct, than, for any t, the probability that the generator output byte at time t is defined by $f_2(x_1, x_2)$ is equal to $\left(\frac{255}{256}\right)^2 = 0.9922$. Since 9922 is 0.39% greater than 9883, the generated sequence will be more similar to the given one, so that a discrimination between incorrect and correct hypothesis is possible.
- The analog techniques can be employed for the initial states recovering of LFSR4 and LFSR5.

6   Conclusions

This paper yields two alerts relevant for nonlinear combination keystream generators over $GF(q)$ and the related schemes, and it points out: (i) a possibility for *malicious* selection of the LFSRs feedback polynomials in order to install a trap-door for the cryptanalysis; (ii) a weakness of the construction of the resilient functions over $GF(q)$ proposed in [2]-[3]. On the other hand the results are novel general elements for design of keystream generators over $GF(q)$. More precisely, the results of this paper can be summarized as follows.

Certain characteristics of LFSRs over $GF(q)$ based on the matrix characterization are discussed related to the behaviour of the different powers of the LFSR state transition matrix and it is pointed out the possibility of choosing the feedback polynomial, among all primitive polynomials of a given degree over $GF(q)$, which has a behaviour very far from the expected one, yielding the way for construction of the trapped keystream generator. These characteristic are used for developing the algorithm, Algorithm A, for cryptanalysis of certain nonlinear combination keystream generators. These generators show all characteristics of a secure one but are however trapped and breakable. The derived characteristics and the developed algorithm for cryptanalysis imply a design criterion for employment of LFSRs over $GF(q)$ in certain nonlinear combination keystream generators. The criterion requires checking of the patterns distribution in a sequence of successive powers of the LFSR state transition matrix. Violation of the criterion can result in employment of an LFSR which is the trapped one so that the keystream is breakable when a very short output segment is available.

The developed Algorithm A is an illustration of significance of the proposed criterion, and an efficient algorithm for cryptanalysis of the nonlinear combination generator with two LFSRs and 1-resilient function. The critical observation is that if you can identify some output locations that depend on only a subset of the key, then you can speed-up exhaustive keysearch by guessing only that subset of the key. The developed algorithm has divide-and-conquer nature, and recovering of complete secret key is obtained by independent reconstruction of its parts employing a technique based on the linear finite state machine model of an LFSR over $GF(q)$, and identification of certain subsequence of an LFSR output sequence. Complexity of the cryptanalysis and required length of the keystream sequence are discussed. When two LFSRs have co-prime lengths $L_1 < L_2$ and the primitive characteristic polynomials, the complexity of attack is $O(q^\ell)$, $\ell < L_1$. Particularly, it is pointed out that for certain LFSRs characteristic polynomials, the attack can be performed on very short generator output segments, and such LFSRs are called trapped LFSRs.

The second proposed methods for cryptanalysis, Algorithm B, points out weaknesses in the construction of the resilient functions over $GF(q)$ with optimal nonlinearity order reported in [2]-[3]. It is shown that this method for construction opens a door for attacking the nonlinear combination generator which employs such resilient function based on the method for cryptanalysis proposed in this paper. The developed attack shows how a particular failure of the avalanche property of a function over $GF(q)$ can be employed for the cryptanalysis, and accordingly the attack implies a particular condition necessary for the good avalanche characteristic of the combining function over $GF(q)$.

Algorithm B, the second algorithm for cryptanalysis proposed in this paper, applies when some input variables x of the combining function appear only as x^{q-1} in the algebraic normal form. In that case the function is very close to a function of less input variables (since x^{q-1} takes the value 1 for all non-zero values of x). In [2] a family of resilient functions achieving Siegenthaler's bound was constructed, and these functions have this particular algebraic property: any such n-variable t-resilient function over $GF(q)$ is at low distance from a t-variable function. The second developed algorithm points out that the family of resilient functions proposed in [2] (CRYPTO'96) is not suitable for cryptographic applications even if these functions have the highest possible degree. Most notably, the second algorithm implies a new criterion on the algebraic normal form of the combining function which is specific to q-ary case. In other words, the proposed attack shows how a particular failure of the avalanche property of a function over $GF(q)$ can be employed for the cryptanalysis, and accordingly the attack implies a particular condition necessary for the good avalanche characteristic of the combining function over $GF(q)$.

When n LFSRs over $GF(q)$ have lengths $L_1 < L_2 < \dots < L_n$, and the outputs from LFSR3-LFSRn appear as x^{q-1} in the algebraic normal form, the following is shown: When available keystream output sequence is $O(256^2(\frac{256}{255})^{n-3})$, assuming $n \geq 3$, the complexity of attack is $O(q^{L_1} + \sum_{j=3}^{n} q^{L_j})$, while a direct exhaustive search over all possible secret keys has complexity $O(q^{\sum_{j=1}^{n} L_j})$. In certain cases, and particularly if the LFSRs are the trapped ones, the first algorithm for cryptanalysis can be combined with the second one.

The developed algorithms for cryptanalysis directly imply the design alerts and restrictions on LFSRs characteristic polynomials and resilient functions which are appropriate for nonlinear combination generators over $GF(q)$ and the related schemes. Accordingly, the results of this paper are focused toward some particular problems and, at the same time, they are general guidelines for construction of certain stream ciphers.

Finally note that archiving hidden and nontrivial weaknesses of certain building blocks for keystream generators is an important issue relevant for construction of the secure schemes, as well as for the security evaluation of the proposed ones.

References

1. R. J. Anderson, "A faster attack on certain stream ciphers", *Electronics Letters*, vol. 29, pp. 1322-1323, 22nd July 1993.
2. P. Camion and A. Canteaut, "Generalization of Siegenthaler inequality and Schnorr-Vaudenay multipermutations", Advance in Cryptology - CRYPTO'96, *Lecture Notes in Computer Science*, vol. 1109, pp. 372-386, 1996.
3. P. Camion and A. Canteaut, "Correlation-immune and resilient functions over a finite alphabet and their applications in cryptography", *Design, Codes and Cryptography*, vol 16, pp.103- 116, 1999.
4. P. Camion, M. J. Mihaljević and H. Imai, "On employment of LFSRs over $GF(q)$ in certain stream ciphers", *IEEE Int. Symp. Inform. Theory - ISIT2002*, Lausanne, Switzerland, July 2002, Proceedings, p. 210.
5. A. Canteaut and M. Trabbia, "Improved fast correlation attacks using parity-check equations of weight 4 and 5", Advances in Cryptology - EUROCRYPT 2000, *Lecture Notes in Computer Science*, vol. 1807, pp. 573-588, 2000.
6. V.V. Chepyzhov, T. Johansson and B. Smeets, "A simple algorithm for fast correlation attacks on stream ciphers", Fast Software Encryption 2000, *Lecture Notes in Computer Science*, vol. 1978, pp. 180-195, 2001.
7. P. Chose, A. Joux and M. Mitton, "Fast correlation attacks: An algorithmic point of view", Advances in Cryptology - EUROCRYPT 2002, *Lecture Notes in Computer Science*, vol. 2332, pp. 209-221, 2002.
8. J. Dj. Golić, "On linear complexity of functions of periodic $GF(q)$ sequences", *IEEE Trans. Inform. Theory*, vol. 35, pp. 69-75, Jan. 1989.
9. T. Johansson and F. Jonsson, "Fast correlation attacks through reconstruction of linear polynomials", Advances in Cryptology - CRYPTO 2000, *Lecture Notes in Computer Science*, vol. 1880, pp. 300-315, 2000.

10. F. Jonsson and T. Johansson, "Correlation attacks on stream ciphers over $GF(2^n)$", *2001 IEEE Int. Symp. Inform. Theory - ISIT2001*, Washington DC, June 2001, Proceedings, p. 140.

11. J. L. Massey, "Shift-register synthesis and BCH decoding", *IEEE Trans. Inform. Theory*, vol. IT-15, pp. 122-127, 1969.

12. A. Menezes, P.C. van Oorschot and S.A. Vanstone, *Handbook of Applied Cryptography*. Boca Raton: CRC Press, 1997.

13. W. Meier and O. Staffelbach, "Fast correlation attacks on certain stream ciphers," *Journal of Cryptology*, vol. 1, pp. 159-176, 1989.

14. M. J. Mihaljević, M. P. C. Fossorier and H. Imai, "A low-complexity and high-performance algorithm for the fast correlation attack", Fast Software Encryption - FSE 2000, *Lecture Notes in Computer Science*, vol. 1978, pp. 196-212, 2001.

15. M. J. Mihaljević and J. Golić, "A method for convergence analysis of iterative probabilistic decoding", *IEEE Trans. Inform. Theory*, vol. 46, pp. 2206-2211, Sept. 2000.

16. M. J. Mihaljević, M. P. C. Fossorier and H. Imai, "On decoding techniques for cryptanalysis of certain encryption algorithms", *IEICE Trans. Fundamentals*, vol. E84-A, pp. 919-930, April 2001.

17. M. J. Mihaljević, M.P.C. Fossorier and H. Imai, "Fast correlation attack algorithm with the list decoding and an application", Fast Software Encryption - FSE 2001, *Lecture Notes in Computer Science*, vol 2355, pp. 196-210, 2002.

18. R. A. Rueppel, *Analysis and Design of Stream Ciphers*. Berlin: Springer-Verlag, 1986.

19. T. Siegenthaler, "Decrypting a class of stream ciphers using ciphertext only", *IEEE Trans. Comput.*, vol. C-34, pp. 81-85, 1985.

20. T. Siegenthaler, "Correlation-immunity of nonlinear combining functions for cryptographic applications", *IEEE Trans. Inform. Theory*, vol. IT-30, pp. 776-780, 1984.

Multiples of Primitive Polynomials and Their Products over GF(2)

Subhamoy Maitra, Kishan Chand Gupta, and Ayineedi Venkateswarlu

Applied Statistics Unit, Indian Statistical Institute,
203, B T Road, Calcutta 700 108, INDIA
{subho, kishan_t}@isical.ac.in, ayineedi@yahoo.com

Abstract. A standard model of nonlinear combiner generator for stream cipher system combines the outputs of several independent Linear Feedback Shift Register (LFSR) sequences using a nonlinear Boolean function to produce the key stream. Given such a model, cryptanalytic attacks have been proposed by finding the sparse multiples of the connection polynomials corresponding to the LFSRs. In this direction recently a few works are published on t-nomial multiples of primitive polynomials. We here provide further results on degree distribution of the t-nomial multiples. However, getting the sparse multiples of just a single primitive polynomial does not suffice. The exact cryptanalysis of the nonlinear combiner model depends on finding sparse multiples of the products of primitive polynomials. We here make a detailed analysis on t-nomial multiples of products of primitive polynomials. We present new enumeration results for these multiples and provide some estimation on their degree distribution.

Keywords : *Primitive Polynomials, Galois Field, Polynomial Multiples, Cryptanalysis, Stream Cipher.*

1 Introduction

Linear Feedback Shift Registers (LFSRs) are used extensively as pseudorandom bit generator in different cryptographic schemes and the connection polynomials of the LFSRs are the polynomials over GF(2) (see [3,12,2] for more details). To get the maximum cycle length these connection polynomials need to be primitive [9]. To resist cryptanalytic attacks, it is important that these primitive polynomials should be of high weight and also they should not have sparse multiples [11,1] (see also [8] and the references in this paper for current research on cryptanalysis in this direction). With this motivation, finding sparse multiples of primitive polynomials has received a lot of attention recently, as evident from [6,4,5].

It has been reported [5] that given any primitive polynomial of degree d, it has exactly $N_{d,t} = \dfrac{\binom{2^d-2}{t-2} - N_{d,t-1} - \frac{t-1}{t-2}(2^d-t+1)N_{d,t-2}}{t-1}$ many t-nomial multiples

K. Nyberg and H. Heys (Eds.): SAC 2002, LNCS 2595, pp. 214–231, 2003.

(having constant term 1) with initial conditions $N_{d,2} = N_{d,1} = 0$. In [5], it has been identified that the distribution of the degrees of t-nomial multiples (having constant term 1) of a degree d primitive polynomial $f(x)$ is very close with the distribution of maximum of the tuples having size $(t - 1)$ in the range 1 to $2^d - 2$. We here provide further experiments to substantiate this claim. In fact we find that the *square of the degrees of t-nomial multiples* and the *square of the maximum of the tuples having size* $(t - 1)$ presents almost similar kind of statistical behaviour. This we discuss in Section 3.

However, in terms of the practical nonlinear combiner model [12,13], it is important to discuss the sparse multiples of *products of primitive polynomials* instead of just a single primitive polynomial. In the nonlinear combiner model, outputs of several LFSRs are combined using a nonlinear Boolean function. To make such a system safe, it is important to use correlation immune Boolean functions with some important cryptographic properties (see [1] and references in this paper for more details). Even if the combining Boolean function satisfies good cryptographic properties and possesses correlation immunity of order m, it is possible to consider product of $(m+1)$ primitive polynomials for cryptanalysis. Generally the degree of the primitive polynomials are taken to be coprime for generation of key stream having better cryptographic properties [9, Page 224]. Hence, if one can find sparse multiples of the product of primitive polynomials, then it is possible to launch cryptanalytic attacks on the nonlinear combiner model of the stream cipher (see [1] for a concrete description of such an attack).

In this direction we concentrate on t-nomial multiples of products of primitive polynomials. Consider k different primitive polynomials $f_1(x), f_2(x), \ldots, f_k(x)$ having degree $d_1, d_2, \ldots, d_k$ respectively, where $d_1, d_2, \ldots, d_k$ are pairwise coprime. Then the number of t-nomial multiples with degree $< (2^{d_1} - 1)(2^{d_2} - 1) \ldots (2^{d_k} - 1)$ of $f_1(x)f_2(x) \ldots f_k(x)$ is at least $((t - 1)!)^{k-1} \prod_{r=1}^{k} N_{d_r,t}$, where $N_{d_r,t}$ is as defined above (see also [5]). In fact, we present a more general result, which works for product of polynomials (may not be primitive) and then as a special case, we deduce the result for products of primitive polynomials. We discuss these issues in Section 4.

In Section 5, we discuss the degree distribution for t-nomial multiples of product of primitive polynomials having degree pairwise coprime. We try to estimate this distribution and support our claim with experimental results. It is observed that the distribution of the degrees of t-nomial multiples (having constant term 1) of product of primitive polynomials is very close with the distribution of maximum of the tuples having size $(t - 1)$. Thus, it is similar to the degree distribution of t-nomial multiples (having constant term 1) of primitive polynomials.

Let us now discuss a few basic concepts in this direction.

2   Preliminaries

The field of 2 elements is denoted by $GF(2)$. $GF(2^d)$ denotes the extension field of dimension d over $GF(2)$. A polynomial is irreducible over a field if it is not the product of two polynomials of lower degree in the field. An irreducible polynomial of degree d is called a primitive polynomial if its roots are the generators of the field $GF(2^d)$. The exponent of the polynomial $f(x)$ (having degree $d \geq 1$, with $f(0) = 1$) is $e \leq 2^d - 1$, which is the least positive integer such that $f(x)$ divides $x^e - 1$. For primitive polynomials $e = 2^d - 1$. By a t-nomial we refer to a polynomial with t distinct non zero terms. For more details on finite fields, the reader is referred to [10,9].

First we revisit some results presented in [5] and show how finding the t-nomial multiples is related to weight enumerator of Hamming codes. This relationship has also been used in [1, Page 580] to estimate the number of parity check equations, but explicit relationship was not investigated.

2.1   Weight Enumerator of Hamming Code and t-nomial Multiples of a Primitive Polynomial

Consider a primitive polynomial $f(x)$ of degree d and its multiples upto degree $2^d - 2$. This constructs a $[2^d - 1, 2^d - d - 1, 3]$ linear code, which is the well known Hamming code [10]. By $N_{d,t}^*$ we denote the number of codewords of weight (number of 1's in the codeword) t in the Hamming code $[2^d - 1, 2^d - d - 1, 3]$. Now we present the following technical result which connects $N_{d,t}$ and $N_{d,t}^*$.

Theorem 1. $N_{d,t}^* = \frac{2^d - 1}{t} N_{d,t}$.

Proof. Consider a primitive polynomial $f(x)$ of degree d over $GF(2)$. Now, $N_{d,t}^*$ is the number of t-nomial multiples with degree $\leq 2^d - 2$ of $f(x)$. Note that, for each of these multiples, the constant term can be either 0 or 1. On the other hand, $N_{d,t}$ is the number of t-nomial multiples having constant term 1 with degree $\leq 2^d - 2$ of $f(x)$.

Let α be a root of $f(x)$. Consider $f(x)$ divides $1 + x^{i_1} + x^{i_2} + \ldots + x^{i_{t-2}} + x^{i_{t-1}}$ for $1 \leq i_1 < i_2 < \ldots < i_{t-2} < i_{t-1} \leq 2^d - 2$. Hence, $1 + \alpha^{i_1} + \alpha^{i_2} + \ldots + \alpha^{i_{t-1}} = 0$. This immediately gives, $\alpha^i(1 + \alpha^{i_1} + \alpha^{i_2} + \ldots + \alpha^{i_{t-1}}) = 0$ for $0 \leq i \leq 2^d - 2$. Thus, there are $(2^d - 1)$ number of distinct t-nomial multiples (having constant term either 0 or 1), corresponding to $1 + x^{i_1} + x^{i_2} + \ldots + x^{i_{t-2}} + x^{i_{t-1}}$. Out of these $(2^d - 1)$ multiples, there are exactly t many multiples having constant term 1. This happens with the original t-nomial and when $i + i_r = 2^d - 1$, for $r = 1, \ldots, t - 1$. Thus, corresponding to each of the $N_{d,t}$ number of multiples *having constant term 1*, we get $\frac{2^d - 1}{t}$ number of distinct t-nomial multiples having constant term either 0 or 1. Hence the result.   □

Some results presented in [5, Section 2] can be achieved using the above theorem.

1. From weight enumerator of Hamming code [10, Page 129]), we get

$$N_{d,t}^* = \frac{\binom{2^d - 1}{t - 1} - N_{d,t-1}^* - (2^d - t + 1)N_{d,t-2}^*}{t - 1}.$$ Hence, using Theorem 1 we obtain

$$N_{d,t} = \frac{\binom{2^d - 2}{t - 2} - N_{d,t-1} - \frac{t-1}{t-2}(2^d - t + 1)N_{d,t-2}}{t - 1}.$$

2. It is easy to see that $N_{d,t}^* = N_{d,2^d-1-t}^*$ which gives

$$\frac{N_{d,t}}{t} = \frac{N_{d,2^d-1-t}}{2^d-1-t}$$

from Theorem 1.

3. Consider a t-nomial multiple $1 + x^{i_1} + x^{i_2} + \ldots + x^{i_{t-2}} + x^{i_{t-1}}$ of a primitive polynomial $f(x)$ having degree d. Now, it is clear that $x^i(1 + x^{i_1} + x^{i_2} + \ldots + x^{i_{t-2}} + x^{i_{t-1}})$ gives $2^d - 2 - i_{t-1}$ many t-nomial multiples of $f(x)$ with constant term 0 for $1 \le i \le 2^d - 2 - i_{t-1}$. Thus, each t-nomial multiple, of the form $1 + x^{i_1} + x^{i_2} + \ldots + x^{i_{t-2}} + x^{i_{t-1}}$ counted in $N_{d,t}$ produces one t-nomial multiple (itself) with constant term 1 and $2^d - 2 - i_{t-1}$ many t-nomial multiples with constant term 0. So, $\sum_{r=1}^{N_{d,t}} (2^d - 1 - d_r) = N_{d,t}^*$, where d_r is the degree of t-nomial multiples with constant term 1. Then using Theorem 1 we get

$$\sum_{r=1}^{N_{d,t}} d_r = \frac{t-1}{t}(2^d - 1)N_{d,t}.$$

3   Degree Distribution of Multiples of Primitive Polynomials

In [5], the distribution of the degrees for the t-nomial multiples of primitive polynomials has been discussed. We consider the multiples with constant term 1. The importance of the constant term being 1 is as follows. We know from [11] that if the connection polynomial (a primitive one) is of low weight, then it is possible to exploit cryptanalytic attacks. In the same direction, it is also clear that if there is a primitive polynomial $f(x)$ of degree d with high weight which has a t-nomial (t small) multiple $f_t(x)$, then the recurrence relation satisfied by $f(x)$ will also be satisfied by $f_t(x)$. It is then important to find t-nomial multiples of low degree for fast cryptanalytic attacks. Note that the recurrence relation induced by the t-nomial $1 + x^{i_1} + x^{i_2} + \ldots + x^{i_{t-2}} + x^{i_{t-1}}$ (constant term 1) is same as the recurrence relation induced by any of the t-nomials $x^i(1 + x^{i_1} + x^{i_2} + \ldots + x^{i_{t-2}} + x^{i_{t-1}})$ (constant term may be zero). Thus, it is important to get distinct t-nomials with constant term 1. This consideration has also been followed in [5].

Given any primitive polynomial $f(x)$ of degree d, it is clear that $f(x)$ has $N_{d,t}$ number of t-nomial multiples having degree $\le 2^d - 2$. Now it is an important question that how many t-nomial multiples are there having degree less than or equal to some c. Since, this result is not settled, in [5], an estimation has been used. In [5], any t-nomial multiple $1 + x^{i_1} + x^{i_2} + \ldots + x^{i_{t-2}} + x^{i_{t-1}}$ has been interpreted as the $(t-1)$-tuple $< i_1, i_2, \ldots, i_{t-2}, i_{t-1} >$. It was also empirically justified using experimental result (considering primitive polynomials of degree 8, 9 and 10, Tables 1, 2, 3 in [5]) that by fixing $f(x)$, if one enumerates all the $N_{d,t}$ different $(t-1)$ tuples, then the distribution of the tuples seems random. Moreover, the distribution of the degrees of the t-nomial multiples seems very close with the distribution of maximum value of each of the ordered tuples $< i_1, i_2, \ldots, i_{t-2}, i_{t-1} >$ with $1 \leq i_1 < i_2 < \ldots < i_{t-2} < i_{t-1} \leq 2^d - 2$.

To analyse the degree distribution of these t-nomial multiples, the random variate X is considered in [5], which is $\max(i_1, i_2, \ldots, i_{t-2}, i_{t-1})$, where $1 + x^{i_1} + x^{i_2} + \ldots + x^{i_{t-2}} + x^{i_{t-1}}$ is a t-nomial multiple of $f(x)$. There are $N_{d,t}$ such multiples. The mean value of the distribution of X is $\frac{t-1}{t}(2^d - 1)N_{d,t}$ divided by $N_{d,t}$, i.e., $\overline{X} = \frac{t-1}{t}(2^d - 1)$ (see [5] and Section 2 of this paper). On the other hand, consider all the $(t-1)$-tuples $< i_1, i_2, \ldots, i_{t-2}, i_{t-1} >$ in the range 1 to $2^d - 2$. There are $\binom{2^d-2}{t-1}$ such tuples. Each tuple is in ordered form such that $1 \leq i_1 < i_2 < \ldots < i_{t-2} < i_{t-1} \leq 2^d - 2$. Consider the random variate Y which is $\max(i_1, i_2, \ldots, i_{t-2}, i_{t-1})$. It has been shown in [5] that the mean of this distribution is $\overline{Y} = \frac{t-1}{t}(2^d - 1)$.

Thus, given any primitive polynomial $f(x)$ of degree d, the average degree of its t-nomial multiples with degree $\leq 2^d - 2$ is equal to the average of maximum of all the distinct $(t-1)$ tuples form 1 to $2^d - 2$. With this result and experimental observations, the work of [5] assumes that the distributions X, Y are very close.

3.1 Sum of Squares

We here provide further experimental results in this direction and strengthen the claim of [5] that the distributions X, Y are very close. For this we first find the sum of squares of $\max(i_1, i_2, \ldots, i_{t-2}, i_{t-1})$ for the distribution Y.

Lemma 1. *The average of squares of the values in Y is $\frac{t-1}{t}(2^d - 1)(\frac{t2^d}{t+1} - 1)$. Moreover, standard deviation of Y is $\frac{1}{t}\sqrt{\frac{t-1}{t+1}(2^d - 1)(2^d - t - 1)}$.*

Proof. Consider the random variate Y which is $\max(i_1, i_2, \ldots, i_{t-2}, i_{t-1})$. We know that $< i_1, i_2, \ldots, i_{t-2}, i_{t-1} >$ is any ordered $(t-1)$-tuple from the values 1 to $2^d - 2$. Note that there is only 1 tuple with maximum value $(t-1)$. There are $\binom{t-1}{t-2}$ tuples with maximum value t, $\binom{t}{t-2}$ tuples with maximum value $t+1$ and so on. Thus, the average of the squares of the values in the distribution Y
$= \sum_{i=t-1}^{2^d-2} i^2 \binom{i-1}{t-2}/\binom{2^d-2}{t-1}$. Now, $\sum_{i=t-1}^{2^d-2} i^2 \binom{i-1}{t-2} = (t-1)t \sum_{i=t-1}^{2^d-2} \binom{i+1}{t} - (t-1)\sum_{i=t-1}^{2^d-2} \binom{i}{t-1} = (t-1)t\binom{2^d}{t+1} - (t-1)\binom{2^d-1}{t}$. Simplifying we get,
$\sum_{i=t-1}^{2^d-2} i^2 \binom{i-1}{t-2}/\binom{2^d-2}{t-1} = \frac{t-1}{t}(2^d - 1)(\frac{t2^d}{t+1} - 1)$. Now standard deviation of Y
$= \sqrt{\frac{t-1}{t}(2^d - 1)(\frac{t2^d}{t+1} - 1) - (\frac{t-1}{t}(2^d - 1))^2} = \frac{1}{t}\sqrt{\frac{t-1}{t+1}(2^d - 1)(2^d - t - 1)}$. □

Let us present some experimental results in Table 1 for multiples of primitive polynomials having degree $d = 4, 5, 6, 7$. We take each of the primitive polynomials and then find the *average of the square of degrees* of t-nomial multiples for $t = 3, 4, 5, 6, 7$. In the last row we present the estimated value $\frac{t-1}{t}(2^d-1)(\frac{t2^d}{t+1}-1)$.

From the above table it is clear that in terms of average of squares, the distributions X, Y are very close. The most interesting observation in this direction

Table 1. Average of *sum of squares for the degrees* of *t*-nomial multiples. Primitive polynomials with degree 4, 5, 6, 7 are considered.

Primitive polynomial	$t = 3$	$t = 4$	$t = 5$	$t = 6$	$t = 7$
$x^4 + x + 1$	110	132.61	148.04	158.96	167.13
$x^4 + x^3 + 1$	110	132.61	148.04	158.96	167.13
Estimated	110	132.75	148	158.92	167.14
$x^5 + x^2 + 1$	475.33	571.48	636.67	682.78	717.40
$x^5 + x^3 + 1$	475.33	571.48	636.67	682.78	717.40
$x^5 + x^3 + x^2 + x + 1$	475.33	571.48	636.43	682.81	717.44
$x^5 + x^4 + x^2 + x + 1$	475.33	571.55	636.41	682.80	717.45
$x^5 + x^4 + x^3 + x + 1$	475.33	571.55	636.41	682.80	717.45
$x^5 + x^4 + x^3 + x^2 + 1$	475.33	571.48	636.43	682.81	717.44
Estimated	475.33	571.95	636.53	682.73	717.42
$x^6 + x + 1$	1974	2371.63	2636.76	2827.51	2969.98
$x^6 + x^4 + x^3 + x + 1$	1974	2371.09	2636.71	2827.54	2969.99
$x^6 + x^5 + 1$	1974	2371.63	2636.76	2827.51	2969.98
$x^6 + x^5 + x^2 + x + 1$	1974	2371.27	2636.46	2827.54	2970.01
$x^6 + x^5 + x^3 + x^2 + 1$	1974	2371.09	2636.71	2827.54	2969.99
$x^6 + x^5 + x^4 + x + 1$	1974	2371.27	2636.46	2827.54	2970.01
Estimated	1974	2371.95	2637.60	2827.50	2970
$x^7 + x + 1$	8043.33	9657.33	10736.02	11505.61	12083.13
$x^7 + x^3 + 1$	8043.33	9656.92	10736.05	11505.62	12083.13
$x^7 + x^3 + x^2 + x + 1$	8043.33	9656.37	10735.46	11505.65	12083.16
$x^7 + x^4 + 1$	8043.33	9656.92	10736.05	11505.62	12083.13
$x^7 + x^4 + x^3 + x^2 + 1$	8043.33	9656.65	10735.77	11505.64	12083.14
$x^7 + x^5 + x^2 + x + 1$	8043.33	9656.66	10735.87	11505.64	12083.14
$x^7 + x^5 + x^3 + x + 1$	8043.33	9657.48	10735.60	11505.61	12083.15
$x^7 + x^5 + x^4 + x^3 + 1$	8043.33	9656.65	10735.77	11505.64	12083.14
$x^7 + x^5 + x^4 + x^3 + x^2 + x + 1$	8043.33	9657.82	10735.71	11505.60	12083.14
$x^7 + x^6 + 1$	8043.33	9657.33	10736.02	11505.61	12083.13
$x^7 + x^6 + x^3 + x + 1$	8043.33	9656.59	10735.42	11505.65	12083.16
$x^7 + x^6 + x^4 + x + 1$	8043.33	9656.59	10735.42	11505.65	12083.16
$x^7 + x^6 + x^4 + x^2 + 1$	8043.33	9657.48	10735.60	11505.61	12083.15
$x^7 + x^6 + x^5 + x^2 + 1$	8043.33	9656.66	10735.87	11505.64	12083.14
$x^7 + x^6 + x^5 + x^3 + x^2 + x + 1$	8043.33	9656.38	10735.47	11505.65	12083.16
$x^7 + x^6 + x^5 + x^4 + 1$	8043.33	9656.37	10735.46	11505.65	12083.16
$x^7 + x^6 + x^5 + x^4 + x^2 + x + 1$	8043.33	9656.38	10735.47	11505.65	12083.16
$x^7 + x^6 + x^5 + x^4 + x^3 + x^2 + 1$	8043.33	9657.82	10735.71	11505.60	12083.14
Estimated	8043.33	9658.35	10735.73	11505.60	12083.14

is the sum of square of the degree of the trinomial multiples. Note that the *average of the squares of the elements of distribution Y* (considering $t = 3$) and *the average of the squares of the degrees of trinomial multiples* are same for all the experiments, which is $\frac{2}{3}(2^d - 1)(3.2^{d-2} - 1)$. Thus we present the following observation (see [14] for formal proof).

Consider any primitive polynomial $f(x)$ of degree d. Consider that the degree of the trinomial multiples (having degree $\leq 2^d - 2$) of $f(x)$ are $d_1, d_2, \ldots, d_{N_{d,3}}$. Then $\sum_{i=1}^{N_{d,3}} d_i^2 = \frac{2}{3}(2^d - 1)(3.2^{d-2} - 1)N_{d,3}$.

3.2   Reciprocal Polynomials

Consider two primitive polynomials $f(x)$ and $g(x)$ of degree d, such that they are reciprocal to each other. That is, if α is a root of $f(x)$, then $\alpha^{-1} = \alpha^{2^d-2}$ is the root of $g(x)$. Consider the multiset $W(f(x), d, t)$, which contains the degree of all the t-nomial multiples (having degree $< 2^d - 1$) of a degree d polynomial $f(x)$. Now we have the following result.

Lemma 2. *Let $f(x)$ and $g(x)$ be two reciprocal primitive polynomials of degree d. Then $W(f(x), d, t) = W(g(x), d, t)$.*

Proof. Note that $f(x)$ divides a t-nomial $x^{i_1} + x^{i_2} + \ldots + x^{i_{t-2}} + x^{i_{t-1}} + 1$ iff $g(x)$ divides a t-nomial $x^{i_1} + x^{i_1 - i_2} + \ldots + x^{i_1 - i_{t-2}} + x^{i_1 - i_{t-1}} + 1$. Without loss of generality, we consider that $i_1 > i_2 > \ldots > i_{t-2} > i_{t-1}$. This gives the proof. $\square$

From Lemma 2 we get that, since $W(f(x), d, t) = W(g(x), d, t)$, the statistical parameters based on $W(f(x), d, t)$ or $W(g(x), d, t)$ are also same. In Table 1, it is clear that the entries corresponding to any primitive polynomial and its reciprocal are same.

4 t-nomial Multiples of Products of Primitive Polynomials

We have already mentioned in the introduction that it is important to find *t-nomial multiples of product of primitive polynomials* instead of *t-nomial multiples of just a single primitive polynomial*. Let us now briefly describe how the exact cryptanalysis works. For more details about the cryptographic properties of the Boolean functions mentioned below, see [1]. Consider $F(X_1, \ldots, X_n)$ is an n-variable, m-resilient Boolean function used in combining the output sequences of n LFSRs S_i having feedback polynomials $c_i(x)$. The Walsh transform of the Boolean function F gives, $W_F(\overline{\omega}) \neq 0$ for some $\overline{\omega}$ with $wt(\overline{\omega}) = m + 1$. This means that the Boolean function F and the linear function $\bigoplus_{i=1}^{n} \omega_i X_i$ are correlated. Let $\omega_{i_1} = \ldots = \omega_{i_{m+1}} = 1$. Now consider the composite LFSR S which produces the same sequence as the XOR of the sequences of the LFSRs $S_{i_1}, \ldots, S_{i_{m+1}}$. The connection polynomial of the composite LFSR will be $\prod_{j=1}^{m+1} c_{i_j}(x)$. Since F and $\bigoplus_{i=1}^{n} \omega_i X_i$ are correlated, the attacks target to estimate the stream generated from the composite LFSR S having the connection polynomial $\psi(x) = \prod_{j=1}^{m+1} c_{i_j}(x)$.

The attack heavily depends on sparse multiples of $\psi(x)$. One such attack, presented in [1], uses t-nomial multiples $t = 3, 4, 5$. In design of this model of stream cipher, generally the degree of the primitive polynomials are taken to be coprime to each other [9, Page 224] to achieve better cryptographic properties. We here take care of that restriction also.

Note that in [1, Page 581], it has been assumed that the approximate count of *multiples of primitive polynomials* and *multiples of products of primitive polynomials* are close. However, this is not always true. In fact, it is possible to find

products of primitive polynomials having same degree which do not have any
t-nomial multiple for some t. The construction of BCH code [10] uses this idea.
On the other hand, if the degree of the primitive polynomials are pairwise coprime, then we show that it is always guaranteed to get t-nomial multiples of
their product, provided each individual primitive polynomial has t-nomial multi-
ple(s). Moreover, in the next section we will show that the approximate count of
the multiples of *a degree d primitive polynomial* and *a degree d polynomial which
is product of some primitive polynomials each having degree d_r*, i.e., $\sum d_r = d$
are close when the degree d_r's are mutually coprime (see Remark 2). So for this
case the assumption of [1, Page 581] is a good approximation. Let us now present
the main theorem.

Theorem 2. *Consider k many polynomials $f_1(x), f_2(x), \ldots, f_k(x)$ over GF(2)
having degrees $d_1, d_2, \ldots, d_k$ and exponents $e_1, e_2, \ldots, e_k$ respectively, with the
following conditions :*

1. *$e_1 \neq e_2 \neq \ldots \neq e_k$ are pairwise coprime,*
2. *$f_1(0) = f_2(0) = \ldots = f_k(0) = 1$,*
3. *$\gcd(f_r(x), f_s(x)) = 1$ for $1 \leq r \neq s \leq k$,*
4. *number of t-nomial multiples (with degree $< e_r$) of $f_r(x)$ is n_r.*

*Then the number of t-nomial multiples with degree $< e_1 e_2 \ldots e_k$ of the product
$f_1(x) f_2(x) \ldots f_k(x)$ is at least $((t-1)!)^{k-1} n_1 n_2 \ldots n_k$.*

Proof. Consider that any polynomial $f_r(x)$ has a t-nomial multiple $x^{i_{1,r}} + x^{i_{2,r}} +
\ldots + x^{i_{t-1,r}} + 1$ of degree $< e_r$. Now we try to get a t-nomial multiple of
$f_1(x) f_2(x) \ldots f_k(x)$ having degree $< e_1 e_2 \ldots e_k$.

   Consider the set of equations $I_1 = i_{1,r} \bmod e_r$, $r = 1, \ldots, k$. Since $e_1, \ldots, e_k$
are pairwise coprime, we will have a unique solution of $I_1 \bmod e_1 e_2 \ldots e_k$ by
Chinese remainder theorem [7, Page 53]. Similarly, consider $I_j = i_{j,r} \bmod e_r$ for
$r = 1, \ldots, k$ and $j = 1, \ldots, t-1$. By Chinese remainder theorem, we get a unique
solution of $I_j \bmod e_1 e_2 \ldots e_k$.

   First we like to show that $f_r(x)$ (for $r = 1, \ldots, k$) divides $x^{I_1} + x^{I_2} + \ldots +
x^{I_{t-1}} + 1$. The exponent of $f_r(x)$ is e_r. So we need to show that $f_r(x)$ divides
$x^{I_1 \bmod e_r} + x^{I_2 \bmod e_r} + \ldots + x^{I_{t-1} \bmod e_r} + 1$. We have $i_{j,r} = I_j \bmod e_r$ for
$r = 1, \ldots, k$, $j = 1, \ldots, t-1$. Thus, $x^{I_1 \bmod e_r} + x^{I_2 \bmod e_r} + \ldots + x^{I_{t-1} \bmod e_r} + 1$
is nothing but $x^{i_{1,r}} + x^{i_{2,r}} + \ldots + x^{i_{t-1,r}} + 1$. Hence $f_r(x)$ (for $r = 1, \ldots, k$)
divides $x^{I_1} + x^{I_2} + \ldots + x^{I_{t-1}} + 1$.

   Here we need to show that $x^{I_1} + x^{I_2} + \ldots + x^{I_{t-1}} + 1$ is indeed a t-nomial,
i.e., $I_j \neq I_l \bmod e_1 \ldots e_k$ for $j \neq l$. If $I_j = I_l$, then it is easy to see that $i_{j,r} =
i_{l,r} \bmod e_r$ and hence, $x^{i_{1,r}} + x^{i_{2,r}} + \ldots + x^{i_{t-1,r}} + 1$ itself is not a t-nomial for
any r, which is a contradiction.

   Moreover, we have $\gcd(f_r(x), f_s(x)) = 1$ for $r \neq s$. Thus, $f_1(x) f_2(x) \ldots f_k(x)$
divides $x^{I_1} + x^{I_2} + \ldots + x^{I_{t-1}} + 1$. Also it is clear that degree of $x^{I_1} + x^{I_2} + \ldots +
x^{I_{t-1}} + 1$ is less than $e_1 e_2 \ldots e_k$.

   Corresponding to the t-nomial multiple of $f_1(x)$, i.e., $x^{i_{1,1}} + x^{i_{2,1}} + \ldots +
x^{i_{t-1,1}} + 1$, we fix the elements in the order $i_{1,1}, i_{2,1}, \ldots, i_{t-1,1}$. Let us name
them $p_{1,1}, p_{2,1}, \ldots, p_{t-1,1}$.

For $r = 2, \ldots k$, the case is as follows. Corresponding to the t-nomial multiple $x^{i_{1,r}} + x^{i_{2,r}} + \ldots + x^{i_{t-1,r}} + 1$ of $f_r(x)$, we use any possible permutation of the elements $i_{1,r}, i_{2,r}, \ldots, i_{t-1,r}$ as $p_{1,r}, p_{2,r}, \ldots, p_{t-1,r}$. Thus we will use any of the $(t-1)!$ permutations for each t-nomial multiple of $f_r(x)$ for $r = 2, \ldots, k$.

Now we use Chinese remainder theorem to get I_j having value $< e_1 e_2 \ldots e_k$ from $p_{j,r}$'s for $r = 1, \ldots, k$. Each $p_{j,r}$ is less than e_r. Here $p_{1,r}, p_{2,r}, \ldots, p_{t-1,r}$ (related to $f_r(x)$) can be permuted in $(t-1)!$ ways and we consider the permutation related to all the t-nomials except the first one.

Corresponding to k many t-nomial multiples (one each for $f_1(x), \ldots, f_k(x)$), we get $((t-1)!)^{k-1}$ many t-nomial multiples (degree $< e_1 e_2 \ldots e_k$) of the product $f_1(x) f_2(x) \ldots f_k(x)$. Using Chinese remainder theorem, it is routine to check that all these $((t-1)!)^{k-1}$ multiples are distinct.

Since, each $f_r(x)$ has n_r distinct t-nomial multiples of degree $< e_r$, the total number of t-nomial multiples of the product $f_1(x) f_2(x) \ldots f_k(x)$ having degree $< e_1 e_2 \ldots e_k$ is $((t-1)!)^{k-1} n_1 n_2 \ldots n_k$.

To accept the above count is a lower bound, one needs to show that the t-nomials generated by this method are all distinct. Consider two collections of t-nomial multiples $x^{a_{1,r}} + x^{a_{2,r}} + \ldots + x^{a_{t-1,r}} + 1$ and $x^{b_{1,r}} + x^{b_{2,r}} + \ldots + x^{b_{t-1,r}} + 1$ of $f_r(x)$ for $r = 1, \ldots, k$. There exists at least one s in the range $1, \ldots, k$ such that $x^{a_{1,s}} + x^{a_{2,s}} + \ldots + x^{a_{t-1,s}} + 1$ and $x^{b_{1,s}} + x^{b_{2,s}} + \ldots + x^{b_{t-1,s}} + 1$ are distinct. Let us consider that one of the common multiples form these two sets of t-nomials are same, say $x^{A_{1,v}} + x^{A_{2,v}} + \ldots + x^{A_{t-1,v}} + 1$ (from the set $x^{a_{1,r}} + x^{a_{2,r}} + \ldots + x^{a_{t-1,r}} + 1$) and $x^{B_{1,v}} + x^{B_{2,v}} + \ldots + x^{B_{t-1,v}} + 1$ (from the set $x^{b_{1,r}} + x^{b_{2,r}} + \ldots + x^{b_{t-1,r}} + 1$).

Without loss of generality we consider $A_{1,v} > A_{2,v} > \ldots > A_{t-1,v}$ and $B_{1,v} > B_{2,v} > \ldots > B_{t-1,v}$. Since these two t-nomials are same, we have $A_{j,v} = B_{j,v} \bmod e_1 e_2 \ldots e_k$. This immediately says that $A_{j,v} = B_{j,v} \bmod e_r$, which implies $a_{j,r} = b_{j,r} \bmod e_r$ for each j in $1, \ldots, t-1$ and each r in $1, \ldots, k$. This contradicts to the statement that $x^{a_{1,s}} + x^{a_{2,s}} + \ldots + x^{a_{t-1,s}} + 1$ and $x^{b_{1,s}} + x^{b_{2,s}} + \ldots + x^{b_{t-1,s}} + 1$ are distinct.

From the above point it is clear that the number of t-nomial multiples with degree $< e_1 e_2 \ldots e_k$ of $f_1(x) f_2(x) \ldots f_k(x)$ is at least $((t-1)!)^{k-1} n_1 n_2 \ldots n_k$.   □

Corollary 1. *Consider k many primitive polynomials $f_1(x), f_2(x), \ldots, f_k(x)$ having degree $d_1, d_2, \ldots, d_k$ respectively, where $d_1, d_2, \ldots, d_k$ are pairwise coprime. Then the number of t-nomial multiples with degree $< (2^{d_1} - 1)(2^{d_2} - 1) \ldots (2^{d_k} - 1)$ of $f_1(x) f_2(x) \ldots f_k(x)$ is at least $((t-1)!)^{k-1} \prod_{r=1}^{k} N_{d_r,t}$, where $N_{d_r,t}$ is as defined in Theorem 1.*

Proof. Since we are considering the primitive polynomials, the exponent $e_r = 2^{d_r} - 1$. Also, given $d_1, d_2, \ldots, d_k$ are mutually coprime, $e_1, e_2, \ldots, e_k$ are also mutually coprime. Moreover, There is no common divisor of any two primitive polynomials. The proof then follows from Theorem 2 putting $n_r = N_{d_r,t}$.   □

Corollary 2. *In Theorem 2, for $t = 3$, the number of trinomial multiples with degree $< e_1 e_2 \ldots e_k$ of $f_1(x) f_2(x) \ldots f_k(x)$ is exactly equal to $2^{k-1} n_1 n_2 \ldots n_k$.*

Proof. Consider a trinomial multiple $x^{I_1} + x^{I_2} + 1$ having degree $< e_1 e_2 \ldots e_k$ of the product $f_1(x)f_2(x) \ldots f_k(x)$. Since, the product $f_1(x)f_2(x) \ldots f_k(x)$ divides $x^{I_1} + x^{I_2} + 1$, it is clear that $f_r(x)$ divides $x^{I_1} + x^{I_2} + 1$. Hence, $f_r(x)$ divides $x^{I_1 \bmod e_r} + x^{I_2 \bmod e_r} + 1$ having degree $< e_r$. Now take, $i_{1,r} = I_1 \bmod e_r$ and $i_{2,r} = I_2 \bmod e_r$, for $r = 1, \ldots, k$. It is clear that $I_1 \neq I_2 \bmod e_r$ (i.e., $i_{1,r} \neq i_{2,r}$), otherwise $f_r(x)$ divides 1, which is not possible.

Also note that either $i_{1,r}$ or $i_{2,r}$ can not be zero, otherwise $f_r(x)$ divides either $x^{i_{2,r}}$ or $x^{i_{1,r}}$, which is not possible. Thus, $f_r(x)$ divides $x^{i_{1,r}} + x^{i_{2,r}} + 1$. Then using the construction method in the proof of Theorem 2, one can get back $x^{I_1} + x^{I_2} + 1$ as the multiple of $f_1(x)f_2(x) \ldots f_k(x)$ which is already considered in the count $2^{k-1} n_1 n_2 \ldots n_k$ as described in the proof of Theorem 2. Hence this count is exact.   □

Corollary 3. *Consider k many primitive polynomials $f_1(x), f_2(x), \ldots, f_k(x)$ having degree $d_1, d_2, \ldots, d_k$ respectively, where $d_1, d_2, \ldots, d_k$ are pairwise co-prime. Then the number of trinomial multiples with degree $< (2^{d_1} - 1)(2^{d_2} - 1) \ldots (2^{d_k} - 1)$ of $f_1(x)f_2(x) \ldots f_k(x)$ is exactly equal to $2^{k-1} \prod_{r=1}^{k} N_{d_r,3}$, where $N_{d_r,3}$ is as defined in Theorem 1.*

Proof. The proof follows from Corollary 1 and Corollary 2.   □

Corollary 2 shows that number of trinomial multiples of $f_1(x)f_2(x) \ldots f_k(x)$ is exactly $2^{k-1} n_1 n_2 \ldots n_k$. However, it is important to mention that for $t \geq 4$, $((t-1)!)^{k-1} n_1 n_2 \ldots n_k$ is indeed a lower bound and not an exact count. The reason is as follows.

Consider $f_r(x)$ has a multiple $x^{a_{1,r}} + x^{a_{2,r}} + \ldots + x^{a_{t-1,r}} + 1$. Note that for $t \geq 5$, we get $(t-2)$-nomial multiples of $f_r(x)$ having degree $< e_r$. Consider the $(t-2)$-nomial multiple as $x^{a_{1,r}} + x^{a_{2,r}} + \ldots + x^{a_{t-3,r}} + 1$. Now, from the $(t-2)$-nomial multiple we construct a multiple $x^{a_{1,r}} + x^{a_{2,r}} + \ldots + x^{a_{t-1,r}} + 1$, where, $a_{t-2,r} = a_{t-1,r} = w$, where, $w < e_r$. Then if we apply Chinese remainder theorem as in Theorem 2, that will very well produce a t-nomial multiple of $f_1(x)f_2(x) \ldots f_k(x)$ which is not counted in Theorem 2. Thus the count is not exact and only a lower bound. For the case of $t = 4$, we can consider the multiples of the form $x^{i_r} + x^{i_r} + 1 + 1$ of $f_r(x)$. These type of multiples of $f_r(x)$'s will contribute additional multiples of the product $f_1(x)f_2(x) \ldots f_k(x)$ which are not counted in Theorem 2.

Corollary 4. *In Theorem 2, for $t \geq 4$, the number of t-nomial multiples with degree $< e_1 e_2 \ldots e_k$ of the product $f_1(x)f_2(x) \ldots f_k(x)$ is strictly greater than $((t-1)!)^{k-1} n_1 n_2 \ldots n_k$.*

Let us consider the product of two primitive polynomials of degree 3, 4, degree 3, 5 and degree 4, 5 separately. Table 2 compares the lower bound given in Theorem 2 and the exact count by running computer program. Note that it is clear that for $t = 3$, the count is exact as mentioned in Corollary 3. On the other hand, for $t \geq 4$, the count is a lower bound (strictly greater than the exact

Table 2. Count for t-nomial multiples of product of primitive polynomials.

t	3	4	5	6	7
Lower bound	42	672	0	0	146160
Exact count	42	1460	35945	717556	11853632

Product of degree 3, 4

t	3	4	5
Lower bound	90	3360	0
Exact count	90	6564	344625

Product of degree 3, 5

t	3	4	5
Lower bound	210	23520	1128960
Exact count	210	32508	3723685

Product of degree 4, 5

count) as mentioned in Corollary 4. In Table 2, for a few cases the lower bound is zero, since $N_{3,5} = N_{3,6} = 0$.

We already know that the lower bound result presented in Corollary 1 is invariant on the choice of the primitive polynomials. We observe that this is also true for the exact count found by computer search. As example, if one chooses any primitive polynomial of degree 3 and any one of degree 4, the exact count does not depend on the choice of the primitive polynomials.

Thus we make the following experimental observation. Consider k many primitive polynomials $f_1(x), f_2(x), \ldots, f_k(x)$ having degree $d_1, d_2, \ldots, d_k$ respectively, where $d_1, d_2, \ldots, d_k$ are pairwise coprime. Then the exact number of t-nomial multiples with degree $< (2^{d_1} - 1)(2^{d_2} - 1) \ldots (2^{d_k} - 1)$ of $f_1(x)f_2(x) \ldots f_k(x)$ is same irrespective of the choice of primitive polynomial $f_r(x)$ of degree d_r.

4.1   Exact Count Vs Lower Bound

Note that the values in the Table 2 shows that there are big differences between the exact count and the lower bound. Note that the lower bound in some cases is zero, since $N_{3,5} = N_{3,6} = 0$. We will now clarify these issues. Let us first present the following result.

Proposition 1. *Consider two primitive polynomials $f_1(x), f_2(x)$ of degree d_1, d_2 (mutually coprime) and exponent e_1, e_2 respectively. Then the exact number of 4-nomial multiples of $f_1(x)f_2(x)$ is $6N_{d_1,4}N_{d_2,4} + (e_1 - 1)(e_2 - 1) + (3(e_1 - 1) + 1)N_{d_2,4} + (3(e_2 - 1) + 1)N_{d_1,4}$.*

Proof. The term $6N_{d_1,4}N_{d_2,4}$ follows from Theorem 2.

Consider $x^i + x^{k_1 e_1} + x^{k_2 e_2} + 1$, where $i < e_1 e_2$, $i \bmod e_1 \neq 0$, $i \bmod e_2 \neq 0$, and $i = k_2 e_2 \bmod e_1 = k_1 e_1 \bmod e_2$, $k_1 < e_2$, $k_2 < e_1$. Thus it is clear that for a fixed i, we will get unique k_1, k_2. Now there are $(e_1 e_2 - 1) - (e_1 - 1) - (e_2 - 1) = (e_1 - 1)(e_2 - 1)$ possible values of i. Note that in each of the cases, $x^i + x^{k_1 e_1} + x^{k_2 e_2} + 1$ is divisible by $f_1(x)f_2(x)$. So this will add to the count.

Fix a multiple $x^i + x^j + x^l + 1$ of $f_2(x)$ where i, j, l are unequal and degree of $x^i + x^j + x^l + 1$ is less than e_2. Now consider a multiple $x^a + x^a + x^0 + 1$ of $f_1(x)$. As a varies from 1 to $e_1 - 1$, for each a, we will get three different multiples of $f_1(x)f_2(x)$ by using Chinese remainder theorem. The reason is as follows. Fix the elements $a, a, 0$ in order. Now i, j, k can be placed in $\frac{3!}{2!} = 3$ ways to get distinct cases. Varying a from 1 to $e_1 - 1$, we get $3(e_1 - 1)$ multiples. Moreover, if $a = 0$, then also $x^a + x^a + x^0 + 1$ and $x^i + x^j + x^l + 1$ will provide only one multiple of $f_1(x)f_2(x)$. Thus, considering each multiple of $f_2(x)$ we get $3(e_1 - 1) + 1$ multiples. Hence the total contribution is $(3(e_1 - 1) + 1)N_{d_2,4}$.

Similarly fixing a multiple $x^i + x^j + x^l + 1$ of $f_1(x)$ and $x^a + x^a + x^0 + 1$ of $f_2(x)$ we get the count $(3(e_2 - 1) + 1)N_{d_1,4}$.

It is a routine but tedious exercise to see that all these 4-nomial multiples of $f_1(x)f_2(x)$ are distinct and there is no other 4-nomial multiples having degree $< e_1 e_2$. □

Note that using this formula of Proposition 1, we get the exact counts for 4-nomial multiples as presented in Table 2. However, extending the exact formula of 4-nomial multiples of product of two primitive polynomials seems extremely tedious. On the other hand, an important question is *do we at all need the exact count for cryptographic purposes?* We answer this as follows.

Consider that $f_1(x)f_2(x) \ldots f_k(x)$ is itself a τ-nomial with constant term 1. From cryptanalytic point of view, it is interesting to find t-nomial multiples of $f_1(x)f_2(x) \ldots f_k(x)$ only when $t < \tau$ (in practical cases, $t \ll \tau$). Now we like to present an interesting experimental observation.

Conjecture 1. Let $x^{I_1} + x^{I_2} + \ldots + x^{I_{t-1}} + 1$ be the least degree t-nomial multiple $(4 \leq t < \tau)$ of $f_1(x)f_2(x) \ldots f_k(x)$ which itself is a τ-nomial. Each polynomial $f_r(x)$ is a primitive polynomial of degree d_r (degrees are pairwise coprime) and exponent $e_r = 2^{d_r} - 1$. Moreover, $N_{d_r,t} > 0$. Then $I_v \neq I_w \bmod e_r$ for any $1 \leq v \neq w \leq t - 1$ and for any $r = 1, \ldots, k$. That is, the least degree t-nomial multiple of $f_1(x)f_2(x) \ldots f_k(x)$ is the one which is generated as described in Theorem 2.

As example, consider $(x^3 + x + 1)(x^4 + x + 1) = x^7 + x^5 + x^3 + x^2 + 1$ which is itself a 5-nomial. Now the least degree 4-nomial multiple of $x^7 + x^5 + x^3 + x^2 + 1$, as generated in the proof of Theorem 2, is $x^9 + x^4 + x^3 + 1$. Note that $x^{9 \bmod 7} + x^{4 \bmod 7} + x^{3 \bmod 7} + 1 = x^2 + x^4 + x^3 + 1$ and $x^{9 \bmod 15} + x^{4 \bmod 15} + x^{3 \bmod 15} + 1 = x^9 + x^4 + x^3 + 1$. Thus the multiple $x^9 + x^4 + x^3 + 1$ is generated as in Theorem 2. On the other hand, the least degree 4-nomial multiple of $x^7 + x^5 + x^3 + x^2 + 1$ is $x^{16} + x^{14} + x^9 + 1$, which is not counted in the proof of Theorem 2. In this case, $x^{16 \bmod 7} + x^{14 \bmod 7} + x^{9 \bmod 7} + 1 = x^2 + x^0 + x^2 + 1$ (basically 0). This supports the statement of Conjecture 1.

We have also checked that the Conjecture 1 is true considering products of two primitive polynomials $f_1(x), f_2(x)$ having degree d_1, d_2 (mutually coprime) for $d_1, d_2 \leq 6$.

Remark 1. Let us once again consider the model where outputs of several LFSRs are combined using a nonlinear Boolean function of n variables to produce the key stream. Consider that the combining Boolean function is $(k - 1)$th order correlation immune (see [1]). Thus it is possible to mount a correlation attack by considering the product of polynomials $f_r(x), r = 1, \ldots, k$ corresponding to k inputs of the Boolean function. Thus to execute the attack one has to consider the

t-nomial multiples of $\prod_{r=1}^{k} f_r(x)$. At this point consider the t-nomial multiples considered in Theorem 2. Once we get a t-nomial multiple $x^{I_1} + x^{I_2} + \ldots + x^{I_{t-1}} + 1$ of $\prod_{r=1}^{k} f_r(x)$, we know when we reduce it as $x^{I_1 \bmod e_r} + x^{I_2 \bmod e_r} + \ldots + x^{I_{t-1} \bmod e_r} + 1$, then we will get a t-nomial multiple (having degree $< e_r$) of $f_r(x)$. On the other hand, if we consider any t-nomial multiple $x^{I_1} + x^{I_2} + \ldots + x^{I_{t-1}} + 1$ of $\prod_{r=1}^{k} f_r(x)$, which is not considered in Theorem 2, then for some r, $x^{I_1 \bmod e_r} + x^{I_2 \bmod e_r} + \ldots + x^{I_{t-1} \bmod e_r} + 1$, will not be a "genuine" t-nomial multiple (having degree $< e_r$) of $f_r(x)$ (i.e., all the terms will not be distinct). That is we will get either some u such that $I_u = 0 \bmod e_r$ or get some $u \neq v$, such that $I_u = I_v \bmod e_r$. Thus from cryptographic point of view, only the multiples considered in Theorem 2 are to be considered.

However, in the next section we will consider all the multiples (not only those referred in Theorem 2) for the degree distribution.

5 Degree Distribution of t-nomial Multiples of Product of Primitive Polynomials

From the cryptanalytic point of view, it is important to find the t-nomial multiples (of product of primitive polynomials) having lower degrees. One way to obtain the minimum degree t-nomial multiple of product of polynomials is to start checking the t-nomials from lower to higher degrees and see when the first time we get one t-nomial multiple. This provides the minimum degree t-nomial multiple of product of the polynomials. Similar method can be continued further to get more multiples. On the other hand, to resist cryptanalytic attack, it is important to select primitive polynomials such that they won't have a t-nomial multiple at lower degree for small t, say $t \leq 10$. Thus it is important to analyse the degree distribution of t-nomial multiples of product of primitive polynomials.

Let us now concentrate on the case when the primitive polynomials are of degree pairwise coprime. We like to estimate how the degree of the t-nomial multiples are distributed. Consider a primitive polynomial $f_r(x)$ of degree d_r. It has $N_{d_r,t}$ many t-nomial multiples of degree $< 2^{d_r} - 1$. Now we like to highlight the following points.

1. Consider t-nomial multiples of the form $x^{p_{1,r}} + x^{p_{2,r}} + \ldots + x^{p_{t-1,r}} + 1$ of a primitive polynomial $f_r(x)$. Note that $p_{1,r}, p_{2,r}, \ldots, p_{t-1,r}$ are not ordered and they are distinct mod e_r. Experimental study shows that the values $p_{1,r}, p_{2,r}, \ldots, p_{t-1,r}$ are uniformly distributed in the range $1, 2, \ldots, 2^{d_r} - 2 = e_r - 1$ for each r.

2. Then using Chinese remainder theorem (see the proof of Theorem 2), we find that $f_1(x) f_2(x) \ldots f_k(x)$ divides $x^{I_1} + x^{I_2} + \ldots + x^{I_{t-1}} + 1$ which has degree $< e_1 e_2 \ldots e_k$. Now in the proof of Theorem 2, it is clear that the value I_j is decided from the values $p_{j,r}$'s for $r = 1, \ldots, k$. Since, $p_{j,r}$'s are uniformly distributed and Chinese remainder theorem provides a bijection from $Z_{e_1} \times Z_{e_2} \times \ldots \times Z_{e_k}$ to $Z_{e_1 e_2 \ldots e_k}$, it is expected that the values $I_1, I_2, \ldots, I_{t-1}$ are uniformly distributed in the range $1, 2, \ldots, e_1 e_2 \ldots e_k - 1$. Here Z_a is the set of integers from 0 to $a - 1$.

3. The distribution of the degrees of the t-nomial multiples of the product $f_1(x)f_2(x)\ldots f_k(x)$ is the distribution of $\max(I_1,\ldots,I_{t-1})$. It can be assumed that the values $I_1, I_2,\ldots, I_{t-1}$ are chosen uniformly from the range $1,\ldots,(2^{d_1}-1)(2^{d_2}-1)\ldots(2^{d_k}-1)-1$.

Table 3. Degree distribution for t-nomial multiples of product of degree 3 and degree 4 primitive polynomials.

Product	< 15	< 25	< 35	< 45	< 55	< 65	< 75	< 85	< 95	< 105
10101101	0.0238	0.0714	0.1429	0.1429	0.2619	0.3571	0.5476	0.6429	0.7857	1.0000
11000111	0.0000	0.0476	0.1190	0.1905	0.3095	0.3810	0.5238	0.6190	0.7857	1.0000
11100011	0.0000	0.0476	0.1190	0.1905	0.3095	0.3810	0.5238	0.6190	0.7857	1.0000
10110101	0.0238	0.0714	0.1429	0.1429	0.2619	0.3571	0.5476	0.6429	0.7857	1.0000
$t = 3$	0.0170	0.0515	0.1047	0.1766	0.2672	0.3764	0.5043	0.6509	0.8161	1.0000
10101101	0.0014	0.0110	0.0329	0.0719	0.1349	0.2295	0.3568	0.5253	0.7370	1.0000
11000111	0.0021	0.0103	0.0308	0.0733	0.1349	0.2288	0.3575	0.5247	0.7370	1.0000
11100011	0.0021	0.0103	0.0308	0.0733	0.1349	0.2288	0.3575	0.5247	0.7370	1.0000
10110101	0.0014	0.0110	0.0329	0.0719	0.1349	0.2295	0.3568	0.5253	0.7370	1.0000
$t = 4$	0.0020	0.0111	0.0329	0.0727	0.1362	0.2288	0.3560	0.5232	0.7361	1.0000
10101101	0.0002	0.0021	0.0095	0.0298	0.0689	0.1388	0.2487	0.4196	0.6644	1.0000
11000111	0.0003	0.0024	0.0100	0.0293	0.0677	0.1378	0.2493	0.4204	0.6644	1.0000
11100011	0.0003	0.0024	0.0100	0.0293	0.0677	0.1378	0.2493	0.4204	0.6644	1.0000
10110101	0.0002	0.0021	0.0095	0.0298	0.0689	0.1388	0.2487	0.4196	0.6644	1.0000
$t = 5$	0.0002	0.0023	0.0101	0.0295	0.0688	0.1382	0.2502	0.4196	0.6632	1.0000
10110101	0.0000	0.0005	0.0030	0.0118	0.0345	0.0829	0.1752	0.3356	0.5968	1.0000
11100011	0.0000	0.0005	0.0031	0.0118	0.0345	0.0829	0.1751	0.3356	0.5968	1.0000
11000111	0.0000	0.0005	0.0031	0.0118	0.0345	0.0829	0.1751	0.3356	0.5968	1.0000
10101101	0.0000	0.0005	0.0030	0.0118	0.0345	0.0829	0.1752	0.3356	0.5968	1.0000
$t = 6$	0.0000	0.0005	0.0030	0.0118	0.0344	0.0829	0.1752	0.3357	0.5969	1.0000
11100011	0.0000	0.0001	0.0009	0.0047	0.0171	0.0494	0.1221	0.2679	0.5365	1.0000
10110101	0.0000	0.0001	0.0009	0.0047	0.0170	0.0494	0.1222	0.2679	0.5365	1.0000
11000111	0.0000	0.0001	0.0009	0.0047	0.0171	0.0494	0.1221	0.2679	0.5365	1.0000
10101101	0.0000	0.0001	0.0009	0.0047	0.0170	0.0494	0.1222	0.2679	0.5365	1.0000
$t = 7$	0.0000	0.0001	0.0009	0.0047	0.0170	0.0494	0.1221	0.2679	0.5366	1.0000

To analyse the degree distribution of these t-nomial multiples of the products of primitive polynomials, let us consider the random variate $X^{(d_1,\ldots,d_k),t}$, which is $\max(I_1,\ldots,I_{t-1})$, where $x^{I_1} + x^{I_2} + \ldots + x^{I_{t-1}} + 1$ is a t-nomial multiple of $f_1(x)f_2(x)\ldots f_k(x)$. Let $\delta = (2^{d_1}-1)(2^{d_2}-1)\ldots(2^{d_k}-1)$. On the other hand, consider all the $(t-1)$-tuples $< I_1,\ldots,I_{t-1} >$, in the range 1 to $\delta - 1$. There are $\binom{\delta-1}{t-1}$ such tuples. Consider the random variate $Y^{(d_1,\ldots,d_k),t}$, which is $\max(I_1,\ldots,I_{t-1})$, where $< I_1,\ldots,I_{t-1} >$ is any ordered t-tuple from the values 1 to $\delta - 1$. With the above explanation and following experimental studies, we consider that the distributions $X^{(d_1,\ldots,d_k),t}$, $Y^{(d_1,\ldots,d_k),t}$ are very close.

Let us first concentrate on the experimental results presented in Table 3. We consider the degree distribution of t-nomial multiples of product of primitive polynomials of degree 3 and 4. The product polynomials of degree 7 are presented in the leftmost column of the table. As example $(x^3+x+1)(x^4+x+1) = x^7 +x^5 +x^3 +x^2 +1$ is represented as 10101101. The exponent of the polynomial $x^7 + x^5 + x^3 + x^2 + 1$ is $(2^3 - 1)(2^4 - 1) = 105$. We present the proportion of t-nomial multiples of degree $< 15, 25, \ldots, 105$, where $t = 3, 4, 5, 6, 7$. Corresponding to each t, we also present the proportion $\binom{c}{t-1} / \binom{\delta-1}{t-1}$ in the last row. Here, $\delta = 105$ and $c = 14, 24, \ldots, 104$. Table 3 clearly identifies the closeness of the distributions $X^{(d_1, \ldots, d_k), t}$, $Y^{(d_1, \ldots, d_k), t}$. Similar support is available from the Table 4 which considers the t-nomial multiples (for $t = 3, 4, 5$) of product of degree 4 and degree 5 primitive polynomials.

Take two sets of primitive polynomials $f_1(x), \ldots, f_k(x)$ and $g_1(x), \ldots, g_k(x)$ of degree $d_1, \ldots, d_k$ (pairwise coprime), such that each $f_r(x)$ and $g_r(x)$ are reciprocal to each other. Consider the multiset $U(f_1(x) \ldots f_k(x), d_1, \ldots, d_k, t)$, which contains the degree of all the t-nomial multiples (having degree $< (2^{d_1} - 1) \ldots (2^{d_k} - 1))$ of $f_1(x) \ldots f_k(x)$. The following result is similar to Lemma 2.

Lemma 3. $U(f_1(x) \ldots f_k(x), d_1, \ldots, d_k, t) = U(g_1(x) \ldots g_k(x), d_1, \ldots, d_k, t)$.

Since, $U(f_1(x) \ldots f_k(x), d_1, \ldots, d_k, t) = U(g_1(x) \ldots g_k(x), d_1, \ldots, d_k, t)$, the statistical parameters based on the multisets $U(f_1(x) \ldots f_k(x), d_1, \ldots, d_k, t)$, and $U(g_1(x) \ldots g_k(x), d_1, \ldots, d_k, t)$ are exactly same. In Table 3, it is clear that the entries corresponding to the multiples $f_1(x)f_2(x)$ and $g_1(x)g_2(x)$ are same where $f_1(x), g_1(x)$ are reciprocal and and $f_2(x), g_2(x)$ are also reciprocal. Thus, in Table 4, we put only one row corresponding to each such pair. Now we present the following result. The proof is similar to that of Lemma 1.

Table 4. Degree distribution for t-nomial multiples of product of degree 4 and degree 5 primitive polynomials.

Product	< 30	< 65	< 115	< 165	< 215	< 265	< 315	< 365	< 415	< 465
1101011101	0.0000	0.0286	0.0571	0.1238	0.2095	0.3238	0.4524	0.6095	0.7905	1.0000
1111110001	0.0048	0.0190	0.0619	0.1143	0.2238	0.3238	0.4333	0.6238	0.7952	1.0000
1011111111	0.0000	0.0143	0.0619	0.1333	0.2190	0.3238	0.4619	0.6095	0.7810	1.0000
1001010011	0.0048	0.0190	0.0667	0.1143	0.2190	0.3286	0.4524	0.6286	0.7952	1.0000
1110100111	0.0095	0.0190	0.0571	0.1286	0.2286	0.3238	0.4571	0.6095	0.7952	1.0000
1000000101	0.0095	0.0143	0.0524	0.1286	0.2000	0.3190	0.4571	0.6190	0.7952	1.0000
$t = 3$	0.0040	0.0188	0.0600	0.1244	0.2122	0.3232	0.4575	0.6150	0.7959	1.0000
1101011101	0.0002	0.0023	0.0145	0.0434	0.0969	0.1835	0.3090	0.4819	0.7099	1.0000
1111110001	0.0002	0.0025	0.0142	0.0434	0.0969	0.1834	0.3083	0.4820	0.7099	1.0000
1011111111	0.0002	0.0025	0.0146	0.0433	0.0977	0.1832	0.3091	0.4820	0.7097	1.0000
1001010011	0.0002	0.0023	0.0146	0.0428	0.0973	0.1835	0.3088	0.4820	0.7100	1.0000
1110100111	0.0003	0.0023	0.0145	0.0434	0.0973	0.1830	0.3093	0.4821	0.7099	1.0000
1000000101	0.0004	0.0022	0.0142	0.0433	0.0966	0.1829	0.3086	0.4820	0.7098	1.0000
$t = 4$	0.0002	0.0025	0.0145	0.0436	0.0974	0.1833	0.3089	0.4819	0.7098	1.0000
1101011101	0.0000	0.0003	0.0035	0.0152	0.0446	0.1038	0.2085	0.3774	0.6328	1.0000
1111110001	0.0000	0.0003	0.0035	0.0153	0.0445	0.1037	0.2086	0.3773	0.6328	1.0000
1011111111	0.0000	0.0003	0.0035	0.0152	0.0445	0.1038	0.2084	0.3774	0.6329	1.0000
1001010011	0.0000	0.0003	0.0035	0.0153	0.0445	0.1037	0.2085	0.3773	0.6328	1.0000
1110100111	0.0000	0.0003	0.0035	0.0152	0.0445	0.1037	0.2084	0.3774	0.6328	1.0000
1000000101	0.0000	0.0003	0.0035	0.0152	0.0446	0.1038	0.2084	0.3774	0.6328	1.0000
$t = 5$	0.0000	0.0003	0.0035	0.0152	0.0446	0.1038	0.2084	0.3774	0.6328	1.0000

Lemma 4. Let $\delta = (2^{d_1} - 1)(2^{d_2} - 1) \ldots (2^{d_k} - 1)$. The average of the values in $Y^{(d_1, \ldots, d_k), t}$ is $\frac{t-1}{t}\delta$. Moreover, the average of squares of the values in $Y^{(d_1, \ldots, d_k), t}$ is $\frac{t-1}{t}\delta(\frac{t(\delta+1)}{t+1} - 1)$.

Table 5. Average of degree and average of degree square of t-nomial multiples for product of primitive polynomials.

Product polynomial	$t = 3$	$t = 4$	$t = 5$
10110101	70.00, 5530.00	78.75, 6595.27	84.00, 7335.44
11100011	70.00, 5530.00	78.75, 6595.15	84.00, 7334.90
Estimated	70.00, 5495.00	78.75, 6599.25	84.00, 7336.00
101000111	144.67, 23580.67	162.75, 28212.40	173.60, 31363.62
100110011	144.67, 23580.67	162.75, 28214.39	173.60, 31362.93
100001001	144.67, 23580.67	162.75, 28213.60	173.60, 31363.82
110101111	144.67, 23580.67	162.75, 28213.88	173.60, 31363.46
111100001	144.67, 23580.67	162.75, 28214.15	173.60, 31362.90
111100001	144.67, 23580.67	162.75, 28216.71	173.60, 31363.33
Estimated	144.67, 23508.33	162.75, 28220.85	173.60, 31363.73
1101011101	310.00, 108190.00	348.75, 129651.90	372.00, 144087.34
1101011101	310.00, 108190.00	348.75, 129659.90	372.00, 144087.41
1101011101	310.00, 108190.00	348.75, 129656.72	372.00, 144086.58
1101011101	310.00, 108190.00	348.75, 129652.81	372.00, 144087.51
1101011101	310.00, 108190.00	348.75, 129652.43	372.00, 144087.20
1101011101	310.00, 108190.00	348.75, 129657.92	372.00, 144087.93
Estimated	310.00, 108035.00	348.75, 129665.25	372.00, 144088.00

In the Table 5, we present the exact data for multiples of products of primitive polynomials. We consider the product of primitive polynomials having degree (3, 4), (3, 5) and (4, 5). The product polynomials are presented in the leftmost column of the table. In each cell, we present the experimental values for the distribution $X^{(d_1,d_2),t}$. We present the *average of the degrees* and *average of the squares of the degrees* of t-nomial multiples in the same cell of the table. We also present the estimated values in the tables which gives the results related to the distribution $Y^{(d_1,d_2),t}$. It is clear from the table that for the set of experiments we have done, the results related to the distributions $X^{(d_1,d_2),t}$ and $Y^{(d_1,d_2),t}$ are very close. We like to present the following observations (see [14] for formal proof) from the Table 5, which is related to the distribution $X^{(d_1,\ldots,d_k),t}$.

1. The average of degree of the t-nomial multiples of $\prod_{r=1}^{k} f_r(x)$ is fixed and it is equal to $\frac{t-1}{t}\delta$, where δ is the exponent of $\prod_{r=1}^{k} f_r(x)$.

2. The average of the square of degree of the trinomial multiples of $\prod_{r=1}^{k} f_r(x)$ is fixed but not exactly equal to the estimated value.

From [5, Section 2], it is possible to approximate $N_{d_r,t}$ as $\frac{1}{(t-1)!}2^{d_r(t-2)}$. Now let us estimate considering the count as the lower bound $((t-1)!)^{k-1} \prod_{r=1}^{k} N_{d_r,t}$ mentioned in Theorem 2. After approximating $N_{d_r,t}$ as $\frac{1}{(t-1)!}2^{d_r(t-2)}$, we get

$$((t-1)!)^{k-1} \prod_{r=1}^{k} N_{d_r,t} \approx ((t-1)!)^{k-1} \prod_{r=1}^{k} \frac{1}{(t-1)!}2^{d_r(t-2)} = \frac{2^{\left(\sum_{r=1}^{k} d_r\right)(t-2)}}{(t-1)!} =$$

$\frac{1}{(t-1)!}2^{d(t-2)}$, where $d = \sum_{r=1}^{k} d_r$, is the degree of $\prod_{r=1}^{k} f_r(x)$.

Remark 2. Consider a primitive polynomial $f(x)$ having degree d and a polynomial $g(x)$, which is product of k different primitive polynomials with degree $d_1, \ldots, d_k$ (pairwise coprime), where $d = d_1 + \ldots + d_k$. From the above discussion, it follows that the approximate count of the t-nomial multiples of $f(x)$ and $g(x)$ are close.

From the distribution, it is expected that there are $\left(\binom{c}{t-1} / \binom{\delta}{t-1}\right) \prod_{r=1}^{k} N_{d_r,t}$ number of t-nomial multiples having degree $\leq c$. Consider that we need the lowest degree t-nomial multiple (a single one) of $\prod_{r=1}^{k} f_r(x)$. Thus we expect $\left(\binom{c}{t-1} / \binom{\delta}{t-1}\right) \prod_{r=1}^{k} N_{d_r,t} \approx 1$, i.e., $\left(\binom{c}{t-1} / \binom{\delta}{t-1}\right) \frac{1}{(t-1)!} 2^{d(t-2)} \approx 1$. Now $\delta = \prod_{r=1}^{k} (2^{d_r} - 1) \approx 2^d$. Then we get that $c \approx 2^{\frac{d}{t-1}}$.

Note that the attacks presented by finding t-nomial multiples of product of primitive polynomials require at least one t-nomial multiple. Consider a scheme using primitive polynomials of degree > 128. If the designer uses an 8-input, 3-resilient Boolean function, then attacker has to consider product of at least 4 primitive polynomials. Thus the degree of the product polynomial will be > 512. In such a scenario, the degree of the lowest degree t-nomial multiple (of the product polynomial) will be approximately as large as $2^{256}, 2^{170}, 2^{128}$ for $t = 3, 4, 5$ respectively. This shows that in such a situation the attacks presented in this direction (see for reference [1]) will not succeed in practical sense. However, for $t = 17$, the approximate degree of the lowest degree t-nomial multiple will be 2^{32}, which is at a much lower degree. Thus, the work presented in this paper clearly identifies how the parameters should be chosen for safe design of stream cipher systems based on nonlinear combiner model. On the other hand, existing systems can also be revisited to see whether those are still secured given the computational power available now a days and the analysis presented in this paper.

Acknowledgment : This work has been supported partially by the ReX program, a joint activity of USENIX Association and Stichting NLnet. The authors also like to acknowledge Dr. Palash Sarkar of Indian Statistical Institute for his valuable suggestions towards some analysis in Section 5.

References

1. A. Canteaut and M. Trabbia. Improved fast correlation attacks using parity-check equations of weight 4 and 5. In *EUROCRYPT 2000*, number 1807 in Lecture Notes in Computer Science, pages 573–588. Springer Verlag, 2000.
2. C. Ding, G. Xiao, and W. Shan. *The Stability Theory of Stream Ciphers*. Number 561 in Lecture Notes in Computer Science. Springer-Verlag, 1991.
3. S. W. Golomb. *Shift Register Sequences*. Aegean Park Press, 1982.
4. K. C. Gupta and S. Maitra. Primitive polynomials over GF(2) – A cryptologic approach. In *ICICS 2001*, number 2229 in LNCS, Pages 23–34, November 2001.
5. K. C. Gupta and S. Maitra. Multiples of primitive polynomials over GF(2). IN-DOCRYPT 2001, number 2247 in LNCS, Pages 62–72, December 2001.
6. K. Jambunathan. On choice of connection polynomials for LFSR based stream ciphers. INDOCRYPT 2000, number 1977 in LNCS, Pages 9–18, 2000.
7. G. A. Jones and J. M. Jones. *Elementary Number Theory*. Springer Verlag London Limited, 1998.

8. T. Johansson and F. Jonsson. Fast correlation attacks through reconstruction of linear polynomials. In *Advances in Cryptology - CRYPTO 2000*, number 1880 in Lecture Notes in Computer Science, pages 300–315. Springer Verlag, 2000.

9. R. Lidl and H. Niederreiter. Introduction to finite fields and their applications. Cambridge University Press, 1994.

10. F. J. MacWillams and N. J. A. Sloane. *The Theory of Error Correcting Codes.* North Holland, 1977.

11. W. Meier and O. Stafflebach. Fast correlation attacks on certain stream ciphers. *Journal of Cryptology*, 1:159–176, 1989.

12. T. Siegenthaler. Correlation-immunity of nonlinear combining functions for cryptographic applications. *IEEE Transactions on Information Theory*, IT-30(5):776–780, September 1984.

13. T. Siegenthaler. Decrypting a class of stream ciphers using ciphertext only. *IEEE Transactions on Computers*, C-34(1):81–85, January 1985.

14. A. Venkateswarlu and S. Maitra. Further results on multiples of primitive polynomials and their products over GF(2). Accepted in *ICICS 2002*, to be published in Lecture Notes in Computer Science, Springer Verlag.

A New Cryptanalytic Attack for PN-generators Filtered by a Boolean Function

Sabine Leveiller[1,2], Gilles Zémor[2], Philippe Guillot[3], and Joseph Boutros[2]

[1] Thales Communication
66, rue du Fossé Blanc, 92231 Genevilliers, FRANCE
[2] Ecole Nationale Supérieure des Télécommunications
46, rue Barrault, 75013 Paris, FRANCE
{leveille, zemor, boutros}@enst.fr
[3] Canal-Plus Technologies
34, place Raoul Dautry, 75015 Paris, FRANCE
pguillot@canal-plus.fr

Abstract. We present a new cryptanalytic attack on PN-generators filtered by a Boolean function. The key-idea is to jointly combine the knowledge of the Boolean function and the LFSR structure so as to introduce a new iterative decoding technique. The results we obtained prove to be very good: indeed, even in the case of systems for which classical iterative algorithms appear powerless, our scheme enables us to recover the LFSR initial state with a very low error probability. The latter is such that ending the algorithm by an exhaustive search among sequences of limited length is hardly needed. Therefore, the overall complexity of our scheme remains very small and the algorithm appears as an excellent candidate for cryptanalysis of filtered PN-generators.

Keywords: Boolean functions, stream ciphers, APP decoding, Fourier transform.

1 Introduction

The original paper on correlation attacks by Meier and Staffelbach [16] together with the invention of turbo codes [2] and the rediscovery of iterative decoding [6,23,14] produced an extensive effort to improve correlation attacks on stream ciphers [10,11,3,18,12,19,20]. These attacks are mainly based on powerful channel decoding techniques, such as iterative APP decoding of low density parity-check codes, trellis decoding (Viterbi algorithm) of large memory convolutional codes, iterative APP decoding of turbo codes, or maximum likelihood channel decoding [4]. In this paper, we address the case when the keystream is a non-linearly filtered generator [21]. Attacks on filter generators fall into two classes: deterministic attacks, mainly [1,8,13], and correlation attacks. All correlation attacks to be found in the literature on such systems model the filtering Boolean function [17,22] as a memoryless binary symmetric channel (BSC) [5]. Hence, all known performance results and statements are obtained in the idealized case when the

K. Nyberg and H. Heys (Eds.): SAC 2002, LNCS 2595, pp. 232–249, 2003.
© Springer-Verlag Berlin Heidelberg 2003

pseudo-noise (PN) sequence [9] runs through a BSC rather than a Boolean function.

In this paper, we consider both the true structure of a filter generator without any BSC modeling and we infer the original key value (the LFSR initial state) by jointly combining the knowledge of the Boolean function and the LFSR characteristics. The linear feedback shift register (LFSR) followed by a Boolean function is illustrated in Fig.1.

This paper is organized as follows: after presenting the key-idea of the algorithm in section 2, section 3 describes the new probabilistic attack we call SOJA (Soft Output Joint Algorithm) and gives the mathematical expression of the *a posteriori* probabilities generated by the SOJA. Section 4 deals with a less complex but approximated version of the SOJA. In section 5, we focus on a specific type of Boolean function, namely plateaued functions, and we analyze the performance of both algorithms. Finally, numerical results showing the performance of the SOJA attacks are given in section 6.

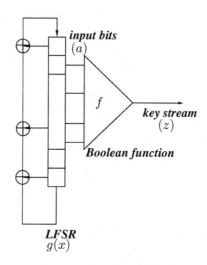

Fig. 1. The key stream filter generator

Notation. The following notation is used in this manuscript:

- K is the degree of the LFSR feedback polynomial g and N is the length of the key-stream sequence z, also called received sequence in channel decoding terminology
- the original PN-sequence is denoted a, where $\{a_t\}$ are also called input bits
- f denotes the n-input filtering Boolean function
- $X(t) = (X_1(t), \ldots, X_n(t))$ is the input vector of the function at time t

- $\forall u \in \{0,1\}^n$, ϕ_u denotes the linear form: $\phi_u : x \longrightarrow (u.x)$ where $u.x = \sum_i u_i x_i$ is the usual scalar product. Applying such a linear form to the initial sequence (a) will provide us with a new sequence denoted (a^{ϕ_u}). Note that any linear form of the initial sequence satisfies the same parity-check equations as the latter.

- $\widehat{f}$ denotes the Fourier Transform of f:

$$\forall u \in \{0,1\}^n, \quad \widehat{f}(u) = \sum_{x \in \{0,1\}^n} f(x)(-1)^{u.x}$$

- f_χ denotes the sign function associated to f:

$$\forall x \in \{0,1\}^n, \quad f_\chi(x) = (-1)^{f(x)}$$

- $r_f : x \longrightarrow \sum_y (-1)^{f(y)+f(y+x)}$ denotes the auto-correlation function

2 An Overall View over the Proposed Algorithms

In this section, we derive the basic and general principles of the SOJA algorithms, and we look into more details in sections 3 and 4.

The attack we propose hereafter requires the knowledge of the Boolean function table, the feedback polynomial, and a set of d-weight parity-check equations satisfied by the initial PN sequence. For instance, these might be provided by square elevations of the feedback polynomial as mentioned in [16] or a table lookup algorithm as described in [3], [7].

Let us introduce further notation: we call $\mathcal{E}^b(t)$ the set of parity-checks

$$a_{t_1} + a_{t_2} + \ldots + a_{t_d} = 0$$

to which bit a_t belongs. An element of $\mathcal{E}^b(t)$, e, is a set of d bits, among which a_t, that sum to zero. The sequence (a) can be seen as a codeword of the (N, K) code generated by the LFSR. This code being cyclic, its dual is also cyclic and every single parity-check shifted n times gives rise to a vectorial one: let $\mathcal{E}^v(t) = \{E\}$ such that E is a set of d input vectors, $X(t_1), \ldots, X(t_d)$, among which $X(t)$, that sum to zero. Note that, if μ denotes the average cardinality of $\mathcal{E}^v(t)$, that is the average number of parity-checks to which $X(t)$ belongs, then the average cardinality of $\mathcal{E}^b(t)$ is $n\mu$.

Our joint attack consists in combining the Boolean function constraints and the information provided by PN parity-check equations to compute *a posteriori* probabilities $APP(a_t)$ on the input bits $\{a_t\}$. Sections 3 and 4 propose two ways of deriving the APP's. Both these SOJA versions use the list of constraints satisfied by the d vectors of every vectorial check E, namely

- $X(t_1) + \ldots + X(t_d) = 0_n$
- their image by the Boolean function f is the received d-tuple $z_{t_1}, \ldots, z_{t_d}$

0_n being the all-zero vector.

Hence, we have a $d \times n$ constrained system written as:

$$z_{t_1} = f\left(X_1(t_1), X_2(t_1), \ldots, X_n(t_1)\right)$$
$$z_{t_2} = f(X_1(t_2), X_2(t_2), \ldots, X_n(t_2)) \tag{1}$$
$$\ldots$$
$$z_{t_d} = f(X_1(t_d), X_2(t_d), \ldots, X_n(t_d))$$
$$\text{with} \quad 0_n = \sum_i X(t_i)$$

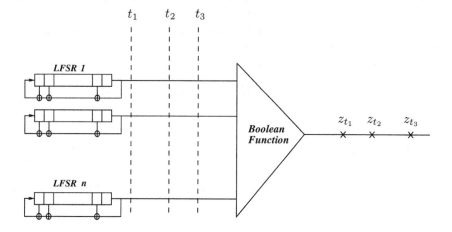

Fig. 2. Alternative representation of the key stream generator with $X(t_1) + X(t_2) + X(t_3) = 0$

To illustrate our purpose, Fig.2 gives an equivalent, but more appropriate representation of Fig.1 with a weight-3 parity-check equation: $X(t_1) + X(t_2) + X(t_3) = 0$. The PN generator is replaced by n parallel PN generators with identical feedback polynomials but different initial states. The 3 input vectors, $X(t_1) = (X_1(t_1), \ldots, X_n(t_1))$, $X(t_2) = (X_1(t_2), \ldots, X_n(t_2))$, $X(t_3) = (X_1(t_3), \ldots, X_n(t_3))$ sum to zero, while their images through f are z_{t_1}, z_{t_2}, and z_{t_3} respectively.

Basically the general principle of the SOJA is to use the knowledge of the Boolean function jointly with vectorial parity-checks to estimate $P(X(t) = x)$ that is further used to get the APP probabilities $\Lambda_{\phi_u}(t) = P_{app}(a_t^{\phi_u})$, where $a_t^{\phi_u}$ is a linear form of the input sequence that is chosen according to the Boolean function properties.

The overall decoding algorithm can be written in the following way:

1. *Inputs*: $g(X)$, f, $\{\mathcal{E}^v(t)\}$ and\or $\{\mathcal{E}^b(t)\}$, (z)
2. *Processing steps*:
   - Generate the APP's using SOJA-1 (see section 3) or SOJA-2 (see section 4).
   - Once the APP's are computed, cryptanalyze the system using either SOJA-Gallager or SOJA-threshold described hereafter.
3. *Output* : initial state of the PN generator.

Let us describe both decoding strategies in more details:

- **SOJA-Gallager**: iterative decoding using these SOJA APPs as channel observations.
  We briefly recall a simplified version of Gallager's probabilistic decoding algorithm [6]: let $APP^\theta(a_t^{\phi_u})$ be the APP of bit $a_t^{\phi_u}$ at iteration θ produced by the probabilistic decoder, and $Obs(a_t^{\phi_u})$ be the channel observation. Assuming that for all t, the bits among $\mathcal{E}_b^t$ are statistically independent, the simplified Gallager algorithm is:

  1. $\theta = 0$: $\forall t \in [1, N]$, $APP^{(0)}(a_t^{\phi_u}) = Obs(a_t^{\phi_u}) = \Lambda_{\phi_u}(t)$
  2. $\theta > 0$: $\forall t \in [1, N]$,

$$APP^{(\theta)}(a_t^{\phi_u}) \propto Obs(a_t^{\phi_u}) \times \prod_{e \in \mathcal{E}_t^b} Prob(a_t^{\phi_u} = 1 \text{ in } e \text{ at iteration } \theta)$$

$$\propto Obs(a_t^{\phi_u}) \times \prod_{e \in \mathcal{E}_t^b} \frac{1 - \prod_{a_j^{\phi_u} \in e, j \neq t} \left(1 - 2APP^{(\theta-1)}\left(a_j^{\phi_u}\right)\right)}{2}$$

  3. If $APP^{\theta_{max}}(a_t^{\phi_u}) > \frac{1}{2}$, $a_t^{\phi_u}$ is decoded as 1, else $a_t^{\phi_u}$ is decoded as 0.

  where $\propto$ stands for "proportional to" (the proportionality factor depending on the considered bit). Steps (2) and (3) include a normalization phase of the APP of each bit so that $\forall t$, $\forall \theta$, $APP^{(\theta)}(a_t^{\phi_u} = 1) + APP^{(\theta)}(a_t^{\phi_u} = 0) = 1$. The above algorithm is a simplification of the initial Gallager decoder, since it doesn't handle extrinsic information [2]. The incoming *a priori* probability is taken to be equal to the previous APP.

- **SOJA-Threshold**: a threshold decoding on SOJA APPs.
  The *a posteriori* probability $0 \leq \Lambda(a_t^{\phi_u}) \leq 1$ produced by the SOJA is considered to be reliable when its value is close to 0 or 1 and unreliable if $|\Lambda(a_t^{\phi_u}) - 0.5|$ is small. Hence, we can select the most reliable bits, decode them by comparing their APP with $\frac{1}{2}$, and invert the PN sequence system so as to provide the initial state of the PN generator. Finally, we check that the solution is correct by re-encoding the sequence.
  To apply this strategy, we select the K most reliable and linearly independent bits and we proceed as follows:

- if $\Lambda(a_t^{\phi_u}) - 0.5 > 0$, $a_t^{\phi_u}$ is decoded as 1,
- if $0.5 - \Lambda(a_t^{\phi_u}) > 0$, $a_t^{\phi_u}$ is decoded as 0.

3 New Probabilistic Attack: Soft Output Joint Attack, SOJA-1

3.1 Algorithm Description

A restricted set of input vectors jointly satisfy the constrained system (1) and this provides accurate information on the input vectors: for a given output d-tuple $z_{t_1}, \ldots, z_{t_d}$, we can enumerate all vectors in the truth table of the function f whose image matches the output (first constraint), and that sum to zero (second constraint). Let us define the set $z^{\mathcal{E}}$ of all observed bits z_s such that $X(s)$ is in some vectorial check E of $\mathcal{E}^v(t)$ and z^E the bits z_s such that s belongs to the support of E, i.e. $z^{\mathcal{E}} = \bigcup_{E \in \mathcal{E}^v(t)} z^E$. We also define:

$$\Gamma^t(x) = P(X(t) = x \text{ in } E \mid z^E, f) \tag{2}$$

as the proportion of arrays (see (1)) such that $X(t) = x$; $x \in \{0,1\}^n$ and E is a vectorial parity-check in $\mathcal{E}^v(t)$. Assuming that the only vector common to every pair of elements of the set $\mathcal{E}^v(t)$ is precisely $X(t)$, that is, assuming $\mathcal{E}^v(t)$, seen as a Tanner graph, doesn't contain any cycle of length 4, we can write:

$$\forall t, \; P(X(t) = x \mid z^{\mathcal{E}}, f) = \frac{\prod_{E \in \mathcal{E}^v(t)} \Gamma^t(x)}{\sum_y \prod_{E \in \mathcal{E}^v(t)} \Gamma^t(y)}$$

and then $\forall \, u \in \{0,1\}^n$

$$\Lambda_{\phi_u}(t) = P(u.X(t) = 1 \mid z, f) = \sum_{x/\phi_u(x)=1} \frac{\prod_{E \in \mathcal{E}^v(t)} \Gamma^t(x)}{\sum_y \prod_{E \in \mathcal{E}^v(t)} \Gamma^t(y)}$$

As noted before, according to the function properties, we might decode a linear form of the input sequence.

3.2 Mathematical Expression of SOJA-1

Let us derive the expression of Γ^t in more details.
The only assumption that we make on the Boolean function is that it is balanced. The particular case of plateaued functions is viewed later in section 5.

Proposition 1. *Given a received d-tuple $(z_1, \ldots, z_d)$, we can write*

$$\Gamma(x) = \mathbb{1}_{\{f(x)=z_1\}}(x) \times \frac{2^{(d-1)n+1} + (-1)^{\sum_{i=2}^d z_i}\, 2.\widehat{g}(x)}{2^{dn} + (-1)^{\sum_{i=1}^d z_i}\, \widehat{h}(0)}$$

where Γ was defined in (2) (the time index is omitted for the sake of simplicity), $g = \widehat{f_\chi}^{d-1}$ and $h = \widehat{f_\chi}^{d}$.

Proof. See Appendix A, prop. 1.

The above expression deals with the antecedent of z_1, but it holds for the other input vectors by permuting them in the formula. This expression also shows that the quantity Γ needs to be computed for all $x \in \{0,1\}^n$ and for a given parity of $\sum_{i=2}^{d} z_i$. The most efficient way to proceed is then to build a table in which we store the values of Γ; assuming the function is balanced, we must store 2^n values. Each computation requires at most $\mathcal{O}(n2^{n+1})$ elementary operations. Recall that μ is the average cardinality of $\mathcal{E}^v(t)$; the overall complexity of the computation of the APP's is in $\mathcal{O}(n2^{2n+1} + N\mu2^{n-1})$.

Remarks

– When the weight of the parity-checks equals 3, we get

$$\Gamma(x) \propto \left[2^n + (-1)^{z_2+z_3} r_f(x)\right]$$

The value of $\Gamma(x)$ is then directly related to the auto-correlation function associated to f.

Moreover the case when $d = 3$ is very interesting because it enables us to detect the all-zero vector with a very high probability. More precisely, let us consider one of the checks to which X belongs and let us write it as: $X + Y_2 + Y_3 = 0_n$. Assume $X = 0_n$; then $Y_2 = Y_3$ and the corresponding received bits are equal, that is $z_2 = f(Y_2) = f(Y_3) = z_3$. The interesting point is that this equality also stands in all other equations in which X is involved, as depicted on Fig. 3. From the cryptanalyst's point of view, such an equality between two bits within all parity-checks is very rare: if μ denotes the cardinality of the set of equations of X, and if the function f takes the values 0 and 1 equiprobably, the probability of such an event is in $1/2^\mu$. Therefore, using the SOJA is a very efficient way to detect the event of having the all-zero vector at the input. This can be extended to parity-checks of higher weight if cycles among the equations can be found.

– Earlier, we mentioned the fact that, according to the properties of the Boolean function, we could try to decode a particular linear form of the input sequence. However, when the spacings between the function inputs are coprime, decoding the "one-weight" linear form of the type $\phi_i : x \longrightarrow x_i$ often guarantees much better performance. As a matter of fact, these linear forms are the only ones that can be "shifted", *i.e.* which are involved in n input vectors successively on each component of the input, while each bit of a non-trivial linear form of the input is involved in the generation of only one output bit. Then instead of having one quantity $\Lambda_{\phi_u}(t)$ associated to one bit of the sequence to be decoded, we have n quantities.

Next we propose a lower complexity SOJA algorithm, which actually results from an approximation of the above version.

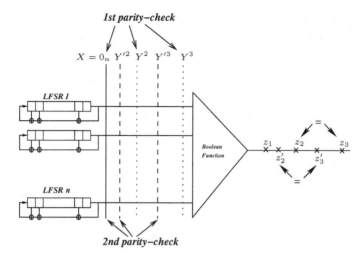

Fig. 3. Detection of the all-zero vector in the particular case of 3-weight parity checks

4   An Approximated SOJA Version, SOJA-2

The approximated version of the SOJA that we propose hereafter relies on the assumption that the bits among an input vector are independent: from a parity check, we directly deduce informations on the vector components of the sequence to be decoded, and, for a given bit, the scalar probabilities brought by all its parity-checks are multiplied together as if they were independent. This new scheme appears less complex than SOJA-1, but its major drawback is to give poor results when applied to non-trivial linear forms of the input sequence. Therefore, we will only consider the case when one strives to decode the original sequence (a), and not a linear form of it.

A paradox is that this simplified scheme works best when the function is resilient that is when the independence assumption of the input bits is the most justified.

4.1   Algorithm Description

The basic principle is identical to that of the SOJA-1: considering a parity-check $X(t_1) + X(t_2) + \ldots + X(t_d) = 0_n$, we enumerate the input vectors that jointly satisfy the parity-check and correspond to the received bits $z_{t_1} \ldots z_{t_d}$. Then, on each components, we can evaluate the proportions of 1s and 0s, and we deduce probabilities on each of these components; we obtain individual a posteriori probabilities on the input bits: for all m, j, one computes:

$$\mathcal{A}_{j,m} = P\left(X_m(t_j) = 1 \mid \forall i \in [1,d] \; f\left(X\left(t_i\right)\right) = z_{t_i} \text{ and } X(t_1) + \ldots + X(t_d) = 0_n \right)$$

$$= P\left(X_m(t_j) = 1 \mid \forall i \in [1, d-1] \; f(X(t_i)) = z_{t_i}, f(\sum_{\ell=0}^{d-1} X(t_\ell)) = z_{t_d} \right)$$

$m \in [1, n]$, $j \in [1, d]$.

This quantity represents the partial APP of the bit that coincides with the m-th component of the antecedent of z_{t_j}. We notice that this probability only depends on the value of the vector $(z_{t_1}, \ldots, z_{t_d})$; therefore the computation of these partial APPs is made once for every 2^d possible d-tuples, and stored in a $2^d \times d \times n$ table. Another simplification is to be noted: the computations have to be done for each $(z_{t_1}, \ldots, z_{t_d})$ of a given weight, and the rest of the table is completed by appropriate permutations on the input. Then, using this table, the received vectors that correspond to each parity-check equation will provide additional information on the components of their antecedents.

Assuming that the information brought by all equations are independent, we get the *a posteriori* probabilities, Λ, generated by the SOJA-2, namely:

$$\forall t \in [1, N], \quad \Lambda(a_t = 1) \propto \prod_{e \in \mathcal{E}^s(t)} A_{j,m} \tag{3}$$

Note that the superscript ϕ_u is omitted because, as noted before, SOJA-2 is only used to decode trivial linear forms of weight one. Once these APP's are evaluated, we suggest to apply one of the two decoding strategies presented in section 2.

We will now derive a mathematical expression of the above probabilities.

4.2   Mathematical Expression of SOJA-2

Let $v = (0, \ldots, 0, v_m = 1, 0, \ldots) \in \{0, 1\}^n$, where v is a pointer at the m-th input of the Boolean function, *i.e.* the m-th canonical vector.

For a given received d-tuple $(z_1, \ldots, z_d)$, we define the correlation coefficient, for $1 \leq j \leq d$,

$$c^j(v) = \frac{\Omega^j(v)}{\Omega^j(0_n)} = 2A_{j,m} - 1 \tag{4}$$

where

$$\Omega^j(v) = \sum_{Y^1} \sum_{Y^2} \cdots \sum_{Y^{d-1}} \mathbb{1}_{\{f(Y^1)=z_1\}}(Y^1) \mathbb{1}_{\{f(Y^2)=z_2\}}(Y^2) \cdots$$
$$\times \mathbb{1}_{\{f(\sum_{\ell=1}^{d-1} Y^\ell)=z_d\}} \left(\sum_{\ell=1}^{d-1} Y^\ell \right) (-1)^{v.Y^j} \tag{5}$$

and 0_n is the all-zero vector, and $\forall \ell, Y^\ell \in \{0, 1\}^n$. Developing the above expressions, we can state the following proposition:

Proposition 2. *For a given received d-tuple $(z_1, \ldots, z_d)$, $\Omega^j(v)$ is given by*

$$\Omega^j(v) = \frac{1}{2^d 2^n} \sum_s \left[2^n \mathbb{1}_{\{s=v\}}(s) + (-1)^{z_j} \widehat{f_\chi}(s+v) \right]$$
$$\times \prod_{\ell \neq i} \left[2^n \mathbb{1}_{\{s=0_n\}}(s) + (-1)^{z_\ell} \widehat{f_\chi}(s) \right] \tag{6}$$

If we further assume that f is balanced, and correlation immune (i.e. f is resilient) whatever its nonzero order of resiliency, $c^j(v)$ takes the very simple expression:

$$c^j(v) = \frac{(-1)^{\sum_\ell z_\ell} \sum_s \widehat{f_\chi}(v+s)\widehat{f_\chi}^{d-1}(s)}{2^{dn} + (-1)^{\sum_\ell z_\ell}\widehat{h}(0)} \tag{7}$$

where $h = \widehat{f_\chi}^d$.

As noted before, it clearly appears that the value of $c^j(v)$ needs only to be computed for a given weight of the output vector: all the other probabilities can be derived by appropriate permutations. When the function f is resilient as in (7), the correlation coefficient $c^j(v)$ depends on the parity of the output vector and it does not depend on the time position j.

Moreover, expression (6) enables a quick evaluation of the SOJA complexity: in general, for any f, each correlation roughly takes $n \times 2^n$ computation steps in the Fourier transform. Therefore, the overall complexity is: $\mathcal{O}(n \times 2^n + Nn\mu)$.

5   The Effect of Plateaued Functions

We have tried to envisage what Boolean functions f would make our attack least effective. In [24], Zheng and Zhang introduced the notion of *plateaued functions*: a function f is said to be plateaued iff

$$\exists\, r \ \text{such that} \ \forall u, \ \widehat{f_\chi}^2(u) = 0 \ \text{or} \ 2^{2n-r}$$

From the cryptanalyst's point of view, such functions are very embarrassing, because the linear forms of the initial sequence that have non-zero input-output correlation are all equidistant from the keystream z (considering the complement of the received sequence z when the correlation is negative). Therefore, a BSC decoder will tend to oscillate between them. We will show that using plateaued functions affects our SOJA algorithm performance when the parity-checks are even weight.

5.1   The Effect of Plateaued Functions on the SOJA-1

Proposition 3. *If the function f is plateaued and the parity-checks are odd-weighted, we have*

$$\Gamma(x) = [1 + (-1)^{f(x)+z_1}]\frac{2^{(d-1)n} + (-1)^{\sum_2^d z_i} \times 2^{(2n-r)(p-1)}r_f(x)}{2^{dn} + (-1)^{\sum_1^d z_i} \times 2^{(2n-r)p+n}f_\chi(0)}$$

where $d = 2p+1$, and $Sp(f_\chi) = \{0, \pm\, 2^{n-\frac{r}{2}}\}$.

Proof. See Appendix A, prop. 3.

Proposition 4. *If the function is plateaued and if the parity-checks are even-weighted, we don't gain anything over the classical initialization, which uses the function non-zero correlations .*

Proof. See Appendix A, prop.4 .

5.2   Effect of Plateaued Resilient Functions on SOJA-2

Proposition 5. *For any plateaued function f,*

$$\forall (p,q) \in \mathbb{N}, \forall v \neq 0_n \in \{0,1\}^n, \quad \sum_s \widehat{f_\chi}^{2p+1}(v+s)\widehat{f_\chi}^{2q+1}(s) = 0$$

Proof. See Appendix A, prop. 5.

Corollary 1. *If f is a plateaued resilient Boolean function, only odd-weight parity-check equations are usable when applying the SOJA.*

If f is resilient, the correlation values are given by equation (7). Then, if the parity-check equation weight is even, by applying the above proposition with $d = 2p$ and $q = 0$, we find that all correlations are zero.

6   Results and Comments

6.1   The Experiment

We present two different sets of results, obtained with the two resilient plateaued Boolean functions written below.

   For each function, we compare:

- classical simplified Gallager iterative decoding (see the first decoding strategy in section 2) applied to z with the Boolean function modeled as a BSC.
- classical simplified Gallager iterative decoding applied to a genuine BSC with the same transition probability; this is to underline the limitations of BSC modeling.
- (SOJA-1)-Gallager algorithm, (SOJA-1)- threshold algorithm.
- (SOJA-2)-Gallager algorithm, (SOJA-2)- threshold algorithm.

When the Boolean function is considered, the spacings between its input are taken to be coprime. Moreover, in both cases (SOJA-1 and SOJA-2), we chose to decode the trivial linear form that corresponds to a single input of the Boolean function, because, as noted before, when the spacings are coprime, the latter is the only linear form that is involved in n output bits.

The results are summarized in tables 1 and 2. For different values of the length N of observation z, we present the results obtained with the above decoding schemes. The second and third rows feature the average success percentage of Gallager decoding with a BSC channel (simplest model) and a Boolean function respectively (with the same corresponding transition probability). The last four rows contain the results obtained with our algorithms: in the fourth row we present the average success of the (SOJA-1)-Gallager algorithm and in the fifth one, the results obtained when using (SOJA-2)-algorithm. The last two rows contain the results obtained with the SOJA-threshold algorithms, SOJA-1 and SOJA-2, that is the average error rate among the K decoded bits, ρ_{av}.

First Application In this section, the results are obtained with the 3-resilient 7-input plateaued function

$$f(x) = 1 + x_1 + x_2 + x_3 + x_4 + x_5 + x_6 + x_1 x_7 + x_2(x_3 + x_7) +$$
$$x_1 x_2(x_3 + x_6 + x_7)$$

with $r = 4$ that is equivalent transition probability $p = 0.375$. The polynomial is $g(x) = 1 + X + X^3 + X^5 + X^9 + X^{11} + X^{12} + X^{17} + X^{19} + X^{21} + X^{25} + X^{27} + X^{29} + X^{32} + X^{33} + X^{38} + X^{40}$, and the weight-5 parity-check equations are obtained with the algorithm developed in [3]. Moreover the spacings between the inputs of the Boolean function are taken to be coprime. The results are presented in table 1.

Decoding strategy	N= 11000	N= 17000
real BSC ($p = 0.375$) + Gallager	no convergence	85%
f modeled as a BSC + Gallager	no convergence	19%
f + (SOJA-2)-Gallager	no convergence	36%
f + (SOJA-1)-Gallager	no convergence	100%
f + (SOJA-2)-threshold	$p_{av} = 0.226$	$p_{av} = 0.02$
f + (SOJA-1)-threshold	$p_{av} = 0.096$	$p_{av} < 10^{-4}$

Table 1. K=40, 7-input 3-resilient plateaued function

Second Application Here, we consider the system where the PN-sequence is generated by $g(X) = 1 + X^{37} + X^{100}$ and filtered by the 8-input 2-resilient plateaued function

$$f(x) = x_1 + x_4 + x_5 + x_6 + x_7 + x_1(x_2 + x_7) + x_2 x_6 + x_3(x_6 + x_8)$$
$$+ x_1 x_2(x_4 + x_6 + x_7 + x_8) + x_1 x_3(x_2 + x_6) + x_1 x_2 x_3(x_4 + x_5 + x_8)$$

with $r = 6$, that is nonzero correlation equal to $c = \frac{1}{8}$ or equivalent transition probability in the BSC representation equal to $p = 0.4375$. We worked with weight-3 parity-check equations, obtained by successive square elevations of the weight-3 feedback polynomial. The spacings between the Boolean function are taken coprime and span the whole memory of the PN generator. The corresponding results are featured in table 2.

6.2   Comments on the 3 Variations on Gallager Decoding

We mentioned the results obtained with Gallager simplified iterative decoding applied in different situations. It clearly appears in table 1 that iterative algorithms converge worst when applied to a Boolean function rather than to the corresponding BSC model (with same transition probability). The function we used is a plateaued function, which might not act in favor of iterative decoding

Decoding strategy	N = 5000	N= 11000	N= 30000
real BSC model (p=0.4375) **+ Gallager**	no convergence	no convergence	no convergence
f **modeled as a BSC + Gallager**	no convergence	no convergence	no convergence
f + (**SOJA-2**)-**Gallager**	no convergence	no convergence	no convergence
f + (**SOJA-1**)-**Gallager**	1%	42%	86%
f + (**SOJA-2**)-**threshold**	$\rho_{av} = 0.245$	$\rho_{av} = 0.165$	$\rho_{av} = 0.08$
f + (**SOJA-1**)-**threshold**	$\rho_{av} = 0.004$	$\rho_{av} < 10^{-4}$	$\rho_{av} < 10^{-4}$

Table 2. K=100, 8-input 2-resilient plateaued function

as all non-zero correlations are equal in absolute value. Note however that even (SOJA-2)-Gallager improves over classical Gallager iterative decoding.

In the second application, table 2 shows that classical iterative decoding doesn't work in the considered situation. We even tried higher values of N (up to 200,000) and didn't observe any convergence. Recall that in this particular example, the parity-check equations were obtained by successive squarings of the (low-weight) feedback polynomial. Unlike the table lookup algorithm [3] (which would require unreasonable complexity to be applied here), this provides very few parity check equations, not enough to enable iterative algorithm to converge.

Finally, it is to be noted that the approximated version of the SOJA, SOJA-2, doesn't give as good results as the true version: while in the first example, a slight increase of the length N of the received sequence tends to justify the utility of SOJA-2 the performance of the latter is far behind those of SOJA-1 in the second example, specially as regards SOJA-Gallager. A trade-off must be found between the system parameters and the available computational ability.

6.3   The Efficiency of SOJA-Threshold

In both applications, the SOJA-threshold algorithm appears as the most efficient way to decrypt the system. In some cases when most iterative algorithms don't converge, the SOJA-threshold gives good results.

The most striking result is obtained in the second application: the SOJA-threshold gives significantly better results than other algorithms with very few required bits and enables us to recover the initial state of the sequence with a complexity which is much lower than that of the SOJA-Gallager. One might expect that the SOJA-threshold decoding should be followed by an exhaustive search among all sequences of K bits to correct the wrongly decoded bits. Yet, as illustrated in both tables, a slight increase of N enables to lower significantly the remaining error rate. The global complexity of the SOJA is therefore limited.

Conclusion

In this paper, we derived a new algorithm for filtered LFSR cryptanalysis: our attack jointly takes advantage of the knowledge of both the Boolean function and the LFSR structure to provide better information on the input bits. Next, we proposed two decoding strategies, and surprisingly, the less complex is very often the most efficient one. We obtained very good results and extend the range of cryptanalysis to systems for which Gallager's algorithm cannot hope to converge, mostly because the Boolean function is plateaued and because of the lack of parity-check equations when the degree of the feedback polynomial is too high. However, if the SOJA gives better results than more usual iterative algorithms, it must be pointed out that this algorithm needs low-weight parity-checks to be processed which is an important issue; still, the number of parity-checks required for convergence is not as high as the number required for classical iterative algorithms. Besides parity-checks, the properties of the Boolean function also play an important part: it would be interesting to derive criterions on Boolean functions that would describe their resistance to such attacks.

References

1. R.J. Anderson, "Searching for the optimum correlation attack," *Fast Software Encryption -Leuven 94*, Lectures Notes in Computer Science, vol. 1008, pp. 137-143, Springer-Verlag, 1995.
2. C. Berrou, A. Glavieux and P. Thitimajshima: "Near Shannon limit error-correcting coding and decoding: turbo-codes," *Proceedings of ICC'93*, Geneva, pp. 1064-1070, May 1993.
3. A. Canteaut and M. Trabbia: "Improved fast correlation attacks using parity-check equations of weight 4 and 5," *Advances in Cryptology - EUROCRYPT 2000*, Lecture Notes in Computer Science, vol. 1807, pp. 573-588, Springer Verlag, 2000.
4. V. V. Chepyzhov, T. Johansson and B. Smeets," A simple algorithm for fast correlation attacks on stream ciphers," *Fast Software Encryption 2000*, Lecture Notes in Computer Science, vol. 1978, pp. 181-195, Springer Verlag, 2001.
5. T.M. Cover and J.A. Thomas: *Elements of information theory*. Wiley series in Telecommunications, 1991.
6. R.G. Gallager: *Low Density Parity check codes*. MIT Press, Cambridge, MA, 1963.
7. J.Dj. Golic, "Computation of low-weight parity-check polynomials," *Electronics Letters*, vol. 32, pp. 1981-1982, 1996.
8. J.Dj. Golic, A. Clark and E. Dawson, "Generalized Inversion Attack on Nonlinear Filter Generators," *IEEE Transactions on computers*, vol.49, No. 10, October 2000.
9. S.W. Golomb: *Shift register sequences*. Holden-Day, San Francisco, 1967.
10. T. Johansson and F. Jönsson: "Improved fast correlation attack on stream ciphers via convolutional codes," *Advances in Cryptology - EUROCRYPT'99*, Lecture Notes in Computer Science, vol. 1592, pp. 347-362, Springer Verlag, 1999.
11. T. Johansson and F. Jönsson: "Fast correlation attacks based on turbo code techniques," *Advances in Cryptology - CRYPTO'99*, in Lecture Notes in Computer Science, vol. 1666, pp. 181-197, Springer Verlag, 1999.
12. T. Johansson and F. Jönsson, "Fast correlation attacks through reconstruction of linear polynomials," *Advances in Cryptology - CRYPTO'2000*, Lecture Notes in Computer Science, vol. 1880, pp. 300-315, Springer Verlag, 2000.
13. S. Leveiller, J.J. Boutros, P. Guillot, G. Zémor, "Cryptanalysis of nonlinear filter generators with {0, 1}-metric Viterbi decoding," *IMA International Conference 2001*, Lecture Notes in Computer Science, vol. 2260, pp. 402-414, Springer Verlag, 2001.

14. D.J.C MacKay: "Good Error-Correcting Codes based on Very Sparse Matrices," *IEEE Transactions on Information Theory*, vol. 45, March 1999.

15. J.L. Massey: *Threshold Decoding*. MIT Press, Cambridge, MA, 1963.

16. W. Meier and O. Staffelbach: " Fast correlation attack on certain stream ciphers," *Journal of Cryptology*, pp. 159-176, 1989.

17. W. Meier and O. Staffelbach: "Nonlinearity Criteria for Cryptographic Functions," *Advances in Cryptology - EUROCRYPT'89*, Lecture Notes in Computer Science, vol. 434, pp. 549-562, Springer Verlag, 1990.

18. M.J. Mihaljević, M.P.C. Fossorier and H. Imai, "On decoding techniques for cryptanalysis of certain encryption algorithms", *IEICE Transactions on Fundamentals*, vol. E84-A, pp. 919-930, Apr. 2001.

19. M.J. Mihaljević, M.P.C. Fossorier and H. Imai, "A low-complexity and high-performance algorithm for the fast correlation attack", *Fast Software Encryption 2000*, Lecture Notes in Computer Science, vol. 1978, pp. 196-212, Springer Verlag, 2001.

20. M.J. Mihaljević, M.P.C. Fossorier and H. Imai, "Fast correlation attack algorithm with the list decoding and an application", *Fast Software Encryption 2001*, Lecture Notes in Computer Science, vol. 2355, pp. 196-210, Springer Verlag, 2002.

21. R.A. Rueppel: *Analysis and Design of Stream Ciphers*. Berlin: Springer-Verlag, 1986.

22. T. Siegenthaler: "Correlation-Immunity of Nonlinear Combining Functions for Cryptographic Applications," *IEEE Transactions on Information Theory*, vol. IT-30, pp. 776-780, 1984.

23. R.M. Tanner: "A recursive approach to low complexity codes," *IEEE Transactions on Information Theory*, vol. IT-27, Sept 1981.

24. Y. Zheng and X.-M. Zhang: "Plateaued Functions," *2nd International Conference on Information and Communications Security*, ICISC'99, Lecture Notes in Computer Science, vol. 1758, pp. 284-300, Springer-Verlag, 1999.

Appendix A

Let us recall that the basic assumption made upon the Boolean function is its balanceness.

Proposition 1 *Given a received d-tuple $(z_1, \ldots, z_d)$, we can write*

$$\Gamma(x) = \mathbb{1}_{\{f(x)=z_1\}}(x) \times \frac{2^{(d-1)n+1} + (-1)^{\sum_{i=2}^{d} z_i} 2.\widehat{g}(x)}{2^{dn} + (-1)^{\sum_{i=1}^{d} z_i} \widehat{h}(0)}$$

where Γ, g, and h were defined in (2).

Proof. Let us define

$$\gamma(x) = card \ \{(Y^2, \ldots, Y^{d-1}) \text{ satisfying}$$

$$f(x) = z_1, \ f(Y^2) = z_2, \ \ldots f(X + \sum_{i=2}^{d-1} Y^i) = z_d \ \}$$

Then $\Gamma(x) = \frac{\gamma(x)}{\sum_y \gamma(y)}$.

$$\gamma(x) = \frac{1}{2^d}\left[1 + (-1)^{f(x)+z_1}\right] \times$$
$$\sum_{Y^2} \cdots \sum_{Y^{d-1}} \left[1 + (-1)^{f(Y^2)+z_2}\right]\left[1 + (-1)^{f(Y^{d-1})+z_{d-1}}\right]\left[1 + (-1)^{f(x+\sum_i Y^i)+z_d}\right]$$

When developing the above expression, we get:

$$\gamma(x) = \frac{1}{2^{n+d}}\left[1 + (-1)^{f(x)+z_1}\right]\left[2^{(d-1)n} + (-1)^{\sum_2^d z_i}\sum_s \widehat{f_\chi}^{d-1}(s)(-1)^{s.x}\right]$$

Then

$$\sum_x \gamma(x) = \frac{1}{2^{n+d}}\left[2^{dn} + (-1)^{\sum_{i=1}^d z_i}\sum_s \widehat{f_\chi}^{d}(s)\right]$$

and

$$\Gamma(x) = \left[1 + (-1)^{f(x)+z_1}\right]\frac{2^{(d-1)n} + (-1)^{\sum_2^d z_i}\widehat{g}(x)}{2^{dn} + (-1)^{\sum_{i=1}^d z_i}\widehat{h}(0)}$$

$\square$

Proposition 3 *If the function f is plateaued and the parity-checks are odd-weighted, we have*

$$\Gamma(x) = [1 + (-1)^{f(x)+z_1}]\frac{2^{(d-1)n} + (-1)^{\sum_2^d z_i} \times 2^{(2n-r)(p-1)}r_f(x)}{2^{dn} + (-1)^{\sum_1^d z_i} \times 2^{(2n-r)p+n}f_\chi(0)}$$

where $d = 2p + 1$, and $Sp(f_\chi) = \{0, \pm 2^{n-\frac{r}{2}}\}$

Proof. Let us recall the expression of $\Gamma(x)$:

$$\Gamma(x) = \left[1 + (-1)^{f(x)+z_1}\right]\frac{2^{(d-1)n} + (-1)^{\sum_2^d z_i}\widehat{g}(x)}{2^{dn} + (-1)^{\sum_{i=1}^d z_i}\widehat{h}(0)}$$

where $g = \widehat{f_\chi}^{d-1}$ and $h = \widehat{f_\chi}^{d}$.
If we assume that the weight of the parity-checks is odd, that is $d = 2p+1$, then

$$\widehat{g}(x) = \sum_s \widehat{f_\chi}^{d-1}(s)$$
$$= \sum_s \widehat{f_\chi}^{2p}(s)$$
$$= [2^{2n-r}]^{p-1}r_f(x)$$

and

$$\widehat{h}(0) = \sum_s \widehat{f_\chi}^d(s)$$

$$= \sum_s \widehat{f_\chi}^{2p+1}(s)$$

$$= [2^{2n-r}]^p \times 2^n f_\chi(0)$$

then

$$\Gamma(x) = [1 + (-1)^{f(x)+z_1}]\frac{2^{(d-1)n} + (-1)^{\sum_2^d z_i} \times 2^{(2n-r)(p-1)}r_f(x)}{2^{dn} + (-1)^{\sum_1^d z_i} \times 2^{(2n-r)p+n}f_\chi(0)}$$

□

Proposition 4 *If the function is plateaued and if the parity-checks are even-weighted, we don't gain anything over the initialisation using the correlations.*

Proof. If the weight of the parity-checks is even, $d = 2p$, using the same tricks as above, and using the fact that $\Gamma(x) \neq 0$ iff $f(x) = z_1$ iff $f_\chi(x) = (-1)^{z_1}$, we show that:

$$\Gamma(x) = 0 \text{ if } f(x) \neq z_1$$

$$= \frac{1}{2^{n-1}} \text{ otherwise}$$

Then, suppose $f(X(t)) = 1$ and recall that the Boolean function is balanced

$$\Lambda_{\phi_u}(t) = P(u.X(t) = 1|z, f) = \sum_{x/\phi_u(x)=1} \frac{\prod_{E \in \mathcal{E}^v(t)} \Gamma^t(x)}{\sum_y \prod_{E \in \mathcal{E}^v(t)} \Gamma^t(y)}$$

$$= \sum_{x/u.x=1} \frac{(\frac{1}{2^{n-1}})^\mu f(x)}{2^{n-1} \times (\frac{1}{2^{n-1}})^\mu}$$

$$= \frac{1}{2^{n-1}} \sum_{x/u.x=1} f(x)$$

$$= \frac{1}{2} - \frac{\widehat{f}(u)}{2^n}$$

which is the probability of the equivalent BSC channel modeling the Boolean function. Therefore, when the Boolean function is plateaued, and the parity-checks even weighted, the SOJA is of no use.

□

Proposition 5 *For any plateaued function f,*

$$\forall (p,q) \in \mathbb{N}, \forall v \neq 0_n \in \{0,1\}^n, \quad \sum_s \widehat{f_\chi}^{2p+1}(v+s)\widehat{f_\chi}^{2q+1}(s) = 0$$

Proof. Suppose $p = 0$, $q = 0$. Then,

$$\sum_s \widehat{f_\chi}(v + s)\widehat{f_\chi}(s) = \sum_s \sum_x \sum_y (-1)^{f(x)+f(y)+s.(x+y)+v.x}$$

$$= \sum_x \sum_y (-1)^{f(x)+f(y)+v.x} \times 2^n \mathbb{1}_{\{x=y\}}$$

$$= 2^{2n} \delta_{0_n}(v)$$

$$= 0$$

because v is a nonzero vector.
f is assumed to be a plateaued function; $sp(f_\chi) = \{0, \pm A\}$, $A = 2^{n-\frac{r}{2}}$
Hence,

$$\sum_s \widehat{f_\chi}(v + s)\widehat{f_\chi}(s) = \sum_{s \in Supp(\widehat{f_\chi}) \cap Supp(\widehat{f_\chi} \circ \tau_v)} (-1)^{sgn(\widehat{f_\chi}(s)) + sgn(\widehat{f_\chi}(s+v))} \times A^2$$

$$= A^2 \sum_{s \in Supp(\widehat{f_\chi}) \cap Supp(\widehat{f_\chi} \circ \tau_v)} (-1)^{sgn(\widehat{f_\chi}(s)) + sgn(\widehat{f_\chi}(s+v))}$$

$$= 0$$

Let p, q be any positive integers,

$$\sum_s \widehat{f_\chi}^{2p+1}(v + s)\widehat{f_\chi}^{2q+1}(s)$$

$$= A^{2(p+q+1)} \times \sum_{s \in Supp(\widehat{f_\chi}^{2p+1}) \cap Supp(\widehat{f_\chi}^{2q+1} \circ \tau_v)} (-1)^{sgn(\widehat{f_\chi}^{2p+1}(s)) + sgn(\widehat{f_\chi}^{2q+1}(s+v))}$$

$$= 0$$

because

$$Supp(\widehat{f_\chi}^{2p+1}) = Supp(\widehat{f_\chi})$$
$$Supp(\widehat{f_\chi}^{2q+1} \circ \tau_v) = Supp(\widehat{f_\chi} \circ \tau_v)$$
$$\forall s, sgn\left(\widehat{f_\chi}^{2p+1}(s)\right) = sgn\left(\widehat{f_\chi}(s)\right)$$

where τ_v denotes the translation function:

$$\tau_v : \{0,1\}^n \longrightarrow \{0,1\}^n$$
$$x \longrightarrow x + v$$

$\square$

White-Box Cryptography and an AES Implementation

Stanley Chow, Philip Eisen, Harold Johnson, and Paul C. Van Oorschot

Cloakware Corporation, Ottawa, Canada
{stanley.chow, phil.eisen, harold.johnson, paulv}@cloakware.com

Abstract. Conventional software implementations of cryptographic algorithms are totally insecure where a hostile user may control the execution environment, or where co-located with malicious software. Yet current trends point to increasing usage in environments so threatened. We discuss encrypted-composed-function methods intended to provide a practical degree of protection against *white-box* (total access) *attacks* in untrusted execution environments. As an example, we show how AES can be implemented as a series of lookups in key-dependent tables. The intent is to hide the key by a combination of encoding its tables with random bijections representing compositions rather than individual steps, and extending the cryptographic boundary by pushing it out further into the containing application. We partially justify our AES implementation, and motivate its design, by showing how removal of parts of the recommended implementation allows specified attacks, including one utilizing a pattern in the AES *SubBytes* table.

1 Introduction and Overview

There has been tremendous progress in the uptake of cryptography within computer and network applications over the past ten years. Unfortunately, the attack landscape in the real world has also changed. In many environments, the standard cryptographic model — assuming that end-points are trusted, mandating a strong encryption algorithm, and requiring protection of only the cryptographic key — is no longer adequate. Among several reasons is the increasing penetration of commercial applications involving cryptography into untrusted, commodity host environments. An example is the use of cryptography in content protection for Internet distribution of e-books, music, and video. The increasing popularity of the Internet for commercial purposes illustrates that users wish to execute, and vendors will support, sensitive software-based transactions on physically insecure system components and devices. This sets the stage for our work.

The problem we seek to address is best illustrated by considering the software implementation of a standard cryptographic algorithm, such as RSA or AES [15], on an untrusted host. At some point in time, the secret keying material is in memory. Malicious software can easily search memory to locate keys, looking for randomness characteristics distinguishing keys from other values [26]. These keys can then be e-mailed at will to other addresses, as illustrated by the Sircam

K. Nyberg and H. Heys (Eds.): SAC 2002, LNCS 2595, pp. 250–270, 2003.

virus-worm [7]. An even easier attack in our context is to use a simple debugger to directly observe the cryptographic keying material at the time of use. We seek cryptographic implementations providing protection in such extremely exposed contexts, which we call the *white-box attack context* or WBAC (§2). This paper discusses methods developed and deployed for doing so.

A natural question is: if an attacker has access to executing decryption software, why worry about secret-key extraction — the attacker could simply use the software at hand to decrypt ciphertext. Protection methods in §2.2 make this hard, and even if such protections were compromised, our techniques are targeted at applications such as software-based cryptographic content protection for Internet media, rather than more traditional communications security. In such applications, the damage is often relatively small if an attacker can make continued use of an already-compromised platform, but cannot extract keying material allowing software protection goals to be bypassed on other machines, or publish keys or software sub-components allowing 'global cracks' to defeat security measures across large user-bases of installed software. Our solutions can also be combined with other software protection approaches, such as node-locking techniques tying software use to specific hardware devices.

Relevant Applications. There are many applications for which our approach is clearly inappropriate in its current form, including applications in which symmetric keys are changed frequently (such as secure e-mail or typical file encryption applications which randomly select per-use keys). Our approach also results in far slower and bulkier code than conventional cryptographic implementations, ruling out other applications. Nonetheless, we have been surprised at the range of applications for which slow speed and large size can be accommodated, through a combination of careful selection of applications and crypto operations, and careful application engineering. For example, key management involving symmetric key-encrypting keys consumes only a negligible percentage of overall computation time, relative to bulk encryption, so use of white-box cryptography here has little impact on overall performance. Examples of relevant applications include copy protection for software, conditional access markets (e.g. set-top boxes for satellite pay-TV and video-on-demand), and applications requiring distribution control for protected content playback.

Limitations on Expected Security. In the face of such an extreme threat environment, there are naturally limits to practically achievable security. In *all* environments, however, our white-box implementations provide *at least* as much security as a typical black-box implementation (see §2.1). Moreover on hostile platforms, for conventional (black-box) implementations of even the theoretically strongest possible algorithms, typically-claimed "crypto" levels of security (e.g. 2^{128} operations, 10^{20} years, etc.) fall essentially to zero (0) as the key is directly observable by an attacker. Therefore when considering white-box security, a useful comparison is the commercial use of cryptographic implementations on smartcards: an inexpensive circuit mounted on plastic, with embedded secret keys, is widely distributed in essentially uncontrolled environments. This is hardly wise from a security standpoint, and successful attacks on smart cards are regularly reported. However for many applications smartcards provide a reasonable level of added security at relatively low cost (*vs.* crypto hardware solutions), and a practical compromise among cost, convenience, and security. (Such trade-offs have long been recognized: e.g., see Cohen [11].) Our motivation is similar: we do not seek the ultimate level of security, on which a theoretical cryptographer might insist, but rather to provide an increased degree of protection given the constraints of a software-only solution and the hostile-host reality.

Theoretical Feasibility of Obfuscation. The theoretical literature on software obfuscation appears somewhat contradictory. The NP-hardness results of Wang [27] and PSPACE-hardness results of Chow *et al.* [10] provide theoretical evidence that code transformations can massively increase the difficulty of reverse-engineering. In contrast, the impossibility results of Barak *et al.* [3], essentially show that a software *virtual black box generator*, which can protect *every* program's code from revealing more than the program's input-output behavior reveals, cannot exist. Of greater interest to us is whether this result applies to programs of practical interest, or whether cryptographic components based on widely-used families of block ciphers are programs for which such a virtual black box *can* be generated. Lacking answers to these questions, we pursue practical virtual boxes which are, so to speak, a usefully dark shade of gray.

It seems safe to conjecture that no perfect long-term defense against white-box attacks exists. We therefore distinguish our goals from typical cryptographic goals: we seek neither perfect protection nor long-term guarantees, but rather a practical level of protection in suitable applications, sufficient to make use of cryptography viable under the constraints of the WBAC. The theoretical results cited above leave room for software protection of significant practical value.

Overview of White-Box AES Approach. This paper describes generation and composition of WBAC-resistant AES components, analogous in some ways to the encrypted-composed-function approach (see Sander and Tschudin [24,25], and Algesheimer et al. [1] for an update and comments). This converts AES-128 into a series of lookups in key-dependent tables. The key is hidden by (1) using tables for compositions rather than individual steps; (2) encoding these tables with random bijections; and (3) extending the cryptographic boundary beyond the algorithm itself further out into the containing application, forcing attackers (reverse engineers) to understand significantly larger code segments.

Organization. We discuss white-box cryptography and the white-box attack context (WBAC) in §2. §3 outlines a strategy and provides details for generating white-box AES implementations, including key-embedding, construction and composition of lookup tables implementing AES steps, insertion of random bijections, and size-performance issues. §4 includes security comments on white-box AES, with partial justification showing how removing portions of our design allows specified attacks. One of the attacks described in §4.4 employs patterns in the AES *SubBytes* table which may be of independent interest. Concluding remarks are in §5.

2   White-Box Cryptography and Attack Context

Hosts may be untrusted for various reasons, including the economics and logistics of the Internet. Often software is distributed to servers where access control enforcement cannot be guaranteed, or sites beyond the control of the distributor. This happens for mobile code [24,25], and where software tries to constrain what end-users may do with content — as in digital rights management for software-based web distribution of books, periodicals, music, movies, news or sports events. This may allow a *direct attack* by an otherwise legitimate end-user with hands-on access to the executing image of the target software. Hosts may also be rendered effectively hostile by viruses, worm programs, Trojan horses, and remote attacks on vulnerable protocols. This may involve an *indirect attack* by a remote attacker or automated attack tools, tricking users into opening malicious e-mail attachments, or exploiting latent software flaws such as buffer overflow vulnerabilities. Online shopping, Internet banking and stock trading software are all susceptible to these hazards. This leads to what we call the *white-box attack context* (WBAC) and *white-box cryptography* (i.e., cryptography designed for WBAC-resistance). First we briefly review related approaches.

2.1   Black-Box, Gray-Box, and White-Box Attack Contexts

In traditional *black-box* models (as in: black-box testing), one is restricted to observing input-output or external behavior of software. In the cryptographic context, progressive levels of black-box attacks are known. Passive attacks (e.g. known-plaintext attacks, exhaustive key search) are restricted to observation only; active attacks (e.g. chosen-plaintext attacks) may involve direct interaction; adaptive attacks (e.g. chosen plaintext-ciphertext attacks) may involve interaction which depends upon the outcome of previous interactions.

True black-box attacks are generic and do not rely on knowing internal details of an algorithm. More advanced attacks appear to be 'black-box' at the time of execution, but in fact exploit knowledge of an algorithm's internal details. Examples include linear and differential cryptanalysis (e.g. see [15]). These have remnants of a *gray-box attack*. Other classes of cryptographic attacks that have a 'gray' aspect are so-called *side-channel attacks* or *partial-access attacks*, including timing, power, and fault analysis attacks [2,4,5,6,12,13,18,19]. These clearly illustrate that even partial access or visibility into the inner workings, side-effects, or execution of an algorithm can greatly weaken security.

White-Box Attack Context.   The *white-box attack context* (WBAC), in contrast, contemplates threats which are far more severe. It assumes that:

1. fully-privileged attack software shares a host with cryptographic software, having complete access to the implementation of algorithms;
2. dynamic execution (with instantiated cryptographic keys) can be observed;
3. internal algorithm details are completely visible and alterable at will.

The attacker's objective is to extract the cryptographic key, e.g. for use on a standard implementation of the same algorithm on a different platform. WBAC includes the previously studied *malicious host* attack context [24,25] and the hazards of unwittingly importing malicious software (e.g., see Forrest *et al.* [16]). The black-box attack model and its gray-box variations are far too optimistic for software implementations on untrusted hosts.

Security requirements for WBAC-resistance are greater than for resistance to gray-box attacks on smartcards. The WBAC assumes the attacker has complete access to the implementation, rendering typical smartcard defenses insufficient, and typical smartcard attacks obsolete. For example, an attacker has no interest in the power profile of computations if computations themselves are accessible, nor any need to introduce hardware faults if software execution can be modified at will. The smartcard experience highlights that when the attacker has internal information about a cryptographic implementation, *choice of implementation is the sole remaining line of defense* [5,6,8,12,13,20,22] — and this is precisely what white-box cryptography pursues.

On the other hand, implementations addressing the WBAC such as the white-box AES implementation proposed herein, are less constrained, in the sense that implementations may employ resources far more freely than in smartcard environments, including flexibility in processing power and memory. Among other available approaches, WBAC-resistant cryptographic components can also (and are often recommended to) employ a strategy of regular software updates or replacements (cf. Jakobsson and Reiter [17]). When appropriate, such a design requires that protection need only withstand attacks for a limited period of time — thus counterbalancing the extreme threats faced, and the resulting limits on the level of protection possible.

2.2   White-Box Attack-Resistance at the Cryptographic Interface

Any key input by a cryptographic implementation is completely exposed to privileged attack software sharing its host. Two ways to avoid this follow. (1) *Dynamic key approach*: input encrypted and/or otherwise encoded key(s); this is the subject of ongoing white-box research. (2) *Fixed key approach*: embed the key(s) in the implementation by partial evaluation with respect to the key(s), so that key input is unnecessary. Since such key-customized software implementations can be transmitted wherever bits can, keys may still be changed with reasonable frequency. This approach is appropriate in selected applications (see §1), and is the subject of the remainder of this paper. We begin with a definition.

Definition 1 (encoding) *Let X be a transformation from m to n bits. Choose an m-bit bijection F and an n-bit bijection G. Call $X' = G \circ X \circ F^{-1}$ an encoded version of X. F is an* input encoding *and G is an* output encoding.

A potential problem with the fixed-key approach is that a key-specific implementation might be extracted and used instead of its key, permitting an adversary to encrypt or decrypt any message for which the legitimate user had such capabilities. However, cryptography is seldom stand-alone; it is typically a component of a larger system. Our solution is to have this containing system provide the input to the cryptographic component in a manipulated or encoded form (see §3.4 for AES-specific details) for which the component is designed, but which an adversary will find difficult to remove. Further protection is provided by producing the output in another such form, replacing a key-customized encryption function E_K by the composition $E'_K = G \circ E_K \circ F^{-1}$. Here F and G are (external) input and output encodings, both randomly selected bijections independent of K. E'_K no longer corresponds to encryption with key K; this protects against key-extraction as no combination of implementation components computes E_K in isolation.

The recommended implementation makes G^{-1} and F available only on a computing platform separate from the platform running E'_K (the attack platform). Additionally, when possible, some prior and subsequent computational steps (e.g. xors, binary shifts, and bit-field extractions and insertions, conveniently representable as linear operations on vectors over GF(2)) of the host system are composed with the initial and final operations implementing E'_K. This adds further protection by arranging that no precise boundary for E'_K exists within the containing system (boundaries lie in the 'middle' of compositions represented as table lookups).

2.3   Concatenated Encoding and Networked Encoding

In what follows, to avoid huge tables, we can construct an input or output encoding as the *concatenation* of smaller bijections. Consider bijections F_i of size n_i, where $n_1 + n_2 + \ldots + n_k = n$. Let $\|$ denote vector concatenation.

Definition 2 *The function concatenation $F_1\|F_2\|\ldots\|F_k$ is the bijection F such that $F(b) = F_1(b_1,\ldots,b_{n_1})\|F_2(b_{n_1+1},\ldots,b_{n_1+n_2})\|\ldots\|F_k(b_{n_1+\ldots+n_{k-1}+1},\ldots,b_n)$ for any n-bit vector $b = (b_1, b_2, \ldots, b_n)$. Plainly, $F^{-1} = F_1^{-1}\|F_2^{-1}\|\ldots\|F_k^{-1}$.*

Encodings generally make use of random bijections (cf. Definition 1). To make results meaningful, the output encoding of one encoded transformation will generally be matched with the input encoding of the next, as follows.

Definition 3 *A networked encoding for computing $Y \circ X$ (i.e. transformation X followed by transformation Y) is an encoding of the form*

$$Y' \circ X' = (H \circ Y \circ G^{-1}) \circ (G \circ X \circ F^{-1}) = H \circ (Y \circ X) \circ F^{-1} .$$

Note that internally, $Y \circ X$ is computed. By separately representing the steps as tables corresponding to Y' and X', the bijections F, G, and H may be hidden.

3   Constructing White-Box AES Implementations

In the white-box attack context, each cryptographic step might leak information. Our strategy is to break each AES round into a number of steps, and compose the steps after inserting randomly chosen bijections serving as *internal* encodings (in addition to the *external* encodings enveloping an overall cipher, as in $G \circ E_K \circ F^{-1}$ above). This randomness, intended to be difficult to separate from the step itself, introduces 'ambiguity' (see §4.2) — many possible $\langle key, bijection \rangle$ combinations might correspond to the same encoded step (composed function); cf. the 'diversity' which it also introduces (see §4.1).

To facilitate such encoding, we represent each AES component as a lookup table (an array of 2^m n-bit vectors, mapping m-bit inputs to n-bit outputs). An AES *implementation generator* program takes as input an AES key and a random seed, and outputs a key-customized WBAC-resistant AES implementation. Composition of lookup tables is straightforward, and done by the implementation generator. The resulting implementation consists entirely of encoded lookup tables, with functionalities shown in Fig. 1 (to be discussed).

Taken to an unrealistic extreme, one could use a single lookup table of about 5.4×10^{39} bytes representing the 128×128 bit AES bijection from plaintext to ciphertext for a given key. This could be attacked only as a black box. We attempt to approximate this with tables of very much smaller size, as follows.

3.1   Partial Evaluation with Respect to the AES Key

Using standard terminology [15,23], AES consists of N_r rounds; $N_r = 10$ for AES-128. A basic round has four parts: *SubBytes*, *ShiftRows*, *MixColumns*, and *AddRoundKey*. An *AddRoundKey* operation occurs before the first round; the *MixColumns* operation is omitted from the final round. Blocks of 128 bits are processed, and each round updates a set of 16 8-bit AES cells. To generate key-customized instances of AES-128, we integrate the key into the *SubBytes* transformation by creating 160 8×8 (i.e. 8-bit in, 8-bit out) lookup tables $\mathbf{T}_{i,j}^r$ defined as follows (one per cell per round):

$$\mathbf{T}_{i,j}^r(x) = S(x \oplus k_{i,j}^{r-1}) \qquad i = 0, \ldots, 3, \ j = 0, \ldots, 3, \ r = 1, \ldots, 9 \ . \qquad (1)$$

Here S is the AES S-box (an invertible 8-bit mapping), and $k_{i,j}^r$ is the AES subkey byte in position i, j at round r. These 'T-boxes' compose the *SubBytes* step with the previous round's *AddRoundKey* step.

The round 10 T-boxes also absorb the post-whitening key as follows:

$$\mathbf{T}_{i,j}^{10}(x) = S(x \oplus k_{i,j}^9) \oplus k_{sr(i,j)}^{10} \qquad i = 0, \ldots, 3, \ j = 0, \ldots, 3 \ , \qquad (2)$$

where $sr(i, j)$ denotes the new location of cell i, j after the *ShiftRows* step.

Remark. Of itself, partial evaluation provides little security: the key is easily recovered from T-boxes because the S-box is publicly known. Further (networked) encoding is used to make partial evaluation useful.

3.2   Applying Encodings to Large Linear Transformations

To efficiently implement the wide function (32-bit) *MixColumns* step, we use standard matrix blocking, combined with concatenated and networked encodings

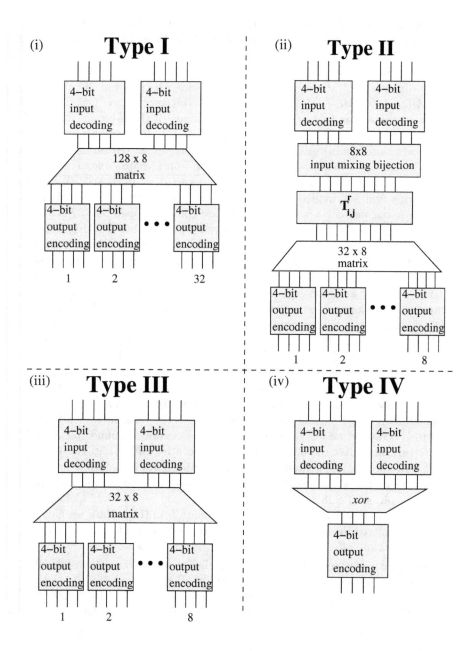

Fig. 1. Functionality of four table types in white-box AES implementation. Type I tables compute strips corresponding to the external encoding (§3.4). Tables of types II and III respectively compute strips in the first and second half of AES round transformations. Type IV tables are used to compute certain GF(2) additions (*xors*).

for white-box protection. *MixColumns*, which operates on the AES state a column (four 8-bit cells) at a time, can be implemented [23] by multiplying a 4×4 matrix over $GF(2^8)$ and a 4×1 vector. We use a 32×32 matrix MC times a 32×1 vector over $GF(2)$, using four copies of MC to operate on the full 128-bit state.

We consider MC 'strips' (see Fig. 2): we block MC into four 32×8 sections, MC_0, MC_1, MC_2, MC_3. Multiplication of a 32-bit vector $x = (x^0, \ldots, x^{31})$ by MC is considered as four separate multiplications of the 8-bit $(x^{4i}, \ldots, x^{4i+7})$ by MC_i (yielding four 32-bit vectors y_0, y_1, y_2, y_3), followed by three 32-bit binary additions (xors) giving the final 32-bit result y. We further subdivide the additions into twenty-four 4-bit xors with appropriate concatenation (e.g. $((y_0^0, y_0^1, y_0^2, y_0^3) + (y_1^0, y_1^1, y_1^2, y_1^3))\|((y_0^4, y_0^5, y_0^6, y_0^7) + (y_1^4, y_1^5, y_1^6, y_1^7))\| \ldots)$. By using these strips and subdivided xors, each step is represented by a small lookup table. In particular, for $i = 0 \ldots 3$, the y_i are computed using 8×32 tables Ty_i (Fig. 1(ii)), while the 4-bit xors become twenty-four 8×4 tables (Fig. 1(iv)).

Note that the xor tables, regardless of their order of use, take in 4 bits from each of two previous (e.g. partial y_i) computations. The output encodings of those computations must be matched by the input encodings for the xor tables. It turns out that as a consequence of pulling in 4-bit pieces from two separate computations (lookups), we require the use of concatenated 4-bit encodings for type IV tables; this imposes similar limitations on all other types, i.e. the use of 4-bit bijections. In particular, we use concatenated encodings both for the 32-bit output encodings to Ty_i and the 8-bit input encodings to the xor tables.

The T-boxes and 8×32 Ty_i's could be represented as separate lookup tables. Instead, we compose them creating new Ty_i's computing the *SubBytes* and *AddRoundKey* transformations as well as part of *MixColumns*. This saves both space (to store the T-boxes) and time (to perform the table lookups). Following our broad strategy, we insert input and output encodings around the xor tables (Fig. 1(iv)), and after the 32×8 matrix incorporating MC_i (Fig. 1(ii)).

ShiftRows is implemented by providing appropriately shifted input data (plaintext) to the generated tables, i.e. by run-time code during each round. The composition of *SubBytes* and *MixColumns*, and use of 8×32 lookup tables, resembles a proposed Rijndael implementation (§5 in [14]). Here we have composed also the *AddRoundKey* part and inserted encodings for added benefits of WBAC-protection, offset by the cost of being much larger and slower.

Remark. Ideally for security, we would explicitly avoid linear transformations. But randomly choosing bijections, essentially all will be non-linear: of the $2^n!$ n-bit bijections, $2^n \prod_{i=0}^{n-1}(2^n - 2^i)$ are affine — so for $n = 4$, of $16! \approx 2.09 \times 10^{13}$, only $322\,560$ (less than $.000\,002\%$) are affine (i.e. linear or translations thereof).

3.3   Insertion of Mixing Bijections

So far, we have used only (internal) encodings which are non-linear (or very likely so). Considering encodings as encipherments of AES intermediate values, such encodings are confusion steps. To further disguise the underlying operations, we now introduce linear transformations as diffusion steps, and for this reason

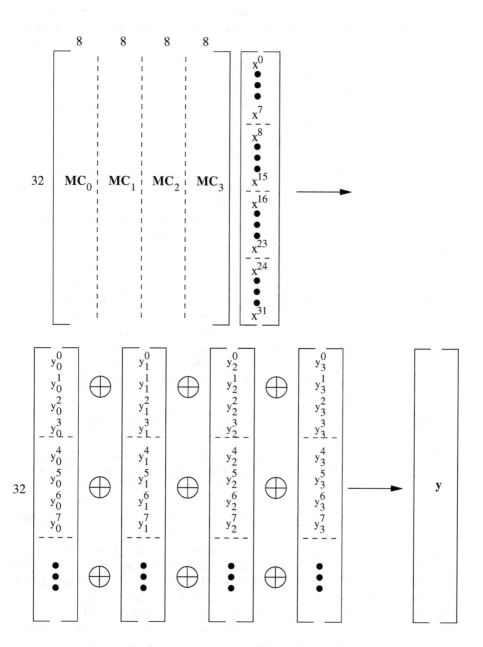

Fig. 2. Multiplication by *MC* (AES *MixColumns* operation)

refer to a linear bijection as a *mixing bijection*. Since linear transformations are representable as matrices, we think of mixing bijections as matrices over GF(2).

We use 8×8 (input) mixing bijections (Fig. 1(ii)) to diffuse the T-box inputs (technically, the inputs to the combined T-box/*MixColumns* step); these are inverted by an earlier computation. Moreover, before splitting MC into MC_i as above, we pre-multiply MC (i.e., left-multiply, yielding $MB \cdot MC$, so MC operates on data first) by a 32×32 mixing bijection MB chosen as a non-singular matrix with 4×4 submatrices of full rank. (See Xiao and Zhou [28] for a way to generate such matrices.) This design decision is related to using 4-bit encodings above.

To invert MB, an extra set of tables is used to calculate MB^{-1}, similar in form to those calculating MC. In type III tables, MB^{-1} is pre-multiplied by the inverses of the appropriate four input mixing bijections, and split into four 32×8 blocks. Implementing these via 8×32 tables[1] diffuses the 8×8 mixing bijections over several lookup tables. Corresponding *xor* tables are also needed; for appropriate applications, the detrimental size and speed implications are offset by MB's security benefits.

Summary. A set of tables is used for each of four 32-bit strips of state in an AES round. For each strip, a type II table combines a T-box (a partial evaluation of the *SubBytes* function with respect to a key byte) with three transformations: input mixing bijections, MC, MB; type IV *xor* (GF(2) addition) tables follow. Then a type III table combines MB^{-1} with the inverse of the input mixing bijections for the next round's T-boxes; again type IV *xor* tables follow. The type II, III and IV tables are all encoded using concatenated 4-bit (internal) input- and output-encodings in a networked fashion (see §2.2, §2.3).

3.4   Input and Output Data Manipulations (External Encoding)

As described in §2.2, our implementation takes input in a manipulated form, and produces output in another manipulated form, making the WBAC-resistant AES harder to separate from its containing application. The techniques described in previous sections, intended to securely handle both small non-linear steps (e.g. S-boxes) and large linear steps (e.g. *MixColumns*), are again used here to combine linear and non-linear components in the external encoding.

The idea is to have the first steps of the implementation undo a previous manipulation performed elsewhere in the program or at another site. Thus, while it is more straightforward to describe what these first steps of AES might look like, note that it is actually the inverse of steps done earlier; similarly the last steps will be undone at a later stage. The net result is a functionally equivalent, and WBAC-resistant, AES computation obtained by embedding a non-standard AES implementation in a correspondingly non-standard usage context.

The following is one suggestion for data manipulation, essentially corresponding to the input and output encodings F, G in §2.2. Select two 128×128 mixing

---

[1] For a 32×8 (8-bit in, 32-bit out) matrix A, the corresponding 8×32 (8-bit in, 32-bit out) lookup table is defined by $B[x] = A \cdot x$.

bijections U^{-1} and V in which all aligned 4×4 submatrices are of full rank. Insert U^{-1} prior to the first AES *AddRoundKey* operation; insert V after the last AES *AddRoundKey* operation. Pre-multiply U^{-1} by the inverted input mixing bijections for $\mathbf{T}^1$. Matrix-block the result into 128×8 strips; precede and follow these by concatenated 4-bit networked input and output encodings. These output encodings are inverted by the usual set of type IV *xor* tables. To complete the networking, the output encodings on the last stage of *xor* tables supporting U^{-1} invert the input decodings of round 1. We also compose tables representing $\mathbf{T}^{10}$ with tables computing the strips of V (cf. §3.3). This external encoding is implemented in type I tables (see Fig. 1(i)). Where the context of the generated implementation permits, we can further compose operations immediately preceding U^{-1} or following V into the U^{-1} and V tables as per §2.2.

3.5   Overall Implementation

The AES implementation now consists entirely of table lookups. Sixteen 8×128 type I tables implement an input mixing bijection over the full state, along with supporting type IV tables. Each of the first 9 rounds is then performed by a series of type II and III lookup tables, plus supporting type IV tables. Sixteen 8×128 type I tables are used to combine the final round with the output mixing bijection, again supported by corresponding type IV tables.

As shown in Fig. 1, type I tables represent two 4-bit decodings, a 128×8 matrix, and 32 4-bit encodings. Type II tables represent two 4-bit decodings, an 8×8 (input) mixing bijection, a T-box, a 32×8 matrix representing $(MB \cdot MC)_i$, and 8 4-bit encodings. Type III tables represent two 4-bit decodings, a 32×8 matrix, and 8 4-bit encodings. Type IV tables represent two 4-bit decodings, the known *xor* operation, and a 4-bit output encoding.

3.6   Size and Performance

The total size of lookup tables in the resulting implementation is $770\,048$ bytes[2], and there are $3\,104$ lookups during each execution.[3] A fair comparison is the AES implementation of Daemen and Rijmen [14], which requires $4\,352$ bytes for lookup tables, and approximately 300 operations (lookups and *xors*) in total. The expected increase in the size of an implementation is thus about $177\times$. (The performance slowdown is not as easy to measure; our implementation showed a slowdown of $55\times$, but this is presumably sensitive to the layout of the tables in memory and the size of the cache.) While WBAC-protection is important in hostile environments, it does come at quite a substantial price. Thus careful choices must be made as to where and how to employ white-box AES (see §1).

---

[2]   Type II and III: $9 \times 2 \times 4 \times 4 = 288$ 8×32 tables $= 294\,912$ bytes;
 type IV supporting II, III: $9 \times 2 \times 4 \times 8 \times 3 = 1\,728$ 8×4 tables $= 221\,184$ bytes;
 type I tables: $2 \times 16 = 32$ 8×128 tables $= 131\,072$ bytes;
 type IV supporting I: $2 \times 32 \times 15 = 960$ 8×4 tables $= 122\,880$ bytes.

[3]   Type II and III: 288 lookups; type IV supporting II, III: $1\,728$ lookups;
 type I tables: $32 \times 4 = 128$ lookups; type IV supporting I: 960 lookups.

4   Preliminary Security Comments on White-Box AES

Some immediate security observations are made in §1. Beyond these, an obvious question is: *can use of (external) encodings F and G as per §2.2 weaken the ordinary black-box security of E_K?* This seems unlikely — if with any significant probability, these key-independent, random bijections render $G \circ E_K \circ F^{-1}$ weaker than E_K, then intuitively one expects the cipher E itself is seriously flawed.

4.1   White-Box Diversity

We assume that encodings are random and independent, except for those which are inverses of each other; choosing the encodings is one-time per implementation work. Keyspace provides an upper bound on the security of a cryptographic algorithm. Analogously, if encodings 'encrypt' implementation steps, we can count the possible encoded steps, and call this metric *white-box diversity*. The white-box diversity of table types in Fig. 1 is the number of distinct *constructions* (or equivalently, distinct *decompositions*) — for type II tables, this includes varying the key — which exist for all possible tables of that type; this exceeds the number of distinct tables. (E.g., if constructing a table requires n independent choices to be made, and the ith choice has c_i alternatives, then the white-box diversity of the table is $\prod_{i=1}^{n} c_i$.) White-box diversity measures variability among implementations, which is useful in foiling pre-packaged attacks against specific instances. Implementations may differ both in time at a single site, and in space across sites (cf. [11,16]). The *white-box diversity* for the table types of Fig. 1 (see also §3.5) is:

Type I:[4] $(16!)^2 \times 20\,160^{64} \times (16!)^{32} \approx 2^{2\,419.7}$
Type II:[5] $(16!)^2 \times 256 \times 2^{62.2} \times 2^{256} \times (16!)^8 \approx 2^{768.7}$
Type III: $(16!)^2 \times 2^{256} \times (16!)^8 \approx 2^{698.5}$
Type IV: $(16!)^2 \times 16! \approx 2^{132.8}$

This is vastly more than needed for a diversity defense (see Forrest *et al.* [16]), but does not measure the resistance to key extraction from a specific instance.

4.2   White-Box Ambiguity

A far more important metric is the *white-box ambiguity* of a table type, which estimates the number of distinct *constructions* which produce *exactly the same table* of that type, computed by dividing its white-box diversity (see §4.1) by the (usually much smaller) number of distinct tables of that type. This gives an average measure of how many alternative interpretations (meanings) exist for an instance of a specific table type; certain white-box attacks must disambiguate

---

[4]   There are $20\,160$ nonsingular 4×4 matrices over $\mathrm{GF}(2)$.

[5]   The number of 8×8 mixing bijections is roughly $2^{62.2}$. The actual number of type II tables is slightly lower, as not every 8×32 matrix can be produced as a product of MC and mixing bijections.

among these. (E.g., since for a type II table, changing its T-box key-byte and changing its input encoding can have the same effect, the ambiguity of a type II table includes all possible key bytes.) Type IV tables have the lowest ambiguity. Ambiguity is intended as a defense against *disambiguation*, in the sense that greater ambiguity is likely to make disambiguation more difficult:[6]

Definition 4 (disambiguation) *To* disambiguate *a table is to narrow its set of possible constructions below the cardinality given by the* white-box ambiguity *for its table type, restricting its potential decompositions. Disambiguation is* total *if the set of possible constructions contains one element; otherwise, it is* partial.

Finding a rigorous and tractable way to compute white-box ambiguity appears difficult. We have made estimates by extrapolating from smaller tables preserving our basic structure, and assuming that the constructions are equiprobable (which is only approximately true).

For estimation purposes, assume type I tables are built from 128×8 matrices having all aligned 4×4 blocks of full rank, and 2-bit input and output encodings. We modelled them by combinatorially more tractable 4×4 matrices with all aligned 2×2 blocks of full rank, computing the number of distinct constructions. We carried out these constructions and counted the number of distinct resulting tables. We observed that for a given scaled-down such table, its two input encodings together with one of its $b \times b$ (here, $b = 2$) blocks in each aligned set of b rows uniquely determines the other $b \times b$ block in the aligned set of b rows and the output encodings. This observation also held for $b = 2$ and 6×4 matrices, and we conjecture that it holds for the real $b = 4$, 128×8 matrices. By this reasoning, the ambiguity of a type I table is $(16!)^2 \times 20\,160^{32} \approx 2^{546.1}$.

Type II and III tables are more complex: the matrix blocks may not have full rank. We discuss only construction of type III tables here. The rank of each block is a function of the the table, as follows. Consider the components needed to compute a single, fixed nybble of each entry in a type III table. We have two 4-bit input decodings, each feeding into a 4×4 block of the 32×8 matrix, and finally a 4-bit output encoding. If we arrange the 256 32-bit outputs in a 16×16 array, the effect of the first input decoding is to permute the array rows, while the second input decoding permutes its columns. The rank of the first block can be determined by taking the base 2 logarithm of the number of distinct entries in any array column; the rank of the second by taking the base 2 logarithm of the number of distinct entries in any array row. (E.g., a rank 3 block preserves 3 bits of information; over all 16 inputs it yields 8 distinct outputs; $\log_2 8 = 3$.)

The simplest sub-case to analyze is one where both blocks have rank 0. Here, the resulting table reveals no information about the input encodings (as any row and column permutation of a single entry table will look identical) and also reveals no information about the output encoding of any value except 0.

---

[6] For example, the greatest possible ambiguity would be achieved by an implementation of AES-128, with input and output data manipulation, as a single (infeasibly) immense table. At this limiting point, the power of a white-box attacker is reduced to that of the black-box attacker.

Therefore, the number of components which could have produced such a table is $(16!)^2 \times 15! \approx 2^{128.8}$. Of course, it is entirely possible that the other blocks in the 32×8 matrix reveal more information about the encodings.

For full-rank blocks, the blocks uniquely determine the output encodings. Since there are at most $20\,160^2$ possible such blocks, an upper bound for the number of components which could produce a given table is $(16!)^2 \times 20\,160^2 \approx 2^{117}$. In other cases, we could construct similar upper bounds (taking into account parts of the output encoding that cannot be determined).

The type IV tables have the smallest white-box ambiguity by far. One input decoding, together with the value to which 0 decodes for the other input decoding, uniquely determines the remaining encodings, so the number of constructions yielding a given type IV table is $16! \times 16 \approx 2^{48.2}$. It is not clear, however, how an attacker could determine which of these alternatives corresponds to the generated AES implementation. Total disambiguation of the eight type IV tables feeding into a set of type II tables (see §3.3 *Summary*) would permit removal of decodings for that set of type II tables, allowing the attack of §4.3.

Of course, keyspace-like security measures are appropriate only in the absence of efficient attacks which bypass much of the search space. We now consider what form such an attack might take.

4.3   A Generic Square-like Attack

We describe a generic attack, possible only in the white-box context where the attacker has full control of the key-instantiated AES implementation, and when all input encoding is removed (i.e., $\mathbf{T}^r_{i,j}$ inputs are fully exposed) for the set of four type II tables performing a round transformation for one column. (§4.4 shows how to perform such removal for weakened variants of our AES implementation.) While we can send arbitrary texts through these simplified tables, whose inputs are unencoded inputs to the *AddRoundKey* and *SubBytes* steps, the outputs are still obscured by the *MB* transformation and the output encoding.

Consider the value of an AES cell after our two-part round transformation. It has undergone an 8-bit mixing bijection and two concatenated 4-bit random bijections. This encoding is local to the cell, and therefore has the following property: *two texts having the same encoded value in a cell, have the same unencoded value in that cell*. In other words, while we cannot in general determine the unencoded xor difference of two texts, we *can* determine when it is zero.

Our goal is to find two 32-bit texts which have a non-zero input difference in each of the four cells, and a zero output difference in all but one cell (called a 'three-cell collision'). This can be recognized as the strategy in the first round of the Square attack on AES [14]. Suppose we find such texts, denoted $w = (w_0, w_1, w_2, w_3)$ and $x = (x_0, x_1, x_2, x_3)$. Let the key which is embedded in the type II tables be $k = (k_0, k_1, k_2, k_3)$. Let $y = (y_0, y_1, y_2, y_3)$ be the mod 2 difference between the two texts after the *SubBytes* transformation, i.e.

$$y_i = S(w_i \oplus k_i) \oplus S(x_i \oplus k_i) . \tag{3}$$

Then we have three equations in four unknowns y_i, with hexadecimal coefficients determined by the *MixColumns* matrix [23]:

$$01 \cdot y_0 \ \oplus \ 02 \cdot y_1 \ \oplus \ 03 \cdot y_2 \ \oplus \ 01 \cdot y_3 \ = \ 00 \ , \tag{4}$$

$$01 \cdot y_0 \ \oplus \ 01 \cdot y_1 \ \oplus \ 02 \cdot y_2 \ \oplus \ 03 \cdot y_3 \ = \ 00 \ , \tag{5}$$

$$03 \cdot y_0 \ \oplus \ 01 \cdot y_1 \ \oplus \ 01 \cdot y_2 \ \oplus \ 02 \cdot y_3 \ = \ 00 \ , \tag{6}$$

or some variant thereof, depending on which cells 'collide' and which cell differs. The above system has the solution

$$y_0 = \mathsf{ec} \cdot y_3 \ , \quad y_1 = \mathsf{9a} \cdot y_3 \ , \quad y_2 = \mathsf{b7} \cdot y_3 \ .$$

Thus, the choice-count for k has been reduced to at most 256 (by equation (3)). Exhaustive search now finds k.

Based on the probability of a three-cell collision ($\binom{4}{1}$ cells in which to occur $\times$ probability $\frac{255}{256}$ of a non-collision $\times$ probability $(\frac{1}{256})^3$ of three collisions $\approx 2^{-22}$) and a birthday-paradox counting argument, the expected work to find an entire round key is approximately 2^{11} texts $\times$ four 32-bit columns $= 2^{13}$ one-round encryptions for this weakened variant.

4.4 Partial Design Justification by Examining Weakened Variants

We show here that removing certain aspects of our design destroys its security.

Need for Input and Ouptut Data Manipulation. The weakened WBAC-resistant AES variant without input and output data manipulation (see §3.4), beyond suffering the problem discussed in §2.2, has no input encoding for the first set of type II tables, and is thus vulnerable to the attack in §4.3. Thus such manipulations are necessary for security.

Need for Internal Mixing Bijections. Diffusion (cf. §3.3) is crucial to the security of white-box implementations: without it, patterns in the underlying tables allow disambiguation, as we illustrate in the attack methods below. Hence, mixing bijections are essential in the intermediate steps of the cipher.

Consider an implementation in which T-boxes are not preceded by input mixing bijections (see Fig. 1(ii)) nor followed by MB, thus having no type III tables. Each of its type II tables implements two 4-bit decodings, followed by a T-box, then a known 32×8 matrix, and finally eight 4-bit encodings. Within such a 32×8 matrix, two 8×8 blocks are identities (multiplications by the 01 polynomial), so considering only parts of the output coming from such an identity, we can read an encoded version of the underlying T-box from the type II table, computing a function of the form $T' = (G_1 \| G_2) \circ T \circ (F_1^{-1} \| F_2^{-1})$, where T is some $\mathbf{T}_{i,j}^r$ function *per* equation (1) or (2). We can rewrite this as $T' = (B_1 \| B_2) \circ S \circ (A_1 \| A_2)$ where S is the *SubBytes* function, each B_i is an output nybble encoding (rounds 1–9) or such an encoding composed with a post-whitening nybble *xor* (round 10), and each A_i is a nybble *xor* (from *AddRoundKey*) composed with an input decoding (rounds 1–10).

By ignoring nybble values *per se*, and considering only left and right nybble frequencies described below, we can recover output encodings for the T' for each type II table in rounds 1–9, where $B_1 = G_1$ and $B_2 = G_2$. Since the A_i and B_i are 4×4 bijections, a table for T' can be derived from the 16×16 *SubBytes* table (see [23] p. 16, Fig. 7) by row (due to A_1) and column (due to A_2) permutation, together with bijective left (due to B_1) and right (due to B_2) renumbering of entry nybbles. (Random choice of nybble swapping in table elements or the table input affords no further protection, as shown below.) We disambiguate as follows.

Definition 5 (frequency signature) *Let L be an $n \times n$ array of byte entries. L has n^2 cells $L[rc]$ where r is the row and c is the column. For a sequence of left (respectively, right) nybbles in a row (respectively, column) of L, its* frequency signature *is the sequence of n occurrence frequencies for values 0–F, sorted into descending order, written as a string of n digits in a sufficiently large base.*

E.g., F 0 1 3 A B 0 7 3 A F 3 2 1 2 6 has the frequency signature 3222221110000000.

Definition 6 (cell signature) *For an $n \times n$ array L of byte entries, the* cell signature *of a cell $L[rc]$ in row r and column c is the $4n$-digit concatenation of the frequency signatures for (a) row r left nybbles; (b) row r right nybbles; (c) column c left nybbles; and (d) column c right nybbles.*

For example, in the *SubBytes* table above, the *SubBytes*[00] cell signature is 4421111110000000 4311111111100000 3222221110000000 4222211110000000.

There are 192 distinct cell signatures in *SubBytes*. 160 apply to unique cells. Each of the remaining 32 applies to a 3-set of cells with indices $[rc]$ of the form $[xd]$, $[yd]$, and $[zd]$, where among 3-sets, d ranges over all hex digits and either (a) $x = 4$, $y = 6$, and $z = 9$ or (b) $x = 5$, $y = 7$, and $z = F$.[7]

This 3-set co-ordinates pattern is invariant under any combination of: (a) column permutation; (b) bijective renumbering of entry left nybbles or right nybbles; and (c) swapping left and right nybbles in all entries. A row permutation bijectively renumbers the rows and the corresponding alternatives for x, y, z above, but otherwise preserves the 3-set pattern above. Swapping input nybbles is easily identified: it interchanges rows and columns in the pattern. Entry nybble swapping is identified by the numerically highest signature, which has different values for swapped and unswapped.

Given a 16×16 T' table for a T' function, for any table cell $T'[r'c']$ there is a corresponding cell *SubBytes*[rc] with the same cell signature. After correcting for entry or input nybble swapping, 160 T' cells are identified immediately with *SubBytes* cells having their signatures. Every left and right nybble occurs in a unique-signatured *SubBytes* (and hence T') table cell: comparing corresponding

---

[7] The *SubBytes* shared-cell-signature n-set pattern is atypical: of 10 000 16×16 S-boxes filled with pseudo-randomly selected permutations of the byte values from 0 to 255 using L'Ecuyer's recommended generator [21] with its default seeds, just 4.6% contained any, and just 1.7% contained only, such n-sets with n divisible by 3.

entries, we find B_1 and B_2. Then the T' table's row and column permutations (relative to *SubBytes*) define A_1 and A_2, and thus reveal the function T.

In rounds 1–9, B_1 and B_2 are the identity-block output encodings for T'. Non-identity blocks are known (corresponding to multiplications by 02 and 03 polynomials), so correcting for these known bijective blocks, we obtain output codings for the non-identity blocks. We can thus find a round's type II table output codings, from which we know all succeeding type IV tables input codings. Since these encode *xors*, we can then determine their output codings. We proceed in a similar fashion until we reach the next round's type II table input codings, which are the inverses of the (now known) output codings of the immediately preceding type IV tables. We can then remove them, creating the conditions necessary to launch the Square-like attack of §4.3.

Round-Pair Attack. A simpler and faster attack on this weakened variant (without internal mixing bijections) is as follows. We perform the above disambiguation process on two successive rounds in the range 2–9. For the second round of the round-pair, as noted above, we then know the input encodings, and the previous disambiguation techniques give us the output encodings. We can write any round 2–9 T' function as

$$T' = (G_1 \| G_2) \circ S \circ (X_1 \| X_2) \circ (F_1^{-1} \| F_2^{-1}) , \qquad (7)$$

where the G_i are the output nybble encodings, S is the *SubBytes* function, the F_i are the input nybble encodings, and the X_i denote *xors* with *AddRoundKey* nybbles. Given the corresponding type II table in the second round of the round-pair, we can now identify G_1, G_2, F_1 and F_2. Removing these encodings, we derive the function $T = S \circ (X_1 \| X_2)$, where $T(x) = S(x \oplus k)$ for any byte x by equation (1), and k is the key-byte hidden in T by partial evaluation (see §3.1). This allows key extraction directly from (weakened) type II tables, without any encryption operations (required in the Square-like attack). However, it requires absence of mixing in two successive rounds.

Summary. The mixing bijections thwart the above attacks by diffusing information over bytes instead of nybbles for both inputs and outputs of type II tables: they make it impossible to write their input encodings as concatenations of nybble-to-nybble bijection pairs, thereby causing them to have T' cell signatures unlike those of the *SubBytes* table, and they eliminate identity blocks in the 32×8 matrices of the type II tables, thereby making it hard for an attacker to separate the effects of their output encodings from those of the matrices.

5   Conclusions and Future Work

The white-box attack context (WBAC) reflects both the capabilities of an adversary who can introduce malicious code, and the reality of untrusted hosts. Traditional implementations of cryptographic algorithms, including AES, are completely insecure in the face of these threats. As is well-known with smartcards, in practice the security of a cipher is dependent on its environment and implementation, as well as its mathematical underpinnings.

As a proposal for pragmatically acceptable white-box attack-resistance, we present a new way of implementing AES using lookup tables representing encoded compositions. Such implementations are far larger and slower than reference code, but arguably allow cryptographic computation to take place with a useful degree of security, for a period of time, even in the presence of an adversary who can observe and modify every step. As a bonus feature, aside from white-box strength, generated AES implementation instances provide a diversity defense against pre-packaged attacks on particular instances of executable software.

Further security analysis is needed, and we encourage the wider cryptographic community to participate. In this paper, we consider the concept of component disambiguation, a Square-like attack, and attacks on weakened variants. The issues of attacks on multiple components at once, or on multiple implementations sharing a key, remain to be investigated. For example, white-box ambiguity for a *sub-network* of tables in our implementation may differ depending on where its boundaries lie.

Although AES implementations using optimized versions of the techniques in this paper have been found acceptable in several commercial applications, their large size and low speed limit general applicability. Efficiency improvements would be most welcome. We also encourage the extension of white-box techniques to other algorithms (cf. Chow *et al.* [9]).

Acknowledgements. We thank Alexander Shokurov for suggesting the ambiguity metric of §4.2 in another context, and anonymous reviewers.

References

1. J. Algesheimer, C. Cachin, J. Camenisch, G. Karjoth, *Cryptographic Security for Mobile Code*, pp. 2–11 in Proceedings of the 2001 IEEE Symposium on Security and Privacy, May 2001.
2. R.J. Anderson, M.G. Kuhn, *Low Cost Attacks on Tamper-Resistant Devices*, pp. 125–136, 5th International Workshop on Security Protocols (LNCS 1361), Springer 1997.
3. B. Barak, O. Goldreich, R. Impagliazzo, S. Rudich, A. Sahai, S. Vadhan, K. Yang, *On the (Im)possibility of Obfuscating Programs*, pp. 1–18, Advances in Cryptology – Crypto 2001 (LNCS 2139), Springer-Verlag, 2001.
4. E. Biham, A. Shamir, *Differential Fault Analysis of Secret Key Cryptosystems*, pp. 513–525, Advances in Cryptology – Crypto '97 (LNCS 1294), Springer-Verlag, 1997. *Revised*: Technion - C.S. Dept. - Technical Report CS0910-revised, 1997.
5. E. Biham, A. Shamir, *Power Analysis of the Key Scheduling of the AES Candidates*, presented at the 2nd AES Candidate Conference, Rome, Mar. 22–23 1999.
6. D. Boneh, R.A. DeMillo, R.J. Lipton, *On the Importance of Eliminating Errors in Cryptographic Computations*, J. Cryptology 14(2), pp. 101–119, 2001.
7. CERT Advisory CA-2001-22 W32/Sircam Malicious Code, 25 July 2001 (revised 23 August 2001), http://www.cert.org/advisories/CA-2001-22.html.
8. S. Chari, C. Jutla, J.R. Rao, P. Rohatgi, *A Cautionary Note Regarding Evaluation of AES Candidates on Smart-Cards*, presented at the Second AES Candidate Conference, Rome, Italy, March 22–23, 1999.

9. S. Chow, P. Eisen, H. Johnson, P.C. van Oorschot, *A White-Box* DES *Implementation for* DRM *Applications*, Proceedings of DRM 2002 – 2nd ACM Workshop on Digital Rights Management, Nov. 18, 2002 (Springer-Verlag LNCS, to appear).

10. S. Chow, Y. Gu, H. Johnson, V.A. Zakharov, *An Approach to the Obfuscation of Control-Flow of Sequential Computer Programs*, pp. 144–155, Proceedings of ISC 2001 – Information Security, 4th International Conference (Malaga, Spain, 1–3 October 2001), LNCS 2200, Springer-Verlag, 2001.

11. F. Cohen, *Operating System Protection Through Program Evolution*, Computers and Security 12(6), 1 Oct. 1993, pp. 565–584.

12. J. Daemen, V. Rijmen, *Resistance Against Implementation Attacks: A Comparative Study of the* AES *proposals*, presented at the Second AES Candidate Conference, Rome, Italy, March 22–23, 1999.

13. J. Daemen, M. Peeters, G. van Assche, *Bitslice Ciphers and Power Analysis Attacks*, pp. 134–149, 7th International Workshop on Fast Software Encryption – FSE 2000 (LNCS 1978), Springer-Verlag, 2000.

14. J. Daemen, V. Rijmen, AES *Proposal: Rijndael,* http://csrc.nist.gov/encryption/aes/rijndael/Rijndael.pdf, 1999.

15. J. Daemen, V. Rijmen, *The Design of Rijndael:* AES *– The Advanced Encryption Standard*, Springer, 2001.

16. S. Forrest, A. Somayaji, D. H. Ackley, *Building Diverse Computer Systems*, pp. 67–72, Proceedings of the 6th Workshop on Hot Topics in Operating Systems, IEEE Computer Society Press, 1997.

17. M. Jakobsson, M.K. Reiter, *Discouraging Software Piracy Using Software Aging*, pp. 1–12, Security and Privacy in Digital Rights Management – ACM CCS-8 Workshop DRM 2001 (LNCS 2320), Springer-Verlag, 2002.

18. P.C. Kocher, *Timing Attacks against Implementations of Diffie-Hellman,* RSA*,* DSS*, and Other Systems*, pp. 104–113, Advances in Cryptology – Crypto '96 (LNCS 1109), Springer-Verlag, 1996.

19. P. Kocher, J. Jaffe, B. Jun, *Differential Power Analysis*, pp. 388–397, Advances in Cryptology – Crypto '99 (LNCS 1666), Springer-Verlag, 1999.

20. O. Kömmerling, M.G. Kuhn, *Design Principles for Tamper-Resistant Smartcard Processors*, pp. 9–20, Proceedings of the USENIX Workshop on Smartcard Technology (Smartcard '99), USENIX Association, ISBN 1-880446-34-0, 1999.

21. P. L'Ecuyer, *Efficient and Portable Combined Random Number Generators*, Communications of the ACM 31(6), pp. 742–749, 1988.

22. National Institute of Standards and Technology (NIST), *Round 2 Discussion Issues for the* AES *Development Effort*, November 1, 1999. http://csrc.nist.gov/encryption/aes/round2/Round2WhitePaper.htm.

23. National Institute of Standards and Technology (NIST), *Advanced Encryption Standard* (AES), FIPS Publication 197, 26 Nov. 2001. http://csrc.nist.gov/publications/fips/fips197/fips-197.pdf

24. T. Sander, C.F. Tschudin, *Towards Mobile Cryptography*, pp. 215–224, Proceedings of the 1998 IEEE Symposium on Security and Privacy.

25. T. Sander, C.F. Tschudin, *Protecting Mobile Agents Against Malicious Hosts*, pp. 44–60, Mobile Agent Security (LNCS 1419), Springer-Verlag, 1998.

26. N. van Someren, A. Shamir, *Playing Hide and Seek with Keys*, pp. 118–124, Financial Cryptography '99 (LNCS 1648), Springer-Verlag, 1999.

27. C. Wang, *A Security Architecture for Survivability Mechanisms*, Doctoral thesis, University of Virginia, October 2000.
28. J. Xiao, Y. Zhou, *Generating Large Non-Singular Matrices over an Arbitrary Field with Blocks of Full Rank*, Cryptology ePrint Archive (http://eprint.iacr.org), no. 2002/096.

Luby-Rackoff Ciphers: Why XOR Is Not So Exclusive

Sarvar Patel[1], Zulfikar Ramzan[2*], and Ganpathy S. Sundaram[1]

[1] Bell Labs, Lucent Technologies
{sarvar, ganeshs}@bell-labs.com
[2] IP Dynamics, Inc.
zramzan@ipdynamics.com

Abstract. This work initiates a study of Luby-Rackoff ciphers when the bitwise exclusive-or (XOR) operation in the underlying Feistel network is replaced by a binary operation in an arbitrary finite group. We obtain various interesting results in this context:

- First, we analyze the security of three-round Feistel ladders over arbitrary groups. We examine various Luby-Rackoff ciphers known to be insecure when XOR is used. In some cases, we can break these ciphers over arbitrary *Abelian groups* and in other cases, however, the security remains an open problem.
- Next, we construct a four round Luby-Rackoff cipher, operating over *finite groups of characteristic greater than 2*, that is not only completely secure against *adaptive* chosen plaintext and ciphertext attacks, but has better time / space complexity and uses fewer random bits than all previously considered Luby-Rackoff ciphers of equivalent security in the literature. Surprisingly, when the group is of characteristic 2 (i.e., the underlying operation on strings is bitwise exclusive-or), the cipher can be completely broken in a constant number of queries.

Notably, for the former set of results dealing with three rounds (where we report no difference) we need new techniques. However for the latter set of results dealing with four rounds (where we prove a new theorem) we rely on a generalization of known techniques albeit requires a new type of hash function family, called a *monosymmetric hash function family*, which we introduce in this work. We also discuss the existence (and construction) of this function family over various groups, and argue the necessity of this family in our construction. Moreover, these functions can be very easily and efficiently implemented on most current microprocessors thereby rendering the four round construction very practical.

1 Introduction

MOTIVATION. Let X be the n-bit string which represents the integer $2^n - 1$, and let Y be the n-bit string representing 1. Observe that, when we replace X

---

* Work done while this author was at Lucent Technologies and the Massachusetts Institute of Technology. This author would like to acknowledge DARPA grant DABT63-96-C-0018 and an NSF graduate fellowship.

K. Nyberg and H. Heys (Eds.): SAC 2002, LNCS 2595, pp. 271–290, 2003.
© Springer-Verlag Berlin Heidelberg 2003

by $X + Y$ modulo 2^n we get the "zero" string whereas when we replace X by $X \oplus Y$ we get the string with $n - 1$ leading 1's and a 0 in the least significant position. In the former, all the bits of the orginial string X are affected, and in the latter only the least significant bit is affected. Surprisingly, this naive observation contributes to the complexity of various computational problems.

Consider, for example, the *subset sum problem*. This problem is known to be $\mathcal{NP}$-hard when the inputs are treated as elements in the group of integers modulo 2^n [6], [9]. Yet, when we treat the inputs as elements of $\mathrm{GF}(2^n)^+$ the subset sum problem can be efficiently solved via a system of linear equations.

Yet another example is the problem of factoring a bit string treated as an integer. This problem is believed to be hard and is central to various cryptosystems proposed in the past few decades (RSA and its variants). On the other hand, the same bit string treated as a polynomial in one variable over a binary field can be very easily factored; for example via Berlekamp's algorithm [2].

This idea of examining binary operations between bit strings has also been considered in the context of block ciphers. For example, Biham and Shamir [3] show that replacing some of the exclusive-or operations in DES with additions modulo 2^n, makes their differential attack less powerful. Carter, Dawson, and Nielsen [4] show a similar phenomenon when addition in DES is replaced by addition using a particular Latin Square. While these results show resistance to one particular type of attack, they are more ad-hoc since they do not demonstrate provable security against *all attacks*. Motivated by these examples, we embark on a formal study of the impact of the underlying binary operation on block ciphers. We focus our attention on three and four round *Luby-Rackoff ciphers*.

LUBY-RACKOFF CIPHERS AND VARIANTS. Luby and Rackoff [10] formalize the notion of a provably-secure block cipher as a *Pseudorandom Permutation* (PRP) family (indexed by the key). They achieve a construction satisfying this definition which relies on the existence of one-way functions. This seminal piece of work has received a lot of attention, and ciphers based on this principle are now called *Luby-Rackoff ciphers*. A Luby-Rackoff cipher involves the use of a *Feistel permutation* which sends a $2n$-bit string (L, R) to $(R, L \oplus f(R))$ where f is a length-preserving function on n bit strings and $\oplus$ represents the XOR operation on bit strings. The Feistel permutation appears in a number of well-known block cipher constructions such as DES. Luby and Rackoff show that composing three Feistel permutations with independently keyed pseudorandom functions, which we denote as $\Psi(f_1, f_2, f_3)$, yields a cipher secure against chosen plaintext attacks. They also show that composing four Feistel permutations with independent keys, denoted as $\Psi(f_1, f_2, f_3, f_4)$, yields a cipher secure against adaptive chosen plaintext and ciphertext attacks. This path-breaking work, has stimulated much research which can be broadly classified as follows:

- Reducing the number of independent functions in the three or four round construction, and examine which constructions continue to guarantee pseudorandomness or super pseudorandomness, (example, [15], [17]).

- Replacing the outer rounds of the four round construction by various flavors of universal hash functions, and examine which constructions continue to guarantee super pseudorandomness, (example, [11]).

- Increasing the number of rounds to enhance the security guarantees, (example, [12], [13]).

Our work fits in the first two broad areas of research to obtain variants of Luby-Rackoff constructions where the number of different functions used in the 3 or 4 rounds is minimized. The kind of questions asked by this research are, for example: is the three-round variant $\Psi(f, f, f)$ pseudorandom? Alternatively, is the four-round variant $\Psi(f_1, f_2, f_2, f_1)$ strongly pseudorandom?

The answer to these questions are important not just because of the apparent savings of key material achieved by minimizing different pseudorandom functions, but also because of the insight they provide into the design of secure block ciphers. In this context, negative results are also very useful. *For example, knowing that $\Psi(f, f, f)$ is not a pseudorandom permutation for any pseudorandom function f means that block cipher designers should avoid such symmetrical structures independent of what is being used for f.* Also the description of the specific attack which works on $\Psi(f, f, f)$ is useful to the designer because he can check if that attack or similar attacks may also work with many more feistel rounds used in practical block ciphers. Thus the question of security of variants of Luby-Rackoff ciphers is fundamental. Similarly variants of Luby-Rackoff ciphers where the first and last rounds are replaced by universal hash functions, should be considered; for example, is $\Psi(h, f, f, h)$ strongly pseudorandom?

OUR CONTRIBUTIONS. All of the previous constructions rely on the bitwise exclusive-or (XOR) operation. We depart from this paradigm and we hope that utilizing different operations, with different algebraic properties, may yield new more powerful constructions. A more direct motivation is the result in [14], where the authors optimize a Naor-Reingold variant using "non-XOR" operations. Naor and Reingold proved that $\Psi(h_1, f, f, h_2)$ using XOR is super pseudorandom where the universal hash functions h_1 and h_2 work on $2n$ bits. Following this Patel, Ramzan, and Sundaram, [14] optimized this construction by using specialized hash functions and working over addition mod 2^n to make h_1 and h_2 work over n bits. Although, they proved an interesting optimization, their construction did not further minimize the different kinds of functions when compared to the constructions in the Naor-Reingold construction [11]. Both require h in round 1 and 4 to be different. Thus it remained an open question whether there are Luby-Rackoff variants which are secure when a non-XOR operation is used and are insecure when XOR is used.

Our efforts focus on both three-round and four-round Feistel networks that permute $2n$-bits of data as in the original Luby-Rackoff construction and some of its variants discussed above. Our point of departure is that we treat the n-bit strings as elements in an arbitrary algebraic structure which is not necessarily

$GF(2^n)^+$.[1] This idea seems to open up new lines of research and we obtain results which are both surprising and useful. Specifically:

- We examine various three-round Luby-Rackoff ciphers known to be insecure over $GF(2^n)^+$. In some cases, we can break these ciphers over arbitrary *Abelian groups* – though we have to employ different attacks. In other cases, however, the security remains an open problem.
- Next we construct a Luby-Rackoff style cipher, whose Feistel ladder operates over various *finite groups* of characteristic greater than 2, that is not only super-pseudorandom, but has better time/space complexity and uses fewer random bits than all previously considered Luby-Rackoff ciphers of equivalent security in the literature. Interestingly, when we use the bit-wise exclusive-or operation instead, we can distinguish the cipher from random with near certainty using only two queries.
- We show that the requirements on our construction are precise when operations are performed in a *finite field*. In particular, eliminating one of the statistical requirements on the hash function used in the first and last round results in the cipher becoming distinguishable from random with near certainty using only a small constant number of queries.

The four-round construction is fairly interesting since one can then construct a Luby-Rackoff cipher that can be broken with two plaintext/ciphertext queries when the bit-wise exclusive-or is the group operation; yet, if one simply changes four of those bit-wise exclusive-or operations to, for example, additions mod 2^n, the cipher becomes completely secure against both adaptive chosen plaintext and ciphertext attacks. Note that both operations can be implemented very efficiently on most current microprocessors, and both are frequently used in popular block ciphers. A more careful analysis shows that we only need to change the exclusive-or operation in the first and last round to addition mod 2^n to achieve security. Thus, in some sense, there are two very simple operations at the heart of the cipher's security. Our construction utilizes the notion of a *monosymmetric* universal hash function, which we intoduce in this work. In particular the monosymmetric property does not really hold in groups of characteristic 2, which explains why our constructions fail to be secure in this case. In addition we discuss the existence and necessity of this hash function family in our construction.

ORGANIZATION. The next section provides relevant definitions and reviews prior art on Luby-Rackoff ciphers; we focus on results that are relevant to this paper. In sections three and four we analyze three and four-round Luby-Rackoff ciphers over arbitrary groups. Section five discusses monosymmetric hash functions.

2 Definitions and Prior Work

NOTATION. We let I_n denote the set of bit strings of length n. For a bit string x, if x has even length, then x^L and x^R denote the left and right halves of

---

[1] Recall that $GF(2^n)^+$ refers to the additive group attached to the field $GF(2^n)$. The addition of two elements in this group amounts to computing their bit-wise exclusive-or.

the bits respectively; we sometimes write $x = (x^L, x^R)$ or $x^L \cdot x^R$. If S is a set whose elements can be sampled according to some pre-specified underlying probability distribution, then $x \xleftarrow{R} S$ denotes the process of picking an element x from S according to this distribution. Unless otherwise specified, the underlying distribution is assumed to be uniform. We let $|x|$ denote its length.

If n is a positive integer, we let $\mathrm{GF}(2^n)$ denote the Galois Field of order 2^n, and we let $\mathrm{GF}(2^n)^+$ denote the additive group attached to the field $\mathrm{GF}(2^n)$. Recall that elements of $\mathrm{GF}(2^n)$ can be represented as bit strings of length n, and that the addition operation on two elements merely amounts to taking their bit-wise exclusive-or.

By a finite function (permutation) family $\mathcal{F}$, we mean a set of functions (permutations) on a fixed domain and range. If k and l are positive integers, then $\mathsf{Rand}^{k \to l}$ denotes the set of all functions going from I_k to I_l. Similarly, Perm^l denotes the set of all permutations on the set I_l. We call a finite function (permutation) family keyed if every function in it can be specified (not necessarily uniquely) by a key a. We denote the function corresponding to a as f_a. For a given keyed function family, a key can be any string from I_s, where s is known as the "key length." While it is possible to consider key spaces other than I_s, we avoid doing so for clarity of exposition. For functions f and g, where the range of f is contained in the domain of g, we let $g \circ f$ denote their functional composition; i.e. $x \mapsto g(f(x))$. If S is a set contained in a universe U, then S^C denotes the set-theoretic complement of S – that is the set of elements of U that are not in S.

MODEL OF COMPUTATION. The adversary $\mathcal{A}$ is modeled as a program for a *Random Access Machine* (RAM) that has black-box access to some number k of oracles, each of which computes some specified function. The adversary $\mathcal{A}$ will have a one-bit output. If $(f_1, \ldots, f_k)$ is a k-tuple of functions, then $\mathcal{A}^{f_1, \ldots, f_k}$ denotes a k-oracle adversary who is given black-box oracle access to each of the functions $f_1, \ldots, f_k$. We define $\mathcal{A}$'s "running time" to be the number of time steps it takes plus the length of its description (to prevent one from embedding arbitrarily large lookup tables in $\mathcal{A}$'s description). This convention was used by Bellare, Kilian, and Rogaway [1].

Sometimes we abuse notation by listing an entire function family as the oracle, rather than just a single function. In this case, the oracle is considered to be a function (or some set of functions) chosen from the family, according to some induced probability distribution. That is, we can think of the oracle as a random variable, which denotes a function, and outputs the value of the function on any input queries it receives. For example, $\mathcal{A}^{\mathsf{Rand}^{n \to n}}$ would be used to denote an adversary whose oracle computes a function chosen at random from the set of all functions with domain and range I_n. Similarly, it may be the case that an adversary has access to multiple oracles, all of which are drawn from the same family. For example, if we deal with oracles chosen from the family Perm^n, we could conceive of giving oracle access to the permutations $f, f^{-1} \in \mathsf{Perm}^n$. These kinds of scenarios apply when we talk about attacks on block ciphers. We also remark that oracles need not simply represent deterministic functions.

Instead there could be some degree of randomness in their answers. In this case the oracle's output is determined by the input together with some internal coin tosses. Both deterministic and randomized oracles are used in this paper.

PSEUDORANDOM FUNCTIONS AND BLOCK CIPHERS. The pseudorandomness of a keyed function family $\mathcal{F}$ with domain I_k and range I_l captures its computational indistinguishability from $\mathsf{Rand}^{k \to l}$. This definition is a slightly modified version of the one given by Goldreich, Goldwasser and Micali [7].

Definition 1. *Let $\mathcal{F}$ be a keyed function family with domain $\mathcal{D}$ and range $\mathcal{R}$. Let $\mathcal{A}$ be a 1-oracle adversary. Then we define $\mathcal{A}$'s advantage in distinguishing between $\mathcal{F}$ and $\mathsf{Rand}^{\mathcal{D} \to \mathcal{R}}$ as $\mathsf{Adv}^{\mathsf{prf}}_{\mathcal{F}}(\mathcal{A}) = \Pr[a \overset{R}{\leftarrow} \mathsf{Keys}(\mathcal{F}) : \mathcal{A}^{f_a} = 1] - \Pr[f \overset{R}{\leftarrow} \mathsf{Rand}^{\mathcal{D} \to \mathcal{R}} : \mathcal{A}^f = 1]$. For any integers $q, t \geq 0$, we define an insecurity function $\mathsf{Adv}^{\mathsf{prf}}_{\mathcal{F}}(q,t)$: $\mathsf{Adv}^{\mathsf{prf}}_{\mathcal{F}}(q,t) = \max_{\mathcal{A}}\{\mathsf{Adv}^{\mathsf{prf}}_{\mathcal{F}}(\mathcal{A})\}$, where the maximum is taken over choices of adversary $\mathcal{A}$ such that $\mathcal{A}$ makes at most q queries to its oracle, and the running time of $\mathcal{A}$, plus the time necessary to select the key a, and answer $\mathcal{A}$'s queries, is at most t.*

We are now ready to formally define security for a block cipher. The first notion we consider is that of a pseudorandom permutation. This notion, which is due to Luby and Rackoff [10], captures the pseudorandomness of a permutation family on I_l in terms of its indistinguishability from Perm^l, where the adversary is given access to the forward diretion of the permutation. In other words, it measures security of a block cipher against adaptive chosen plaintext attacks.

Definition 2. *Let $\mathcal{F}$ be a keyed permutation family with domain and range $\mathcal{D}$. Let $\mathcal{A}$ be a 1-oracle adversary. Then we say that $\mathcal{A}$ is an ϵ pseudorandom permutation distinguisher for $\mathcal{F}$ if $\mathsf{Adv}^{\mathsf{prp}}_{\mathcal{F}}(\mathcal{A}) = \Pr[a \overset{R}{\leftarrow} \mathsf{Keys}(\mathcal{F}) : \mathcal{A}^{f_a} = 1] - \Pr[f \overset{R}{\leftarrow} \mathsf{Perm}^{\mathcal{D}} : \mathcal{A}^f = 1] \leq \epsilon$. For any integers $q, t \geq 0$, we define an insecurity function $\mathsf{Adv}^{\mathsf{prp}}_{F}(q,t)$ just like the one in definition 1. We say that $\mathcal{F}$ is a (t, q, ϵ)-secure pseudorandom permutation family if $\mathsf{Adv}^{\mathsf{prp}}_{\mathcal{F}}(q,t) \leq \epsilon$.*

Luby and Rackoff [10] also define the notion of a *super pseudorandom* permutation which captures the pseudorandomness of a permutation family on I_l in terms of its indistinguishability from Perm^l, where the adversary is given access to *both* directions of the permutation thereby measuring the security of a block cipher against adaptive interleaved chosen plaintext and ciphertext attacks.

Definition 3. *Let $\mathcal{F}$ be a keyed permutation family with domain and range $\mathcal{D}$. Let $\mathcal{A}$ be a 2-oracle adversary. Then we define $\mathcal{A}$'s advantage in distinguishing between $\mathcal{F}$ and $\mathsf{Perm}^{\mathcal{D}}$ as $\mathsf{Adv}^{\mathsf{sprp}}_{\mathcal{F}}(\mathcal{A}) = \Pr[a \overset{R}{\leftarrow} \mathsf{Keys}(\mathcal{F}) : \mathcal{A}^{f_a, f_a^{-1}} = 1] - \Pr[f \overset{R}{\leftarrow} \mathsf{Perm}^{\mathcal{D}} : \mathcal{A}^{f, f^{-1}} = 1]$. For any integers $q, t \geq 0$, we define an insecurity function $\mathcal{A}^{\mathsf{sprp}}_{F}(q,t)$ similar to the one in definition 1. We say that $\mathcal{F}$ is a (t, q, ϵ)-secure super pseudorandom permutation family if $\mathsf{Adv}^{\mathsf{sprp}}_{\mathcal{F}}(q,t) \leq \epsilon$.*

UNIVERSAL HASH FUNCTIONS. We define various families of universal hash functions, which appear in many of the constructions in this paper. Stinson [16] prepared an excellent note accurately outlining the history and evolution of these function families.

Definition 4. *Let H be a keyed function family with domain $\mathcal{D}$, range $\mathcal{R}$, and key space $\mathcal{K}$. We assume that the elements of the key space $\mathcal{K}$ are picked according to some underlying distribution. We also assume that the elements of $\mathcal{R}$ form a group with additive notation ('+' and '-'). Let $\epsilon_1, \epsilon_2, \epsilon_3, \epsilon_4 \geq 1/|\mathcal{R}|$. Then, H is an ϵ_1-uniform family of hash functions if for all $x \in \mathcal{D}, z \in \mathcal{R}$, $\Pr[a \xleftarrow{R} \mathcal{K} : h_a(x) = z] \leq \epsilon_1$. H is ϵ_2-almost-Δ-universal if for all $x \neq y \in \mathcal{D}, z \in \mathcal{R}$, $\Pr[a \xleftarrow{R} \mathcal{K} : h_a(x) - h_a(y) = z] \leq \epsilon_2$. H is ϵ_3-monosymmetric if for all $x, y \in \mathcal{D}$ (here we allow $x = y$) and $z \in \mathcal{R}$, $\Pr[a \xleftarrow{R} \mathcal{K} : h_a(x) + h_a(y) = z] \leq \epsilon_2$. H is ϵ_4-universal if for all $x \neq y \in \mathcal{D}$, $\Pr[a \xleftarrow{R} \mathcal{K} : h_a(x) = h_a(y)] \leq \epsilon_4$.*

We remark that the notion of monosymmetric hash function families is a novel contribution of this paper. An example of a family that has all four properties for $\epsilon_1 = \cdots = \epsilon_4 = 1/|\mathcal{R}|$ is a family keyed by a random pair $a = (a_1, a_2)$ with $a_1 \in \mathcal{Z}_p^*$, $a_2 \in \mathcal{Z}_p$, and $h_a(x) = a_1 x + a_2 \bmod p$ where p is a prime, $\mathcal{Z}_p^*$ is the multiplicative group of nonzero integers modulo p, and $\mathcal{Z}_p$ is the additive group of integers modulo p. We also remark that we use the phrase "h is a Δ-universal (monosymmetric) hash function" to mean "h is drawn from a Δ-universal (monosymmetric) family of hash functions."

CONSTRUCTIONS OF LUBY-RACKOFF CIPHERS. We now formally define Feistel ladders which are the main tool for constructing pseudorandom permutations on $2n$-bit strings from length-preserving functions on n-bits strings. Feistel ladders have been used in a large number of popular block cipher such as DES.

Definition 5 (Feistel Ladders). *Let f be a mapping from I_n to I_n. Let $x = (x^L, x^R)$ with $x^L, x^R \in I_n$. We denote by $\overline{f}$ the basic Feistel permutation on I_{2n} defined as $\overline{f}(x) = (x^R, x^L \oplus f(x^R))$. Note that it is a permutation because $\overline{f}^{-1}(y) = (y^R \oplus f(y^L), y^L)$, which can be computed if the function f is known. If $f_1, \ldots, f_s$ are mappings with domain and range I_n, then we denote by $\Psi(f_1, \ldots, f_s)$ the Feistel ladder, which is a permutation on I_{2n} defined by $\Psi(f_1, \ldots, f_s) = \overline{f_s} \circ \cdots \circ \overline{f_1}$.*

Note that this definition (although stated using exclusive-or) easily extends to any binary group operation. We also note that, we will often need to talk about the intermediate stages of the computation in Feistel ladders as plaintext is transformed to ciphertext (and vice-versa). We denote the right halves of the values attained, as each successive basic Feistel permutations is applied, by the letters S, T, V, and W respectively. In addition, we refer to the left half and right halves of the plaintext input to the cipher as L and R respectively. Similarly, we refer to the left and right halves of the ciphertext output as V and W respectively. We can, for example, describe $\Psi(f_1, f_2, f_3, f_4)$ by:

$$S = L \oplus f_1(R);$$
$$T = R \oplus f_2(S);$$
$$V = S \oplus f_3(T);$$
$$W = T \oplus f_4(V).$$

Observe that a Feistel ladder is invertible since it is simply a composition of basic Feistel permutations. Sometimes we refer to Feistel ladders as *Feistel networks*.

Luby and Rackoff [10] show that three independently-keyed pseudorandom functions in a Feistel ladder yields a pseudorandom permutation, whereas four independently-keyed pseudorandom functions yields a super pseudorandom permutation. Here by *key* to a pseudorandom permutation we mean the concatenation of the individual keys of the underlying pseudorandom functions. The main theorem in their paper is:

Theorem 1 (Luby-Rackoff). *Let $f_1, \ldots, f_4$ be independently-keyed functions from $\mathsf{Rand}^{n \to n}$. Let $\mathcal{B}_1$ be the family of permutations on I_{2n} consisting of permutations of the form $P = \Psi(f_1, f_2, f_3)$. Then $\mathsf{Adv}_{\mathcal{B}}^{\mathsf{prp}}(q, t) \leq \binom{q}{2} \left(2^{-n+1} + 2^{-2n} \right)$. Let $\mathcal{B}_2$ be the family of permutations on I_{2n} with key consisting of permutations of the form $P = \Psi(f_1, f_2, f_3, f_4)$. Then $\mathsf{Adv}_{\mathcal{B}}^{\mathsf{sprp}}(q, t) \leq \binom{q}{2} \left(2^{-n+1} + 2^{-2n} \right)$.*

We remark that in the original Luby-Rackoff paper, the main theorem statement is written using complexity-theoretic security; we have recast the statement to the concrete security setting. Also, our treatment is in the information-theoretic case, where our functions are chosen from $\mathsf{Rand}^{n \to n}$. It is straightforwad to translate these results to the computational case, where the functions might be chosen from a finite function family $\mathcal{F}$, using a hybrid argument [11]. These same remarks apply for the remaining theorems given in this paper.

Naor and Reingold [11] optimize the above construction by replacing the first and last rounds in the Feistel ladder with strongly universal hash functions. Here the underlying hash function family must consist of permutations to ensure that the cipher is invertible. Their construction is more efficient since universal hash functions only involve specific statistical properties, so can typically be implemented much faster than pseudorandom functions. Also, universal hash function constructions do not require making any cryptographic assumption or conjecture. By reducing the number of pseudorandom function invocations from four to two, Naor and Reingold achieve a significant savings.

Theorem 2 (Naor-Reingold). *Let f_1 and f_2 be independently-keyed functions from $\mathsf{Rand}^{n \to n}$. Let h_1, h_2 be strongly-universal hash functions, keyed independently of each other and of f_1, f_2, from a keyed permutation family H with domain and range I_{2n}. Let $\mathcal{B}$ be the family of permutations on I_{2n} consisting of permutations of the form $P = h_2^{-1} \circ \Psi(f_1, f_2) \circ h_1$. Then $\mathsf{Adv}_{\mathcal{B}}^{\mathsf{sprp}}(q, t) \leq \binom{q}{2} \left(2^{-n+1} + 2^{-2n} \right)$.*

Naor and Reingold gave two improvements to their construction. Patel, Ramzan, and Sundaram [14] observed that trying to securely achieve both simultaneously requires different conditions on the universal hash functions:

Theorem 3 (Patel-Ramzan-Sundaram). *Let f be a function from $\mathsf{Rand}^{n \to n}$. Let h_1, h_2 be ϵ_1-bisymmetric ϵ_2-almost Δ-universal hash functions, keyed independently of each other and of f, from a keyed function family H with domain and range I_n. Let $\mathcal{B}$ be the family of permutations on I_{2n} consisting* of permutations of the form $P = \Psi(h_1, f, f, h_2)$. Then $\mathsf{Adv}_\mathcal{B}^{\mathsf{sprp}}(q,t) \leq q^2\epsilon_1 + \binom{q}{2}\left(2\epsilon_2 + 2^{-2n}\right)$.

3 Three-Round Luby-Rackoff Ciphers

Various negative results (for example, [10], [15], and [17]) were known regarding conventional XOR-based three-round Luby-Rackoff ciphers. We explore the validity of these results in the more general context of Feistel networks over Abelian groups. Overall, we reach the same conclusions between XOR-based Feistel constructions and the non-XOR constructions. Notably, for the most part, the techniques we need to obtain the various attacks are subtly different.

3.1 Attacking $\Psi(f_1, f_2, f_1)$

Rueppel [15] shows that $\Psi(f, f, f)$, the three-round Feistel cipher in which all the round functions are identical, is not even pseudorandom when the operation in the Feistel ladder is the bit-wise exclusive-or. The idea behind his attack is that when we use the same function f in all three rounds and addition is performed in a group of characteristic 2, $\Psi(f, f, f)$ has certain involution-like properties. Rueppel left open the problem of generalizing his attack to Feistel ladders that operate over other algebraic structures.

When operations are performed over an arbitrary algebraic structure, the involution-like properties that Rueppel exploits in his original attack no longer seem to hold. It turns out that this cipher is still insecure, but requires a subtly different type of attack. In fact, the new attack is applicable not only to $\Psi(f, f, f)$ over any Abelian group but also applies to $\Psi(f_1, f_2, f_1)$ where f_1 and f_2 are picked independently (and hence applies to the case of $f_1 = f_2 = f$). We present this attack here.

1. Query for the encryption of $0 \cdot 0$ and call the result $T_1 \cdot V_1$.
2. Query for the encryption of $0 \cdot T_1$ and call the result $T_2 \cdot V_2$.
3. Query for the encryption of $(V_1 - V_2) \cdot T_2$ and call the result $T_3 \cdot V_3$.
If $T_3 == T_1 + T_2$ **then** return that the cipher is not random
else return that the cipher is random.

This attack allows the adversary to distinguish $\Psi(f_1, f_2, f_1)$ from a random permutation with very high probability. We omit the analysis since it is similar to the analysis for the next attack.

3.2 Attacking $\Psi(f^i, f^j, f^k)$ When k Is a Multiple of $i + j$

Another interesting class of ciphers is $\Psi(f^i, f^j, f^k)$ where f is a pseudorandom function, and f^i represents the i-fold composition of f with itself. Zheng, Matsumoto, and Imai [17] show how to break this class of ciphers for arbitrary i, j, k, when working over $\mathrm{GF}(2^n)^+$. The attack more heavily depends on the involutory properties of $\mathrm{GF}(2^n)^+$. When considering arbitrary finite groups, we know how to break the cipher only when i, j, and k satisfy certain relations; in particular, when k is a multiple of $i + j$. Our attack is much different than the original one. We are unable to produce an attack that works in all cases, nor are we able to prove security for most other cases. We describe the attack.

1. Let $\alpha = k/(i + j)$.
2. Query the encryption of $(0, 0)$; call the result (T_1, V_1).
3. Query the encryption of $(0, T_1)$; call the result (T_2, V_2).
4. Initialize $X_1 = 0$, and $X_2 = T_1$.
5. **For** $l = 3$ to $\alpha + 1$ **do**
    5a. Set $X_l = T_{l-1} - X_{l-1}$.
    5b. Query the encryption of $(0, X_l)$; call the result (T_l, V_l).
6. Query the encryption of $(T_{\alpha+1} - X_{\alpha+1} - V_1, 0)$; call the result $(T_{\alpha+2}, V_{\alpha+2})$.
7. Query the encryption of $(-T_1, T_{\alpha+2})$; call the result $(T_{\alpha+3}, V_{\alpha+3})$.
If $T_{\alpha+3} = 2 \times T_{\alpha+2}$ **then** return that the cipher is not random
else return that the cipher is random.

The above attack gives the adversary a distinguishing advantage which is exponentially close to one. The analysis follows. It is not hard to see that if the cipher were truly random, then the attack algorithm would return the correct answer with probability extremely close to 1. We now claim that if the cipher is of the form $\Psi(f^i, f^j, f^k)$ with $k = \alpha(i + j)$ then the attack will always output that the cipher is not random. The proof follows the same notation in the attack; in particular we let $X_1 = 0$, and $X_l = T_{l-1} - X_{l-1}$, for all $l > 1$. In other words, X_l is the alternating telescoping sum of all the previous T_i. First, consider what happens when we encrypt $0 \cdot 0$: $S_1 = f^i(0); T_1 = f^{i+j}(0); V_1 = f^i(0) + f^{i+j+k}(0)$.

Next, consider what happens when we encrypt $0 \cdot T_1$: $S_2 = f^i(T_1); T_2 = f^{i+j}(T_1) + T_1; V_2 = f^i(T_1) + f^k(f^{i+j}(T_1) + T_1)$. Thus, $T_2 - T_1 = f^{i+j}(T_1) = f^{2(i+j)}(0)$. In general, when we encrypt $0 \cdot x$: $S = f^i(x); T = f^{i+j}(x) + x; V = S + f^k(f^{i+j}(x) + x)$. Thus, $T - x = f^{i+j}(x)$. Using this observation, when we set $x = X_{\alpha+1}$, we see: $T_{\alpha+1} - X_{\alpha+1} = f^{(i+j)(\alpha+1)}(0) = f^{(i+j)\alpha+(i+j)}(0) = f^{i+j+k}(0)$. Thus $T_{\alpha+1} - X_{\alpha+1} - V_1 = -f^i(0)$. During query $\alpha + 2$ this value is on the left hand side of the encryption, and 0 is on the right hand side. The result of this encryption is: $S_{\alpha+2} = 0; T_{\alpha+2} = f^j(0); V_{\alpha+2} = f^{k+j}(0)$. Finally, when we encrypt $(-T_1, T_{\alpha+2})$, we get: $S_{\alpha+3} = 0; T_{\alpha+3} = f^j(0) + f^j(S_{\alpha+3}); V_{\alpha+3} = f^k(f^j(0) + T_{\alpha+2})$. Which implies that $T_{\alpha+3} = f^j(0) + f^j(0) = T_{\alpha+2} + T_{\alpha+2}$.

3.3   Attacking the Super Pseudorandom Property of $\Psi(f_1, f_2, f_3)$

Luby and Rackoff show that the three-round variant of their cipher $\Psi(f_1, f_2, f_3)$ is pseudorandom, but not super pseudorandom [10]. In particular, one can distinguish the cipher from random with high probability by making two plaintext queries, and one ciphertext query. We generalize their attack to work when the operation in the Feistel ladder is addition over an arbitrary Abelian group G. We stress that the cipher is still pseudorandom over these other algebraic structures – it is just not super pseudorandom. We describe the attack.

1. Choose a random plaintext: $(L_1, R_1) \overset{R}{\leftarrow} G \times G$.
2. Query for the encryption of $L_1 \cdot R_1$ and call the result $T_1 \cdot V_1$.
3. Choose a value L_2 at random: $L_2 \overset{R}{\leftarrow} G$.
4. If $L_2 = L_1$ repeat the above step.
5. Query for the encryption of $L_2 \cdot R_1$ and call the result $T_2 \cdot V_2$.
6. Query for the decryption of $T_2 \cdot (V_2 + L_1 - L_2)$, and call the result $L_3 \cdot R_3$.
If $R_3 = T_2 + R_1 - T_1$ **then** return that the cipher is not super pseudorandom **else** return that the cipher is super pseudorandom.

If the cipher is a three-round Luby-Rackoff cipher, then the above test is always correct. On the other hand, if the cipher is a truly random permutation, the above test is wrong with negligibly small probability. We omit the analysis since it is similar to the analysis of the previous attack.

One can see that our attack makes use of the fact that the underlying group is Abelian. We are unable to develop an attack that works for non-Abelian groups, in general. At the same time, we note that in certain cases, there are non-Abelian groups which are still very "commutative." Consider, for example, the dihedral group D_{2n}, which represents the group of symmetries (rotations and flips) of a regular n-gon [8]. In this case, any two rotations with no flips commute. Thus, if two elements are picked uniformly at random from D_{2n}, they commute with probability at least $1/4$. In fact, the probability is higher since other randomly chosen pairs of elements commute; for example, every element commutes with itself and the identity. The above attack thus works for Dihedral groups, though the success probability diminishes by a constant factor.

4   Four-Round Luby Rackoff Ciphers

In this section we construct a four-round Luby-Rackoff cipher that is secure when the underlying operation is addition in certain algebraic structures, but is broken easily when addition is performed in $GF(2^n)^+$.

We describe our construction. Let G be a group (with binary operation '+'). Let f be a function drawn from a family $\mathcal{F}$, with domain and range G. Let h be drawn from an ϵ_1-monosymmetric ϵ_2-almost Δ-universal family of hash functions. *Then, our construction is $\Psi(h, f, f, h)$ where addition in the underlying Feistel ladder is performed in the group G.* Note that $\Psi(h, f, f, h)$ can be viewed as a permutation on $G \times G$. The security of this construction can be related in a precise manner to the parameters ϵ_1 and ϵ_2, and the pseudorandomness of the function family $\mathcal{F}$. It turns out that if this group G has characteristic 2, then $\epsilon_1 = 1$, and the cipher can easily be broken. On the other hand, for various other groups, the construction is provably secure. We now make some important observations about this construction:

- The hash functions in the first and fourth rounds have the same randomly chosen key. Alternatively, we can replace h by f_2, where f_2 is a pseudorandom function keyed independently of f. Hence we also obtain the new result that $\Psi(f_2, f, f, f_2)$ is strongly pseudorandom as a corollary.

- The pseudorandom functions in the second and third rounds have the *same* randomly chosen key (though this key should be chosen independently from the key for the hash functions).
- If addition is performed over a group of characteristic 2 (e.g. $G = \mathrm{GF}(2^n)^+$), then this cipher has involution-like properties, so it can easily be distinguished from random.

The cipher $\Psi(h, f, f, h)$ is very efficient: only two calls to the *same* pseudorandom function are made, the universal hash functions operate on half the input block, and the *same* universal hash function is used in the first and fourth rounds, which saves additional key material. We cite our main theorem:

Theorem 4. *Let G be a group, and let f be a function chosen from $\mathsf{Rand}^{G \to G}$. Let $h \in H$ be an ϵ_1-monosymmetric ϵ_2-almost Δ-universal hash function over the group G. Let $\mathcal{P}$ be the family of permutations on $G \times G$ consisting of permutations of the form $P = \Psi(h, f, f, h)$. Then: $\mathsf{Adv}_{\mathcal{P}}^{\mathsf{sprp}}(q, t) \leq q^2 \epsilon_1 + \binom{q}{2} \left(2\epsilon_2 + |G|^{-2} \right)$.*

We remark that although Δ-universal hash functions are traditionally defined over Abelian groups one could easily extend the definition to hold over non-Abelian groups, and our above result would continue to hold. Also, by modifying the appropriate definitions we can model cases in which each individual round involves a possibly different group operation. Using our techniques in this general model we can easily prove, for example, that $\Psi(h, f, f, h)$ is secure if the second and third rounds involve exclusive-or, but the first and fourth perform addition in certain other groups (for example the integers modulo 2^n). This result is surprising since if we simply change two operations by making the first and fourth round use exclusive-or, then the cipher can be distinguished from random using only two queries.

The proof of theorem 4 follows the framework of Naor and Reingold [11]. We start by recasting the original setting into the more general context of arbitrary finite groups. As usual, our adversary $\mathcal{A}$ is modeled as a program for a random access machine that gets black-box access to either a permutation uniformly sampled from $\mathsf{Perm}^{G \times G}$ or one sampled from the set of ciphers $\mathcal{P} = \Psi(h, f, f, h)$. As was done previously, the adversary will have access to two oracles – one for computing each direction of the permutation. We denote a query for the forward direction of the permutation by $(+, x)$. Such a query asks to obtain the value $\mathcal{P}(x)$. Similarly, we denote query in the reverse direction by $(-, y)$. Such a query asks to obtain the value for $\mathcal{P}^{-1}(y)$. Like before, we write $L \cdot R$ to denote the left and right halves of the plaintext respectively, and we write $V \cdot W$ to denote the left and right halves of the ciphertext respectively. In this case, however, L and R are each elements of the group G, and we can think of $L \cdot R$ as an element of $G \times G$. Also, in the following proof we make the standard assumption that the adversary $\mathcal{A}$ is deterministic. Under this assumption, the ith query made by $\mathcal{A}$ can be determined from the first $i - 1$ query-answer pairs in $\mathcal{A}$'s transcript. We consider the notion of a function C which can determine the adversary's next query given the previous queries and answers as well as the notion of which transcripts can possibly be generated.

Definition 6. *Let $C_{\mathcal{A}}[\{\langle x_1, y_1 \rangle, \ldots, \langle x_{i-1}, y_{i-1} \rangle\}]$ denote the ith query $\mathcal{A}$ makes as a function of the first $i-1$ query-answer pairs in $\mathcal{A}$'s transcript. The output of $\mathcal{A}$ as a function of its transcript is denoted by $C_{\mathcal{A}}[\{\langle x_1, y_1 \rangle, \ldots, \langle x_q, y_q \rangle\}]$.*

Definition 7. *Let σ be a sequence $\{\langle x_1, y_1 \rangle, \ldots, \langle x_q, y_q \rangle\}$, where for $1 \leq i \leq q$ we have that $\langle x_1, y_1 \rangle \in (G \times G) \times (G \times G)$. Then, σ is a consistent $\mathcal{A}$-transcript if for every $1 \leq i \leq q : C_{\mathcal{A}}[\{\langle x_1, y_1 \rangle, \ldots, \langle x_{i-1}, y_{i-1} \rangle\}] \in \{(+, x_i), (-, y_i)\}$.*

We now consider a special random process for $\mathcal{A}$'s queries that will be useful to us. This random process is analogous to the one given in the security proof of the Naor-Reingold construction [11].

Definition 8. *The random process $\tilde{R}$ answers the ith query of $\mathcal{A}$ as follows:*

- *If $\mathcal{A}$'s query is $(+, x_i)$ and for some $1 \leq j < i$ the jth query-answer pair is $\langle x_i, y_i \rangle$, then $\tilde{R}$ answers with y_i. If more than one such query-answer pair exists, we pick the one with the smallest index.*
- *If $\mathcal{A}$'s query is $(-, y_i)$ and for some $1 \leq j < i$ the jth query-answer pair is $\langle x_i, y_i \rangle$, then $\tilde{R}$ answers with x_i. If more than one such query-answer pair exists, we pick the one with the smallest index.*
- *If neither of the above happens, then $\tilde{R}$ answers with a uniformly chosen pair $(g_1, g_2) \in G \times G$.*

As before, we note that $\tilde{R}$'s answers may not be consistent with any function, let alone any permutation. We formalize this concept.

Definition 9. *Let $\sigma = \langle (x_1, y_1), \ldots, (x_q, y_q) \rangle$ be any possible $\mathcal{A}$-transcript. We say that σ is inconsistent if for some $1 \leq j < i \leq q$ the corresponding query-answer pairs satisfy: $x_i = x_j$ and $y_i \neq y_j$, or $x_i \neq x_j$ and $y_i = y_j$.*

Fortunately, the process $\tilde{R}$ often "behaves" exactly like a permutation over $G \times G$. If $\mathcal{A}$ is given oracle access to either $\tilde{R}$ or $\text{Perm}^{G \times G}$, then it will have a negligible advantage in distinguishing between the two. Naor and Reingold prove this when the group is $\text{GF}(2^n)^+$. We generalize their proof to the case of any algebraic structure. Before proceeding, recall that we denote by the random variables $T_{\mathcal{P}}$, $T_{\text{Perm}^{G \times G}}$, and $T_{\tilde{R}}$ the transcript seen by $\mathcal{A}$ when its oracle queries are answered by $\mathcal{P}$, $\text{Perm}^{G \times G}$, and $\tilde{R}$ respectively.

Proposition 1. *Let $\mathcal{A}$ be a 2-oracle adversary restricted to making a total of at most q queries to its oracles. Then: $\Pr_{\tilde{R}}[C_{\mathcal{A}}(T_{\tilde{R}}) = 1] - \Pr_{\text{Perm}^{G \times G}}[C_{\mathcal{A}}(T_{\text{Perm}^{G \times G}}) = 1] \leq \binom{q}{2} \cdot |G|^{-2}$.*

Proof. First, let Con denote the event that $T_{\tilde{R}}$ is consistent, and let $\neg\text{Con}$ denote the complement. For any possible and consistent $\mathcal{A}$-transcript σ we have that:

$$\Pr_{\text{Perm}^{G \times G}}[T_{\text{Perm}^{G \times G}} = \sigma] = \frac{(|G| - q)!}{|G|!} = \Pr_{\tilde{R}}[T_{\tilde{R}} = \sigma \mid \text{Con}].$$

Thus $T_{\mathsf{Perm}^{G \times G}}$ and $T_{\tilde{R}}$ have the same distribution conditioned on the event Con. We now bound the probability of $\neg$Con. Recall that $T_{\tilde{R}}$ is inconsistent if there exists an i and j with $1 \leq j < i \leq q$ for which $x_i = x_j$ and $y_i \neq y_j$, or $x_i \neq x_j$ and $y_i = y_j$. For a particular i and j this event happens with probability $|G|^{-2}$. So, $\Pr_{\tilde{R}}[\neg\mathsf{Con}] \leq \binom{q}{2} \cdot |G|^{-2}$. We complete the proof via a standard argument: $\Pr_{\tilde{R}}[C_{\mathcal{A}}(T_{\tilde{R}}) = 1] - \Pr_{\mathsf{Perm}^{G \times G}}[C_{\mathcal{A}}(T_{\mathsf{Perm}^{G \times G}}) = 1] =$

$$\left(\Pr_{\tilde{R}}[T_{\tilde{R}} = \sigma \mid \mathsf{Con}] - \Pr_{\mathsf{Perm}^{G \times G}}[C_{\mathcal{A}}(T_{\mathsf{Perm}^{G \times G}}) = 1] \right) \cdot \Pr_{\tilde{R}}[\mathsf{Con}] +$$

$$\left(\Pr_{\tilde{R}}[T_{\tilde{R}} = \sigma \mid \mathsf{Con}] - \Pr_{\mathsf{Perm}^{G \times G}}[C_{\mathcal{A}}(T_{\mathsf{Perm}^{G \times G}}) = 1] \right) \cdot \Pr_{\tilde{R}}[\neg\mathsf{Con}]$$

$$\leq \Pr_{\tilde{R}}[\neg\mathsf{Con}] \leq \binom{q}{2} \cdot |G|^{-2}.$$

We now proceed to obtain a bound on the advantage $\mathcal{A}$ will have in distinguishing between $T_{\mathcal{P}}$ and $T_{\tilde{R}}$. It turns out that $T_{\mathcal{P}}$ and $T_{\tilde{R}}$ are identically distributed unless some event depending on the choice of h in $\mathcal{P}$ occurs. We call this event Bad and obtain a bound on the probability that it actually occurs. Intuitively, Bad occurs whenever the internal function f in $\mathcal{P}$ would be evaluated on the exact same point twice for two distinct oracle queries – that is, whenever there is an internal collision. We formalize this concept as follows.

Definition 10. *For every specific monosymmetric ϵ-almost-Δ-universal hash function h, define $\mathsf{Bad}(h)$ to be the set of all possible and consistent $\mathcal{A}$-transcripts $\sigma = \langle (L_1 \cdot R_1, V_1 \cdot W_1), \ldots, (L_q \cdot R_q, V_q \cdot W_q) \rangle$ satisfying:*

 - *Event B1: there exists $1 \leq i < j \leq q$ such that $h(R_i) + L_i = h(R_j) + L_j$, or*
 - *Event B2: there exists $1 \leq i < j \leq q$ such that $W_i - h(V_i) = W_j - h(V_j)$, or*
 - *Event B3: there exists $1 \leq i, j \leq q$ such that $h(R_i) + L_i = W_j - h(V_j)$.*

Proposition 2. *Let $h \in H$ be an ϵ_1-monosymmetric ϵ_2-almost-Δ-universal hash function. Then, for any possible and consistent $\mathcal{A}$-transcript $\sigma = \langle (L_1 \cdot R_1, V_1 \cdot W_1), \ldots, (L_q \cdot R_q, V_q \cdot W_q) \rangle$, we have that $\Pr_h[\sigma \in \mathsf{Bad}(h)] \leq 2\binom{q}{2} \cdot \epsilon_2 + q^2 \cdot \epsilon_1$.*

Proof. Recall that a transcript $\sigma \in \mathsf{Bad}(h)$ if event B1, event B2, or event B3 occurs. We can determine an upper bound on the individual probabilities of each of these events separately using the fact that they are ϵ_1-monosymmetric, ϵ_2-almost-Δ-universal, and obtain an upper bound on the overall probability by taking the sum. □

The following key lemma for proving theorem 4 shows that the distribution of possible and consistent transcripts generated by $T_{\mathcal{P}}$ given that the bad conditions do not occur is identical to the distribution of possible and consistent transcripts generated by $T_{\tilde{R}}$. This lemma will be useful when we try to determine a bound on the advantage our adversary $\mathcal{A}$ will have when trying to distinguish between these two cases in general.

Lemma 1. *Let σ be any possible and consistent $\mathcal{A}$ – transcript, then $\Pr_{\mathcal{P}}[T_{\mathcal{P}} = \sigma | \sigma \notin \mathsf{Bad}(h)] = \Pr_{\tilde{R}}[T_{\tilde{R}} = \sigma]$.*

Proof. First observe that $\Pr_{\tilde{R}}[T_{\tilde{R}} = \sigma] = |G|^{-2q}$. This equality follows since $\tilde{R}$ picks elements from $G \times G$. Thus for a given fixed transcript entry, the probability that $\tilde{R}$ could generate it is $1/|G \times G|$ which equals $|G|^{-2}$. Now, for q consistent transcript entries, $\tilde{R}$ would generate them by picking q elements independently from $G \times G$, which gives us the desired probability of $|G|^{-2q}$.

Since σ is a possible $\mathcal{A}$-transcript, it follows that $T_{\mathcal{P}} = \sigma$ if and only if $V_i \cdot W_i = P(L_i \cdot R_i)$ for all $1 \leq i \leq q$. Next, suppose h is an ϵ_1-monosymmetric ϵ_2-almost-Δ-universal hash function for which $\sigma \notin \mathsf{Bad}(h)$. Now, we know that $L_i \cdot R_i$ and $V_i \cdot W_i$ must satisfy the following series of equations:

$$S_i = L_i + h(R_i);$$
$$T_i = R_i + f(S_i);$$
$$V_i = S_i + f(T_i);$$
$$W_i = T_i + h(V_i).$$

So, in particular $(V_i, W_i) = P(L_i, R_i) \Leftrightarrow f(S_i) = T_i - R_i$ and $f(T_i) = V_i - S_i$. Now observe that for all $1 \leq i < j \leq q$, $S_i \neq S_j$ and $T_i \neq T_j$ (otherwise $\sigma \in \mathsf{Bad}(h)$). Similarly, for all $1 < i, j < q$, $S_i \neq T_j$. So, if $\sigma \notin \mathsf{Bad}(h)$ all the inputs to f are distinct. Since f is a random function, for every specific choice of h such that $\sigma \notin \mathsf{Bad}(h)$ the probability that $T_{\mathcal{P}} = \sigma$ is exactly $|G|^{-2q}$. Therefore: $\Pr_{\mathcal{P}}[T_{\mathcal{P}} = \sigma | \sigma \notin \mathsf{Bad}(h)] = |G|^{-2q}$. $\square$

To complete the proof we use the above lemma as well as propositions 1 and 2 in a probability argument. Letting Γ be the set of all possible and consistent transcripts σ such that $C_{\mathcal{A}}(\sigma) = 1$:

$$\Pr_{\mathcal{P}}[\mathcal{A}^{\mathcal{P}, \mathcal{P}^{-1}} = 1] - \Pr_{R}[\mathcal{A}^{R, R^{-1}} = 1]$$
$$= \Pr_{\mathcal{P}}[C_{\mathcal{A}}(T_{\mathcal{P}}) = 1] - \Pr_{R}[C_{\mathcal{A}}(T_R) = 1]$$
$$\leq \Pr_{\mathcal{P}}[C_{\mathcal{A}}(T_{\mathcal{P}}) = 1] - \Pr_{\tilde{R}}[C_{\mathcal{A}}(T_{\tilde{R}}) = 1] + \binom{q}{2} \cdot |G|^{-2}$$

The last inequality follows from the previous by proposition 1. Now, let $\mathcal{T}$ denote the set of all possible transcripts (whether or not they are consistent), and let Δ denote the set of all possible inconsistent transcripts σ such that $C_{\mathcal{A}}(\sigma) = 1$. Notice that $\Gamma \cup \Delta$ contains all the possible transcripts such that $C_{\mathcal{A}}(\sigma) = 1$, and $\mathcal{T} - (\Gamma \cup \Delta)$ contains all the possible transcripts such that $C_{\mathcal{A}}(\sigma) = 0$. Then $\Pr_{\mathcal{P}}[C_{\mathcal{A}}(T_{\mathcal{P}}) = 1] - \Pr_{\tilde{R}}[C_{\mathcal{A}}(T_{\tilde{R}}) = 1] =$

$$\sum_{\sigma \in \mathcal{T}} \Pr_{\mathcal{P}}[C_{\mathcal{A}}(\sigma) = 1] \cdot \Pr_{\mathcal{P}}[T_{\mathcal{P}} = \sigma] - \sum_{\sigma \in \mathcal{T}} \Pr_{\tilde{R}}[C_{\mathcal{A}}(\sigma) = 1] \cdot \Pr_{\tilde{R}}[T_{\tilde{R}} = \sigma]$$
$$= \sum_{\sigma \in \Gamma} (\Pr_{\mathcal{P}}[T_{\mathcal{P}} = \sigma] - \Pr_{\tilde{R}}[T_{\tilde{R}} = \sigma]) + \sum_{\sigma \in \Delta} (\Pr_{\mathcal{P}}[T_{\mathcal{P}} = \sigma] - \Pr_{\tilde{R}}[T_{\tilde{R}} = \sigma])$$
$$\leq \sum_{\sigma \in \Gamma} (\Pr_{\mathcal{P}}[T_{\mathcal{P}} = \sigma] - \Pr_{\tilde{R}}[T_{\tilde{R}} = \sigma])$$

The last expression follows from the previous since for any *inconsistent* transcript σ, $\Pr_{\mathcal{P}}[T_{\mathcal{P}} = \sigma] = 0$. To bound the above expression observe that it equals:

$$\sum_{\sigma \in \Gamma} (\Pr_{\mathcal{P}}[T_{\mathcal{P}} = \sigma | \sigma \in \mathsf{Bad}(h)] - Pr_{\tilde{R}}[T_{\tilde{R}} = \sigma]) \cdot \Pr_{\mathcal{P}}[\sigma \in \mathsf{Bad}(h))]$$

$$+ \sum_{\sigma \in \Gamma} (\Pr_{\mathcal{P}}[T_{\mathcal{P}} = \sigma | \sigma \notin \mathsf{Bad}(h)] - \Pr_{\tilde{R}}[T_{\tilde{R}} = \sigma]) \cdot \Pr_{\mathcal{P}}[\sigma \notin \mathsf{Bad}(h)]$$

Now, we can apply Lemma 1 to get that the last term of the above expression is equal to 0. All that remains is to find a bound for the first term:

$$\sum_{\sigma \in \Gamma} (\Pr_{\mathcal{P}}[T_{\mathcal{P}} = \sigma | \sigma \in \mathsf{Bad}(h))] - \Pr_{\tilde{R}}[T_{\tilde{R}} = \sigma]) \cdot \Pr_{\mathcal{P}}[\sigma \in \mathsf{Bad}(h))]$$

$$\leq \max_{\sigma} \Pr_{\mathcal{P}}[\sigma \in \mathsf{Bad}(h)] \times$$

$$\max \left\{ \sum_{\sigma \in \Gamma} (\Pr_{\mathcal{P}}[T_{\mathcal{P}} = \sigma | \sigma \in \mathsf{Bad}(h)], \sum_{\sigma \in \Gamma} \Pr_{\tilde{R}}[T_{\tilde{R}} = \sigma]) \right\}.$$

Note that the last two sums of probabilities are both between 0 and 1, so the above expression is bounded by $\max_{\sigma} \Pr_{\mathcal{P}}[\sigma \in \mathsf{Bad}(h)]$, which is, by Proposition 2, bounded by $2\binom{q}{2} \cdot \epsilon_2 + q^2 \cdot \epsilon_1$. We combine the above computations to complete the proof:

$$\Pr_{\mathcal{P}}[\mathcal{A}^{\mathcal{P}, \mathcal{P}^{-1}} = 1] - \Pr_{R}[\mathcal{A}^{R, R^{-1}} = 1] \leq 2\binom{q}{2} \cdot \epsilon_2 + q^2 \cdot \epsilon_1 + \binom{q}{2} \cdot |G|^{-2}.$$

5 Monosymmetric Δ-Universal Hash Functions

The security of the construction in the previous section rests upon the pseudo-randomness of the round function f, and the parameters ϵ_1, ϵ_2 associated with the hash function h. This section focuses on constructing monosymmetric universal hash functions and argues that they are necessary for our constructions.

CONSTRUCTIONS. We initially demonstrate that over certain algebraic structures, small values of ϵ_1, ϵ_2 are easy to attain. Next, we show that in other groups, the value of ϵ_1 will always be quite large. Our first example concerns the family $\mathsf{Rand}^{G \to G}$, for a group G.

Lemma 2. *Suppose G has no element of order 2. Then, the set of all possible functions $\mathsf{Rand}^{G \to G}$ is $1/|G|$-monosymmetric $1/|G|$-almost-Δ-universal.*

Proof. First we show that $\mathsf{Rand}^{G \to G}$ is $1/|G|$-almost-Δ-universal. Consider three values $x, y, \delta \in G$, with $x \neq y$. The values $f(x)$ and $f(y)$ are uniformly distributed when $f \xleftarrow{R} \mathsf{Rand}^{G \to G}$. Thus, their difference is uniformly distributed, and takes on any value in the range G with equal probability. Consequently, $\forall x \neq y \in G, \forall \delta \in G : \Pr[f \xleftarrow{R} \mathsf{Rand}^{G \to G} : f(x) - f(y) = \delta] = 1/|G|$.

Now we examine the monosymmetric property. Again, pick values $x, y, \delta \in G$. There are two cases. If $x \neq y$, then using an argument very similar to the one above, we get: $\forall x \neq y \in G, \forall \delta \in G : \Pr[f \xleftarrow{R} \mathsf{Rand}^{G \to G} : f(x) + f(y) = \delta] = 1/|G|$. The only remaining case is when $x = y$. Then, $f(x) + f(y) = 2f(x)$ and we are then left with an equation of the form $2f(x) = \delta$. We claim that at most one value of $f(x)$ that satisfies this equation. If this claim were true, then we are done since $f(x)$ is uniformly distributed over the choice of f. We now prove the claim by contradiction. Suppose that there are two values x_1, x_2 such that $2f(x_1) = 2f(x_2) = \delta$, but $f(x_1) \neq f(x_2)$. It follows that $2(f(x_1) - f(x_2)) = 0$. However, $f(x_1) - f(x_2) \in G$, and $f(x_1) - f(x_2) \neq 0$ contradicting the assumption that G does not contain any element of order 2. $\qquad \square$

Unfortunately, it is difficult to efficiently sample from $\mathsf{Rand}^{G \to G}$ because it contains $|G|^{|G|}$ elements, which is quite large for our purposes. If one looks at the proof of the above lemma, it is not hard to see that we did not need truly random functions. Instead, strongly universal families of functions suffice since they appear random whenever one considers only two input / output pairs. Therefore:

Corollary 1. *Suppose G has no element of order 2. Then any strongly universal family of functions is $1/|G|$-monosymmetric $1/|G|$-almost-Δ-universal.*

EXAMPLE. If G is the additive group attached to a finite field F, then one such family of strongly universal hash functions is the linear congruential hash family: $h_{a,b}(x) = ax + b$ where arithmetic is performed in F.

Since finite fields, of characteristic greater than 2 with size p^k exist for any odd prime p and any natural number k, we can construct good monosymmetric Δ-universal hash function families for sets of these size. We now show how to construct reasonably good families of such hash functions for sets of *any* size.

Lemma 3. *Let m be a natural number, and let G be the cyclic group $\mathcal{Z}_m$. Let p be the smallest prime such that $m \leq p$. Let H be any ϵ_1-monosymmetric ϵ_2-almost-Δ-universal hash function family over the additive group attached to the finite field F_p. Consider the family of functions H', which is defined as follows: $H' = \{h'_a : \mathcal{Z}_m \to \mathcal{Z}_m \mid a \in \mathsf{Keys}(H)\}$, where the functions h'_a are defined as: $h'_a(x) = h_a(x) \bmod m$. Here h_a is chosen from H according to key a. We are also using the natural representation of elements in $\mathcal{Z}_m$ and $\mathcal{Z}_p$ whereby we utilize the smallest non-negative integer. Then H' is $4\epsilon_1$-monosymmetric $4\epsilon_2$-almost-Δ-universal over the group $\mathcal{Z}_m$.*

Proof. We first start with Bertrand's postulate, which states that for each integer $m \geq 2$, there is a prime number p with $m \leq p < 2m$. First, we examine the Δ-universal property. Let $x, y, \delta \in \mathcal{Z}_m$ be chosen arbitrarily, with $x \neq y$. Let a be a key such that $h'_a(x) - h'_a(y) = \delta$. Equivalently, $(h_a(x) - h_a(y)) \bmod m = \delta$.

Now, since H operates over the additive group attached to the finite field F_p, it follows that $h_a(x), h_a(y) \in \{0, \ldots, p - 1\}$. Combining this fact with the previous observation, we see $h_a(x) - h_a(y) \in \{\delta, \delta + m, \delta - m, \delta + 2m, \delta - 2m, \ldots\}$.

Since the set of possible differences is finite there must be some minimum element which we can denote by l_0. It must be of the form $l_0 = \delta + im$, for some integer i. Consider values of the form $l_r = \delta + (i+r)m$, where $r \geq 4$. Observe that $l_r - l_0 = rm \geq 4m > 2p$. Since there are at most $2p$ values in the range, l_r cannot appear as the difference of h applied to two inputs for $r \geq 4$. Thus, $\Pr[a \xleftarrow{R} \mathsf{Keys}(H) : h'_a(x) - h'_a(y) = \delta] \leq \Pr[a \xleftarrow{R} \mathsf{Keys}(H') : h_a(x) - h_a(y) \in \{l_0, l_1, l_2, l_3\}] \leq 4\epsilon_2$ which follows by applying the union bound and observing that h is ϵ_2-almost-Δ-universal. With the same technique we can show that H' is $4\epsilon_1$-monosymmetric.   □

In specific cases we can get tighter bounds by exploiting either the algebraic structure of the hash function itself or the relationship between p and m (for example, if $m < p \leq 3m/2$, then we can achieve values of $3\epsilon_1$ and $3\epsilon_2$). For the case $m = 2^n$, these functions are interesting since addition modulo 2^n is easily implemented on most processors. Therefore, our constructions have practical implications. Another very efficient family of monosymmetric ϵ-almost-Δ-universal hash functions for which ϵ is small $(=2/2^n)$ is the square hash family [5].

We now consider groups for which no good families of monosymmetric-Δ universal hash functions exist. The most striking example occurs in the additive group of the Galois Field of order 2^n, $GF(2^n)^+$.

EXAMPLE. If H is *any* family of functions whose range is $GF(2^n)^+$ (i.e. characteristic 2), then $\Pr_{h \in H}[h(x) + h(y) = \delta] = 1$ whenever $x = y$ and $\delta = 0$. Thus, it is not possible to get a value of ϵ_1 smaller than 1 for the monosymmetry property.

Another case in which a group may not possess good monosymmetry properties is the *multiplicative* group modulo m, $\mathcal{Z}_m^*$. If we set $x = y$, then the expression $\Pr_{h \in H}[h(x) \cdot h(y) = \delta]$ may be high if δ has many square roots. For example, if the prime factorization of m consists of k distinct odd primes $p_1, \ldots, p_k$ then it follows from the Chinese Remainder Theorem that certain elements of $\mathcal{Z}_m^*$ may have up to 2^k square roots.

NECESSITY. We give evidence that our minimal-key construction is fairly optimal and that the monosymmetry property is needed. Specifically, we show that $\Psi(h_1, f, f, h_2)$ is not necessarily secure if h_1 and h_2 are independently keyed Δ-universal hash functions that do not satisfy the additional monosymmetry property. Note that in this case, we consider a cipher for which h_1 and h_2 may be different hash functions, so our attack is more general. The attack also works if they are the same hash function. Patel, Ramzan, and Sundaram [14] show that this particular cipher can be broken when operations were performed in $GF(2^n)^+$; we now extend the result to the case when operations are performed over arbitrary *finite fields* and resort to different techniques to do so. We note that this result is shown only for finite fields. Extending it to hold for arbitrary groups is left as an open problem.

We describe the attack. Suppose that h_1 and h_2 are taken from the linear hash family. That is $h_1(x) = a_1 \cdot x$ and $h_2(x) = a_2 \cdot x$, where multiplication is performed with respect to the underlying finite field. This family is known to be Δ-universal. Pick values α, α' at random (with $\alpha \neq \alpha'$), and obtain both the encryption of $x = \alpha \cdot 0$ and the decryption of $0 \cdot \alpha$. Next, obtain the encryption of $\alpha' \cdot 0$ and the decryption of $0 \cdot \alpha'$. Working through the equations for the encryption of $x = \alpha \cdot 0$: $S_1 = h_1(R_1) + L_1 = h_1(0) + \alpha = 0 + \alpha = \alpha; T_1 = f(S_1) + R_1 = f(\alpha); V_1 = f(T_1) + S_1 = f^2(\alpha) + \alpha; W_1 = h_2(V_1) + T_1 = a_2 \cdot V_1 + f(\alpha)$. Now we work through the equations for *decrypting* $V_2 \cdot W_2 = 0 \cdot \alpha$: $T_2 = W_2 - h_2(V_2) = \alpha - 0 = \alpha; S_2 = V_2 - f(T_2) = 0 - f(\alpha) = -f(\alpha); R_2 = T_2 - f(S_2) = \alpha - f(-f(\alpha)); L_2 = S_2 - h_1(R_2) = -f(\alpha) - a_1 \cdot R_2$. Next, let $A_1 = L_2 + W_1$. Observe that $A_1 = L_2 + W_1 = a_2 \cdot V_1 - a_1 \cdot R_2$.

Now, we repeat the same process as above. In particular, we ask for the encryption of $L_3 \cdot R_3 = \alpha' \cdot 0$ and call the result $V_3 \cdot W_3$. We also ask for the decryption of $V_4 \cdot W_4 = 0 \cdot \alpha'$ and call the result $L_4 \cdot R_4$. Let A_2 denote $L_4 + W_3$. By an argument similar to the one given above, $A_2 = a_2 \cdot V_3 - a_1 \cdot R_4$. We now have a system of equations: $-a_1 \cdot R_2 + a_2 \cdot V_1 = A_1; -a_1 \cdot R_4 + a_2 \cdot V_3 = A_2$.

Since we know $R_2, R_4, V_1, V_3, A_1, A_2$ the only unknowns are a_1, a_2. With high probability, this system of equations has full rank, and we can solve for a_1 and a_2. If $h_1 = h_2 = h$, then $a_1 = a_2 = a$ and the function is an involution that can easily be distinguished from random. The above procedure allows us to compute the keys to the hash functions in the first and fourth rounds. Knowing these keys reduces the problem to distinguishing the two-round Luby-Rackoff cipher $\Psi(f, f)$ from random, which can easily be done in two queries [10].

6   Conclusion

This paper initiated a study of Luby-Rackoff ciphers over arbitrary finite algebraic structures. To our surprise, we discovered that certain Luby-Rackoff cipher constructions are secure when the Feistel operation is taken over particular groups but are insecure when operations are taken with respect to other groups. For example, when we replace bit-wise exclusive-or by addition modulo 2^n we turn an insecure cipher into a provably secure one. Precisely, we prove that $\Psi(h, f, f, h)$ is a super pseudorandom permutation where h is a mono-symmetric hash function and that such hash functions do not apply to XOR-based groups. We also gave attacks on various well-known three-round constructions over general Abelian groups. We proved that:

- $\Psi(f_1, f_2, f_1)$ and consequently $\Psi(f, f, f)$ are not pseudorandom.
- $\Psi(f^i, f^j, f^k)$ is not pseudorandom, when k is a multiple of $i + j$.
- $\Psi(f_1, f_2, f_3)$ is not super pseudorandom.

Our results spawn new areas for research and motivate a need to re-examine the literature on Luby-Rackoff ciphers to determine the extent to which the old results hold when we look at arbitrary finite algebraic structures. More generally, this work opens up the possibility of security advantages with non-XOR operations for almost any cryptographic primitive and not just block ciphers.

References

1. M. Bellare, J. Kilian, and P. Rogaway. The security of cipher block chaining. In Yvo G. Desmedt, editor, *Advances in Cryptology—CRYPTO '94*, volume 839 of *Lecture Notes in Computer Science*, pages 341–358. Springer-Verlag, 21–25 August 1994.

2. E. R. Berlekamp. Factoring polynomials over large finite fields. *Mathematics of Computation*, 24:713–735, 1970.

3. E. Biham and A. Shamir. *Differential Cryptanalysis of the Data Encryption Standard.* Springer Verlag, 1993. ISBN: 0-387-97930-1, 3-540-97930.

4. G. Carter, E. Dawson, and L. Nielsen. DESV: A Latin Square variation of DES. In *Proceeding of Workshop on Selected Areas of Cryptography*, 1995.

5. M. Etzel, S. Patel, and Z. Ramzan. Square hash: Fast message authentication via optimized universal hash functions. In *Proc. CRYPTO 99*, Lecture Notes in Computer Science. Springer-Verlag, 1999.

6. M.R. Garey and D.S. Johnson. *Computers and Intractability: A Guide to the Theory of NP-Completeness.* W.H. Freeman, 1979.

7. O. Goldreich, S. Goldwasser, and S. Micali. How to construct random functions. *Journal of the ACM*, 33(4):792–807, October 1986.

8. I. N. Herstein. *Topics in Algebra.* Blaisdell Publishing Company, 1964.

9. R. Karp. Reducibility among combinatorial problems. in Complexity of Computer Computations, 1972.

10. M. Luby and C. Rackoff. How to construct pseudorandom permutations and pseudorandom functions. *SIAM J. Computing*, 17(2):373–386, April 1988.

11. M. Naor and O. Reingold. On the construction of pseudo-random permutations: Luby-Rackoff revisited. *J. of Cryptology*, 12:29–66, 1999. Preliminary version in: *Proc. STOC 97.*

12. J. Patarin. New results on pseudorandom permutation generators based on the DES scheme. In *Proc. CRYPTO 91*, Lecture Notes in Computer Science. Springer-Verlag, 1991.

13. J. Patarin. Improved security bounds for pseudorandom permutations. In *4th ACM Conference on Computer and Communications Security*, pages 140–150, 1997.

14. S. Patel, Z. Ramzan, and G. Sundaram. Towards making Luby-Rackoff ciphers optimal and practical. In *Proc. Fast Software Encryption 99*, Lecture Notes in Computer Science. Springer-Verlag, 1999.

15. R. A. Rueppel. On the security of Schnorr's pseudo random generator. In *Proc. EUROCRYPT 89*, Lecture Notes in Computer Science. Springer-Verlag, 1989.

16. D. R. Stinson. Comments on definitions of universal hash families, August 2000. Available from: http://cacr.math.uwaterloo.ca/~dstinson/.

17. Y. Zheng, T. Matsumoto, and H. Imai. Impossibility and optimality results on constructing pseudorandom permutations. In *Proc. EUROCRYPT 89*, Lecture Notes in Computer Science. Springer-Verlag, 1989.

New Results on Unconditionally Secure Distributed Oblivious Transfer

(Extended Abstract)

Carlo Blundo[1], Paolo D'Arco[2], Alfredo De Santis[1], and Douglas R. Stinson[3]

[1] Dipartimento di Informatica ed Applicazioni
Università di Salerno, 84081 Baronissi (SA), Italy
{carblu, ads}@dia.unisa.it
[2] Department of Combinatorics and Optimization
University of Waterloo, Waterloo Ontario, N2L 3G1, Canada
pdarco@cacr.math.uwaterloo.ca
[3] School of Computer Science
University of Waterloo, Waterloo Ontario, N2L 3G1, Canada
dstinson@cacr.math.uwaterloo.ca

Abstract. This paper is about the Oblivious Transfer in the distributed model recently proposed by M. Naor and B. Pinkas. In this setting a Sender has n secrets and a Receiver is interested in one of them. During a set up phase, the Sender gives information about the secrets to m servers. Afterwards, in a recovering phase, the receiver can compute the secret she wishes by interacting with k of them. More precisely, from the answers received she computes the secret in which she is interested but she gets no information on the others and, at the same time, any coalition of $k - 1$ servers can neither compute any secret nor figure out which one the receiver has recovered.

We present an analysis and new results holding for this model: lower bounds on the resources required to implement such a scheme (i.e., randomness, memory storage, communication complexity); some impossibility results for one-round distributed oblivious transfer protocols; two polynomial-based constructions implementing 1-out-of-n distributed oblivious transfer, which generalize the two constructions for 1-out-of-2 given by Naor and Pinkas; as well as new one-round and two-round distributed oblivious transfer protocols, both for threshold and general access structures on the set of servers, which are optimal with respect to some of the given bounds. Most of these constructions are basically combinatorial in nature.

1 Introduction

Introduced by Rabin in [27], and subsequently defined in different forms [18,8], the *oblivious transfer* (OT, for short) has found many applications in cryptographic studies and protocol design. Basically, such a protocol enables one party to transfer knowledge to another in an "oblivious" way. Rabin's definition, for

K. Nyberg and H. Heys (Eds.): SAC 2002, LNCS 2595, pp. 291–309, 2003.

example, enables a Sender to transmit a message to a Receiver in such a way that the Receiver with probability $\frac{1}{2}$ gets the message while, with the same probability, she does not, and the Sender does not know which situation has happened. Rabin showed how this transfer can be used in order to exchange secrets, and subsequently several other researchers have shown some useful applications of this concept. The protocol proposed by Rabin was later strengthened in [19].

The second OT definition was given in [18]. In this form, the Sender has two secrets and the Receiver is interested in one of them. After the execution of the protocol, the receiver gets the secret she wishes to recover, obtaining at the same time no information on the other, while the Sender does not know which secret the receiver has recovered. The author of [18] showed a first application to signing contracts.

The last and more general form of OT was introduced in [8], under the name of *all-or-nothing Disclosure of Secrets*, even if the same concept was born in an artificial intelligence context [33], under the name of *multiplexing*. Here the Sender has n secrets and the Receiver is interested in one of them. After the execution of the protocol, the receiver gets the secret she wishes to recover, obtaining at the same time no information on the others, while the Sender does not know which secret the receiver has recovered.

All these forms were shown to be equivalent [9,7,13], and Kilian in [24] showed that the OT is a complete primitive, in the sense that it can be used as building block for any secure function evaluation (multi-party computation).

A variety of slightly different definitions and implementations can be found in the literature as well as papers addressing issues such as the relation of the OT with other cryptographic primitives, the assumptions required to implement such a concept, reductions among "more complex" forms of OT to "simpler ones" and applicative environments (e.g., [13,9,17,16,3,14,23,26,22], just to name few examples).

Our Contribution. In this paper we study *unconditionally secure distributed oblivious transfer protocols*, introduced in [25] in order to strengthen the security of protocols designed for electronic auctions [26]. We present an analysis and some new results: lower bounds on the resources required by an implementation such as randomness, memory storage, and communication complexity; some impossibility results for one-round protocols; two polynomial-based constructions implementing 1-out-of-n distributed oblivious transfer which generalize the two constructions for 1-out-of-2 schemes given by M. Naor and B. Pinkas; as well as new one-round and two-round distributed oblivious transfer protocols, both for threshold and general access structures on the set of servers, which are optimal with respect to some of the given bounds. Most of these constructions are basically combinatorial in nature.

Related Work. In the literature there are many papers that address problems related to 1-out-of-n distributed oblivious transfer. In [1], for example, the authors show how to distribute a function between several servers, in such a way that a user can compute the function by interacting with the servers; the servers cannot find out which values of the function the user computes, but the user can compute the function in *more than* one point. Another very close area is represented by PIR (Private Information Retrieval) Schemes, introduced in [11]. A PIR scheme enables a user to retrieve an item of information from a public accessible database in such a way that the database manager cannot figure out from the query which item the user is interested in. However, the user can get information about more than one item. On the other hand, in SPIR (Symmetric Private Information Retrieval) schemes [20], the user can get information about *one and only one* item, i.e. even the privacy of the database is considered. In PIR and SPIR schemes, the emphasis is placed on the *communication complexity* of the interaction of user and servers. Notice that a SPIR Scheme can be seen as a *communication-efficient* 1-out-of-n oblivious transfer scheme and the protocols given in [20] represent the first 1-round distributed implementation of 1-out-of-n oblivious transfer. However, the main differences between the model we are going to consider and (information theoretic) SPIR schemes are that in SPIR schemes the receiver communicates with k out of k servers in order to retrieve an item while in our setting the receiver can choose k out of m servers, where $k \leq m$. Moreover, in SPIR schemes, the security of the sender against *coalitions* of receiver and servers is not of concern. Other PIR papers of interest, for the distribute OT scenario we consider, are [2,21,15].

Finally, Rivest's model in [28], where a trusted initializer participates *only* during the set up phase of the system (see also [6]), provides a very close setting to the one described in [25] and considered in this paper. A very recent paper which deals with distributed oblivious transfer implementations, close to the setting introduced in [25] (but not unconditionally secure) is [32].

In our constructions we use secret sharing schemes. Secret sharing were introduced in 1979 by Blakley [4] and Shamir [29], and have been extensively studied during the last years. The reader can find an introduction in [31] and references to the literature in [30].

2   The Distributed Model

Let us define the model we are going to consider. We assume that the Sender holds n secrets and the receiver is interested in one of them. Hence, we are concerned with a 1-out-of-n distributed oblivious transfer.

2.1   An Informal Description

In the distributed setting, the sender S does not directly interact with the receiver R in order to carry out the oblivious transfer. Rather, he *delegates* m servers to accomplish this task for him. More precisely, we consider the following scenario:

Initialization Phase. Let $S_1, \ldots, S_m$ be m servers. The sender S generates m programs $P_1, \ldots, P_m$, and, for $i = 1, \ldots, m$ sends, *in a secure way*, program P_i to server S_i.

Oblivious Transfer Phase. The receiver $\mathcal{R}$ holds a program which enables her to interact with a subset $\{\mathcal{S}_{i_1}, \ldots, \mathcal{S}_{i_k}\}$ of the servers at her choice. Using the knowledge acquired by exchanging messages with the servers, $\mathcal{R}$ recovers the secret in which she is interested, but receives no information on the other secrets. At the same time, no subset of $k-1$ servers, gains any information about the secret she has recovered. More precisely, a distributed (k, m)-DOT-$\binom{n}{1}$ must guarantee:

1. **Reconstruction.** If the receiver gets information from k out of the m servers, she can compute the secret.
2. **Sender's Privacy.** Given any k values, the receiver must gain information about a single secret, and no information about the others.
3. **Receiver's Privacy.** No coalition of less than k servers gains information about which secret the receiver has recovered.
4. **Receiver-servers Collusion.** A coalition of the receiver with $k-1$ corrupt servers cannot learn about the n secrets more than can be learned by the receiver herself.

Notice that, in [25], properties 3. and 4. are only guaranteed with respect to a threshold t and a threshold ℓ, respectively, which should be as close to k as possible.

2.2   A Formal Model

Assume that $\mathcal{S}$ holds a program S to generate m programs $P_1, \ldots, P_m$ enabling $\mathcal{S}_1, \ldots, \mathcal{S}_m$ and $\mathcal{R}$ to perform a (k, m)-DOT-$\binom{n}{1}$ oblivious transfer of his n secrets. $\mathcal{R}$ holds an associated program R for interacting with the servers. The $m + 1$ programs $P_1, \ldots, P_m$ and R, specify[1] the computations to be performed to achieve (k, m)-DOT-$\binom{n}{1}$. In order to model dishonest behaviors, where a coalition of at most $k-1$ servers tries to figure out which secret $\mathcal{R}$ has recovered from the transfer, we assume that cheating servers $\mathcal{S}_{i_1}, \ldots, \mathcal{S}_{i_{k-1}}$ hold a modified version of the programs, denoted by $\overline{P_{i_1}}, \ldots, \overline{P_{i_{k-1}}}$. These programs could have been generated either by a dishonest $\mathcal{S}$, who holds a cheating generating program $\overline{S}$, or they could have been modified by the dishonest servers. Similarly, a cheating $\mathcal{R}$, who tries to gain some information about other secrets, holds a modified version of the program $\overline{R}$. These programs can be described by random variables and will be represented in bold face type.

An execution of the protocol can be described by using the following additional random variables: for $j = 1, \ldots, m$, let $\mathbf{C}_j$ be the transcript of the communication between $\mathcal{R}$ and S_j. Let W be the set of all length n sequences of secrets, and, for any $w \in W$, let w_i be the i-th secret of the sequence. Denoting by $\mathbf{W}$ the random variable that represents the choice of an element in W, and by $\mathbf{T}$ the random variable representing the choice of an index i in $T = \{1, \ldots, n\}$,

---

[1]   If we are interested in a reduction of a more complex form of DOT to a simpler available one, we can simply assume that these programs encapsulate, as *black box*, a smaller (k, m)-DOT-$\binom{n'}{1}$. Hence, during the execution, $\mathcal{S}_1, \ldots, \mathcal{S}_m$ and $\mathcal{R}$ are able to carry out many times unconditionally secure (k, m)-DOT-$\binom{n'}{1}$.

we can define the conditions that a (k, m)-DOT-$\binom{n}{1}$ oblivious transfer protocol must satisfy as follows[2]:

Definition 1. *The sequence of programs* $[S, P_1, \ldots P_m, R]$ *is correct for* (k, m)-DOT-$\binom{n}{1}$ *if for any* $i \in T$ *and* $j = 1, \ldots, m$, *it holds that*

$$H(\mathbf{C}_j | \mathbf{P}_j \, \mathbf{T} \, \mathbf{R}) = 0, \tag{1}$$

and, for any $w \in W$ *and for any* $\{i_1, \ldots, i_k\} \subseteq \{1, \ldots, m,\}$ *it holds that*

$$H(\mathbf{W}_T | \mathbf{C}_{i_1} \ldots \mathbf{C}_{i_k}) = 0. \tag{2}$$

Notice that the definition means that, given the program of server S_j and the program of the receiver and her choices, the transcript of the communication is completely determined. Moreover, after interacting with k servers, an honest receiver always recovers the secret in which she is interested.

Assuming that both $\mathcal{S}$ and $\mathcal{R}$ are aware of the joint probability distribution $\mathcal{P}_{W,T}$ on W and T, the probability with which $\mathcal{S}$ chooses the secrets in W and $\mathcal{R}$ chooses an index $i \in T$, the privacy property of (k, m)-DOT-$\binom{n}{1}$ can be defined as follows:

Definition 2. *The sequence of programs* $[S, P_1, \ldots P_m, R]$ *is private for* (k, m)-DOT-$\binom{n}{1}$ *if*

- *for any set of indices* $\{i_1, \ldots, i_{k-1}\} \subset \{1, \ldots, m\}$, *it holds that*

$$H(\mathbf{T} | \overline{\mathbf{P}}_{i_1}, \ldots, \overline{\mathbf{P}}_{i_{k-1}} \mathbf{C}_{i_1}, \ldots, \mathbf{C}_{i_{k-1}}) = H(\mathbf{T}). \tag{3}$$

- *for any program* $\overline{R}$, *for any* $i \in T$ *and for any set of indices* $\{i_1, \ldots, i_k\} \subset \{1, \ldots, m\}$, *it holds that*

$$H(\mathbf{W} \setminus \mathbf{W}_T | \mathbf{T} \overline{\mathbf{R}} \mathbf{C}_{i_1} \ldots \mathbf{C}_{i_k} \mathbf{W}_T) = H(\mathbf{W} \setminus \mathbf{W}_T). \tag{4}$$

- *for any set of indices* $\{i_1, \ldots, i_{k-1}\} \subset \{1, \ldots, m\}$, *for any* $i \in T$, *and for any* $\overline{R}$, *it holds that*

$$H(\mathbf{W} | \mathbf{T} \overline{\mathbf{R}} \mathbf{C}_{i_1} \ldots \mathbf{C}_{i_{k-1}} \overline{\mathbf{P}}_{i_1}, \ldots, \overline{\mathbf{P}}_{i_{k-1}}) = H(\mathbf{W}). \tag{5}$$

- *for any sets of indices* $\{i_1, \ldots, i_{k-1}\} \subseteq \{1, \ldots, m\}$ *and* $\{j_1, \ldots, j_k\} \subseteq \{1, \ldots, m\}$, *for any* $i \in T$, *and for any* $\overline{R}$, *it holds that*

$$H(\mathbf{W} \setminus \mathbf{W}_T | \mathbf{T} \overline{\mathbf{R}} \overline{\mathbf{P}}_{i_1}, \ldots, \overline{\mathbf{P}}_{i_{k-1}} \mathbf{C}_{j_1} \ldots \mathbf{C}_{j_k} \mathbf{W}_T) = H(\mathbf{W} \setminus \mathbf{W}_T). \tag{6}$$

Conditions (3) and (4) ensure that a dishonest coalition of servers does not gain information about $\mathcal{R}$'s index; and a dishonest $\mathcal{R}$ infers at most one secret among the ones held by $S_1, \ldots, S_m$. Condition (5) takes into account the possibility of an attack against $\mathcal{S}$ performed either by at most $k - 1$ servers alone or with the cooperation of $\mathcal{R}$. The condition states that such coalitions do not gain

---

[2] Since we focus our attention on unconditionally secure DOT protocols, we use the entropy function, which leads to a compact and concise description. The reader is referred to the Appendix for a short introduction to entropy and information theory.

any information about the secrets held by $\mathcal{S}$. Finally, condition (6) states that a coalition of $k-1$ servers and the receiver, once the receiver has obtained a secret, cannot compute any information about the other secrets. In the following, we will show that this condition cannot be achieved if the DOT protocol provides only one round of interaction. On the other hand, with two rounds of interaction, this level of security can be obtained. Notice that, in our model, conditions (4) and (6) are not independent: indeed, (6) implies (4). To simplify the description and the analysis of the security we have chosen to state two different conditions.

3 Lower Bounds and Impossibility Results

Using some information theory tools, we can prove bounds on the memory storage, on the communication complexity and on the randomness needed by a DOT scheme. Moreover, we can show that with one-round protocols condition (6) of the DOT definition cannot be achieved. Actually, we can prove that *a single* server can help the receiver to recover all the secrets, once the receiver has legally retrieved the first one. Due to this result, we will refer to schemes achieving all but condition (6), as to *weak* DOT schemes.

The following bounds (see Table 1) hold for both weak DOT schemes and for DOT schemes, since condition (6) is not used in the proofs that, due to lack of space, will appear in the full version of the paper.

Theorem 1. (Memory Storage.) In any (k,m)-DOT-$\binom{n}{1}$ scheme for each $j = 1,\ldots,m$, it holds that
$$H(\mathbf{P}_j) \geq H(\mathbf{W}).$$

Theorem 2. (Randomness to Set Up the Scheme.) In any (k,m)-DOT-$\binom{n}{1}$ scheme, it holds that
$$H(\mathbf{P}_1\ldots\mathbf{P}_m) \geq kH(\mathbf{W}).$$

Theorem 3. (Complexity of each Interaction.) In any (k,m)-DOT-$\binom{n}{1}$ scheme, for each $j = 1,\ldots,m$, it holds that
$$H(\mathbf{C}_j) \geq H(\mathbf{W}_T).$$

Theorem 4. (Randomness of the whole Communication.) In any (k,m)-DOT-$\binom{n}{1}$ scheme, for any $1 \leq i_1 < \ldots, < i_k \leq n$, it holds that
$$H(\mathbf{C}_{i_1}\ldots\mathbf{C}_{i_k}) \geq kH(\mathbf{W}_T).$$

Table 1. Bounds holding on the Model

Notice that if the protocol is one-round, then $C_j = (Q_j, A_j)$, the query of the receiver and the answer of the server. Therefore, condition (1) can be re-phrased saying that for $j = 1, \ldots, m$

$$H(\mathbf{Q}_j | \mathbf{R}\,\mathbf{T}) = 0 \quad \text{and} \quad H(\mathbf{A}_j | \mathbf{Q}_j \mathbf{P}_j) = 0. \tag{7}$$

With this notation, we can prove the following impossibility result:

Theorem 5. *In any one-round scheme for (k, k)-DOT-$\binom{n}{1}$, once the receiver has legally recovered a secret, a single corrupt server and the receiver can recover all the others.*

Proof. Let $q_1, \ldots, q_k$ be the queries sent by the receiver when $T = i$, and let $a_1, \ldots, a_k$ be the answers that $S_1 \ldots, S_k$ send back to the receiver. The Receiver's security property (3) with respect to $k - 1$ servers, say $S_2, \ldots, S_k$, implies that there exist queries q_1^s and answers a_1^s, for any $s \neq i$, such that if

$$H(\mathbf{W}_i | \mathbf{Q}_1 = q_1\, \mathbf{Q}_2 = q_2 \ldots \mathbf{Q}_k = q_k, \mathbf{A}_1 = a_1\, \mathbf{A}_2 = a_2 \ldots \mathbf{A}_k = a_k) = 0$$

then

$$H(\mathbf{W}_s | \mathbf{Q}_1 = q_1^s\, \mathbf{Q}_2 = q_2 \ldots \mathbf{Q}_k = q_k, \mathbf{A}_1 = a_1^s\, \mathbf{A}_2 = a_2 \ldots \mathbf{A}_k = a_k) = 0$$

Since the answer given by S_1 depends only on his own program P_1 and on the received query (i.e., $H(\mathbf{A}_1 | \mathbf{Q}_1 \mathbf{P}_1) = 0$), it holds that

$$H(\mathbf{W} | \mathbf{P}_1 \mathbf{A}_2 \ldots \mathbf{A}_k, \mathbf{Q}_2 \ldots \mathbf{Q}_k \mathbf{R}) = 0.$$

Indeed

$$H(\mathbf{W} | \mathbf{P}_1 \mathbf{A}_2 \ldots \mathbf{A}_k, \mathbf{Q}_2 \ldots \mathbf{Q}_k \mathbf{R}) \leq \sum_{t\ T} H(\mathbf{W}_t | \mathbf{P}_1 \mathbf{A}_2 \ldots \mathbf{A}_k, \mathbf{Q}_2 \ldots \mathbf{Q}_k \mathbf{R}, \mathbf{T} = t)$$

and

$$H(\mathbf{W}_t | \mathbf{P}_1 \mathbf{A}_2 \ldots \mathbf{A}_k \mathbf{Q}_2 \ldots \mathbf{Q}_k \mathbf{R}, \mathbf{T} = t) \leq H(\mathbf{W}_t | \mathbf{P}_1 \mathbf{A}_2 \ldots \mathbf{A}_k \mathbf{Q}_1 \mathbf{Q}_2 \ldots \mathbf{Q}_k)$$
$$\leq H(\mathbf{W}_t | \mathbf{A}_1 \mathbf{A}_2 \ldots \mathbf{A}_k \mathbf{Q}_1 \mathbf{Q}_2 \ldots \mathbf{Q}_k) = 0$$

Therefore, the receiver and S_1 can recover all the secrets and the result holds[3].
□

A consequence of this impossibility result for one-round protocols is that the highest security level aimed in [26] with this approach cannot be achieved.

Notice that the model is quite general. If we consider one-round weak DOT schemes such that a sequence of k queries determines $\mathbf{T}$ *uniquely*, i.e.,

---

[3] Notice that the result can easily be extended to general (k, m)-DOT-$\binom{n}{1}$ and to $\mathcal{A}$-DOT-$\binom{n}{1}$ schemes for general access structures on the set of servers. Moreover, applying the same argument, it is possible to show that, if the receiver's security property (3) must hold, in the threshold case, against a coalition *of size at most t*, then the receiver, after having legally recovered one secret, can recover *all* the others if she colludes with $k - t$ servers.

$$H(\mathbf{T}|\mathbf{Q}_{i_1} \ldots \mathbf{Q}_{i_k}) = 0, \tag{8}$$

then we can show a bound on the randomness of the receiver. All the known constructions and the new ones we introduce enjoy this property, which in general is not guaranteed or required by the conditions defining our model.

Theorem 6. *In any one-round weak (k, m)-DOT-$\binom{n}{1}$ scheme satisfying (8) it holds that*

$$H(\mathbf{R}) \geq (k - 1)H(\mathbf{T}).$$

4 Protocols Implementing Weak (k, m)-DOT-$\binom{n}{1}$

Two protocols for weak (k, m)-DOT-$\binom{2}{1}$ have been proposed in [25]. Their general structure is given in Table 2.

A General Protocol for a weak (k, m)-DOT-$\binom{2}{1}$ Implementation.
Let $w_0, w_1 \in GF(q)$ be $\mathcal{S}$'s secrets, and let $\sigma \in \{0, 1\}$ be $\mathcal{R}$'s index.

- $\mathcal{S}$ generates a bivariate polynomial $Q(x, y)$ with values in $GF(q)$ such that $Q(0, 0) = w_0$ and $Q(0, 1) = w_1$.
- Then, for $i = 1, \ldots, m$, he sends the univariate polynomial $Q(i, \cdot)$ to the server $\mathcal{S}_i$.
- $\mathcal{R}$ chooses a random polynomial Z such that $Z(0) = \sigma$, and defines a univariate polynomial $V(x) = Q(x, Z(x))$. The degree of V is $k - 1$.
- Then, she asks server $\mathcal{S}_i$ for the value $V(i) = Q(i, Z(i))$.
- After receiving k values of V, $\mathcal{R}$ interpolates V and computes $V(0)$.

Table 2. A General Protocol for a weak (k, m)-DOT-$\binom{2}{1}$

The first protocol uses a *sparse* bivariate polynomial. The second one uses a *full* bivariate polynomial and is secure against coalitions between $\mathcal{R}$ and several servers (under the weaker condition (3)). The constructions can be transformed in an *unconditionally secure* form, by replicating the basic scheme given in Table 2, and using some ad hoc coefficients [25]. Moreover, we can use weak (k, m)-DOT-$\binom{2}{1}$ as a black box to construct "more complex" forms of oblivious transfer in the same distributed model (see [16] for some unconditionally secure reductions). In this situation, any improvement in the design of the available weak (k, m)-DOT-$\binom{2}{1}$, yields an improvement of the performance of the more complex protocols.

In this section, we propose a protocol, based on polynomial interpolation, implementing weak (k, m)-DOT-$\binom{n}{1}$ oblivious transfer. This protocol is a generalization of the weak (k, m)-DOT-$\binom{2}{1}$ protocol proposed in [25]. The protocol is described in Table 3.

First Protocol for a weak (k, m)-DOT-$\binom{n}{1}$.

Let $s_0, s_1, \ldots, s_{n-1} \in GF(q)$ be $\mathcal{S}$'s secrets, and let $i \in \{0, \ldots, n-1\}$ be $\mathcal{R}$'s index.

- $\mathcal{S}$ generates an n-variate polynomial $Q(x, y_1, \ldots, y_{n-1})$ with values in $GF(q)$ such that $Q(0, 0, \ldots, 0) = s_0, Q(0, 1, 0, \ldots, 0) = s_1, \ldots, Q(0, 0, \ldots, 1) = s_{n-1}$. More precisely,

$$Q(x, y_1, \ldots, y_{n-1}) = \sum_{j=1}^{k-1} a_j x^j + b_0 + b_1 y_1 + \cdots, b_{n-1} y_{n-1},$$

  where $s_0 = b_0$ and, for $i = 1, \ldots, n-1$, $s_i = b_0 + b_i$.
- Then, for $i = 1, \ldots, m$, he sends the $n-1$-variate polynomial $Q(i, y_1, \ldots, y_{n-1})$ to the server $\mathcal{S}_i$.
- $\mathcal{R}$ chooses $n-1$ random polynomials $Z_{y_1}(x) \ldots, Z_{y_{n-1}}(x)$ of degree $k-1$ such that $(Z_{y_1}(0) \ldots, Z_{y_{n-1}}(0))$ is an $(n-1)$-tuple of zeroes having at most one 1 in position i, the position corresponding to the secret in which she is interested, and defines a univariate polynomial V to be $V(x) = Q(x, Z_{y_1}(x), \ldots, Z_{y_{n-1}}(x))$. The degree of V is $k-1$.
- Then, she asks server $\mathcal{S}_{i_j}$ for the value $V(i_j) = Q(i_j, Z_{y_1}(i_j), \ldots, Z_{y_{n-1}}(i_j))$.
- After receiving k values of V, say $V(i_1), \ldots V(i_k)$, $\mathcal{R}$ interpolates V and computes $V(0)$.

Table 3. First Protocol for weak (k, m)-DOT-$\binom{n}{1}$.

Correctness. Let $Z_{y_i}(x) = s_{y_i}^0 + \sum_{j=1}^{k-1} s_{y_i}^j x^j$ be the polynomials generated by $\mathcal{R}$, random up to $s_{y_i}^0$. The polynomial $V(x)$ interpolated by $\mathcal{R}$,

$$V(x) = Q(x, Z_{y_1}(x), \ldots, Z_{y_{n-1}}(x)),$$

can be written in explicit form as

$$\sum_{j=1}^{k-1} a_j x^j + b_0 + b_1(s_{y_1}^0 + \sum_{j=1}^{k-1} s_{y_1}^j x^j) + \cdots, b_{n-1}(s_{y_{n-1}}^0 + \sum_{j=1}^{k-1} s_{y_{n-1}}^j x^j),$$

which can be re-arranged as

$$\sum_{j=1}^{k-1}(a_j + b_1 s_{y_1}^j + \cdots b_{n-1} s_{y_{n-1}}^j) x^j + b_0 + b_1 s_{y_1}^0 + \cdots + b_{n-1} s_{y_{n-1}}^0.$$

For $x = 0$, and assuming that the $n-1$-tuple $(s_{y_1}^0, \ldots, s_{y_{n-1}}^0) = (0, \ldots, 1, \ldots, 0)$ (i.e., having at most one 1 in position i, where $i \in \{1, \ldots, n-1\}$), then $V(0) = b_i + b_0 = s_i$.

$\square$

It is possible to show that, in the above form, the receiver can learn *a single* linear combination of the secrets, extending the proof given by Naor and Pinkas [25] for two secrets. Moreover, along the same line as [25], the protocol can be used as a building block to set up an unconditionally secure weak DOT that meets the bounds given by Theorems 1 and 2. Indeed, these bounds still hold for weak DOT schemes, since they are obtained without making any use of condition (6). As well as, we can use full n-variate polynomials to set up a protocol which is secure against t servers and a coalition among the receiver and $\ell \leq k - t$ servers. Details will be given in the full version of the paper.

5   Combinatorial Constructions

In this section we propose some combinatorial constructions for distributed oblivious transfer. Some of these constructions require trivial computations once the scheme has been set up by the Sender, and the one-round protocols meet the lower bound on the number of random bits the receiver must use to set up the queries, given by Theorem 6. However, they are not so efficient in terms of memory server storage and communication complexity.

5.1   One-Round Constructions

We start by giving protocols which require one round of interaction to recover a secret. The constructions are based on well-known combinatorial structures used in secret sharing. The first protocol is given in Table 4:

A Weak (k, k)-DOT-$\binom{n}{1}$.

Let $s_0, s_1, \ldots, s_{n-1} \in GF(q)$ be $\mathcal{S}$'s secrets, and let $A[p, j]$ be a $k \times n^k$ matrix of values in $GF(q)$ such that, for $j \in \{0, \ldots, n^k - 1\}$, the sum of the values of column $A[j]$ is s_i if, assuming that $c_1^j \cdots c_k^j$ is the representation in base n of j, the sum $\sum_{\ell=1}^{k} c_\ell^j \bmod n = i$.

- $\mathcal{S}$ sends the p-th row $A[p]$ of $A[p, j]$ to the server S_p
- The receiver chooses a value $j \in \{0, \ldots, n^k - 1\}$ such that the $\sum_{\ell=1}^{k} c_\ell^j \bmod n = i$, where i is the index of the secret she wishes to recover. Then, for $p = 1, \ldots, k$ she sends the digit c_p^j to server S_p.
- Server S_p sends to the receiver, for $q = 0, \ldots, n^k - 1$, the value $A[p, q]$ if and only if the p-th digit of the n-ary representation of q is equal to c_p^j.
- The receiver sums up the values $A[1, j], \ldots, A[k, j]$, recovering the secret.

Table 4. A Weak (k, k)-DOT-$\binom{n}{1}$ Construction

Example. For 3 secrets and 2 servers, suppose that we use the protocol described in Table 4.

Let $A[2, 3^2]$ be the following matrix with values in $GF(q)$:

$$\begin{bmatrix} a_{1,0} & a_{1,1} & a_{1,2} & a_{1,3} & a_{1,4} & a_{1,5} & a_{1,6} & a_{1,7} & a_{1,8} \\ a_{2,0} & a_{2,1} & a_{2,2} & a_{2,3} & a_{2,4} & a_{2,5} & a_{2,6} & a_{2,7} & a_{2,8} \end{bmatrix}$$

The representations of $\{0, 1, \ldots, 8\}$ in base 3 are:

$$\begin{array}{ccccccccc} 0 & 1 & 2 & 3 & 4 & 5 & 6 & 7 & 8 \\ 00 & 01 & 02 & 10 & 11 & 12 & 20 & 21 & 22 \end{array}$$

Columns $0, 5$ and 7 encrypt s_0, $1, 3$ and 8 encrypt s_1, and $2, 4$ and 6 encrypt s_2.

To recover s_1, the receiver chooses, for example, column 8, and sends $c_1 = 2$ to server 1 and $c_2 = 2$ to server 2, receiving the values $a_{1,6}, a_{1,7}, a_{1,8}$ and $a_{2,2}, a_{2,5}, a_{2,8}$. □

Using some well-known combinatorial structures, we can generalize the above construction, in order to set up a weak (k, m)-DOT-$\binom{n}{1}$. More precisely, let t be an integer such that $1 \leq t \leq q$ and $r \geq 2$. An *orthogonal array* $OA_\lambda(t, q, r)$ is a $\lambda r^t \times q$ array A of r symbols, such that within any t columns of A, every possible t-tuple of symbols occurs in exactly λ rows of A. Using an orthogonal array and a collection of secret sharing schemes we can set up a weak (k, m)-DOT-$\binom{n}{1}$ (see Table 5).

Example. We present a weak $(2, 3)$-DOT-$\binom{3}{1}$ using the protocol described in Table 5.
Let us consider the following $OA_1(2, 4, 3)$:

$$A[4, 9] = \begin{bmatrix} 0 & 0 & 0 & 1 & 1 & 1 & 2 & 2 & 2 \\ 0 & 1 & 2 & 0 & 1 & 2 & 0 & 1 & 2 \\ 0 & 1 & 2 & 2 & 2 & 0 & 2 & 0 & 1 \\ 0 & 1 & 2 & 2 & 0 & 1 & 1 & 2 & 0 \end{bmatrix}$$

Suppose that $\mathcal{R}$ wishes to recover the secret s_0. Hence, she chooses for example the first column, $c = 0$, she chooses a subset of 2 servers, say S_2 and S_3, and she sends 0 to S_2 and 0 to S_3. The contacted servers reply by sending the following values

- S_2 sends $(0, sh_{2,0}), (5, sh_{2,5})$ and $(7, sh_{2,7})$
- S_3 sends $(0, sh_{3,0}), (4, sh_{3,4})$ and $(8, sh_{3,8})$.

Therefore, the receiver can recover s_0 using $(0, sh_{2,0})$ and $(0, sh_{3,0})$. □

Complete proofs of correctness and privacy for the above protocols will appear in the full version of the paper.

A Weak (k, m)-DOT-$\binom{n}{1}$

Let $s_0, s_1, \ldots, s_{n-1} \in GF(q)$ be $\mathcal{S}$'s secrets, and let $A[m+1, n^k]$ be an orthogonal array $OA_1(k, m+1, n)$. The first row $A[0]$ of the (public) orthogonal array $A[m+1, n^k]$ establishes "which column encrypts which secret". More precisely, we have the following:

Set up Phase.

- The Sender $\mathcal{S}$, for each $0 \leq c \leq n^k - 1$, shares $s_{A[0,c]}$ according to a (k, m)-threshold scheme. Let us denote such sharing by $sh_{1,c}, \ldots, sh_{m,c}$.
- Then, for $i = 1, \ldots, m$, $\mathcal{S}$ sends $sh_{i,0}, \ldots, sh_{i,n^k-1}$ to server S_i.

Suppose that $\mathcal{R}$ wishes to reconstruct the secret s_ℓ, for some $\ell \in \{0, \ldots, n-1\}$.

Recovering Phase.

- $\mathcal{R}$ chooses a random column c of the matrix A such that $A[0, c] = \ell$, picks a k-subset of $\{1, \ldots, m\}$, say $p_1, \ldots, p_k$, and, for $1 \leq j \leq k$, sends the value $y_j = A[p_j, c]$ to server S_{p_j}.
- For $1 \leq j \leq k$, server S_{p_j} sends $(d, sh_{p_j,d})$ to the receiver $\mathcal{R}$, for all d such that $A[p_j, d] = y_j$. $\mathcal{R}$ gets n shares from each of the k servers.
- Finally, $\mathcal{R}$ uses $sh_{p_1,c}, \ldots, sh_{p_k,c}$ to reconstruct the secret s_ℓ.

Table 5. A Weak (k, m)-DOT-$\binom{n}{1}$ Construction

Protocol for General Access Structures. The main idea underlying the combinatorial schemes is that an orthogonal array is used as an *indexing structure* for several sharings of the secrets[4]. We can pursue the same idea in order to support general access structures. To explain the protocol and how to construct the *indexing structure*, let us consider a simple case. Let S_1, S_2, S_3 and S_4 be four servers, and let $\mathcal{P}_3 = \{\{S_1, S_2\}, \{S_2, S_3\}, \{S_3, S_4\}\}$ be an access structure on the set of servers. This access structure is well-studied in secret sharing scheme theory and its (optimal) information rate ρ is equal to $\frac{2}{3}$ (see [10]). Assume that the secret is a pair of values (k_1, k_2) belonging to $GF(q') \times GF(q')$. It can be shared among $\mathcal{P}_3$ as follows:

S_1	x	z	
S_2	$k_1 + x$	$k_2 + z$	w
S_3	$k_1 + w$	$k_2 + y$	z
S_4	w	y	

---

[4] Indeed, notice that even the constructions given in Table 4, can be re-phrased along the same line of the protocol described in Table 5. In this case the orthogonal array used is an $OA_1(k, m+1, n)$.

The values x, y, z, and w are random values in $GF(q')$. The dealer computes the above shares and sends to each server a row of the matrix.

We can construct a weak $\mathcal{P}_3$-DOT using the above secret sharing scheme as a building block. More precisely, each secret is shared many times with different instances of the secret sharing scheme. At the same time, an indexing matrix which represents all these sharings can be set up filling in the entries of each column using the same secret sharing scheme.

To exemplify, assume that we have $9 = 3^2$ secrets. Each secret (k_i, k_j) can be indexed by $(i, j) \in GF(3) \times GF(3)$. An indexing matrix can be set up, considering 3^4 sharings for each value of the key (i.e., the number of possible choices for x, y, z, and w when seen as elements belonging to $GF(3)$). For example, the restriction of the indexing matrix to the key (k_1, k_2), indexed by $(1, 2)$, is:

0	(1,2)		$\cdots$	(1,2)	
1	0	0	$\cdots$	2	2
2	$1+0$	$2+0$ 0	$\cdots$	$1+2$	$2+2$ 2
3	$1+0$	$2+0$ 0	$\cdots$	$1+2$	$2+2$ 2
4	0	0	$\cdots$	2	2

Each of the 3^4 columns indexed by $(1, 2)$ represents a sharing of $(k_1, k_2) \in GF(q') \times GF(q')$. The receiver can choose one of those columns and can ask a subset $B \in \mathcal{P}_3$ to get the shares whose indices match the entries of the columns of the matrix corresponding to the servers in B. In our example the receiver, to retrieve (k_1, k_2), can choose the first column and can send $(1, 2, 0)$ to S_3 and $(0, 0)$ to S_4, receiving from S_3 all the shares corresponding to the fourth row of the matrix whose indices are $(1, 2, 0)$ (and, among these, is $(sh_1^{(1,2)}, sh_2^{(1,2)}, sh_0^{(1,2)})$) and from S_4 all the shares corresponding to the fifth row of the matrix whose indices are $(0, 0)$ (and, among these, is $(sh_0^{(1,2)}, sh_0^{(1,2)})$), where each $sh_j^{(1,2)} \in GF(q')$.

It is not difficult to see that the construction is correct, due to the reconstruction property of the secret sharing scheme. In our example $(sh_1^{(1,2)}, sh_2^{(1,2)})$ and $(sh_0^{(1,2)}, sh_0^{(1,2)})$ enable the receiver to recover (k_1, k_2). Moreover the scheme is secure since, for each subset of servers belonging to $\mathcal{P}_3$ and for each pair of different keys, say (k_i, k_j) and $(k_{i'}, k_{j'})$, looking at the restriction of the matrix to the columns indexed by the pairs (i, j) and (i', j'), there is no sequence of queries that enables to recover both secrets: *at least one* of the queries the receiver has to send to the servers to recover the second secret must be different in *at least one* of the entries from the queries that enable to recover the first one[5]. On the other hand, a forbidden subset of servers $F \notin \mathcal{P}_3$ neither get information about the secret $\mathcal{R}$ wishes to recover from the queries sent by her nor can they compute information about any secret, due to the security property of the secret sharing scheme. Notice that, if we have $n = q^2$ secrets, the construction

---

[5] Arguing by contradiction it is possible to show that if there exists a sequence of queries (in our example a sequence of two queries) which enables to recover two different secrets (k_i, k_j) and $(k_{i'}, k_{j'})$ then $i = i$ and $j = j$.

seen before requires q^4 sharings for each secret, and an indexing matrix with q^6 columns.

At this point it is not difficult to figure out how the same strategy can be applied to any access structure. In this extended abstract, without going into details that will be given in the full paper, we would like just to point out the use of secret sharing schemes for the construction of both the indexing structure and the subsequent sharing of the secrets. Perhaps this design technique can be applied successfully to other cryptographic protocols.

5.2   Two-Round Constructions

It is possible to gain in terms of security and reduce the complexity if we allow an additional round of interaction between the receiver and the servers. A simple protocol is described in Table 6.

A (k, k)-DOT-$\binom{2}{1}$ with one addressing bit
Let $s_0, s_1 \in GF(q)$ be $\mathcal{S}$'s secrets.

- $\mathcal{S}$ chooses k random bits r_i, and computes the bit r, by xoring the r_i's. Then, he sets up two vectors with entries in Z_q, v_0 and v_1, by choosing the first $k-1$ entries at random and computing

$$v_0[k] = s_r - \sum_{i=1}^{k-1} v_0[i] \bmod q, \text{ and } v_1[k] = s_{(1-r)} - \sum_{i=1}^{k-1} v_1[i] \bmod q.$$

- Then, for $i = 1, \ldots, k$, he sends the bit r_i and the values $v_0[i]$ and $v_1[i]$ to server S_i.
- In a first round of communication, $\mathcal{R}$ asks each server for the bit r_i and computes r. Then, for $i = 1, \ldots, k$, if $\mathcal{R}$ is interested in s_0 and $r = 0$, she asks server S_i for the value $v_0[i]$; otherwise, if $r = 1$, she asks for $v_1[i]$. Symmetrically, to recover s_1, if $r = 1$, she asks for $v_0[i]$, while if $r = 0$, she asks for $v_1[i]$.
- Then, she sums up the received values $\bmod q$.

Table 6. Two-Round (k, k)-DOT-$\binom{2}{1}$

An easy check shows that the receiver always recovers the secret in which is interested and she gets no information on the other secret, since it is encrypted by the values of the other column. Moreover, a coalition of $k-1$ servers cannot find out which secret $\mathcal{R}$ has recovered, since the "label" specifying which secret each column encrypts can be recovered *only* by *all* the k servers. Finally, a coalition of $k-1$ servers cannot compute *any* secret since the coalition misses the value held by the k-th server.

It is worthwhile to point out that the two-round construction above described enjoys the further security property that is impossible to achieve using a one-round protocol: indeed, a coalition of $k - 1$ servers and the receiver, after the latter has recovered one of the secret, still cannot compute the other without the help of the last server.

Notice that, if we compress the above protocol into one round, we can obtain a *random* DOT where the receiver *can recover one secret but she cannot choose which one*. This functionality can be realized if the servers simply send to the receiver the "addressing bits" and *all but one* of the values $v_0[i]$ and $v_1[i]$, for $i = 1, \ldots, k$. For example, one of the servers, say S_i, chooses uniformly at random which of the two values $v_0[i], v_1[i]$ to send to $\mathcal{R}$.

The above protocol can be extended to realize a DOT for a *general access structure* on the set of servers as well as a DOT for any number of secrets. The extensions can be done as follows: in order to implement a DOT for a general access structure $\mathcal{A}$ on the set of servers, say an $\mathcal{A}$-DOT-$\binom{2}{1}$, the bit r, which establishes which vector hides s_0, is shared among the m servers, according to a secret sharing scheme for $\mathcal{A}$. Then, if $r = 0$, the secret s_0 is shared by the first vector and s_1 by the second, according to a secret sharing scheme for $\mathcal{A}$; otherwise, s_0 is shared by the second vector and s_0 by the first. Once the receiver has recovered the value of r, contacting a subset of servers belonging to $\mathcal{A}$, she can recover one of the secret by sending a request for shares to a subset of servers (perhaps the same ones that were contacted before) belonging to $\mathcal{A}$. On the other hand, a (k, k)-DOT-$\binom{n}{1}$ requires that, instead of a bit r_i, each server has a value $r_i \in \{0, \ldots, n-1\}$, and, instead of two vectors sharing s_0 and s_1, there are exactly n vectors $v_0, \ldots, v_{n-1}$, sharing the secrets $s_0, \ldots, s_{n-1}$, respectively. The value $r = \sum r_j \mod n$ establishes the correspondence between vectors and the n secrets. In other words, if $r = 2$ then the third vector v_2 shares s_0, the fourth shares s_1, and so on, following a cyclic order modulo n. Applying the same argument described before for the case of two secrets, it is not difficult to show that even this is correct and secure.

6   Conclusions

In this paper, we have studied unconditionally secure distributed oblivious transfer protocols. We have presented lower bounds on the resources required to implement such schemes, some impossibility results for one-round schemes, and new constructions which are optimal with respect to some of the given bounds. Moreover, we have shown that, with a second round of interaction, the highest possible security level in this model can be achieved with, at the same time, a suitable reduction of resources (randomness, memory storage and communication complexity). It is worthwhile to notice that the same effect can be achieved modifying the model for DOT by allowing the Sender to send information during the set up phase even to the receiver. In this case the two-round protocol we have shown in the previous section can be simply transformed in a one-round protocol. This is another example of a tradeoff.

Interesting open problems include the design of a single protocol meeting all the bounds given by the information theoretic analysis, as well as to find out settings which can benefit from the application of this distributed primitive. Along this line, in the full version of the paper, we will discuss some applications mainly related to contexts in which the privacy (anonymity) of the user must be guaranteed.

Acknowledgment

D.R. Stinson's research is supported by NSERC grants IRC #216431-96 and RGPIN #203114-02. The authors would like to thank the referees for valuable suggestions and references.

References

1. D. Beaver, J. Feigenbaum, J. Kilian, and P. Rogaway, *Locally Random Reductions: Improvements and Applications*, Journal of Cryptology 10 (1), pp. 17-36, 1997.
2. A. Beimel, Y. Ishai, and T. Malkin, *Reducing the Servers Computation in Private Information Retrieval: PIR with Preprocessing*, Advances in Cryptology: Proceedings of Crypto 2000, Springer-Verlag, vol. 1880, pp. 55-73, 2000.
3. M. Bellare and S. Micali, *Non-interactive Oblivious Transfer and Applications*, Advances in Cryptology: Crypto '89, Springer-Verlag, pp. 547-559, 1990.
4. G.R. Blakley. Safeguarding Cryptographic Keys. Proceedings of AFIPS 1979 National Computer Conference, Vol. 48, pp. 313–317, 1979.
5. M. Blum, *How to Exchange (Secret) Keys*, ACM Transactions of Computer Systems, vol. 1, No. 2, pp. 175-193, 1993.
6. C. Blundo, B. Masucci, D.R. Stinson and R. Wei, *Constructions and Bounds for Unconditionally Secure Non-Interactive Commitment Schemes*, Designs, Codes, and Cryptography, Vol. 26, pp. 97–110, 2002.
7. G. Brassard, C. Crepéau, and J.-M. Roberts, *Information Theoretic Reductions Among Disclosure Problems*, Proceedings of 27th IEEE Symposium on Foundations of Computer Science, pp. 168-173, 1986.
8. G. Brassard, C. Crepéau, and J.-M. Roberts, *All-or-Nothing Disclosure of Secrets*, Advances in Cryptology: Crypto '86, Springer-Verlag, vol. 263, pp. 234-238, 1987.
9. G. Brassard, C. Crepéau, and M. Sántha, *Oblivious Transfer and Intersecting Codes*, IEEE Transaction on Information Theory, special issue in coding and complexity, Vol. 42, No. 6, pp. 1769-1780, 1996.
10. R.M. Capocelli, A. De Santis, L. Gargano and U. Vaccaro, *On the Size of the Shares in Secret Sharing Schemes*, Advances in cryptology - CRYPTO'91, Lecture Notes in Computer Science, vol. 576, pp. 101–113, 1992.
11. B. Chor, O. Goldreich, E. Kushilevitz, and M. Sudan, *Private Information Retrieval*, Proc. 36th IEEE Symposium on Foundations of Computer Science (FOCS), 1995, 41-50.
12. T. M. Cover and J. A. Thomas, **Elements of Information Theory**, John Wiley & Sons, 1991.
13. C. Crepéau, *Equivalence between to flavors of oblivious transfers*, Advances in Cryptology: Proceedings of Crypto '87, vol. 293, pp. 350-354, Springer Verlag, 1988.

14. C. Crepéau, *A Zero-Knowledge Poker Protocol that achieves confidentiality of the players' strategy or how to achieve an electronic poker face*, Advances in Cryptology: Proceedings of Crypto '86, Springer-Verlag, pp. 239-247, 1987.

15. G. Di Crescenzo, Y. Ishai, and R. Ostrovsky, *Universal Service-Providers for Database private Information Retrieval*, Proc. of Seventeenth Annual ACM Symposium on Principles of Distributed Computing (PODC), 1998.

16. P. D'Arco and D.R. Stinson, *Generalized Zig-zag Functions and Oblivious Transfer Reductions*, Selected Areas in Cryptography SAC 2001, vol. 2259, pp. 87-103, 2001.

17. Y. Dodis and S. Micali, *Lower Bounds for Oblivious Transfer Reduction*, Advances in Cryptology: Proceedings of Eurocrypt '99, vol. 1592, pp. 42-54, Springer Verlag, 1999.

18. S. Even, O. Goldreich, and A. Lempel, *A Randomized Protocol for Signing Contracts*, Communications of the ACM 28, pp. 637-647, 1985.

19. M. Fisher, S. Micali, and C. Rackoff, *A Secure Protocol for the Oblivious Transfer*, Journal of Cryptology, vol. 9, No. 3, pp. 191-195, 1996.

20. Y. Gertner, Y. Ishai, E. Kushilevitz, and T. Malkin, *Protecting Data Privacy in Private Information Retrieval Schemes*, Proc. of the 30th Annual ACM Symposium on Theory of Computing (STOC), 1998, pp. 151-160.

21. Y. Gertner, S. Goldwasser, and T. Malkin, *A Random Server Model for Private Information Retrieval or How to Achieve Information Theoretic PIR Avoiding Database Replication*, RANDOM 1998, Lecture Notes in Computer Science, Vol. 1518, pp. 200-217, 1998.

22. Y. Gertner, S. Kannan, T. Malkin, O. Reingold, and M. Viswanathan, *The Relationship between Public Key Encryption and Oblivious Transfer*, Proceedings of the 41st Annual Symposium on Foundations of Computer Science (FOCS 2000), pp. 325-339, 2000.

23. O. Goldreich, S. Micali, and A. Wigderson, *How to play ANY mental game or: A Completeness Theorem for Protocols with Honest Majority*, Proceedings of 19th Annual Symposium on Theory of Computing, pp. 20-31, 1987.

24. J. Kilian, *Founding Cryptography on Oblivious Transfer*, Proceedings of 20th Annual Symposium on Theory of Computing, pp. 20-31, 1988.

25. M. Naor and B. Pinkas, *Distributed Oblivious Transfer*, Advances in Cryptology: Proceedings of Asiacrypt '00, Springer-Verlag, pp. 205-219, 2000.

26. M. Naor, B. Pinkas, and R. Sumner, *Privacy Preserving Auctions and Mechanism Design*, ACM Conference on Electronic Commerce, 1999 available at http://www.wisdom.weizmann.ac.il/ naor/onpub.html

27. M. Rabin, *How to Exchange Secrets by Oblivious Transfer*, Technical Memo TR-81, Aiken Computation Laboratory, Harvard University, 1981.

28. R. Rivest, *Unconditionally Secure Committment and Oblivious Transfer Schemes Using Private Channels and a Trusted Initializer*, manuscript. Available: http://theory.lcs.mit.edu/~rivest/publications.html

29. A. Shamir. How to Share a Secret. Communications of ACM, vol. 22, n. 11, pp. 612–613, 1979.

30. D.R. Stinson. Bibliography on Secret Sharing Schemes. http://www.cacr.math.uwaterloo.ca/~dstinson/ssbib.html.

31. D.R. Stinson. An explication of secret sharing schemes. Des. Codes Cryptogr., 2, 357–390, 1992.

32. W. Tzeng, *Efficient 1-out-of-n Oblivious Transfer Schemes*, Proceedings of PKC 2002, Lecture Notes in Computer Science, Vol. 2274, pp. 159-171, 2002.

33. S. Wiesner, *Conjugate Coding*, SIGACT News 15, pp. 78-88, 1983.

A   Information Theory Elements

In this section we give some basic concepts about Information Theory. However, the reader is referred to [12] for a complete treatment of the subject.

Let $\mathbf{X}$ be a random variable taking values on a set X according to a probability distribution $\{P_{\mathbf{X}}(x)\}_{x \in X}$. The *entropy* of $\mathbf{X}$, denoted by $H(\mathbf{X})$, is defined as

$$H(\mathbf{X}) = - \sum_{x \in X} P_{\mathbf{X}}(x) \log P_{\mathbf{X}}(x),$$

where the logarithm is relative to the base 2. The entropy satisfies $0 \leq H(\mathbf{X}) \leq \log |X|$, where $H(\mathbf{X}) = 0$ if and only if there exists $x_0 \in X$ such that $Pr(\mathbf{X} = x_0) = 1$; whereas, $H(\mathbf{X}) = \log |X|$ if and only if $Pr(\mathbf{X} = x) = 1/|X|$, for all $x \in X$. The entropy of a random variable is usually interpreted as

- a measure of the "equidistribution" of the random variable
- a measure of the amount of information given on average by the random variable

Given two random variables $\mathbf{X}$ and $\mathbf{Y}$, taking values on sets X and Y, respectively, according to a probability distribution $\{P_{\mathbf{XY}}(x, y)\}_{x \in X, y \in Y}$ on their Cartesian product, the *conditional entropy* $H(\mathbf{X}|\mathbf{Y})$ is defined as

$$H(\mathbf{X}|\mathbf{Y}) = - \sum_{y \in Y} \sum_{x \in X} P_{\mathbf{Y}}(y) P_{\mathbf{X}|\mathbf{Y}}(x|y) \log P_{\mathbf{X}|\mathbf{Y}}(x|y).$$

It is easy to see that

$$H(\mathbf{X}|\mathbf{Y}) \geq 0. \tag{9}$$

with equality if and only if X is a function of Y. The conditional entropy is a measure of the amount of information that $\mathbf{X}$ still has, once given $\mathbf{Y}$.

The *mutual information* between $\mathbf{X}$ and $\mathbf{Y}$ is given by

$$I(\mathbf{X}; \mathbf{Y}) = H(\mathbf{X}) - H(\mathbf{X}|\mathbf{Y}).$$

Since, $I(\mathbf{X}; \mathbf{Y}) = I(\mathbf{Y}; \mathbf{X})$ and $I(\mathbf{X}; \mathbf{Y}) \geq 0$, it is easy to see that

$$H(\mathbf{X}) \geq H(\mathbf{X}|\mathbf{Y}), \tag{10}$$

with equality if and only if $\mathbf{X}$ and $\mathbf{Y}$ are independent. The mutual information is a measure of the common information between $\mathbf{X}$ and $\mathbf{Y}$.

Given $n + 1$ random variables, $\mathbf{X}_1 \ldots \mathbf{X}_n \mathbf{Y}$, the entropy of $\mathbf{X}_1 \ldots \mathbf{X}_n$ given $\mathbf{Y}$ can be written as

$$H(\mathbf{X}_1 \ldots \mathbf{X}_n | \mathbf{Y}) = H(\mathbf{X}_1|\mathbf{Y}) + H(\mathbf{X}_2|\mathbf{X}_1\mathbf{Y}) + \cdots + H(\mathbf{X}_n|\mathbf{X}_1 \ldots \mathbf{X}_{n-1}\mathbf{Y}). \tag{11}$$

Therefore, for any sequence of n random variables, $\mathbf{X}_1 \ldots \mathbf{X}_n$, it holds that

$$H(\mathbf{X}_1 \ldots \mathbf{X}_n) = \sum_{i=1}^{n} H(\mathbf{X}_i | \mathbf{X}_1 \ldots \mathbf{X}_{i-1}) \leq \sum_{i=1}^{n} H(\mathbf{X}_i). \tag{12}$$

Moreover, the above relation implies that, for each $k \leq n$,

$$H(\mathbf{X}_1 \ldots \mathbf{X}_n) \geq H(\mathbf{X}_1 \ldots \mathbf{X}_k). \tag{13}$$

Given three random variables, $\mathbf{X}$, $\mathbf{Y}$, and $\mathbf{Z}$, the *conditional mutual information* between $\mathbf{X}$ and $\mathbf{Y}$ given $\mathbf{Z}$ can be written as

$$I(\mathbf{X}; \mathbf{Y}|\mathbf{Z}) = H(\mathbf{X}|\mathbf{Z}) - H(\mathbf{X}|\mathbf{Z}\,\mathbf{Y}) = H(\mathbf{Y}|\mathbf{Z}) - H(\mathbf{Y}|\mathbf{Z}\,\mathbf{X}) = I(\mathbf{Y}; \mathbf{X}|\mathbf{Z}). \tag{14}$$

Since the conditional mutual information $I(\mathbf{X}; \mathbf{Y}|\mathbf{Z})$ is always non-negative we get

$$H(\mathbf{X}|\mathbf{Z}) \geq H(\mathbf{X}|\mathbf{Z}\,\mathbf{Y}). \tag{15}$$

Efficient Identity Based Signature Schemes Based on Pairings

Florian Hess

Dept. Computer Science,
University of Bristol,
Merchant Venturers Building,
Woodland Road,
Bristol, BS8 1UB
florian@cs.bris.ac.uk

Abstract. We develop an efficient identity based signature scheme based on pairings whose security relies on the hardness of the Diffie-Hellman problem in the random oracle model. We describe how this scheme is obtained as a special version of a more general generic scheme which yields further new provably secure identity based signature schemes if pairings are used. The generic scheme also includes traditional public key signature schemes. We further discuss issues of key escrow and the distribution of keys to multiple trust authorities. The appendix contains a brief description of the relevant properties of supersingular elliptic curves and the Weil and Tate pairings.

Keywords: Identity based signatures, Weil pairing, Tate pairing, key escrow.

1 Introduction

Digital signatures are one of the most important security services offered by cryptography. In traditional public key signature algorithms the public key of the signer is essentially a random bit string picked from a given set. This leads to a problem of how the public key is associated with the physical entity which is meant to be performing the signing. In these traditional systems the binding between the public key and the identity of the signer is obtained via a digital certificate. As noticed by Shamir [18] it would be more efficient if there was no need for such a binding, in that the users identity would be their public key, more accurately, given the users identity the public key could be easily derived using some public deterministic algorithm.

An identity based signature scheme based on the difficulty of factoring integers is given in [18], and it remained an open problem to develop an identity based encryption scheme. In 2001 two such schemes were given, the first by Cocks [7] was based on the quadratic residuosity problem, whilst the second given by Boneh and Franklin [3] was based on the bilinear Diffie-Hellman problem with respect to a pairing, e.g. the Weil pairing.

K. Nyberg and H. Heys (Eds.): SAC 2002, LNCS 2595, pp. 310–324, 2003.
© Springer-Verlag Berlin Heidelberg 2003

Originally the existence of the Weil pairing was thought to be a bad thing in cryptography. For example in [10] it was shown that the discrete logarithm problem in supersingular elliptic curves was reducible to that in a finite field using the Weil pairing. This led supersingular elliptic curves to be dropped from cryptographic use. The situation changed with the work of Joux [9], who gave a simple tripartite Diffie-Hellman protocol based on the Weil pairing on supersingular curves. Since Joux's paper a number of other applications have arisen, including an identity based encryption scheme [3] and a general signature algorithm [4]. The extension to higher genus curves and abelian varieties has also recently been fully explored in [8,16]. This new work has resulted in a rekindling of cryptographic interest in supersingular elliptic curves.

In [17] an identity based public key signature algorithm is given which uses the Weil pairing and other identity based signature schemes [5,14] have recently been proposed.

In this paper we present an identity based signature scheme whose security is based on the Diffie-Hellman problem in the domain of the pairing. Furthermore, we describe a generic scheme in a more general underlying situation and relate its security to a computational problem. Instantiations of this scheme using pairings then yield further new identity based signature schemes with security again based on the above Diffie-Hellman problem. These schemes are different from [5,14,17] and we argue that they can offer advantages over those schemes. Furthermore it appears possible that there are other instantiations of the general scheme, using for example RSA one way functions instead of pairings similar to Shamir's scheme [18]. Finally we address issues regarding key escrow and the distribution of keys to multiple trust authorities and discuss in the appendix how our schemes can be realized using elliptic curves and the Weil or Tate pairings.

2   An Identity Based Signature Scheme

Let $(G, +)$ and $(V, \cdot)$ denote cyclic groups of prime order l, $P \in G$ a generator of G and let $e : G \times G \to V$ be a pairing which satisfies the following conditions.

1. Bilinear: $e(x_1 + x_2, y) = e(x_1, y)e(x_2, y)$ and $e(x, y_1 + y_2) = e(x, y_1)e(x, y_2)$.
2. Non-degenerate: There exists $x \in G$ and $y \in G$ such that $e(x, y) \neq 1$.

We also assume that $e(x, y)$ can be easily computed while, for any given random $b \in G$ and $c \in V$, it should be infeasible to compute $x \in G$ such that $e(x, b) = c$. We remark that the pairing e is not required to be symmetric or antisymmetric. Furthermore we define the hash functions

$$h : \{0, 1\}^* \times V \to (\mathbb{Z}/l\mathbb{Z})^\times, \quad H : \{0, 1\}^* \to G^*$$

where $G^* := G\backslash\{0\}$. We also abbreviate $V^* := V\backslash\{1\}$.

The identity based signature scheme consists of four algorithms, **Setup**, **Extract**, **Sign** and **Verify**. There are three parties in the system, the trust authority (or TA), the signer and the verifier.

Scheme 1.

Setup : The TA picks a random integer $t \in (\mathbb{Z}/l\mathbb{Z})^{\times}$, computes $Q_{TA} = tP$ and publishes Q_{TA} while t is kept secret.

Extract : This algorithm is performed by the TA when a signer requests the secret key corresponding to their identity. Suppose the signer's identity is given by the string ID. The secret key of the identity is then given by $S_{ID} = tH(ID)$, which is computed by the TA and given to the signer.

The extraction step is typically done once for every identity and uses the same setup data for many different identities.

Sign : To sign a message m the signer chooses an arbitrary $P_1 \in G^*$, picks a random integer $k \in (\mathbb{Z}/l\mathbb{Z})^{\times}$ and computes:

1. $r = e(P_1, P)^k$.
2. $v = h(m, r)$.
3. $u = vS_{ID} + kP_1$.

The signature is then the pair $(u, v) \in (G, (\mathbb{Z}/l\mathbb{Z})^{\times})$.

Verify : On receiving a message m and signature (u, v) the verifier computes:

1. $r = e(u, P) \cdot e(H(ID), -Q_{TA})^v$.
2. Accept the signature if and only if $v = h(m, r)$.

It is straightforward to check that the verification equation holds for a valid signature.

We discuss some general performance enhancements for Scheme 1. The signing operation can be further optimized by the signer precomputing $e(P_1, P)$ for a P_1 of his choice, for example $P_1 = S_{ID}$, and storing this value with the signing key. For $P_1 = S_{ID}$ this means that the signing operation involves one exponentiation in the group V, one hash function evaluation and one multiplication involving an element in the group G.

The verification operation requires one exponentiation in V, one hash function evaluation and two evaluations of the pairing. One of the pairing evaluations can be eliminated, if a large number of verifications are to be performed for the same identity, by precomputing $e(H(ID), -Q_{TA})$.

For the security of Scheme 1 we have the following theorem. The attack model is explained in section 5.

Theorem 1. *In the random oracle model, suppose that an adaptive adversary A exists which makes at most $n_1 \geq 1$ queries of an identity hash and extraction oracle, at most $n_2 \geq 1$ queries of a message hash and signature oracle and which succeeds within time T_A of making an existential forgery with probability*

$$\varepsilon_A \geq \frac{a\, n_1 n_2^2}{l}$$

for some constant $a \in \mathbb{Z}^{\geq 1}$. Then there is another probabilistic algorithm C and a constant $c \in \mathbb{Z}^{\geq 1}$ such that C solves the Diffie-Hellman problem with respect to

$$(P, Q_{TA}, R)$$

on input of any given $R \in G^*$, in expected time

$$T_C \leq \frac{c\, n_1 n_2 T_A}{\varepsilon_A}.$$

Proof. Follows from Theorem 2 and Example 1 in section 5. See also the remarks after Theorem 2.

If G is represented as a subgroup of another group $\hat{G}$ the definition of H might be difficult in practice. Just as in section 4.3 and Theorem 4.7 of the full version of [3] one can relax this requirement on the hash function H that it produces elements in G by using admissible encodings, without affecting the above security theorem.

3   Comparison to Other Identity Based Schemes

We compare Scheme 1 to the three most recent schemes [5,14,17] which are also based on pairings.

First, the setup and extraction steps are virtually identical for all four schemes and compatible with the identity based encryption scheme in [3]. Next we compare the efficiency. In the following table we denote by E an exponentiation in V, by M a scalar multiplication in G, by SM a simultaneous scalar multiplication of the form $\lambda P + \mu Q$ in G and by P a computation of the pairing. We do not take hash evaluations into account.

	Scheme 1	[5]	[14]	[17]
Signing	1E + 1M	2M	1M + 1SM	2M
Verifying	1E + 2P / 1E + 1P	1M + 2P	2E + 2P / 2E + 1P	3P / 2P
Signature	$G \times (\mathbb{Z}/l\mathbb{Z})^{\times}$	$G \times G$	$G \times G$	$G \times G$

The pairing computation is the operation which by far takes the most running time. The verifying step in Scheme 1 and the scheme of [14] can be optimized to 1E + 1P and 2E + 1P respectively if the same identities occur frequently, thus roughly taking half the runtime of [5]. The scheme in [17] requires 3P (2P in the optimized version) and is hence the slowest. In terms of communication requirements Scheme 1 is at least as efficient as the other two since an element in G requires at least as much memory as an element in $(\mathbb{Z}/l\mathbb{Z})^{\times}$ (remember $\#G = l$). Often one would actually need to apply special compression techniques in G.

In terms of provable security Scheme 1 and the scheme of [5] rely on the hardness of the Diffie-Hellman problem in G. There is no formal reduction to an underlying hard problem in [14,17].

We conclude that Scheme 1 can offer advantages in runtime, communication requirements and provable security over the schemes [5,14,17].

4   Key Escrow

In this section we pause to discuss the issue of key escrow. The generalization of Scheme 1 will then be given in the next section.

One criticism against identity based signature schemes, as opposed to identity based encryption schemes, is that the trust authority has access to the signer's private key and hence can sign messages as if they came from the signer. This escrow facility is deemed a great draw back for signature schemes, whereas one could debate that such an escrow facility for encryption may be desirable.

All previous identity based signature schemes have this built in escrow property. By using multiple trust authorities however the threat from escrowing the private key can be reduced. For Shamir's original scheme [18] one would for example need to produce an RSA modulus N and a public exponent e such that no individual trust authority knows the factors of N and each trust authority has a share d_i of the private exponent d. Protocols exist for this problem, see for example [1], [2] and [6]. In order to distribute shares of the private key, a secret sharing scheme has also been applied in [3] in the identity based encryption setting. In general such a strategy would require a third party which computes the shares of the private key and distributes them to the trust authorities, together with some other data (e.g. appropriate Lagrange coefficients) allowing a signer to reconstruct his private key given the private partial information he obtains from sufficiently many trust authorities. In the case of an (n,n)-threshold secret sharing scheme the third party can however be dropped resulting in a similar, more efficient technique as follows.

Suppose we have the trust authorities TA_i for $1 \leq i \leq n$. We can trivially "distribute" the master secret t among the n trusted authorities in the following way. Each TA_i generates their own private key t_i independently of each other and publishes $Q_{TA_i} = t_i P$. The master private key is defined to be $t = \sum_{i=1}^{n} t_i$, a quantity completely unknown to any of the participants in the scheme. The master public key is $Q_{TA} = \sum_{i=1}^{n} Q_{TA_i}$. A signer obtains a share of its private key from each TA_i via $S_{ID}^{(i)} = t_i Q_{ID}$. The signer's secret key is then computed by the signer via $S_{ID} = \sum_{i=1}^{n} S_{ID}^{(i)}$. For the trust authorities to determine the signer's private key they would all need to collude, providing the (n,n)-threshold secret sharing scheme.

There is the possibility of one or several trust authorities cheating and not responding with the correct value of $S_{ID}^{(i)}$, with respect to Q_{TA_i}, for a given signer's key extraction request. This would have the effect of producing an invalid private key for the signer. A signer can check whether some trust authorities have responded with incorrect values, and which trust authorities have been involved, in one of the two following ways.

1. The signer tries to sign and verify a message using only the data provided by each TA_i in turn. This method clearly requires $O(n)$ signing operations.
2. The signer could detect the incorrect value by forming and checking the various subkeys of the form $\sum_i S_{ID}^{(i)}$, using a binary search method. This is a technique which will require $O(\log n)$ signing operations to determine an i with an incorrect value of $S_{ID}^{(i)}$.

5   A Generic Signature Scheme

In this section we explain the general principle behind Scheme 1 thereby obtaining the generic scheme and further identity based signature schemes. We relate the security of these schemes to a computational problem which specializes to the Diffie-Hellman problem in G if pairings are used. Finally the key escrow problem is discussed briefly and some examples are given.

Let $(G, +)$, $(G_1, +)$ and $(V, \cdot)$ denote cyclic groups of prime order l and $p : G \to V$ an efficiently computable monomorphism. We define a hash function

$$h : \{0,1\}^* \times V \to (\mathbb{Z}/l\mathbb{Z})^\times \times (\mathbb{Z}/l\mathbb{Z})^\times$$

with image size greater than or equal to l. There will be various choices for h as described later. We further define a full hash function

$$H : \{0,1\}^* \to G_1^*$$

where $G_1^* := G_1 \backslash \{0\}$. We also abbreviate again $G^* := G \backslash \{0\}$ and $V^* := V \backslash \{1\}$.

The general signature scheme consists of four algorithms, **Setup, Extract, Sign** and **Verify**. There are three parties in such a system, the trust authority (or TA), the signer and the verifier.

Scheme 2.

Setup : The TA chooses efficiently computable monomorphisms $s : G_1 \to G$ and $q : G_1 \to V$ with $p(s(x)) = q(x)$ for all $x \in G_1$ and publishes q, while s is kept secret.

Extract : This algorithm is performed by the TA when a signer requests the secret key corresponding to their identity. Suppose the signer's identity is given by the string ID. The secret key of the identity is then given by $a = s(H(ID))$, which is computed by the TA and given to the signer.

The extraction step is typically done once for every identity and uses the same setup data for many different identities. The public key of the signer is

$y = q(H(ID))$ which can be computed by the verifier using the identity of the signer.

Sign : To sign a message m the signer picks a random $k \in G^*$ and then computes:

1. $r = p(k)$
2. $(v, w) = h(m, r)$
3. $u = va + wk$

The signature is the pair $(u, r) \in G \times V^*$.

Verify : On receiving a message m and signature (u, r) the verifier computes:

1. $(v, w) = h(m, r)$
2. $y = q(H(ID))$
3. Accept the signature if and only if $p(u) = y^v r^w$.

That this verification equation holds for a valid signature follows from the following algebra:

$$
\begin{aligned}
p(u) &= p(va + wk) \\
&= p(a)^v p(k)^w \\
&= p(s(H(ID)))^v p(k)^w \\
&= q(H(ID))^v p(k)^w \\
&= y^v r^w.
\end{aligned}
$$

ElGamal Variations and Schnorr Version

There are a number of variations of Scheme 2. First of all, the signer and verifier could compute $(w, v) = h(m, r)$ instead of $(v, w) = h(m, r)$. If $G = (\mathbb{Z}/l\mathbb{Z})^+$ they could additionally assign $h(m, r)$ to any of the six combinations $(u, v), (u, w), \dots$ and the signer would solve for the remaining variable in the equation $u = va + wk$. The signature consists then of the value of this remaining variable together with r. We remark that the case $G = (\mathbb{Z}/l\mathbb{Z})^+$ does however not lead to true identity based schemes. These variations are equally secure (in the random oracle model) since the respective tuples (u, v, w) are computationally indistinguishable, because of $a, k \neq 0$. These variations correspond to the well known six variations of the modified ElGamal scheme, see [11,13].

There are various possibilities for the definition of h. If $h_1 : \{0, 1\}^* \to (\mathbb{Z}/l\mathbb{Z})^\times$, $h_2 : V \to (\mathbb{Z}/l\mathbb{Z})^\times$ and $h_3 : \{0, 1\}^* \times V \to (\mathbb{Z}/l\mathbb{Z})^\times$ are hash functions we can for example consider $h(m, r) := (h_1(m), h_2(r))$ or $h(m, r) := (h_3(m, r), 1)$. The choice $h(m, r) := (h(m), r)$ would however not be admissible. The case $h(m, r) := (h_3(m, r), 1)$ is of particular interest. Namely, in Scheme 2 we then have $w = 1$ and the verification equation is $p(u) = y^v r$. This means we can solve $r = p(u)y^{-v}$. It is hence equivalent giving (u, v) as a signature instead of (u, r) and depending on V this might take less memory. The modification of the signing and verification steps is straightforward and yields a general version of Schnorr signatures (compare also with Scheme 1).

Security

We proceed with the security discussion. We consider an adversary A which is assumed to be a (polynomial time) probabilistic Turing machine which besides the global scheme parameters takes as input q and a random tape. The adversary's goal is to produce an existential forgery of a signature by a signer ID of its choice. To aid the adversary we allow it to query four oracles:

Identity Hash Oracle : For any given identity ID this oracle will produce the corresponding hash value $H(ID)$.

Extraction Oracle : For any given identity ID this oracle will produce the corresponding secret key $s(H(ID))$.

Message Hash Oracle : For any given message m and $r \in V^*$ this oracle will produce the corresponding hash value $h(m, r)$.

Signature Oracle : For any given message m and identity ID this oracle will produce a signature from the user with identity ID on the message m.

Of course the output of the adversary A should not be a signature such that the secret key of the corresponding identity or the signature itself have been asked of the oracles.

Theorem 2. *In the random oracle model, suppose that an adaptive adversary A exists which makes at most $n_1 \geq 1$ queries of the identity hash and extraction oracle, at most $n_2 \geq 1$ queries of the message hash and signature oracle and which succeeds within time T_A of making an existential forgery with probability*

$$\varepsilon_A \geq \frac{a\, n_1 n_2^2}{l}$$

for some constant $a \in \mathbb{Z}^{\geq 1}$. Then there is another probabilistic algorithm C and a constant $c \in \mathbb{Z}^{\geq 1}$ such that C computes

$$s(R)$$

on input of any given $P, R \in G_1^*$ and $Q \in G^*$ with $Q = s(P)$, in expected time

$$T_C \leq \frac{c\, n_1 n_2 T_A}{\varepsilon_A}.$$

Proof. We assume familiarity with [15] and their proof technique. Let $P, R \in G_1^*$ and $Q \in G^*$ be generators such that $Q = s(P)$ and hence $p(Q) = q(P)$. We first explain how the oracle queries of A are simulated. For the i-th identity hash or extraction query for ID_i we return $H(ID_i) := \lambda_i P$ and, if requested, $s(H(ID_i)) = \lambda_i Q$ where $\lambda_i \in (\mathbb{Z}/l\mathbb{Z})^\times$ and $\lambda = (\lambda_i)_{i=1,2,\dots}$ constitutes a random tape. A query for the hash value $h(m, r)$, if not yet defined, is answered by a random $(v, w) = \delta_i \in (\mathbb{Z}/l\mathbb{Z})^\times \times (\mathbb{Z}/l\mathbb{Z})^\times$ which is successively taken from a random tape $\delta = (\delta_i)_{i=1,2,\ldots}$. To sign a message m for ID we issue the hash query $H(ID)$ ourselves and generate a random $u \in G^*$ and a random vector $(v,w) \in (\mathbb{Z}/l\mathbb{Z})^\times \times (\mathbb{Z}/l\mathbb{Z})^\times$ where $u = \gamma_\nu$ and $(v,w) = \delta_j$ are successively taken from the random tapes $\gamma = (\gamma_\nu)$ and $\delta = (\delta_j)$ respectively. Let $y := q(H(ID))$. We then compute $r := (p(u)/y^v)^{1/w}$. We remark that r is a random element in V since γ and δ are random and independent. We define the hash value $h(m,r) := (v,w)$ and return the signature (u,r). This procedure fails if $r = 1$ or $h(m,r)$ is already defined (the adversary could for example make a large number of queries $h(m,r)$ without us computing and recording the associated signatures). Since r is random the probability for a simulation failure during the n_2 message hash and signing queries is less than $2n_2^2/l$. The simulation is indistinguishable since (u,r) is random.

Running A and answering its oracle queries in the described way depends deterministically on λ, δ, γ and the random tape ω the adversary A is provided with. Because of the assumption on A, the indistinguishability and the low failure probability of the simulation, providing random values and running A results in a signature in time T_A with probability at least $\varepsilon_A - 2n_2^2/l \geq \varepsilon_A/2$ (true for $a = 14$), using at most n_1 identity and extraction queries, n_2 message hash and signature queries. This reduces the discussion to the case of a "passive" adversary, depending deterministically on λ, δ, γ and ω.

We now want to apply the forking lemma technique of [15] to control the identity hash and message hash values for which the adversary computes forged signatures.

We can proceed almost verbatim as in [15, Lemma 8] and its proof: Since the probability of guessing the hash value of an identity is $1/l$ and $\varepsilon_A/2 \geq 7n_1/l$ (true for $a = 14$), running A repeatedly with random input yields a signature for the hash value $H(ID_\beta) = \lambda_\beta P$ and (finite) index β after (expected) $4/\varepsilon_A$ executions with probability at least $4/5$. Next, with probability $1/4$ we have that a replay of A with the same δ, γ, ω, and $\lambda = (\lambda_i)$ unchanged for $i < \beta$ and randomly chosen for $i \geq \beta$, yields a signature with probability at least $(\varepsilon_A/2)/(14n_1)$, for the now different $H(ID_\beta) = \lambda_\beta P$ but same β. The point is that we may as well answer the β-th identity hash query of A by values μR for random $\mu \in (\mathbb{Z}/l\mathbb{Z})^\times$ since this is as random as $H(ID_\beta)$ and A does not issue an extraction query for this identity, which we could not answer. As an aside, note that if we have an identity hash collision $H(ID_{\beta'}) = H(ID_\beta) = \mu R$ we have solved the discrete logarithm problem $R = \lambda P$, namely $\lambda = \lambda_{\beta'}/\mu$.

We combine these steps similar to [15, Lemma 8]. Replaying A an at most $(14n_1)/(\varepsilon_A/2)$ (expected) times and answering the β-th identity hash query with random values μR results in a signature for some μR with probability at least $3/5$. We thus obtain a machine B which on input of δ, γ and the random tape ω' returns a signature for an identity hash μR in time $T_B \leq (4/\varepsilon_A + (14n_1)/(\varepsilon_A/2))T_A \leq 32n_1T_A/\varepsilon_A$ with probability $\varepsilon_B \geq 1/9$, where μ depends on δ, γ, ω' and is drawn from a set of $(14n_1)/(\varepsilon_A/2)$ candidates which depends only on ω'. Furthermore at most $32n_1n_2/\varepsilon_A$ values are taken from δ

and the message hash $h(m, r)$ of the signature equals one of the last n_2 queried values of δ.

We apply the forking lemma a second time, now to B and with respect to δ (and regarding γ, ω' as one random tape). The conditions of [15, Lemma 8] are satisfied because we may assume that $\varepsilon_B \geq 1/9 \geq 7n_2/l$ (this is true for $a = 63$). Feeding δ, γ, ω', the input to B, from a random tape ω'' we obtain a machine C which on input of ω'' replays B at most $2/\varepsilon_B + 14n_2/\varepsilon_B$ times and returns two signatures (u_1, r) and (u_2, r) with message hash values $h_1(m, r)$ and $h_2(m, r)$ for the same m, r and identity hash values $\mu_1 R$ and $\mu_2 R$, in time $T_C \leq 16n_2 T_B/\varepsilon_B$ and with probability $\varepsilon_C \geq 1/9$. The value of m, r is the same since up to the query of $h_1(m, r)$ and $h_2(m, r)$ identical operations are carried out by the replays of B, as $\delta = (\delta_j)$ for $j < \beta$ for some fixed index β and γ, ω' remain unchanged. Furthermore, the $h_i(m, r)$ are randomly chosen from the set of successful hash values δ_β for the given fixed γ, ω' which has cardinality $\geq \varepsilon_B/(14n_2)(l - 1)^2$ and can be partitioned into $\geq \varepsilon_B/(14n_2)(l - 1)$ classes of linearly dependent vectors. Also, the μ_i are chosen from a set of $(14n_1)/(\varepsilon_A/2)$ candidates. Let $(v_1, w_1) = h_1(m, r)$ and $(v_2, w_2) = h_2(m, r)$. The pairs $(\mu_1 v_1, w_1)$, $(\mu_2 v_2, w_2)$ are hence linearly dependent with probability $\leq (14n_1)/(\varepsilon_A/2)/(\varepsilon_B/(14n_2)(l - 1)) \leq 3528n_1 n_2/(\varepsilon_A(l - 1)) \leq 2/3$ (true for $a = 7056$ and $l \geq 5$). Thus C returns linearly independent $(\mu_1 v_1, w_1)$, $(\mu_2 v_2, w_2)$ in time $T_C \leq 16n_2 T_B/\varepsilon_B \leq 4608n_1 n_2 T_A/\varepsilon_A$ with probability $\geq 1/27$.

By dividing the two signing equations $p(u_i) = y_i^{v_i} r^{w_i}$ for $y_i = q(\mu_i R)$ we obtain the equation

$$p(u_1 - (w_1/w_2)u_2) = q(R)^{\mu_1 v_1 - (w_1/w_2)\mu_2 v_2}.$$

Since the $(\mu_i v_i, w_i)$ are linearly independent we have $\mu_1 v_1 - (w_1/w_2)\mu_2 v_2 \neq 0$. Hence

$$p((\mu_1 v_1 - (w_1/w_2)\mu_2 v_2)^{-1}(u_1 - (w_1/w_2)u_2)) = q(R)$$

so that we have solved $p(x) = q(R)$ and thus computed $x = s(R)$ in time $\leq 4608n_1 n_2 T_A/\varepsilon_A$ with probability $\geq 1/27$. This yields the constants $a = 7056$ and $c = 27 \cdot 4608 = 124416$.

Finally, we observe that the expected number of replays of A and B might not be explicitly known so that B and C cannot be given in the form above. In this case we can apply the same technique as in [15, Thm. 10] for B and C. Here B would have expected running time $T_B \leq 84480n_1 T_A/(\varepsilon_A/2)$ and thus succeeds with probability $\geq 1/2$ in time $2T_B$. The expected running time of C is then $T_C \leq 84480n_2 2T_B/(1/2) \leq 8 \cdot 84480^2 n_1 n_2 T_A/\varepsilon_A$, resulting in $c = 2 \cdot 168960^2$.

The constants in the proof can be optimized when l is chosen large with respect to n_1 and n_2. Also, the assumption $\varepsilon_A \geq a\, n_1 n_2^2/l$ of the theorem can be replaced by weaker assumptions as used in the proof.

Theorem 2 says in other words that, given p, q and one or several equations $Q = s(P)$, for the signature scheme to be secure it should be infeasible to compute other values $s(R)$. If this is the case then the TA's secret knowledge of s thus provides a generalized trap door with respect to p and q.

Multiple Trust Authorities

The general signature scheme can be extended to multiple trust authorities TA_i in the following way. Suppose $s_i : G_1 \to G$ and $q_i : G_1 \to V$ are the secret and public monomorphisms of TA_i for $1 \leq i \leq n$. We can then form a virtual trust authority TA defined by the monomorphisms $s(x) := \sum_{i=1}^{n} s_i(x)$ and $q(x) := \prod_{i=1}^{n} q_i(x)$ such that $p(s(x)) = q(x)$ for all $x \in G_1$. Note that since the s_i are random and independent, the probability of s and q not to be injective is $1/l$. The signer computes his private key via $s(H(ID)) = \sum_i s_i(H(ID))$ where he obtains the $s_i(H(ID))$ from each TA_i in turn. The verifier determines the signer's public key via $q(H(ID)) = \prod_i q_i(H(ID))$ where he computes the $q_i(H(ID))$ using the public monomorphisms q_i of each TA_i.

Let $I \cup J = \{1, \ldots, n\}$ and $I \cap J = \{\}$. An existential forgery with respect to the virtual trust authority TA under collusion of the TA_i for $i \in I$ is equivalent to an existential forgery with respect to the virtual trust authority obtained by combining the TA_i for $i \in J$, for which we can apply Theorem 2.

Examples

Example 1. The pairing based signature scheme Scheme 1 is obtained from the general Scheme 2 in the following way. We let $(G_1, +) = (G, +)$ and define $p(x) := e(x, P)$, $q(x) := e(x, Q_{TA})$ and $s(x) := tx$. Since P and Q_{TA} are public, $p(x)$ and $q(x)$ can be computed by all parties. As t is known to the TA it can compute $s(x)$. The steps of Scheme 1 are obtained from the steps of Scheme 2 together with the slight modification outlined in the remarks about Schnorr signatures. Other schemes can be obtained from the variations of hash functions and the parameter order as described above. With respect to the security we have $p(Q_{TA}) = q(P)$ which we need for the assumptions of Theorem 2. It follows that if there is an adversary, we can compute $s(x)$ without knowing t. Now, if we are given (P, Q_{TA}, R) we can thus compute $s(R) = tR$ where $Q_{TA} = tP$, thereby solving the Diffie-Hellman problem in G. This proves Theorem 1.

Example 2. The usual public key signature schemes are obtained as follows. Let $(G_1, +) = (V, \cdot)$ and q be the identity. The trust authority is now identical to the signer and there are no other signers associated. The signer chooses $a \in G^*$ at random and computes $y = p(a)$. The monomorphism s is the inverse of p. A typical example would be $p(x) = g^x$ such that s is the discrete logarithm map with respect to the element g. In the attack model we would artificially require $q(H(ID)) = H(ID) = y$ and that precisely one H-query is made. As a consequence, $n_1 = 1$ and Theorem 2 implies the standard security of the schemes in the single user setting, relating it to the inversion of p.

Example 3. If we take $(G, +) = (G_1, +) = (V, \cdot) = (\mathbb{Z}/n\mathbb{Z})^\times$ for n an RSA-modulus we essentially recover versions of the identity based signature scheme in [18]. Note that we have defined our general scheme only for cyclic groups of prime order whereas $(\mathbb{Z}/n\mathbb{Z})^\times$ is in general not cyclic of prime order. Thus

Theorem 2 cannot readily be applied. Since $(\mathbb{Z}/n\mathbb{Z})^{\times}$ is not too far from being cyclic it might be possible to adapt Scheme 2 and Theorem 2 towards this case.

6   Conclusion

We have described a generic signature scheme which gives rise to efficient identity based signature schemes if pairings are used. The security of these schemes follows from the security of the generic scheme in the random oracle model and is based on the Diffie-Hellman problem in the domain of the used pairing. Other instantiations of the generic scheme include traditional public key signature schemes in cyclic groups. In addition we have discussed key escrow and the distribution of keys to multiple trust authorities.

7   Acknowledgements

I would like to thank D. Kohel, J. Malone-Lee, K. Paterson and especially N. P. Smart for helpful discussions.

References

1. S. Blackburn, S. Blake-Wilson, M. Burmester and S. D. Galbraith. Shared Generation of Shared RSA Keys. University of Waterloo technical report, CORR 98-19 (1998).
2. D. Boneh and M. Franklin. Efficient Generation of Shared RSA Keys. In *Advances in Cryptology - CRYPTO '97*, Springer-Verlag LNCS 1294, 425–439, 1997.
3. D. Boneh and M. Franklin. Identity-based encryption from the Weil pairing. In *Advances in Cryptology - CRYPTO 2001*, Springer-Verlag LNCS 2139, 213–229, 2001.
4. D. Boneh, B. Lynn and H. Shacham. Short signatures from the Weil pairing. In *Advances in Cryptology - ASIACRYPT 2001*, Springer-Verlag LNCS 2248, 514–532, 2001.
5. J. Cha and J. Cheon. An Identity-Based Signature from Gap Diffie-Hellman Groups *IACR preprint server*, submission 2002/018, 2002.
6. C. Cocks. Split knowledge generation of RSA parameters. In *Cryptography and Coding*, Springer-Verlag LNCS 1355, 89–95, 1997.
7. C. Cocks. An identity based encryption scheme based on quadratic residues. In *Cryptography and Coding*, Springer-Verlag LNCS 2260, 360–363. 2001.
8. S. D. Galbraith. Supersingular curves in cryptography. In *Advances in Cryptology - ASIACRYPT 2001*, Springer-Verlag LNCS 2248, 495-513, 2001.
9. A. Joux. A one round protocol for tripartite Diffie-Hellman. In *Algorithmic Number Theory Symposium, ANTS-IV*, Springer-Verlag LNCS 1838, 385–394, 2000.
10. A. J. Menezes, T. Okamoto and S. Vanstone. Reducing elliptic curve logarithms to logarithms in a finite field. *IEEE Trans. Info. Th.*, **39**, 1639–1646, 1993.
11. A. J. Menezes, P. C. Oorschot and S. Vanstone. Handbook of Applied Cryptography. CRC Press, 1996.
12. V. Miller. Short programs for functions on curves. Unpublished manuscript, 1986.

13. K. Nyberg and R. A. Rueppel. Message recovery for signature schemes based on the discrete logarithm problem. *Designs, Codes and Cryptography*, **7(1/2)**, 61-81, 1996.
14. K. G. Paterson. ID-based signatures from pairings on elliptic curves *IACR preprint server*, submission 2002/003, 2002.
15. D. Pointcheval and J. Stern. Security arguments for digital signatures and blind signatures. *Journal of Cryptology*, **13**, 361–396, 2000.
16. K. Rubin and A. Silverberg. The best and worst of supersingular abelian varieties in cryptology. *IACR preprint server*, submission 2002/006, 2002.
17. R. Sakai, K. Ohgishi and M. Kasahara. Cryptosystems based on pairing. In *SCIS 2000*, 2000.
18. A. Shamir. Identity-based cryptosystems and signature schemes. In *Advances in Cryptology - CRYPTO '84*, Springer-Verlag LNCS 196, 47–53, 1984.
19. J. H. Silverman. *The Arithmetic of Elliptic Curves*. GTM 106, Springer-Verlag, 1986.

Appendix

Realization of the Identity Based Signature Schemes

In order use the identity based schemes described in the paper we need to find suitable groups G, V and pairings $e : G \times G \to V$. These groups are provided by finite fields and elliptic curves over finite fields, and the pairings are derived from the Weil or Tate pairing, as for example in [3].

More precisely G will be a point subgroup on an elliptic curve over a finite field and V a subgroup of the cyclic group of a larger finite field. We remark that elements in G can be represented in compressed form. Also, in Scheme 1 the signature consists of $v \in (\mathbb{Z}/l\mathbb{Z})^\times$ instead of $r \in V$, resulting in a more bandwidth efficient scheme.

The Weil and Tate Pairings on Elliptic Curves

We shall summarize the properties we require of the Weil pairing, much of the details can be found in [3], [10] and [19]. We also present the Tate pairing since it is more efficient to compute than the Weil pairing.

Let E be an elliptic curve defined over $\mathbb{F}_q$ and let G be a subgroup of $E(\mathbb{F}_q)$ of prime order l. For simplicity we will assume that $l^2 \nmid \#E(\mathbb{F}_q)$ so $G = E(\mathbb{F}_q)[l]$. We define α to be the smallest integer such that

$$l \mid (q^\alpha - 1).$$

The full l-torsion group $E[l]$ is defined over a unique minimal extension field $\mathbb{F}_{q^k}$,

$$E[l] \subseteq E(\mathbb{F}_{q^k}).$$

In practical implementations we will require k and α to be small. Let G' be a subgroup of $E[l]$ such that $E[l] = G \oplus G'$.

The Weil pairing is a non-degenerate, bilinear and antisymmetric pairing

$$e_l : E[l] \times E[l] \to \mathbb{F}_{q^k}^\times.$$

We cannot use it immediately for our purpose since $e_l(P, Q) = 1$ for any $P, Q \in G$. To overcome this problem one possibility is to consider an (injective) non $\mathbb{F}_q$-rational endomorphism $\phi : G \to G'$. We define

$$e : G \times G \to \mathbb{F}_{q^k}, \quad e(P, Q) := e_l(P, \phi(Q)).$$

This yields a pairing of the required properties since P and $\phi(Q)$ are linearly independent. Such non rational endomorphisms are known to exist for supersingular elliptic curves. They do not exist for ordinary elliptic curves since the Frobenius acts trivially on G. From the non degeneracy of the Weil pairing we have $k \geq \alpha$.

The Tate pairing is a non-degenerate, bilinear pairing

$$t_l : E(\mathbb{F}_{q^\alpha})[l] \times E(\mathbb{F}_{q^\alpha})/lE(\mathbb{F}_{q^\alpha}) \to \mathbb{F}_{q^\alpha}^\times / (\mathbb{F}_{q^\alpha}^\times)^l.$$

For $\alpha = 1$ we have $E(\mathbb{F}_q)[l] = G$ and $E(\mathbb{F}_q)/lE(\mathbb{F}_q) \cong G$. Using this isomorphism we can define

$$e : G \times G \to \mathbb{F}_{q^\alpha}^\times, \quad e(P, Q) := t_l(P, Q)^{(q-1)/l}.$$

For $\alpha > 1$ we have $E(\mathbb{F}_{q^\alpha})[l] = E[l]$, $E(\mathbb{F}_{q^\alpha})/lE(\mathbb{F}_{q^\alpha}) \cong E[l]$ and $k = \alpha$ from the non-degeneracy of t_l. Here we again need a non rational endomorphism $\phi : G \to G'$ since t_l is trivial on G. Using the isomorphism we define

$$e : G \times G \to \mathbb{F}_{q^\alpha}^\times, \quad e(P, Q) := t_l(P, \phi(Q))^{(q^\alpha - 1)/l}.$$

Both cases yield pairings with the required properties.

If there are no non rational endomorphisms we could use any group homomorphism $\phi : G \to G'$ defined by $P \mapsto P'$ for an arbitrary $P' \in G' \backslash \{0\}$. The computation of the pairing in the signature schemes only requires the evaluation of ϕ at P and Q_{TA} which means that the two additional points $P' = \phi(P)$ and $Q'_{TA} = \phi(Q_{TA})$, to be computed by the trust authority, have to be publicly known.

The Weil and Tate pairings are efficiently computable by an unpublished, but much referenced, algorithm of Miller [12]. Suppose given $P, Q \in G$ we wish to compute $e_l(P, \phi(Q))$ or $t_l(P, \phi(Q))$. We first compute, via Miller's algorithm, the functions f_P and $f_{\phi(Q)}$ whose divisors are given by

$$(f_P) = l(P + X) - l(X)$$

and

$$(f_{\phi(Q)}) = l(\phi(Q)) - l(\mathcal{O}),$$

where $X \in G$ is randomly chosen such that $\#\{\mathcal{O}, \phi(Q), X, P + X\} = 4$. Note, that since $P \in G \subseteq E(\mathbb{F}_q)$ we have

$$f_P \in \mathbb{F}_q(x, y)$$

whilst since $\phi(Q) \in G'$ we have

$$f_{\phi(Q)} \in \mathbb{F}_{q^r}(x,y)$$

where $r = k$ or $r = \alpha$ respectively. This means that computing f_P is easier than computing $f_{\phi(Q)}$. The Weil pairing is then given by

$$e_l(P,\phi(Q)) = \frac{f_P((\phi(Q)) - (\mathcal{O}))}{f_{\phi(Q)}((P+X)-(X))}$$

and the Tate pairing is computed via

$$t_l(P,\phi(Q)) = f_P((\phi(Q)) - (\mathcal{O})).$$

We see that not only is the Tate pairing easier to compute, since we do not need to compute $f_{\phi(Q)}$, but the single function we need to compute, namely f_P, is easier to compute than $f_{\phi(Q)}$ since one can work over $\mathbb{F}_q$ instead of $\mathbb{F}_{q^k}$. These facts together make computing the Tate pairing around fifty percent more efficient than the Weil pairing. On the other hand the value of the Tate pairing has to be raised to the power of $(q^\alpha - 1)/l$ to obtain the final result, and $f_{\phi(Q)}$ can be computed as $\phi(f_Q)$ using much more operations over $\mathbb{F}_q$ than over $\mathbb{F}_{q^k}$.

Supersingular Elliptic Curves

Only supersingular elliptic curves provide non $\mathbb{F}_q$-rational endomorphisms. The following table lists the essential examples, the parameter α and a non $\mathbb{F}_q$-rational endomorphism ϕ.

Field	Curve	$\#E$	α	ϕ
$\mathbb{F}_{2^p}$	$y^2 + y = x^3$	$2^p + 1$	2	$(x,y) \rightarrow (x+1, y+x+\xi)$
$\mathbb{F}_{2^p}$	$y^2 + y = x^3 + x$	$2^p + 1 + t_2(p)$	4	$(x,y) \rightarrow (\xi^2 x + \zeta^2, y + \xi^2 \zeta x + \mu)$
$\mathbb{F}_{2^p}$	$y^2 + y = x^3 + x + 1$	$2^p + 1 - t_2(p)$	4	$(x,y) \rightarrow (\xi^2 x + \zeta^2, y + \xi^2 \zeta x + \mu)$
$\mathbb{F}_{3^p}$	$y^2 = x^3 + x$	$3^p + 1$	2	$(x,y) \rightarrow (-x, iy)$
$\mathbb{F}_{3^p}$	$y^2 = x^3 - x + 1$	$3^p + 1 + t_3(p)$	6	$(x,y) \rightarrow (-x + \tau_1, iy)$
$\mathbb{F}_{3^p}$	$y^2 = x^3 - x - 1$	$3^p + 1 - t_3(p)$	6	$(x,y) \rightarrow (-x + \tau_{-1}, iy)$
$\mathbb{F}_p$	$y^2 = x^3 + b$	$p + 1$	2	$(x,y) \rightarrow (\xi x, y)$
$\mathbb{F}_p$	$y^2 = x^3 + ax$	$p + 1$	2	$(x,y) \rightarrow (-x, iy)$

Here p denotes a prime ≥ 5 and

$$t_2(p) = \begin{cases} 2^{(p+1)/2} & \text{for } p \equiv \pm 1, \pm 7 \bmod 24 \equiv \pm 1 \bmod 8, \\ -2^{(p+1)/2} & \text{for } p \equiv \pm 5, \pm 11 \bmod 24 \equiv \pm 3 \bmod 8, \end{cases}$$

$$t_3(p) = \begin{cases} 3^{(p+1)/2} & \text{for } p \equiv \pm 1 \bmod 12, \\ -3^{(p+1)/2} & \text{for } p \equiv \pm 5 \bmod 12. \end{cases}$$

Furthermore, ϕ is a non rational endomorphism with

$$\xi^2 + \xi + 1 = 0, \qquad \zeta^4 + \zeta + \xi + 1 = 0,$$
$$\mu^2 + \mu + \zeta^6 + \zeta^2 = 0, \qquad \tau_s^3 - \tau_s - s = 0,$$

and $i^2 + 1 = 0$. In order that $\xi \notin \mathbb{F}_p$ we need $p \equiv 2 \bmod 3$ and for $i \notin \mathbb{F}_p$ we need $p \equiv 3 \bmod 4$.

The Group Diffie-Hellman Problems

Emmanuel Bresson[1], Olivier Chevassut[2,3], and David Pointcheval[1]

[1] École normale supérieure, 75230 Paris Cedex 05, France
{Emmanuel.Bresson,David.Pointcheval}@ens.fr,
http://www.di.ens.fr/~{bresson,pointche}.
[2] Lawrence Berkeley National Laboratory, Berkeley, CA 94720, USA,
OChevassut@lbl.gov.,
http://www.itg.lbl.gov/~chevassu.
[3] Université Catholique de Louvain, 31348 Louvain-la-Neuve, Belgium.

Abstract. In this paper we study generalizations of the Diffie-Hellman problems recently used to construct cryptographic schemes for practical purposes. The *Group Computational* and the *Group Decisional Diffie-Hellman assumptions* not only enable one to construct efficient pseudo-random functions but also to naturally extend the Diffie-Hellman protocol to allow more than two parties to agree on a secret key. In this paper we provide results that add to our confidence in the GCDH problem. We reach this aim by showing exact relations among the GCDH, GDDH, CDH and DDH problems.

1 Introduction

The theoretical concepts of public-key cryptography go back to Diffie and Hellman in 1976 [11] whereas the first public-key cryptosystem appeared only two years later to Rivest, Shamir and Adleman [14]. In their seminal paper *New Directions in Cryptography*, Diffie and Hellman provided a method whereby two principals communicating over an insecure network can agree on a secret key: a key that a (computationally bounded) adversary cannot recover by only eavesdropping on the flows exchanged between the two principals.

Given a prime order cyclic group $\mathbb{G}$ and a generator g, the Diffie-Hellman protocol works as follows. Two principals U_1, U_2 first pick at random $x_1, x_2 \in [1, |\mathbb{G}|]$ and exchange the values g^{x_1}, g^{x_2} over the network. Principal U_1 (U_2 resp.) then computes the Diffie-Hellman secret $g^{x_1 x_2}$ upon receiving the flow from principal U_2 (U_1 resp.). The motivation for running this protocol is to use the Diffie-Hellman secret as input of key derivation function mapping elements of the cyclic group to the space of either a MAC and/or a symmetric cipher.

The security of Diffie-Hellman schemes has thus far been based on two intractability assumptions. Schemes analyzed in the random-oracle model [4] generally rely on the *Computational Diffie-Hellman assumption* (CDH-assumption) which states that given the two values g^{x_1} and g^{x_2} a computationally bounded adversary cannot recover the Diffie-Hellman secret $g^{x_1 x_2}$ [2,3]. Strong security for schemes analyzed in the standard model usually relies on a stronger assumption

K. Nyberg and H. Heys (Eds.): SAC 2002, LNCS 2595, pp. 325–338, 2003.

than the CDH one [3,15], the so-called *Decisional Diffie-Hellman assumption* (DDH-assumption). It states that given g^{x_1} and g^{x_2} a computationally bounded adversary cannot distinguish the Diffie-Hellman secret $g^{x_1 x_2}$ from a random element g^r in the group. This latter assumption is also useful to prove the security of ElGamal-based encryption schemes [12,10].

With the advance of multicast communication the Diffie-Hellman method has been extended to allow more than two principals to agree on a secret key [17]. In the case of three parties, for example, each principal picks at random a value $x_i \in [1, |\mathbb{G}|]$ and they exchange the set of values $g^{x_i}, g^{x_i x_j}$, for $1 \leq i < j \leq 3$, to compute the common group Diffie-Hellman secret $g^{x_1 x_2 x_3}$.

The security of group Diffie-Hellman schemes has thus far been based on generalizations of the Diffie-Hellman assumptions. Schemes analyzed in the random-oracle model [4] have been proved secure under the *Group Computational Diffie-Hellman assumption* (GCDH-assumption) which states that given the values $g^{\prod x_i}$, for *some* choice of proper subsets of $\{1, \ldots, n\}$, a computationally bounded adversary cannot recover the group Diffie-Hellman secret [6,7,9]. This assumption has also found application in the context of pseudo-random functions [13]. Schemes for group Diffie-Hellman key exchange analyzed without the random-oracle model achieve strong security guarantees under the *Group Decisional Diffie-Hellman assumption* (GDDH-assumption) which states that given the values $g^{\prod x_i}$ the adversary cannot distinguish the group Diffie-Hellman secret from a random element in the group [8].

Motivated by the increasing applications of the group Diffie-Hellman assumptions to cryptography we have studied their validity. Although we cannot prove the equivalence between the CDH and the GCDH in this paper, we are able to show that the GCDH can be considered to be a standard assumption. We reach this aim by relating the GCDH to both the CDH-assumption and the DDH-assumption. The GCDH was furthermore believed to be a weaker assumption than the GDDH but it was not proved until now. In this paper we prove this statement by comparing the quality of the reduction we obtain for the GCDH and the one we carry out to relate the GDDH to the DDH. The results we obtain in this paper add to our confidence in the GCDH-assumption.

This paper is organized as follows. In Section 2 we summarize the related work. In Section 3 we formally define the group Diffie-Hellman assumptions. In Section 4 we show the relationship between the GDDH and the DDH. In Section 5 we carry out a similar treatment to relate the GCDH to both the CDH and DDH.

2   Related Work

The *Generalized* GDDH-assumption, defined in terms of the values $g^{\prod x_i}$ formed from *all* the proper subsets of $\{1, \ldots, n\}$, first appeared in the literature in the paper by Steiner et al. [17]. They exhibited an asymptotic reduction to show that the DDH-assumption implies the *Generalized* GDDH-assumption. In his PhD thesis [16], Steiner later quantified this reduction and showed that relating the *Generalized* GDDH problem to the DDH problem leads to very inefficient reductions, especially because a *Generalized* GDDH instance is exponentially large.

In practice, it is fortunately possible to improve on the quality of the reductions since only some of the proper subsets of indices are used in the key exchange protocol flows. These are special forms of the *Generalized* GDDH or even the *Generalized* GCDH. To prove secure protocols for static group Diffie-Hellman key exchange [6,9], we used the special structure of basic trigon (see Figure 1). To prove secure protocols for dynamic group Diffie-Hellman key exchange [7,8], we used the special structure of extended basic trigon (see Figure 2).

The first attempts to relate the *Generalized* GCDH to the CDH is due to Biham et al. [1]. Their results gave some confidence in the *Generalized* GCDH in the multiplicative group $\mathbb{Z}_n^*$ (where n is composite) by relating it to factoring, but our group DH key exchange schemes [6,7,8,9] use large groups of known prime order so that the proofs can benefit from the multiplicative random self-reducibility (see below). Therefore in this paper we focus on this latter case only.

3   Complexity Assumptions

This section presents the group Diffie-Hellman assumptions by first introducing the notion of group Diffie-Hellman distribution and using it to define the group computational Diffie-Hellman assumption (GCDH-assumption) and the group decisional Diffie-Hellman assumption (GDDH-assumption). For the remainder of the paper we fix a cyclic group $\mathbb{G} = \langle g \rangle$ of prime order q.

3.1   Group Diffie-Hellman Distribution

The group Diffie-Hellman distribution (GDH-distribution) of size an integer n is the set of elements $g^{\prod_{j \in J} x_j}$ for some proper subsets $J \subsetneq I_n = \{1, .., n\}$. We formally write it using the set $\mathcal{P}(I_n)$ of all subsets of I_n and any subset Γ_n of $\mathcal{P}(I_n) \backslash \{I_n\}$, as follows:

$$\mathsf{GDH}_{\Gamma_n} = \{ \mathcal{D}_{\Gamma_n}(x_1, \ldots, x_n) \,|\, x_1, \ldots, x_n \in_R \mathbb{Z}_q \},$$

where

$$\mathcal{D}_{\Gamma_n}(x_1, \ldots, x_n) = \left\{ \left(J, g^{\prod_{j \in J} x_j} \right) \,\Big|\, J \in \Gamma_n \right\}.$$

Since this distribution is a function of the parameters n and Γ_n it could be instantiated with any of the following special forms:

- If $n = 2$ and $\Gamma_2 = \{\{1\}, \{2\}\}$, the GDH-distribution is the usual Diffie-Hellman distribution.
- If Γ_n has the following triangular structure $\mathcal{T}_n$, the GDH-distribution is the basic trigon depicted in Figure 1:

$$\mathcal{T}_n = \bigcup_{1 \le j \le n} \left\{ \{i \,|\, 1 \le i \le j, i \ne k\} \,|\, 1 \le k \le j \right\}$$

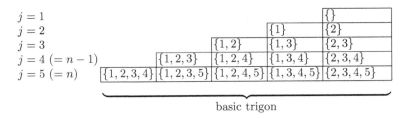

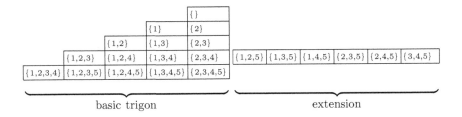

Fig. 1. Basic GDH-distribution (Example when $n = 5$ and $\Gamma_n = \mathcal{T}_5$)

- If Γ_n has the following structure $\mathcal{E}_n$, the GDH-distribution is the extended trigon depicted in Figure 2:

$$\mathcal{E}_n = \bigcup_{1 \le j \le n-2} \big\{ \{i \mid 1 \le i \le j, i \ne l\} \mid 1 \le l \le j \big\}$$

$$\bigcup \big\{ \{i \mid 1 \le i \le n, i \ne k, l\} \mid 1 \le k, l \le n \big\}$$

Fig. 2. Extended GDH-distribution (Example when $n = 5$ and $\Gamma_n = \mathcal{E}_5$)

- If $\Gamma_n = \mathcal{P}(I_n) \backslash \{I_n\}$, the GDH-distribution is the *Generalized* GDH-distribution since we have *all* the proper subsets of $\{1, \ldots, n\}$.

The γ function denotes the cardinality of any structure Γ:

- For $\mathcal{T}_n$, we have $\tau_n = \gamma(\mathcal{T}_n) = \sum_{i=1}^{n} i = n(n+1)/2$ since the i-th "line" of this structure has exactly i elements.
- And the cardinality of $\mathcal{E}_n$ is $\varepsilon_n = \gamma(\mathcal{E}_n) = \gamma(\mathcal{T}_n) + \binom{n-2}{n} - n + 1 = n^2 - n + 1$ since the extension of the $n-1$-th line of this structure has exactly $\binom{n-2}{n} - (n-1)$ elements.
- It is also worthwhile to mention that the cardinality of the *Generalized* one is $2^n - 2$.

The later is exponential in n, while the two others are quadratic.

3.2   Good Structure Families

For any indexed structure $\Gamma = \{\Gamma_n\}$, we consider an auxiliary structure $\hat{\Gamma} = \{\hat{\Gamma}_n\}$, where $\hat{\Gamma}_n$ is built from the set $\{0, 3, \ldots, n+1\}$ in the same way Γ_n is built from the set I_n through the map $1 \to 0,\ 2 \to 3,\ \ldots,\ n \to n+1$.

Definition 1 (Good Structure Family). *A family $\Gamma = \{\Gamma_n\}$ is **good** if for any integer n greater than 3 the following four conditions are satisfied:*

1. $\forall J \in \Gamma_n, \{1, 2\} \subseteq J \Rightarrow J_{12} \cup \{0\} \in \hat{\Gamma}_{n-1}$
2. $\forall J \in \Gamma_n, 1 \notin J, 2 \in J \Rightarrow J_2 \in \hat{\Gamma}_{n-1}$
3. $\forall J \in \Gamma_n, 1 \in J, 2 \notin J \Rightarrow J_1 \in \hat{\Gamma}_{n-1}$
4. $\forall J \in \Gamma_n, 1 \notin J, 2 \notin J \Rightarrow J \in \hat{\Gamma}_{n-1}$

where for any J, we denote by J_1, J_2 and J_{12} the sets $J\backslash\{1\}$, $J\backslash\{2\}$ and $J\backslash\{1, 2\}$ respectively.

In other words, this means that

$$\Gamma_n \subseteq \left\{ J_0 \cup \{1, 2\} \,\middle|\, J \in \hat{\Gamma}_{n-1}, 0 \in J \right\} \bigcup \left\{ J \cup \{2\}, J \cup \{1\}, J \,\middle|\, J \in \hat{\Gamma}_{n-1}, 0 \notin J \right\},$$

where for any J, we denote by J_0 the set $J\backslash\{0\}$.

Note 2. The basic trigon $\mathcal{T} = \{\mathcal{T}_n\}$ and extended trigon $\mathcal{E} = \{\mathcal{E}_n\}$ are *good structure families.*

3.3   Group Diffie-Hellman Assumptions

Definition 3 (The Group Computational Diffie-Hellman assumption). *A (T, ε)-GCDH$_{\Gamma_n}$-attacker in $\mathbb{G}$ is a probabilistic Turing machine Δ running in time T such that*

$$\mathsf{Succ}_{\mathbb{G}}^{\mathrm{gcdh}\,\Gamma_n}(\Delta) = \Pr_{x_i}\left[\Delta(\mathcal{D}_{\Gamma_n}(x_1, \ldots, x_n)) = g^{x_1 \cdots x_n}\right] \geq \varepsilon.$$

*The GCDH$_{\Gamma_n}$-problem is (T, ε)-**intractable** if there is no (T, ε)-GCDH$_{\Gamma_n}$-attacker in $\mathbb{G}$. The GCDH$_\Gamma$-assumption states this is the case for all polynomial T and non-negligible ε, for a family $\Gamma = \{\Gamma_n\}$.*

Let us define two additional distributions from the GDH-distribution:

$$\mathsf{GDH}_{\Gamma_n}^{\star} = \left\{ \mathcal{D}_{\Gamma_n}^{\star}(x_1, \ldots, x_n) \,|\, x_1, \ldots, x_n \in_R \mathbb{Z}_q \right\},$$

$$\mathsf{GDH}_{\Gamma_n}^{\$} = \left\{ \mathcal{D}_{\Gamma_n}^{\$}(x_1, \ldots, x_n, r) \,|\, x_1, \ldots, x_n, r \in_R \mathbb{Z}_q \right\},$$

where

$$\mathcal{D}_{\Gamma_n}^{\star}(x_1, \ldots, x_n) = \mathcal{D}_{\Gamma_n}(x_1, \ldots, x_n) \cup \{(I_n, g^{x_1 \cdots x_n})\}$$

$$\mathcal{D}_{\Gamma_n}^{\$}(x_1, \ldots, x_n, r) = \mathcal{D}_{\Gamma_n}(x_1, \ldots, x_n) \cup \{(I_n, g^r)\}$$

A GDDH$_{\Gamma_n}$-distinguisher in $\mathbb{G}$ is a probabilistic Turing machine trying to distinguish GDH$_{\Gamma_n}^{\star}$ from GDH$_{\Gamma_n}^{\$}$.

Definition 4 (The Group Decisional Diffie-Hellman assumption). *A (T, ε)-GDDH$_{\Gamma_n}$-distinguisher in $\mathbb{G}$ is a probabilistic Turing machine Δ running in time T such that its advantage $\mathsf{Adv}_{\mathbb{G}}^{\mathsf{gddh}_{\Gamma_n}}(\Delta)$ defined by*

$$\left| \Pr_{x_i}\left[\Delta\big(\mathcal{D}_{\Gamma_n}^{\star}(x_1, \ldots, x_n)\big) = 1\right] - \Pr_{x_i, r}\left[\Delta\big(\mathcal{D}_{\Gamma_n}^{\$}(x_1, \ldots, x_n, r)\big) = 1\right] \right|$$

is greater than ε.
The GDDH$_{\Gamma_n}$-*problem is (T, ε)-**intractable** if there is no (T, ε)-GDDH$_{\Gamma_n}$-distinguisher in $\mathbb{G}$. The* GDDH$_{\Gamma}$-*assumption states this is the case for all polynomial T and non-negligible ε, for a family $\Gamma = \{\Gamma_n\}$.*

3.4   The Random Self-Reducibility

The Diffie-Hellman problems have the nice property of random self-reducibility. Certainly the most common is the additive random self-reducibility, which works as follows. Given, for example, a GCDH-instance $\mathcal{D} = (g^a, g^b, g^c, g^{ab}, g^{bc}, g^{ac})$ for any a, b, c it is possible to generate a random instance

$$\mathcal{D}' = (g^{(a+\alpha)}, g^{(b+\beta)}, g^{(c+\gamma)}, g^{(a+\alpha).(b+\beta)}, g^{(b+\beta).(c+\gamma)}, g^{(a+\alpha).(c+\gamma)})$$

where α, β and γ are random numbers in $\mathbb{Z}_q$, whose solution may help us to solve $\mathcal{D}$. Indeed, given the solution $z = g^{(a+\alpha).(b+\beta).(c+\gamma)}$ to the instance $\mathcal{D}'$ it is possible to recover the solution g^{abc} to the random instance $\mathcal{D}$ (i.e. $g^{abc} = z(g^{ab})^{-\gamma}(g^{ac})^{-\beta}(g^{bc})^{-\alpha}(g^a)^{-\beta\gamma}(g^b)^{-\alpha\gamma}(g^c)^{-\alpha\beta}g^{-\alpha\beta\gamma}$). However the cost of such a computation may be high; furthermore it is easily seen that such a reduction works for the *Generalized* DH-distribution only and thus its cost increases exponentially with the size of $\mathcal{D}$.

On the other hand, the multiplicative random self-reducibility works for any form of the GDH-problems in a prime order cyclic group. Given, for example, a GCDH-instance $\mathcal{D} = (g^a, g^b, g^{ab}, g^{ac})$ for any a, b, c it is easy to generate a random instance $\mathcal{D}' = (g^{a\alpha}, g^{b\beta}, g^{ab\alpha\beta}, g^{ac\alpha\gamma})$ where α, β and γ are random numbers in $\mathbb{Z}_q^*$. And given the solution K' to the instance $\mathcal{D}'$, we directly get the solution $K = K'^{\delta}$, where $\delta = (\alpha\beta\gamma)^{-1} \bmod q$, to the instance $\mathcal{D}$. Such a reduction is efficient and only requires a linear number of modular exponentiations.

4   The Group Decisional Diffie-Hellman Problem

In this section we provide a reduction of the Decisional Diffie-Hellman (DDH) problem to the group Decisional Diffie-Hellman (GDDH) problem, but for the good structure families only.

4.1   The Main Result

Theorem 5. *Let $\mathbb{G}$ be a cyclic multiplicative group of prime order q and $t_{\mathbb{G}}$ the time needed for an exponentiation in $\mathbb{G}$. For any integer n and any good structure family $\Gamma = \{\Gamma_n\}$ of cardinality $\gamma = \{\gamma_n\}$, we have:*

$$\mathsf{Adv}_{\mathbb{G}}^{\mathsf{gddh}\,\Gamma_n}(t) \leq (2n-3)\mathsf{Adv}_{\mathbb{G}}^{\mathsf{ddh}}(t') \;\; where \; t' \leq t + t_{\mathbb{G}} \sum_{i=3}^{n} \gamma_i.$$

The proof of this theorem results, by induction, from the following two lemmas 6 and 7 which lead to

$$\mathsf{Adv}_{\mathbb{G}}^{\mathsf{gddh}\,\Gamma_n}(t) \leq \mathsf{Adv}_{\mathbb{G}}^{\mathsf{gddh}\,\Gamma_{n-1}}(t + \gamma_n t_{\mathbb{G}}) + 2\mathsf{Adv}_{\mathbb{G}}^{\mathsf{ddh}}(t + \gamma_n t_{\mathbb{G}}).$$

However before to prove it let's plug in some numerical values for the time of computation:

- for the structure of basic trigon $\mathcal{T}_n$, the time t' is less than $t + n^3 t_{\mathbb{G}}/3$;
- for the structure of extended trigon $\mathcal{E}_n$, the time t' is less than $t + 2n^3 t_{\mathbb{G}}/3$.

For proving this result, we need to alter Group Diffie-Hellman tuples, introducing some randomness. This leads to the *group random distributions* (the *group random adversaries* resp.) where some elements are independently random in the *group Diffie-Hellman distributions* (the *group Diffie-Hellman problems* resp.).

4.2 Group Random Distributions

Let us split in two parts instances $\mathcal{D}_{\Gamma_n}(x_1, \ldots, x_n)$:

$$= \left\{ \left(J, g^{\prod_{j \in J} x_j} \right) \Big| J \in \Gamma_n, \{1,2\} \not\subseteq J \right\} \cup \left\{ \left(J, g^{\prod_{j \in J} x_j} \right) \Big| J \in \Gamma_n, \{1,2\} \subseteq J \right\}$$

$$= \left\{ \left(J, g^{\prod_{j \in J} x_j} \right) \Big| \{1,2\} \not\subseteq J \right\} \cup \left\{ \left(J, g^{x_1 x_2 \prod_{j \in J_{12}} x_j} \right) \Big| \{1,2\} \subseteq J \right\}.$$

We can now define an additional distribution:

$$\mathsf{GR}_{\Gamma_n} = \left\{ \mathcal{V}_{\Gamma_n}(x_1, \ldots, x_n, \alpha) \,|\, x_1, \ldots, x_n, \alpha \in_R \mathbb{Z}_q \right\},$$

where

$$\mathcal{V}_{\Gamma_n}(x_1, \ldots, x_n, \alpha) = \left\{ \left(J, g^{\prod_{j \in J} x_j} \right) \Big| J \in \Gamma_n, \{1,2\} \not\subseteq J \right\}$$
$$\bigcup \left\{ \left(J, g^{\alpha \prod_{j \in J_{12}} x_j} \right) \Big| J \in \Gamma_n, \{1,2\} \subseteq J \right\}.$$

Similarly to above, we define $\mathcal{V}_{\Gamma_n}^{\star}(x_1, \ldots, x_n, \alpha)$ and $\mathcal{V}_{\Gamma_n}^{\$}(x_1, \ldots, x_n, \alpha, r)$, the extensions of $\mathcal{V}_{\Gamma_n}(x_1, \ldots, x_n, \alpha)$ where one appends $\{(I_n, g^{\alpha x_3 \cdots x_n})\}$ and $\{(I_n, g^r)\}$ respectively. Then,

$$\mathsf{GR}_{\Gamma_n}^{\star} = \left\{ \mathcal{V}_{\Gamma_n}^{\star}(x_1, \ldots, x_n, \alpha) \,|\, x_1, \ldots, x_n, \alpha \in_R \mathbb{Z}_q \right\},$$
$$\mathsf{GR}_{\Gamma_n}^{\$} = \left\{ \mathcal{V}_{\Gamma_n}^{\$}(x_1, \ldots, x_n, \alpha, r) \,|\, x_1, \ldots, x_n, \alpha, r \in_R \mathbb{Z}_q \right\}.$$

We note that under the constraint $\alpha = x_1 x_2$, for any $x_1, \ldots, x_n, r \in_R \mathbb{Z}_q$, one has,

$$\mathcal{V}_{\Gamma_n}(x_1, \ldots, x_n, \alpha) = \mathcal{D}_{\Gamma_n}(x_1, \ldots, x_n)$$
$$\mathcal{V}_{\Gamma_n}^{\star}(x_1, \ldots, x_n, \alpha) = \mathcal{D}_{\Gamma_n}^{\star}(x_1, \ldots, x_n)$$
$$\mathcal{V}_{\Gamma_n}^{\$}(x_1, \ldots, x_n, \alpha, r) = \mathcal{D}_{\Gamma_n}^{\$}(x_1, \ldots, x_n, r)$$

and thus,

$$\mathsf{GR}_{\Gamma_n} \equiv \mathsf{GDH}_{\Gamma_n} \quad \mathsf{GR}^\star_{\Gamma_n} \equiv \mathsf{GDH}^\star_{\Gamma_n} \quad \mathsf{GR}^\$_{\Gamma_n} \equiv \mathsf{GDH}^\$_{\Gamma_n}.$$

4.3   Group Random Adversaries

A (T, ε)-GCR_{Γ_n}-attacker in $\mathbb{G}$ is a probabilistic Turing machine Δ running in time T such that

$$\mathsf{Succ}_{\mathbb{G}}^{\mathsf{gcr}\,\Gamma_n}(\Delta) = \Pr_{x_i, \alpha}\left[\Delta(\mathcal{V}_{\Gamma_n}(x_1, \ldots, x_n, \alpha)) = g^{\alpha x_3 \cdots x_n}\right] \geq \varepsilon.$$

A (T, ε)-GDR_{Γ_n}-distinguisher in $\mathbb{G}$ is a probabilistic Turing machine Δ running in time T such that its advantage $\mathsf{Adv}_{\mathbb{G}}^{\mathsf{gdr}\,\Gamma_n}(\Delta)$ defined by

$$\left| \Pr_{x_i, \alpha}\left[\Delta(\mathcal{V}^\star_{\Gamma_n}(x_1, \ldots, x_n, \alpha)) = 1\right] - \Pr_{x_i, \alpha, r}\left[\Delta(\mathcal{V}^\$_{\Gamma_n}(x_1, \ldots, x_n, \alpha, r)) = 1\right] \right|$$

is greater than ε.

4.4   Proof

Lemma 6. *For any integer n and any structure Γ_n, we have*

$$\mathsf{Adv}_{\mathbb{G}}^{\mathsf{gddh}\,\Gamma_n}(t) \leq \mathsf{Adv}_{\mathbb{G}}^{\mathsf{gdr}\,\Gamma_n}(t) + 2\mathsf{Adv}_{\mathbb{G}}^{\mathsf{ddh}}(t + \gamma_n t_{\mathbb{G}}).$$

Proof. We consider an adversary $\mathcal{A}$ against the GDDH_{Γ_n} problem. Such an adversary, on input a distribution depending on a bit b, replies with a bit b' which is a guess for b. We assume that $\mathcal{A}$ runs in maximal time t, in particular it always terminates, even if the input comes from neither $\mathsf{GDH}^\star_{\Gamma_n}$ nor from $\mathsf{GDH}^\$_{\Gamma_n}$. Then we define the following two games: $\mathbf{G}_0$, $\mathbf{G}_1$ and consider the event S_i in game $\mathbf{G}_i$ as $b = b'$.

Game $\mathbf{G}_0$. In this game, we are given a Diffie-Hellman triple $(A, B, C) = (g^{x_1}, g^{x_2}, g^{x_1 x_2})$. Then we choose at random $(x_3, \ldots, x_n)$ in $\mathbb{Z}_q^*$ and compute a tuple U_n which follows the distribution GDH_{Γ_n}, as follows

$$\mathsf{U}_n = \left\{ \left(J, g^{\prod_{j \in J} x_j}\right) \middle| J \in \Gamma_n, 1 \notin J, 2 \notin J \right\}$$
$$\bigcup \left\{ \left(J, A^{\prod_{j \in J_1} x_j}\right) \middle| J \in \Gamma_n, 1 \in J, 2 \notin J \right\}$$
$$\bigcup \left\{ \left(J, B^{\prod_{j \in J_2} x_j}\right) \middle| J \in \Gamma_n, 1 \notin J, 2 \in J \right\}$$
$$\bigcup \left\{ \left(J, C^{\prod_{j \in J_{12}} x_j}\right) \middle| J \in \Gamma_n, \{1, 2\} \subseteq J \right\}.$$

Then if $b = 1$, one appends to U_n the value $C^{x_3 \cdots x_n}$; and if $b = 0$, one appends to U_n a value g^r, where r is a random exponent: the computed tuple follows exactly the distribution $\mathsf{GDH}^\star_{\Gamma_n}$ (resp. $\mathsf{GDH}^\$_{\Gamma_n}$) if $b = 1$ (resp. $b = 0$). Thus by definition, if we feed the attacker $\mathcal{A}$ with this tuple, we have

$$\Pr[S_0] = \frac{\mathsf{Adv}_{\mathbb{G}}^{\mathsf{gddh}\,\Gamma_n}(\mathcal{A}) + 1}{2}.$$

Game G_1. Game G_1 is the same as game G_0 except that we are given a tuple $(A, B, C) = (g^{x_1}, g^{x_2}, g^\alpha)$, where α is a random exponent. It is easy to see that the tuple given to the attacker $\mathcal{A}$ follows the distribution $\mathsf{GR}^\star_{\Gamma_n}$ (resp. $\mathsf{GR}^\$_{\Gamma_n}$) if $b = 1$ (resp. $b = 0$). Then,

$$\Pr[S_1] = \frac{\mathsf{Adv}_{\mathbb{G}}^{\mathsf{gdr}\,\Gamma_n}(\mathcal{A}) + 1}{2} \le \frac{\mathsf{Adv}_{\mathbb{G}}^{\mathsf{gdr}\,\Gamma_n}(t) + 1}{2}.$$

Also, the difference in the probability distributions in the two games is upper-bounded by:

$$\Pr[S_0] \le \Pr[S_1] + \mathsf{Adv}_{\mathbb{G}}^{\mathsf{ddh}}(t + \gamma_n t_{\mathbb{G}}).$$

The lemma follows. $\qquad\square$

Lemma 7. *For any good structure family $\Gamma = \{\Gamma_n\}$ and any integer n, we have*

$$\mathsf{Adv}_{\mathbb{G}}^{\mathsf{gdr}\,\Gamma_n}(t) \le \mathsf{Adv}_{\mathbb{G}}^{\mathsf{gddh}\,\Gamma_{n-1}}(t + \gamma_n t_{\mathbb{G}}).$$

Proof. We consider a GDR_{Γ_n}-distinguisher $\mathcal{A}$ running in time t and we use it to built a $\mathsf{GDDH}_{\Gamma_{n-1}}$-distinguisher. To reach that goal, we receive as input a tuple drawn from either $\mathsf{GDH}^\star_{\Gamma_{n-1}}$ or $\mathsf{GDH}^\$_{\Gamma_{n-1}}$. We use $\mathcal{A}$ to guess the underlying bit b. In the given tuple, we denote by (I_{n-1}, u_{n-1}) the last value and by U_{n-1} the first values of this input tuple:

$$\mathsf{U}_{n-1} = \left\{ \left(J, g^{\prod_{j \in J} x_j}\right) \Big| J \in \Gamma_{n-1} \right\} = \mathcal{D}_{\Gamma_{n-1}}(x_1, \ldots, x_{n-1}) \in \mathsf{GDH}_{\Gamma_{n-1}}$$

$$u_{n-1} = g^{x_1 \cdots x_{n-1}} \text{ if } b = 1, \text{ or } g^r \text{ if } b = 0.$$

We split the tuple U_{n-1} in two blocks, depending whether $1 \in J$:

$$\mathsf{U}_{n-1} = \left\{ \left(J, g^{x_1 \prod_{j \in J_1} x_j}\right) \Big| J \in \Gamma_{n-1}, 1 \in J \right\} \cup \left\{ \left(J, g^{\prod_{j \in J} x_j}\right) \Big| J \in \Gamma_{n-1}, 1 \notin J \right\}.$$

Now we write this tuple by renaming the variables $x_1, \ldots, x_{n-1}$ to be respectively $X_0, X_3, \ldots, X_n$. It then follows that the elements of U_{n-1} are indexed by the elements of $\hat{\Gamma}_{n-1}$ rather than Γ_{n-1}:

$$\left\{ \left(J, g^{X_0 \prod_{j \in J_0} X_j}\right) \Big| J \in \hat{\Gamma}_{n-1}, 0 \in J \right\} \cup \left\{ \left(J, g^{\prod_{j \in J} X_j}\right) \Big| J \in \hat{\Gamma}_{n-1}, 0 \notin J \right\}.$$

Now we pick at random two values X_1, X_2 in $\mathbb{Z}_q^\star$ and use them to construct the following tuple, in which the last block in the above equation is split in the last three blocks of W_{n-1}:

$$\mathsf{W}_{n-1} = \left\{ \left(J, g^{X_0 \prod_{j \in J_0} X_j}\right) \Big| J \in \hat{\Gamma}_{n-1}, 0 \in J \right\}$$
$$\cup \left\{ \left(J, g^{X_2 \prod_{j \in J} X_j}\right) \Big| J \in \hat{\Gamma}_{n-1}, 0 \notin J \right\}$$
$$\cup \left\{ \left(J, g^{X_1 \prod_{j \in J} X_j}\right) \Big| J \in \hat{\Gamma}_{n-1}, 0 \notin J \right\}$$
$$\cup \left\{ \left(J, g^{\prod_{j \in J} X_j}\right) \Big| J \in \hat{\Gamma}_{n-1}, 0 \notin J \right\}.$$

Remember that Γ is a "good" structure family:

$$\Gamma_n \subseteq \left\{ J_0 \cup \{1,2\} \,\middle|\, J \in \hat{\Gamma}_{n-1}, 0 \in J \right\} \bigcup \left\{ J \cup \{2\}, J \cup \{1\}, J \,\middle|\, J \in \hat{\Gamma}_{n-1}, 0 \notin J \right\}.$$

Then one can build the following tuple V_n which is also included in W_{n-1}:

$$V_n = \left\{ \left(J, g^{X_0 \prod_{j \in J_{12}} X_j} \right) \,\middle|\, J \in \Gamma_n, \{1,2\} \subseteq J \right\}$$
$$\bigcup \left\{ \left(J, g^{\prod_{j \in J} X_j} \right) \,\middle|\, J \in \Gamma_n, \{1,2\} \not\subseteq J \right\}.$$

We note that

$$V_n = \mathcal{V}_{\Gamma_n}(X_1, \ldots, X_n, X_0) \in \mathsf{GR}_{\Gamma_n}.$$

Then V_n is appended (I_n, u_{n-1}) and given to $\mathcal{A}$. The latter returns a bit b' that we relay back as an answer to the original $\mathrm{GDDH}_{\Gamma_{n-1}}$ problem. The computation time needed to properly generate V_n from the input U_{n-1} is at most $\gamma_n t_{\mathbb{G}}$.

Thus, we have

$$\mathsf{Adv}_{\mathbb{G}}^{\mathrm{gddh}\,\Gamma_{n-1}}(t + \gamma_n t_{\mathbb{G}}) \geq \mathsf{Adv}_{\mathbb{G}}^{\mathrm{gdr}\,\Gamma_n}(t).$$

$\square$

Putting all together, we obtain:

$$\mathsf{Adv}_{\mathbb{G}}^{\mathrm{gddh}\,\Gamma_n}(t) \leq \mathsf{Adv}_{\mathbb{G}}^{\mathrm{gdr}\,\Gamma_n}(t) + 2\mathsf{Adv}_{\mathbb{G}}^{\mathrm{ddh}}(t + \gamma_n t_{\mathbb{G}})$$
$$\leq \mathsf{Adv}_{\mathbb{G}}^{\mathrm{gddh}\,\Gamma_{n-1}}(t + \gamma_n t_{\mathbb{G}}) + 2\mathsf{Adv}_{\mathbb{G}}^{\mathrm{ddh}}(t + \gamma_n t_{\mathbb{G}})$$
$$\leq \mathsf{Adv}_{\mathbb{G}}^{\mathrm{ddh}}\left(t + \sum_{i=3}^{n} \gamma_i t_{\mathbb{G}} \right) + 2 \sum_{i=3}^{n} \mathsf{Adv}_{\mathbb{G}}^{\mathrm{ddh}}\left(t + \sum_{j=i}^{n} \gamma_j t_{\mathbb{G}} \right)$$
$$\leq (2n-3)\mathsf{Adv}_{\mathbb{G}}^{\mathrm{ddh}}(t') \text{ where } t' \leq t + t_{\mathbb{G}} \sum_{i=3}^{n} \gamma_i.$$

5   The Group Computational Diffie-Hellman Problem

In this section we show the GCDH is a standard assumption by relating it to both the CDH and the DDH.

Theorem 8. *Let $\mathbb{G}$ be a cyclic multiplicative group of prime order q and $t_{\mathbb{G}}$ the time needed for an exponentiation in $\mathbb{G}$. Then for any integer n and any good structure family $\Gamma = \{\Gamma_n\}$ of cardinality $\gamma = \{\gamma_n\}$ we have:*

$$\mathsf{Succ}_{\mathbb{G}}^{\mathrm{gcdh}\,\Gamma_n}(t) \leq \mathsf{Succ}_{\mathbb{G}}^{\mathrm{cdh}}(t') + (n-2)\mathsf{Adv}_{\mathbb{G}}^{\mathrm{ddh}}(t') \text{ where } t' \leq t + \sum_{i=3}^{n} \gamma_i t_{\mathbb{G}}.$$

As for the previous theorem, the result comes, by induction, from both

$$\mathsf{Succ}_{\mathbb{G}}^{\mathsf{gcdh}\,\Gamma_n}(t) \leq \mathsf{Succ}_{\mathbb{G}}^{\mathsf{gcr}\,\Gamma_n}(t)$$

$$\mathsf{Succ}_{\mathbb{G}}^{\mathsf{gcr}\,\Gamma_n}(t) \leq \mathsf{Succ}_{\mathbb{G}}^{\mathsf{gcdh}\,\Gamma_{n-1}}(t + \gamma_n t_{\mathbb{G}}) + \mathsf{Adv}_{\mathbb{G}}^{\mathsf{ddh}}(t + \gamma_n t_{\mathbb{G}}).$$

Proof. We consider an adversary $\mathcal{A}$ against the GCDH$_{\Gamma_n}$ problem. Such an adversary, on input a tuple drawn from the GDH$_{\Gamma_n}$ distribution, replies with a single value which is a guess for the corresponding secret. We assume that $\mathcal{A}$ runs in maximal time t, in particular it always terminates, even if the input does not come from GDH$_{\Gamma_n}$.

We then define a sequence of games $\mathbf{G}_0$, $\mathbf{G}_1$, ... In each game, given a triple (A, B, C) and $n - 2$ random elements $(x_3, \ldots, x_n)$ in $\mathbb{Z}_q^*$ (which are not necessarily known), we consider S_i as the event that the adversary $\mathcal{A}$ outputs $C^{x_3 \cdots x_n}$.

Game $\mathbf{G}_0$. In this game, we are given a Diffie-Hellman triple $(A, B, C) = (g^{x_1}, g^{x_2}, g^{x_1 x_2})$. Then by randomly choosing $(x_3, \ldots, x_n)$ we can compute:

$$\mathsf{U}_n = \left\{ \left(J, g^{\prod_{j \in J} x_j} \right) \,\middle|\, J \in \Gamma_n, 1 \notin J, 2 \notin J \right\}$$
$$\bigcup \left\{ \left(J, A^{\prod_{j \in J_1} x_j} \right) \,\middle|\, J \in \Gamma_n, 1 \in J, 2 \notin J \right\}$$
$$\bigcup \left\{ \left(J, B^{\prod_{j \in J_2} x_j} \right) \,\middle|\, J \in \Gamma_n, 1 \notin J, 2 \in J \right\}$$
$$\bigcup \left\{ \left(J, C^{\prod_{j \in J_{12}} x_j} \right) \,\middle|\, J \in \Gamma_n, \{1, 2\} \subseteq J \right\}.$$

It is easy to see that $\mathsf{U}_n = \mathcal{D}_{\Gamma_n}(x_1, \ldots, x_n)$, and thus follows exactly the distribution GDH$_{\Gamma_n}$. Then the tuple U_n is provided to the adversary. By definition, since $C^{x_3 \cdots x_n} = g^{x_1 \cdots x_n}$, we have

$$\Pr[S_0] = \mathsf{Succ}_{\mathbb{G}}^{\mathsf{gcdh}\,\Gamma_n}(\mathcal{A}).$$

Game $\mathbf{G}_1$. Game $\mathbf{G}_1$ is the same as game $\mathbf{G}_0$ except that we are given a tuple $(A, B, C) = (g^{x_1}, g^{x_2}, g^{\alpha})$, where α is a random element in $\mathbb{Z}_q^*$. We then perform the same operations as in game $\mathbf{G}_0$ to obtain a tuple which follows the distribution GR$_{\Gamma_n}$: $\mathsf{U}_n = \mathcal{V}_{\Gamma_n}(x_1, \ldots, x_n, \alpha)$. This tuple is provided to the adversary, which computes $g^{\alpha x_3 \cdots x_n}$. By definition, we have:

$$\Pr[S_1] = \mathsf{Succ}_{\mathbb{G}}^{\mathsf{gcr}\,\Gamma_n}(\mathcal{A}) \leq \mathsf{Succ}_{\mathbb{G}}^{\mathsf{gcr}\,\Gamma_n}(t).$$

In both games the computation time needed for generating the tuple from the input a triple (A, B, C) is at most $(\gamma_n - 1) t_{\mathbb{G}}$ where $t_{\mathbb{G}}$ is the time required for an exponentiation in $\mathbb{G}$. Another exponentiation is needed to compute $C^{x_3 \cdots x_n}$. Clearly the computational distance between the games is upper-bounded by $\mathsf{Adv}_{\mathbb{G}}^{\mathsf{ddh}}(t + \gamma_n t_{\mathbb{G}})$, then:

$$\mathsf{Succ}_{\mathbb{G}}^{\mathsf{gcdh}\,\Gamma_n}(\mathcal{A}) \leq \mathsf{Succ}_{\mathbb{G}}^{\mathsf{gcr}\,\Gamma_n}(t) + \mathsf{Adv}_{\mathbb{G}}^{\mathsf{ddh}}(t + \gamma_n t_{\mathbb{G}}).$$

Game G_2. Game G_2 is the same as game G_1 except that we choose x_1 and x_2 by ourselves. Therefore $(A, B, C) = (g^{x_1}, g^{x_2}, g^\alpha)$ where x_1 and x_2 are known, but α is not. The remaining of this game is distributed exactly as in the previous one, so $\Pr[S_2] = \Pr[S_1]$.

Game G_3. Game G_3 is the same as game G_2 except that we do not know the elements $(x_3, \ldots, x_n)$. Instead, we are given an instance U_{n-1} of the GCDH$_{\Gamma_{n-1}}$ problem, built from the (unknown) exponents $(\alpha, x_3, \ldots, x_n)$, where α is the same than the underlying (hidden) exponent in C. By operating as in the previous section, granted the property of good structure family, we can complete the given tuple by using x_1 and x_2 (which are known) to obtain a tuple V_n following the distribution GR$_{\Gamma_n}$.

The variables are distributed exactly as in the previous game, so we have $\Pr[S_3] = \Pr[S_2]$. Note that since we do not know $x_3, \ldots, x_n$, we are no longer able to decide whether the value the adversary outputs is $C^{x_3 \cdots x_n}$. But it is not a problem since the two games are *perfectly* identical.

Anyway, since $C^{x_3 \cdots x_n} = g^{\alpha x_3 \cdots x_n}$ is the Diffie-Hellman secret associated to the given GCDH$_{\Gamma_{n-1}}$ instance, the adversary outputs $C^{x_3 \cdots x_n}$ with probability at most $\mathsf{Succ}_\mathbb{G}^{\mathsf{gcdh}_{\Gamma_{n-1}}}(t + \gamma_n t_\mathbb{G})$:

$$\Pr[S_3] \le \mathsf{Succ}_\mathbb{G}^{\mathsf{gcdh}_{\Gamma_{n-1}}}(t + \gamma_n t_\mathbb{G}).$$

Putting all these together gives us

$$\Pr[S_0] = \mathsf{Succ}_\mathbb{G}^{\mathsf{gcdh}_{\Gamma_n}}(\mathcal{A}) \le \Pr[S_1] + \mathsf{Adv}_\mathbb{G}^{\mathsf{ddh}}(t + \gamma_n t_\mathbb{G})$$

$$\le \Pr[S_3] + \mathsf{Adv}_\mathbb{G}^{\mathsf{ddh}}(t + \gamma_n t_\mathbb{G}) \le \mathsf{Succ}_\mathbb{G}^{\mathsf{gcdh}_{\Gamma_{n-1}}}(t + \gamma_n t_\mathbb{G}) + \mathsf{Adv}_\mathbb{G}^{\mathsf{ddh}}(t + \gamma_n t_\mathbb{G})$$

Since it is true for any adversary running within time t,

$$\mathsf{Succ}_\mathbb{G}^{\mathsf{gcdh}_{\Gamma_n}}(t) \le \mathsf{Succ}_\mathbb{G}^{\mathsf{gcdh}_{\Gamma_{n-1}}}(t + \gamma_n t_\mathbb{G}) + \mathsf{Adv}_\mathbb{G}^{\mathsf{ddh}}(t + \gamma_n t_\mathbb{G}).$$

By induction, it follows:

$$\mathsf{Succ}_\mathbb{G}^{\mathsf{gcdh}_{\Gamma_n}}(t) \le \mathsf{Succ}_\mathbb{G}^{\mathsf{gcdh}_{\Gamma_{n-1}}}(t + \gamma_n t_\mathbb{G}) + \mathsf{Adv}_\mathbb{G}^{\mathsf{ddh}}(t + \gamma_n t_\mathbb{G})$$

$$\le \mathsf{Succ}_\mathbb{G}^{\mathsf{gcdh}_{\Gamma_{n-2}}}(t + (\gamma_n + \gamma_{n-1})t_\mathbb{G})$$

$$+ \mathsf{Adv}_\mathbb{G}^{\mathsf{ddh}}(t + (\gamma_n + \gamma_{n-1})t_\mathbb{G}) + \mathsf{Adv}_\mathbb{G}^{\mathsf{ddh}}(t + \gamma_n t_\mathbb{G})$$

$$\le \cdots$$

$$\le \mathsf{Succ}_\mathbb{G}^{\mathsf{cdh}}\left(t + \sum_{i=3}^{n} \gamma_i t_\mathbb{G}\right) + \sum_{i=3}^{n} \mathsf{Adv}_\mathbb{G}^{\mathsf{ddh}}\left(t + \sum_{j=i}^{n} \gamma_j t_\mathbb{G}\right)$$

$$\le \mathsf{Succ}_\mathbb{G}^{\mathsf{cdh}}(t') + (n-2)\mathsf{Adv}_\mathbb{G}^{\mathsf{ddh}}(t') \quad \text{where } t' \le t + \sum_{i=3}^{n} \gamma_i t_\mathbb{G}.$$

$\square$

6   Conclusion

In this paper, we have shown that breaking the Group Computational Diffie-Hellman problem is at least as hard as breaking either the Computational or Decisional (two-party) Diffie-Hellman problems. This result is particularly relevant in practice since when engineers and programmers choose a protocol for authenticated group Diffie-Hellman key exchange [6,7,8,9] they are ensured that the intractability assumptions underlying the security of this protocol have been deeply studied, and thus, well accepted by the cryptographic community. Furthermore providing implementers with an exact measurement of these relations gives them the ability to compare the security guarantees achieved by the protocol in terms of tightness of the reduction. An open problem is to still show whether breaking the GCDH problem is as hard as breaking the CDH problem.

7   Acknowledgments

The second author was supported by the Director, Office of Science, Office of Advanced Scientific Computing Research, Mathematical Information and Computing Sciences Division, of the U.S. Department of Energy under Contract No. DE-AC03-76SF00098. This document is report LBNL-50775. Disclaimer available at http://www-library.lbl.gov/disclaimer.

References

1. E. Biham, D. Boneh, and O. Reingold. Breaking generalized Diffie-Hellman modulo a composite is no easier than factoring. In *Information Processing Letters (IPL)*, volume 70(2), pages 83–87. Elsevier Science, April 1999.
2. S. Blake-Wilson, D. Johnson, and A. Menezes. Key agreement protocols and their security analysis. In M. Darnell, editor, *Proc. of 6th IMA International Conference on Crypotography and Coding*, volume 1355 of *LNCS*, pages 30–45. Springer-Verlag, 1997.
3. S. Blake-Wilson and A. Menezes. Authenticated Diffie-Hellman key agreement protocols. In H. Meijer and S. Tavares, editors, *Proc. of Selected Areas in Cryptography SAC '98*, volume 1556 of *LNCS*, pages 339–361. Springer-Verlag, August 1998.
4. Bellare, M., Rogaway, P.: Random oracles are practical: a paradigm for designing efficient protocols. In *Proc. of ACM CCS '93*, pages 62–73. ACM Press, November 1993.
5. D. Boneh. The decision Diffie-Hellman problem. In J. P. Buhler, editor, Proc. of the *3rd ANTS Symposium*, volume 1423 of *LNCS*, pages 48–63, Portland, OR, USA, June 1998. Springer-Verlag.
6. E. Bresson, O. Chevassut, D. Pointcheval, and J.-J. Quisquater. Provably authenticated group Diffie-Hellman key exchange. In P. Samarati, editor, *Proc. of ACM CCS '01*, pages 255–264. ACM Press, November 2001.
7. E. Bresson, O. Chevassut, and D. Pointcheval. Provably authenticated group Diffie-Hellman key exchange – the dynamic case. In C. Boyd, editor, *Proc. of Asiacrypt '01*, volume 2248 of *LNCS*, pages 290–309. Springer-Verlag, December 2001. Full Version available at http://www.di.ens.fr/users/pointche.

8. E. Bresson, O. Chevassut, and D. Pointcheval. Dynamic group Diffie-Hellman key exchange under standard assumptions. In L. R. Knudsen, editor, *Proc. of Eurocrypt '02*, volume 2332 of *LNCS*, pages 321–336. Springer-Verlag, May 2002. Full Version available at http://www.di.ens.fr/users/pointche.

9. E. Bresson, O. Chevassut, and D. Pointcheval. Group diffie-hellman key exchange secure against dictionary attacks. In Y. Zheng, editor, *Proc. of Asiacrypt '2002*. Springer, December 2002. Full Version available at http://www.di.ens.fr/users/pointche.

10. R. Cramer and V. Shoup. A practical public key cryptosystem provably secure against adaptive chosen ciphertext attack. In H. Krawczyk, editor, *Proc. of Crypto '98*, volume 1462 of *LNCS*, pages 13–25. Springer-Verlag, August 1998.

11. W. Diffie and M. E. Hellman. New directions in cryptography. *Transactions on Information Theory*, IT-22(6):644–654, November 1976.

12. T. ElGamal. A public key cryptosystem and a signature scheme based on discrete logarithms. In *Proc. of Crypto '84*, LNCS 196, pp. 10–18.

13. M. Naor and O. Reingold. Number-theoretic constructions of efficient pseudo-random functions. In *Proc. of FOCS '97*, pages 458–467. IEEE Computer Society Press, October 1997.

14. R. L. Rivest, A. Shamir, and L. M. Adleman. A method for obtaining digital signatures and public-key cryptosystems. *Communications of the ACM*, 21(2):120–126, February 1978.

15. V. Shoup. On formal models for secure key exchange. Technical Report RZ 3120, IBM Zürich Research Lab, November 1999.

16. M. Steiner, B. Pfitzmann, and M. Waidner. A formal model for multi-party group key agreement. PhD Thesis RZ 3383, IBM Research, April 2002.

17. M. Steiner, G. Tsudik, and M. Waidner. Diffie-Hellman key distribution extended to group communication. In *Proc. of ACM CCS '96*, pages 31–37. ACM Press, March 1996.

Secure Block Ciphers Are Not Sufficient for One-Way Hash Functions in the Preneel-Govaerts-Vandewalle Model

Shoichi Hirose

Graduate School of Informatics, Kyoto University, Kyoto, 606–8501 JAPAN
hirose@i.kyoto-u.ac.jp

Abstract. There are many proposals of unkeyed hash functions based on block ciphers. Preneel, Govaerts and Vandewalle, in their CRYPTO'93 paper, presented the general model of unkeyed hash functions based on block ciphers such that the size of the hashcode is equal to the block size and is almost equal to the key size. In this article, it is shown that, for every unkeyed hash function in their model, there exist block ciphers secure against the adaptive chosen plaintext attack such that the unkeyed hash function based on them is not one-way. The proof is constructive: the secure block ciphers are explicitly defined based on which one-way unkeyed hash functions cannot be constructed. Some of the block ciphers presented are secure even against the adaptive chosen plaintext/ciphertext attack.

1 Introduction

Hash functions are very important primitives in cryptography. Hash functions in cryptography are classified in two types: unkeyed hash functions and keyed hash functions. The former ones are also called manipulation detection codes (MDCs). They are used for message digest in signature schemes. The latter ones are also called message authentication codes (MACs). Excellent surveys are presented in [4,8]. Unkeyed hash functions are discussed in this article.

There are many proposals of unkeyed hash functions. One of the approaches is to construct them based on block ciphers. Some of the proposals following this approach are found in [2,3,6,7]. The main motivation of this approach is the minimization of design and implementation effort, which is supported by the expectation that secure unkeyed hash functions can be constructed from secure block ciphers.

Secure unkeyed hash functions are classified in two types: one-way hash functions and collision resistant hash functions. One-way hash functions are further classified in preimage resistant hash functions and second-preimage resistant hash functions. Informally, preimage resistance means that, given an output, it is infeasible to obtain an input which produces the output. Second-preimage resistance means that, given an input, it is infeasible to obtain another input which produces the same output as the given input. Collision resistance means that it is infeasible to obtain two different inputs which produce the same output.

K. Nyberg and H. Heys (Eds.): SAC 2002, LNCS 2595, pp. 339–352, 2003.

Preneel, Govaerts and Vandewalle studied the unkeyed hash functions based on block ciphers such that the size of the hashcode is equal to the block size and is almost equal to the key size [9]. They presented the general model of such hash functions. There are 64 schemes in their model. Let us call them PGVHFs. They considered the security of all PGVHFs against the existing five important attacks and concluded that 12 schemes are secure assuming that the underlying block cipher is ideal. However, "ideal" means that the block cipher is a keyed random permutation, which is quite impractical in a strict sense.

On the other hand, for collision resistance, Simon's result [10] implies that no provable construction of a collision resistant hash function exists based on a "black box" one-way permutation, which means that the one-way permutation is used as a subroutine, that is, the internal structure is not used. PGVHFs are constructed based on a "black box" block cipher, and a block cipher can be constructed based on a "black box" one-way permutation.

It is still open if there exist any provable one-way PGVHFs based on secure block ciphers. In this article, a negative result is given to this problem. It is shown that, for every PGVHF, there exist block ciphers secure against the adaptive chosen plaintext attack such that the PGVHF based on them is not one-way. Some of the block ciphers presented are secure against the adaptive chosen plaintext/ciphertext attack. The proof is constructive: the secure block ciphers are explicitly defined based on which one-way PGVHFs cannot be constructed. These block ciphers have a small amount of non-randomness. Though the non-randomness cannot be used by adversaries of a block cipher, they can be used to break one-wayness of PGVHFs. Informally, the reason is that block ciphers have a secret input (secret key) randomly chosen, while unkeyed hash functions do not have any secret input.

Actually, it is mentioned, for example in [4], that some kinds of non-randomness of underlying block ciphers such as weak keys or fixed points may facilitate adversarial manipulation of PGVHFs. The contribution of this article is that it shows explicitly that security of block ciphers against the adaptive chosen plaintext(/ciphertext) attack is not sufficient for one-wayness of PGVHFs.

This article is organized as follows. Section 2 gives the definitions and basic notations necessary for subsequent discussions. The main result of this article is presented in Section 3. Further considerations are given in Section 4. Section 5 concludes the article with a few open questions.

2   Preliminaries

Let $\{0,1\}^{\leq k} = \cup_{i=1}^{k}\{0,1\}^{i}$. For $b \in \{0,1\}$, let b^n represent the sequence of n b's. For a $\{0,1\}$-sequence x, let $|x|$ represent the length of x. For two $\{0,1\}$-sequences x, y, let $x \cdot y$ represent the concatenation of x and y. For two $\{0,1\}$-sequences x, y such that $|x| = |y|$, $x \oplus y$ represents bit-wise addition modulo 2.

Let $\mathbb{Z}^+$ be the set of non-negative integers and $\mathbb{R}^+$ be the set of non-negative reals. A function $\varepsilon : \mathbb{Z}^+ \to \mathbb{R}^+$ is said to be negligible, if, for every $c > 0$, there exists some $n_c > 0$ such that $\varepsilon(n) < n^{-c}$ for all $n > n_c$. A function $\sigma : \mathbb{Z}^+ \to \mathbb{R}^+$ is said to be non-negligible if it is not negligible.

2.1   Hash Functions

In this article, unkeyed hash functions are simply called hash functions. A hash function is a function which maps an input of arbitrary length to an output of fixed length.

Definition 1. A function $H = \{h_n \mid h_n : \{0,1\}^{\leq \ell(n)} \to \{0,1\}^n\}$ is called a hash function if

1. $\ell(n) = n^{O(1)}$ and $\ell(n) > n$,
2. the length of the description of h_n is $n^{O(1)}$,
3. there exists a polynomial-time algorithm H such that $\mathsf{H}(1^n, h_n, x) = h_n(x)$ for every $x \in \{0,1\}^{\leq \ell(n)}$. □

The length of the input is polynomially bounded by the length of the output. This is because only polynomially bounded adversary will be considered in the following discussion.

In this article, the description of a function is denoted by its name as in the above definition; the description of the function h_n is also denoted by h_n.

Three kinds of notions are provided with the security of a hash function; preimage resistance, second-preimage resistance, and collision resistance. Informally, preimage resistance means that, given a hash function and its output, it is intractable to find a preimage which produces the output. Second-preimage resistance means that, given a hash function and its input, it is intractable to find another preimage which produces the same output as the given input. Collision resistance means that, given a hash function, it is intractable to find two inputs which produce the same output.

In this article, only preimage resistance and second-preimage resistance are considered. Formal definitions are given below.

Definition 2. A hash function $H = \{h_n \mid h_n : \{0,1\}^{\leq \ell(n)} \to \{0,1\}^n\}$ is preimage resistant if, for every probabilistic polynomial-time algorithm F,

$$\Pr[\mathsf{F}(1^n, h_n, y) = x' \in \{0,1\}^{\leq \ell(n)} \wedge h_n(x') = y]$$

is negligible, where $y = h_n(x)$ such that x is selected uniformly from $\{0,1\}^{\leq \ell(n)}$. The probability is taken over the random selection of x and the random choices of F. □

Definition 3. A hash function $H = \{h_n \mid h_n : \{0,1\}^{\leq \ell(n)} \to \{0,1\}^n\}$ is second-preimage resistant if, for every probabilistic polynomial-time algorithm F,

$$\Pr[\mathsf{F}(1^n, h_n, x) = x' \in \{0,1\}^{\leq \ell(n)} \wedge x' \neq x \wedge h_n(x') = h_n(x)]$$

is negligible, where x is selected uniformly from $\{0,1\}^{\leq \ell(n)}$ and the probability is taken over the random selection of x and the random choices of F. □

A hash function is usually defined with a round function with fixed length of inputs, which is applied to the input iteratively to produce the output. Thus, this kind of hash function is called an iterative hash function.

Definition 4. A hash function $H = \{h_n \mid h_n : \{0,1\}^{\leq \ell(n)} \to \{0,1\}^n\}$ is called an iterative hash function if h_n is specified with

- a round function $f_n : \{0,1\}^n \times \{0,1\}^{m(n)} \to \{0,1\}^n$, where $\ell(n) > m(n) > \lceil \log_2(\ell(n)+1) \rceil$,
- a padding rule Pad, and
- an initial-value generator IV.

A padding rule Pad is a deterministic polynomial-time algorithm which takes 1^n and $x \in \{0,1\}^{\leq \ell(n)}$ and outputs z defined below. It first divides x into $l = \lceil |x|/m(n) \rceil$ blocks $x_1, x_2, \ldots, x_l$ such that $|x_i| = m(n)$ for $i = 1, \ldots, l-1$ and $1 \leq |x_l| \leq m(n)$. Then it outputs $z = (z_1, z_2, \ldots, z_{l+1})$ such that

$$
z_i = \begin{cases} x_i & \text{for } i = 1, 2, \ldots, l-1, \\ x_l \cdot 0^{m(n)-|x_l|} & \text{for } i = l, \\ bin(|x|) & \text{for } i = l+1, \end{cases}
$$

where $bin(|x|)$ is the binary representation of the length of x.

An initial-value generator IV is a deterministic polynomial-time algorithm which takes 1^n for input and outputs $IV \in \{0,1\}^n$.

For $x \in \{0,1\}^{\leq \ell(n)}$, let $z = (z_1, \ldots, z_{l+1})$ be the corresponding padded input. $h_n(x)$ is defined as follows: $h_n(x) = v_{l+1}$, where $v_0 = IV$ and $v_i = f_n(v_{i-1}, z_i)$ for $i = 1, 2, \ldots, l+1$. □

As the padding rule in the above definition, adding a block which contains the length of the input is called MD-strengthening after Merkle [5] and Damgård [1].

For the sake of generality, the initial-value generator is assumed in the above definition. The results presented in the next section is independent of the initial value.

2.2   Block Ciphers

In this article, for block ciphers, it is assumed that the length of a plaintext or a ciphertext is equal to that of the secret key.

Definition 5. A pair of functions $B = (E, D)$ is called a block cipher if

1. $E = \{e_n \mid e_n : \{0,1\}^n \times \{0,1\}^n \to \{0,1\}^n\}$ and for every $k \in \{0,1\}^n$, $e_n(k, \cdot) : \{0,1\}^n \to \{0,1\}^n$ is a one-to-one mapping,
2. $D = \{d_n \mid d_n : \{0,1\}^n \times \{0,1\}^n \to \{0,1\}^n\}$ and for every $k \in \{0,1\}^n$ and $x \in \{0,1\}^n$, $d_n(k, e_n(k, x)) = x$,
3. the length of the description of e_n and d_n is $n^{O(1)}$,
4. there exists a polynomial-time algorithm B such that $B(1^n, e_n, k, x) = e_n(k, x)$ and $B(1^n, d_n, k, x) = d_n(k, x)$.

E is called an encryption function and D is called a decryption function.   □

In the following, security of a block cipher is defined. Adversaries are assumed to make the adaptive chosen plaintext attack or the adaptive chosen plaintext/ciphertext attack. The security goal is indistinguishability of encryption against the attacks.

Definition 6. An adversary $\mathcal{A}$ making the adaptive chosen plaintext attack is defined as follows:

$\mathcal{A}$ is a probabilistic polynomial-time algorithm with an oracle $\mathcal{B}$. Both $\mathcal{A}$ and $\mathcal{B}$ take 1^n and e_n, d_n for input. Before the execution of $\mathcal{A}$, $\mathcal{B}$ uniformly selects $k \in \{0,1\}^n$. First, $\mathcal{A}$ selects and asks $x_i \in \{0,1\}^n$ to $\mathcal{B}$, which replies $e_n(k, x_i)$ for $i = 1, 2, \ldots, q$. These queries are adaptive; $\mathcal{A}$ may select and ask x_{i+1} after it receives $e_n(k, x_i)$. Then, $\mathcal{A}$ chooses $x^{(0)}, x^{(1)} \in \{0,1\}^n$ such that $x^{(0)} \neq x^{(1)}$ and $x^{(0)}, x^{(1)} \notin \{x_1, \ldots, x_q\}$ and sends them to $\mathcal{B}$. $\mathcal{B}$ selects $b \in \{0,1\}$ at random and replies $e_n(k, x^{(b)})$. $\mathcal{A}$ outputs the guess of b.

The advantage of an adversary $\mathcal{A}$ is $|\Pr[\mathcal{A}(1^n, e_n, d_n) = b] - 1/2|$, where the probability is taken over the random choices of $\mathcal{A}$ and $\mathcal{B}$.   □

Based on the above definition, a block cipher secure against the adaptive chosen plaintext attack is defined in the following way.

Definition 7. A block cipher is secure against the adaptive chosen plaintext attack if, for every adversary making the adaptive chosen plaintext attack, its advantage is negligible.   □

Definition 8. An adversary $\mathcal{A}$ making the adaptive chosen plaintext/ciphertext attack is defined as follows:

$\mathcal{A}$ is a probabilistic polynomial-time algorithm with an oracle $\mathcal{B}$. Both $\mathcal{A}$ and $\mathcal{B}$ take 1^n and e_n, d_n for input. Before the execution of $\mathcal{A}$, $\mathcal{B}$ uniformly selects $k \in \{0,1\}^n$. First, $\mathcal{A}$ selects and asks (x_i, s_i) to $\mathcal{B}$ such that $x_i \in \{0,1\}^n$ and $s_i \in \{0,1\}$ for $i = 1, 2, \ldots, q$. Then, $\mathcal{B}$ replies $e_n(k, x_i)$ if $s_i = 0$ and $d_n(k, x_i)$ if $s_i = 1$. These queries are adaptive; $\mathcal{A}$ may select and ask (x_{i+1}, s_{i+1}) after it receives the answer to (x_i, s_i). Then, $\mathcal{A}$ chooses $x^{(0)}, x^{(1)} \in \{0,1\}^n$ and $s \in \{0,1\}$ such that $x^{(0)} \neq x^{(1)}$ and

$$x^{(0)}, x^{(1)} \notin \begin{cases} \{x_i \mid s_i = 0\} \cup \{d_n(k, x_j) \mid s_j = 1\} & \text{if } s = 0 \\ \{x_i \mid s_i = 1\} \cup \{e_n(k, x_j) \mid s_j = 0\} & \text{if } s = 1 \end{cases}$$

and sends them to $\mathcal{B}$. $\mathcal{B}$ selects $b \in \{0,1\}$ at random and replies $e_n(k, x^{(b)})$ if $s = 0$ or $d_n(k, x^{(b)})$ if $s = 1$. $\mathcal{A}$ outputs the guess of b.

The advantage of an adversary $\mathcal{A}$ is $|\Pr[\mathcal{A}(1^n, e_n, d_n) = b] - 1/2|$, where the probability is taken over the random choices of $\mathcal{A}$ and $\mathcal{B}$.   □

Based on the above definition, a block cipher secure against the adaptive chosen plaintext/ciphertext attack is defined in the following way.

Definition 9. A block cipher is secure against the adaptive chosen plaintext/ciphertext attack if, for every adversary making the adaptive chosen plaintext/ciphertext attack, its advantage is negligible.   □

2.3   Iterative Hash Functions Based on Block Ciphers

The general model of iterative hash functions considered in this article is defined. This model was first defined by Preneel, Govaerts and Vandewalle [9].

Definition 10. An iterative hash function based on a block cipher is in the general model by Preneel, Govaerts and Vandewalle if its round function

$$f_n(v_{i-1}, z_i) \stackrel{\text{def}}{=} e_n(k, x) \oplus y,$$

where

1. $E = \{e_n \mid e_n : \{0,1\}^n \times \{0,1\}^n \rightarrow \{0,1\}^n\}$ is the encryption function of a block cipher, and
2. $k, x, y \in \{v_{i-1}, z_i, v_{i-1} \oplus z_i\} \cup \{0,1\}^n$. $\qquad\qquad\square$

Let us call the iterative hash functions defined above PGVHFs. With a block cipher, 64 kinds of PGVHFs are defined. Let a PGVHF be denoted by $\mathrm{HF}_E^{(k,x,y)}$ if its round function is defined by $e_n(k,x) \oplus y$, where $E = \{e_n \mid e_n : \{0,1\}^n \times \{0,1\}^n \rightarrow \{0,1\}^n\}$. For example, $\mathrm{HF}_E^{(z_i, v_{i-1}, v_{i-1})}$ is a PGVHF with the round function $f_n(v_{i-1}, z_i) = e_n(z_i, v_{i-1}) \oplus v_{i-1}$. This is known as the Davies-Meyer scheme.

3   Secure Block Ciphers Are Not Sufficient for PGVHFs

In this section, the following statement is disproved:

> There exists some PGVHF such that, for every secure block cipher B, it is one-way if constructed with B.

The proof is constructive: for each PGVHF, some block cipher is explicitly defined such that the PGVHF is not one-way if it is constructed with the block cipher.

3.1   Secure Block Ciphers Used to Construct Counterexamples

Let $B^* = (E^*, D^*)$ be a block cipher, where $E^* = \{e_n^* \mid e_n^* : \{0,1\}^n \times \{0,1\}^n \rightarrow \{0,1\}^n\}$ and $D^* = \{d_n^* \mid d_n^* : \{0,1\}^n \times \{0,1\}^n \rightarrow \{0,1\}^n\}$. For even n and $x = (x_1, \ldots, x_n) \in \{0,1\}^n$, let $x^{\mathrm{L}} = (x_1, \ldots, x_{n/2})$ and $x^{\mathrm{R}} = (x_{n/2+1}, \ldots, x_n)$. Let $W(x)$ denote the Hamming weight of $x \in \{0,1\}^n$. $(0,0,\ldots,0) \in \{0,1\}^n$ is simply denoted by 0.

Eight block ciphers B^{A0}, B^{A1}, B^{B0}, B^{B1}, B^{C0}, B^{C1}, B^{D0}, B^{D1} are defined in the following way based on B^*. Only the definitions of the encryption functions are presented. The definitions of the decryption functions can be derived easily from those of the corresponding encryption functions.

$$e_n^{\mathrm{A0}}(k, x) = \begin{cases} x & \text{if } W(k) \leq 1, \\ e_n^*(k, x) & \text{otherwise.} \end{cases}$$

$$e_n^{A1}(k, x) = \begin{cases} k \oplus x & \text{if } W(k) \leq 1, \\ e_n^*(k, x) & \text{otherwise.} \end{cases}$$

if $k = 0$, then $e_n^{B0}(k, x) = x$,

otherwise $e_n^{B0}(k, x) = \begin{cases} k & \text{if } x = k, \\ e_n^*(k, k) & \text{if } x = d_n^*(k, k), \\ e_n^*(k, x) & \text{otherwise.} \end{cases}$

if $k = 0$, then $e_n^{B1}(k, x) = x$,

otherwise $e_n^{B1}(k, x) = \begin{cases} 0 & \text{if } x = k, \\ e_n^*(k, k) & \text{if } x = d_n^*(k, 0), \\ e_n^*(k, x) & \text{otherwise.} \end{cases}$

if $k = 0$, then $e_n^{C0}(k, x) = (x^L \oplus x^R) \cdot x^L$,

otherwise $e_n^{C0}(k, x) = \begin{cases} k & \text{if } x = k, \\ e_n^*(k, k) & \text{if } x = d_n^*(k, k), \\ e_n^*(k, x) & \text{otherwise.} \end{cases}$

if $k = 0$, then $e_n^{C1}(k, x) = (x^L \oplus x^R) \cdot x^L$,

otherwise $e_n^{C1}(k, x) = \begin{cases} 0 & \text{if } x = k, \\ e_n^*(k, k) & \text{if } x = d_n^*(k, 0), \\ e_n^*(k, x) & \text{otherwise.} \end{cases}$

$$e_n^{D0}(k, x) = \begin{cases} x & \text{if } W(k \oplus x) \leq 1, \\ e_n^*(k, e_n^*(k, x)) & \text{if } W(k \oplus e_n^*(k, x)) \leq 1, \\ e_n^*(k, x) & \text{otherwise.} \end{cases}$$

$$e_n^{D1}(k, x) = \begin{cases} k \oplus x & \text{if } W(k \oplus x) \leq 1, \\ e_n^*(k, k \oplus e_n^*(k, x)) & \text{if } W(e_n^*(k, x)) \leq 1, \\ e_n^*(k, x) & \text{otherwise.} \end{cases}$$

B^{A0} and B^{A1} have $(n + 1)$ weak keys. The Hamming weight of the weak keys are at most 1. B^{B0}, B^{B1} have a weak key $k = 0$. B^{B0} and B^{C0} as well as B^{B1} and B^{C1} are different from each other only when $k = 0$. B^{C0} and B^{C1} are defined only if n is even.

To simplify the definitions of B^{D0} and B^{D1}, it is assumed that $\{\hat{x} \mid W(k \oplus \hat{x}) \leq 1\} \cap \{\tilde{x} \mid W(k \oplus e_n^*(k, \tilde{x})) \leq 1\} = \phi$ and $\{\hat{x} \mid W(k \oplus \hat{x}) \leq 1\} \cap \{\tilde{x} \mid W(e_n^*(k, \tilde{x})) \leq 1\} = \phi$ for every $k \in \{0, 1\}^n$. In general, it is not restrictive for secure encryption functions.

For the security of the block ciphers defined above, the following two lemmas can be obtained.

Lemma 1. If B^* is secure against the adaptive chosen plaintext attack, then $B^{A0}, B^{A1}, B^{B0}, B^{B1}, B^{C0}, B^{C1}, B^{D0}, B^{D1}$ are secure against the adaptive chosen plaintext attack.

(Proof) It is obvious that both B^{A0} and B^{A1} are secure against the adaptive chosen plaintext attack because the probability that the weak keys are selected is $(n + 1)/2^n$ and negligible.

In the following part of this proof, it is only proved that B^{B0} and B^{B1} are secure against the adaptive chosen plaintext attack. It can be proved that B^{C0}, B^{C1}, B^{D0} and B^{D1} are secure against the adaptive chosen plaintext attack almost in the same way.

Suppose that $\mathcal{A}$ is an adversary against B^* and let $X = \{x_i \mid x_i \in \{0,1\}^n$ for $i = 1, \ldots, q\}$ be the set of plaintexts $\mathcal{A}$ asks to the oracle, where q is bounded by some polynomial in n.

If the probability that $\{k, d_n^*(k, k)\} \cap X \neq \phi$ is non-negligible, then $\mathcal{A}$ can guess k correctly with non-negligible probability, which contradicts the assumption that B^* is secure against the adaptive chosen plaintext attack. If the probability that $d_n^*(k, 0) \in X$ is non-negligible, then the following adversary $\mathcal{A}'$ against B^* can be constructed.

1. $\mathcal{A}'$ guess j such that $x_j = d_n^*(k, 0)$.
2. $\mathcal{A}'$ simulates $\mathcal{A}$ and asks $x_1, \ldots, x_{j-1}$ to the oracle.
3. When $\mathcal{A}$ generates x_j, $\mathcal{A}'$ terminates the simulation of $\mathcal{A}$. $\mathcal{A}'$ does not ask x_j to the oracle.
4. $\mathcal{A}'$ randomly selects $x^{(0)}$ and sends $x^{(0)}$ and $x^{(1)} = x_j$ to the oracle.
5. If the reply from the oracle is equal to 0, then $\mathcal{A}'$ outputs 1. Otherwise, $\mathcal{A}'$ randomly selects a bit and outputs it.

The advantage of $\mathcal{A}'$ is non-negligible, which contradicts the assumption that B^* is secure against the adaptive chosen plaintext attack. Thus, for any adversary, the probability that $\{k, d_n^*(k, k), d_n^*(k, 0)\} \cap X \neq \phi$ is negligible. Thus, any adversary for B^{B0} can ask k or $d_n^*(k, k)$ to the oracle only with negligible probability because $e_n^{\mathrm{B0}}(k, x) = e_n^*(k, x)$ for every $x \notin \{k, d_n^*(k, k)\}$. Any adversary for B^{B1} can ask k or $d_n^*(k, 0)$ to the oracle only with negligible probability because $e_n^{\mathrm{B1}}(k, x) = e_n^*(k, x)$ for every $x \notin \{k, d_n^*(k, 0)\}$. Thus, any adversary for B^{B0} or B^{B1} is only as powerful as the most powerful adversary for B^*. Consequently, both B^{B0} and B^{B1} is secure against the adaptive chosen plaintext attack.   □

The next lemma is presented without proof because it can be proved in the same way as the above lemma.

Lemma 2. If B^* is secure against the adaptive chosen plaintext/ciphertext attack, then $B^{\mathrm{A0}}, B^{\mathrm{A1}}, B^{\mathrm{B0}}, B^{\mathrm{C0}}, B^{\mathrm{D0}}$ are secure against the adaptive chosen plaintext/ciphertext attack.   □

It is obvious that B^{B1}, B^{C1} and B^{D1} is not secure against the chosen plaintext/ciphertext attack even if B^* is secure against the chosen plaintext/ciphertext attack. For these block ciphers, if an adversary asks the ciphertext 0 to the oracle, then it can obtain the secret key.

In the following parts of this section, it is proved that each PGVHF is not one-way if its round function is composed with at least one of $B^{\mathrm{A0}}, B^{\mathrm{A1}}, B^{\mathrm{B0}}, B^{\mathrm{B1}}, B^{\mathrm{C0}}, B^{\mathrm{C1}}, B^{\mathrm{D0}}, B^{\mathrm{D1}}$.

3.2 Counterexamples

In the following discussion, for $\mathrm{HF}_E^{(k,x,y)}$, when k, x or y are constant, they are always regarded as 0. This is just for simplicity of the discussion. The following discussion can be easily modified so as to be applied to the case when they are non-zero constant.

Table 1 summarizes the results. It shows with which encryption function each PGVHF is not second-preimage resistant. "-" represents that the PGVHF is not second-preimage resistant with any encryption function.

Theorem 1. The following PGVHFs are not second-preimage resistant:

i. $\mathrm{HF}_{E\mathrm{A1}}^{(v_{i-1}\oplus z_i,0,v_{i-1})}$, $\mathrm{HF}_{E\mathrm{A0}}^{(v_{i-1}\oplus z_i,0,z_i)}$, $\mathrm{HF}_{E\mathrm{A1}}^{(v_{i-1}\oplus z_i,v_{i-1},0)}$, $\mathrm{HF}_{E\mathrm{A0}}^{(v_{i-1}\oplus z_i,v_{i-1},v_{i-1}\oplus z_i)}$,
$\mathrm{HF}_{E\mathrm{A0}}^{(v_{i-1}\oplus z_i,z_i,0)}$, $\mathrm{HF}_{E\mathrm{A1}}^{(v_{i-1}\oplus z_i,z_i,v_{i-1}\oplus z_i)}$, $\mathrm{HF}_{E\mathrm{A0}}^{(v_{i-1}\oplus z_i,v_{i-1}\oplus z_i,v_{i-1})}$
$\mathrm{HF}_{E\mathrm{A1}}^{(v_{i-1}\oplus z_i,v_{i-1}\oplus z_i,z_i)}$

ii. $\mathrm{HF}_{E\mathrm{B0}}^{(z_i,v_{i-1}\oplus z_i,v_{i-1})}$, $\mathrm{HF}_{E\mathrm{B1}}^{(z_i,v_{i-1}\oplus z_i,v_{i-1}\oplus z_i)}$, $\mathrm{HF}_{E\mathrm{B0}}^{(v_{i-1}\oplus z_i,z_i,v_{i-1})}$, $\mathrm{HF}_{E\mathrm{B1}}^{(v_{i-1}\oplus z_i,z_i,z_i)}$,

iii. $\mathrm{HF}_{E\mathrm{C0}}^{(v_{i-1},z_i,z_i)}$, $\mathrm{HF}_{E\mathrm{C1}}^{(v_{i-1},z_i,v_{i-1}\oplus z_i)}$, $\mathrm{HF}_{E\mathrm{C1}}^{(v_{i-1},v_{i-1}\oplus z_i,z_i)}$, $\mathrm{HF}_{E\mathrm{C0}}^{(v_{i-1},v_{i-1}\oplus z_i,v_{i-1}\oplus z_i)}$,

iv. $\mathrm{HF}_{E\mathrm{D1}}^{(z_i,v_{i-1},v_{i-1})}$, $\mathrm{HF}_{E\mathrm{D0}}^{(z_i,v_{i-1},v_{i-1}\oplus z_i)}$, $\mathrm{HF}_{E\mathrm{D1}}^{(v_{i-1}\oplus z_i,v_{i-1},v_{i-1})}$, $\mathrm{HF}_{E\mathrm{D0}}^{(v_{i-1}\oplus z_i,v_{i-1},z_i)}$.

(Proof) For each PGVHF listed above and a given preimage, a second preimage will be presented which is of the same length as the given preimage. It is apparent from the following proof that second preimages can be easily found for almost all given preimages.

Let $a_1, a_2, \ldots, a_m \in \{0,1\}^n$ be a padded input corresponding to the given preimage. Let $b_j = f_n(b_{j-1}, a_j)$ for $j = 1, \ldots, m$, where b_0 is the initial value. Let $\alpha^{(l)} = (\alpha_1^{(l)}, \ldots, \alpha_n^{(l)}) \in \{0,1\}^n$ such that

$$\alpha_j^{(l)} = \begin{cases} 1 \text{ if } j = l \\ 0 \text{ otherwise,} \end{cases}$$

for $1 \leq l \leq n$.

(i) For $\mathrm{HF}_{E\mathrm{A1}}^{(v_{i-1}\oplus z_i,0,v_{i-1})}$, $\mathrm{HF}_{E\mathrm{A0}}^{(v_{i-1}\oplus z_i,0,z_i)}$, $\mathrm{HF}_{E\mathrm{A1}}^{(v_{i-1}\oplus z_i,v_{i-1},0)}$, $\mathrm{HF}_{E\mathrm{A0}}^{(v_{i-1}\oplus z_i,v_{i-1},v_{i-1}\oplus z_i)}$,
$\mathrm{HF}_{E\mathrm{A0}}^{(v_{i-1}\oplus z_i,z_i,0)}$, $\mathrm{HF}_{E\mathrm{A1}}^{(v_{i-1}\oplus z_i,z_i,v_{i-1}\oplus z_i)}$, $\mathrm{HF}_{E\mathrm{A0}}^{(v_{i-1}\oplus z_i,v_{i-1}\oplus z_i,v_{i-1})}$ and
$\mathrm{HF}_{E\mathrm{A1}}^{(v_{i-1}\oplus z_i,v_{i-1}\oplus z_i,z_i)}$,

$$v_i = f_n(v_{i-1}, z_i) = \begin{cases} v_{i-1} & \text{if } z_i = v_{i-1}, \\ v_{i-1} \oplus \alpha^{(l)} & \text{if } z_i = v_{i-1} \oplus \alpha^{(l)}. \end{cases}$$

Suppose $m \geq n + 2$. Let $\delta = (\delta_1, \ldots, \delta_n) = b_0 \oplus b_n$. Let $a'_1, \ldots, a'_n, b'_0, \ldots, b'_{n-1} \in \{0,1\}^n$ such that $b'_0 = b_0$, $b'_j = f_n(b'_{j-1}, a'_j)$ and

$$a'_j = \begin{cases} b'_{j-1} & \text{if } \delta_j = 0, \\ b'_{j-1} \oplus \alpha^{(j)} & \text{if } \delta_j = 1 \end{cases}$$

for $j = 1, \ldots, n$. Then, $b'_n = b_n$. Thus, $a'_1, \ldots, a'_n, a_{n+1}, \ldots, a_m$ is a second preimage if $(a'_1, \ldots, a'_n) \neq (a_1, \ldots, a_n)$.

(ii) Suppose $m \geq 4$. For $\mathrm{HF}_{E\mathrm{B0}}^{(z_i, v_{i-1} \oplus z_i, v_{i-1})}$ and $\mathrm{HF}_{E\mathrm{B1}}^{(z_i, v_{i-1} \oplus z_i, v_{i-1} \oplus z_i)}$, let $a'_j = 0$ and $a'_{j+1} = b_{j+1}$ for some $j \leq m - 3$. Then,

$$
\begin{aligned}
f(f(b_{j-1}, a'_j), a'_{j+1}) &= f(f(b_{j-1}, 0), b_{j+1}) \\
&= f(0, b_{j+1}) \\
&= b_{j+1}.
\end{aligned}
$$

For $\mathrm{HF}_{E\mathrm{B0}}^{(v_{i-1} \oplus z_i, z_i, v_{i-1})}$ and $\mathrm{HF}_{E\mathrm{B1}}^{(v_{i-1} \oplus z_i, z_i, z_i)}$, let $a'_j = b_{j-1}$ and $a'_{j+1} = b_{j+1}$ for some $j \leq m - 3$. Then,

$$
\begin{aligned}
f(f(b_{j-1}, a'_j), a'_{j+1}) &= f(f(b_{j-1}, b_{j-1}), b_{j+1}) \\
&= f(0, b_{j+1}) \\
&= b_{j+1}.
\end{aligned}
$$

Thus, for the above four PGVHFs, $a_1, \ldots, a_{j-1}, a'_j, a'_{j+1}, a_{j+2}, \ldots, a_m$ is a second preimage if $(a'_j, a'_{j+1}) \neq (a_j, a_{j+1})$.

(iii) Suppose $m \geq 4$. For $\mathrm{HF}_{E\mathrm{C0}}^{(v_{i-1}, z_i, z_i)}$ and $\mathrm{HF}_{E\mathrm{C1}}^{(v_{i-1}, z_i, v_{i-1} \oplus z_i)}$, let $a'_j = b_{j-1}$ and $a'_{j+1} = (b^{\mathrm{L}}_{j+1} \oplus b^{\mathrm{R}}_{j+1}) \cdot b^{\mathrm{L}}_{j+1}$ for some $j \leq m - 3$. Then,

$$
\begin{aligned}
f(f(b_{j-1}, a'_j), a'_{j+1}) &= f(0, a'_{j+1}) \\
&= (b^{\mathrm{R}}_{j+1} \cdot (b^{\mathrm{L}}_{j+1} \oplus b^{\mathrm{R}}_{j+1})) \oplus ((b^{\mathrm{L}}_{j+1} \oplus b^{\mathrm{R}}_{j+1}) \cdot b^{\mathrm{L}}_{j+1}) \\
&= b_{j+1}.
\end{aligned}
$$

For $\mathrm{HF}_{E\mathrm{C1}}^{(v_{i-1}, v_{i-1} \oplus z_i, z_i)}$ and $\mathrm{HF}_{E\mathrm{C0}}^{(v_{i-1}, v_{i-1} \oplus z_i, v_{i-1} \oplus z_i)}$, let $a'_j = 0$ and $a'_{j+1} = (b^{\mathrm{L}}_{j+1} \oplus b^{\mathrm{R}}_{j+1}) \cdot b^{\mathrm{L}}_{j+1}$ for some $j \leq m - 3$. Then,

$$
f(f(b_{j-1}, a'_j), a'_{j+1}) = f(0, a'_{j+1}) = b_{j+1}.
$$

Thus, for the above four PGVHFs, $a_1, \ldots, a_{j-1}, a'_j, a'_{j+1}, a_{j+2}, \ldots, a_m$ is a second preimage if $(a'_j, a'_{j+1}) \neq (a_j, a_{j+1})$.

(iv) Suppose $m \geq n + 2$. Let $\delta = (\delta_1, \ldots, \delta_n) = b_0 \oplus b_n$.
    For $\mathrm{HF}_{E\mathrm{D1}}^{(z_i, v_{i-1}, v_{i-1})}$ and $\mathrm{HF}_{E\mathrm{D0}}^{(z_i, v_{i-1}, v_{i-1} \oplus z_i)}$,

$$
v_i = f_n(v_{i-1}, z_i) = \begin{cases} v_{i-1} & \text{if } z_i = v_{i-1}, \\ v_{i-1} \oplus \alpha^{(l)} & \text{if } z_i = v_{i-1} \oplus \alpha^{(l)}. \end{cases}
$$

Let $a'_1, \ldots, a'_n, b'_0, \ldots, b'_{n-1} \in \{0,1\}^n$ such that $b'_0 = b_0$, $b'_j = f_n(b'_{j-1}, a'_j)$ and

$$
a'_j = \begin{cases} b_{j-1} & \text{if } \delta_j = 0, \\ b_{j-1} \oplus \alpha^{(j)} & \text{if } \delta_j = 1 \end{cases}
$$

for $j = 1, \ldots, n$. Then, $b'_n = b_n$.
    For $\mathrm{HF}_{E\mathrm{D1}}^{(v_{i-1} \oplus z_i, v_{i-1}, v_{i-1})}$ and $\mathrm{HF}_{E\mathrm{D0}}^{(v_{i-1} \oplus z_i, v_{i-1}, z_i)}$,

$$
v_i = f_n(v_{i-1}, z_i) = \begin{cases} v_{i-1} & \text{if } z_i = 0, \\ v_{i-1} \oplus \alpha^{(l)} & \text{if } z_i = \alpha^{(l)}. \end{cases}
$$

Let $a'_1, \ldots, a'_n, b'_0, \ldots, b'_{n-1} \in \{0,1\}^n$ such that $b'_0 = b_0$, $b'_j = f_n(b'_{j-1}, a'_j)$ and

$$a'_j = \begin{cases} 0 & \text{if } \delta_j = 0, \\ \alpha^{(j)} & \text{if } \delta_j = 1 \end{cases}$$

for $j = 1, \ldots, n$. Then, $b'_n = b_n$.

Thus, for the above four PGVHFs, $a'_1, \ldots, a'_n, a_{n+1}, \ldots, a_m$ is a second preimage if $(a'_1, \ldots, a'_n) \neq (a_1, \ldots, a_n)$. □

Theorem 2. The following PGVHFs are not preimage resistant:

i. $\mathrm{HF}_E^{(0,v_{i-1}\oplus z_i, z_i)}$ if $E \in \{E^{\mathrm{A0}}, E^{\mathrm{A1}}\}$,

ii. $\mathrm{HF}_{E^{\mathrm{A1}}}^{(z_i, v_{i-1}-1, 0)}$, $\mathrm{HF}_{E^{\mathrm{A0}}}^{(z_i, v_{i-1}, z_i)}$, $\mathrm{HF}_{E^{\mathrm{A0}}}^{(z_i, v_{i-1}\oplus z_i, 0)}$, $\mathrm{HF}_{E^{\mathrm{A1}}}^{(z_i, v_{i-1}\oplus z_i, z_i)}$,

iii. $\mathrm{HF}_E^{(v_{i-1}\oplus z_i, v_{i-1}\oplus z_i, v_{i-1})}$ and $\mathrm{HF}_E^{(v_{i-1}\oplus z_i, v_{i-1}\oplus z_i, z_i)}$ if $E \in \{E^{\mathrm{B0}}, E^{\mathrm{C0}}\}$.

(Proof) (i) It is obvious that $\mathrm{HF}_E^{(0,v_{i-1}\oplus z_i, z_i)}$ is not preimage resistant if $E \in \{E^{\mathrm{A0}}, E^{\mathrm{A1}}\}$, because the round function $f_n(v_{i-1}, z_i) = e_n(0, v_{i-1}\oplus z_i)\oplus z_i = v_{i-1}$ for any v_{i-1}, z_i if $e_n \in \{e_n^{\mathrm{A0}}, e_n^{\mathrm{A1}}\}$.

(ii) In this part, a procedure is presented to compute a preimage of a given output only for $\mathrm{HF}_{E^{\mathrm{A0}}}^{(z_i, v_{i-1}, z_i)}$. Preimages can be obtained in the same way for the other three PGVHFs.

Let b_{n+2} be the given output. The padded input $a_1, \ldots, a_{n+2}$, which consists of $n + 2$ blocks, is obtained in the following way.

1. Fix a_{n+2} and a_{n+1}. a_{n+2} is the binary representation of the length of the preimage. Without loss of generality, suppose that the length of the preimage is $n^2 + 1$. Then, $a_{n+1} \in \{(0,0,\ldots,0), (1,0,\ldots,0)\}$.
2. Compute $b_{n+1} = d^{\mathrm{A0}}(a_{n+2}, b_{n+2} \oplus a_{n+2})$ and $b_n = d^{\mathrm{A0}}(a_{n+1}, b_{n+1} \oplus a_{n+1})$.
3. Let $\delta = (\delta_1, \ldots, \delta_n) = b_0 \oplus b_n$, where b_0 is the initial value of the PGVHF. For $j = 1, \ldots, n$, let

$$a_j = \begin{cases} 0 & \text{if } \delta_j = 0, \\ \alpha^{(j)} & \text{if } \delta_j = 1. \end{cases}$$

It can be verified easily that $a_1, \ldots, a_{n+2}$ is a padded input which produces the output b_{n+2} from the fact that

$$v_i = f_n(v_{i-1}, z_i) = \begin{cases} v_{i-1} & \text{if } z_i = 0, \\ v_{i-1} \oplus \alpha^{(l)} & \text{if } z_i = \alpha^{(l)} \end{cases}$$

for $\mathrm{HF}_{E^{\mathrm{A0}}}^{(z_i, v_{i-1}, z_i)}$.

(iii) It is obvious that $\mathrm{HF}_E^{(v_{i-1}\oplus z_i, v_{i-1}\oplus z_i, v_{i-1})}$ and $\mathrm{HF}_E^{(v_{i-1}\oplus z_i, v_{i-1}\oplus z_i, z_i)}$ are not preimage resistant if $E \in \{E^{\mathrm{B0}}, E^{\mathrm{C0}}\}$. If $e_n \in \{e_n^{\mathrm{B0}}, e_n^{\mathrm{C0}}\}$, then, for any v_{i-1}, z_i, the round function of $\mathrm{HF}_E^{(v_{i-1}\oplus z_i, v_{i-1}\oplus z_i, v_{i-1})}$ is $e_n(v_{i-1}\oplus z_i, v_{i-1}\oplus z_i)\oplus v_{i-1} = z_i$ and that of $\mathrm{HF}_E^{(v_{i-1}\oplus z_i, v_{i-1}\oplus z_i, z_i)}$ is $e_n(v_{i-1} \oplus z_i, v_{i-1} \oplus z_i) \oplus z_i = v_{i-1}$. □

Table 1. With which block cipher each PGVHF is not second-preimage resistant. Especially, $^\sharp$ represents that the corresponding PGVHF is not preimage resistant with the specified block cipher. "-" represents that the corresponding PGVHF is not second-preimage resistant with any block cipher.

k	x	y			
		0	v_{i-1}	z_i	$v_{i-1} \oplus z_i$
0	0	-	-	-	-
0	v_{i-1}	-	-	-	-
0	z_i	-	-	-	-
0	$v_{i-1} \oplus z_i$	-	-	A0$^\sharp$, A1$^\sharp$	-
v_{i-1}	0	-	-	-	-
v_{i-1}	v_{i-1}	-	-	-	-
v_{i-1}	z_i	-	-	C0	C1
v_{i-1}	$v_{i-1} \oplus z_i$	-	-	C1	C0
z_i	0	-	-	-	-
z_i	v_{i-1}	A1$^\sharp$	D1	A0$^\sharp$	D0
z_i	z_i	-	-	-	-
z_i	$v_{i-1} \oplus z_i$	A0$^\sharp$	B0	A1$^\sharp$	B1
$v_{i-1} \oplus z_i$	0	-	A1	A0	-
$v_{i-1} \oplus z_i$	v_{i-1}	A1	D1	D0	A0
$v_{i-1} \oplus z_i$	z_i	A0	B0	B1	A1
$v_{i-1} \oplus z_i$	$v_{i-1} \oplus z_i$	-	A0, B0$^\sharp$, C0$^\sharp$	A1, B0$^\sharp$, C0$^\sharp$	-

4   Discussion

In this section, a few considerations are given to the results obtained in the previous section.

Twelve Schemes Secure against the Existing Attacks. It is interesting that only for PGVHFs regarded as secure by Preneel, Govaerts and Vandewalle [9], some non-randomness other than weak keys is required for block ciphers to disprove their second-preimage resistance. These are the PGVHFs whose corresponding entries in Table 1 include B0, B1, C0, C1, D0, or D1 without $^\sharp$. Other PGVHFs may not be one-way with any block cipher or block ciphers only with some weak keys.

Preimage Resistance. For some of the PGVHFs in Theorem 1, preimages may be found for given outputs. However, it seems infeasible to find a preimage with polynomial length for such PGVHFs.

Example 1. For $\mathrm{HF}_{E^{\mathrm{C0}}}^{(v_{i-1}, z_i, z_i)}$, a preimage can be found for a given output by the following algorithm.

1. Let $b_m \in \{0,1\}^n$ be the given output.
2. Let $b_{m-1} = 0$ and $a_m = (b_m^{\mathrm{L}} \oplus b_m^{\mathrm{R}}) \cdot b_m^{\mathrm{L}}$. Then, $f_n(b_{m-1}, a_m) = b_m$.
3. Select arbitrarily a_{m-1} such that it ends with at least $n - (len \bmod n)$ consecutive 0's, where len is the length of the input represented by a_m. Let $b_{m-2} = a_{m-1}$. Then, $f_n(b_{m-2}, a_{m-1}) = b_{m-1} = 0$.
4. Select $a_1, a_2, \ldots, a_{m-4}$ arbitrarily, and compute b_{m-4}.
5. Compute a_{m-3}, a_{m-2} for b_{m-4}, b_{m-2} with the technique used in the proof of Theorem 1.

However, if $E^{\mathrm{C}0}$ is random enough except for some non-randomness provided, then b_m is also random. Thus, the probability is negligible that the length of the preimage obtained by the above algorithm is polynomial in n.   □

Padding Rules. In the above discussions, only the padding rule with MD-strengthening is considered. Thus, the length of every second preimage obtained in the proof of Theorem 1 is equal to that of the corresponding first preimage. Fixed points of the round function f_n such as $f_n(v_{i-1}, z_i) = v_{i-1}$ are not used in that proof. If the padding rules without MD-strengthening are adopted, that is, the padded inputs do not contain the length of the original inputs, then it is much easier to find the examples which are not one-way for some of PGVHFs using fixed points.

Example 2. For $\mathrm{HF}_E^{(v_{i-1}, v_{i-1} \oplus z_i, z_i)}$, if $E = E^{\mathrm{B}0}$ or $E^{\mathrm{C}0}$, then $f_n(v_{i-1}, 0) = v_{i-1}$ for every v_{i-1}. Thus, for every input x, second preimages such as $0 \cdot x$ can be found easily.   □

5 Conclusion

In this article, it has been shown that, for every PGVHF, there exist block ciphers secure against the adaptive chosen plaintext attack such that the PGVHF based on them is not one-way. The secure block ciphers have been explicitly defined based on which one-way PGVHFs cannot be constructed. Some of them are secure against the adaptive chosen plaintext/ciphertext attack.

The followings are some open questions.

- Are the following PGVHFs second-preimage resistant if their round functions are composed with any block cipher secure against the adaptive chosen plaintext/ciphertext attack?
  $\mathrm{HF}_E^{(v_{i-1}, z_i, v_{i-1} \oplus z_i)}$, $\mathrm{HF}_E^{(v_{i-1}, v_{i-1} \oplus z_i, z_i)}$, $\mathrm{HF}_E^{(z_i, v_{i-1}, v_{i-1})}$,
  $\mathrm{HF}_E^{(z_i, v_{i-1} \oplus z_i, v_{i-1} \oplus z_i)}$, $\mathrm{HF}_E^{(v_{i-1} \oplus z_i, v_{i-1}, v_{i-1})}$, $\mathrm{HF}_E^{(v_{i-1} \oplus z_i, z_i, z_i)}$.
- Are the following PGVHFs preimage resistant if their round functions are composed with any block cipher secure against the adaptive chosen plaintext attack?
  $\mathrm{HF}_E^{(v_{i-1}, z_i, z_i)}$, $\mathrm{HF}_E^{(v_{i-1}, v_{i-1} \oplus z_i, v_{i-1} \oplus z_i)}$, $\mathrm{HF}_E^{(z_i, v_{i-1}, v_{i-1} \oplus z_i)}$,
  $\mathrm{HF}_E^{(z_i, v_{i-1} \oplus z_i, v_{i-1})}$, $\mathrm{HF}_E^{(v_{i-1} \oplus z_i, v_{i-1}, z_i)}$, $\mathrm{HF}_E^{(v_{i-1} \oplus z_i, z_i, v_{i-1})}$.

Acknowledgements

The author would like to thank the anonymous reviewers for their valuable comments.

References

1. I. B. Damgård. A design principle for hash functions. In *CRYPTO'89*, pages 416–427, 1990. Lecture Notes in Computer Science 435.
2. D. Davies and W. L. Price. Digital signatures, an update. In *Proceedings of the 5th International Conference on Computer Communication*, pages 845–849, 1984.
3. S. M. Matyas, C. H. Meyer, and J. Oseas. Generating strong one-way functions with cryptographic algorithm. *IBM Technical Disclosure Bulletin*, 27:5658–5659, 1985.
4. A. Menezes, P. van Oorschot, and S. Vanstone. *Handbook of Applied Cryptography*. CRC Press, 1996.
5. R. C. Merkle. A fast software one-way hash function. *Journal of Cryptology*, 3:43–58, 1990.
6. C. H. Meyer and M. Schilling. Secure program load with manipulation detection code. In *Proceedings of the 6th Worldwide Congress on Computer and Communications Security and Protection (SECURICOM'88)*, pages 111–130, 1988.
7. B. Preneel. *Analysis and Design of Cryptographic Hash Functions*. PhD thesis, Katholieke Universiteit Leuven, 1993.
8. B. Preneel. The state of cryptographic hash functions. In *Lectures on Data Security*, pages 158–182, 1998. Lecture Notes in Computer Science 1561.
9. B. Preneel, R. Govaerts, and J. Vandewalle. Hash functions based on block ciphers: A synthetic approach. In *CRYPTO'93*, pages 368–378, 1994. Lecture Notes in Computer Science 773.
10. D. R. Simon. Finding collisions on a one-way street: Can secure hash functions be based on general assumptions? In *EUROCRYPT'98*, pages 334–345, 1998. Lecture Notes in Computer Science 1403.

An Efficient MAC for Short Messages

Sarvar Patel

Bell Labs, Lucent Technologies
67 Whippany Rd, Whippany, NJ 07981, USA
sarvar@bell-labs.com

Abstract. HMAC is the internet standard for message authentication [BCK96,KBC97]. What distinguishes HMAC from other MAC algorithms is that it provides proofs of security assuming that the underlying cryptographic hash (e.g. SHA-1) has some reasonable properties. HMAC is efficient for long messages, however, for short messages the nested constructions results in a significant inefficiency. For example to MAC a message shorter than a block, HMAC requires at least two calls to the compression function rather than one.
This inefficiency may be particularly high for some applications, like message authentication of signaling messages, where the individual messages may all fit within one or two blocks. Also for TCP/IP traffic it is well known that a large number of packets (e.g. acknowledgement) have sizes around 40 bytes which fit within a block of most cryptographic hashes. We propose an enhancement that allows both short and long messages to be message authenticated more efficiently than HMAC while also providing proofs of security. In particular, for a message smaller than a block our MAC only requires one call to the compression function.

1 Introduction

MESSAGE AUTHENTICATION. The goal in message authentication is for one party to efficiently transmit a message to another party in such a way that the receiving party can determine whether or not the message he receives has been tampered with. The setting involves two parties, Alice and Bob, who have agreed on a pre-specified secret key k. There are two algorithms used: a signing algorithm S_k and a verification algorithm V_k. If Alice wants to send a message M to Bob then she first computes a message authentication code, or MAC, $\mu = S_k(M)$. She sends (M, μ) to Bob, and upon receiving the pair, Bob computes $V_k(M, \mu)$ which returns 1 if the MAC is valid, or returns 0 otherwise. In other words, without knowledge of the secret key k, it is next to impossible for an adversary to construct a message and corresponding MAC that the verification algorithm will be accept as valid.

The formal security requirement for a Message Authentication Code was defined in [BKR94]. This definition was an analog to the formal definition of security for digital signatures [GMR88]. In particular, we say that an adversary forges a MAC if, when given oracle access to (S_k, V_k), where k is kept secret, the adversary can come up with a valid pair (M^*, μ^*) such that $V_k(M^*, \mu^*) = 1$ but the message M^* was never made an input to the oracle for S_k.

K. Nyberg and H. Heys (Eds.): SAC 2002, LNCS 2595, pp. 353–368, 2003.
© Springer-Verlag Berlin Heidelberg 2003

CRYPTOGRAPHIC HASH FUNCTION APPROACH. One common approach to message authentication commonly seen in practice involves the use of cryptographic hash functions such as $MD5$ and SHA-1. These schemes are practical because they use fast and secure cryptographic building blocks. Creating a MAC from a hash function may seem deceptively easy. It seems all one needs to do is to put a key somewhere in the hash function. An easy way to accomplish this is to prepend the key to the data before hashing. Unfortunately, this is not secure and one can forge MACs on unseen messages as we described next. To forge a MAC for the prepend key construction, we begin with a previously MACed message x and its tag $MAC_k(x)$. We create a new message z by appending any message y to x, z = (x,y). To create the tag $MAC_k(z)$ we use $MAC_k(x)$ as the chaining variable and hash y, making sure to set the length of the message to be the length of z. The result will be $MAC_k(z)$. Thus we have forged the MAC for z.

HMAC, the internet standard for message authentication, uses the cryptographic hash approach. What distinguishes HMAC from other cryptographic hash based MACs is its formal security analysis. The analysis provides a proof of security of HMAC assuming the underlying cryptographic hash is (weakly) collision resistant and that the underlying compression function is a secure MAC when both are appropriately keyed.

There are other approaches to message authentication, each having a different tradeoff between efficiency, requiring larger keys, and making stronger security assumptions about the cryptographic primitive. The cipher block chaining approach of [BKR94] does not require a nested construction but makes the stronger assumption about the underlying primitive, namely, that it is a pseudorandom permutation rather than a MAC. The universal hashing approach of Wegman and Carter [WC81] can provide very efficient MACing algorithms, however, they often require much larger keys than other approaches and require the underlying cryptographic primitive to be a pseudorandom generarator or a pseudorandom function. This paper solely deals with the cryptographic hash based approach for MACs.

THIS WORK. HMAC is efficient for long messages, however, for short messages the nested constructions results in a significant inefficiency. For example to MAC a message shorter than a block, HMAC requires at least two calls to the hash function rather than one. This inefficiency may be particularly high for some applications, like message authentication of signaling messages, where the individual messages may all fit within one or two blocks. Also for TCP/IP traffic it is well known that a large number of packets (e.g. acknowledgement) have sizes around 40 bytes which fit within a block of most cryptographic hashes. We propose an enhancement that allows both short and long messages to be message authenticated more efficiently than HMAC while also providing proofs of security. For a message smaller than a block our MAC only requires one call to the hash function. A version of the enhanced MAC algorithm presented here has been accepted as a message authentication algorithm for CDMA 2000 [ECAB].

2   Preliminaries

CRYPTOGRAPHIC HASH FUNCTIONS Cryptographic hash functions, $F(x)$, are public, keyless, and collision-resistant functions which map inputs, x, of arbitrary lengths into short outputs. Collision-resistance implies that it should be computationally infeasible to find two messages x_1 and x_2 such that $F(x_1) = F(x_2)$. MD5, SHA-1, and RIPE-MD are widely used cryptographic hash functions. Along with collision-resistance, the hash functions are usually designed to have other properties both inorder to use the function for other purposes and to increase the likelihood of collision-resistance.

ITERATED CRYPTOGRAPHIC HASH FUNCTIONS Most cryptographic hash functions like MD5 and SHA-1 use an iterated construction where the input message is processed block by block. The basic building block is called the compression function, f which takes two inputs of size l and b and maps into a shorter output of length l. The l sized input is called the chaining variable and the b sized input is used to actually process the message b bits at a time. The hash function $F(x)$ then is formed by iterating the compression function f over the message m using these steps:

1. Use an appropriate procedure to append the message length and pad to make the input a multiple of the block size b. The input can be broken into block size pieces $x = x_1, \ldots, x_n$.
2. $h_0 = IV$, a fixed constant.
3. For $i = 1$ to n
   $h_i = f(h_{i-1}, x_i)$
4. output h_n as $F(x)$.

KEYED HASH FUNCTIONS Cryptographic hash functions by design are keyless. However, since message authentication requires the use of a secret key, we need a method to key the hash function. The method we use in this paper is the same as that used by NMAC [BCK96] where a secret key is used instead of the fixed and known IV. In this case the key k replaces the chaining variable in the compression function $f(chainingvariable, x)$ to form $f_k(x) = f(k, x)$ where x is of block size b. The iterated hash function $F(IV, x)$ is modified by replacing the fixed IV with the secret key k to form $F_k(x) = F(k, x)$. Collision resistance for keyed function is different because the adversary cannot evaluate $F_k(x)$ at any points without querying the user. This requirement is weaker than the standard collision requirement and hence we will call the function $F_k(x)$ to be weakly collision-resistant [BCK96] .

3   NMAC and HMAC

HMAC is a practical variant of the NMAC construction defined in [BCK96]. The formal security proofs are given for NMAC and its relation to HMAC is described. First we describe the NMAC construction and state the theorem proved in [BCK96].

3.1   The NMAC Function

The message authentication function NMAC is defined as

$$NMAC_k(x) = F_{k_1}(F_{k_2}(x)).$$

where the cryptographic hash function is first keyed with the secret key k_2 instead of IV and the message x is hashed to the short output. This output is then padded to a block size according to the padding scheme of F and then F is keyed with secret key k_1 and hashed. Thus the NMAC key k has two parts $k = (k_1, k_2)$. The following theorem relating the security of NMAC to the security of the underlying cryptographic hash function is proved in [BCK96]:

Theorem 1. *In t steps and q queries if the keyed compression function f is an ϵ_f secure MAC, and the keyed iterated hash F is ϵ_F weakly collision-resistant then the NMAC function is $(\epsilon_f + \epsilon_F)$ secure MAC.*

3.2   Efficiency of NMAC

The NMAC construction makes two calls to F, the inner call to $F_{k_2}(x)$ has the same cost as the keyless hash function $F(x)$. Thus the outer call to $F_{k_1}()$ is an extra call beyond that required by the keyless hash function. The outer function call is basically a call to the keyed compression function $f_{k_1}()$ since the l size output of $F_{k_2}(x)$ can fit in the b size input to the compression function. For large x consisting of many blocks the cost of the extra outer compression call is not significant. However, for small sized messages x the extra compression function can in terms of percentage result in a significantly high inefficiency when compared to the unkeyed hash function. Figure 1 shows the inefficiency for small x for the SHA-1 hash function. The number of compressions calls needed by the underlying hash function and by NMAC are compared for various small x, increasing in 30 byte increments. The inefficiency of NMAC with respect to the underlying hash function is also noted in the figure.

As can be seen the penalty for small messages can be large. In particular, for messages which fit within a block, the penalty is 100% because two compression function calls are required in NMAC versus one call by the underlying cryptographic hash function.

3.3   The HMAC Function

HMAC is a practical variant of NMAC for those implementations which do not have access to the compression function, but can only call the cryptographic hash function F with the message. That is the key cannot be placed in the chaining variable and the function F with the fixed and known IV is called.

$$HMAC_k(x) = F(\bar{k} \oplus opad, F(\bar{k} \oplus ipad, x))$$

where $\bar{k}$ is the padding of k with zeroes to complete the b block size of the iterated hash function. Also ipad and opad are fixed constants, see [BCK96] for details.

x in 240 bit increments	# of f in $F(x)$	# of f in NMAC	% inefficiency
240	1	2	100%
480	2	3	50%
720	2	3	50%
960	3	4	33%
1200	3	4	33%
1440	3	4	33%
1680	4	5	25%
1920	4	5	25%
2160	5	6	20%
2400	5	6	20%

Fig. 1. Comparison in number of compression calls for short messages of various sizes.

HMAC requires 4 calls to the compression function, the first time its evaluated. If the intermediate keys can be cached and loaded directly into the chaining variable then HMAC subsequently requires at least two calls. If direct loading of the keys into the chaining variable is not possible then HMAC continues to require at least 4 calls to the compression function. HMAC's security relies on an added assumption that the compression function has some pseudorandom properties.

4   ENMAC: Enhanced NMAC

We present a MAC construction which is not only significantly more efficient than NMAC for short messages but is also somewhat more efficient for longer messages. Recall that $f_k(x)$ is the compression function whose input block size is b bits and the output size is l bits, also the size of the chaining variable and hence the key size also is l bits.

$$ENMAC_k(x) = f_{k_1}(x, pad, 1) \qquad\qquad if\ |x| <= b - 2\ bits$$

$$= f_{k_1}(x_{pref}, F_{k_2}(x_{suff}), 0) \quad else$$

where in the first case the first $b - 2$ bits in the block are used to hold the message x. If the message x does not fill the block completely, then padding is required and the remaining block, except the last bit, is filled with a mandatory 1 followed by 0s, possibly none. In the case that the message is $b - 2$ bits long, the $b - 1th$ bit is set to 1. The last bit of the block, indicates whether a single compression call is used for ENMAC. The last bit of the block is set to 1 in the single compression call case, and is set to 0 when multiple compression calls are required which we describe next. The padding scheme for the single block case is unambiguous in the sense that every message, x, less than or equal to $b - 2$ bits is uniquely mapped to a b bit string.

In the second case where things will not fit in one block, the string x is broken into two pieces x_{pref} and x_{suff}, where

$$x_{pref} = x_1 \ldots x_{b-l-1}$$

$$x_{suff} = x_{b-l} \ldots x_{|x|}$$

First x_{suff} is hashed using k_2 to produce the l bit tag. Then an outer compression call is performed using k_1 where the first $b - l - 1$ bits are set to x_{pref} and the next l bits are set to the tag $F_{k_2}(x_{suff})$, and the last bit is set to 0.

4.1   SHA-1-ENMAC

The ENMAC construction, described abstractly above, may become clearer when we look at the concrete case of using SHA-1 as the underlying cryptographic hash function.

1. If $|x| \leq 510$ bits then goto next step else goto step 7.
2. The 512 bit payload of $f_{k_1}()$ is formed by loading x into the first 510 bits.
3. Append a 1 to x.
4. Append as few 0s (possibly none) as needed to fill 511 bits. If $|x|$ is less than 510 bits than zeroes will be padded beyond the 1 or else if $|x|$ is 510 bits then no zeroes are padded and only a single 1 is added at the 511-th bit position.
5. The last 512-th bit is set to 1, to indicate the message fits in a single block.
6. Apply the keyed compression function on the payload and output the result.
7. Split x into two pieces x_{pref} and x_{suff} where $x_{pref} = x_1 \ldots x_{351}$ and $x_{suff} = x_{352} \ldots x_{|x|}$.
8. Apply the keyed hash function $F_{k_2}(x_{suff})$.
9. Form the 512 bit payload of f_{k_1} by setting the last bit to 0.
10. Set the first 351 bits to be x_{pref}.
11. Set the next 160 bits to be $F_{k_2}(x_{suff})$ calculated in step 8.
12. Apply the keyed compression function on the payload and output the result.

4.2   Efficiency of ENMAC

Figure 2 below compares the number of compression calls required by the underlying hash function, SHA-1, and by ENMAC for short messages varying in sizes of 30 byte increments.

We can see a significant difference between this figure and the previous figure which compared plain NMAC. For many of the short sizes ENMAC has the same efficiency as the underlying hash function, For larger messages the efficiency of NMAC, ENMAC and the underlying hash function will not be significantly different from each other. For message of size 480 bits the entry in figure 2 surprisingly indicates that the ENMAC is more efficient than the underlying hash function! This anomaly occurs because the underlying SHA-1 function reserves 64 bits for size information while ENMAC reserves only 2 bits for messages less than 510 bits. Thus the savings resulting from using ENMAC are significant for messages that fit in one or few blocks.

x in 240 bit increments	# of f in $F(x)$	# of f in ENMAC	% inefficiency
240	1	1	0%
480	2	1	-50%
720	2	2	0%
960	3	3	0%
1200	3	3	0%
1440	3	4	33%
1680	4	4	0%
1920	4	5	25%
2160	5	5	0%
2400	5	6	20%

Fig. 2. Comparison in number of compression calls for short messages of various sizes.

4.3   Security of ENMAC

MOTIVATION If we were to use a different key k_3 to MAC messages which fit in one block and use key $k = (k_1, k_2)$ to MAC larger messages using NMAC then we could argue the system would be secure. Essentially, this is what is being done, but instead of using a different key to create a different MAC, the trailing bit is being set to 1 if the message fits in one block and its set to 0 for the other case. Secondly, whereas NMAC pads the payload of the outer compression call with zeroes, we fit part of the message in the outer call. Our security results are similar to NMAC and we state our security theorem and prove it next.

Theorem 2. *In t steps and q queries if the keyed compression function f is an ϵ_f secure MAC, and the keyed iterated hash F is ϵ_F weakly collision-resistant then the ENMAC function is $(\epsilon_f + \epsilon_F)$ secure MAC.*

Proof: Suppose an adversary A_E is successful against ENMAC with probability ϵ_E assuming t time steps and q adaptively chosen queries to the ENMAC function. We will use this adversary to build another adversary A_f which will forge a MAC associated with the keyed compression function on a previously unqueried message. We will bound this probability of breaking the MAC in terms of ϵ_E and ϵ_F, where ϵ_F is the best probability of an adversary finding a collision in the hash function F in time t and q queries. We know that the probability of breaking the MAC in this particular way, using A_E, has to be less than the best probability of breaking the MAC in any way, ϵ_f. We use this in turn to get a bound on ϵ_E. Figure 3 outlines the algorithm A_f which we describe next.

A_f algorithm will attack the MAC f by first querying it on $x_1 \ldots x_q$ and get $f_{k1}(x_1) \ldots f_{k1}(x_q)$. Inside A_f, the algorithm A_E is being run; A_E itself will want to query the ENMAC function before it attacks the ENMAC. Actually there is no real ENMAC function that we are attacking, the real thing we want to attack is the MAC $f_{k1}()$. So we are simulating an ENMAC function to the A_E algorithm by answering its query correctly. We have picked a random k_2, and when A_E asks us to form ENMAC of messages x_i we will use the key k_2 to form the inside calculation part $F_{k2}()$, and for the outer part of ENMAC, which is $f_{k1}()$, we actually call the real MAC that we want to attack. When the A_E queries for $ENMAC(x_i)$ we see if x_i will fit in a single block or requires multiple block. If it fits in a single block then we just make a call to the real MAC function $f_{k1}()$ with the arguments $(x_i, pad, 1)$. The indicator bit is used here and set to 1. On the other hand if multiple blocks will be used then we first evaluate $F_{k2}(x_{i,suff})$ then we make a call to the real MAC with the arguments $(x_{i,pref}, F_{k2}(x_{i,suff}), 0)$. The indicator bit is set to zero.

Now suppose the A_E algorithm has forged an ENMAC tag y on an unseen, unqueried message x and the message fits in one block. ENMAC tag on a small message x is equivalent to $f_{k1}()$ MAC tag on unseen message $(x, pad, 1)$. Now this is the crucial role about the indicator bit. The pair $(x, y = ENMAC(x))$ was never queried or requested by the A_E algorithm inside the A_f algorithm. Thus all the previous calls to the real $f_{k1}()$ MAC made on behalf of the A_E queries never made the real MAC call with argument $(x, pad, 1)$! This we see because the only calls to the real MAC that were made were either $f_{k1}(...., 1)$ on behalf of single block ENMAC queries or $f_{k1}(...., 0)$ on behalf of multiple block ENMAC queries, no other calls to the real MAC were made. So the indicator bit creates an independence from the multiple block ENMAC case, and allows us to just see that among all the single block queries, none was made with x, thus this is a new forged MAC pair. By our direct assumption that we cannot forge new message MAC pair on $f_{k1}()$, this is a contradiction. Hence there could not have been an attack on ENMAC for single block. We also note that the unambiguous padding scheme used in ENMAC guarantees that for every message x queried by $ENMAC(x)$ means there is a unique message $(x, pad, 1)$ queried by the real MAC $f_{k1}(x, pad, 1)$. If the multiple block ENMAC was what was forged first by A_E then we have to show that this allows A_f to forge new messages and MAC pair on $f_{k1}()$. We formally prove the theorem below, but first we define some useful events and their probabilities:

```
Choose random k₂
For i = 1 ... q do
    A_E → x_i
    If x_i ≤ b − 2
        A_E ← f_{k₁}(x_i, pad, 1)
    else
        A_E ← f_{k₁}(x_{i,pref}, F_{k₂}(x_{i,suff}), 0)
A_E → (x, y)
If x ≤ b − 2
    output (x, pad, 1), y
else
    output (x_{pref}, F_{k₂}(x_{suff}), 0), y
```

Fig. 3. A_f algorithm to forge the keyed compression MAC

A_f forges : the event where A_f correctly forges a mac of $f_{k1}()$

      E : the event where A_E correctly forges a mac of $ENMAC()$

      $\bar{E}$: the event where A_E fails to correctly forge a mac of $ENMAC()$

      E_1 : the event where A_E correctly forges $(x, y = ENMAC(x))$ and message x fits in a single block

      E_+ : the event where A_E correctly forges $(x, y = ENMAC(x))$ and message x requires multiple blocks

$E_{+,pref\neq}$: the event where A_E correctly forges $(x, y = ENMAC(x)$ and message x requires multiple blocks and $x_{pref} \neq x_{i,pref}$ of any queried messages $x_i \in x_1 \dots x_q$

$E_{+,pref=}$: the event where A_E correctly forges $(x, y = ENMAC(x)$ and message x requires multiple blocks and $x_{pref} = x_{i,pref}$ of some queried message $x_i \in x_1 \dots x_q$

    ϵ_E : $P(E)$

    ϵ_{E_1} : $P(E_1)$

    ϵ_{E_+} : $P(E_+)$

$\epsilon_{E_+,pref\neq}$: $P(E_{+,pref\neq})$

$\epsilon_{E_+,pref=}$: $P(E_{+,pref=})$

We note that $\epsilon_E = \epsilon_{E_1} + \epsilon_{E_+}$ where E_1 is the event and ϵ_{E_1} is the probability that ENMAC is attacked and the ENMAC message forged by A_E is about one block size, or to be precise less than $b - 2$ bits. And let E_+ be the event and ϵ_{E_+} be the probability that ENMAC is attacked and the ENMAC message forged by A_E is larger than one block size. Furthermore, $\epsilon_{E_+} = \epsilon_{E_+,pref\neq} + \epsilon_{E_+,pref=}$ where $\epsilon_{E_+,pref\neq}$ is the probability that the ENMAC is forged with a multi block message and the prefix of the message does not equal the prefix of any of the messages previously queried by A_E. And $\epsilon_{E_+,pref=}$ is the probability that the ENMAC is forged with a multi block message and the prefix of the message is equal to prefix of some previously queried messages by A_E. In this case we know the suffix of the forged message has to be different than the suffix of the messages with the same prefix. We begin the proof:

$$P[A_f\ forges] = P[A_f forges \cap E] + P[A_f\ forges \cap \bar{E}] \qquad (1)$$
$$= P[A_f forges \cap E] \qquad (2)$$

In equation 1, $P[A_f\ forges \cap \bar{E}] = 0$ because when A_E fails and outputs a message/tag pair (x, y) where $y \neq ENMAC(x)$ then A_f will also output incorrect message/tag pair. In the case of a single block message, A_f will output the message/tag pair $([x, pad, 1], y)$ but since $y \neq ENMAC(x)$ and $ENMAC(x) = f_{k1}(x, pad, 1)$ then $y \neq f_{k1}(x, pad, 1)$, thus A_f has also output an incorrect message/tag pair. Similarly, for the multi block case if A_f will output the (message,tag) pair $([x_{pref}, F_{k2}(x_{suff}), 0], y)$ but since $y \neq ENMAC(x)$ and $ENMAC(x) = f_{k1}(x_{i,pref}, F_{k2}(x_{i,suff}), 0)$ then $y \neq f_{k1}(x_{i,pref}, F_{k2}(x_{i,suff}), 0)$, thus A_f has also output an incorrect message/tag pair.

$$P[A_f \ forges] = P[A_f \ forges \cap E_1] + P[A_f \ forges \cap E_+] \tag{3}$$
$$= P[A_f \ forges \cap E_1] + P[A_f \ forges \cap E_{+,pref \neq}] +$$
$$P[A_f forges \cap E_{+,pref=}] \tag{4}$$
$$= P[A_f \ forges \mid E_1] \ P[E_1] +$$
$$P[A_f \ forges \mid E_{+,pref \neq}] \ P[E_{+,pref \neq}] +$$
$$P[A_f \ forges \cap E_{+,pref=}] \tag{5}$$
$$= 1 \cdot \epsilon_{E_1} + 1 \cdot \epsilon_{E_+,pref \neq} + P[A_f \ forges \cap E_{+,pref=}] \tag{6}$$
$$= \epsilon_{E_1} + \epsilon_{E_+,pref \neq} + P[A_f \ forges \cap E_{+,pref=}] \tag{7}$$

In equation 5, $P[A_f \ forges \mid E_1] = 1$ because when A_E correctly outputs the message/tag pair (x, y) where $y = ENMAC(x)$ then A_f outputs $([x, pad, 1], y)$ where $y = f_{k1}(x, pad, 1)$. The indicator bit 1 means we have to only consider the previously queried single block messages since the multi block messages will have the indicator bit set to 0. Among the single block messages queried by A_E, none equal x because A_E has correctly forged a new message. Thus none of the previous queries $(x_i, pad, 1)$ to $f_{k1}(x_i, pad, 1)$ would equal $(x, pad, 1)$ and hence A_f would have correctly forged a new message/tag pair. Similarly in equation 5 $P[A_f \ forges \mid E_{+,pref \neq}] = 1$ because when A_E correctly outputs the message/tag pair (x, y) where $y = ENMAC(x)$ and x is multiple blocks long then A_f outputs the message/tag pair $([x_{pref}, F_{k2}(x_{suff}), 0], y)$ where $y = f_{k1}(x_{i,pref}, F_{k2}(x_{i,suff}), 0)$. The indicator bit 0 means we have to only consider the previously queried multi block messages. Furthermore, the probability in question is conditioned on the multi block message being of the sort where $x_{pref} \neq x_{i,pref}$, the prefix of any previously queried message. Thus this will be a new prefix x_{pref} and independently of what the suffix is, the message/tag pair $([x_{pref}, F_{k2}(x_{suff}), 0], y = f_{k1}(x_{i,pref}, F_{k2}(x_{i,suff}), 0))$ is new and correct.

$P[A_f \ forges]$
$$= \epsilon_{E_1} + \epsilon_{E_+,pref \neq}$$
$$+ P[(\forall j \epsilon S_{pref=} \ (\ F_{k2}(x_{suff}) \neq F_{k2}(x_{j,suff}) \ ) \ ) \cap E_{+,pref=}] \tag{8}$$
$$\text{where } S_{pref=} \text{ is the set of } x_i \epsilon \ x_1 \ldots x_q \text{ such that } x_{i,pref} = x_{pref}$$
$$= \epsilon_{E_1} + \epsilon_{E_+,pref \neq} + P[E_{+,pref=}]$$
$$- P[(\exists j \epsilon S_{pref=} \ s.t. \ (F_{k2}(x_{suff}) = F_{k2}(x_{j,suff}))) \cap E_{+,pref=}] \tag{9}$$
$$= \epsilon_E$$
$$- P[(\ \exists j \epsilon S_{pref=} \ s.t. \ (\ F_{k2}(x_{suff}) = F_{k2}(x_{j,suff}) \ ) \ ) \cap E_{+,pref=}] \tag{10}$$

Equation 7 is transformed to equation 8 because the event $A_f \ forges \cap E_{+,pref=}$ will happen when $E_{+,pref=}$ happens and $F_{k2}(x_{suff})$ is not equal to $F_{k2}(x_{i,suff})$, the suffix of any other previously queried x_i whose prefix $x_{i,pref} = x_{pref}$. To repeat, in that case even when the prefixes are the same, $F_{k2}(x_{suff})$ is not equal to any other previously queried $F_{k2}(x_{i,suff})$. Thus we see that the message $(x_{pref}, F_{k2}(x_{suff}), 0)$ would not have been queried before and A_f would have correctly forged a new mac $f_{k1}()$. In equation 8, the last term is really stating the probability of no collision in x_{suff} and $S_{pref=}$. In equation 9, the last term is really stating the probability of a collision in x_{suff} and $S_{pref=}$. Equation 9 can be derived from equation 8 by noting that:

$$P[E_{+,pref=}] = P[no\ collision\ in\ x_{suff}\ and\ S_{pref=} \cap E_{+,pref=}]$$
$$+P[collision\ in\ x_{suff}\ and\ S_{pref=} \cap E_{+,pref=}]$$
$$or\ more\ formally$$
$$= P[(\ \forall j \epsilon S_{pref=}\ (\ F_{k2}(x_{suff}) \neq F_{k2}(x_{j,suff})\ )\ ) \cap E_{+,pref=}] +$$
$$P[(\ \exists j \epsilon S_{pref=}\ s.t.\ (F_{k2}(x_{suff}) = F_{k2}(x_{j,suff}))\ )\ \cap E_{+,pref=}]$$

To bound $P[(\ \exists j \epsilon S_{pref=}\ s.t.\ (\ F_{k2}(x_{suff}) = F_{k2}(x_{j,suff}))\ )\ \cap E_{+,pref=}]$ value in equation 10, we will use the lemma below:

Lemma 1. $P[(\ \exists j \epsilon S_{pref=}\ (\ F_{k2}(x_{suff}) = F_{k2}(x_{j,suff})\ )\ )\ \cap E_{+,pref=}] < \epsilon_F$

Proof: In Appendix A.

Using the lemma to substitute in equation 10, we get the inequality in equation 11.

$$P[A_f\ forges] > \epsilon_E - \epsilon_F \qquad (11)$$

$$\epsilon_f \geq P[best\ (t,q)\ algorithm\ forges\ f_{k1}()) \geq P[A_f\ forges] > \epsilon_E - \epsilon_F \quad (12)$$
$$\epsilon_f > \epsilon_E - \epsilon_F \qquad (13)$$
$$\epsilon_E < \epsilon_f + \epsilon_F \qquad (14)$$

Equation 12 simply restates the definition of ϵ_f and notes that probability of success of A_f, a particular kind of algorithm, has to be less than or equal to probability of success by the best mac attacking algorithm. This completes the proof of theorem 1. An alternate proof of theorem 1 is presented in Appendix B which more closely follows the NMAC proof style.

4.4   Practical Implementations

In the case of multiple block ENMAC, forming x_{suff}, beginning at a non-word boundary may cause us to re-align all the words in x_{suff}. We can avoid this case by using this variant (presented in the bit processing mode) of ENMAC:

$$ENMAC_k(x) = f_{k_1}(x, pad, 1) \qquad\qquad if\ |x| <= b - 2\ bits$$

$$= f_{k_1}(F_{k_2}(x_{pref}), x_{suff}, 0) \quad else$$

where for SHA

$$x_{pref} = x_1 \ldots x_{|x|-351}$$

$$x_{suff} = x_{|x|-350} \ldots x_{|x|}$$

A similar security proof described in the last section applies to this variant since the independence of the single block compression call and multiple block compression call is preserved by the last indicator bit, and in the single block case unambiguous padding is used. Other variants are possible where the single block indicator bit is placed in a different location, for example, as the first bit of the block. Also since in practice data is often processed in bytes, it may be appropriate to perform the single block case when the message $|x|$ is less than $b - 8$ bits rather than the $b - 2$ bits we specified.

4.5   One Key ENMAC

A variant of NMAC would be to use a keyless hash function in the inner call rather than a keyed hash function. Similar security proofs will work if one makes the assumption that the hash function is not only weakly collision resistant but also simply collision resistant.

$$One\ key\ ENMAC_k(x) = f_{k_1}(x, pad, 1) \qquad\qquad if\ |x| <= b - 2\ bits$$

$$= f_{k_1}(F(x_{pref}), x_{suff}, 0) \qquad else$$

where for SHA

$$x_{pref} = x_1 \ldots x_{|x|-351}$$

$$x_{suff} = x_{|x|-350} \ldots x_{|x|}$$

5   EHMAC: Enhanced HMAC

HMAC, as previously described, is a variant of NMAC which does not require the direct loading of the key in to the chaining variable of the compression function, but only makes call to the hash function. A straightforward adaptation of ENMAC to EHMAC would be to prepend HMAC type preprocessing, but we have to now change the message size that can be processed by a single block because the SHA-1 hash function appends its own padding and length values. We specify the straightforward EHMAC function using SHA-1 hash function:

$$EHMAC_k(x) = F(\bar{k} \oplus opad, x, pad, 1) \qquad\qquad if\ |x| <= 445\ bits$$

$$= F(\bar{k} \oplus opad, F(\bar{k} \oplus ipad, x_{pref}), x_{suff}, 0) \qquad else$$

where for SHA

$$x_{pref} = x_1 \ldots x_{|x|-286}$$

$$x_{suff} = x_{|x|-285} \ldots x_{|x|}$$

The key k is appended with enough zeroes to expand k to 512 bit value $\bar{k}$. The 512 bit values of opad and ipad are different from each other and for example are specified in [BCK96]. Since the underlying hash function SHA-1 appends its own 64 bit length value and a mandatory padding bit, the largest possible string that can be fed to F in the SHA-1 case is 447 bits. As specified for the single block case of ENMAC, we reserve the last 447th bit as a single block indicator bit which is set to 1 for the single block case and set to 0 for the multiple block case. Also the single block padding scheme "pad" described in the ENMAC case is used here, hence one more bit is reserved for padding. Thus if the message is less than or equal to 445 bits then we treat it as a single block case. Even for the single block case two calls to the compression are needed, first to process the 512 bit value $\bar{k} \oplus opad$ and then the actual (445 or less) message x. If we look upon $k_1 = f(IV, \bar{k} \oplus opad)$ then the relationship of EHMAC to ENMAC seems more apparent.

For the multiple block case similar HMAC preprocessing is added, but the length of x_{suff} that can be loaded in the outer call has to be reduced to accommodate the length and pad appending of the underlying SHA-1 hash function.

A variant of EHMAC which is slightly more efficient for the single block case is possible where instead of specifying a pad scheme, a "1" is appended to x in the single block case and a "0" is appended in the multiple block case. The security is preserved because SHA-1 hash function itself has an unambiguous method of padding.

6   Conclusion

NMAC and HMAC are efficient for long messages, however, for short messages the nested constructions results in a significant inefficiency. For example to MAC a message shorter than a block, HMAC requires at least two calls to the hash function rather than one. We proposed an enhancement that allows both short and long messages to be message authenticated more efficiently than HMAC while also providing proofs of security. For a message smaller than a block our MAC only requires one call to the hash function. We discuss various variants of our constructions.

7   Acknowledgements

I would like to thank Phil MacKenzie for providing helpful comments on an earlier version of the draft, and Frank Quick for suggesting to include presentation of security proofs (Appendix B) which closely follow the presentation in the HMAC paper.

References

[BCK96] M. Bellare, R. Canetti, and H. Krawczyk. Keying hash functions for message authentication. CRYPTO 96.

[KBC97] H. Krawczyk, M. Bellare, and R. Canetti. HMAC: Keyed-hash functions for message authentication, IETF RFC-2104, Feb 1997.

[BKR94] M. Bellare, J. Kilian and P. Rogaway. The security of cipher block chaining. CRYPTO 94

[ECAB] Enhanced Cryptographic Algorithms, Rev. B, TR45.AHAG.

[FIPS180] National Bureau of Standards, FIPS publication 180-1: Secure Hash Standard, 1995. Federal Information Processing Standards Publications 180-1.

[GMR88] O. Goldwasser, S. Micali, and R. Rivest. A digital Signature Scheme Secure Against Adaptive Chosen-Message Attacks. Siam Journal of Computing, 1988, pg 281-308.

[PV95] B. Preneel and P.C. van Oorschot. MD-x MAC and building fast MACs from hash functions, CRYPTO 95.

[R92] R. Rivest. The MD5 message digest algorithm. IETF RFC-1321, 1992.

[WC81] M. Wegman and L. Carter. New hash funcitons and their use in authentication and set equality. Journal of Computer and System Sciences, 22:265-279, 1981.

A   Lemma 1

Lemma 1 states that the joint probability of the event that $E_{+,pref=}$ happens where A_E forges a multi block message with its prefix, x_{pref}, being equal to prefix of some previously queried message, $x_{i,pref}$, and there is a collision of x_{suff} and a message in set $S_{pref=}$ is less than ϵ_F. Suppose that the probability of $P[(\ \exists j\epsilon S_{pref=}\ s.t.\ (\ F_{k2}(x_{suff}) = F_{k2}(x_{j,suff})\ )\ )\ \cap\ E_{+,pref=}]$ is significant then we can, similar to A_f, create an algorithm A_F which will find collisions on the hash function $F_{k2}()$. This particular way of finding collisions we know is bounded above by ϵ_F, the probability that the best algorithm finds a collision. We now describe the algorithm A_F shown in figure 4.

Instead of choosing a random k_2 as in A_f, we choose a random key k_1 since we are trying to break the collision resistant function F_{k2} and not the mac function f_{k1}. The algorithm A_E will ask to see the ENMAC on various messages x_i. We answer these queries correctly, as was done in A_f, so to A_E it looks like the answers are coming from a true ENMAC function. To calculate ENMAC on x_i we check if its a single block message, if it is then A_F itself calculates $f_{k1}(x_i, pad, 1)$ since it knows the key k_1. If x_i is a multi block message then A_F first makes a query call to the real hash function $F_{k2}()$ with the argument $x_{i,suff}$. A_F takes this answer and uses key k_1 to form the mac of $f_{k1}(x_{i,pref}, F_{k2}(x_{i,suff}), 0)$ and gives to A_E. When A_E gives a forgery (x, y), we see if its a multi block message and whether its x_{pref} equals $x_{i,pref}$ for some previously queried x_i. If it doesn't then A_F says no collision found. If the set $S_{pref=}$ is not empty then we query

Choose random k_1
For $i = 1 \ldots q$ do
    $A_E \to x_i$
    If $x_i \leq b - 2$
        $A_E \leftarrow f_{k_1}(x_i, pad, 1)$
    else
        $A_E \leftarrow f_{k_1}(x_{i,pref}, F_{k_2}(x_{i,suff}), 0)$
$A_E \to (x, y)$
If $(x > b - 2)$ and $(x_{pref}$ equals some $x_{i,pref})$
    query $F_{k_2}(x_{suff})$
    If $F_{k_2}(x_{suff}$ equals $F_{k_2}(x_{j,suff})$ for some j in $S_{pref=}$
        output x_{suff} and $x_{j,suff}$ as collision points and stop
output no collisions found

Fig. 4. A_F algorithm to find collisions in keyed hash $F_{k_2}()$

$F_{k_2}(x_{suff})$ and see if it equals $F_{k_2}(x_{j,suff})$ for some j in $S_{pref=}$. If it does then we output the pair x_{suff} and $x_{j,suff}$ as collision points and stop.

    The probability of A_F finding a collision this way has to be less than the probability of finding collision by the best algorithm which is ϵ_F. But we also see that the probability of A_F finding a collision is the same as the event in A_f of ($\exists j \epsilon S_{pref=}$ s.t. ($F(x_{suff}) = F(x_{j,suff})$)) $\cap$ $E_{+,pref=}$. Thus this will also be bounded by ϵ_F.

B   Alternate Security Proof of ENMAC

In this alternate proof we proceed from the probability of A_f failing to forge a correct mac of $f_{k_1}()$ rather than the $P[A_f\ forges]$ as done in the main proof.

$$P[A_f\ fails] = P[A_f\ fails \cap E] + P[A_f\ fails \cap \bar{E}] \tag{15}$$
$$= P[A_f\ fails \cap E] + P[A_f\ fails \mid \bar{E}]\ P[\bar{E}] \tag{16}$$
$$= P[A_f\ fails \cap E] + 1 \cdot (1 - \epsilon_E) \tag{17}$$
$$= P[A_f\ fails \cap E] + 1 - \epsilon_E \tag{18}$$

    In equation 17, the $P[A_f\ fails \mid \bar{E}]$ is set to 1 because whether in the single block or multi block case, if A_E was unsuccessful in forging a valid ENMAC on x then A_f output would also not be a valid mac.

$$P[A_f\ fails]$$
$$= P[A_f\ fails \cap E_1] + P[A_f\ fails \cap E_+] + 1 - \epsilon_E \tag{19}$$
$$= P[A_f\ fails \mid E_1]\ P[E_1] + P[A_f\ fails \cap E_+] + 1 - \epsilon_E \tag{20}$$
$$= 0 \cdot P[E_1] + P[A_f\ fails \cap E_+] + 1 - \epsilon_E \tag{21}$$

$$= P[A_f \ fails \cap E_{+,pref \neq}] + P[A_f \ fails \cap E_{+,pref=}] + 1 - \epsilon_E \quad (22)$$

$$= P[A_f \ fails \mid E_{+,pref \neq}] \ P[E_{+,pref \neq}]$$
$$+ P[A_f \ fails \cap E_{+,pref=}] + 1 - \epsilon_E \quad (23)$$

$$= 0 \cdot P[E_{+,pref \neq}] + P[A_f \ fails \cap E_{+,pref=}] + 1 - \epsilon_E \quad (24)$$

$$= P[A_f \ fails \cap E_{+,pref=}] + 1 - \epsilon_E \quad (25)$$

In equation 20, $P[A_f \ fails \mid E_1]$ is zero because if A_E has forged a correct $(x, y = ENMAC(x))$ pair then A_f would have forged a correct message/tag pair, $([x, pad, 1], f_{k1}(x, pad, 1))$. Similarly in equation 23 the $P[A_f \ fails \mid E_{+,pref \neq}]$ is zero because if a correct pair was forged with a prefix different then any previously queried then this prefix will be a new input to the message/tag pair output by A_f which is $(x_{pref}, F_{k2}(x_{suff}), 0)$ as message and $f_{k1}(x_{pref}, F_{k2}(x_{suff}), 0)$ as tag.

$$P[A_f \ fails] \quad (26)$$
$$= P[(\ \exists j \epsilon S_{pref=} \ s.t. \ (\ F_{k2}(x_{suff}) = F_{k2}(x_{j,suff})\ )\ )\ \cap \ E_{+,pref=}] + 1 - \epsilon_E$$

$$P[A_f \ fails] < \epsilon_F + 1 - \epsilon_E \quad (27)$$
$$1 - \epsilon_f < P[best \ (t, q) \ algorithm \ fails \ in \ forging \ mac \ f_{k1}()]$$
$$\leq \ P[A_f \ fails] < \epsilon_F + 1 - \epsilon_E \quad (28)$$
$$1 - \epsilon_f < \epsilon_F + 1 - \epsilon_E \quad (29)$$
$$\epsilon_E < \epsilon_f + \epsilon_F \quad (30)$$

Equation 26 equates the $P[A_f \ fails \cap E_{+,pref=}]$ in equation 25 with the probability of finding a collision in $F_{k2}(x_{suff})$ and another $F_{k2}(x_{j,suff})$ where x_j is from the set $S_{pref=}$. Lemma 1 deals exactly with this probability and we use Lemma 1 to bound this collision probability in equation 27. Equation 28 restates the fact that even the best algorithm will fail to forge with probability greater than $1 - \epsilon_f$. And in turn the particular algorithm A_f will fail to forge with probability greater than or equal to that. In equation 30 we complete the alternate proof of theorem 1.

Optimal Extension Fields for XTR

Dong-Guk Han[1*], Ki Soon Yoon[1], Young-Ho Park[2], Chang Han Kim[3], and Jongin Lim[1]

[1] Center for Information and Security Technologies(CIST),
Korea University, Anam Dong, Sungbuk Gu, Seoul, KOREA
{christa,ksyoon}@cist.korea.ac.kr,
jilim@tiger.korea.ac.kr
[2] Dept. of Information Security & System Engineering,
Sejong Cyber Univ., Seoul, KOREA
youngho@cybersejong.ac.kr
[3] Dept. of Information Security, Semyung Univ., Jechon, KOREA
chkim@venus.semyung.ac.kr

Abstract. Application of XTR in cryptographic protocols leads to substantial savings both in communication and computational overhead without compromising security [6]. XTR is a new method to represent elements of a subgroup of a multiplicative group of a finite field $GF(p^6)$ and it can be generalized to the field $GF(p^{6m})$ [6,9]. This paper proposes optimal extension fields for XTR among Galois fields $GF(p^{6m})$ which can be applied to XTR. In order to select such fields, we introduce a new notion of Generalized Optimal Extension Fields(GOEFs) and suggest a condition of prime p, a defining polynomial of $GF(p^{2m})$ and a fast method of multiplication in $GF(p^{2m})$ to achieve fast finite field arithmetic in $GF(p^{2m})$. From our implementation results, $GF(p^{36}) \rightarrow GF(p^{12})$ is the most efficient extension fields for XTR and computing $Tr(g^n)$ given $Tr(g)$ in $GF(p^{12})$ is on average more than twice faster than that of the XTR system[6,10] on Pentium III/700MHz which has 32-bit architecture.

Keywords XTR public key system, Pseudo-Mersenne prime, Karatsuba's method.

1 Introduction

Almost all public key systems have a large key size except Elliptic Curve Cryptosystem(ECC). This is impractical in many applications such as smart card and wireless telecommunication of which power and bandwidth are limited. So many cryptographers think that ECC is one of the most efficient public key systems applicable to many hardwares with limited environments.

---

* This work was supported by both Ministry of Information and Communication and Korea Information Security Agency, Korea, under project 2002-130

K. Nyberg and H. Heys (Eds.): SAC 2002, LNCS 2595, pp. 369–384, 2003.

The XTR public key system was introduced at Crypto 2000[6]. From a security point of view XTR is a traditional subgroup discrete logarithm system. But it uses a non-standard way to represent and compute subgroup elements to achieve substantial computational and communication advantages over traditional representations. It is the first method we are aware of that uses $GF(p^2)$ arithmetic to achieve $GF(p^6)$ security, without requiring explicit construction of $GF(p^6)$. As shown in [6], XTR of security equivalent to 1024-bit RSA achieves speed comparable to cryptosystems based on random elliptic curves over random prime fields (ECC) and of equivalent security. Here the XTR public keys are only twice as large as ECC keys, but parameter initialization from scratch for XTR takes a negligible amount of computing time, unlike RSA and ECC. So XTR is an excellent alternative to either RSA or ECC in applications such as smart card and wireless telecommunications. Therefore finding the optimized extension fields for XTR is very significant.

It was mentioned very briefly that XTR can be generalized in a straightforward way using the extension field of the form $GF(p^{6m})$ and systematic design of this generalization was proposed in [9]. But they did not propose optimized extension fields for XTR.

In this paper, we suggest optimized extension fields among several extension fields $GF(p^{6m})$ at 32-bit word system. It is sufficient to look around following five extension fields for XTR according to a size of prime p.

☐   Generalized extension fields for XTR : $GF(p^{6m}) \to GF(p^{2m})$

- $GF(p^6) \to GF(p^2)$, the size of prime p is about 170 bits and $m = 1$.
- $GF(p^{12}) \to GF(p^4)$, the size of prime p is about 85 bits and $m = 2$.
- $GF(p^{18}) \to GF(p^6)$, the size of prime p is about 64 bits and $m = 3$.
- $GF(p^{36}) \to GF(p^{12})$, the size of prime p is about 32 bits and $m = 6$.
- $GF(p^{66}) \to GF(p^{22})$, the size of prime p is about 16 bits and $m = 11$.

We compare complexities of elementary operations of above five extension fields and select optimal extension fields for XTR. Moreover, we consider the cost of computing XTR single exponentiation that is to compute $Tr(g^n)$ given $Tr(g), n \in Z$. The most frequently performed operations in XTR[6,9] are the following three types:

$$x^2, xy, xz - yz^{p^m} \text{ for } x, y, z \in GF(p^{2m})$$

These three operations play an important role to speed up XTR single exponentiation. To optimize elementary operations in $GF(p^{2m})$ we stipulate the following properties on the choice of p and defining polynomial:

1. Choose p to be a pseudo-Mersenne prime, that is, of the form $2^n \pm c$ for some $\log_2 c \le \frac{1}{2}n$ to allow for efficient subfield modular reduction.

2. Choose a defining polynomial that is a binomial or $2m$-th all-one-polynomial (AOP) for efficient extension field modular reduction.

3. Choose p to be less than but close to the word size of the processor so that all subfield operations take advantage of the processor's fast integer arithmetic.

To meet the third condition, we choose m large enough. And then we can select p to be less than but close to the word size of the processor. On the other hand, a number of subfield multiplications and additions in $GF(p)$ required for polynomial multiplicaton in $GF(p^{2m})$ would increase rapidly. As customary we do not count the cost of additions in $GF(p)$, however, when p is small and m is large the cost of additions in $GF(p)$ is not negligible. In this paper, we use Karatsuba-like method at polynomial multiplicaton in $GF(p^{2m})$ to reduce the number of subfield multiplications and modify the Karatsuba-like method to reduce the cost of additions in $GF(p)$. Due to the above considerations for prime p and fast polynomial multiplication method, our proposed system is on average more than twice faster than the XTR[6,10] to compute a single exponentiation.

As the construction in this paper, there are fewer appropriate prime p than XTR case. This means that users may share the same extension field. But Elliptic Curve Cryptosystems has this property.

The rest of the paper is organized as follows. In Section 2 we shall briefly review on the XTR Public Key Cryptosystems[6,9,10]. In Section 3 and 4 deal with Generalized Optimal Extension Field(GOEF) and an efficient arithmetic in GOEF, respectively. In Section 5 we present our implementation results and propose the optimized extension field for XTR. The final Section contains our conclusions to the present work.

2   Review on the XTR Public Key Cryptosystems

In this section we review some of the results from [6,9,10].

Definition 1. *The trace $Tr(h)$ over $GF(p^{2m})$ of $h \in GF(p^{6m})$ is the sum of the conjugates over $GF(p^{2m})$ of h, i.e.,*

$$Tr(h) = h + h^{p^{2m}} + h^{p^{4m}}.$$

For constructing XTR, primes p, q and positive integer m must satisfy following conditions :

- p and $2m+1$ are prime numbers, $p \pmod{2m+1}$ is a primitive element in Z_{2m+1}.
- $\Phi_{6m}(p)$ has a prime factor q whose the size is more than 160 bits.

Note that $\Phi_n(X)$ is $n-th$ cyclotomic polynomial for a positive integer n. The first above condition guarantees $GF(p^{2m})$ has an optimal normal basis of type I[11, Theorem 5.2]. The subgroup with order q cannot be embedded in the multiplicative group of any true subfield of $GF(p^{6m})$ by the second condition[7, Lemma 2.4].

Definition 2. For $c \in GF(p^{2m})$ let $F(c, X)$ be the polynomial $X^3 - cX^2 + c^{p^m}X - 1 \in GF(p^{2m})[X]$ with (not necessarily distinct) roots h_0, h_1, h_2 in $GF(p^{6m})$, and let $c_n = h_0^n + h_1^n + h_2^n$ for $n \in Z$.

Note. If $F(c, X)$ is irreducible over $GF(p^{2m})$ then c_n is equal to $Tr(h_0^n)$.

Lemma 1 (9, Lemma 2.1).

  i. $c = c_1$.
 ii. $h_0 h_1 + h_1 h_2 + h_0 h_2 = c^{p^m}$.
iii. $h_0 h_1 h_2 = 1$.
 iv. $c_n = c_{np^m} = c_n^{p^m}$ for $n \in Z$.
  v. Either all h_i have order dividing $p^{2m} - p^m + 1$ and > 3 or all $h_i \in GF(p^{2m})$.
 vi. $(c_n)_t = c_{nt} = (c_t)_n$.
vii. $c_n \in GF(p^{2m})$ for $n \in Z$. [6, Lemma 2.3.2]

Corollary 1 (9, Lemma 2.3). Let c, c_{n-1}, c_n and c_{n+1} be given.

  i. $c_{2n} = c_n^2 - 2c_n^{p^m}$.
 ii. $c_{n+2} = c * c_{n+1} - c^{p^m} * c_n + c_{n-1}$.
iii. $c_{2n-1} = c_{n-1} * c_n - c^{p^m} * c_n^{p^m} + c_{n+1}^{p^m}$.
 iv. $c_{2n+1} = c_n * c_{n+1} - c * c_n^{p^m} + c_{n-1}^{p^m}$.

In XTR, an algorithm to compute $Tr(g^n)$ given $Tr(g)$ and $n \in Z$ is needed like that to compute g^n in public key system based on discrete logarithm problem. The size of n depends on the size of the order g.

Definition 3. Let $S_n(c) = (c_{n-1}, c_n, c_{n+1}) \in GF(p^{2m})^3$

To compute $S_n(c)$ from any given $c \in GF(p^{2m})$, $m \in Z^+$, the algorithm 2.3.7[6] for $m = 1$ and the algorithm 4.2 [9] were proposed. Another XTR single exponentiation method [10] is on average more than 35% faster than the algorithm 2.3.7[6]. The most frequently performed operation in the algorithm to compute $S_n(c)$[6,9,10] was organized with Corollary 1 i,iii,iv. Thus the complexity of the algorithm computing $S_n(c)$ depends on the complexity of computing $x^2, xy, xz - yz^{p^m}$ for $x, y, z \in GF(p^{2m})$.

Lemma 2 (10, Lemma 2.2). $x, y, z \in GF(p^2)$ with $p \equiv 2 \bmod 3$.

  i Computing x^p is free.
 ii Computing x^2 takes two multiplications in $GF(p)$.
iii Computing xy costs the same as two and a half multiplications in $GF(p)$.
 iv Computing $xz - yz^p$ costs the same as three multiplications in $GF(p)$.

Lemma 3 (9, Lemma 4.3). *Let p and $2m + 1$ be prime numbers, where $p \pmod{2m + 1}$ is a primitive element in Z_{2m+1}. Then for $x, y, z \in GF(p^{2m})$,*

   i *Computing x^{p^m} is free.*
   ii *Computing x^2 takes 80% of the complexity taken for multiplications in $GF(p^{2m})$.*
   iii *Computing xy takes $4m^2$ multiplications in $GF(p)$.*
   iv *Computing $xz - yz^{p^m}$ takes $4m^2$ multiplications in $GF(p)$.*

Remark 1. In $GF(p^2)$, $S_n(c)$ can be computed in $7 \log_2 n$ multiplications in $GF(p)$ [10].

Theorem 1. *Let $c \in GF(p^{2m})$ and a positive integer n be given. Then it takes $(2a + b) \log_2 n$ multiplications in $GF(p)$ to compute $S_n(c)$, where a is the number of multiplications in $GF(p)$ to compute x^2 for $x \in GF(p^{2m})$ and b is the number of multiplications in $GF(p)$ to compute $xz - yz^{p^m}$ for $x, y, z \in GF(p^{2m})$.*

3 Generalized Optimal Extension Field

The performance of field arithmetic in $GF(p^m)$ mainly depends on the choice of parameters for extension field, such as a prime p and a defining polynomial. The reduction step in multiplication has the biggest time complexity. So there are many methods proposed as follows to reduce complexity in reduction steps.

Definition 4. *Let c be a positive rational integer. A pseudo-Mersenne prime is a prime number of the form $2^n \pm c$, $\log_2 c \leq \lfloor \frac{1}{2} n \rfloor$.*

Definition 5. *[3] An Optimal Extension Field(OEF) is a finite field $GF(p^m)$ such that:*

   1. p is a pseudo-Mersenne prime,
   2. An irreducible binomial $P(x) = x^m - \omega$ exists over $GF(p)$.

Theorem 2. *[11] Let $m \geq 2$ be an integer and $\omega \in GF(p)^*$. Then the binomial $x^m - \omega$ is irreducible in $GF(p)[x]$ if and only if the following two conditions are satisfied:*

   i. each prime factor of m divides the order e of ω over $GF(p)$, but not $(p-1)/e$,
   ii. $p \equiv 1 \bmod 4$ if $m \equiv 0 \bmod 4$.

There are two special cases of OEF which yield additional arithmetic advantages. A Type I OEF which has $p = 2^n \pm 1$ allows for subfield modular reduction with very low complexity. Type II OEF which has an irreducible binomial $x^m - 2$ allows for a reduction in the complexity of extension field modular reduction.

There is another method to reduce the complexity of extension field modular reduction.

Definition 6. *We call f_m the m-th all-one-polynomial(AOP) if*

$$f(x) = \Phi_{m+1}(x) = \frac{x^{m+1} - 1}{x - 1} = x^m + x^{m-1} + \cdots + x + 1.$$

The following theorem shows when AOP is irreducible [11].

Theorem 3. *Let p be a prime. $f_m(x)$ is irreducible over $GF(p)$ if and only if $m + 1$ is a prime and p is primitive in Z_{m+1}.*

Theorem 4. *If $m+1$ is a prime and p is primitive in Z_{m+1}, where p is a prime or prime power. Let α be a root of m-th AOP then $\{\alpha, \alpha^p, \cdots, \alpha^{p^{m-1}}\}$ is a basis of $GF(p^m)$ over $GF(p)$. Furthermore $\{\alpha, \alpha^p, \cdots, \alpha^{p^{m-1}}\} = \{\alpha, \alpha^2, \cdots, \alpha^m\}$.*

Proof. The first assertion is from [11]. To prove the second, it is sufficient to show that $\{1, p, p^2, \cdots, p^{m-1}\} = \{1, 2, \cdots, m\}$ in Z_{m+1}. Suppose $0 \leq j \leq i \leq m - 1$ and $p^i \equiv p^j \mod (m + 1)$ then $p^j(p^{i-j} - 1) \equiv 0 \mod (m + 1)$. Thus $p^{i-j} \equiv 1 \mod (m + 1)$ and order of p divides $i - j$. But the order of p is m and $i - j < m$. Therefore $i = j$. Hence $\{1, p, p^2, \cdots, p^{m-1}\}$ are all distinct and $\{1, p, p^2, \cdots, p^{m-1}\} = \{1, 2, \cdots, m\}$.

Definition 7. *If a set $A = \{\alpha, \alpha^2, \cdots, \alpha^m\}$ in $GF(p^m)$ is a basis over $GF(p)$ then we call it a non-conventional basis of $GF(p^m)$ over $GF(p)$.*

In this paper, we use a non-conventional basis representation for $GF(p^m)$ whose defining polynomial is AOP. Because the property that is $\alpha^{m+1} = 1$ and $1 = -\alpha - \alpha^2 - \cdots - \alpha^m$ can be used to speed up extension field modular reduction in a non-conventional basis. The detail explanation can be covered in the section 4.3.

We introduce a new type of Galois field.

Definition 8. *Generalized Optimal Extension Field(GOEF) is a finite field $GF(p^m)$ such that:*

1. *p is a pseudo-Mersenne prime,*
2. *Either an binomial $x^m - \omega$ or $m - th$ AOP is irreducible.*

The construction of GOEF can be achieved from a pair of a pseudo-Mersenne prime and an irreducible polynomial. Either a binomial or an AOP must be chosen as the irreducible polynomial to construct GOEF. But in GOEF, determination of irreducible polynomial is related to the choice of a pseudo-Mersenne prime. The choice of defining polynomial determines the complexity of the operations required to perform the extension field modular reduction. And the selection of a pseudo-Mersenne prime affects the complexity in subfield modular reduction. So it is very important to make a pair of a pseudo-Mersenne prime and a defining polynomial. We consider a polynomial basis or normal basis representation of a field element $A \in GF(p^m)$ depending on f.

$$A(\alpha) = a_{m-1}\alpha^{m-1} + \cdots + a_1\alpha + a_0, \text{ when } f(x) \text{ is binomial.}$$

or

$$A(\alpha) = a_{m-1}\alpha^m + \cdots + a_1\alpha^2 + a_0\alpha, \text{ when } f(x) \text{ is AOP.}$$

where $a_i \in GF(p)$ and α is a root of $f(x)$. Note that since we choose p to be less than the processor's word size, we can represent $A(x)$ with m registers.

4 Efficient Arithmetic in GOEF

This section describes a basic construction for arithmetic in fields $GF(p^m)$, of which GOEF is a special case.

4.1 Addition and Subtraction

Addition and subtraction of two field elements are implemented in a straightforward manner by adding or subtracting the coefficients of their polynomial or normal basis representation and if necessary, performing a modular reduction by subtracting or adding p once from the intermediate result.

4.2 Multiplication

Field multiplication can be performed in two steps. First, we perform a multiplication of two field elements $A(\alpha)$ and $B(\alpha)$. If we use $f(x)$ as a binomial and polynomial basis, then resulting in an intermediate product $C'(\alpha)$ of degree less than or equal to $2m - 2$.

$$C'(\alpha) = A(\alpha)B(\alpha) = c'_{2m-2}\alpha^{2m-2} + \cdots + c'_1\alpha + c'_0 \text{ where } c'_i \in GF(p).$$

When AOP is used, the intermediate product $C'(\alpha)$'s degree is less than or equal to $2m$.

$$C'(\alpha) = A(\alpha)B(\alpha) = c'_{2m-2}\alpha^{2m} + \cdots + c'_1\alpha^3 + c'_0\alpha^2 \text{ where } c'_i \in GF(p).$$

The schoolbook method to calculate the coefficients $c'_i, i = 0, 1, \cdots, 2m - 2$, requires m^2 multiplications and $(m - 1)^2$ additions in the subfield $GF(p)$.

Since field multiplication is the time critical task in many public-key algorithms, in this paper, we use Karatsuba-like Method[5] to calculate the coefficients which requires $O(m^{1.59})$ cost for multiplication at the cost of more subfield additions[1]. Using this method gives considerable advantages to the cost of multiplication in the subfield. In general, the costs of addition and subtraction in $GF(p)$ do not be counted. But if m is chosen such that the size of p is as small as the word size of common processors, the complexity of addition and subtraction must be considered. For example, it is required 62 additions, subtractions and 18 multiplications in a base field to compute a multiplication in $GF(p^6)$, but the number of additions,subtractions and multiplications in a base field increases to 722 and 147 in $GF(p^{22})$, respectively. From the results in Table 6, $T_{mul}/T_{add+sub} = 5.76$ in $GF(p^6)$ and $T_{mul}/T_{add+sub} = 1.7$ in $GF(p^{22})$ where T_{mul} is the time required for a subfield multiplication and $T_{add+sub}$ for a subfield addition and subtraction. The detail description of Karatsuba-like method won't be covered here for the lack of space. Instead we give an example to compute multiplication in $GF(p^{12})$ by our modified Karatsuba-like method in Appendix.

Also, there is Schonhage-Strassen FFT based Method which requires $O(m$ $(\log_2 m)(\log_2 \log_2 m))$ complexity for multiplication. But this method is better than the classical method approximately when $m \geq 300[2]$.

In Section 4.3 we present an efficient method to calculate the residue $C(\alpha) \equiv C'(\alpha) \mod f(\alpha), C(\alpha) \in GF(p^m)$.

4.3   Extension Field Modular Reduction

After performing a multiplication of field elements in a polynomial representation, we obtain the intermediate result $C'(\alpha)$. In general, the degree of $C'(\alpha)$ will be greater than or equal to m when $f(x)$ is a binomial, and $m + 1$ when AOP is used. In this case, we need to perform a modular reduction. The canonical method to carry out this calculation is long division with remainder by the defining polynomial. However, defining polynomials of special form allow for computational efficiencies in the modular reduction.

When the Defining Polynomial Is Binomial : $x^m - \omega$

Theorem 5. *[3] Given a polynomial $C'(\alpha)$ over $GF(p)$ of degree less than or equal to $2m - 2$, $C'(\alpha)$ can be reduced module $f(x) = x^m - \omega$ requiring at most $m - 1$ multiplications by ω and $m - 1$ additions, where both of these operations are performed in $GF(p)$.*

A general expression for the reduced polynomial is given by :

$$C(\alpha) \equiv c'_{m-1}\alpha^{m-1} + [\omega c'_{2m-2} + c'_{m-2}]\alpha^{m-2} + \cdots + [\omega c'_m + c'_0] \mod f(\alpha).$$

As an optimization, when possible we choose those fields with an irreducible binomial $x^m - 2$, allowing us to implement the multiplications as shifts.

When the Defining Polynomial Is AOP : $x^m + x^{m-1} + \cdots + x + 1$

Theorem 6. *Given a polynomial $C'(\alpha)$ over $GF(p)$ of degree less than or equal to $2m$, $C'(\alpha)$ can be reduced module $f(x) = x^m + x^{m-1} + \cdots + x + 1$ requiring at most $m - 2$ additions and m subtractions, where both of these operations are performed in $GF(p)$.*

Using the property that is $\alpha^{m+1} = 1$ *and* $1 = -\alpha - \alpha^2 - \cdots - \alpha^m$ then a general expression for the reduced representation is given by :

$$C(\alpha) \equiv [c'_{m-2} - c'_{m-1}]\alpha^m + [c'_{m-3} - c'_{m-1} + c'_{2m-2}]\alpha^{m-1} + \cdots$$
$$+ [c'_0 - c'_{m-1} + c'_{m+1}]\alpha^2 + [c'_m - c'_{m-1}]\alpha \; mod \; f(\alpha).$$

Comparison : In general, multiplication is more expensive than subtraction. In Theorem 5, modular reduction requires at most $m - 1$ multiplications by ω. If ω is 2 then the complexity of reduction of the above two methods is almost equal. When ω is greater than 2, however, extension field modular reduction using AOP is more efficient.

Combining or Postponing the Reduction Steps : For a regular multiplication of $a, b \in GF(p)$, an integer multiplication step and an integer reduction step are needed.

Generally, extension field multiplication using Schoolbook method takes m^2 multiplications in a base field. That is m^2 integer reduction step must be performed. If m is large, the cost of reduction step is very high. So a method which reduces the number of reduction step, contributes to the overall performance. We can reduce the number of reduction step by combining individual product terms as many as possible, and then reducing the accumulated sum $mod \; p$ only once. Therefore, only m reduction step is needed. Because the intermediate results are greater than p^2 in absolute value when p is selected as a prime near the word size, the cost of the resulting final reductions is higher than that of the original reductions. According to the our implementation results, the case when p is word size and m is large is not attractive. Because modern workstation CPUs are optimized to perform integer arithmetic on operands of size up to the width of their registers and a double or triple-word integer arithmetic generated in combining stage is considerably less efficient than single-word integer arithmetic. Combining or postponing the reduction steps is not at all new. See for instance [4] for much earlier applications.

4.4   Fast Subfield Multiplication with Modular Reduction

In general, fast subfield multiplication is essential for fast multiplication in $GF(p^m)$. Subfield arithmetic in $GF(p)$ is implemented with standard modular integer techniques. For efficient implementation of GOEF arithmetic, optimization of subfield arithmetic is critical to performance. Modern workstation CPUs are optimized to perform integer arithmetic on operands of size up to the width of their registers. GOEF takes advantage of this fact by constructing subfields whose elements may be represented by integers in a single register.

We perform multiplication of two single-word integers and in general obtain a double-word integer result. In order to finish the calculation, we must perform a modular reduction. It is well known that fast modular reduction is possible with moduli of the form $2^n \pm c$, where c is a *small* integer[12]. Integers of this form allow modular reduction without division. The operators $<<$ and $>>$ mean **left shift** and **right shift**, respectively.

Algorithm : Reduction modulo $p = 2^m - c$, where $\log_2 c \leq \frac{1}{2} n$.

INPUT : a base 2 positive integer $x < p^2$ and a modulus p.

OUTPUT : $r \equiv x \bmod p$.

---

1. $q_0 \leftarrow (x >> n)$, $r_0 \leftarrow x - (q_0 << n)$, $r \leftarrow r_0$, $i \leftarrow 0$.
2. While $q_i > 0$ do the following:
    2.1 $q_{i+1} \leftarrow q_i c >> n$, $r_{i+1} \leftarrow q_i c - (q_{i+1} << n)$.
    2.2 $i \leftarrow i + 1$, $r \leftarrow r + r_i$.
3. While $r \geq p$ do: $r \leftarrow r - p$.
4. Return(r).

Remark 2. Algorithm 1 can be modified if $p = 2^n + c$ for some positive integer c such that $\log_2 c \leq \frac{1}{2} n$: in step 2.2, replace $r \leftarrow r + r_i$ with $r \leftarrow r + (-1)^i r_i$.

The Algorithm 1 terminates after a maximum of two iterations of the while loop, so we require at the most two multiplications by c. In practice, this leads to a dramatic performance enhancement over performing explicit division with remainder. If $p = 2^n + c$ is used then the number of iterations of the second while loop is smaller than that of $p = 2^n - c$ used in step 3. Since Algorithm 1 is organized with shift, addition, subtraction and multiplication by c, and if c is well chosen then multiplication by c can be substituted by shift the reduction of the number of subtraction is meaningful.

5   Implementation Results

We have implemented various field and XTR arithmetic using the techniques presented in previous Sections on typical microprocessors: Pentium III/700MHz (32-bit μP; Windows 2000, MSVC).

5.1   Application to XTR

In this Section 5.1,first,we propose optimized parameters for XTR such as prime p and a defining polynomial in Table 1. For the convenience to find primes, we give the prime p with the size of prime q is greater than 160bit. But we can also find prime p such that the size of prime q is as large as the original XTR.

In this paper, we used Karatsuba-like Method to achieve the efficiency of multiplication in $GF(p^{2m})$. Table 2 shows the number of multiplication, addition and subtraction in $GF(p)$ required to compute multiplication in $GF(p^{2m})$. Here, the defining polynomial is used as AOP. Note that values in the parenthesis are the numbers when Schoolbook method is used.

extension field	characteristic p	$f(x)$	the size q
$GF(p^6) \rightarrow GF(p^2)$	$2^{174} + 7$	AOP	323 bit
$GF(p^{12}) \rightarrow GF(p^4)$	$2^{88} + 7$	AOP	234 bit
$GF(p^{18}) \rightarrow GF(p^6)$	$2^{61} + 15$	AOP	354 bit
$GF(p^{36}) \rightarrow GF(p^{12})$	$2^{30} + 3$	AOP	302 bit
$GF(p^{66}) \rightarrow GF(p^{22})$	$2^{16} - 17$	AOP	320 bit

Table 1. Construction of extension fields for XTR

extension field	Mul in $GF(p)$	Add in $GF(p)$	Sub in $GF(p)$
$GF(p^6) \rightarrow GF(p^2)$	3	5	2
$GF(p^{12}) \rightarrow GF(p^4)$	9(16)	12(11)	12(4)
$GF(p^{18}) \rightarrow GF(p^6)$	18(36)	39(29)	23(6)
$GF(p^{36}) \rightarrow GF(p^{12})$	54(144)	130(131)	118(12)
$GF(p^{66}) \rightarrow GF(p^{22})$	147(484)	345(461)	377(22)

Table 2. Multiplication in $GF(p^{2m})$ by using Karatsuba-like Method

In Table 3 we give the results of computing the linear recurrence $S_n(c)$ over $GF(p^{2m})$ from the values in Table 1,2,6.

extension field	prime p	$S_n(c)$ (msec)
$GF(p^6) \rightarrow GF(p^2)$	$2^{174} + 7$	10.174
$GF(p^{12}) \rightarrow GF(p^4)$	$2^{88} + 7$	28.393
$GF(p^{18}) \rightarrow GF(p^6)$	$2^{61} + 15$	50.276
$GF(p^{36}) \rightarrow GF(p^{12})$	$2^{30} + 3$	4.932
$GF(p^{66}) \rightarrow GF(p^{22})$	$2^{16} - 17$	6.789

Table 3. Comparison of $S_n(c)$ performance

It can be seen that $GF((2^{30} + 3)^{12})$ yields XTR single exponentiation speeds which are more than twice as fast as the original XTR single exponentiation[10].

From the results of Table 4, we can see the need for a pseudo-Mersenne prime and Karatsuba-like Method to speed up XTR single exponentiation.

Finally, we recommend parameters of GOEF for XTR in Table 5.

6   Conclusion

We presented various speed-up techniques for field arithmetic in $GF(p^m)$ and introduced a class of finite fields, known as Generalized Optimal Extension Fields, which take advantage of well-known optimizations for finite field arithmetic on

extension field	prime p	Method of multiplication	$f(x)$	$S_n(c)$ (msec)
$GF(p^6)$	general	Karatsuba method[10]	AOP	11.910
$\Rightarrow GF(p^2)$	$2^{174}+7$	Karatsuba method[10]	AOP	10.174
$GF(p^{36})$	general	Schoolbook method	AOP	129.338
	general	Karatsuba method(Appendix)	AOP	67.822
$\Rightarrow GF(p^{12})$	$2^{30}+3$	Schoolbook method	AOP	8.218
	$2^{30}+3$	Karatsuba method(Appendix)	AOP	4.932

Table 4. Comparison XTR in $GF(p^2)$ [6,10] with XTR in $GF(p^{12})$

extension field	prime p	$f(x)$	the size q
	$2^{30}+3$	$x^{12}-2$	302 bit
	$2^{30}+7, (7=2^3-1)$	AOP	355 bit
$GF(p^{36})$	$2^{30}+129, (129=2^7+1))$	AOP	351 bit
$\Rightarrow GF(p^{12})$	$2^{30}-257, (257=2^8+1))$	AOP	269 bit
	$2^{30}-513, (513=2^9+1)$	AOP	341 bit
	$2^{30}-513$	$x^{12}-3$	341 bit

Table 5. Recommended primes and $f(x)$ for $GF(p^{12})$

microprocessors. The main improvements presented in this paper consist of optimization in field multiplication and careful choices of field parameters to speed up field arithmetic. With above results, we proposed the optimized extension field for XTR that is $GF(p^{36}) \rightarrow GF(p^{12})$. The defining polynomial of $GF(p^{12})$ is the 12-th AOP and a candidate of nice prime is $2^{30}+3$. From our implementation results, our proposed field is about twice faster than the XTR[6] to compute $Tr(g^n)$. The key size of it is equal as that of the original XTR system. So our proposed optimal extension field for XTR is the more excellent alternative to either RSA or ECC than XTR[6] in applications such as SSL/TLS(Secure Sockets Layer, Transport Layer Security), public key smartcards, WAP/WTLS(Wireless Application Protocol, Wireless Transport Layer Security).

References

1. Aho,A.,Hopcroft,J.,Ullman,J., *The Design and Analysis of Computer Algorithms.*, Addison-Wesley,Reading Mass,1974.
2. Bach,E, Shallit,J., *Algorithmic Number Theory.*, Vol 1, The MIT Press, Mass, 1996.
3. Bailey. D.V. and Paar C, *Optimal extension fields for fast arithmetic in public-key algorithms.*, Crypto '98, Springer-Verlag pp.472-485, 1998.
4. H.Cohen, A.K. Lenstra, *Implementation of a new primality test.*, Math.Comp.48 (1987) 103-121.
5. D.E. Knuth, *The art of computer programming.*, Volume 2, Seminumerical Algorithms, second edition, Addison-Wesley, 1981.
6. A.K. Lenstra, E.R. Verheul, *The XTR public key system.*, Proceedings of Crypto 2000, LNCS 1880,Springer-Verlag, 2000,1-19; available from www.ecstr.com.

7. A.K. Lenstra, *Using Cyclotomic Polynomials to Construct Efficient Discrete Logarithm Cryptosystems over Finite Fields.*, Proceedings of ACISP 1997, LNCS 1270,Springer-Verlag, 1997,127-138.

8. A.K. Lenstra, *Lip 1.1*, available at www.ecstr.com.

9. Seongan Lim, Seungjoo Kim, Ikkwon Yie, Jaemoon Kim, Hongsub Lee, *XTR Extended to GF(p^{6m})*. Procee dings of SAC 2001,317-328, LNCS 2259, Springer-Verlag, 2001,125-143.

10. Martijn Stam, A.K. Lenstra, *Speeding Up XTR*. Proceedings of Asiacrypt 2001, LNCS 2248, Springer-Verlag, 2001,125-143; available from www.ecstr.com.

11. A.J Menezes, *Applications of Finite Fields.*, Waterloo, 1993.

12. S.B.Mohan and B.S.Adiga, *Fast Algorithms for Implementating RSA Public Key Cryptosystem.*, Electronics Letters, 21917):761,1985.

13. S.Oh, S.Hong,D.Cheon,C.Kim,J.Lim and M.Sung, *An Extension Field of Characteristic Greater than Two and its Applicatins.* Technical Report 99-2, CIST,1999. Available from http://cist.korea.ac.kr/.

Appendix

A. Comparison of Arithmetic Performance in $GF(p)$

The first three results were made with freelip version 1.1 [8] and the last two were made by our own hands.

extension field	prime p	Mul (μsec)	Add (μsec)	Sub (μsec)
$GF(p^6) \to GF(p^2)$	$2^{174} + 7$	7.884	0.761	0.431
$GF(p^{12}) \to GF(p^4)$	$2^{88} + 7$	4.095	0.53	0.67
$GF(p^{18}) \to GF(p^6)$	$2^{61} + 15$	3.365	0.5	0.31
$GF(p^{36}) \to GF(p^{12})$	$2^{30} + 3$	0.131	0.006	0.006
$GF(p^{66}) \to GF(p^{22})$	$2^{16} - 17$	0.0507	0.006	0.006

Table 6. GOEF arithmetic timings on a 700 MHz

B. Karatsuba-like Multiplication of Two Elements with Degree 12

For a prime p and $A, B \in GF(p^{12})$, let $A = a_1 x + a_2 x^2 + \cdots + a_{12} x^{12}$ and $B = b_1 x + b_2 x^2 + \cdots + b_{12} x^{12}$

Now, we shall compute $AB = C = c_1 x + c_2 x^2 + \cdots + c_{12} x^{12} \bmod 1 + x + \cdots + x^{12}$ using Karatsuba-like multiplication where $a_i, b_i \in GF(p)$.

We previously compute the followings.

Step 1

$$G_1 = a_1 b_1 \qquad\qquad G_2 = a_2 b_2 \qquad\qquad\qquad G_3 = G_{17}G_{18}$$
$$G_4 = G_3 - G_1 - G_2 \qquad G_5 = a_3 b_3 \qquad\qquad\qquad G_6 = a_4 b_4$$
$$G_7 = G_{19}G_{20} \qquad\qquad G_8 = G_7 - G_5 - G_6 \qquad\qquad G_9 = (a_1 + a_3)(b_1 + b_3)$$
$$G_{10} = (a_2 + a_4)(b_2 + b_4) \quad G_{11} = (G_{17} + G_{19})(G_{18} + G_{20}) \quad G_{12} = G_9 - G_1 - G_5$$
$$G_{13} = G_{11} - G_4 - G_8 \qquad G_{14} = G_{10} - G_2 - G_6 \qquad\qquad G_{15} = G_{12} + G_2$$
$$G_{16} = G_{14} + G_5 \qquad\qquad G_{17} = a_1 + a_2 \qquad\qquad\qquad G_{18} = b_1 + b_2$$
$$G_{19} = a_3 + a_4 \qquad\qquad G_{20} = b_3 + b_4$$

Step 2

$$H_1 = a_5 b_5 \qquad\qquad H_2 = a_6 b_6 \qquad\qquad\qquad H_3 = H_{17}H_{18}$$
$$H_4 = H_3 - H_1 - H_2 \qquad H_5 = a_7 b_7 \qquad\qquad\qquad H_6 = a_8 b_8$$
$$H_7 = H_{19}H_{20} \qquad\qquad H_8 = H_7 - H_5 - H_6 \qquad\qquad H_9 = (a_5 + a_7)(b_5 + b_7)$$
$$H_{10} = (a_6 + a_8)(b_6 + b_8) \quad H_{11} = (H_{17} + H_{19})(H_{18} + H_{20}) \quad H_{12} = H_9 - H_1 - H_5$$
$$H_{13} = H_{11} - H_4 - H_8 \qquad H_{14} = H_{10} - H_2 - H_6 \qquad\qquad H_{15} = H_{12} + H_2$$
$$H_{16} = H_{14} + H_5 \qquad\qquad H_{17} = a_5 + a_6 \qquad\qquad\qquad H_{18} = b_5 + b_6$$
$$H_{19} = a_7 + a_8 \qquad\qquad H_{20} = b_7 + b_8$$

Step 3

$$I_1 = I_{17}I_{18} \qquad\qquad I_2 = I_{21}I_{22} \qquad\qquad\qquad I_3 = (G_{17} + I_{17})(G_{18} + I_{18})$$
$$I_4 = I_3 - I_1 - I_2 \qquad I_5 = I_{19}I_{20} \qquad\qquad\qquad I_6 = I_{23}I_{24}$$
$$I_7 = I_{25}I_{26} \qquad\qquad I_8 = I_7 - I_5 - I_6 \qquad\qquad I_9 = I_{27}I_{28}$$
$$I_{10} = I_{29}I_{30} \qquad\qquad I_{11} = (I_{27} + I_{29})(I_{28} + I_{30}) \qquad I_{12} = I_9 - I_1 - I_5$$
$$I_{13} = I_{11} - I_4 - I_8 \qquad I_{14} = I_{10} - I_2 - I_6 \qquad\qquad I_{15} = I_{12} + I_2$$
$$I_{16} = I_{14} + I_5 \qquad\qquad I_{17} = a_1 + a_5 \qquad\qquad\qquad I_{18} = b_1 + b_5$$
$$I_{19} = a_3 + a_7 \qquad\qquad I_{20} = b_3 + b_7 \qquad\qquad\qquad I_{21} = a_2 + a_6$$
$$I_{22} = b_2 + b_6 \qquad\qquad I_{23} = a_4 + a_8 \qquad\qquad\qquad I_{24} = b_4 + b_8$$
$$I_{25} = G_{19} + I_{19} \qquad\qquad I_{26} = G_{20} + I_{20} \qquad\qquad\qquad I_{27} = I_{17} + I_{19}$$
$$I_{28} = I_{18} + I_{20} \qquad\qquad I_{29} = I_{21} + I_{23} \qquad\qquad\qquad I_{30} = I_{22} + I_{24}$$

Step 4

$$J_1 = a_9 b_9 \qquad\qquad J_2 = a_{10} b_{10} \qquad\qquad\qquad J_3 = J_{17}J_{18}$$
$$J_4 = J_3 - J_1 - J_2 \qquad J_5 = a_{11} b_{11} \qquad\qquad\qquad J_6 = a_{12} b_{12}$$
$$J_7 = J_{19}J_{20} \qquad\qquad J_8 = J_7 - J_5 - J_6 \qquad\qquad J_9 = J_{21}J_{22}$$
$$J_{10} = J_{23}J_{24} \qquad\qquad J_{11} = (J_{17} + J_{19})(J_{18} + J_{20}) \qquad J_{12} = J_9 - J_1 - J_5$$
$$J_{13} = J_{11} - J_4 - J_8 \qquad J_{14} = J_{10} - J_2 - J_6 \qquad\qquad J_{15} = J_{12} + J_2$$
$$J_{16} = J_{14} + J_5 \qquad\qquad J_{17} = a_9 + a_{10} \qquad\qquad\qquad J_{18} = b_9 + b_{10}$$
$$J_{19} = a_{11} + a_{12} \qquad\qquad J_{20} = b_{11} + b_{12} \qquad\qquad\qquad J_{21} = a_9 + a_{11}$$
$$J_{22} = b_9 + b_{11} \qquad\qquad J_{23} = a_{10} + a_{12} \qquad\qquad\qquad J_{24} = b_{10} + b_{12}$$

Step 5

$$K_1 = K_{17}K_{18}$$
$$K_2 = K_{21}K_{22}$$
$$K_3 = K_{29}K_{30}$$
$$K_4 = K_3 - K_1 - K_2$$
$$K_5 = K_{19}K_{20}$$
$$K_6 = K_{23}K_{24}$$
$$K_7 = K_{31}K_{32}$$
$$K_8 = K_7 - K_5 - K_6$$
$$K_9 = K_{25}K_{26}$$
$$K_{10} = K_{27}K_{28}$$
$$K_{11} = (K_{25} + K_{27})(K_{26} + K_{28})$$
$$K_{12} = K_9 - K_1 - K_5$$
$$K_{13} = K_{11} - K_4 - K_8$$
$$K_{14} = K_{10} - K_2 - K_6$$
$$K_{15} = K_{12} + K_2$$
$$K_{16} = K_{14} + K_5$$
$$K_{17} = a_1 + a_9$$
$$K_{18} = b_1 + b_9$$
$$K_{19} = a_3 + a_{11}$$
$$K_{20} = b_3 + b_{11}$$
$$K_{21} = a_2 + a_{10}$$
$$K_{22} = b_2 + b_{10}$$
$$K_{23} = a_4 + a_{12}$$
$$K_{24} = b_4 + b_{12}$$
$$K_{25} = K_{17} + K_{19}$$
$$K_{26} = K_{18} + K_{20}$$
$$K_{27} = K_{21} + K_{23}$$
$$K_{28} = K_{22} + K_{24}$$
$$K_{29} = K_{17} + K_{21}$$
$$K_{30} = K_{18} + K_{22}$$
$$K_{31} = K_{19} + K_{23}$$
$$K_{32} = K_{20} + K_{24}$$

Step 6

$$L_1 = (K_{17}+a_5)(K_{18}+b_5)$$
$$L_2 = (K_{21}+a_6)(K_{22}+b_6)$$
$$L_3 = (K_{29}+H_{17})(K_{30}+H_{18})$$
$$L_4 = L_3 - L_1 - L_2$$
$$L_5 = (K_{19}+a_7)(K_{20}+b_7)$$
$$L_6 = (K_{23}+a_8)(K_{24}+b_8)$$
$$L_7 = (K_{31}+H_{19})(K_{32}+H_{20})$$
$$L_8 = L_7 - L_5 - L_6$$
$$L_9 = L_{17}L_{18}$$
$$L_{10} = L_{19}L_{20}$$
$$L_{11} = (L_{17}+L_{19})(L_{18}+L_{20})$$
$$L_{12} = L_9 - L_1 - L_5$$
$$L_{13} = L_{11} - L_4 - L_8$$
$$L_{14} = L_{10} - L_2 - L_6$$
$$L_{15} = L_{12}+L_2$$
$$L_{16} = L_{14}+L_5$$
$$L_{17} = I_{27}+J_{21}$$
$$L_{18} = I_{28}+J_{22}$$
$$L_{19} = I_{29}+J_{23}$$
$$L_{20} = I_{30}+J_{24}$$

Step 7

$$M_1 = I_1 - G_1 - H_1 + G_{16}$$
$$M_2 = I_4 - G_4 - H_4 + G_8$$
$$M_3 = I_{15} - G_{15} - H_{15} + G_6$$
$$M_4 = I_{16} - G_{16} - H_{16} + H_1$$
$$M_5 = I_8 - G_8 - H_8 + H_4$$
$$M_6 = I_6 - G_6 - H_6 + H_{15}$$
$$Q = H_{13} + K_{13} - G_{13} - J_{13}$$

Step 8

The following are the table of the coefficients of multiplication of two polynomials after reduction $mod\ 1 + x + \cdots + x^{12}$.

Degree	Coefficients	Addition	Subtraction
1	$H_{16} + K_{16} + L_1 - K_1 - H_1 - M_1 - J_{16} - Q$	2	5
2	$G_1 + H_8 + K_8 + L_4 - K_4 - H_4 - M_2 - J_8 - Q$	3	5
3	$G_4 + H_6 + K_6 + L_{15} - K_{15} - H_{15} - M_3 - J_6 - Q$	3	5
4	$G_{15} + L_{13} - K_{13} - H_{13} - I_{13} + G_{13} + H_{13} - Q$	3	4
5	$G_{13} + H_1 + L_{16} - K_{16} - H_{16} - M_4 + J_1 - Q$	3	4
6	$M_1 + H_4 + L_8 - K_8 - H_8 - M_5 + J_4 - Q$	3	4
7	$M_2 + H_{15} + L_6 - K_6 - H_6 - M_6 + J_{15} - Q$	3	4
8	$M_3 + J_{13} - Q$	1	1
9	$I_{13} - G_{13} - H_{13} + J_{16} - Q$	1	3
10	$K_1 - G_1 - J_1 + M_4 + J_8 - Q$	2	3
11	$K_4 - G_4 - J_4 + M_5 + J_6 - Q$	2	3
12	$K_{15} - G_{15} - J_{15} + M_6 - Q$	1	3
Sum		**27**	**44**

Table 7. Amount of operation in a reduction step

Step	1	2	3	4	5	6	7	8	Total
Multiplication	9	9	9	9	9	9	0	0	54
Addition	12	12	20	12	20	20	7	27	130
Subtraction	10	10	10	10	10	10	14	44	118

Table 8. Total amount of operation

On Some Attacks on Multi-prime RSA

M. Jason Hinek, Mo King Low, and Edlyn Teske

University of Waterloo
Department of Combinatorics and Optimization
Waterloo, Ontario, N2L 3G1 Canada
{mjhinek,eteske}@uwaterloo.ca, mklow@fastmail.ca

Abstract. Using more than two factors in the modulus of the RSA cryptosystem has the arithmetic advantage that the private key computations can be speeded up using Chinese remaindering. At the same time, with a proper choice of parameters, one does not have to work with a larger modulus to achieve the same level of security in terms of the difficulty of the integer factorization problem. However, numerous attacks on specific instances on the RSA cryptosystem are known that apply if, for example, the decryption or encryption exponent are chosen too small, or if partial knowledge of the private key is available. Little work is known on how such attacks perform in the multi-prime case. It turns out that for most of these attacks it is crucial that the modulus contains exactly two primes. They become much less effective, or fail, when the modulus factors into more than two distinct primes.

1 Introduction

The RSA cryptosystem, due to Rivest, Shamir and Adleman [RSA78], is one of the most popular public key cryptosystems and widely used to ensure privacy and authenticity of electronic data. In the first place, the security of RSA is based on the difficulty of the following Integer Factorization Problem (IFP): given an integer N that is the product of two primes p and q of approximately the same size, find p and q. As a consequence, the choice of RSA parameters to achieve a certain level of security is based on the estimated current and future performance of integer factorization algorithms. On the other hand, numerous attacks have been developed that are unrelated to the IFP and show vulnerabilities of specific instances of the RSA cryptosystem. Boneh [Bon99] gives an excellent survey on this matter.

Little work has been reported on how such attacks apply to multi-prime RSA, i.e., where N is a product of more than two primes. Of most practical interest are the cases of 3- and 4-prime RSA. Commercial implementations of 3-prime RSA [CHLS97] exist. The use of more than two primes in the RSA cryptosystem has the advantage that the private key operations can be speeded up using the Chinese Remainder Theorem. An easy calculation shows that compared with 2-prime RSA, the theoretical speed-up is by a factor of 9/4 for 3-prime RSA, and 4 for 4-prime RSA. (In practice, a speed-up of 1.73 for 3-prime RSA has been

K. Nyberg and H. Heys (Eds.): SAC 2002, LNCS 2595, pp. 385–404, 2003.

achieved [BS02].) This is under the assumption that the size of the modulus N is the same in all systems. In fact, as long as the running time for the Elliptic Curve Method to find the smallest factor of $N = \prod_{i=1}^{r} p_i$ exceeds the running time for the Number Field Sieve to factor N, multi-prime RSA does not require a larger modulus. For example, we can conclude from [Len01, Tab. 3] that currently a 2048-bit modulus $N = pq$ offers roughly the same level of security against factoring algorithms as a 2048-bit modulus for 3-prime RSA.

In this report, we take selected attacks discussed in [Bon99] and examine whether and how efficiently they can be applied to multi-prime RSA. We now briefly describe multi-prime RSA in a simplified version, which works about just the same as RSA. Throughout this paper, we use the notation as follows. Let r be an integer ≥ 2, and let N be the product of r pairwise distinct large primes $p_1, \ldots, p_r$ of roughly the same size. For convenience, if $r = 2$ we work with $p := p_1$ and $q := p_2$. The bitsize of N is always denoted by n. Let $\phi(N) = \prod_{i=1}^{r}(p_i - 1)$ be the order of the multiplicative group $\mathbb{Z}_N^*$, and let e, d be two integers satisfying $ed \equiv 1 \pmod{\phi(N)}$. We call N the *modulus*, e the *encryption* (or: *public*) *exponent* and d the *decryption* (or: *private*) *exponent*. The pair (N, e) is the *public key*, the pair (N, d) is the *private key*. To encrypt a message $M \in \mathbb{Z}_N^*$, one computes the ciphertext $C = M^e \bmod N$, which then can be decrypted by computing $C^d = M^{ed} = M \bmod N$. When RSA is used for signing, the private key is used to generate a digital signature $S = M^d \bmod N$ of the message $M \in \mathbb{Z}_N^*$, and the public key is used for verification, where it is checked that $S^e \equiv M \pmod{N}$. As said, this description of the RSA encryption and signature algorithms is highly simplified. In practice, proper padding and, for signature generation, hashing are indispensable.

Just as in the case of 2-prime RSA, factoring the modulus is equivalent to exposing the private key for 3- and 4-prime RSA (see Section 3). In particular, this means that the common modulus attack can be mounted in these cases as well. On the other hand, most of the attacks discussed in [Bon99] make such extensive use of the fact that the modulus is a product of exactly two primes that they become much less effective in the multi-prime case, or don't seem to work at all. For example, in Section 4 we study low private exponent attacks based on continued fractions and on lattice reduction. For the continued fraction attack, we show that the bound on the size of the decryption exponent for the attack to work is $O(N^{1/2r})$, and a similar behaviour can be observed for the lattice based attacks. Another example is the following: while 2-prime RSA with small encryption exponent can leak half of the most significant bits of the decryption exponent, this fraction goes down to $1/r$ for r-prime RSA. See Section 5. In 2-prime RSA, if the public exponent is small, a polynomial time method by Boneh, Durfee and Frankel exists that completely recovers the private exponent once it is partially exposed. However, in the 3- and 4-prime case these methods become totally ineffective, as we show in Section 5.1. A partial key exposure attack for a medium public exponent (i.e., $e < \sqrt{N}$), also by Boneh, Durfee and Frankel, fails in the multi-prime case because instead of solving a quadratic congruence, solving congruences of degree r where not all coefficients are known is required.

Another, weaker, partial key exposure attack by the same authors carries over, but is applicable only for public exponents up to $N^{1/r}$ rather than $\sqrt{N}$. See Section 5.2. These results suggest that multi-prime RSA does not only allow for faster decryption using Chinese remaindering, but is also somewhat more secure than 2-prime RSA.

Our paper is organized as follows. First we introduce and discuss precise conditions on the relative sizes of the prime factors; these conditions correspond to the usual assumptions in the 2-prime case. We also provide some background needed for lattice-based attacks. Then, in Section 3, we discuss the equivalence of factoring and finding the secret key. Low decryption exponent attacks are the subject of Section 4. In Section 5 we study partial key exposure attacks. We conclude with Section 6.

2 Preliminaries

We introduce some more notation. We call the congruence $ed \equiv 1 \pmod{\phi(N)}$ the *public/private key relation*. If $0 < d, e < \phi(N)$, there exists a unique integer k, $0 < k < \min\{e, d\}$, such that

$$ed - k\phi(N) = 1 . \tag{1}$$

This equation is called the *public/private key equation*, and in the sequel, k is always the value defined through (1).

Throughout this work we make the following assumptions on the primes in the RSA modulus. First, the primes are labeled in increasing order. That is,

$$p_i < p_{i+1} \tag{2}$$

for all $i \geq 1$. Second, the primes satisfy

$$4 < N^{1/r}/2 < p_1 < N^{1/r} < p_r < 2N^{1/r} . \tag{3}$$

This second assumption guarantees that we have *balanced primes*. That is, all primes in the modulus are of roughly the same size and thus are equally hard to find by the Elliptic Curve Method. On the other hand, other factoring algorithms (esp. the Number Field Sieve) cannot exploit (2), (3) for speed-ups.

For an r-prime RSA modulus N, (2) and (3) imply that

$$N - \phi(N) < (2r - 1)N^{1-1/r} . \tag{4}$$

This is because with Euler's phi function,

$$\phi(N) = N - \sum_{i=1}^{r} N/p_i + \sum_{\substack{i,j=1 \\ i<j}}^{r} N/(p_i p_j) - \sum_{\substack{i,j,k=1 \\ i<j<k}}^{r} N/(p_i p_j p_k) + \cdots + (-1)^r , \tag{5}$$

we have $N - \phi(N) < \sum_{i=1}^{r} N/p_i$. Now, since $p_r > N^{1/r}$ and $p_i \geq p_1 > N^{1/r}/2$ for $i = 1, \ldots, r - 1$, we have that $N/p_r < N^{1-1/r}$, and $N/p_i < 2N^{1-1/r}$ for

$i = 1, \ldots, r - 1$. Combining these inequalities gives (4). Further, since N is an n-bit modulus, we can express (4) as

$$N - \phi(N) < (2r)2^{n(1-1/r)} = 2^{n-n/r+1+\log_2 r} \, . \tag{6}$$

Some of the attacks we consider use lattices and lattice reduction algorithms. We now give some notation and facts, for which we follow [DN00] and [BD00].

Let $u_1, \ldots, u_w \in \mathbb{Z}^m$ with $w \leq m$. The set $L = \{\sum_{i=1}^{w} a_i u_i \,|\, a_i \in \mathbb{Z}\}$ of all integer linear combinations of the u_i's is a lattice. It is called the lattice *spanned* by $\langle u_1, \ldots, u_w \rangle$. Further, if the vectors $u_1, \ldots, u_w$ are linearly independent over $\mathbb{Z}$, then $\langle u_1, \ldots, u_w \rangle$ is called a *basis* of L. There are an infinite number of bases for each lattice L. All bases for a given lattice share two common parameters: the lattice rank and the lattice volume. The lattice *rank* (or *dimension*) is the number, w, of vectors in the basis. The lattice *volume* (or *determinant*), denoted by $\mathrm{vol}(L)$, is the w-dimensional volume of the parallelepiped spanned by the u_i's. If $w = m$ the lattice is said to have full rank. In the full rank case, the volume is equal to the absolute value of the determinant of any basis.

Given any basis $\langle u_1, \ldots, u_w \rangle$ of a lattice, we can use the LLL lattice reduction algorithm [LLL82] to create a new basis such that the vectors, say $\langle b_1, \ldots, b_w \rangle$, of the new basis are in some way "small". This new basis is called an *LLL-reduced* basis. The main features of any LLL-reduced basis $\langle b_1, \ldots, b_w \rangle$ of a lattice L spanned by $\langle u_1, \ldots, u_w \rangle$ in $\mathbb{Z}^m$ are:

1. $\|b_1\| \leq 2^{w/2}\mathrm{vol}(L)^{1/w}$ and $\|b_2\| \leq 2^{(w-1)/2}\mathrm{vol}(L)^{1/(w-1)}$.
2. The basis can be computed in time $O(mw^5 \log(\max\{\|u_i\|_\infty\}))$.

We will treat the LLL lattice reduction algorithm as a black box.

Boneh, Durfee and Frankel showed how to use lattice reduction to factor a 2-prime RSA modulus given that the $n/4$ least significant bits of one of the factors are known.

Theorem 1 ([BDF98]). *Let $N = pq$ be an n-bit RSA modulus. Let $s \geq 2^{n/4}$ be given and suppose $p \bmod s$ is known. Then it is possible to factor N in time polynomial in n.*

The runtime of the algorithm needed to factor the modulus in Theorem 1 will be denoted by $T_C(n)$. The C is in reference to the fact that the above result follows from Coppersmith's work on finding small roots of bivariate polynomials [Cop97].

3   Equivalence of Factoring and Exposing the Private Key

In 2-prime RSA, computing the decryption exponent d from the public key is equivalent to factoring N. This result can be extended to $r = 3, 4$. Given the public and private exponents, we find a multiple of $\phi(N)$ from (1). This multiple $k\phi(N)$ is fed into a Las Vegas algorithm that produces a factor of N by calculating non-trivial square roots of 1 modulo N. This works as follows:

We write $k\phi(N) = 2^t u$ with u odd. Then, for a randomly chosen integer $w \in [2, N-2]$ we compute $w^{2^s u}$ for $s = 0, 1, \ldots$, until $w^{2^s u} \equiv 1 \pmod{N}$. If that happens already for $s = 0$, the algorithm outputs FAILURE. If $s \geq 1$ and $w^{2^{s-1}u} \not\equiv -1 \pmod{N}$, then $w^{2^{s-1}u}$ is a non-trivial square root of 1 mod N and thus $\gcd(N, w^{2^{s-1}u} + 1)$ is a non-trivial factor of N. If $w^{2^{s-1}u} \equiv -1 \pmod{N}$, the output is FAILURE.

In the 2-prime case, an analysis in [Sti95] shows that the probability of finding a (prime) factor of N is at least 0.5. We proceed analogously for an r-prime modulus N $(r \geq 2)$, and estimate the number of integers $w \in [2, N-2]$ that cause FAILURE. For this, we write $p_i - 1 = 2^{h_i} q_i$ with q_i odd. Then there exist $\prod_{i=1}^r q_i$ integers $w \in [1, N-1]$ for which $w^u \equiv 1 \pmod{N}$, and at most $\left(\prod_{i=1}^r q_i\right) \sum_{i=0}^{h-1} 2^{ri}$ integers $w \in [1, N-1]$ for which $w^{2^{s-1}u} \equiv -1 \pmod{N}$ for some integer $s \in [1, t]$, where $h = \min\{h_i : i = 1, \ldots, r\}$. The total number of values of w that cause FAILURE can then easily be bounded by $N/2^{r-1}$ (see [Sti95, Low02] for details). Thus, the probability that the above algorithm outputs a factor of N is at least $1 - 1/2^{r-1}$. In the 2-prime case, disclosure of one factor leads to the complete factorization of N.

3.1   3-Prime RSA

The probability of finding a factor p of N with the above algorithm is at 0.75. Then either p or N/p is prime, and the problem of factoring N can be reduced to the 2-prime case.

3.2   4-Prime RSA

The probability of finding a factor x of N is at least 0.875. However, it may occur that both x and N/x are composite. We consider this event a FAILURE since then the 4-prime case cannot be reduced to a smaller-prime case: we cannot determine a multiple of $\phi(x)$ or $\phi(N/x)$. To guarantee a sufficient probability that a *prime* factor is revealed, we put $x_s = \gcd(w^{2^{s-1}u} + 1, N)$ and j such that $h_j = \max\{h_i : i = 1, \ldots, 4\}$, and we give a lower bound on the number of $w \in [1, N-1]$ for which $x_s = p_j$ for some integer $s \in [1, t]$. From the Chinese Remainder Theorem,

$$\left.\begin{array}{c} w^{2^s u} \equiv 1 \pmod{N} \\ \text{and} \\ x_s = p_j \end{array}\right\} \iff \left\{\begin{array}{ll} w^{2^{s-1}u} \equiv -1 \pmod{p_j} \\ \text{and} \\ w^{2^{s-1}u} \equiv 1 \pmod{p_i} \text{ for } i \neq j . \end{array}\right. \tag{7}$$

Note that if our Las Vegas algorithm chooses an integer w for which (7) holds for some s, then its output will indeed be x_s. Now let $s = h_j$. Then the number of w modulo p_j for which $w^{2^{s-1}u} \equiv -1 \pmod{p_j}$ is $2^{s-1}q_j = (p_j - 1)/2$. Since $s = h_j \geq h_i$, the number of w modulo p_i $(i \neq j)$ for which $w^{2^{s-1}u} \equiv 1 \pmod{p_i}$ is at least $(p_i - 1)/2$. Thus, the number of w mod N for which (7) holds for $s = h_j$ is at least $\phi(N)/16$. By (5), $\phi(N) > N - 7N^{3/4}$, so that the probability that the output of our algorithm is a prime factor is at least $\frac{1}{16} - \frac{7}{16N^{1/4}}$, which is > 0.0624 for $N > 2^{49}$. Of course, this lower bound is far away from being sharp, but sufficient for our purpose: we expect to find a prime factor of N with probability at least $1 - 10^{-6}$ after trying at most 215 values of w. Once a prime factor of N is found, the 4-prime case can be reduced to the 3-prime case.

4   Low Private Exponent Attacks

An advantage of choosing a low private exponent, d, is that decryption or digital signatures can be made faster (the cost for modular exponentiation grows linearly in $\log d$). This is important especially in constrained environments such as smartcards. But a private exponent that is too small is insecure because it leads to the factorization of the modulus, as we discuss in Sections 4.1 and 4.2.

4.1   Continued Fractions Attack

A result of Wiener [Wie90] implies that if $N = pq$ and the private exponent $d < \frac{1}{3}N^{1/4}$, then, given the public key (N, e) the prime factors of N can be recovered in time polynomial in N. The underlying attack [Bon99] is based on the following property of approximation using continued fractions: If α, β are integers and x is a real number, and $|\alpha/\beta - x| < 1/(2\beta^2)$, then α/β is a convergent of x [HW60]. Convergents of x are computed using the continued fraction algorithm, which is based on Euclid's algorithm.

We generalize Wiener's attack to the multi-prime case. Let k be as in (1). Then

$$0 < \frac{k}{d} - \frac{e}{N} = \frac{k(N - \phi(N)) - 1}{dN} .$$

Using (4) and that $k < d$, we find that the right-hand side is strictly less than $(2r - 1)/N^{1/r}$. Now

$$(2r - 1)/N^{1/r} < 1/(2d^2) \qquad \Longleftrightarrow \qquad d < N^{1/2r}/\sqrt{2(2r - 1)} .$$

Thus, if the last inequality holds, then on applying the continued fraction algorithm to e/N, we will obtain k/d as one of the convergents. To obtain the private exponent, an adversary simply has to test all convergents k'/d' of e/N. In fact, only the convergents with even index need to be tested (where the expansion begins with $q_0 = \lfloor e/N \rfloor$), since these convergents are exactly those for which $k'/d' > e/N$ [Old63]. Note that all convergents, as well as k/d, are in their lowest terms. Now one substitutes k', d' into (1) to produce ϕ', a candidate for $\phi(N)$. In the 2-prime case one now can solve the quadratic equation $(x - p)(x - q) = x^2 - (N - \phi' + 1)x + N = 0$. If $\phi' = \phi(N)$, the roots of this equation will be p, q. If N is an r-prime modulus with $r > 2$, we use that $\phi(N)$ is divisible by 2^r. Only if this is the case for a candidate ϕ', one proceeds with testing d'. For this, let M be a random element in $\mathbb{Z}_N$. If $(M^e)^{d'} \equiv M \pmod{N}$, then there is a high probability that $d' = d$, which can be verified using the techniques from Section 3.

Since the continued fraction algorithm is polynomial time, and the number of convergents of the fraction e/N is $O(\log N)$, and the test for each candidate k'/d' costs polynomial time, the decryption exponent can be found in polynomial time. We thus have proven

Theorem 2. *Let N be an r-prime modulus and $d < N^{1/2r}/\sqrt{2(2r-1)}$. Given (N, e), the decryption exponent can be recovered in time polynomial in $n = \log N$.*

Experimental results show that the attack is effective even if d is slightly larger than $N^{1/2r}/\sqrt{2(2r-1)}$. Using Shoup's NT Library [Sho], we implemented Wiener's attack and applied it in the 3-prime case. We generated three 512-bit primes to produce a modulus of 1534 to 1536 bits. Thus, for d of 256 and more bits, the bound of Theorem 2 does not hold. Nevertheless, among 1000 trials with randomly chosen primes and 256-bit private exponents, the correct value of k/d was among the convergents of e/N in 344 cases. For 257-bit d, the success rate still was 93/1000, while for 258 and 259 bits the rates were 23/1000 and 7/1000, respectively. (The number of convergents was always less than 1000. Among the successful runs, the correct value of d was found after an average of 150 convergents.) Nevertheless, the continued fraction attack is outperformed by the lattice-based attacks by Boneh and Durfee, which we discuss next.

We conclude by noting that just as in the 2-prime case, a method of defense against the continued fraction attack is to work with a public exponent $e' = e + t\phi(N)$ for some large t. In the 2-prime case, $e' > N^{3/2}$ is sufficient to defeat the attack. This bound decreases as r increases. In fact, generalizing Wiener's analysis [Wie90] to the r-prime case gives the following theorem.

Theorem 3. *Let N be an RSA modulus and $e > N^{(r+1)/r}$. Given (N, e), the attack underlying Theorem 2 cannot reveal the decryption exponent, independent of the size of d.*

4.2   Lattice Based Attacks

A low private exponent attack by Boneh and Durfee [BD00] uses lattice reduction techniques. This attack renders 2-prime RSA insecure when the private exponent is less than N^δ, where, in the most efficient variant of the attack, $\delta = 0.292$ as $N \to \infty$. We show how the Boneh-Durfee attack and a modified approach due to Blömer and May [BM01] generalize to r-prime RSA, and obtain corresponding asymptotic upper bounds on the private exponent. Moreover, for $r = 2, 3, 4$ and various fixed sizes of N, we give explicit upper bounds on the private exponent for which the attack is guaranteed to work.

Following [BD00], with slight modifications, we begin with the public/private key equation $ed - k\phi(N) = 1$. Letting $s = \phi(N) - N$ and $A = N$, we get $ed - k(A + s) = 1$, and reduction modulo e yields $-k(A + s) \equiv 1 \pmod{e}$. Our aim is to solve this equivalence relation with two unknowns. In fact, if we knew s, then we could immediately compute the private exponent $d = e^{-1} \mod \phi(N)$, and factor N. We let $\alpha, \delta \in \mathbb{R}^+$ such that

$$e = N^\alpha \qquad \text{and} \qquad d < N^\delta (= e^{\delta/\alpha}).$$

Then
$$k = (ed - 1)/\phi(N) < ed/\phi(N) < 2ed/N = 2e^{1+(\delta-1)/\alpha} , \qquad (8)$$

where we used that $\phi(N) > N/2$. Also, by (4), we have $|s| < (2r-1)e^{(1-1/r)/\alpha}$. Letting $a_r = 1 - 1/r$ we obtain

$$|s| < (2r - 1)e^{a_r/\alpha} . \qquad (9)$$

Thus, with $\epsilon_2 = \ln 2$ and $\epsilon_r = \ln(2r - 1)$, we are trying to solve the following *small inverse problem*: find integers k and s satisfying

$$-k(A + s) \equiv 1 \pmod{e} , \quad |k| < e^{1+(\delta-1)/\alpha+\epsilon_2} \quad \text{and} \quad |s| < e^{a_r/\alpha+\epsilon_r} . \qquad (10)$$

In order to be able to efficiently find $s = \phi(N) - N$ among the solutions of the small inverse problem, we need an efficient method to find all solutions, and we need that the number of solutions is sufficiently small.

Solving the Small Inverse Problem. In the following, identify a polynomial and its associated coefficient vector. In particular, we define the *norm* of a polynomial $h(x, y) = \sum_{i,j} a_{i,j} x^i y^j$ by $\|h(x, y)\| = (\sum_{i,j} |a_{i,j}|^2)^{1/2}$.

The small inverse problem (10) can be restated as follows: given a polynomial $f(x, y) = x(A + y) - 1$, find (x_0, y_0) such that

$$f(x_0, y_0) \equiv 0 \pmod{e} , \quad |x_0| < X , \quad |y_0| < Y , \qquad (11)$$

where $X = e^{1+\frac{\delta-1}{\alpha}+\epsilon_2}$, and $Y = e^{\frac{a_r}{\alpha}+\epsilon_r}$. Notice that $(-k, s)$ is a root of $f(x, y)$ mod e. Now, a result of Howgrave-Graham allows us to transform the modular equation in (11) into an integer equation.

Theorem 4 ([HG97]). *Let $h(x, y) \in \mathbb{Z}[x, y]$ be a polynomial which is a sum of at most w monomials, and let $X, Y \in \mathbb{N}$. Suppose that $h(x_0, y_0) \equiv 0 \pmod{e^m}$ for some positive integer m, where $|x_0| < X$ and $|y_0| < Y$. Then, if $\|h(xX, yY)\| < e^m/\sqrt{w}$, the equation $h(x_0, y_0) = 0$ holds over the integers.*

Our goal now is to construct a small norm polynomial that has $(-k, s)$ as a root modulo e^m for some m. To this end, given a positive integer m, define the polynomials

$$g_{i,k}(x, y) := x^i f^k(x, y) e^{m-k} \quad \text{and} \quad h_{j,k}(x, y) := y^j f^k(x, y) e^{m-k} . \qquad (12)$$

Now let (x_0, y_0) be a root of $f(x, y)$ modulo e. Then $g_{i,k}(x_0, y_0) \equiv h_{j,k}(x_0, y_0) \equiv 0 \pmod{e^m}$ for all $i, j, k \geq 0$. Thus, if we construct a lattice L using $g_{i,k}$ and $h_{j,k}$ as basis vectors, for various i, j, k, then all polynomials in the lattice have (x_0, y_0) as a root modulo e^m. Now recall from Section 2 that the first two polynomials b_1 and b_2 in an LLL-reduced basis satisfy $\|b_1\| \leq 2^{w/2}\text{vol}(L)^{1/w}$ and $\|b_2\| \leq 2^{(w-1)/2}\text{vol}(L)^{1/(w-1)}$. Therefore, if our lattice L satisfies

$$2^{(w-1)/2}\text{vol}(L)^{1/(w-1)} < e^m/\sqrt{w} , \qquad (13)$$

then b_1 and b_2 have norm small enough to satisfy Theorem 4, so that all small roots of b_1 and b_2 modulo e^m are also roots over the integers. This gives us two bivariate equations over the integers, which have at least one common small root, (x_0, y_0). Further, if these two polynomials are also algebraically independent, we can use the resultant of b_1 and b_2 to find their common roots (see [BD00] for details).

We now focus on generating a lattice with sufficiently small volume.

The Boneh-Durfee Lattice [BD00, Section 4]. Given integers $m \geq 1$ and $t \geq 0$, we construct the lattice as follows. For each $k = 0, \ldots, m$, use $g_{i,k}(xX, yY)$ for $i = 0, \ldots, m - k$ and $h_{j,k}(xX, yY)$ for $j = 0, \ldots, t$ as the basis vectors, with $g_{i,k}$ and $h_{j,k}$ as in (12). The lattice and basis will be denoted by $L_{BD}(m,t)$ and $B_{BD}(m,t)$, respectively. By construction, $L_{BD}(m,t)$ has full rank, and so the volume of the lattice equals the absolute value of determinant of the matrix generated by $B_{BD}(m,t)$. The dimension of the lattice is

$$w = (m+1)(m+2)/2 + t(m+1) .$$

Also, since this matrix is triangular, the determinant computation is straightforward and we have $\mathrm{vol}(L_{BD}(m,t)) = \det_x \cdot \det_y$, where $\det_x$ and $\det_y$ are the determinants of the submatrices corresponding to the $g_{i,k}$ and the $h_{j,k}$, respectively. We have

$$\det_x = e^{m(m+1)(m+2)/3} \cdot X^{m(m+1)(m+2)/3} \cdot Y^{m(m+1)(m+2)/6} , \tag{14}$$
$$\det_y = e^{tm(m+1)/2} \cdot X^{tm(m+1)/2} \cdot Y^{t(m+1)(m+t+1)/2} . \tag{15}$$

Substituting $X = e^{1+\frac{\delta-1}{\alpha}+\epsilon_2}$ and $Y = e^{\frac{a_r}{\alpha}+\epsilon_r}$ into (14) and (15) we obtain

$$\det_x = e^{(2+\frac{\delta-1}{\alpha}+\epsilon_2+(\frac{a_r}{\alpha}+\epsilon_r)/2)m(m+1)(m+2)/3} ,$$
$$\det_y = e^{(2+\frac{\delta-1}{\alpha}+\epsilon_2)tm(m+1)/2+(\frac{a_r}{\alpha}+\epsilon_r)t(m+1)(m+t+1)/2} .$$

Thus, $\mathrm{vol}(L_{BD}(m,t)) = e^C$, where

$$\begin{aligned}
C &= C(m,t,\alpha,\delta,r) \\
&= (2+(\delta-1)/\alpha + \epsilon_2 + (a_r/\alpha + \epsilon_r)/2)m(m+1)(m+2)/3 \\
&\quad + (2+(\delta-1)/\alpha + \epsilon_2)tm(m+1)/2 + (a_r/\alpha + \epsilon_r)t(m+1)(m+t+1)/2 .
\end{aligned}$$

We now need to find values for m and t so that (13) holds. That is, we require m and t to satisfy

$$e^{C(m,t,\alpha,\delta,r)} < \frac{e^{m(w-1)}}{2^{(w-1)^2/2}w^{(w-1)/2}} . \tag{16}$$

Finding integer values for m and t that allow for the largest δ in (16) is a difficult problem, as (16) is highly nonlinear, α and e are variables, and we require $m \geq 1$ and $t \geq 0$. In the case $r = 2$, Boneh and Durfee [BD00] approximate the right-hand side of (16) by $e^{m(w-1)}$ and then find that $t = t_{\mathrm{opt}} = m(1-2\delta)/2$ minimizes the left-hand side of $C(m, t, \alpha, \delta, r) - m(w - 1) < 0$. By letting $m \to \infty$ in this inequality, they obtain an upper bound $\delta_{\max}$ on δ such that, for N large, the attacks works if $d < N^{\delta_{\max}}$. For $\alpha = 1$, they obtain $\delta_{\max} = 7/6 - \sqrt{7}/3 \approx 0.2847$. Using [May02, Lemma 7] and [BD00], we can generalize this asymptotic bound and find that for arbitrary $\alpha > 0$ and $r = 2, 3, 4, \ldots$,

$$\delta_{\max}(\alpha, a_r) = 1 + \frac{1}{3} a_r - \frac{2}{3} \sqrt{a_r(a_r + 3\alpha)}. \tag{17}$$

(Recall that $a_r = 1 - 1/r$.) Next, we want to find upper bounds for δ for explicit values of N and α. For this, in a tedious but elementary computation we transform (16) to an inequality of the form $\delta < G(m, t, \alpha, r, N)$ (recall that $e = N^\alpha$) and numerically maximize G over $(m, t) \in \mathbb{N} \times \mathbb{N}_0$, for $r = 2, 3$, and 4. We show the results for $\alpha = 1$ (which represents the most common case in practice) in Table 1. We see that for r fixed and N increasing, the bounds converge to the

Table 1. Upper bounds for δ with $\alpha = 1$ using the Boneh-Durfee lattice. Last row: bounds from Section 4.1.

$\alpha = 1$	2-prime RSA				3-prime RSA				4-prime RSA			
N (bits)	$\delta_{\max}$	t_{opt}	m_{opt}	w_{opt}	$\delta_{\max}$	t_{opt}	m_{opt}	w_{opt}	$\delta_{\max}$	t_{opt}	m_{opt}	w_{opt}
1000	0.257	4	23	396	0.156	2	24	375	0.109	1	24	350
2000	0.267	6	31	720	0.165	3	32	660	0.118	2	33	663
4000	0.273	9	45	1495	0.170	4	41	1071	0.123	3	44	1170
6000	0.275	10	50	1836	0.172	5	49	1525	0.125	3	47	1320
8000	0.277	12	59	2550	0.173	6	57	2059	0.126	4	57	1943
10000	0.278	12	59	2912	0.174	7	65	2673	0.127	4	59	2070
$\vdots$	$\vdots$				$\vdots$				$\vdots$			
∞	0.285	∞	∞	∞	0.180	∞	∞	∞	0.132	∞	∞	∞
Wiener	0.250				0.167				0.125			

asymptotic bounds (17), which are given in the penultimate row. Moreover, just as in the case of Wiener's continued fractions attack whose bounds are given in the last row, the upper bounds on δ decrease as the number of prime factors of N increases.

Table 2 illustrates how $\delta_{\max}$ varies with α. Here we give data for the 3-prime case with a 2000-bit modulus, which reflects the typical behaviour. We see that, roughly, $\delta \sim 1/\alpha$. Hence, with increasing public exponent $e = N^\alpha$, a smaller private exponent $d = N^\delta$ is required for the attack to work, up to a point (here: $\alpha = 1.4$) where the attack is not guaranteed to work for any d. For 2-prime RSA and 2000-bit N, we have $\delta_{\max}(\alpha = 0.6) = 0.441$, while for 4-prime RSA and 2000-bit N, we have $\delta_{\max}(\alpha = 0.6) = 0.315$. See Figure 1(a) for a plot. Comprehensive data covering the 1000- to 10000-bit range for N are given in [Hin02].

Table 2. Upper bounds for δ for 2000-bit 3-prime N using the Boneh-Durfee lattice.

α	0.6	0.7	0.8	0.9	1.0	1.1	1.2	1.3	1.4	1.5
δ_{max}	0.357	0.307	0.257	0.210	0.165	0.121	0.079	0.039	0.000	-0.038
t_{opt}	0	0	1	2	3	4	5	7	8	9
m_{opt}	25	27	30	31	32	33	33	37	37	37
w_{opt}	26	28	62	96	132	170	204	304	342	380

Figure 1. Upper bound on δ for 2-, 3-, and 4-prime RSA with 2000-bit N.

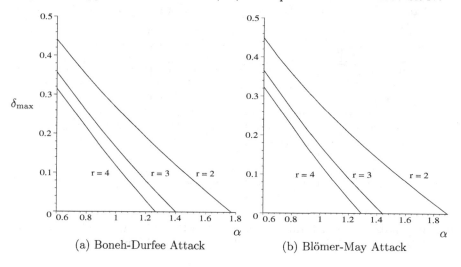

(a) Boneh-Durfee Attack   (b) Blömer-May Attack

Extending the Boneh-Durfee Lattice. By construction, the matrix that represents the basis $B_{BD}(m, t)$ for the Boneh-Durfee lattice is triangular. Thus, the volume of the lattice is simply the product of the diagonal elements. Boneh and Durfee [BD00] observed that some of these diagonal elements contribute more to the volume than others, and suggested to remove those. This complicates the computation of the lattice volume, since one now has to work with a lattice that does not have full rank. But using the concept of geometrically progressive matrices, one nevertheless can bound the volume of the new lattice. Applied to the case $r = 2$ and $\alpha = 1$, this gives a larger upper bound on δ, namely $\delta_{max} = 1 - \sqrt{2}/2 \approx 0.2929$. As before, this bounds holds as $N \to \infty$.

The Blömer-May Lattice. Another extension of the Boneh-Durfee lattice is given by Blömer and May [BM01]. Again, certain rows of $B_{BD}(m, t)$ are removed that contribute too much to the volume. But now also certain columns are removed, to ensure that the new basis has full rank and the matrix is triangular. Blömer and May find that, asymptotically, $\delta_{max} = (\sqrt{6} - 1)/5 \approx 0.2899$

for 2-prime N with $\alpha = 1$. As before, we can generalize this and find that for arbitrary $\alpha > 0$ and $r = 2, 3, \ldots$ the Blömer-May lattice yields an asymptotic upper bound on δ that is given by

$$\delta_{\max}(\alpha, a_r) = 1 - \frac{6}{5} a_r - \frac{3}{5}\alpha + \frac{2}{5}\sqrt{\alpha^2 - a_r\,\alpha + 4\,a_r^2}\,. \qquad (18)$$

As with the Boneh-Durfee lattice, we present some bounds on δ when $\alpha = 1$ for 2-, 3-, and 4-prime RSA for various modulus sizes in Table 3. These were determined in the same manner as for the Boneh-Durfee attack. Upper bounds on δ for varying α are shown in Figure 1(b). From Table 3 and more extensive

Table 3. Upper bounds for δ with $\alpha = 1$ using the Blömer-May lattice.

$\alpha = 1$	2-prime				3-prime				4-prime			
N (bits)	$\delta_{\max}$	t_{opt}	m_{opt}	w_{opt}	$\delta_{\max}$	t_{opt}	m_{opt}	w_{opt}	$\delta_{\max}$	t_{opt}	m_{opt}	w_{opt}
1000	0.271	14	30	465	0.167	10	43	484	0.120	8	62	567
2000	0.277	19	39	800	0.172	14	54	825	0.125	11	68	828
4000	0.281	26	51	1404	0.175	19	68	1380	0.128	16	86	1479
6000	0.283	31	60	1952	0.177	23	80	1944	0.129	19	98	1980
8000	0.284	36	69	2590	0.177	26	89	2430	0.129	21	106	2354
10000	0.285	39	74	3000	0.178	28	95	2784	0.130	23	115	2784
$\vdots$	$\vdots$				$\vdots$				$\vdots$			
∞	0.290	∞	∞	∞	0.181	∞	∞	∞	0.132	∞	∞	∞

data in [Hin02] we see that this attack allows for larger δ than Boneh and Durfee's attack in Section 4.2, but behaves in the same general way.

4.3 Chinese Remainder Theorem Attack

As the previous sections show, the private exponent must not be chosen too small. To still achieve fast private key computations, one can perform modular exponentiations by $d_i := d \bmod (p_i - 1)$ modulo the prime factors p_i of N and then recombine the results using Chinese remaindering. Of course, the smaller d_i, the faster the private key computations. However, although the attacks of the previous sections do not apply to small d_i, one can find a factor of N in time $O(\sqrt{d_{\mathrm{SL}}} \log^2 N)$, where d_{SL} denotes the *second* largest value among the d_i. This attack is an immediate generalization of the corresponding attack in the 2-prime case.

Let $m = \log d_{\mathrm{SL}}$, and let g be a random number modulo N. Let

$$G(X) = \prod_{k=0}^{2^{\lceil m/2 \rceil}-1} \left(g^{e \cdot 2^{m/2} \cdot k} X - g\right) \quad \bmod N\,.$$

Using fast Fourier transform techniques, for $j = 1, 2, \ldots, 2^{m/2}$ evaluate $G(X)$ at $X_j = g^{ej}$. Now assume $d_i \leq d_{\mathrm{SL}}$. Then, since d_i can be written in the form

$d_i = 2^{m/2}A_i + B_i$ for some $0 \le A_i < 2^{m/2}$, $0 < B_i \le 2^{m/2}$, and since $ed_i \equiv 1$ (mod $(p_i - 1)$), we find that

$$g^{e(2^{m/2} \cdot A_i + B_i)} - g = g^{ed_i} - g \equiv 0 \pmod{p_i},$$

so that $\gcd(G(g^{eB_i}), N) > 1$. If $d_i \not\equiv d_l \pmod{2^{m/2}}$ for $i \ne l$, then $G(g^{eB_i}) \not\equiv 0$ (mod p_l) and the event $\gcd(G(g^{eB_i}), N) > 1$ indeed reveals a prime factor of N.

Using FFT methods to evaluate a polynomial of degree σ at σ points with co-efficients modulo N requires time $O(\sigma \log \sigma)$ for the transforms and $O(\sigma \log^2 N)$ or the σ multiplications [Tur82]. Thus, in running time $O(2^{m/2} \log^2 N) = O(\sqrt{d_{\mathrm{SL}}} \log^2 N)$ the modulus can be factored.

5   Partial Key Exposure Attacks

A *partial key exposure* attack is an attack in which some bits of the decryption exponent are known and are used to try to extract the rest of the bits. We discuss selected partial key exposure attacks on 2-prime RSA when the encryption exponent is either of small or medium size, and extend these attacks to r-prime RSA with $r > 2$.

Let us first point out that the assumption of partial knowledge of the private exponent is quite realistic. For example, if the public exponent is small, then 2-prime RSA leaks half of the most significant bits of the private exponent [Bon99]. More generally, r-prime RSA leaks $1/r$ of the most significant bits of d. This works as follows. Assume we know k from (1). Let $d_k = \lfloor (kN + 1)/e \rfloor$. Then, with (1) and since $1 \le k < e$,

$$d_k - d \le \frac{k}{e}(N - \phi(N)) < N - \phi(N).$$

Applying (6) to the right-hand side, we get

$$d_k - d < 2^{n - n/r + 1 + \log_2 r}.$$

That is, at least $n/r - 1 - \log_2(r)$ of the most significant bits of d_k and d agree. Of course, an attacker does not know k, but since $1 \le k < e$, there are only $e - 1$ candidates for d_k. Thus, r-prime RSA with an n-bit modulus leaks $n/r + O(1)$ of the most significant bits of d once the correct value of d_k is identified. In many cases, the latter can be done using techniques discussed later in this section.

Boneh [Bon99] points out that if $e = 3$, then always $k = 2$. This is also true for multi-prime RSA.

Lemma 1. *Let N be the product of two or more distinct primes each greater than 3, and $d \equiv 3^{-1} \pmod{\phi(N)}$. Then $3d - 2\phi(N) = 1$.*

Proof. Let $N = \prod_{i=1}^{r} p_i$ with $p_i > 3$ prime. Then $p_i - 1 \not\equiv 2 \pmod 3$ for $i = 1, \ldots, r$. Also, since the inverse of 3 modulo $\phi(N)$ exists, we have $\gcd(p_i - 1, 3) = 1$ for $i = 1, \ldots, r$ and thus $p_i - 1 \not\equiv 0 \pmod 3$ for all i. Therefore, $p_i - 1 \equiv 1 \pmod 3$ for all i, and hence $\phi(N) = \prod_{i=1}^{r}(p_i - 1) \equiv 1 \pmod 3$. Now, reducing (1) (with $e = 3$) modulo 3 gives $-k \equiv 1 \pmod 3$, or $k \equiv 2 \pmod 3$. Since $1 \le k < 3$, this implies $k = 2$. $\qquad\square$

Consequently, when $e = 3$ in an r-prime RSA system, about $1/r$ of the most significant bits of the decryption exponent can be immediately disclosed. Although this is less bits than in the 2-prime case, the conclusion is that $e = 3$ (and small values of e in general) should be avoided in r-prime RSA as well.

5.1   Low Public Exponent Attack

When the public exponent is small (such that a running time $O(e \log e)$ is manageable) and the $n/4$ *least* significant bits of d are known, the remaining bits of the private exponent of a 2-prime RSA system can be recovered.

In brief, this attack works as follows (see [BDF98]). Assume the $n/4$ least significant bits of d are known. Let $d_0 = d \bmod 2^{n/4}$. Reducing (1) modulo $2^{n/4}$ and substituting $\phi(N) = N - (p + N/p) + 1$ yields the congruence

$$k'x^2 + (ed_0 - 1 - k'(N+1))x + k'N \equiv 0 \pmod{2^{n/4}}, \tag{19}$$

where $k' = k$ and $x = p \bmod 2^{n/4}$. If we knew $p \bmod 2^{n/4}$, then we could apply Theorem 1 to factor N in time $T_C(n)$. Thus, in the actual attack, for each integer k', $1 \le k' < e$, one computes all solutions $\bmod 2^{n/4}$ of (19) and attempts to factor N with each such candidate for $p \bmod 2^{n/4}$.

For the attack to be effective, it is important that the number of solutions of (19) is small if $k = k'$. Steinfeld and Zheng [SZ01] give a bound on this number that is exponential in the number of common least significant bits of the prime factors p and q of N, and which leads to the following result.

Theorem 5 ([SZ01]). *Let t_{p-q} denote the number of common least significant bits of p and q. Then, given the $n/4$ least significant bits of d, an attack by Boneh, Durfee, and Frankel [BDF98] factors N in time $O(T_{\mathrm{BDF}}(n))$, where*

$$T_{\mathrm{BDF}}(n) \le \begin{cases} 2e \log e \cdot 2^{t_{p-q}+1} T_C(n), & \text{if } 2(t_{p-q} - 1) < n/4, \\ 2e \log e \cdot 2^{n/8} T_C(n), & \text{if } 2(t_{p-q} - 1) \ge n/4. \end{cases}$$

The attack works best if $p \not\equiv q \pmod 4$, in which case a total number of at most $4e\lceil \log_2 e \rceil$ candidates for $p \bmod 2^{n/4}$ need to be tested (cf. [BDF98]).

We now consider this attack in the 3-prime case. Again, we start from (1), substitute $\phi(N)$ using (5), replace p_3 by $N/(p_1 p_2)$ and write $k' = k$ to obtain that $(x, y) = (p_1 \bmod 2^{n/4}, p_2 \bmod 2^{n/4})$ is a solution of the congruence $F_{k'}(x, y) \equiv 0 \pmod{2^{n/4}}$, where

$$F_{k'}(x, y) = \tag{20}$$
$$k'x^2y^2 - k'(x^2y + xy^2) + ((ed_0 - 1) - k'(N - 1))xy + k'N(x + y) - k'N.$$

With k' unknown, the idea is as above, namely to try all solutions $(x, y) \bmod 2^{n/4}$ for each $1 \le k' < e$, by applying a lattice reduction algorithm to factor N. For this approach to be of any use, the number of candidates for $(p_1 \bmod 2^{n/4}, p_2 \bmod 2^{n/4})$ must be small enough such that exhaustive search is feasible. To estimate the number of solutions of $F_{k'}(x, y) \equiv 0 \pmod{2^{n/4}}$, let

$$F(x, y) = x^2y^2 + ax^2y + bxy^2 + cxy + dx + ey + f, \tag{21}$$

and $h_x(y) = by^2 + cy + d$ and $h_y(x) = ax^2 + cx + e$. Then a straightforward computation shows that for integers x_0, y_0 and for $\nu \in \mathbb{N}$,

$$F(x + x_0 2^\nu, y + y_0 2^\nu) \equiv F(x, y) + 2^\nu(x_0 h_x(y) + y_0 h_y(x)) \pmod{2^{\nu+1}}.$$

Now, if $(\hat{x}, \hat{y})$ is a particular solution to $F(x, y) \equiv 0 \pmod{2^\nu}$, this solution can possibly be lifted to a solution modulo $2^{\nu+1}$, and any lifted solution (if it exists) will be of the form $(x, y) = (\hat{x} + x_0 2^\nu, \hat{y} + y_0 2^\nu)$, where $x_0, y_0 \in \{0, 1\}$. In fact, it is easy to see (cf. [Hin02]) that

$$F(\hat{x} + x_0 2^\nu, \hat{y} + y_0 2^\nu) \equiv 0 \pmod{2^{\nu+1}}$$

$$\text{iff} \tag{22}$$

$$x_0 h_x(\hat{y}) + y_0 h_y(\hat{x}) \equiv F(\hat{x}, \hat{y})/2^\nu \pmod{2}.$$

We now make the following substitutions in (21):

$$a = b = -1 \ , \ c = \phi(N) - N + 1 \ , \ d = e = N \ , \ f = -N \ ,$$

and denote the corresponding function by $\overline{F}(x, y)$. Then the corresponding $\overline{h}_x(y)$ and $\overline{h}_y(x)$ satisfy $\overline{h}_x(y) \equiv y^2 + 1 \pmod{2}$ and $\overline{h}_y(x) \equiv x^2 + 1 \pmod{2}$. From this, we easily obtain

Lemma 2 ([Hin02]). *If $(\hat{x}, \hat{y})$ is a solution of $\overline{F}(x, y) \equiv 0 \pmod{2^\nu}$ with $\hat{x}, \hat{y} \equiv 1 \pmod{2}$ then $(\hat{x}, \hat{y})$ lifts to either 4 solutions modulo $2^{\nu+1}$ or does not lift to any solution modulo $2^{\nu+1}$.*

This lemma together with (22) allows us to generate all solutions of $\overline{F}(x, y) \equiv 0 \pmod{2^\nu}$ for any $\nu > \eta$ provided we know all solutions modulo 2^η. Now observe that, conveniently, $k\overline{F}(x, y) \equiv F_k(x, y) \pmod{2^{n/4}}$ and $p, q \equiv 1 \pmod{2}$. Thus, if $k = 2^t u$ where u odd, then every solution to $\overline{F}(x, y) \equiv 0 \pmod{2^{n/4-t}}$ is also a solution to $F_k(x, y) \equiv 0 \pmod{2^{n/4}}$. This allows us to conjecture a lower bound for the number of solutions to the latter congruence.

Conjecture 1. For a random 3-prime RSA modulus N, the number of solutions to $F_k(x, y) \equiv 0 \pmod{2^{n/4}}$ is exponential in n.

Rationale. Let $(\hat{x}, \hat{y})$ be a solution of $\overline{F}(x, y) \equiv 0 \pmod{2^\nu}$, for some $\nu \in \mathbb{N}$. This solution lifts to 4 solutions mod $2^{\nu+1}$ if and only if $\overline{F}(\hat{x}, \hat{y})/2^\nu$ is even. Which, under the reasonable assumption that $\overline{F}(\hat{x}, \hat{y})/2^\nu$ behaves like a random integer, happens with probability $1/2$. Thus, *on average, each $(\hat{x}, \hat{y})$ lifts to 2 solutions,* and, on average, the number of solutions modulo $2^{\nu+1}$ will be twice as high as the number of solutions modulo 2^ν. Thus the average number of solutions modulo $2^{\nu+1}$ will be 2^ν times the number of solutions modulo 2. □

Using (22) and Lemma 2, we carried out some experiments to obtain experimental evidence on the average number of solutions of (20). We generated a random 3-prime RSA modulus N, and then computed all solutions of $F_k(x, y) \equiv 0 \pmod{2^\nu}$ for $2 \leq \nu \leq 10$, starting with the known solution $(1, 1)$ modulo 2.

Table 4. Number of solutions of $F_k(x, y) \equiv 0 \pmod{2^\nu}$ with random 150-bit 3-prime RSA modulus N, for $2 \leq \nu \leq 10$. σ denotes the standard deviation. (*) when the number of solutions exceeded 73728, the implementation terminated with a memory error.

Modulo	Number of Solutions for $e = 3$ (2000 trials)			Number of Solutions for $e = 2^{16} + 1$ (1500 trials)		
	ave $\pm \sigma$	min	max	ave $\pm \sigma$	min	max
2^2	4 ± 0	4	4	4 ± 0	4	4
2^3	16 ± 0	16	16	16 ± 0	16	16
2^4	64 ± 0	64	64	58 ± 13	16	64
2^5	205 ± 64	64	256	191 ± 64	64	256
2^6	592 ± 188	256	768	554 ± 302	64	1024
2^7	1431 ± 705	256	2304	1504 ± 1175	256	4096
2^8	3162 ± 1936	1024	6144	3868 ± 4081	256	16384
2^9	6856 ± 4853	1024	15360	9610 ± 13405	1024	65536
2^{10}	14273 ± 11306	4096	43008	*	1024	73728*

This was done for 2000 and 1500 values of N, using public exponents $e = 3$ and $e = 2^{16} + 1$, respectively. The results of these experiments are given in the Table 4. We see that indeed, the number of solutions to $F_k(x, y) \equiv 0 \pmod{2^\nu}$ is $\Omega(2^\nu)$. This supports our conjecture that the number of solutions to $F_k(x, y) \equiv 0 \pmod{2^{n/4}}$ is exponential in the bitsize of the RSA modulus N, which makes the Boneh-Durfee-Frankel attack [BDF98] completely ineffective for 3-prime RSA.

Extending the attack to 4-prime RSA yields similar results. Here we look for solutions to the multivariate modular equation in three unknowns: $G_{k'}(x, y, z) \equiv 0 \pmod{2^{n/4}}$, where

$$G_{k'}(x, y, z) = k'(x^2 y^2 z^2 - (x^2 y^2 z + x^2 y z^2 + x y^2 z^2) + (x^2 y z + x y^2 z + x y z^2))$$
$$+ (ed_0 - 1 - k'(N+1))xyz + k'N(xy + xz + yz) - k'N(x + y + z) + k'N .$$

Note that $(p_1 \bmod 2^{n/4}, p_2 \bmod 2^{n/4}, p_3 \bmod 2^{n/4})$ is a solution of $G_{k'}(x, y, z) \equiv 0 \pmod{2^{n/4}}$ if $k' = k$. Here we find, for the corresponding function $\overline{G}(x, y, z)$, that

Lemma 3 ([Hin02]). If $(\hat{x}, \hat{y}, \hat{z})$ is a solution of $\overline{G}(x, y, z) \equiv 0 \pmod{2^\nu}$ with $\hat{x}, \hat{y}, \hat{z} \equiv 1 \bmod 2$ then $(\hat{x}, \hat{y}, \hat{z})$ either lifts to 8 solutions modulo $2^{\nu+1}$ or does not lift to any solution modulo $2^{\nu+1}$.

We also obtain similar experimental results, this time conducted with random 200-bit 4-prime moduli N and $e = 3$ and $\nu \leq 6$. We conclude that also in the 4-prime case the number of solutions of the corresponding modular equation is exponential in the size of the RSA modulus and the partial key attack is not feasible for 4-prime RSA.

Given the result by Steinfeld and Zheng, it is interesting to examine a possible dependence between the number of solutions to $\overline{F}(x, y) \equiv 0 \pmod{2^\nu}$ and common least significant bits of the p_i. To this end, for $l = 1, \ldots, 10$, we generated 100 random 150-bit 3-prime RSA moduli for which p_1, p_2, p_3 had exactly the l least significant bits in common. For $e = 3$ and $\nu = 1, \ldots, 10$, and $e = 2^{16} + 1$ and $\nu = 1, \ldots, 9$, we counted the number of solutions of $\overline{F}(x, y) \equiv 0 \pmod{2^\nu}$. Table 5 shows our experimental results for $e = 3$ and $\nu = 10$, which captures the general behaviour of the data. There is obviously a pattern, but certainly the

Table 5. Frequency of the number of solutions of $\overline{F}(x, y) \equiv 0 \pmod{2^{10}}$ with respect to the number of common least significant bits of p_1, p_2, p_3.

# solutions	# common bits									
	1	2	3	4	5	6	7	8	9	10
4096	0	0	0	64	55	53	42	46	54	52
6144	56	55	50	0	0	0	0	0	0	0
10240	0	0	0	22	29	27	29	22	16	20
12288	11	0	0	0	0	0	0	0	0	0
18432	14	19	26	0	0	0	0	0	0	0
24576	6	0	0	0	0	0	0	0	0	0
34816	0	7	24	14	16	20	29	32	30	28
36864	12	0	0	0	0	0	0	0	0	0
43008	1	19	0	0	0	0	0	0	0	0

number of solutions is not determined by the number of common least significant bits alone, as it was the case for 2-prime RSA.

5.2 Medium Public Exponent Attack

Next we discuss an attack by Boneh, Durfee, and Frankel [BDF98] that applies when $e < \sqrt{N}$ and a certain fraction of the *most* significant bits of d is known. It first computes a small-size interval that contains the unique integer k that satisfies (1), and then uses these candidates to determine d. This works as follows.

Using (4), we can immediately generalize Lemma 4.2 and Theorem 4.1 from [BDF98] to the r-prime case ($r \geq 2$).

Lemma 4. *Let* $N = \prod_{i=1}^{r} p_i$ *and suppose* d_0 *is given such that, for positive integers* c_1 *and* c_2, $|e(d - d_0)| < c_1 N$ *and* $e d_0 < c_2 N^{1+1/r}$. *Let* $\Delta = 2(2r - 1)c_2 + 2c_1$ *and* $\tilde{k} = (e d_0 - 1)/N$. *Then the integer* k *satisfying* (1) *lies in* $(\tilde{k} - \Delta, \tilde{k} + \Delta) \cap \mathbb{Z}$.

Proof. With $\tilde{k} = (e d_0 - 1)/N$ and $k = (e d - 1)/\phi(N)$ we have

$$|k - \tilde{k}| = \left| (e d_0 - 1)\left(\frac{1}{\phi(N)} - \frac{1}{N} \right) + \frac{e(d - d_0)}{\phi(N)} \right|$$

$$< c_2 N^{1+1/r} \left(\frac{N - \phi(N)}{N\phi(N)} \right) + c_1 \frac{N}{\phi(N)}.$$

Using (4) and that $\phi(N) > N/2$, we obtain $|k - \tilde{k}| < 2(2r - 1)c_2 + 2c_1$. $\square$

Theorem 6. *Let t be an integer, $0 \le t \le n/r$, and assume $2^t < e < 2^{t+1}$. Given the t most significant bits of d, there is an efficiently computable set of integers A_r such that $k \in A_r$ and $|A_r| \le 16((2r-1)2^{1/r}+1)$.*

Proof. Given the t most significant bits of d, we can construct an integer $d_0 < 2^n$ such that $|d - d_0| < 2^{n-t}$. Then, since $2^{n-1} < N < 2^n$, we have $|e(d - d_0)| < 2^{n+1} < 4N$ and $ed_0 < 2^{n+n/r+1} < 2^{2+1/r}N^{1+1/r}$. Thus, Lemma 4 holds with $c_1 = 4$ and $c_2 = 2^{2+1/r}$. So let $\Delta_r = 8(2r-1)2^{1/r}+8$ and $\tilde{k} = (ed_0 - 1)/N$ and $A_r = (\tilde{k} - \Delta_r, \tilde{k} + \Delta_r) \cap \mathbb{Z}$. Then $k \in A_r$ and $|A_r| \le 2\Delta_r$. $\square$

Note that for $r = 2$, the cardinality of A_2 differs from the value given in [BDF98], which is 40. On the one hand, we were able to derive a sharper bound on $N - \phi(N)$ from our assumption (3) on the relative sizes of the prime factors (while (3) is actually equivalent with the corresponding condition (1) of [BDF98]). But on the other hand, for the n-bit number N we used the estimate $2^{n-1} < N$ rather than $2^n < N$.

Not only does the range of suitable e in Theorem 6 decrease for $r > 2$, we also run into problems in the attempt to identify the correct value of k among the integers in A_r.

In the 2-prime case, if $n/4 \le t \le n/2$ and if the public exponent is prime, one proceeds as follows ([BDF98]): Let $k' \in A_2$. If $k' \ge e$, discard k'. Otherwise, let $s = N + 1 + (k')^{-1} \mod e$, and compute a root x_0 of $x^2 - sx + N \equiv 0 \pmod{e}$. If $k' = k$ then, from (1), $(k')^{-1} \equiv -\phi(N) \pmod{e}$ and $s \equiv N + 1 - \phi(N) \pmod{e}$. Thus, $s \equiv p + q \pmod{e}$ and $x_0 \equiv p \pmod{e}$ or $x_0 \equiv q \pmod{e}$ so that Theorem 1 applies (observe that $e > 2^{n/4}$) and it is possible to factor N in time polynomial in n. If $k \ne k'$, then Theorem 1 fails to factor N and k' can be discarded. This technique can also be adapted to the case that e is composite with known prime factorization.

In the r-prime case ($r > 2$), the above approach to test the elements of A_r does not work. To find p_i modulo e in a similar way, we would need to solve the degree-r congruence $\prod_{i=1}^{r}(x - p_i) \equiv 0 \pmod{e}$. However, not all coefficients in this equation are known! For example, if $r = 3$, we might want to put $s = N - 1 + (k')^{-1} \mod e$. Then, if $k = k'$, we have $s \equiv p_1 p_2 + p_1 p_3 + p_2 p_3 - (p_1 + p_2 + p_3) \pmod{e}$. But this leaves us only with the congruence $x^3 - (p_1 + p_2 + p_3)x^2 + (s + p_1 + p_2 + p_3)x - N \equiv 0 \pmod{e}$, with $\sum_{i=1}^{3} p_i$ unknown.

That means that 2-prime RSA can be broken if the public exponent is prime or of known prime factorization, if e has $t + 1$ bits and the t most significant bits of the private exponent are known and $n/4 \le t \le n/2$, but for multi-prime RSA with $r > 2$ factors no corresponding attack is known.

Another, weaker, result from [BDF98] that requires knowledge of significantly more bits of the private exponent does generalize to the r-prime case. This result does not require knowledge of the prime factorization of e, but we need that k is not significantly smaller than e. (The latter is not a significant restriction, see [BDF98]).

Theorem 7. *Let N be an r-prime RSA modulus and suppose $2^t < e < 2^{t+1}$ where $0 \le t \le n/r$ is an integer. Also, assume that $k > \epsilon \cdot e$ for $1 > \epsilon > 0$. Given* *the $n - t$ most significant bits of d, the remaining bits of d can be recovered in time $O(rn^3/\epsilon)$.*

Proof. Using the $n - t$ most significant bits of d we can construct an integer d_0 such that $d - d_0 < 2^t$. Let $\tilde{k} = (ed_0 - 1)/N$. Then Theorem 6 applies with $A_r = (\tilde{k} - \Delta_r, \tilde{k} + \Delta_r) \cap \mathbb{Z}$ where $\Delta_r = 16((2r - 1)2^{1/r} + 1)$. So we know that $k \in A_r$. Now, for each $k' \in A_r$ that is coprime with e, we do the following: for each integer $v \in [0, 1/\epsilon)$, let $d' = d_0 + k'v$; then check if d' is the correct private exponent, by testing if $(M^e)^{d'} \equiv M \pmod{N}$ for random $M \in \mathbb{Z}_N$. This method succeeds because if $k = k'$, then $d = d_0 + k(d - d_0)/k$, and $(d - d_0)/k < 1/\epsilon$ by our assumption on k and construction of d_0. Testing each candidate (k', v) through modular exponentiations of n-bit integers takes $O(n^3)$ time. There are $1/\epsilon$ candidates for v' and $O(r)$ candidates for k'. Hence, the total running time to recover d is $O(rn^3/\epsilon)$.   □

Theorem 7 implies that, paradoxically, the smaller e is, the more bits of d are required to completely recover the private exponent. For example, if e is approximately $N^{1/3}$, then we need $2/3$ of the most significant bits of d to mount the attack, while if e is close to $N^{1/4}$, as many as $3/4$ of the bits of d are needed. Note that the bound on the public exponent for which the attack works becomes smaller with more prime factors in the modulus.

6   Conclusion

We have examined how selected attacks on RSA can be extended to the multi-prime case, and how they perform in the new setting. We have shown that as the numbers of primes factors in the modulus increases, the attacks become more complex, which results in that the attacks apply in fewer instances, or become totally ineffective, or do not seem to extend at all. While our results suggest that thus multi-prime RSA is less vulnerable to current attacks on RSA, it is important to now look for attacks that specifically exploit the fact that the modulus factors into three, or four, primes.

Acknowledgements. The authors would like to thank Dan Boneh for help with Section 4.3, and Shuhong Gao for help with Section 5.1. We also thank Don Coppersmith, Glenn Durfee and Alexander May for helpful explanations.

References

[BD00]   D. Boneh and G. Durfee. Cryptanalysis of RSA with private key d less than $N^{0.292}$. *IEEE Transactions on Information Theory*, 46(4):1339–1349, 2000.

[BDF98]   D. Boneh, G. Durfee, and Y. Frankel. Exposing an RSA private key given a small fraction of its bits. In *Advances in Cryptology - ASI-ACRYPT '98*, volume 1514 of *Lecture Notes In Computer Science*, pages 25–34. Springer-Verlag, 1998. Revised and extended version available from http://crypto.stanford.edu/ dabo/pubs.html.

[BM01]   J. Blömer and A. May. Low secret exponent RSA revisited. In *Cryptography and Lattices - Proceedings of CALC '01*, volume 2146 of *Lecture Notes In Computer Science*, pages 4–19. Springer-Verlag, 2001.

[Bon99]   D. Boneh. Twenty years of attacks on the RSA cryptosystem. *Notices of the American Mathematical Society*, 46(2):203–213, 1999.

[BS02]   D. Boneh and H. Shacham. Fast variants of RSA. *CryptoBytes (The technical newsletter of RSA laboratories)*, 5(1):1–9, 2002.

[CHLS97]   T. Collins, D. Hopkins, S. Langford, and M. Sabin. Public Key Cryptography Apparatus and Method. US Patent #5,848,159, Jan. 1997.

[Cop97]   D. Coppersmith. Small solutions to polynomial equations, and low exponent RSA vulnerabilities. *Journal of Cryptology*, 10(4):233–260, 1997.

[DN00]   G. Durfee and P. Q. Nguyen. Cryptanalysis of the RSA schemes with short secret exponent from Asiacrypt '99. In *Advances in Cryptology - ASIACRYPT 2000*, volume 1976 of *Lecture Notes In Computer Science*, pages 14–29. Springer-Verlag, 2000.

[HG97]   N.A. Howgrave-Graham. Finding small roots of univariate modular equations revisited. In *Cryptography and Coding*, volume 1355 of *Lecture Notes In Computer Science*, pages 131–142. Springer-Verlag, 1997.

[Hin02]   M. J. Hinek. Low public exponent partial key and low private exponent attacks on multi-prime RSA. Master's thesis, University of Waterloo, Dept. of Combinatorics and Optimization, 2002.

[HW60]   G. H. Hardy and E. M. Wright. *An Introduction to the Theory of Numbers*. Oxford University Press, fourth edition, 1960.

[Len01]   A. K. Lenstra. Unbelievable security : Matching AES security using public key systems. In *Advances in Cryptology - ASIACRYPT 2001*, volume 2248 of *Lecture Notes In Computer Science*, pages 67–86. Springer-Verlag, 2001.

[LLL82]   A. Lenstra, H. Lenstra, and L. Lovász. Factoring polynomials with rational coefficients. *Mathematische Annalen*, 261:515–534, 1982.

[Low02]   M.K. Low. Attacks on multi-prime RSA with low private exponent or medium-sized public exponent. Master's thesis, Univ. of Waterloo, Dept. of Combinatorics and Optimization, 2002.

[May02]   A. May. Cryptanalysis of unbalanced RSA with small CRT-exponent. In *Advances in Cryptology - CRYPTO 2002*, Lecture Notes In Computer Science. Springer-Verlag, 2002.

[Old63]   C. D. Olds. *Continued Fractions*. Random House, Inc., 1963.

[RSA78]   R. L. Rivest, A. Shamir, and L. Adleman. A method for obtaining digital signatures and public-key cryptosystems. *Communications of the ACM*, 21(2):120–126, 1978.

[Sho]   V. Shoup. Number theory library (NTL), Version 5.2. http://www.shoup.net/ntl.

[Sti95]   D. R. Stinson. *Cryptography : Theory and Practice*. CRC Press LLC, 1995.

[SZ01]   R. Steinfeld and Y. Zheng. An advantage of low-exponent RSA with modulus primes sharing least significant bits. In *Proceedings RSA Conference 2001, Cryptographer's Track*, volume 2020 of *Lecture Notes in Computer Science*, pages 52–62. Springer-Verlag, 2001.

[Tur82]   J. W. M. Turk. Fast arithmetic operations on numbers and polynomials. In H.W. Lenstra, Jr. and R. Tijdeman, editors, *Computational Methods in Number Theory, Part I*. Mathematisch Centrum, Amsterdam, 1982.

[Wie90]   M. J. Wiener. Cryptanalysis of short RSA secret exponents. *IEEE Transactions on Information Theory*, 36(3):553–558, 1990.

Author Index

Black, John, 62
Blundo, Carlo, 291
Boutros, Joseph, 232
Bresson, Emmanuel, 325

Camion, Paul, 196
Chang, Donghoon, 160
Charpin, Pascale, 175
Chevassut, Olivier, 325
Chow, Stanley, 250
Ciet, Mathieu, 21

D'Arco, Paolo, 291
Demirci, Hüseyin, 147

Eisen, Philip, 250
Ekdahl, Patrik, 47

Furuya, Soichi, 94

Guillot, Philippe, 232
Gupta, Kishan Chand, 214

Han, Dong-Guk, 369
Hatano, Yasuo, 129
Hawkes, Philip, 37
Hess, Florian, 310
Hinek, M. Jason, 385
Hirose, Shoichi, 339

Imai, Hideki, 196

Johansson, Thomas, 47
Johnson, Harold, 250
Jonsson, Jakob, 76

Kaneko, Toshinobu, 129
Kim, Chang Han, 369
Kim, Dongryeol, 13

Lee, Sangjin, 160
Leveiller, Sabine, 232

Lim, Jongin, 160, 369
Lim, Seongan, 13
Low, Mo King, 385

Maitra, Subhamoy, 214
Malone-Lee, John, 1
Mihaljević, Miodrag J., 196

Oorschot, Paul C. Van, 250

Park, Young-Ho, 369
Pasalic, Enes, 175
Patel, Sarvar, 271, 353
Pointcheval, David, 325

Quisquater, Jean-Jacques, 21

Ramzan, Zulfikar, 271
Reichardt, Ben, 110
Rogaway, Phillip, 62
Rose, Gregory G., 37

Sakurai, Kouichi, 94
Santis, Alfredo De, 291
Sekine, Hiroki, 129
Shrimpton, Thomas, 62
Sica, Francesco, 21
Smart, Nigel P., 1
Stinson, Douglas R., 291
Sundaram, Ganapathy S., 271
Sung, Jaechul, 160
Sung, Soohak, 160

Teske, Edlyn, 385

Venkateswarlu, Ayineedi, 214

Wagner, David, 110

Yoon, Ki Soon, 369

Zémor, Gilles, 232

Lecture Notes in Computer Science

For information about Vols. 1–2514

please contact your bookseller or Springer-Verlag

Vol. 2515: F. Boavida, E. Monteiro, J. Orvalho (Eds.), Protocols and Systems for Interactive Distributed Multimedia. Proceedings, 2002. XIV, 372 pages. 2002.

Vol. 2516: A. Wespi, G. Vigna, L. Deri (Eds.), Recent Advances in Intrusion Detection. Proceedings, 2002. X, 327 pages. 2002.

Vol. 2517: M.D. Aagaard, J.W. O'Leary (Eds.), Formal Methods in Computer-Aided Design. Proceedings, 2002. XI, 399 pages. 2002.

Vol. 2518: P. Bose, P. Morin (Eds.), Algorithms and Computation. Proceedings, 2002. XIII, 656 pages. 2002.

Vol. 2519: R. Meersman, Z. Tari, et al. (Eds.), On the Move to Meaningful Internet Systems 2002: CoopIS, DOA, and ODBASE. Proceedings, 2002. XXIII, 1367 pages. 2002.

Vol. 2521: A. Karmouch, T. Magedanz, J. Delgado (Eds.), Mobile Agents for Telecommunication Applications. Proceedings, 2002. XII, 317 pages. 2002.

Vol. 2522: T. Andreasen, A. Motro, H. Christiansen, H. Legind Larsen (Eds.), Flexible Query Answering. Proceedings, 2002. XI, 386 pages. 2002. (Subseries LNAI).

Vol. 2523: B.S. Kaliski Jr., Ç.K. Koç, C. Paar (Eds.), Cryptographic Hardware and Embedded Systems – CHES 2002. Proceedings, 2002. XIV, 612 pages. 2002.

Vol. 2525: H.H. Bülthoff, S.-Whan Lee, T.A. Poggio, C. Wallraven (Eds.), Biologically Motivated Computer Vision. Proceedings, 2002. XIV, 662 pages. 2002.

Vol. 2526: A. Colosimo, A. Giuliani, P. Sirabella (Eds.), Medical Data Analysis. Proceedings, 2002. IX, 222 pages. 2002.

Vol. 2527: F.J. Garijo, J.C. Riquelme, M. Toro (Eds.), Advances in Artificial Intelligence – IBERAMIA 2002. Proceedings, 2002. XVIII, 955 pages. 2002. (Subseries LNAI).

Vol. 2528: M.T. Goodrich, S.G. Kobourov (Eds.), Graph Drawing. Proceedings, 2002. XIII, 384 pages. 2002.

Vol. 2529: D.A. Peled, M.Y. Vardi (Eds.), Formal Techniques for Networked and Distributed Sytems – FORTE 2002. Proceedings, 2002. XI, 371 pages. 2002.

Vol. 2531: J. Padget, O. Shehory, D. Parkes, N. Sadeh, W.E. Walsh (Eds.), Agent-Mediated Electronic Commerce IV. Proceedings, 2002. XVII, 341 pages. 2002. (Subseries LNAI).

Vol. 2532: Y.-C. Chen, L.-W. Chang, C.-T. Hsu (Eds.), Advances in Multimedia Information Processing – PCM 2002. Proceedings, 2002. XXI, 1255 pages. 2002.

Vol. 2533: N. Cesa-Bianchi, M. Numao, R. Reischuk (Eds.), Algorithmic Learning Theory. Proceedings, 2002. XI, 415 pages. 2002. (Subseries LNAI).

Vol. 2534: S. Lange, K. Satoh, C.H. Smith (Ed.), Discovery Science. Proceedings, 2002. XIII, 464 pages. 2002.

Vol. 2535: N. Suri (Ed.), Mobile Agents. Proceedings, 2002. X, 203 pages. 2002.

Vol. 2536: M. Parashar (Ed.), Grid Computing – GRID 2002. Proceedings, 2002. XI, 318 pages. 2002.

Vol. 2537: D.G. Feitelson, L. Rudolph, U. Schwiegelshohn (Eds.), Job Scheduling Strategies for Parallel Processing. Proceedings, 2002. VII, 237 pages. 2002.

Vol. 2538: B. König-Ries, K. Makki, S.A.M. Makki, N. Pissinou, P. Scheuermann (Eds.), Developing an Infrastructure for Mobile and Wireless Systems. Proceedings 2001. X, 183 pages. 2002.

Vol. 2539: K. Börner, C. Chen (Eds.), Visual Interfaces to Digital Libraries. X, 233 pages. 2002.

Vol. 2540: W.I. Grosky, F. Plášil (Eds.), SOFSEM 2002: Theory and Practice of Informatics. Proceedings, 2002. X, 289 pages. 2002.

Vol. 2541: T. Barkowsky, Mental Representation and Processing of Geographic Knowledge. X, 174 pages. 2002. (Subseries LNAI).

Vol. 2542: I. Dimov, I. Lirkov, S. Margenov, Z. Zlatev (Eds.), Numerical Methods and Applications. Proceedings, 2002. X, 174 pages. 2003.

Vol. 2543: O. Bartenstein, U. Geske, M. Hannebauer, O. Yoshie (Eds.), Web Knowledge Management and Decision Support. Proceedings, 2001. X, 307 pages. 2003. (Subseries LNAI).

Vol. 2544: S. Bhalla (Ed.), Databases in Networked Information Systems. Proceedings 2002. X, 285 pages. 2002.

Vol. 2545: P. Forbrig, Q, Limbourg, B. Urban, J. Vanderdonckt (Eds.), Interactive Systems. Proceedings 2002. XII, 574 pages. 2002.

Vol. 2546: J. Sterbenz, O. Takada, C. Tschudin, B. Plattner (Eds.), Active Networks. Proceedings, 2002. XIV, 267 pages. 2002.

Vol. 2547: R. Fleischer, B. Moret, E. Meineche Schmidt (Eds.), Experimental Algorithmics. XVII, 279 pages. 2002.

Vol. 2548: J. Hernández, Ana Moreira (Eds.), Object-Oriented Technology. Proceedings, 2002. VIII, 223 pages. 2002.

Vol. 2549: J. Cortadella, A. Yakovlev, G. Rozenberg (Eds.), Concurrency and Hardware Design. XI, 345 pages. 2002.

Vol. 2550: A. Jean-Marie (Ed.), Advances in Computing Science – ASIAN 2002. Proceedings, 2002. X, 233 pages. 2002.

Vol. 2551: A. Menezes, P. Sarkar (Eds.), Progress in Cryptology – INDOCRYPT 2002. Proceedings, 2002. XI, 437 pages. 2002.

Vol. 2552: S. Sahni, V.K. Prasanna, U. Shukla (Eds.), High Performance Computing – HiPC 2002. Proceedings, 2002. XXI, 735 pages. 2002.

Vol. 2553: B. Andersson, M. Bergholtz, P. Johannesson (Eds.), Natural Language Processing and Information Systems. Proceedings, 2002. X, 241 pages. 2002.

Vol. 2554: M. Beetz, Plan-Based Control of Robotic Agents. XI, 191 pages. 2002. (Subseries LNAI).

Vol. 2555: E.-P. Lim, S. Foo, C. Khoo, H. Chen, E. Fox, S. Urs, T. Costantino (Eds.), Digital Libraries: People, Knowledge, and Technology. Proceedings, 2002. XVII, 535 pages. 2002.

Vol. 2556: M. Agrawal, A. Seth (Eds.), FST TCS 2002: Foundations of Software Technology and Theoretical Computer Science. Proceedings, 2002. XI, 361 pages. 2002.

Vol. 2557: B. McKay, J. Slaney (Eds.), AI 2002: Advances in Artificial Intelligence. Proceedings, 2002. XV, 730 pages. 2002. (Subseries LNAI).

Vol. 2558: P. Perner, Data Mining on Multimedia Data. X, 131 pages. 2002.

Vol. 2559: M. Oivo, S. Komi-Sirviö (Eds.), Product Focused Software Process Improvement. Proceedings, 2002. XV, 646 pages. 2002.

Vol. 2560: S. Goronzy, Robust Adaptation to Non-Native Accents in Automatic Speech Recognition. Proceedings, 2002. XI, 144 pages. 2002. (Subseries LNAI).

Vol. 2561: H.C.M. de Swart (Ed.), Relational Methods in Computer Science. Proceedings, 2001. X, 315 pages. 2002.

Vol. 2562: V. Dahl, P. Wadler (Eds.), Practical Aspects of Declarative Languages. Proceedings, 2003. X, 315 pages. 2002.

Vol. 2566: T.Æ. Mogensen, D.A. Schmidt, I.H. Sudborough (Eds.), The Essence of Computation. XIV, 473 pages. 2002.

Vol. 2567: Y.G. Desmedt (Ed.), Public Key Cryptography – PKC 2003. Proceedings, 2003. XI, 365 pages. 2002.

Vol. 2568: M. Hagiya, A. Ohuchi (Eds.), DNA Computing. Proceedings, 2002. XI, 338 pages. 2003.

Vol. 2569: D. Gollmann, G. Karjoth, M. Waidner (Eds.), Computer Security – ESORICS 2002. Proceedings, 2002. XIII, 648 pages. 2002. (Subseries LNAI).

Vol. 2570: M. Jünger, G. Reinelt, G. Rinaldi (Eds.), Combinatorial Optimization – Eureka, You Shrink!. Proceedings, 2001. X, 209 pages. 2003.

Vol. 2571: S.K. Das, S. Bhattacharya (Eds.), Distributed Computing. Proceedings, 2002. XIV, 354 pages. 2002.

Vol. 2572: D. Calvanese, M. Lenzerini, R. Motwani (Eds.), Database Theory – ICDT 2003. Proceedings, 2003. XI, 455 pages. 2002.

Vol. 2574: M.-S. Chen, P.K. Chrysanthis, M. Sloman, A. Zaslavsky (Eds.), Mobile Data Management. Proceedings, 2003. XII, 414 pages. 2003.

Vol. 2575: L.D. Zuck, P.C. Attie, A. Cortesi, S. Mukhopadhyay (Eds.), Verification, Model Checking, and Abstract Interpretation. Proceedings, 2003. XI, 325 pages. 2003.

Vol. 2576: S. Cimato, C. Galdi, G. Persiano (Eds.), Security in Communication Networks. Proceedings, 2002. IX, 365 pages. 2003.

Vol. 2578: F.A.P. Petitcolas (Ed.), Information Hiding. Proceedings, 2002. IX, 427 pages. 2003.

Vol. 2580: H. Erdogmus, T. Weng (Eds.), COTS-Based Software Systems. Proceedings, 2003. XVIII, 261 pages. 2003.

Vol. 2581: J.S. Sichman, F. Bousquet, P. Davidsson (Eds.), Multi-Agent-Based Simulation II. Proceedings, 2002. X, 195 pages. 2003. (Subseries LNAI).

Vol. 2583: S. Matwin, C. Sammut (Eds.), Inductive Logic Programming. Proceedings, 2002. X, 351 pages. 2003. (Subseries LNAI).

Vol. 2585: F. Giunchiglia, J. Odell, G. Weiß (Eds.), Agent-Oriented Software Engineering III. Proceedings, 2002. X, 229 pages. 2003.

Vol. 2587: P.J. Lee, C.H. Lim (Eds.), Information Security and Cryptology – ICISC 2002. Proceedings, 2002. XI, 536 pages. 2003.

Vol. 2588: A. Gelbukh (Ed.), Computational Linguistics and Intelligent Text Processing. Proceedings, 2003. XV, 648 pages. 2003.

Vol. 2589: E. Börger, A. Gargantini, E. Riccobene (Eds.), Abstract State Machines 2003. Proceedings, 2003. XI, 427 pages. 2003.

Vol. 2590: S. Bressan, A.B. Chaudhri, M.L. Lee, J.X. Yu, Z. Lacroix (Eds.), Efficiency and Effectiveness of XML Tools and Techniques and Data Integration over the Web. Proceedings, 2002. X, 259 pages. 2003.

Vol. 2594: A. Asperti, B. Buchberger, J.H. Davenport (Eds.), Mathematical Knowledge Management. Proceedings, 2003. X, 225 pages. 2003.

Vol. 2595: K. Nyberg, H. Heys (Eds.), Selected Areas in Cryptography. Proceedings, 2002. XI, 405 pages. 2003.

Vol. 2597: G. Păun, G. Rozenberg, A. Salomaa, C. Zandron (Eds.), Membrane Computing. Proceedings, 2002. VIII, 423 pages. 2003.

Vol. 2598: R. Klein, H.-W. Six, L. Wegner (Eds.), Computer Science in Perspective. X, 357 pages. 2003.

Vol. 2600: S. Mendelson, A.J. Smola, Advanced Lectures on Machine Learning. Proceedings, 2002. IX, 259 pages. 2003. (Subseries LNAI).

Vol. 2601: M. Ajmone Marsan, G. Corazza, M. Listanti, A. Roveri (Eds.) Quality of Service in Multiservice IP Networks. Proceedings, 2003. XV, 759 pages. 2003.

Vol. 2602: C. Priami (Ed.), Computational Methods in Systems Biology. Proceedings, 2003. IX, 214 pages. 2003.

Vol. 2604: N. Guelfi, E. Astesiano, G. Reggio (Eds.), Scientific Engineering for Distributed Java Applications. Proceedings, 2002. X, 205 pages. 2003.

Vol. 2607: H. Alt, M. Habib (Eds.), STACS 2003. Proceedings, 2003. XVII, 700 pages. 2003.

Vol. 2609: M. Okada, B. Pierce, A. Scedrov, H. Tokuda, A. Yonezawa (Eds.), Software Security – Theories and Systems. Proceedings, 2002. XI, 471 pages. 2003.

Vol. 2614: R. Laddaga, P. Robertson, H. Shrobe (Eds.), Self-Adaptive Software: Applications. Proceedings, 2001. VIII, 291 pages. 2003.